EDUCATION,

ECONOMY,

and SOCIETY

EDUCATION,

ECONOMY,

and SOCIETY

A Reader in the Sociology of Education

Edited by

A. H. HALSEY, JEAN FLOUD,

and C. ARNOLD ANDERSON

The Free Press of Glencoe, Inc.

A DIVISION OF THE CROWELL-COLLIER PUBLISHING COMPANY

Foreword

A VOLUME of the kind presented here, narrowly focused on the connection of education in modern society with the economy and the class structure, is perhaps liable to be misunderstood. As the authors of the Crowther Report aptly say, children are "individual human beings and the primary concern of the schools should not be with the living they will earn but with the life they will lead"; and we should not like it to be thought that we hold otherwise. We hope, however, that the following essays will induce readers to agree with us that no apology is needed for our attempt in assembling them to elucidate and illustrate the contribution that sociology can make to the understanding of education in modern society, by analyzing important aspects of the wider social setting in which policy-makers, administrators, and teachers must work.

We wish to thank Mrs. Suzanne Heintz and Mrs. Isabel Ross for their translations of chapters 4, 16, 29, 39, and 40, although we naturally take full responsibility for the edited form in which they appear.

A. H. HALSEY
JEAN FLOUD
C. ARNOLD ANDERSON

Contents

PART III THE SELECTION PROCESS IN EDUCATION

PART IV SOCIAL FACTORS IN EDUCATIONAL ACHIEVEMENT

PART V THE CHANGING SOCIAL FUNCTIONS OF SCHOOLS AND UNIVERSITIES

EDUCATION,

ECONOMY,

and SOCIETY

1   *Introduction*

JEAN FLOUD and A. H. HALSEY

I

EDUCATION is a crucial type of investment for the exploitation of modern technology. This fact underlies recent educational development in all the major industrial societies. Despite idiosyncrasies of national history, political structure, and social tradition, in every case the development of education bears the stamp of a dominant pattern imposed by the new and often conflicting pressures of technological and economic change. This collection of essays has been assembled to illustrate and discuss the modern interrelationship of economy, society and education, which, if not in itself entirely novel, is so at least in its prevailing intensity under conditions of advanced industrialism.

We shall try in this introductory essay first to picture the broad features of educational development involved by the movement toward what might be called a technological society, and second to discuss the sociological problems to which it gives rise, as they are illustrated by the work of our contributors.

In an advanced industrial society, it is inevitable that the educational system should come into very close relationship with the economy. Modern industrial technology, based on the substitution of electrical and atomic for other forms of power and introducing new and more intricate forms of the division of labor, transforms the scale of production, the economic setting of enterprise, and the productive and social role of labor. It is dependent to an unprecedented extent on the results of scientific research, on the supply of skilled and responsible manpower, and consequently on the efficiency of the educational system.

The enhanced scale and complexity of the productive unit reinforces the growth of the tertiary, at the expense of the primary, sector of the economy. The proportion of the total labor force engaged in the direct production of goods and services falls still further than in the earlier stage of industrialism; and bureaucratic, administrative, liaison, maintenance, and communication functions proliferate. More strikingly, an expansionist tendency, inherent in production on this scale and with this degree of complexity—quite apart from the exigencies of military competition—involves heavy investment in research and innovation. The proportion of the labor force engaged in manual —particularly unskilled manual work—declines; the demand for white-collar, professional, and managerial workers rises; above all, there develops a characteristically insatiable demand for scientists and technologists. The new technology, based on the invention of these men, integrates labor into a unified process of machine production. The traditional structure of production, in which bodies of skilled craftsmen, aided by laborers or apprentices, work under the supervision of foremen, yields to a more complex structure. The skill required of labor is up-graded and differentiated. A select group of skilled workers become, in effect, junior technicians—the setters-up and maintenance-men of machines operated by a much enlarged group of semi-skilled workers, dependent on dexterity more than special skill, and working under workshop supervisors—another enlarged group of workers, indeterminantly situated somewhere between the lower grades of management and the main body of skilled craftsmen.

Thus, modern industrial societies are distinguished in their structure and development from others of comparable complexity, principally by the institutionalization of innovation—that is to say, by the public and private organization, on an increasingly large scale, of scientific research in the service of economic and military growth. Their occupational structures are characteristically diversified, with relatively high educational qualifications for employment at all levels but the lowest. Education attains unprecedented economic importance as a source of technological innovation, and the educational system is bent increasingly to the service of the labor force, acting as a vast apparatus of occupational recruitment and training. Social selection is added to its traditional function of social differentiation: it must promote new, as well as maintain old, elites. Furthermore, it must cater to the new educational needs of the mass of population, deriving from the changed status of labor in modern processes of mass production.

Education becomes, then, a major form of investment for the economy as a whole, and old educational forms turn themselves willy-nilly to the new purposes of the modern economy. Secondary schools, colleges, and universities expand in number and in scope. The process of democratization affects their membership—the selection of students and recruitment of teachers; their curricula; their perception of themselves as institutions; their structure and functioning as going concerns; and, in their classrooms and lecture halls, the very learning process itself.

These developments do not take place easily in institutions for the most part deeply involved with outmoded, but by no means moribund, political and class structures. Conflict and friction are endemic in the movement toward a technological society and show themselves whether education is studied macroscopically, as an institutional complex in relation to the total structure of society, or whether it is studied microscopically, as the interaction processes of a single educational organization. Thus, at the macroscopic level, Jeffersonian and Jacksonian principles of educational provision, and elite and populist theories of educational opportunity, confront each other; there is controversy over what proportion of the population can profit from university education, and over the issues of desegregation and *apartheid*. Similar conflicts express themselves at the microscopic level in school or college. There is the perennial clash between "classical" and "modern" curricula; between intellectual and "social," or "personality," requirements for admission; between consolidation or expansion in schools with traditions of social or academic exclusiveness. As Margret Mead points out (in Chapter 30) a prevailing theme in the history of theory or practice in American education is "the conflict between the school oriented to the past (the private academy) and the school oriented to the future (the city school), with the seldom obtainable dream of the school which would hold the world steady."

Whatever the difficulties or delays in adaptation, there is no mitigation of the underlying pressures on education; and the traditional business of education with the process of cultural transmission is performed in quite new terms under the new conditions of technological society. No longer is it a question of handing on an unchanging, or only slowly changing, body of knowledge and belief. On the contrary, education in modern societies has more to do with changing knowledge than with conserving it, and more to do with diffusing culture to wider social circles, or from one society to another, than with preserving and transmitting the particular culture of a particular group.

II

This, then, is the broad picture of the process by which, as the economies of the advanced countries are increasingly dominated by scientific and technological innovation, education and economy become more closely geared, until the educational system occupies a strategic place as a central determinant of the economic, political, social, and cultural character of a society.

This description of the developing and changing relations of education, economy, and society raises a number of problems that are illuminated by our contributors.

THE CONTRIBUTION OF INVESTMENT IN EDUCATION TO ECONOMIC GROWTH

Drucker (Chapter 2) offers a graphic account of education's emergence from a consumption luxury to a productive investment. The pressures of economic change are such, he asserts, that "the highly educated man has become the central resource of today's society"; and Professor Schultz (Chapter 6) calculates that, as a proportion of all productive capital in America, human capital has risen between 1950 and 1957 from 22 to 42 per cent. There can be little doubt, indeed, that differences in educational provision, whether between nations, regions, or classes, do reflect differences in the movement toward prosperity on the basis of modern technology; educational inequalities become, in effect, fundamentally determinant of all social inequality. For the fortunate nations, technological advance seems to have brought us in sight of a state of affairs foreseen by Alfred Marshall, where unskilled work is minimal and highly paid, and education—i.e., investment in human resources—is the foundation of an elevated civilization.

Yet, the precise contribution of education to economic growth remains an open question. Although it must be primarily one for the economists to answer, we have included some discussion of it here, as it seems important to show that there are limitations to generalization from the generally high individual and social return to educational investment. Two of our contributors are cautious; Vaizey and Debeauvais show (in Chapter 5) that the relation is complex and shifting, according to the stage of economic development and the social and cultural context. Anderson (Chapter 21) goes further, and produces evidence to contradict the assumption that a productive economy necessarily requires high levels of educational provision. He reminds us that the mobilization of skilled human resources for economic growth is by no means a simple question of the scale of formal educational organization.

However that may be, the expansion and democratization of educational provision proceeds apace in all the industrial countries. There can be little doubt that the need to respond to technological and economic pressures is as much responsible as more liberal views of the natural rights of citizenship. Expansion raises many problems, of which only a few are considered in this volume. These concern changes in the social structure and development of educational institutions concomitant with expansion; and we will remark on these and others that seem to us to have been so far neglected by sociologists when we come to discuss the sociology of schools, colleges, and universities.

Meantime, we may consider the second major problem underlying our account of educational development in technological society, that is, the rationalization of the educational system in the service of the modern labor market.

EDUCATION AND SOCIAL MOBILITY

The notion that an advanced industrial economy requires a well-educated, adaptable, and fluid—i.e., geographically and occupationally mobile—labor force is implicit in our account of the growing involvement of education and economy. Ideally, runs the implication, talent should find its own level in the market, and the only guarantees that it may possibly do so lie in a high rate of social mobility and the minimizing or elimination of social factor in educational selection and occupational recruitment.

It is worth noting, in the first place, that we have no very clear idea either of the amount of mobility actually imposed by the movement toward technological society or of the part played in this process by education. Havighurst (Chapter 11) assumes that mobility must increase with economic development. However, evidence that "the overall pattern of social mobility appears to be much the same in the industrial societies in various Western countries" has been interpreted by Bendix and Lipset in terms of a "threshold" theory of more or less constant rates of mobility beyond a certain stage of economic development.[1] In any case, the extent to which education fosters mobility remains limited. Variations in economic development or social structure notwithstanding, "as the economy becomes more tertiary (and even as University attendance expands), there is at most a sluggish tendency for the more disadvantaged sectors of the population to contribute an increasing relative proportion of students" (Anderson, Chapter 21). Moreover, Anderson argues further, on the basis of American, British, and Swedish evidence, that ability—genetic or acquired—plays an important part in mobility independently of schooling.

The truth is that the schools and universities function badly as selectors and promotors of talent. This problem is discussed in general terms by Marshall (14) and Schelsky (29). Schools and universities were not designed for the selection processes thrust upon them in a modern economy by the tightening bond of schooling with occupation, and hence with social class, nor were they designed to act as agencies of social justice, distributing "life chances" according to some meritocratic principle in face of the social claims of parents for their children. In the past, education has had only conservative functions; as Becker reminds us (10), this is still true in many areas of the world, where education bears no relationship to social mobility and serves only to transmit an unchanging culture. Education has also traditionally been one of the signs of status. It differentiated people socially, but it did not on the whole create the differences it indicated. Concerning social mobility, it had what Havighurst aptly terms *symbolic* value—that is to say, it put the stamp on the outcome of the upward climb by conferring the symbols of the newly acquired status. That it should also be required to take on a *functional* value, to be the very agent or avenue of mobility, is a disrupting novelty.

Yet, as it seems, the school must select; and it is a fascinating exercise in comparative sociology to account for the obvious differences between the United States and Britain in its manner of responding to the task—legitimized in both cases in the same terms of "equality of educational opportunity." Turner (12) distinguishes *modes* of social mobility, which are reflected in contrasting strategies of educational selection. Where aristocratic conditions underlie the contemporary class structure, as in Britain, mobility is *sponsored,* and educational selection is overt, systematic, and prompt in the school career of an age-group of children, from which an able minority is chosen for education as an elite. In the more democratic atmosphere of American society, on the other hand, the organizing norm of *contest* mobility is preserved, with the aid of a tacit, belated, and prolonged selection, through "drop-out" and "cooling-out" (see Burton Clark's Chapter 36) from college rather than schools.

The modern trend, nevertheless, is from "sponsored" to "contest" mobility, and from "symbolic" to "functional" education for mobility. Despite differences in modes of mobility, education both in America and Britain confers on the individual training for an occupational function from which he derives his general place in society. The old elites were based on birth and wealth, which ensured to their members a distinctive education. The elites of a technological society, however, are based on education and wealth; they tend to share a common education rather than a common class or caste—and herein lie the crucial sociological problems of the selection process in education.

THE SELECTION PROCESS IN EDUCATION

Before turning to these problems, however, we may ask whether the differences we have discussed, in modes of mobility and strategies in educational selection, result in differences in the efficiency with which ability is matched with opportunity in America and Britain. The comparison is not a simple one, in that for all but the highest levels of ability the United States offers much more opportunity than any other country. The U. S. Census of 1950 (cf. Chapter 19) showed that over three-quarters of American Negroes, ages fourteen through seventeen, were enrolled in school, whereas this was true for less than a quarter of English fifteen- to seventeen-year-olds in 1957–58.[2] The vast extension of American higher education means also that the category of college student is a markedly heterogenous one by comparison with its European counterpart. There are some American colleges in which the student with the highest measured intelligence has a lower score than the least intelligent student at one of the more rigorously selective colleges.

Nevertheless, there is clear evidence for all industrialized countries of systematic selection for ability, as measured by intelligence tests, at each step up the educational ladder. Thus, Wolfle shows (19) for America that the average AGCT score rises, as the total population (100) is drawn into high school (105), graduates from high school (110), and into college (115), until it reaches 121 for the college graduate. Similarly, Macpherson's analysis of a representative national sample of an age-group of Scottish children (Chapter 17) shows that the percentage of those with I.Q.'s between 105 and 114 who completed a five-year course of secondary schooling was 12; for the I.Q. range 120–44, it rose to 41; and for those with 150 I.Q. or more, it was 96.

Equally remarkable, however, is the fact that, for all the variety of structure and method in the educational systems of the industrial world, there is universal inefficiency in the prevention of "wasted" ability. Thus, Wolfle's study indicates that over half of the most able 5 per cent of American high school graduates did not graduate from college; and this was true of 57 per cent of those classified in the top 20 per cent of high school graduates by grade. Similarly, in England, a recent enquiry revealed that 42 per cent of the most able one-tenth of English boys leave school by the age of 16.[3]

Educational systems did not develop historically, nor are they now designed single-mindedly, as sieves of ability. The distribution of educational facilities in all countries is but loosely related to the distribution of ability. The scale and quality of education are considerably affected by the vagaries of geography and demography, as well as by the unusual economic and political power of different nations, classes, and ethnic groups. The essays in Part III offer detailed illustration of these factors. Thus, the proportion of American college-age youths actually in college varies, from 30 per cent in Utah to 10 per cent in North Carolina (Chapter 19); and Natalie Rogoff (Chapter 30) shows similar variations for children according to the type of local community in which they happen to be brought up. Girard's essay (16) on France indicates the existence of similar differences between metropolitan, suburban, and rural districts; and it is a notorious feature of British education that grammar-school provision varies from over 50 per cent in a Welsh county to 10 per cent in a Northern industrial town. Again, as may be seen from Chapter 18, quite small fluctuations in birthrates and migration may result in important changes—from one year or one district to another—in the ability demanded for a given type of education.

These factors, together with the fact that the costs of education, especially beyond the primary stage, are partly born by private families, either directly or as earnings foregone, produce a correlation between educational attainment and socio-economic status that is as impressive as its relation to ability.

THE "SOCIOLOGY OF TALENT"

Unequal life-chances are both cause and effect of unequal educational opportunities; but social factors intrude on the educational process in more subtle ways than implied in this statement, which has by now become a sociological commonplace. Widespread social amelioration since World War II has not removed persistent class and ethnic inequalities in the distribution of ability (potential) and attainment (performance). The emphasis in investigation has shifted in recent years, from study of the material disabilities traditionally underlying these inequalities, to attempts, on the one hand to identify social factors impinging on the intellectual development of individuals and, on the other hand, to explore the social and cultural circumstances affecting their attainment or performance at given level of ability.

Examples of research along both these lines are included in Part IV. The well-established inverse correlation at all social levels between intelligence and family size is explored by John Nisbet, with the hypothesis that belonging to a large family restricts contact with adults, so that verbal development is retarded and intelligence-test performance reduced. Bernstein (Chapter 24) takes us still further by developing the theory that classes differ in the type of language used so as to handicap working-class children in the use of words as vehicles of abstract thought—an essential element in verbal intelligence. Research along this line is beginning to yield an increasingly subtle understanding of what it is about individuals that makes them more or less able.

The parallel line of study may be described as elucidating the environmental determinants of educational attainment. Ability, after all, is not an automatic guarantee of attainment. Indeed, the relation between these two variables is by no means fully known, although a linear association is widely assumed. McClelland[4] has suggested that threshold or curvilinear relationships may, in fact, obtain. For example, Terman and Oden's study of gifted children showed that at very high levels of intelligence the correlation between ability and achievement practically disappears. In any case, there is compelling evidence from many countries that, at any given level of I.Q., socio-economic factors of one kind or another will differentiate the academically successful from the unsuccessful.

One of those factors is the level of motivation induced by the individual's cultural or group attachments; the essays by Strodtbeck (25), Kahl (26), and Coleman (27) exemplify the best kind of relevant modern research. Strodtbeck's study provides an explanation in terms of cultural pressures for the remarkable degree of overachievement found among Jews. Kahl's analysis throws light on the crucial importance of family motivation in deciding the educational fate of talented boys from the working and lower-middle classes. Coleman demonstrates the independent influence of the cultural "climate" of the peer group.

From the point of view of the schools in a class society, class is culture; and education is a process of cultural assimilation through the reconstruction of personalities previously conditioned by class or race. Miss Rogoff points out (Chapter 13) that the Platonic notion of an educational elite "denies all the loyalties, ties, identifications, and memories linking each individual with his own family, clan, race and religion." The exploration of the educational consequences of these links and loyalties is discussed by our contributors in Chapters 16 to 27, and these represent the crucial problems of what the Germans call "the sociology of talent."

It is worth pointing out, however, that an effective sociology of talent must depend heavily on a "sociology of the school." Only some aspects of this important branch of study are represented in this volume, since in making our selection we have confined ourselves, so far as possible, to studies of changes in the structure and functioning of schools and universities that can be traced, in the main, to the economic pressures with which we are predominantly concerned.

EDUCATION AND SOCIAL CONTROL

We have already discussed the modification of the relationship of education to one major aspect of the wider social structure, that is, to the system of stratification. We have seen that a technological society has little use for social-class or other rigidities in the supply of labor, and that the principle of equality of opportunity in education serves an important economic function in such a society. What, in face of this emphasis on innovation and diffusion in education, becomes of its traditional conservative functions? Parsons' analysis (Chapter 31) of American education, assumes a country well advanced toward a technological society, in which the conservative function of transmitting the major cultural values of society is focused in the primary school, and the task of selection and training for different adult occupational roles is assigned to the secondary schools. This is an aspect of the educational problem in a complex modern society that has been neglected since the death of Karl Mannheim. What part do and can the schools play in fostering organic solidarity? Does Durkheim's account of their role in inculcating national and local loyalties and allegiances hold for twentieth-century societies? Do they still educate for leadership and "gentle the masses" in the manner described by Glass (28), in discussing nineteenth-century Britain? How do they equip the unselected majority of pupils for their modest, often underprivileged, adult roles? The problem of education for social consensus and integration is not raised in this volume; but that it is different in at least one purely pedagogical respect in technological society can be inferred from Chapter 7, in which we are reminded that the relations between the generations are upset by the democratization of education, as it introduces marked disparities in the educational experience of the generations, which tend to upset traditional relations of pupilage.

THE CONTENT OF EDUCATION

The striking development of secondary and higher education over the past quarter of a century has been accompanied by a strong trend toward vocationalism. Education increasingly takes on the character of "training"; specialization takes place earlier, is more thorough-going, and is increasingly of a kind directly related to the requirements of modern trades and professions. The extent to which the pressure in this direction is accepted or resisted varies from country to country, as is illustrated by our contributors. Thus, America, as compared with Europe, has moved further and faster than Britain and France, but less fast than Russia, in gearing the content of higher education to the demands of the economy (32). Or, to take a second example, Ashby shows (33) how the introduction of science and technology from the European continent into English university education was delayed and uniquely fashioned by the aristocratic traditions of that country's ancient centers of learning.

However, despite the trend toward vocationalism, there is widespread agreement, at least as far as the schools are concerned, on the overriding need for a general rather than a specialized education. The future is conceived of as inevitably changing and unpredictable in its demands. Employers are said to want "young people with a sound foundation" rather than a vocational training, and it is an advantage if vocational intentions do not have to be crystallized too early, (Ginzburg, Chapter 8). Schelsky (4) points out that modern industry calls for education in generalized and flexible principles of science and technology, so that people can apply their skills to changing demand. What is certain, is that formal instruction is penetrating industry itself, displacing with formal organizations the traditional forms of apprenticeship, and training "on the job" or by experience.

It is regrettable that this whole question of the fate of the content of education should have been relatively so neglected by sociologists. Many questions suggest themselves, to which no answers can as yet be attempted. Is it perhaps the case, after all, that the secondary, like the primary, schools can serve even technological society best by devoting themselves to the traditional business of education with cultural transmission? The current pressure on the secondary schools to select and recruit for adult occupational roles may, after all, be a feature of a period of transition. Schelsky (29) notes the important part played in it by parental pressure deriving from attachment to outmoded symbols of social prestige and transmogrified notions of distributive justice. The corrosive influence on the old class structure and its supporting attitudes, of affluence based on advanced technology, may hold its own release for the schools. It is certain, nevertheless, that they cannot avoid major adjustments in organization and curriculum as the age of schooling is extended and their social composition more closely reflects that of the population at large, whilst the age of marriage falls and the economic status of adolescents improves.

THE SOCIOLOGY OF TEACHING

Substantial changes in the internal structure and functioning of schools and universities are, indeed, already visible; but they are for the most part the unpremeditated results of expansion and democratization of their intake, which has been their immediate response to current pressures.

In the schools, as distinct from the universities, the most obvious changes are in the teaching profession, and we have included a number of essays on various aspects of the sociology of teaching that illustrate these.

The schoolteacher is as much a representative of the differentiation of new middle-class occupations in modern industrial society as he or she is part of the teaching process itself. Indeed, sociological study has so far been directed more to the former aspect of the sociology of teaching than to the latter—i.e., to teachers as an occupational group with a distinctive position in the general social structure, rather than as the staff of the schools.

As with other middle-class groups, the social basis of recruitment to teaching is changing (as is illustrated for England in Chapter 37), and therewith many associated characteristics of the profession, in particular those reflecting the part that it has traditionally played as an avenue of social mobility. Teachers, as a group, are becoming socially more homogeneous, despite the pressures of expansion which have marked the postwar period. The profession tends now to compete for recruits on equal terms with comparable occupations, and no longer relies on attracting able men and women of humble origin "at a discount," as it always has under conditions of more restricted educational opportunity; and it is to an increasing extent self-recruiting.

Recent sociological interest has turned to the study of teachers in their more narrowly professional role, i.e., to the intrinsic peculiarities of their occupation, straddling as it does the two worlds of youths and adults; and especially to the implications for their behavior in school and classroom of their position in the wider society and the pressures deriving from it.

The essays in Part IV contribute in several ways to the analysis of the professional role of the teacher, as does Margaret Mead's broad discussion (30) of the school in the setting of a variety of "ideal typical" social circumstances. Tropp and Baron (38) provide a somewhat more detailed comparison of the pressures exerted by the wider social structure, in particular the authority and power systems, in America and England. Kob (39) discusses the attitudes of German secondary schoolteachers toward their jobs and the formation and distribution among them of the principle stereotypes or "self-pictures" of their professional role. He shows that these attitudes and conceptions can be related both to the nature of teaching as an occupation and to the various social characteristics of teachers—their motives for, and mode of, entering teaching, their social origins, and their professional training.

In the universities, the rationalizing influences of industrialism have had more marked effect on structure and functioning than in the schools, where, as we have seen, the pressures are most clearly reflected in the changed social status of, and basis of recruitment to, the teaching profession. Thus, Clark (36) describes the elaboration of an apparatus of selection in an "open-door" college, and provides a foretaste of the formidable academic and administrative problems confronting a vastly expanded higher educational system, of which the organizing norm, in Turner's phrase, is "contest" rather than "sponsored" mobility. Riesman (34), Caplow and McGee (41), and Goldschmidt (40) all describe the changes in the academic career structure—the lengthening procession of higher learning—for which university expansion is responsible; whilst Trow (42) analyses its effects on the dynamics of recruitment to university teaching. All of these essays make it clear that the response of higher education to the challenge of a technological society implies an unprecedented transformation of traditional conceptions of college and university.

Conclusion

The major theme of this book, then, is the analysis of educational institutions under conditions of rapid social change. In modern society, the major link of education to social structure is through the economy and this is a linkage of both stimulus and response. Contemporary educational organizations stimulate economic change through research and, in turn, they respond to economic change in carrying out the function of selection and training of manpower. The implications for schools and universities, as organizations, are unending. The conditions of recruitment of both teachers and students, the scale of operation, the content of education and the teaching process itself have been, and continue to be, transformed by the advance of industrialism. It is the task of a sociology of education to understand these transformations. In selecting the essays which follow, we have tried to demonstrate both the importance of educational development and the relevance to it of sociological analysis.

NOTES

1. *Social Mobility in Industrial Society* (London: Heinemann, 1959), p. 13.
2. Cf., "*15–18*" Report of the Central Advisory Council for Education (1959), p. 1, Table 6.
3. *Ibid.*, Table 3.
4. D. C. McClelland *et al., Talent and Society* (New York: 1958), p. 13.

PART I

The Consequences of Economic Change

2   *The Educational Revolution*

PETER F. DRUCKER

AN ABUNDANT and increasing supply of highly educated people has become the absolute prerequisite of social and economic development in our world. It is rapidly becoming a condition of national survival. What matters is not that there are so many more individuals around who have been exposed to long years of formal schooling—though this is quite recent. The essential new fact is that a developed society and economy are less than fully effective if anyone is educated to less than the limit of his potential. The uneducated is fast becoming an economic liability and unproductive. Society must be an "educated society" today—to progress, to grow, even to survive.

A sudden, sharp change has occurred in the meaning and impact of knowledge for society. Because we now can organize men of high skill and knowledge for joint work through the exercise of responsible judgment, the highly educated man has become the central resource of today's society, the supply of such men the true measure of its economic, its military and even its political potential.

This is a complete reversal of man's history within the last fifty years or so. Until the twentieth century no society could afford more than a handful of educated people; for throughout the ages to be educated meant to be unproductive.

> A man who is now chief executive of one of America's largest businesses did not dare admit when applying for his first job, in 1916, that he had an advanced degree in economics. "I told the man who hired me that I had been a railroad clerk since I was 14," he says, "otherwise I would have been turned down as too educated for a job in business." Even in the late twenties, when I myself started, commercial firms in England or on the Continent still hesitated before hiring anyone as a junior clerk who had finished secondary school.

It has always been axiomatic that the man of even a little education would forsake the hoe and the potter's wheel and would stop working with his hands. After all our word "school"—and its equivalent in all European languages—derives from a Greek word meaning "leisure."

To support more educated people than the barest minimum required gross exploitation of the "producers," if not strict rules to keep them at work

Reprinted from Peter F. Drucker, *Landmarks of Tomorrow* (New York: Harper and Bros., 1959), pp. 114–25, with the permission of the author and the publisher. (Copyright 1959 by Peter F. Drucker).

and away from education. The short burst of education in the Athens of Pericles rested on a great expansion of slavery, the intellectual and artistic splendor of the Italian Renaissance on a sharp debasement of the economic and social position of peasant and artisan.

Idealists tried to break this "iron law" by combining manual work and education—the tradition goes back to the Rule of St. Benedict with its mixture of farmwork and study. It found its best expression in the mid-nineteenth century, in Emerson's New England farmer who supposedly read Homer in the original Greek while guiding a plow. But this, of course, never worked. The Benedictines—imperiling their salvation to the lasting benefit of mankind—very soon left farming to villeins and serfs and concentrated on study. Long before Emerson's death those New England farmers who cared for the plow had left both Homer and New England for the rich soils of the Midwest, while those few who had cared for Homer had left farming altogether to become lawyers, preachers, teachers or politicians. The "iron law" was indeed inescapable as long as manual labor was the really productive labor.

Thomas Jefferson believed in higher education and in equality as much as any American. He considered the founding of the University of Virginia and the authorship of the Declaration of Independence, rather than the Presidency, his greatest achievements. Yet in his educational master plan he proposed to limit access to higher education to a handful of geniuses. It was obvious that only a few could be spared from manual labor.

Today the dearth of educated people in the formerly colonial areas appears such a handicap as by itself to be adequate condemnation of colonialism and proof of the "wickedness" of the imperialists. But education did not come first in the scale of social needs even fifty years ago; flood control and land boundaries, equitable taxation and improved agriculture, railroads and incorruptible magistrates, all ranked much higher. If the colonial powers were then criticized on the score of education, it was for forcing it on too many, for destroying thereby the native culture, and for creating an unemployable, overeducated proletariat. The educated person was then still a luxury rather than a necessity, and education a preparation for dignified leisure rather than for productive work.

In my own childhood forty years ago, schools still assumed that education was for "nonwork." They preached that the educated man should not despise the honest worker as schools had preached since the days of Seneca in the first century.

The Scale of the Explosion

Thirty years ago only one out of every eight Americans at work had been to high school. Today four out of every five of the young people of high school age in the United States attend high school. Twenty years hence, when today's middle-aged will have retired, practically every working American will be a high school graduate. We have already pased the halfway mark.

Even greater has been the jump in college and university attendance. Thirty years ago it was still an almost negligible 4 per cent or less of the appropriate age group. Today the figure is around 35 per cent for the nation; this takes in groups such as the Southern Negro or the Southern "poor white," for whom going to college is still all but unknown. In the metropolitan areas of the country—even in such predominantly working-class cities as Detroit—the figure is nearly 50 per cent. It will, barring catastrophe, be that high for the nation as a whole in another fifteen years. By then two out of every three young Americans in the metropolitan areas will, regardless almost of income, race or sex, be exposed to higher education.

In the American work force of thirty years ago there were at most three college graduates for every hundred men and women at work. There are eighteen today; the figure will be thirty-five, twenty years hence—even if, contrary to all expectations, going to college becomes no more general than it is already among the two thirds of our people who live in metropolitan areas.

On top of all this, adult education is booming. Fifty years ago only those adults went back to school who had been unable to get a formal education as children. Adult education was for the educationally underprivileged—the immigrant from Southern Europe who wanted to learn English or the man who had gone to work at age fourteen and wanted to improve himself. In England adult education was the "Workers Educational Alliance" or the "Home University Library," both offering standard school subjects to workers and clerks. The German *Volkshochschule* served the same purpose.

Adult education during the last fifteen years has been growing faster in this country than college enrollment. And now increasingly it means advanced education for the already highly educated. It is almost routine for the experienced and successful physician to go back to school for advanced training every two or three years. Refresher courses are increasingly demanded of our teachers. Some fifty universities—in addition to a dozen large companies and professional management associations—offer advanced management courses to successful men in the middle and upper ranks of business, who usually already have college if not advanced degrees. Yet before World War II, only two such programs existed, both new, and both struggling to get students.

The educational revolution has been even more explosive in Soviet Russia. Thirty years ago basic literacy was confined to a small minority—had probably fallen even below the low standards of czarist Russia. The educational push hardly began until the mid-thirties. Today, because of Russia's larger population, the proportion of young people in secondary or higher education is still quite a bit lower than in this country, but the absolute numbers are fast approaching ours.

In the total population of the Soviet Union educated people must still be a small group. Few if any of the top people in the Soviet Union have had more than elementary formal schooling; certainly of those over forty in the Soviet Union, even high school graduates are still only a tiny fraction. But in Russia, too, it has become evident that education is the capital resource of a modern, industrial society. We know now that the Russian achievement does not rest on the Communist tenets of "socialist ownership of productive resources," the "dictatorship of the proletariat," "collectivization of agriculture" or "national planning." Every one of them has been as much an impediment as a help, a source of weakness fully as much as a source of strength. The achievement rests squarely upon the tremendous concentration of resources, time and effort on producing an educated society.

The two outstanding success stories among small nations, Switzerland and Mexico, have nothing in common save extraordinary educational development. Switzerland is the one European country where secondary education, in the last thirty years, has become almost universal. Mexico is the only country in the world that, since the mid-thirties, has spent no money on defense but has instead made education the first charge on its national income. And is it entirely coincidence that the major countries in the Free World that have found the going the roughest since World War II, Great Britain and France, are also the countries in which the educational revolution has advanced the least, in which the supply of educated people, though of high quality, is today still not much larger proportionately than it was in 1930 or even 1913? In England the supply may well be smaller considering the steady emigration of so many of the highly educated young people.

We are undergoing the educational revolution because the work of knowledge is no longer unproductive in terms of goods and services. In the new organization it becomes the specifically productive work. The man who works exclusively or primarily with his hands is the one who is increasingly unproductive. Productive work in today's society and economy is work that applies vision, knowledge and concepts—work that is based on the mind rather than on the hand.

There will therefore be no permanent oversupply of educated people. On the contrary, the more there are, the greater should be the demand for them. Educated people are the "capital" of a developed society. The immediate impact of, say, using physicians instead of barbers is to uncover needs, opportunities and areas of ignorance, leading to the need both for more physicians and for more medical and biological research. The same process can be seen in every other field—and with particular force in the economic field of production and distribution. Every engineer, every chemist, every accountant, every market analyst immediately creates the opportunity and the need for more men who can apply knowledge and concepts, both in his own field and all around it.

This may sound obvious. But it is so new that it is not yet recognized.

Our accountants, for instance, still base their terms and measurements on the eighteenth-century tenet that manual labor creates all value. They still call it "productive labor"; the work of men of knowledge is "nonproductive labor" or "overhead," a term reeking of moral disapproval. When economists talk of "capital" they rarely include "knowledge." Yet this is the only real capital today. The development of educated people is the most important capital formation, their number, quality and utilization the most meaningful index of the wealth-producing capacity of a country.

The Impact on Society

What is today called "automation," that is the rapid substitution of work by knowledge and concept for work by human hands, is a first impact of the educated society. It is a moot question whether the essence of automation lies in specific machinery and technical ideas or whether it lies rather in basic concepts about the nature of work.

But there can be little doubt that the driving force in automation is the fact that people who have been exposed to formal schooling for twelve or sixteen years have expectations in respect to work and jobs which manual work, no matter how well paid, does not fulfill. They increasingly demand jobs in which they can apply knowledge, concepts and system. They increasingly refuse to accept jobs in which they cannot apply what they have learned, namely, to work with their minds. They may be satisfied with a job of little skill—and there are a good many semiskilled knowledge jobs—but they expect work that draws on mental rather than manual faculties.

In the United States, where most of the young people in the metropolitan areas go at least to high school, the assembly line is already obsolete. The labor necessary to run it is becoming scarce. Young people with a high school education do not want to work as human machine tools. Moreover, to use people with that degree of education for the semiskilled and unskilled manual jobs of the assembly line would be a gross waste of valuable, expensive and scarce resources.

Tomorrow everybody—or practically everybody—will have had the education of the upper class of yesterday, and will expect equivalent opportunities. Yet only a small minority can get ahead no matter what work they choose. This is why we face the problem of making every kind of job meaningful and capable of satisfying an educated man. This is why the new organization must create an effective relationship of function, rank, rewards and responsibility, not only for its professionals but for all those employed in knowledge jobs.

How new these expectations are is shown in the field of personnel management. Only forty years old—it began in World War I—the discipline is already outdated in its concepts and its assumptions. Its principles, its rules, its practices and procedures all represent a distillation of experience with unskilled or semiskilled machine workers, largely from the metalworking industries. Today the majority of the personnel employed even in manufacturing industries are no longer of this kind, are rather people doing knowledge work, however unskilled. How far our personnel management theories really applied even to yesterday's machine workers is an open question. For managing tomorrow's employees, the products of the educated society, they are likely to be quite inadequate.

The educational revolution has had an equal impact on the world economy. Educational capacity, as much as natural resources or industrial plants, is becoming a crucial factor in international trade, economic development and economic competition. Educational development, above all, has become a central problem of the poor countries.

Many of these underdeveloped countries spend today a larger proportion of their national income on education than does the United States. Yet where we complain that one fifth of our young people still do not finish high school, many of these countries can barely keep one fifth of their young people in elementary school. They cannot finance the cost of a literate society, let alone that of an educated society.

This educational inequality is a serious international and interracial problem. Its inevitable result is to make inequality greater, to make the rich richer and the poor poorer. Even greater is the danger that it will push poor, underdeveloped countries into the totalitarian camp; for a totalitarian tyranny, so it appears to them, can raise enough money for the rapid development of education even in the poorest. (This is a delusion. Practically all the poor underdeveloped countries are much poorer than Russia was in 1917 and much further behind in education. They are unlikely therefore to repeat her performance in education even by faithfully copying every Russian tenet and action. But this may be found out only when it is too late.)

Here, it would seem, is a highly promising area for international aid and co-operation. There is need—and opportunity—for financial aid to help the underdeveloped countries pay for the rapid expansion of education. There is need for systematic co-operative effort in training and developing people, especially future teachers. There is need—and opportunity—to help think through the purposes, the structure and the methods of education needed in those countries. Above all there is need for the developed countries, and especially for the United States, to accept a national policy of assisting underdeveloped countries in building education.

The Educational Competition

"The Battle of Waterloo," it is said, "was won on the playing fields of Eton." Perhaps; but no one asserts that it was won in Eton's classrooms.

"The Prussian schoolmaster," another saying goes, "defeated France in the War of 1870 that created imperial Germany." But long ago this was exposed as empty boast; the credit belongs to the German railway and the German armaments designers.

With the launching of Russia's Sputnik, however, the old pleasantry became a grim fact. The higher education of a country controls its military, its technological and its economic potential. In an age of superpowers and absolute weapons, higher education may indeed be the only area in which a country can still be ahead, can still gain decisive advantage.

The greatest impact of the educational revolution is therefore on international power and politics. It has made the supply of highly educated people a decisive factor in the competition between powers—for leadership and perhaps even for survival.

The conclusion from this is as simple as it is new: Educational development becomes a priority of national policy.

International leadership is not a matter of power alone. It is as much a matter of policy. Power can never substitute for policy. But purposeful, principled, courageous policy is a potent substitute for power, has again and again given leadership to a weaker rather than to a stronger nation.

Concern for the quantity of educated people is therefore not enough for a national policy in this age of the educational revolution. Numbers of engineers and scientists, of language students and physicians, are not very meaningful in themselves. It is not even enough that national policy aim at the largest possible supply of highly schooled people. It is not enough, in other words, that the graduates know their engineering, their science, their law, languages or medicine. National policy is only possible if these are also highly *educated* people—that is, people who can formulate, understand and support purposeful, principled, courageous policies.

This leads us back to education. And indeed the greatest impact of the educational revolution is on education itself. It raises basic questions about the values, the purposes, the structure and the tools of education. On the one hand, education has become the central capital investment, the highly educated people the central productive resources in such society. On the other hand, education, while "higher" and perhaps "highest," can no longer be limited to an elite, but must be general education.

3 *The Pressure of Economic Change*

OF ALL THE DRIVING FORCES of change in the present day, among the strongest are those that show up in economic form, those that bear upon the amount of money and of other resources that is made available for the educational system, or upon the living the pupils in the schools are looking forward to being able to earn. The essential verities of a sound education are, no doubt, the same from generation to generation. But the particular form that the education takes, the number of pupils who receive it, the number and nature of the schools they attend and the length of time they stay there—all these things are influenced by economic circumstances. We leave aside until the next chapter the question of the economic and financial relationships between the state and the schools. The present chapter is concerned with the impact on the individual of economic changes and the consequences that they can be expected to have for the schools.

The Advance from Poverty

It has hardly yet been generally realised how sharply the average standard of living has risen in the fourteen years since the end of the war. It is useless to quote money figures because of the great rise in prices in the past two decades. But in the broadest of terms, it can be said that the total real output of the United Kingdom (it is impracticable to give figures for England alone) in 1958 was about one-third greater than it had been twenty years earlier. Even after more had been set aside for the needs of the government (especially for defence), for additions to productive and other capital and for exports, there was still enough left over to sustain an increase in consumption. An index number of all forms of consumption by individuals—the best statistical measure of the standard of living of the people—shows an increase of about 10 per cent per head from 1938 to 1958. This great increase in wealth-producing capacity cannot be left out of any consideration of educational policy. As compared, for example, with our predecessors of the Consultative Committee who produced, in 1938, the Spens Report on Secondary Education, we are prescribing for a community that is one-third

---

Reprinted from *A Report of the Central Advisory Council for Education* ("The Crowther Report") (London: H.M.S.O., 1959), chap. v, pp. 45–53.

richer in material wealth. This has a double implication: there should be more real resources available for education; and, since a high level of national productivity can only be sustained by brains and skill, the schools have a higher challenge to meet.

The basis of the great improvement in the standard of living of the average family has, of course, been the full employment that has prevailed for two decades. But it has not been full employment alone, for the combined effect of inflation, of progressive taxation and of the social security schemes of the welfare state has been to divert the larger part of the rise in the national standard of consumption to the lower income groups. They have, therefore, gained proportionately even more than the population as a whole. Those who knew the schools twenty years ago can see the revolution in the faces of the children. The Chief Medical Officer of the Ministry has recently reported that obesity in children is now attracting at least as much attention as under-nutrition. Whether the economic security and prosperity of the 1950's will last through the 1960's, no one can say, and it is certainly no part of the task of this report to venture into economic prophecy. We have, however, based our recommendations on the assumptions, which we trust are reasonable, that at least there will be no sharp and complete reversal; and that, though employment may perhaps from time to time be somewhat less full than it has been in recent years, there will be no relapse into the conditions of the twenty years between the wars. We are thinking here of the state of employment in general and of its effect on the prosperity of the community as a whole. Where the employment of young people is concerned, there is an important reservation to be made, to which we return below.

The transformation in the economic conditions of the people, and particularly of the families in which the great mass of school children are to be found, has had several effects on education, not all of them pointing in the same direction. In the first place, more wealth has meant that more education can be afforded. So far as this relates to public expenditures, it will be dealt with in the next chapter. But even in these days of universal free education, there is still something that a family has to "afford" when it sends its children to school, especially when the legal compulsion to do so has expired and the cost of clothes and meals has to be weighed against the money that might come in from wages. With greater affluence in the family, there is at least less economic compulsion on the sons and daughters to leave school on the earliest day that the law permits. But, secondly, if the father (and mother) can earn better wages, so can the son and daughter. Indeed, in proportion, it is the earnings of young people that have risen most. While the average weekly earnings of adult men in 1958 had risen to 372 per cent of the 1938 figure, and of adult women to 412 per cent, those of boys and girls rose to 429 per cent and 469 per cent respectively. Thus while the economic compulsion to leave school as early as possible has diminished, the economic attraction of doing so has increased. Moreover, not only has the boy or girl who stays on at school after 15 had to resist the lure of an easy job at good wages, he has had to suffer a handicap in his income that lasts for several years. Two of the enquiries made for us have shown, as have many other pieces of evidence, that it is not until the early twenties, and sometimes even later, that the boy who has stayed on at school catches up in earning capacity the boy who left at 15. But, thirdly, it is now much more evident than it has ever been before that he does catch up in the end, and go well ahead. (So does his sister, if she continues in employment.) Not only in the highest grade in intelligence, where the grammar school boy has always been able to look forward to a "career," but well down into the modern schools, it is now (or should be) apparent to all that education pays, always in the long run, and often quite quickly. This also is something new; for in the old days it was never certain, if a boy stayed at school to increase his intellectual attainments, that he would be able to find a job, either at once or for many years, that would match up to the additional qualifications he would obtain. In recent years there has been no such doubt. Not only have there been plenty of jobs for the qualified, there has been a steadily growing list of desirable callings that cannot be entered without a qualification. If, then, there are greater attractions in leaving school early, there are also, for the longer sighted, more prizes to be won by staying on.

On balance—but only on balance—these various effects of prosperity have been favourable to education. The sharp, the almost startling, rise in the numbers of 15 year-old boys and girls staying on to 16 in full-time education, and of 16 year-olds staying on to 18, is the most potent encouragement to further educational progress that can well be imagined. But every headmaster and headmistress can also tell of many promising young people whose development is interrupted by the lure of immediate high wages. The social changes described in the last chapter combine with high juvenile wages to give the young people of today infinitely more independence of their elders than they ever had before. Both in spirit and in purse, they are ready to support themselves. If, therefore, there is a greater demand for education, it is a conditional demand—it is for an education that seems to the boys and girls themselves to be meeting their needs.

The Importance of Being Qualified

The other great force, in addition to growing material wealth, that is transforming the role of education is the rising importance of being properly qualified, to which some reference was made in the last parapragh. To the grammar school boy and girl, this is of course nothing new: qualifications have always been required for the professions. What has been happening in the last twenty years is that the same requirement has been spreading over a much larger field of employment. Not so long ago, there were very few qualifications below those of the professions, save those that could be secured by merely serving in a given status for a stated length of time, as in many apprenticeships. Now there are scores of thousands of boys, and a smaller but steadily growing number of girls, in every type of school, who have a specific qualification of one kind or another in view. Two separate trends have combined to produce the same result. In the first place, there has been a rapid rise in the number of jobs that cannot be performed without some special knowledge or experience. It is difficult to quantify the trend by statistics; it is perhaps most clearly apparent in manufacturing industry, where the onrush of modern technology is yearly creating new jobs that never existed before, each with it special expertise. But it exists also in other technical employments and in commerce, where the old simple broad categories are steadily being split up into more specialised callings, for each of which some qualification is necessary.

In addition to this, however, there is a growing tendency for many occupations, which do not absolutely require a specific expertise for their performance, nevertheless to demand an attested standard of general education for entrance. This tendency is not perhaps to be endorsed without reservation. Admirable though any incentive to continue education is, it is sometimes applied too rigidly, and works harshly on individuals, who are debarred from entering a calling in which they could give good service for lack of some examination result which is not, when isolated by itself, of apparent relevance. But whether because they are really necessary or because they are required by regulation, qualifications are clearly here to stay. We shall have a great deal to say in this report, especially in Part Five, about the principle of specialisation in secondary education. Here it is enough to observe that the qualifications now sought in such large numbers, though they may be specific, are not by any means always specialised. Perhaps the largest aspect of the general phenomenon is the extent to which the General Certificate of Education at Ordinary level is being used as a means of selection for many particular forms of employment and training which did not demand the old School Certificate.

The tendency to seek special qualifications may be reinforced in the years immediately ahead by a special influence. We have been living through a period when juvenile labour has been unusually scarce, and when young people have accordingly found it unusually easy to get jobs. There is at any one time a certain natural shape to the labour market and the number of openings for which boys and girls are sought will tend to be proportional to the size of the whole population of working age. But the numbers of boys and girls available (or potentially available) for the jobs, expressed as a proportion of the total working population, can vary quite considerably. This is shown in Table 1.

Table 1.

Persons aged 15–19 as a Proportion of Total Population of Working Age (England and Wales).

Year	Persons Aged 15–19	Persons Aged 15–64	Column (1) as percentage of Column (2)
	(1)	(2)	(3)
	(000)	(000)	(%)
1901	3,247	20,463	15.9
1911	3,337	23,141	14.4
1921	3,503	25,095	14.0
1931	3,435	27,467	12.5
1951	2,704	29,242	9.2
1956	2,755	29,330	9.4
1958	2,840	29,465	9.6
1963	3,600	30,315	11.9
1968*	3,331	30,515	10.9
1973*	3,361	30,569	11.0
1978*	3,518	30,783	11.4

* Figures for these years are based on the Registrar General's projections, and assume nil net migration.

In the post-war years the ratio of young people to the total population of working age has been abnormally low, and barely more than two-thirds of what it was only a generation ago. But as the "bulge" moves into the population of working age, the ratio is going to rise quite sharply. This means, in all probability, that the supply of young workers is going to rise relatively to the demand for them. The 15 year-olds may be withdrawn from the labour market by a higher school-leaving age, but there will still be relatively more 16 year-olds, 17 year-olds and 18 year-olds seeking employment than there were. And whether or not the country as a whole continues to enjoy full employment, this is likely to mean that jobs for young people are going to be somewhat harder to find than they would otherwise have been. This will have several consequences for education, with some of which we shall be concerned later. The point to be made here is that it can hardly fail to increase the premium on being qualified.

The Impact of Technology

This growth in the importance of qualification is the latest manifestation of the principle of the division of labour, on which the whole of industrial civilisation has been erected. And though, as we have said, it is visible in every part of the field of employment, there can be no doubt that the biggest driving force behind it is that of technology. It is difficult for people whose outlook on the world took shape more than twenty years ago to realise how much the speed of change has increased since then. It is still more difficult to grasp the exciting challenge that it presents for those whose working lives will extend into the twenty-first century. Three brief examples may assist. The population of the world is at present increasing at the rate of at least 130,000 a day, so that in terms of population a new town the size of Derby comes into being every day. Even at present, about half the world's inhabitants are at starvation levels and all man's ingenuity will be needed to meet the challenge posed by his own fertility. The dimensions of another of the problems of the future are given by the comparison between the energy consumed in the United States, which is the equivalent of nine tons of coal per person each year, and the figure for India and great tracts of Africa and Asia, where it is less than five hundredweight. The world's annual demand for energy was 3,200 million tons of coal equivalent in 1950; it may be 7,000 in 1975 and 20,000 by the end of the century. The scientists and the technologists have little more than a generation to develop new sources of energy to meet these needs. Or, finally, there is the problem of endemic and epidemic disease, which there is now, for the first time in the world's history, reason to hope can be brought under control. These are only some of the problems with which the generation now at school will be faced.

To say that the world is living through a scientific revolution has become a truism. For all that, we are not sure that its consequences for education are always rightly drawn. The most obvious and familiar of them is, of course, the need to produce an adequate number of qualified scientists, technologists and technicians. This has been much emphasised in recent years, and we would not wish to say anything that would detract from its imperative character. It is not for us to express any opinion on the numbers of scientists and technologists that should be aimed at. Our concern is with the schools and we wonder whether it is generally realised how sharp has been, and still more will be, the increase in the numbers of boys and girls leaving school and seeking further scientific and higher technological training. There are three forces at work, which have come to be known in educational slang as the "Bulge," the "Trend" and the "Swing"—the increase in the numbers of young people, the crest of which will not reach the age of 18 until 1965; the tendency to stay longer at school—specifically, in this connection, to enter the Sixth Form; and the growing preference for science and mathematics as subjects for specialisation. If all three continue for another few years as they have been going recently, their combined effect will be to produce by the middle of the next decade so many young people qualified to enter upon higher scientific and technological courses that it will be difficult to accuse the schools of not playing their part. The criticism may rather come from the young people themselves, who may find a lack of opportunities in higher education for pursuing the careers they have chosen. When, however, we turn to the technicians—the next grade down—we have considerably more apprehension both about the number of boys and girls between the ages of 15 and 18 who are putting their feet on the lower rungs of the ladder and about the treatment they receive as they climb up it. This is the subject to which Part Six of the report is largely devoted.

Even when the technicians are added to the scientists and the technologists, even when the numbers of all three are made adequate, they will still remain a fraction, and a relatively small fraction, of the total working population. If the first impact of the technological age upon education is to create a need for large numbers of specially trained persons, this is not the way in which the great majority will be affected. In addition to the duty of setting increasing numbers of young people on the road to becoming scientists, technologists and technicians, the schools must also consider what needs to be done to the education of those who are not going to earn their living in these ways, in order to adapt it to the nature of the age in which they will spend their lives. There seem to be three main needs which can be identified. First, there is a need to ensure that the generality of educated men and women can comprehend the impact of technology upon society and to demolish the barrier of language and of modes of thought that tends to separate those who have been trained in the scientific discipline from those who know nothing of it. There is a danger in a further division of society, and in our opinion the community ought to insist that no man or woman should in future complete his or her education in such ignorance both of the dialect and of the philosophy of science as has been customary for so many in this country. To this proposition there is the natural corollary that greater efforts should also be made to see that the scientists and technicians should be exposed to the radiation of humane letters.

If this first requirement is chiefly (but by no means entirely) a matter for abler boys and girls, the second affects all alike. This is that every citizen should be able to use the fruits of technology and to do so intelligently. Not all of our children will be scientists or technicians or even mechanics; but all of them will increasingly use machinery and scientific equipment of all kinds. It is not necessary to know how to make a motor car, or even to be able to repair it, in order to drive it; but to use a machine with intelligence and economy, it is desirable to have some conception of the principles on which it is designed and the limits of its capacities. Just as it is necessary for a craftsman to understand his materials, so it is necessary for every one in the second half of the twentieth century to have a modicum of mechanical common sense. For some, this can be made the foundation on which a sound course can be built; but for all, it needs to be part of the background to their education.

The third aspect of the impact of technology on general education— and, in the long run, undoubtedly the most potent—is the emphasis that it places on the rapidity of change, particularly in the conditions of work. A boy who enters industry today will not retire until well into the next century. In that time, the odds are that he will see at least one complete technological revolution in his industry. The job he will hold when he becomes a grandfather may not exist at all today; it will be concerned with processes not yet invented, using machines still to be designed. This is true not only of the "progressive" industries such as chemicals and electronics. It is probably just as true of agriculture, of older industries such as printing and of services such as transport. It may even be true of large sectors of the retail distributive trades. Clearly, the first quality that is needed to cope with such a world is adaptability.

This need for adaptability exposes an ambiguity in the word "skill," which could otherwise be used to sum up the whole argument. For many centuries, a skilled worker has meant one who in his early years acquired proficiency in a particular specialised form of craftsmanship and spent the rest of his life applying the skill thus acquired. Admittedly, the meaning of the word has been broadening out in recent decades, particularly in the engineering industry. But if one were to say, without further explanation, that what was needed today was an ever larger supply of skilled craftsmen, there is a risk that the conclusion drawn by many people would be that the need could be met by exposing a larger number of boys to the traditional methods of acquiring skill by watching and doing. Watching and doing will always be indispensable, but clearly they are not all that is needed when what the boy will in fact be doing in a few years' time is not now here to be watched. Skill has been thrown back from the actual manufacturing process to the preparatory stages. The transition has been well put by Dr. Kate Liepmann in the report[1] of her enquiry into the present adequacy of the apprenticeship system:

> Fifty or sixty years ago there was, in most industries, a clear-cut distinction between skilled and unskilled jobs. The former required considerable (though not, as a rule, outstanding) intelligence, a very high degree of trained sensitivity of certain senses, highly efficient eye-hand co-ordination, an intuitive knowledge of the properties and behaviour of a limited number of types of fundamentally simple machines, together with literacy and an acquaintance with simple arithmetic . . . Nowadays, the situation is very different . . . the locus of the skill which goes into a product has shifted from the shop-floor to the preparatory stages: to work done by technicians (draughtsmen, production, planning and development engineers), by designers and metallurgists, by works managers, estimating clerks, quantity surveyors and so forth. These are the real skilled occupations in modern industry.

It may be that there will even be a reduced need in the future for "skill" in the old-fashioned sense of the term; what will be needed in ever growing volume will be the quality that can perhaps best be described as "general mechanical intelligence." To say this is not, of course, to assert that training on the job must in future be replaced by an instruction based entirely on books. That would be absurd. But it is to assert that training in the new kind of skill will require an active collaboration between the workshop and the school or college, in which the relative participation of each and the methods they use will need to be kept under the most constant review.

The task of education in the technological age is thus a double one. On the one hand, there is a duty to set young people on the road to acquiring the bewildering variety of qualifications they will need to earn their living. On the other hand, running through and across these vocational purposes, there is also a duty to remember those other objectives of any education, which have little or nothing to do with vocation, but are concerned with the development of human personality and with teaching the individual to see himself in due proportion to the world in which he has been set. In the chapters that follow, we have tried not to lose sight of the economic and vocational purposes that an effective educational system should serve. But children are not the "supply" that meets any "demand" however urgent. They are individual human beings, and the primary concern of the schools should not be with the living they will earn but with the life they will lead.

NOTES

1. Apprenticeship—An Enquiry into its Adequacy under Modern Conditions. Pages 19–20 Kegan & Paul, 1960.

4 Technical Change and Educational Consequences

H. SCHELSKY

WE WILL CONSIDER the occupational structure of industrial society. With the introduction of machinery and factory work in the nineteenth century, there arose first of all a broad stratum of unskilled manual workers, which, in the course of technical development, was soon joined by a steadily growing stratum of skilled workers—mainly former artisans; the modern arrangement for the occupational training of workers developed on this basis. On another level of the factory appeared the group of commercial or clerical occupations, for which the traditional training model was the merchant. The first phase of industrialization—up to World War I—shows three different occupational groups in industry, more or less corresponding to the phases of technical development—unskilled manual workers, skilled workers, and commercial and clerical personnel. The social prestige and income of these groups reflected more or less closely their importance for production; and their training models, at least in the two higher groups, were those of pre-industrial society—the merchant and the artisan.

Since then, technical developments in this century—particularly the introduction of complicated semi-automatic machinery for mass production—have largely changed this pattern. Today, there is a broad stratum of semi-skilled workers, doing varied work and having varied abilities; their modes of work and their social claims no longer relate to pre-industrial forms of production. The semiskilled worker has spilled over into the group of the unskilled as well as of the skilled worker. Furthermore, the shift in emphasis from immediate output to previous planning, as well as the increasing specialization of administration and distribution, have created a stratum of specially trained technical employees, and have so differentiated the remaining clerical occupations that employees in these categories can no longer be regarded as an homogeneous social or occupational group.

Recent and impending changes in production and modes of work—the result, in particular, of the automation of much industrial manufacturing and the mechanization of clerical work—are gradually obliterating the traditional division between unskilled, semiskilled, and skilled occupations

Translated and abridged from H. Schelsky, *Schule und Erziehung in der Industriellen Gesellschaft* Würzburg: Werkbund Verlag, 1957, with the permission of the author and publisher.

and between manual workers and salaried employees. The significance for production of the various industrial occupations is being changed and redistributed. In the course of time, income, security of employment, social mobility, standards of prestige, and consumption will gradually adjust to this development; and the organization and aims of vocational training will have to be changed.

If we illustrate these problems by considering the extreme case of automation, it is not because we believe that automation confronts us with entirely new problems of vocational training. From a technical point of view, automation may constitute a "second industrial revolution." Compared with the first technological phase of the industrial revolution, automation permits the substitution of mechanical devices for managing and directing functions and, in the offices, for schematic intelligence work. I do not think, however, that this technological leap poses entirely new problems and tasks in the social, economic, or cultural areas—for instance, in the field of education. Rather, it implies a reinforcement and intensification of developments and tendencies already under way, the significance of which has not always been recognized. There seems to be no reason to dramatize the social and educational problems posed by automation. On the other hand, automation does make necessary new insights and decisions, which, we may add, are necessitated in any case by other developments.

What are the consequences of automation for the worker? What kind of attitude and achievement does automatic machinery require on his part? For an answer, let us turn to the three levels of automation, or mechanization of industrial techniques, distinguished by Georges Friedmann. First, technology is dominated by *dependent* machinery: the worker must provide the raw materials; he starts the machine, directs it, regulates it, etc., determining thereby the rhythm of work. These machines are still largely like tools; man dominates them as he dominates his arms and legs. The bicycle may be the best example in this context. On the second level are the *semi-independent* machines: work processes are largely, but not entirely, automatic, and the worker still has to lend some assistance. The best known example is the assembly line: the processes of manufacturing are highly differentiated and greatly mechanized, in part already automatized, and the remaining manual tasks have to be adjusted to the rhythm of the machine. Even if the machine has been adapted in many respects to man, man remains essentially part of the machine: he is, indeed, a "slave of the machine." The nearer the approximation to full automation—without reaching it entirely—the more stupid, depressing, and monotonous becomes the work that requires neither technical interest nor skill or initiative.

This state of things changes when full automation is reached. The worker ceases to be a slave of the machine and performs tasks of a very different nature—regulation, supervision, repairs. Most important, the individual worker will have to control a whole complex of automatic machines;

he will be required to supervise measuring instruments and to regulate them, on the basis of his technical knowledge, in an absolutely reliable way. Full automation will relegate, for instance, the assembly line to a mere transitory phase in technical development. Therefore, Friedmann and others see in it a notable progress toward "humanization" of industrial work. However, automation will also bring new burdens. The stress implied by high responsibility and permanently alert attention without action may lead to a kind of dammed-up activity that, in the short run, is experienced as boredom, in the long run as frustration, and that may require new measures in work arrangements.

Thus, automation will create a new type of work and worker—or will at least increase its prevalence, since it already partly exists outside automation. The main requirements will be a high degree of attention and responsibility, technical knowledge, and quick reaction—qualities approximating to those of the technician. Function of control, supervision, and direction are mainly functions of character and intelligence, having little or nothing to do with manual skills or intellectual knowledge; they are the abstract virtues and abilities of industrial and technical work. This fact calls for new ways of training and selecting workers, on the one hand, and creates new occupational interests among workers, on the other, assigning them new professional qualifications.

This in turn will provoke changes among the industrial workers as an occupational or social group. The skilled worker trained according to the model of the artisan will no longer represent the working élite; rather, the stratum of the semiskilled workers *trained in their own factory or plant* will increase, since the complicated and increasingly specific apparatuses of production may hope to profit from their workers only if every major enterprise trains them according to its own specific needs. These semiskilled workers will not be mere auxiliaries but will exercise important functions of controlling automatic processes; thus, their achievement and responsibility will be superior to those of the present-day skilled worker. This new group of workers—even today some of the semiskilled workers earn more and fulfill more important functions than the skilled workers—will lead to an increase in the highly qualified technical occupations and to a reduction in the number of semiskilled auxiliary workers, to whom new occupational and social chances are offered.

Similar structural changes in work requirements and occupational groupings are also apparent in clerical work and will become more obvious with the technical development of business machines. Socially and occupationally, clerical employees—far from uniform even today—will become more and more differentiated. Part of them will continue to do routine work and merely execute orders, while others will be required to display permanent mental initiative and intelligent judgment. The whole group will suffer the impact of machines and mechanization and will in part be transformed

into "clerical technicians"; in part, into mere "clerical workers." The penetration of technology into clerical and administrative occupations will do
away with uniformity even in the lower and middle strata of clerical and
administrative activities. Modes of work in these strata will become more
and more like industrial modes of work outside the office. As is well known,
employees resist this process; typically, they do not defend thereby a specific mode of work but their social position and prestige—although liberation
from the monotony and schematism of so much office work would be as desirable as liberation from the assembly line. The difficulties of this technical
revolution in the modes of work in office and factory are mainly due to the
social structure and its models of prestige. One of the tasks of vocational
training should therefore consist in making people recognize this change in
occupations and prestige order.

Even here it becomes apparent that the technical and social changes in
work and occupations—provoked not only by automation—destroy or
disturb the old and comparatively uniform hierarchy of achievement and
functions. Today, labor legislation, social policy, and industrial organization, as well as vocational training and education, are confronted with the
destruction of the older order. It is not so much progressive specialization
that causes the difficulties of mastering—legally, organizationally, and educationally—the world of industrial occupations; it is rather the fact that attitudes of work and modes of production belonging to different levels and
phases of technical development begin to amalgamate, in such a way that no
simple and distinctive occupational patterns can serve as models to direct
legal, educational, social, and organizational action.

In order to illustrate this difficulty, let us look at the extent of possible
automation of production and its consequences. The questioning of experts
by an American congressional committee (in 1955) about the possibilities
of automation and its consequences for labor policy showed that in the next
twenty years automation will affect around 8 per cent, at best 10 to 12 per
cent of American workers; half of them would retain their positions in the
same branches of industry and in the same enterprises but would have to
change their modes of work, while the other half would be absorbed by
new industries—mainly by the expanding consumption and service industries. Technological recession, so often conjured up in connection with automation, remains a phantom; it is, however, possible that even automation
will not be able to do away with the chronic lack of labor characteristic of
all highly industrialized societies. Two conclusions can be drawn from this:

1. From the point of view of labor policy and vocational training, automation will not bring recession but will require less dramatic if not less
complicated tasks, such as changes of the work place and reorientation of
occupations on a big scale.

2. A relatively considerable number of workers will be absorbed by new
occupations as a result of automation. (It is to be supposed that the as-

sembly line will largely disappear, since semi-automatic manufacturing will become fully so.) But older industrial occupations—the unskilled worker, the semiskilled auxiliary worker, the skilled worker and the artisan, the office clerk and the employee—will retain their old structure; these occupations will be left over on all levels of transition to automatic production.

This is a broad picture of the difficult situation with which vocational training and education are confronted. We will try to summarize these points, focussing our attention on the broad stratum of elementary industrial occupations and leaving aside those professions depending on specialized technical or university training:

1. One of the main characteristics of the situation seems to be the following: vocational training has to take into account not only different occupational branches and the simple scheme of unskilled, semiskilled, and skilled work but also the varying degree of automation; the varying degree of perfection of technical means determines work performance to a greater extent than the manual or intellectual origin of a particular professional knowledge or skill. In other words, *teaching to apply technical means as such* becomes almost more important than a specialized vocational training. Thus, our traditional conception of the term occupation is in jeopardy.

2. The preindustrial occupations of the artisan and the merchant can no longer serve as implicit models for vocational training. In the future, the model for industrial as well as for office work will be the *semiskilled worker,* i.e., the one that up to now has confronted vocational training with the greatest difficulties. The semiskilled worker must no longer be considered merely an intermediate type between unskilled and skilled labor. On the contrary, he will serve as a fundamental model for the development of technical skills and functions among a broad stratum of future industrial and clerical occupations, this, of course, not on the level of the semiskilled auxiliary worker, but on the level of the "semi-skilled technician." Vocational training will have to take into account this fundamentally new situation in industrial work.

3. The demand for greater plasticity and interchangeability of occupations results not only from the change of work place and activity in factory and office, made necessary by automation. These occupational shifts are also connected with people's claims for social security and better living. The educational problem is, therefore, not only to "despecialize" elementary vocational training—as already apparent in various occupations—but also to pay increased attention to the possibilities of transfer and mobility within the industrial bureaucracies—from apprentice to technician and engineer. This view is supported by authors like Georges Friedmann and Eduard Spranger.

4. Modern vocational training should emphasize comparatively *abstract occupational and working qualities.* The worker who controls automatic devices and instruments is required to display concentration, attention, high

responsibility, technical knowledge, quick response, and reliability. These qualities must form in him a kind of permanent latent disposition—a kind of background on which to perform particular activities. Today, mainly abstract qualities are required of workers, such as ability to organize, to handle people and to supervise, self-control, intelligence and reliability, exactitude, keeping up with work-pace, etc., while simple manual or intellectual knowledge and skills become less and less important.

The prevailing urge for specialization should not deceive us. This urge has its origin not in the economy but in the people who look for jobs. Behind it, paradoxically enough, often lies the mistaken idea that the problem of occupational mobility can be solved by applying old means, i.e., by further specializing professional training. The concept of an occupation as a specialized activity evidently needs revising.

Only one thing is certain. These abstract modern qualities cannot be *directly* taught. They can only be acquired by practising and exercising particular occupational skills or knowledge. In spite of this, it seems that one of the important theoretical and practical tasks of vocational education consists in systematically separating these abstract qualities from the concrete context in which they are acquired, i.e., from the particular manual or intellectual training situation. In this way, the accidental character of particular skills—accidental in comparison with the essential achievements in industrial and office work—would become apparent. The vocational training of a baker or hairdresser that makes him despise semiskilled industrial work (if ever he has to do it), in spite of the higher income and security of employment it carries, because he considers it to be socially degrading and denounces it as a "mere job"—such a training has failed to recognize and emphasize the new claims of modern work. The same failure is apparent if replacing artisans, skilled workers, and bookkeepers with machinery leads to a situation where experience is replaced by the mere knowledge of how to handle a switch-board. Responsibility for this is the fact that education is still directed toward the product instead to toward the machine.

I should like to emphasize that these general and abstract qualities of industrial and office work must not be confused with personality and character values. These abstract qualities represent an intermediary behaviorial stratum between specialized occupational skills and knowledge, on the one hand, and general personality formation, on the other; they should be recognized as such and made the aims of vocational training. This intermediate stratum is the one that *gives meaning to behavior in modern work;* in it are found fulfilment and satisfaction, self-affirmation, and acknowledgment of professional and social achievements. Taking all this into account, it is possible to reject the thesis of the meaninglessness of modern industrial and clerical work and to recognize as illusory the coupling of general personality formation with specialized professional training.

5 Economic Aspects of Educational Development

JOHN VAIZEY and MICHAEL DEBEAUVAIS

Introduction

WE LIVE in a time when knowledge is exploding. More knowledge, new techniques, and new abilities have to be given to more and more people because of this fact. Knowledge and techniques are changing the world, and education must change with it. This brutal fact is inescapable. Education has two tasks—to hand on tradition and values and to expand knowledge. The consequence of its success in increasing man's knowledge of his environment and his possibilities of controlling it has been to emphasize the obstructive effects of its role as a channel of tradition. The tension is a familiar one.

In the 1960's, however, education is of overwhelming importance. Many countries are committed to educational reforms that will make heavy demands on finance and resources. At the same time, these countries are concerned to promote economic growth. Their demands for investment in physical capital and for a better standard of living compete with the demands of education for extra resources. As an economy develops, the need for skilled workers, experts, and generally educated people increases almost geometrically. Consequently, education is making new and ever increasing demands on the economy, while the economy is making growing demands on education. In most countries, too, this interaction is taking place in a rapidly changing social environment, where there is a growing demand for an educational structure that will give to all children the equal opportunities promised by the democratic process.

All the evidence suggests that the tide of education is mounting with extraordinary rapidity. Country after country reports higher birth-rates, increased enrollments at all levels of education—particularly at the higher levels—and a marked rise in the interest of ordinary working folk in their children's education. For instance, in the next ten years, the number of

---

This paper, published for the first time in this volume, is extracted from an unpublished report of a conference organized by the International Association of Universities and sponsored by the Ford Foundation, which was held in Italy in July, 1960. The authors, while accepting full responsibility for the report, have tried to summarize what appeared to them to be the main points of consensus among the economists attending the seminar.

French students in higher education will double. In the United Kingdom, university enrollments will almost double. This raises one immediate problem. Are there sufficient people of high ability to benefit from this expansion? Fortunately, evidence shows that the "pool" of talent is nowhere near exhausted. As the Crowther Report[1] suggests, a more efficient pump can reduce the present wastage of talent that exists in every country. Thus, there is no "talent barrier" to the development of education; and more efficient social arrangements in changing school courses to suit those from unacademic backgrounds, and in giving scholarships to poor students, will tend to raise the demand for education still further.

This education will be costly. In Federal Germany, it has been calculated, expenditure on school education will rise from 2.4 per cent of the gross national product in 1960 to 4.4 per cent in 1970; in the United Kingdom, total expenditure on education is likely to rise by at least two-thirds. Obviously, this raises serious problems of finance. Even more serious, perhaps, is the expected increase in *the need for teachers*. In Federal Germany in the 1960's, the numbers of primary and secondary teachers needed to meet existing commitments will rise from 200,000 at present to 370,000 in 1970. In the United Kingdom, a rise in the number of all teachers from 380,000 to 520,000 is required. In France, the number of secondary schoolteachers must double in eight years.

This rise in expenditure is not just a sign of a rise in consumers' expenditure made possible by the rising national incomes of increasingly rich societies. It is to be thought of, rather, as investment—investment in mankind. A nation's wealth is in its people. This trend of thought has recently come to the forefront of economic thinking, and it represents an entirely new attitude to the problem of paying for education. The returns on education, both individually and socially, are at least as high as those in physical capital. More important, the development of the psysical equipment of society may largely be wasted unless there is the trained talent to work it.

This is not an antihumanist point of view. On the contrary, a high level of general culture—as well as being the ultimate end of educational activity —is necessary for the adequate adaptation of the working force to the new economy. The place for the unskilled worker in modern economies is diminishing rapidly. As the economy develops, it needs more, and more diverse, skills that rely upon a general background of education for their development. A growing economy also requires adaptable workers who can quickly and with ease leave one specialty and take up another.

Thus, economists seek from the educational system not only proportionately more people with highly developed skills and abilities and fewer unskilled hands, but also a general and flexible education enabling people to adapt themselves rapidly to changing circumstances. The economic requirements of flexibility and generality coincide with the aims of those who wish to remove the social barriers to education, which exist to a greater or lesser extent everywhere.

Consumption or Investment?

From an economic point of view, education may be regarded both as consumption and as investment. Expenditure per capita has risen with income per capita: for example, in the United Kingdom, it rose from 1 per cent of the gross national product in 1900 to over 2 per cent in 1920, to nearly 3 per cent in 1938, and to 4 per cent in 1958. The same rise may be noted in all countries for which figures are available; in the United States, it appears that the income-elasticity of demand for education is 3.5; as a society grows richer, it spends a larger proportion of its income on education.

What are the deciding factors in establishing this proportion? In absolute terms, the closest relation is between the rise of G.N.P. itself and the rise in educational outlays, but behind this relationship lie others.

First, it appears that the age structure of the population is a relevant, but not necessarily the most important, factor. When the child population rises, there is a choice between expansion and falling standards, and both courses have been chosen at different times. Similarly, when the child population falls, there is a choice between contraction and rising standards; again, both choices have been made at different times.

The next factor is the level of prices. If expenditure is fixed in money terms, then a rise or fall in the price level can lead to unanticipated abundance or shortage. This relationship can become a complicated one when the change in the price level of educational goods and teachers' salaries differs from that of other prices either in direction or rate. Inflation has dominated educational finance in many countries until comparatively recently.

Then there is the actual availability of educational goods. At certain periods, an actual shortage of teachers or of bricks has kept expenditure down to a level below that it would otherwise have reached. It is conceivable that public-works expenditure to counteract a slump might similarly raise expenditure.

Financial resources have often limited the growth of education and are in some respects the crucial link between education and economics. The actual financial costs of education are the main, but not the only, matters to be considered. Of some importance is the cost of not taking part in economic activity that is borne by students and their families. Regardless of income, it is the better-educated parents who most value education.

The growth of education is thus in part a response to the growing wealth of society. The increased production of a growing economy makes educational expansion possible by freeing resources for its use. But education is also a major cause of the growth of output. Hitherto, education has been mainly regarded as consumption. Henceforth, it is primarily to be regarded as investment. This was the view of the participants in the seminar. As the Italian Minister of Education said, in opening the meeting, "education in itself is a fundamental economic fact . . . the highest productivity is in the human capital." Education is investment in mankind.

Economic Growth—a Consequence of Education

The use of the word "investment" in education implies that there is a return to society analogous to that from physical investment, and that education has as one of its main tasks the creation of an efficient working force. If this be allowable, then a number of questions pose themselves. First, how much education is required at different stages of economic growth? Next, where is education most fruitfully to be stimulated—in the universities or primary schools—for girls or for boys? Third, what sort of education is most appropriate for economic development? Fourth, is there in fact a conflict between some important educational ideals and the conditions necessary for economic growth? An appeal may be made to historical experience or to the theory of economic growth for answers to these questions.

The evidence is not overwhelmingly in favor of a generally high level of education as the prime mover of economic growth. The first industrialized nation of the world, Great Britain, has a lower average level of education than some of its European neighbors. On the other hand, Japan, the United States, the U.S.S.R., and Denmark have had high rates of growth and high rates of expenditure. In the Danish case certainly, and in the Soviet case probably, it seems that education played a crucial role. In other cases it might perhaps be more correct to say that there is a correlation between high rates of growth and high rates of expenditure on education, but that this is not necessarily evidence of a causal relationship. Nevertheless, the reverse proposition may be asserted: there is no economic growth without an adequate education system. This might suggest that the clue to the problem is not so much the amount of education as the groups to which it is directed.

Here the historical evidence is less equivocal. In the British case, there is a well-established link between nonconformist academies and the innovating business class. In Germany, Russia, Japan, and America, there is a well-known connection between technical education and the growth of productivity. In Russia and America, there is a connection between the education of the semiskilled and the emergence of the working force.

There is, therefore, some relation between the classes that are educated and economic development, and the character of the education is extremely relevant. In Britain, the education of the nonconformists was more pragmatic that that of the gentry; in the other countries, the development of technical skills has been extremely important.

Finally, the dominant class opposing development has often been traditionally educated: in Russia, the kulaks had a traditional religious education; in Britain, the effects of Oxford and Cambridge on business initiative were alleged to be disastrous; in China, the Mandarins opposed westernization. These differences appear as a conflict of values, although it may be that the traditional education is less concerned with values than with holding on to the seats of power and influence.

So far the argument is rather indefinite. It becomes less so if economic theory is brought to the task.

There is a model that deducts the contributions to growth made by physical capital and increases in the labor force, and leaves the residual to be attributed to a melange of factors, among which education is supposed to be dominant. This depends upon the validity of the calculations on a very broad range of historical data; but even allowing for margins of error it seems that education's contribution is substantial.

There is another model that attributes the additional earnings of the educated to "investment" in education and therefore assesses these earnings as the product of education. This assumes full-employment, competition, and that the correlation between earnings and education indicates a causal relationship—whereas it may indicate a link between social position, education, and economic status. Nevertheless, it seems that after making allowances for this, the returns on education are very high.

A more pragmatic approach recommends itself to "manpower planners." This is to establish precise relationships between certain levels of production, with certain techniques, and the demands for manpower of all grades, which are as a result determinate. This method has the major disadvantage that it overdetermines the solution; manpower of one grade is in fact easily substitutable for one purpose or another. Nevertheless, generally speaking, the indications are clear that skilled people are going to be very scarce in all countries in the next decade.

There is a danger in attempts to formulate the relationship between education and economic growth in narrow terms. Many of the connections are indirect—the influence of women in the home, for example—and may be neglected because they are not easily, or at all, quantifiable. With this reservation, however, it is possible to analyze the contribution of education to "human resources," as the phrase in the new Indian and Pakistani five-year plans has it, and studies made so far suggest that it is considerable.

Certain concrete problems have to be solved before any unequivocal relationship can be established. One is whether education expenditure follows or precedes economic growth. This cannot be settled until internationally comparable figures have been worked out. Then a relationship between various cadres has to be developed. Above all, the problem of "intellectual unemployment" must be recognized; there are many countries now—and it has been true of all countries in the past—where the educated man has been in need of a job. Consequently, the relationship between economic growth and the productive factor of "skill" must take account of employment conditions.

At present, for example, the Egyptian effort in education is many times that of Nigeria. Yet their per capita national incomes are said (for what it is worth) to be equal. It seems likely, however, that in future it will be the unskilled who risk unemployment, not the educated man.

When all these caveats have been entered, the evidence for two propositions seems to be overwhelming: the individual returns to investment in education are at least as high as the returns to investment in physical capital in a market economy like that of the United States; and the social returns, in all economies, are also extremely high.

Furthermore, the changing requirements of the economy for skilled manpower should guide educators on the kind of educational structure that is needed, and the content of the curriculum.

The Labor Force and Education

First, it is clear that any demand for an increase in the number of specialists required for any particular level of economic development is a demand for an increase in a specific branch of education. Thus, in France for example, a demand for engineers to work the third Plan (that of 1961–66) is substantially above the number of expected engineers that might arise from in-service training, promotion from lower levels in industry, immigration, and so on. The greater part of the increase must come from new recruits to industry who are the products of the education system.

To increase any level or branch of education, however, has a multiplying effect on the whole of education. An increase in the number of engineering students requires an expansion of other parts of the universities, in order to keep some balance; the output of the secondary schools has to be increased to allow for an increased recruitment to higher education—this requires more teachers; the increase in teachers in turn requires more training colleges; and so on. The education system is a series of simultaneous equations where a change in one quantity changes all.

Clearly, to have a generously endowed education system gives a national economy certain distinct advantages. For example, in France in recent years 40 per cent of secondary graduates have become school-teachers; despite a need almost to double the teaching force in the next few years, the rate of expansion of the secondary system is such that the proportion of secondary graduates who become teachers can fall to one-sixth and still be adequate. In the United Kingdom, however, if the schools are to be adequately staffed, the proportion of women university graduates entering teaching has to rise from one-third to over two-thirds in ten years. The dangers of not being able to raise this proportion, or starving other occupations of women graduates, are obvious. What is true of the supply of teachers is true of the supply of personnel to other occupations.

The education system should be sufficiently flexible to allow it to respond fairly rapidly to the changing needs of the economy. For example, the movements of the working force between occupations are likely to be considerable as a result of technical change; some traditional industries will diminish—notably coal and agriculture—while service industries will continue to grow in importance. It follows that a flexible system of technical education is especially required. Fewer sons will follow their father's traditional craft or trade; they will need prepartion for the new occupations coming into existence. Moreover, as people change their jobs they will need a high level of general education, which will enable them to be rapidly retrained in new skills. Above all, perhaps, is the striking fact that the former division between a small, highly educated elite and the remainder of society no longer corresponds to the needs of the economy. Industry requires a spectrum of skills.

Education should therefore be relatively abundant, flexible, and capable of producing people with a high general level of culture, which makes them more adaptable to changing economic and social conditions. An increasing emphasis on adult education is necessary if the adult working force is to be prepared to face the risks inherent in the process of economic growth. The interest of the economists in educational reform, however, went further than this: it seemed that the great gap in the supply of labor was less that of the highly qualified specialists than that of the level of skills below this—the well-educated technologist and technician. Consequently, the economists argued against rigid segregation in separate schools of those with high ability from the rest of society, and in favor of a more comprehensive system of education, which brings people of varying abilities together until quite late in their school careers. This reinforced the pedagogical arguments that early segregation is difficult to justify because of the difficulty of accurately discerning talent, and separating those who are stupid from those who are inadequately motivated; it also reinforced the social argument that in an age of rapidly increasing specialization it is necessary for education to try to give a sense of social cohesion by bringing together in the schools people of different abilities, motivation, and background.

The Finances of Education

The current finance of education can be derived from general budgetary funds, local government taxes, fees paid by parents, gifts, repayable loans to students, and remission of taxes that erode the tax base.

Broadly, the private sector is financed mainly from fees, gifts, and tax remission, while the public sector is financed mainly by local and central government funds and fees. In both, the use of loans is not, at present, important, except in Holland and in the United States. Capital is usually financed by loans.

A distinction must be made between *real* and *budgetary* costs. An unemployed man who is put into education as a teacher or a pupil, and whose consumption of other goods does not rise, represents a costless activity. In the socialist economies this sort of development has taken place with remarkable speed. In the market economies, however, there is in fact always a rise in the consumption of the teacher and probably of the pupil, which represents a diversion of resources, arrived at by the use of the budgetary mechanism. Thus, the yield of taxes has to be increased, or a budget deficit incurred, or other government expenditure curtailed to allow for an increase in educational spending. This frequently leads to a lack of use of potential educational facilities.

The necessary education programs will be expensive. Probably by 1970 the advanced western European economies should be spending at least 6 per cent of their G.N.P. on education, compared with between 3 and 4 per cent at present (and over 5 per cent in the U.S.A. and over 7 per cent in the U.S.S.R.). At the same time, many governments are committed to pledges not to increase taxation, or even to reduce it. Obviously, there is here a conflict in social policy. The economists argued strongly that to increase taxes to support education was a wise policy, which would yield high returns. At the same time, they suggested that there was an urgent need to devise new means of finance; probably financial imagination was no less important than imagination in other spheres. Further, the problem was an illusory one in some senses. As these societies grew richer they could afford to pay more for education and their peoples would wish to have more education. The problem of finance was formidable in practice but simple in principle.

The general picture, however, obscures certain important points. One is that in several countries—e.g., U.S.A., U.K., Federal Germany, Switzerland—education is wholly or mainly a local-government responsibility, and local government is tied to the inelastic yields of local taxes, which accentuate, too, the problems of poorer areas. Consequently, the optimistic forecast depends on a resolution of these political difficulties.

There remains the question of the private sector of education. This has denominational significance in France, the United States, and several other countries, and social significance in the United Kingdom and the United States. Financial difficulties tend to affect the denominational but not the other private schools. Private fees for ordinary education should become more freely available as prosperity rises.

The private sector of education includes, in most countries, however, a great deal of higher education. It is here that the financial crisis is likely to occur. There are several points involved. Higher education is very expensive and is likely to become more so as science and technology become more significant. Moreover, its rate of increase is much above the average for education as a whole or G.N.P. and its associated indices. In higher education, too, the demand for income on the part of students is an exceptionally large part of the total expenditure and reflects the high opportunity cost of talented young men and women. How far these costs can be met by repayable loans, earnings of students in their vacations, and grants from industry is a matter for debate. In general, in Europe there is a great hostility to all of these methods and a far greater willingness to put the expenditure on to the central government budget; in the United States the reverse is the case. In the United Kingdom there is particular opposition to the use of part-time earnings. In France there is opposition to the charging of fees.

It becomes clear that the price of higher education and the efficiency with which it is conducted raise fundamental issues of public policy, especially when the supply of teachers is considered.

The reform of education will be financially expensive. It is also costly in terms of the demands it makes on qualified personnel.

Finding the Teachers

The problems of teacher-supply vary from country to country, but certain general principles emerged from the discussions.[2]

First, education is itself a major consumer of highly qualified manpower. Teaching in schools and higher education takes between a sixth and a third or more of the annual output of higher education, and the proportion is still greater if research is included. Consequently, any rapid expansion of the teaching force imposes considerable demands on secondary and higher education.

Second, as education becomes a longer and more complex process, teachers must themselves be more adequately prepared and have at their disposal a greater variety of aids to effective teaching. They will need a broad preparation too, because their mobility between different sectors of the education system is an essential condition of its flexibility and capacity to respond to the rapidly changing requirements of the economy.

Next, adequate forecasting of the requirements for teachers is an essential part of the process of meeting the needs of teachers. Evidence from England, Federal Germany, and France showed disastrous lags in the preparation of plans to train teachers to meet requirements that could, in principle, have been foreseen and easily met.

There were two further problems. One was that the salaries of teachers, linked as they are to the salaries of other employees in the public sector of the economy, tend to lag behind the price that the free play of supply and demand would establish, so that a general shortage of teachers tended to became chronic; the lags in educational development therefore become cumulative. Second, the changing place of women in society meant that they represented both the single most promising source of new teachers, and also (because of the rising popularity of marriage and the falling age of marriage) a source of great instability in the number of teachers. Consequently, the provision of special arrangements for women teachers, especially married women, was essential.

It was further suggested that there were important sources of new teachers among groups of technical workers and specialists, whose skills were urgently needed in the education system. Some part-time teaching could be arranged. There were many people, too, with a vocation for teaching who were anxious to take it up in middle life, and whose maturity and experience could be invaluable for adolescents, for whom special training arrangements were necessary.

The problem of maintaining the quality of the teachers is a central issue that has to be faced. This may involve extra rewards, in cash and prestige, for highly qualified teachers; for if the intellectual standards of the profession are not maintained, or even raised, the expansion of education will be a diffusion of the second-rate.

This means that one of the scarcest resources in education—highly qualified teachers—has to be used efficiently and effectively. Educators ask for more money and for more personnel. They have to give society an account of the use they make of the scarce resources they command.

Effectiveness and Efficiency in Education

The effectiveness of the use of resources in education raises a fundamental issue. It would clearly be wrong to apply simple tests of productivity to education—to judge it as though it were a brain-producing plant. But there are more effective and less effective ways of using resources; and usually the more effective way is the best way culturally and educationally, as well as economically the most efficient.

It is perhaps not often realized that there are different technologies in teaching as there are in any production process. Normally, these may be described as different combinations of manpower: the royal tutor may be highly trained, while the elementary teacher has only eight years of school. There are also, however, different combinations of capital; the capital cost of schools may vary in the world today from $3.00 a pupil to $2,500. There are different items of equipment ranging from a few tattered exercise books to expensive pieces of scientific apparatus. There are, in addition, playing-fields, boarding-houses, school journeys. All these lead to the conclusion that there is a vast range of capital and labor combination in the process of education.

Different methods of teaching require different combinations of capital and labor. The advent of modern psychology, for example, has required far more labor intensive techniques than were previously considered necessary. Furthermore, changes in the curriculum—for example, toward science and technology—may themselves require substantial changes in the use of labor and capital. Changes in the structure of school systems—the greater use of records, greater distances travelled—and so on may also make different demands on economy. Few of these changes have been studied other than from the point of view of education, or perhaps more exactly, from the point of view of educational psychology; the economist has had little or nothing to say about them.

The economist has a bias in favor of precise calculation. One approach that he may suggest is that when there is a choice in teaching methods some attempt should be made to cost these methods, and to cost them not only in money terms but in terms of the demands they make upon, for example, scarce skills or scarce equipment. At present, decisions are taken on the basis of a folklore or on phases of psychological enthusiasm.

The economist asks whether there is the best use of skilled teachers (the scarcest factor in the educational process) and able pupils. Is the school year, or the school day, for example, the correct length to get the results that are needed? Furthermore, he is entitled to ask whether there has been the best possible use made of modern technology, part of whose function is to save skilled manpower. Are machines and television possible aids or substitutes for teachers? Can the principle of division of labor be applied to teaching still further than it has been, to make use of semi-skilled married women, for example, or old-age pensioners, or students?

In these calculations two further points must be made. The first concerns the increased productivity of education. In almost every subject, the amount of knowledge and technical skill required of pupils at any given level is constantly tending to rise. Have we studied sufficiently the means of raising educational productivity? There have been remarkable experiments with the hitherto ineducable. Have we experimented sufficiently with the highly educable? Here the possibilities of genuine international exchange of experience seem rich.

There must also be considered the more obvious problem of the wastage of pupils and teachers. In some parts of some systems of education —e.g., the English part-time educational system or the Pakistani full-time secondary educational system—fewer than one in twenty who begin a course complete it fully. In many cases, this raises the cost of education *per completed pupil* by a factor of five or ten. What we have to ask ourselves is whether the final standards are inappropriate; whether initial selection should be improved; whether the rate of wastage can be reduced by different methods of teaching, student aid, or counselling; and, above all, whether any value can be derived from partly completed courses.

Time Is Money

Lastly, it was emphasized throughout the discussions that a major cost in education is the time of pupils, and the wages that they might have earned had they been at work and not studying. The teacher has a duty not to waste young people's time. This is perhaps the strongest reason for re-examining old pedagogical concepts. By 1970, the number of pupils over fifteen in the United Kingdom will be bigger than the labor force of the coal industry, agriculture, or the armed forces; the same is true elsewhere—education will, in a sense, be the dominant industry. Economically, the productivity of education is important. But the human dignity of the students is the real argument for teaching them well and economically.

Conclusion

We are driven to the conclusion that in order to meet the economic and social needs of the 1960's, Europe will have to give its people what until recently would have been thought of as a luxury education.

This implies that education for many people will become longer, in order to increase their expertise, and that it should also become broader, in order to increase the possibility of contact with others and to guarantee them some freedom of movement as their specialisms become redundant or obsolescent. It should give everybody a general basis of culture, essential for economic growth and human dignity alike.

How to achieve this without overloading the curriculum or making the formal process of education too long seems to be the central educational problem for the gifted. For the less gifted, the problem is to raise their educational status without either imposing intolerable intellectual burdens, or creating a gulf that does not correspond to their place in the spectrum of ability and that replaces the former economic and social division of society by one based on real or supposed talent. This poses complicated educational problems.

Economically, the questions are at least as complex. In the first place, education is part of the expenditure of abundance, which is increasingly child-centered and family-based. In the second place, the economy requires an adequately educated labor force for it productive capacity. In the third place, the bulk of the expenditure falls on to government account and consequently raises problems about the tax burden. Fourth, there is the need to find skilled manpower to provide the teaching force. Fifth, without economic growth, a better education cannot be provided. The relationship between the economy and education is reciprocal.

NOTES

1. "15–18," *A Report of the Central Advisory Council for Education,* Vol. I (London: H.M.S.O., 1959).

2. In the U.K. and U.S.A., teacher-training is a part of higher education; in France, teacher-training for primary schools is part of secondary education, and for secondary and higher education a part of higher education. In this report the convention is adopted that *all* teacher preparation, whether for primary, secondary, or higher education, is itself a part of higher education.

6   *Investment in Education*

T. W. SCHULTZ

IN ORDER to arrive at an adequate sociological understanding of education in differentiated societies, one must appreciate the magnitude of the "educational enterprise." Since it is so often asserted that only a small fraction of national income is spent on education—using only expenditures through taxation—it is important to see a more complete summation of real costs. In this way, one obtains a fuller picture of the extent of the response by contemporary societies to the demands upon education arising out of economic and social changes in recent decades. Even the estimates by Professor Schultz are incomplete, for they do not include the costs of training, paid by industry; adult education programs, paid by fees; etc. The picture given here for the United States would be broadly similar, although the totals relative to income would probably be smaller, for other industrial nations.

Professor Schultz begins his analysis by pointing out that between 1919 and 1957 the output of the American economy grew at the rate of 3 per cent per annum, while the resources put into the economy expanded at the rate of only 1 per cent annually. In questioning the accuracy of previous estimates of the inputs of "human capital," he is led to a dissection of this important category. In tracing the trends during the past half-century, he observes that today postelementary enrollments are nearly two-fifths of elementary enrollment, whereas in 1900 they were only about 6 per cent as large. Obviously, the upper levels of schooling are much more costly, and the cost of teachers does not decline with greater volume, as does, for example, the cost of TV sets. He seeks, therefore, to estimate the human effort going into education in relation to the total labor force. Between 1900 and 1956, the share of teachers in the total labor force rose from 1.86 per cent to 2.34 per cent, but the ratio of students beyond elementary school to the numbers in the labor force rose from 3.5 to 16.5 per cent.

Professor Schultz also relates the cost of schooling to national income and the cost of all resources used in education to the value of physical

Summarized from T. W. Schultz, "Education and Economic Growth," *Sixtieth Yearbook of the National Society for the Study of Education*, 1961, with the permission of the author. A detailed economic assessment of the costs of formal education in the United States has been prepared by Professor Schultz, who kindly allowed this part of his study to be summarized here by C. Arnold Anderson. For the full analysis and an explanation of the estimates, the reader is referred to the original article.

capital used in the economy. In 1900, the total costs of elementary education were 58 per cent of all schooling costs, but by 1956 this lowest stage of schooling was accounting for only 27 per cent of total costs. Meanwhile, over this same period, educational costs rose from 2.9 to 10.3 per cent of total consumer incomes. The population was spending a larger share of its income flow upon education, and to an increasing extent this spending was going to the more advanced levels of schooling.

In order to grasp the full implications of this picture of educational investment, it is helpful briefly to consider the items that make up the costs. A major cost is "foregone earnings," i.e., what students might have earned at going rates of pay if they had not chosen to attend school. He assumes that for elementary pupils this item is negligible. For high-school students in 1956, it is estimated that their foregone earnings for four years total $3,408, as against direct school costs paid by those who finance the public or private secondary schools of only $2,272. For four years of college, the corresponding sums were $7,788 and $5,412; and for three years of graduate or professional study, they totalled $5,841 and $4,059.

But it is necessary also to take account of the growing numbers of Americans who have been attending school. Although it is difficult to measure the improved quality of a year of schooling today compared to 1900, it is possible to allow for the increase in number of days of school per year and the increased number of years attended by the average person. This "equivalent school years" measure—using 1940 as the base year—shows that the average member of the labor force in 1900 had 4.14 years, while in 1957 the typical laborer had 10.45 years. Only a sixth of this schooling was obtained beyond the elementary level in 1900, while in 1957 three-tenths of it was.

Using the cost estimates, Professor Schultz put a price on a typical year of schooling in 1900 and 1956. He then totalled the whole investment made in this way in "human capital." In 1900, the whole population aged 14 and more carried around in its persons an investment of $114 billion; and in 1957, $848 billion (both in 1956 prices). For individuals who belong to the labor force alone, the totals were $63 billion and $535 billion. The value of physical capital for the same two years was $282 billion and $1,270 billion, respectively. Hence, in 1900, the human-capital value of the labor force was 22 per cent of all productive capital, but in 1957 it had risen to 42 per cent of the total. Training, or investment in human resources by education, is clearly becoming a major form of investment in the modern type of economy.

These economic estimates throw fresh light on some of the factors underlying the changes in educational systems, in patterns of selection for education, and upon motives for expansion of school enrollment. They are no less revealing as to the implications of the vast transformation of educational systems in industrialized nations.

It should be pointed out, therefore, that even if no individual gained any private benefit in terms of income from his education above what others with less schooling earned (which of course is contrary to fact), society gains from the impact of the improved quality of the labor force upon productivity, however these gains are distributed.

PART II

Education, Social Mobility, and the Labor Market

7   *Occupation and Education*

EDMUND deS. BRUNNER
and SLOAN WAYLAND

IT IS WELL ESTABLISHED that educational attainment is related to the type of work in which people engage and conversely, that for an increasing number of occupations initial entry is limited to those who have attained a given level of education. The days when a high school graduate could "read" law or medicine with a successful practitioner of these professions and eventually qualify as a lawyer or doctor are over. In five of the 13 major occupational groupings derived from the 1950 Census classification, above average educational status is either required or preferred.[1]

One result of this and perhaps other trends has been a rapid upgrading of the educational status of the American labor force to a degree perhaps little realized. In 1940 males 18 to 64 years of age in the labor force had a median educational attainment of 9.3 years of school. In 1957, according to a Census Bureau survey this had risen to 11.8 years. For females the comparable figures were 10.2 and 12.2 years.[2] In other words the gain in years of schooling among American workers was more rapid than that of the adult population as a whole, which went from 8.6 to 10.3 years for males and 8.7 to 10.9 years for females in the same period. This is perhaps a unique situation. One would expect the education of a nation's labor force to conform to that of the population of which it was a part, especially among males since approximately four-fifth of all adults of this sex are employed.[3]

Education and Unemployment

This raises a question as to whether those in the labor force but unemployed are less well educated than those holding jobs. This was amply demonstrated during the Great Depression but in times of close to full employment may not be the case. In periods of labor scarcity arbitrarily set educational standards might be relaxed as has happened in a number of states with respect to the recruitment of teachers.

From the point of view of answering this question the 1950 Census was

Reprinted from Edmund deS. Brunner and Sloan Wayland, "Occupation, Labor Force Status and Education," *Journal of Educational Sociology,* Vol. XXXII (1958), No. 1, with the permission of the editor.

taken at a fortunate time. About three million persons, 4.8 percent of the labor force were unemployed. This is a large enough number to warrant examination of the association between the unemployed status of this group and their education. There is a positive association.

The findings may be summarized as follows:

1. For any given age level, the median level of educational attainment for the employed is higher than for the unemployed.

2. The difference in educational attainment between the employed and unemployed diminishes as age increases. It is from 1.5 to 2.3 years below age 45; less than one year over that age.

3. The difference in educational attainment between the employed and unemployed is very similar for males and females. Since the educational level of women for any given age level is higher for females, the educational level for unemployed females is almost as high as that of the employed males.

4. For the non-white males, some of the relationships noted above do not obtain. Below 45 years of age, the unemployed non-white had a higher median level of education than the employed. This appears to be a function of the situation in the South. It can be hypothesized that the social structure in this region did not have available for non-whites as many positions requiring above average educational attainment as there were non-whites to fill them, and that some of this group were unwilling to take jobs in which their education would be little utilized. For the non-white female, the employed had a higher median level of education but the difference in education between employed and unemployed was only one half as large as for the total population.

5. Within any particular age group as well as for all persons 25 years old and above, the percentage of the labor force unemployed declined as the educational level increased. The one major exception to this relationship was found in the non-white group where those in the middle education levels experienced higher unemployment than those with low or high education.

Participation or non-participation in the labor force is the result of the interplay of a number of factors of which education is clearly an important one. Especially for women, since far smaller proportions than men are employed, education is a selective factor.

For women marital status is an important determinant of labor force status but regardless of such status for all ages the higher the level of educational attainment, the higher the proportions in the labor force. The increases in these proportions as educational attainment rises is however greater for the unmarried, including widows and divorced, than for married.

College education was a more significant factor in influencing labor force participation for the married than the unmarried. Among the unmarried women, the college graduates participated at only a slightly higher rate than high school graduates. Among the married, the college graduates were in the labor force at a substantially higher rate than the high school graduates, although the high school graduates participated at only a slightly higher rate than eighth-grade or less-than-fifth-grade graduates.

For both the married and unmarried females, the percentage in the labor force increased from the lower age levels to a peak at the 35–44 age level and then declined. This characterized the women at each of the various levels of educational attainment with relatively few exceptions. White high school graduates participated at a higher rate after graduation, and then at a declining rate among the unmarried. Among the married, the rate declined until the age level 35–44, and then increased through age 55.

The strength of the factor of marital status on labor force participation as compared with age and educational status is shown most clearly by the relative levels at which the two marital status groups were available for employment. At most age levels, and particularly over 35 years of age, the highest labor force rate for the married women (college graduates) was near the level of the lowest labor force rate of the non-married (under five years of school).

In general, non-white females conformed to the pattern of relationships described above but for each age and educational level the percentage of non-white women in the labor force is higher than that of the total female population especially among college graduates. For instance, for this group almost six out of eight, 72.2 percent non-white married women 35–44 years of age who were college graduates were in the labor force, as compared with three out of eight for the total females in this category.

Occupational Status and Education

In general the educational status of the major occupational groups is what would be expected, though combining the hundreds of categories used by the Census inevitably conceals some differences. For instance among the 56 occupations in the "Professional, technical and kindred" worker groups, five of the occupations with 50,000 or more persons involved had medians of less than 15 years of schooling; 23 fell in the category of 16 or more.

In Table 1 the median years of school completed by the employed labor force for each major occupational grouping and for color and regional groups is given. This has been arranged in the rank order for median year of school completed for all males.

In general professional and technical workers were at the top, followed

Table 1.

Median Years of School Completed by Males by Major Occupational Grouping by Regions: 1950

Occupational Grouping	U.S. Total	North & West	South	Total Non-white	Southern Non-white
Professional, technical and kindred workers	16 plus	16 plus	16 plus	15.9	16 plus
Sales workers	12.3	12.4	12.1	9.4	8.0
Managers, officials, and proprietors except farm	12.2	12.2	12.0	8.4	7.4
Clerical and kindred workers	12.2	12.2	12.2	12.0	11.0
Craftsmen, foremen and kindred workers	9.3	9.5	8.8	7.8	6.5
Operatives and kindred workers	8.7	8.9	7.9	7.1	6.0
Service workers except private household workers	8.7	8.8	8.2	8.0	7.1
Farmers and farm managers	8.3	8.6	6.8	4.1	4.1
Private household workers	8.1	8.5	6.4	7.0	6.1
Laborers except farm and mine	8.0	8.4	6.0	6.0	5.2
Farm laborers, unpaid family workers	7.9	8.4	6.3	4.5	4.4
Farm laborers except unpaid and farm foremen	7.1	8.3	4.9	4.0	3.8

by white collar workers, blue collar workers, farmers and laborers. This pattern characterized the females as well as the males, although the order within these major categories varied somewhat. The professional and technical occupational group had the most distinctive position. Its median was approximately four years higher than that of the closest group, and in some instances the gap was considerably greater. The gap between the white collar and the blue collar groups was three years or more in most sex and color groups. The differences between the other major occupational groups were not very great. The rank orders for sex and color groups were roughly similar.

For two occupational groups—professional and clerical workers—the median school year completed varies very little for different sex, color, and regional groups. The greatest deviation came among the non-white workers other than those in professional or clerical occupations. Similarly, the non-white workers in agriculture are considerably lower than the white in both the South and the non-South. The occupation group, farm laborers, excluding unpaid family laborers and farm foremen, was consistently at the bottom of each sex, color and regional category even though the median years completed ranged from 3.8 years for non-white southern males to 8.3 years for all males in North and West.

It is interesting also to note that the educational status of sales, clerical and kindred workers in 1950 was slightly higher than for "manager, officials and proprietors." This is almost certainly a function of age since the former group tend to be recruited from the younger, better educated members of the labor force.

Table 2.

Median Years of School Completed by Females

Occupational Grouping	U.S. Total	North & West	South	Total Non-white	Southern Non-White
Professional, technical and kindred workers	15.8	15.6	16 plus	16 plus	16 plus
Sales workers	11.6	11.8	11.1	10.3	9.1
Managers, officials and proprietors except farm	12.1	12.1	11.6	8.6	8.0
Clerical and kindred workers	12.4	12.4	12.5	12.6	12.6
Craftsmen, foremen, and kindred workers	9.9	9.9	10.0	8.9	8.5
Operatives and kindred workers	8.7	8.8	8.3	8.4	7.3
Service workers except private household workers	9.1	9.3	8.8	8.4	7.8
Farmers and farm managers	8.1	8.8	6.4	4.8	4.7
Private household workers	7.9	8.5	6.5	7.0	6.4
Laborers except farm and mine	8.6	8.8	7.6	7.6	6.3
Farm laborers, unpaid family workers	8.4	8.8	6.8	5.7	5.6
Farm laborers except unpaid and farm foremen	6.5	8.7	5.1	4.8	4.6

Age, Occupation, and Education

Several difficulties arise in the analysis of the impact of age on the relationships between education and occupational status. (1) The general level of education has risen over the period of time represented by the current labor force. (2) Education of a type not recorded in the Census, such as industrial training and commercial and vocational courses, may have served the same function for some occupations as education in schools and colleges for other occupations. (3) The variety of occupations within the major occupational groupings may be age selective in such a way that the variation in age and education within a major occupational group may reflect to some degree variation among specific occupations. (4) Changes in the educational level of a major occupational group may not represent a change in the educational level required, but rather an effort on the part of employers to establish a higher level of education as a precondition of employment. For example, a high school education may be required in 1950 for employment in a type of work for which an elementary education was required in an earlier generation, even though the technical level of skill required may not be greatly different. In a sense the relationships between age, education, and occupation described below are probably a resultant of the interplay of these elements.

For the total male population in the employed labor force, the educational attainment level as measured by the median year of school completed declined from 12.0 for the 25–29 age group to 8.4 for the 55–64 age group. This difference of 3.6 years was greater than any major occupational group considered separately. For the professional, technical, and kindred workers group, the median was more than 4 years of college for each age group, and for farmers, sales workers, and private household workers, the young and the old age groups differed by about one year. Only for the craftsmen and service workers were the differences between the young and old workers as much as three years.

For each major occupational group, except the professional workers, the older the worker, the lower the educational median in every sex, color, and regional category, even though in some instances the differences were not very great for different age levels. The increased educational level of the male population over time is not only seen in the higher educational levels in the younger age levels in each major occupational group, but also in the increased proportions of the labor force in the occupations with higher educational levels. During the decade from 1940 to 1950, the male civilian employed labor force increased by 20.1 percent. All of the first seven occupation groups in terms of educational attainment except sales workers increased more than the total rate of increase and of the bottom five occupational groups, four experienced decline of from 16.0 to 35.7 percent and one increased by only 9.5 percent. Professional workers increased by 43.1 percent, and the managers, officials, and proprietors group increased by 34.3 percent. During this same decade the median age of all employed workers increased from 38.3 to 39.3 years. For most of the occupational groups with the lower educational medians, the median age of male workers increased more than the national rate, and the median age of the other occupational groups either declined or increased at less than the national rate.

In the discussion following, the 12 major occupational groups are combined into four categories which are referred to as types of occupational groups. The basis of the classification is a combination of educational characteristics and type of activity involved in the occupations. Since the professional, technical, and kindred workers have a distinctive educational pattern and distinctive occupational status, this major occupational group is considered as a separate type and will be referred to as professional occupations. The second type includes the managers, officials and proprietors; clerical and kindred workers; and sales workers. This group will be referred to as the white collar occupational type. The third type will be referred to as non-farm manual workers and includes skilled and semi-skilled and unskilled workers, as well as private household and other service workers. The fourth type is the series of farming occupations including operators as well as laborers.

Any such classification will bring together some disparate elements. However, this classification is being used primarily for consideration of the factor of age and as will be seen below, seems to be fruitful for that purpose.

Another way to look at the relationship between age, occupation, and education is to compare the type of occupations into which persons go with different educational attainment for the various age levels. For college graduates, the occupational distribution did not vary greatly for different age levels with approximately nine out of ten working in professional and white collar occupations at all age levels. At the other extreme, for those with less than 5 years of education, approximately nine out of ten were in the non-farm manual and farm occupations.

For the middle educational levels, 8 and 12 years of school, the variations by age were not significant for the professional and farming occupations. However, for the white collar and the non-farm manual occupational types, there was a marked shift in the proportions in the different age levels. Among persons with 8 years of school in the 25–29 age level there was one white collar to eight non-farm manual workers as compared with more than one white collar to three non-farm manual workers in the 55–64 age level. For the 12 year graduates the corresponding ratios were one to two for the 25–29 age level and four to three for the 55–64 age level. Since the big increases in relative numbers within the white collar group is in the managers, officials, and proprietor occupations, it would seem that over the life cycle, a portion of workers are moving from the non-farm manual occupations to the white collar occupations with a much greater shift among those with 12 years of schooling than for the 8th year graduates.

The similarities and differences by regions for males will now be examined. As indicated earlier, the median years of school completed for the white collar and professional occupations in the South and in the North and West do not vary greatly. The non-farm manual and the farming occupations in the South are characterized by lower medians and in the North and West by higher medians than the national medians. This relationship between the regions for the total male population characterizes the different age levels as well. In fact the differences between the medians for the South, and for the North and West for the 25–29 age level are larger for several of the major occupational groups than for the 55–64 age level. This is probably a function of two factors: (1) The gains made in the South over a period of time have been more than matched by gains in the non-South, and (2) selective migration has drained out of the South many of its better educated so that the non-South figure is only partly due to the educational advances in that region. For the South the difference in the median number of years of school completed between the 25–29 age level and the 55–64 age level was 2.3 years (7.7 and 10.0) and in the non-South 3.7 years (8.5 and 12.2).

The relationships observed earlier for all males between selected educational levels and basic types of occupations for different ages characterize the males in the two regions with few exceptions. The distribution of college graduates is very similar in the South and the non-South. Among those with less than 5 years of school, fewer are in farm occupations and more in white collar occupations in the North and West than in the South. The relative importance of non-farm manual occupations decreased, and the white collar occupations increased at both 8 and 12 year educational levels with increases in the ages of workers. The rate of change seems to have been somewhat larger in the South than in the North and West.

Non-White Males

The non-white occupational patterns differed from the white in several significant ways. Although the median number of years of school completed for non-white males 25 and over in the labor force was only 6.6 years as compared with 9.5 for the total male population, the medians for non-white professional and for clerical workers were only slightly below the medians for these occupations in the total male labor force. For other major occupational groups, the differences was much greater. For southern non-white males who make up two-thirds of the total non-whites, the median for each occupational group was lower than the median for the total non-white males except for the professional occupations.

Service workers among the non-whites had a higher educational level than craftsmen and operatives in contrast to the pattern for total males. For managers, officials, and proprietors, the educational level for the non-white was substantially lower than the United States total—8.4 to 12.2 years. The educational levels of farmers and farm laborers were only one-half as high as for the total male population. The lower educational level of non-white workers in the major occupational groupings is closely related to the high concentration of the non-white workers in particular kinds of occupations within the major occupational groupings. For example, in the managers, officials, and proprietors group, two out of three were self-employed in such enterprises as retail trade and eating and drinking places, whereas for this entire group only about one-half were in such enterprises. The median incomes for all types of self-employed are substantially lower than for other types of occupations in this broad occupational group, indicating that the enterprises are likely small in size and may be entered by persons of below average education.

Similarly, in the craftsmen, foremen, and kindred workers, and in the operatives and kindred worker groups, relatively few are in the occupations above the median income level for that group, and a large proportion are in the occupations which had median incomes below the median for that group. The educational level of non-whites in the same occupations is therefore not as different as might appear when the related occupations are classified into major occupational groups.

However, in spite of the factors listed, the difference in the median years of school for all males in the labor force and the non-whites (2.9 years) is greater than the difference between these two categories for each major occupational group except for the manager group and the various farm occupations. This indicates that the occupational groups are selective educationally for non-white as well as white. With the movement out of agriculture of many who are the least well educated, it seems important to determine the extent to which upward mobility occupationally is restricted by the lack of education as well as by color.

The examination of the educational characteristics of the non-white by age for major occupational groups reveals examples of both rapid and slow change. (1) The gap in educational attainment between the total and the non-white is greater for the 25–29 year group than for those 55–64—3.9 and 3.3 respectively. While the *percentage* gain of the non-whites —5.1 to 8.1 years—is greater between 25–29 and 55–64, the magnitude of the gain for the total population of this age span—8.4 to 12.0—is such that the non-white group is still at a major disadvantage in an occupational market which is educationally selective.

(2) In the professional and clerical occupations, the non-white workers in the 25–29 age group are very similar to the total workers in their levels of educational attainment. In the managers, officials, and proprietors, and in the sales occupations, the non-white workers are rapidly approaching the level of all workers. In the laborers, except farm and mine, and private household occupations, the differences are diminishing, but in the other occupational groups the differences are still substantial.

Since two-thirds of the non-white workers were in the South, the non-white data for the South and for the United States are similar in most parts. This is particularly true for the professions where essentially national standards apply; for clerical occupations; and for the farm occupations since very few non-white farmers are found outside of the South. For the other occupational groups, the southern non-white educational attainment medians are somewhat lower.

However, the lower southern rates do not account for the lower rates for all non-white. In the youngest age level—25–29—the difference in occupational status by education in the North and West is manifested at each educational level. Among college graduates twice as high a proportion of the non-white were in the non-farm manual occupations—20.9 percent to 10.0 percent. For the high school graduates, almost three out of four (73.5 percent) of the non-white workers were in non-farm manual occupations as compared with less than three out of five (58.0 percent) for all workers.

In this examination of the distribution of all male workers for selected educational levels and selected ages, it was shown that the distribution of college graduates and functional illiterates did not vary much for different age levels, and that the professional and farm occupations tended to hold their relative proportions of each educational level for the different age levels. For the non-white segment of the total, this pattern is also present. However, in the total male labor force there was a marked shift from non-farm manual to white collar in the same educational level as the age increased. While there is some slight change of this in the non-white male labor force, the magnitude of the change is very small as compared with the total male labor force. This lack of mobility is of even greater significance when seen in connection with the data presented above on the initially lower point of entrance into the labor force for the 8th and 12th grade non-white graduate. That is, he comes into the occupational market at a lower position and apparently has not moved up as rapidly as his white peers.

This pattern characterizes also the relationship in the two regions with the following exceptions: a substantially higher proportion of the college graduates at each level are in the professions in the South than in the North and West. For the 25–29 age level 70.6 percent of the college graduates in the South were in the professions as compared with only 52.1 percent in the North and West. For the lower educational levels the workers are split between farming and non-farm manual occupations in the South, but are highly concentrated in the latter occupations in the North and West.

Females in the Labor Force

As was shown in the section above on labor force and education, females in the labor force as a group have a much higher educational attainment level than males (11.3 to 9.5 years). Not only do females in and out of the labor force have a higher educational level, but also participation in the labor force is educationally selective in favor of those with more education. However, when the females are classified by major occupational groupings, this favorable position is seen as largely related to the types of occupations in which women engage. In six of the major occupational groups, males had a higher median number of years completed, in five females were higher, and in one they were the same. In all occupational groups the differences by sex were relatively small.

A somewhat different rank order of the major occupational groups by median educational level exists for females. After the professions, the second highest was the clerical and kindred workers, followed by managers, officials and proprietors, and then by sales workers. In comparison with the male workers, the service workers had a higher median than operatives, and private household workers dropped to a position just above farm laborers. This rank order characterized the regions and color groups except for a shift of the farming occupations to the bottom for the non-white segment of the female labor force.

Close to four out ten (39.6 percent) of the females were in the two major occupational groups ranking one and two in median years of school completed, and over one-half (52.4 percent) were in the top four groups. For males, the corresponding figure was three out of ten (30.8 percent) for these top four occupational groups. Between 1940 and 1950 the percent of all females in these four occupational groups increased from 45.4 percent to the 52.4 percent cited above, whereas the large increases in females in the labor force since 1950, and the educationally selective characteristics identified earlier, the favorable position of females has probably been extended.

Age and Occupational Status

For females in the labor force, the median year of school completed was 3.4 years higher for those in the age group 25–64 than for those 55–64. Among the major occupation groups, the difference was less than one year in five of the twelve, and over three years in only one case. The educational levels for females were much more homogeneous for the different ages than for males. The range among female clerical workers for the United States, and for the two regions for the different age levels was from 12.1 to 12.6.

The regional patterns were similar to the national pattern with several exceptions. The professional workers in the South had a higher educational attainment level than the North and West. Below the white collar level, the South had consistently lower medians for each age level in each major occupational group. This difference was greatest in the farming occupations, and in private household occupations.

Another way of looking at the relationship of age to occupation and education is the examination of the types of occupation engaged in by persons at specified educational levels. Among the female functional illiterates, for the United States, approximately three out of four worked in non-farm manual occupations, and one-half of the others worked in farming occupations. This did not vary greatly by age although there was a slight increase in this proportion in the non-farm manual occupations at the older ages, and a decline in the proportion in the farming occupations. At the other end, seven out of ten of the college graduates were in the professions, and this held constant for the different ages. This is a considerably higher proportion than the males, more of whom went into managerial and proprietary occupations. In the earlier analysis it was shown that the proportion in the non-farm manual occupations for a given educational level tended to decline with age, and the proportions in non-professional white collar occupations tended to increase. However, this was true among females only for the 8th grade graduate, and the rate of increase was not as great as for males. This would suggest that the movement to higher status occupations is not as open for females as for males, although the entrance level is in general at a higher point.

The relationships described above characterize the two regions as well as the nation with two exceptions. (1) Among the eighth grade graduates in the South, the rate of decline in non-farm manual occupations with increased age and the increase in the white collar occupations is much greater than in the North and West, and is of the same order as the male shifts. (2) Functional illiterates in the North and West are found to a greater degree (24.1 percent at the 25–29 age level) in the white collar occupations than in the South (5.4 percent). The farming occupations in the South attract those who do not work as non-farm manual workers.

Non-White Females

The major proportion of the female non-white population in the labor force is found in the operative, service, and household worker occupations. However, those in the professions and in clerical work had higher levels of educational attainment than the total female population in these occupations.

In the three farming occupations the non-white females were considerably below all females in those occupations, but in the three major occupational groups in which most of the non-white females were found, the educational level of non-white and total females were not greatly different, particularly at the younger ages.

The higher proportion of college graduates who enter the professions, noted in the data on all females, is even higher for the non-white females. For the 25–29 group, over three out of four (76.1 percent) were in this category, and a roughly similar proportion was found at the other age levels. Of the high school graduates, few were in the professional and white collar occupations, and three out of four entered the non-farm manual occupations. The proportion of 8th and 12th grade graduates who were in this occupational category did not change significantly in the upper age levels. However, the proportion of high school graduates in the white collar occupations was twice as large for the 25–29 age level as for the 55–64 age level. This might be interpreted as increasing opportunity for the non-white female who has graduated recently in the white collar occupations. Unfortunately, the size of the sample used by the Census did not provide enough cases for reliable percentages for many of the age categories for the regions, and the testing of this relationship is thus not possible. It appears, however, that the patterns in the two regions are very similar to the national picture with the following exception: Over four out of five female non-white college graduates in the South enter the professions, but a smaller proportion of high school graduates enter the white collar occupations.

NOTES

1. Lawrence G. Thomas, *The Occupational Structure and Education,* Englewood Cliffs, New Jersey, Prentice-Hall, 1956. p. 400.

2. Bureau of the Census, *Educational Attainment of Workers: March 1957,* Washington, Bureau of the Census, Series P-50 No. 78—November 1957.

3. There is of course a small measure of incomparability in these data in that the figures for the total population includes those 65 years of age and over and this group has had less education in comparison especially with those under 40 years of age. On the other hand among the 18 to 24 year old cohort those not in the labor force are presumably still in school or college and probably have a higher educational level than those of the same ages who are employed or seeking work.

8   *Education and National Efficiency in the U.S.A.*

ELI GINZBURG

ABOUT TWO YEARS AGO, when the National Manpower Council was engaged in its study of skilled manpower, its staff called a conference of leading American educators to explore the interrelations between secondary education and the way in which young people prepare for work and life. The staff hoped to learn from the educators what, in their opinion, had been the contribution of the schools to the economic progress of the country and how this contribution could be enhanced.

It was a disappointing conference, for the educators were not inclined to move from broad claims to detailed proofs of the ways in which an expanding educational system had contributed to the economy and welfare of society. One participant argued that the subject did not warrant exploration since it was self-evident that the prosperity of the nation was directly dependent upon the American educational system. In support, he pointed out that the expansion of the economy had coincided with the expansion of education.

The purpose of this paper is to probe more deeply into the connexions, past and present, between America's high level of economic productivity and her great and highly diversified educational system. The scale of this system is suggested by the fact that the teaching personnel in elementary and secondary schools numbers over one and a quarter million, and that there are more than eighteen hundred institutions of higher learning in the country, with a total faculty of approximately a quarter of a million. Two additional facts may help to reinforce this picture. In the fall of 1950 there were five and a half million pupils between the ages of 16 and 22 enrolled in all schools, representing 37 per cent of the total population in this age-group. In terms of expenditure, the educational effort of the country amounts to over 11 billion dollars.

It would be difficult to gainsay the conclusions dictated by this data—that Americans are currently investing very substantial resources in the maintenance and operation of a far-reaching educational system. However, impressive though these figures may be, alone they do not make very clear

Reprinted from Eli Ginzburg, "Education and National Efficiency: The United States," *The Yearbook of Education, 1956* (London: Evans Brothers Ltd.; Tarrytown, N.Y., World Book Co., 1956), chap. iii, with the permission of the author and the publishers.

the particular contributions that education has been making to national efficiency. To explore the extent and limits of these contributions, it is necessary, first, to identify some of the outstanding characteristics of the American economy; next, to make explicit the salient features of the American educational effort; and then to study the relationship between the two. Since both the American economy and the American educational system are constantly in a state of flux, it will also be helpful to point to the major directions of likely change. And, finally, it would be well to sort out that part of the American experience which is unique and those lessons which may be transferable—in whole or in part—to other countries, whether industrial or non-industrial, that are struggling to raise the productivity of their economies.

The economist faces a difficult task when he seeks to select for special emphasis a few of the welter of factors responsible for the shape and functioning of the American economy. There is the danger—in fact, the certainty—that by restricting himself to a limited number of factors he will fail to provide himself with an adequate base for interpreting accurately such a highly specialized and productive economy. However, such a selective procedure is permissible when the reader is forewarned that the facets selected represent characteristic and essential elements, and that the author does not pretend to take in all that are of stategic importance. With this warning, three important aspects of the American economy may be briefly considered: the extent to which that economy is driven by the money-making propensities of large numbers of the society; secondly, the extent to which almost the entire society is willing to accept and adjust to change; and, finally, the strong motive power exercised by the prevailing belief in equality—that is, that men should be judged by what they do, not by who their parents were.

The Money-Making Propensity

Without seeking to explain why so many Americans are deeply concerned with the making of money and more money (the simplest explanation might be that the American scene has been unique in terms of the opportunities it has offered people to make money), it would be difficult to deny the potency of this drive and the contribution that it makes to keeping the American economy highly dynamic. Of course, as the distinguished American economist, Frank H. Knight, pointed out many years ago, making money is not only work geared to improving the consumption levels of the individual and his family, but has become in the United States a sort of a game that preempts a man's leisure time as well as his working hours. It is not accidental that much American business is transacted round the luncheon-table, at cocktail bars, and on the golf links.

There is probably no other country in the world where the sons of middle-class and even wealthy parents are so encouraged early in childhood to engage in activities the end of which is the making of money. Here is seen the early and heavy indoctrination with respect to money-making activities. At the some time the extent to which these activities are turned into a game should be noticed. Every society must make a selection among the values it stresses. No society can be equally distinguished in all respects. Economic expansion and the increase of personal and national wealth are unquestionably at the forefront of American life, and have been from the earliest days of colonial settlement. There may come a point in American development when significant re-adjustments will take place, but as yet there is no evidence of this. Men give up the highest positions in government to enter or return to money-making activities. Talented young people turn their backs on academic careers in order to carve out successful niches for themselves in the world of business and so on.

The Value Placed on Change

The progress of a modern economy depends in very large measure on the rate at which improvements in technology take place and, equally important, on the speed with which these improvements are assimilated. An outstanding characteristic of American life is the high value placed upon change, in contrast to the value that other societies place upon custom and tradition. In the major industries of the country, labour has long been willing to accept technological changes, subject only to getting its share of the increases in profit due to increases in productivity. The American consumer is constantly on the look-out for new and improved products and places great faith in even the most modest changes in style or performance To Americans, last year's car is an old car; a house constructed five years ago is an old house.

Another aspect of the American attitude towards change is reflected in the mobility of the population. Millions of people are constantly on the move. Year after year the South sees much of its surplus rural population leave for the major manufacturing cities of the North and, more recently, for the expanding far west. There have also been sizeable movements, although somewhat less spectacular, in the other regions of the country, from rural to urban communities and from one urban community to the next. A new plant located in one of the south-eastern states will find, on the day that it begins hiring, applicants who have come from a distance of a thousand miles. In short, we can see, then, that the employer with a new and improved process need not fear that his labour will refuse to accept it. The manufacturer with a new product need not fear that the public will turn it down simply because it is new; its very newness will give him an edge over competitors. It would be hard to exaggerate the contribution that this cultural desire for the new, this pervasive social acceptance of change, makes to the vitality of the economy.

The Concept of Equality

A third characteristic of the American economy that has contributed greatly to its continuing vitality is summarized by the concept of equality. Americans proceed on the assumption that what some men have done others can do; that success is the result of a combination of brains, initiative, hard work, and luck; and that there is no need to respect a man only because of the accomplishments of his father or his grandfather. The doctrine that a man can be whatever he wants to be if is willing to strive has gone far to unleash the potential that is locked up in many men born into modest circumstances. The ideal of the self-made man, the son of immigrant parents who moves to the top, has substantial validity in a country where literally thousands and tens of thousands of children born into modest, or even poverty-stricken, homes have made their way up the ladder.

Quite another aspect of this doctrine that every man can be as good as any other is reflected in the consumption patterns of the population. With the exception of a few luxuries, there are no items purchased only by a particular class. America is the land of the mass market. The aspiration of the American working man is to provide for his family as many of the good things of life as his employer is able to provide for his family. Automobiles, radios, television sets, college education—all of these and other good things are good not only for the minority, but for all. Much of American prosperity in recent years is the result of the constant growth in demand by the population as a whole for all kinds of consumer goods, consumer durables, and, not least important, for private housing.

There is a further aspect of this equalitarian doctrine which warrants consideration. The family corporation has been replaced in the United States by the public corporation to the extent that nearly every large enterprise in the country is managed by individuals who do not own it. Management is becoming increasingly professionalized, and the decisions of management more and more rationalized. Consequently, no decisions play a larger part in the efficiency of American business than the selection and development of key personnel. Although it would be foolish to argue that all nepotism has been eliminated, or that favouritism and personal factors play no role, it can be said that the personnel practices of large corporations are becoming increasingly objective. This means that a man can anticipate being rewarded and promoted according to his performance. He need not fear that his family or the schools which he attended will limit his progress.

Educational Opportunity and Vocationalism

The first, and undoubtedly the most outstanding, characteristic of the American educational system is the extent to which public funds have been used to support increasingly extended educational preparation for all young people. Within the last two decades there has been a gain of not less than three years in the amount of formal schooling that the average young person receives prior to entering work. At the present time this schooling averages slightly more than twelve years. The important points to note in this connexion are, first, that the support for this schooling comes from public funds and represents no untoward burden upon the poor, other than the very small contribution which they make through taxes, and, secondly, that the educational process has now been extended to provide on the average for more than the completion of high school. Still another point worth mentioning is the extent to which there has been no sex discrimination in the development of American education. Ever since 1870 the number of girls graduating from high school has been greater than the number of boys. At the collegiate and post-graduate level it is true that boys have consistently outnumbered girls, but the gap between the two has been substantially narrowed within recent decades.

The American educational structure has been characterized by a pronounced utilitarianism, in which the responsibility of the schools for preparing individuals for work and life was narrowly and specifically, rather than broadly, defined. The large-scale contributions of the federal government in making grants of land available to the states in the 1860's to facilitate the establishment and expansion of state universities was motivated by the understanding that the embryonic industrial economy of the United States would soon need more engineers and technicians. The importance of vocational education at the high school level was greatly stimulated by shortages of skilled manpower during World War I. Additional evidence of this vocational trend can be found in the great increases in enrollment at the collegiate level in recent decades in such "practical" fields as engineering and business administration. The elaboration of professional schools at university centres is further testimony of the same trend. To-day the larger universities boast schools of journalism, business administration, hospital administration, social work, pharmacy, optometry, and dentistry, as well as the classical triad of law, medicine, and theology.

It is unlikely that up to 25 per cent of the appropriate age-group— in some states it is now as high as 50 per cent—would have entered advanced courses at collegiate or university levels unless such courses had been rather closely geared to preparation for work. There is undoubtedly a close relationship between the vocational orientation of American education and the continued expansion in enrolment.

One of the most striking and perhaps unique features of the American educational system at every level, surely from the secondary level on, has been the difference in quality between institutions and even between departments within the same institution. This reflects the fact that the United States, although a single nation, spans an entire continent, and further reflects that financial support for public education has been exclusively local and by the states. The large variations in wealth and taxing power have been reflected inevitably in the educational systems of the several states and localities. At the collegiate and university level there have been at least three major types of institution: the famous, heavily endowed institutions, few in number but very important in terms of educational leadership; the many state-supported institutions, ranging from outstanding universities to poorly staffed teachers' colleges in states that have been hard-pressed to maintain their position in the expanding economy; and the ubiquitous private smaller colleges, many of which originally were denominational institutions, some well supported and well led, others poorly supported and with little intellectual leadership.

Academic Standards

In the face of the trend to draw ever larger numbers of the population into secondary schools, so that at the present time more than 55 per cent graduate from high school and 25 per cent of the males attend college, it has been next to impossible to maintain rigid standards. Many graduates of the poorer, smaller colleges would have been unable to gain admission to a good college. In turn, many high school graduates from weaker school systems would be unable to match first-year students at strong high schools. The same differences prevail at the upper end of the scale. A Ph.D. degree from one of the weaker universities simply does not represent the same achievements as a Ph.D. degree from a major institution.

Although there are obvious and deep-seated weaknesses in an educational system with this range in standards, there are also some important strengths in the very diversity of the system. Many students who would be unable to gain entrance to a good college are afforded, under this flexible structure, an opportunity not only to enter but to do well at a weaker institution. Many positions in society, even in a society that places as limited value on status and tradition as does the United States, become open to individuals because they have some kind of college degree. Except in the sciences, an individual seeking work is seldom asked what he knows. Emphasis is placed merely upon his satisfactory completion of a required level of education, which often means that he has acquired a bachelor's degree. Moreover, individuals who have been handicapped by inadequate schooling are often able to compensate by an opportunity to continue their education.

Although it is not easy even for a well-endowed student to develop his capacities in the absence of stimulating teachers and a strong curriculum, the fact remains that many are able to do so. Included among the most distinguished American scientists and scholars are a considerable number of men who are graduates of these weaker institutions.

Education and the Economy

We have now considered some major characteristics of the economy and of the American educational system; what connexion and interrelations can be found between the two? More particularly, what can be said about the contribution of the American educational system to the vitality of the American economy? The drive for economic aggrandizement which is found among large numbers of the population is of strategic importance for the American economy; the equalitarian bias of the American educational system strongly supports and encourages this underlying goal. Every youngster who comes to school is told not by a single teacher, but by many, that his future will be what he determines to make it. He learns about presidents who came from humble beginnings. The American school must be given major credit for inspiring the youth of each generation with the model of the self-made man. What this means is well illustrated by a table presented by Dael Wolfle in *America's Resources of Specialized Talent,* in which he estimates the distribution of college graduates according to the occupation of their fathers. Of 100 graduates, only about 40 came from the professional, semi-professional, and managerial classes, while the fathers of the remaining 60 are lower in the socio-economic scale: half are skilled, unskilled, or factory workers; the other half, farmers and clerical and related workers.

It is not necessary to believe that the constant prolongation of education is pure gain, to recognize that there are many advantages in a situation where young people are permitted to find themselves late in their adolescence rather than in a situation of having their life determined for them by their educational accomplishments when they are 10 or 11. My associates and I have shown in our study of occupational choice (*Occupational Choice, An Aproach to a General Theory*) the serious handicaps under which the children of the poor grow up because they leave school before they have reached the emotional and intellectual maturity that enables them to choose their occupations wisely and to prepare themselves in accordance with their choices. At present, young people in certain states can secure their working papers at the age of 14, although 15 or 16 is typical. But it is important to note that the concept of public education is being stretched in the richest states, such as California and New York, to include fourteen years of free education for all. This means that a young person need not make any serious decisions about an occupation until he is 18. In California there is strong pressure to remove all vocational education from the high schools and re-locate it in the junior colleges. This would mean that a young person would not commit himself until his nineteenth year.

The most obvious and direct connexion between the sizeable and constantly expanding American investment in education and the economy is reflected in the levels of education and training that young people have completed at the time when they first look for work. In passing, note must be taken of the fact that this training process has been extended further in recent years by the introduction of compulsory military service, which means that young men serve between two and four years and much of this time is devoted to acquiring some sort of specialized skill. One of the most interesting findings of the National Manpower Council's recent study, *A Policy for Skilled Manpower,* was the extent to which large American corporations have shifted their interest over the last generation or two from young people who have completed a vocational course in high school to young people with substantial control over the fundamentals of mathematics, communications and basic science. This attitude of employers has a simple explanation. They are interested in young people who have acquired a sound foundation; they are willing to undertake the specific skill instruction. It is possible to discount to a considerable extent the official statements of American industry about its serious predicament resulting from the fact that too few young men are graduating in engineering and in the sciences and that a still smaller number are becoming available immediately because of their military service obligations. Yet, there is no denying that American industry around the turn of the century employed one engineer for every 255 workers in manufacturing, mining, construction, transportation, and public utilities; twenty years later the ratio was much higher: it was one for every 78 workers; the most recent data, for 1950, show that industry employs one engineer for every 62 workers. The absorption by American industry of these large numbers of egineers is only one outstanding illustration of the general trend constantly to enlarge the number of staff personnel.

Deficiencies

Significant as the contributions of American education to the expansion of the American economy have been, it would be a serious misreading of the facts to omit to say that this contribution has fallen seriously short in several respects. One of the most striking shortcomings is the extent to which individuals with good intellectual potential are not educated and trained, despite the great public and private investment in education. In the most able sector of the population, not more than one out of every two young persons completes college. Although every young man or woman with the intellectual potential need not necessarily go to college to ensure his own personal development or his place in the economy and the society, the fact that so large a percentage fails to receive advanced training is of major concern to an increasingly large number of Americans. This concern is the deeper because, on the one hand, people have come to recognize the extent to which the progress of the economy and the security of the nation depend upon the development of its brainpower and, on the other, because it runs counter to American principles to admit that in many cases the barrier which prevents young people from going on with their education is financial. Because of the deep belief in the right of every individual to develop his potentialities to the full, the fact that so many are unable to do so because of straitened economic circumstances of their parents is a challenge that will not long remain unanswered.

Other weaknesses that cannot easily be rectified have developed in the secondary school system. Having turned the high school into a common school, the educators have had to develop all types of curricula in order to meet the varying intellectual, emotional, and vocational needs of the vastly expanded student body. In responding to these democratic pressures, many compromises and adjustments have been made which have not necessarily resulted in a sound educational foundation. It is not easy to generalize about any facet of American education because of its great variability. However, many well-informed observers have reached the conclusion that secondary schools need strengthening, and by this they usually mean two things: first, that more stress should be placed upon instruction in mathematics, language, and science; and secondly, that to ensure that students profit from such instruction it is definitely necessary to strengthen the teaching staffs. This, they believe, can be accomplished only if the salaries of teachers and the conditions under which they work are vastly improved. Because of the striking increases in enrolments that loom on the horizon as a result of the much increased birth-rate of the 1940's, this challenge is even more formidable.

World War II revealed one of the more serious consequences of primary and secondary education being originally the responsibility of localities and, now, to a great extent, the states. The well-to-do and highly industrialized regions of the nation suddenly realized that conditions in backward economic areas, such as the south-east and the south-west, had produced substantial numbers of young adults who were either totally illiterate or so poorly educated that the military forces, even during a major emergency, did not accept them for service. As Dr. Bray and I have shown in our book, *The Uneducated*, there is a close relationship between *per capita* income, expenditures for education, and illiteracy rates. Although the over-all problem is complicated in the south-east by the heavy concentration of Negroes, whose schooling has long lagged behind that of the white population, the roots of the problem go deeper. The population of the southeastern states is prolific—the rural South has by far the highest birth-rates in the country, it has lagged far behind most other regions in industrialization, and it has far smaller revenues available for education.

One of the major issues facing the country that is certain to agitate the public and that may well lead to legislative action relates to the advantages of federal aid to education, the level of such aid, and the conditions under which it should be proffered. Were it not for two extraneous issues— whether federal funds should be available to parochial schools and, secondly, whether the granting of federal funds should be made contingent on the introduction of non-segregated practices in the South—there can be little question that substantial federal aid would have been forthcoming long before now. This much is certain; if the legislators can get around these two issues, federal aid of one sort or another will definitely be forthcoming to the states so that they can better cope with the marked rise in enrolments which coincides with a public awareness that education has been less well-nourished than it should have been during the past fifteen years of prosperity.

Within a few years the substantially increased enrolments will press against the facilities available for higher education. A public policy already exists regarding the expansion of state-supported colleges. Recognizing that the major costs of a college education are represented not by tuition but by the cost of living away from home, some of the wealthier and more far-sighted states have moved towards the establishment of junior colleges in communities large enough to provide a student body of reasonable size. At present the junior college can have three distinct objectives. It can represent two years of terminal education beyond high school in liberal arts studies; this type of institution provides half of the usual college course. In other instances it serves as a feeder to the larger colleges and universities in the state, thus reducing the living costs of some young people in acquiring bac-calaureates. Thirdly, it is geared to providing a large number of vocationally oriented courses to prepare people more specifically to enter an occupation. Another objective which is likely to develop is that of providing refresher training and education for older women who will be entering or re-entering the labour market at the age of 35 to 40 after their children are no longer a major demand on their time. During the past few years this particular group of married women has represented one of the most important additions to the labour force, and there is every indication that more and more of them will seek employment in the future. It is no easy matter for a junior college to achieve all these objectives simultaneously; yet concentrating on one or two, leaves other community needs unprovided for.

The great strength of American education has been its expansion so that more and more citizens have acquired the appurtenances of learning. Although the United States has been able to develop at every level a small number of outstanding institutions and a considerable number of strong institutions, the system has also encouraged the survival of a very large number of weak institutions. One consequence of the increasing preoccupation of various leadership groups with education has been to create an increasing awareness that quantity and quality are antithetical concepts. Several of the nation's leading colleges have already announced their intention not to expand their facilities and their staffs to any substantial extent to meet the oncoming rush of students. They plan to maintain standards and do the best job they possibly can with a selected number of students. Another facet of this same awareness is the trend among the best engineering colleges to add a fifth year to the curriculum for the purpose of providing the student body with a broader education in the liberal arts and more fundamental grounding in advanced mathematics and physics. (See the National Manpower Council's *A Policy for Scientific and Professional Manpower.*) Still another piece of evidence is the repeated warnings of leading scientists that the present research and development programme is out of balance because it neglects basic research in favour of applied work.

Clearly most Americans do not exactly understand how an improved educational system can contribute to economic welfare and national security. Nevertheless, there is enough understanding of these interrelations to have built up substantial pressure for constructive action to ensure that a larger number of intellectually able people in the community have an opportunity to go on to college and graduate school; to strengthen the teaching staffs and improve the curriculum of secondary education; to provide financial assistance from the federal government to the poorer states so that they can more readily discharge their obligation to provide a reasonable level of public education for all of their citizens; to expand further the educational plant through the establishment of a larger number of junior or community colleges with the objective of providing more and more citizens with fourteen years of basic education; and, finally, to place more stress than heretofore on raising the quality of American education.

In seeking to understand the reasons that lie behind the phenomenal productivity of the American economy, it would be an error to neglect the unique factors in the American scene, factors that derive from the history of the country. The wealth of natural resources available cannot be overemphasized. Freedom from rigid class structures and traditions, though on occasion a serious disability, has proved a great boon as far as the American economy is concerned, because of the encouragement thus given to individuals to develop their full potential.

The educational system must be given substantial credit for the ways in which it has contributed to the reality of the opportunity story. American schools have encouraged the individual to take his future in his own hands and set high aspirations for himself. Furthermore, the ever greater extension of the educational system has increasingly avoided the wastage which takes place when young people must make occupational decisions at too early an age. Young Americans have had the opportunity to mature emotionally and intellectually before they have had to commit themselves. Finally, the ability of large numbers of individuals to receive specialized training within the educational system at no cost at all, or at a very minimal cost, has prepared them to enter many preferred occupations. In short, the school system itself has been a major source of occupational mobility.

The ability of other countries to profit from the American lesson will depend upon the structure of their society, their economic well-being, and the extent to which their present educational system is developed. But every country in the world can profit by establishing the following as criteria for its educational system: that it should contribute as much as possible to the enlargement of personal opportunities, that it should avoid the necessity for premature commitments, and that it should provide at the lowest possible cost specialized training for all who are capable of profiting from it and who desire it.

9 English Secondary Schools and the Supply of Labour

JEAN FLOUD and A. H. HALSEY

SINCE in a modern economy the quality and efficiency of the working population and the degree of vocational and social mobility very largely depend on the educational system, an analysis of its relation to the occupational structure must naturally dominate any discussion of the economic consequences of educational provision or any attempt to assess the effect of education on the national economy. It is our intention in this essay tentatively to explore the nature of this crucial relationship, and to illustrate it by reference to the present position in England.

Education and Occupational Structure

The efficient division of the working population among occupations requires both that there should be the right number of workers in each occupation and that the qualities of workers in each occupation should be as appropriate as possible—in short, that 'ability' and 'opportunity' should be matched as closely as possible. Education affects the efficiency of the distribution of labour by its influence on both 'ability' and 'opportunity'; the skill of labour at various levels reflects the scale and nature of educational provision, which also exercises a decisive influence on vocational choice and on movement between occupations i.e., on the adjustment of the supply to the demand for trained labour. Thus the relationship between the educational system and occupational structure is not a simple one. Moreover, it changes over time.

In the first place, the range of vocational opportunities and consequently the demands of the economy on the educational system are affected by the growth of industrialism. It is a general feature of most European economies that continuous, often accelerating, technical change constantly calls for the development of new occupations and the modification, decline, or obsolescence of old ones. The structure of opportunity is therefore not only

Reprinted from Jean Floud and A. H. Halsey, "English Secondary Schools and the Supply of Labour," *The Yearbook of Education, 1956* (London: Evans Brothers Ltd.; Tarrytown, N.Y.: World Book Co., 1956), Section iv, Ch. 4, with the permission of the author and the publishers.

heterogeneous but also varies according to the stage of development reached by the economy. Thus, for example, the part played by education in occupational and social selection will be much less pronounced in pre-industrial as against advanced-industrial societies, where the selective functions of education tend to predominate. Similarly, while it was reasonable for Marx to observe of the early stages of industrialism that "a general prohibition of child labour," on which compulsory universal education depended, "is incompatible with the existence of large-scale industry,"[1] it can with equal truth be asserted of present-day technological society that such a prohibition is essential to the continuance of the economy.

In the second place, the relationship is extremely complex from the point of view of causation. Thus, while it may be true that during the past fifty years in England "development within secondary education has had to wait upon changes in the social structure,"[2] it would be naïve in the extreme to see the relationship as one of mechanical adaptation of education to the changing needs of the economy. The opposite position would be even more exposed to criticism, though by no means indefensible. For example, changes in educational provision can influence the distribution of income between occupations. Professor Phelps Brown has pointed out that international comparisons suggest that "save where there is immigrant peasant labour, the extension of education goes with a higher ratio of unskilled earnings to skilled," and has argued that the possibilities of further equalization incomes by further advances in educational opportunity are by no means exhausted.[3]

Moreover, in so far as the technical needs of the economy do mould the educational system, the actual pattern of the influence is mediated through ideological interpretations and the clash of interest groups. Thus, the growth of the dissenting academies reflected the unequal sensitivity of different social groups to the changing technological basis of industry; the growth of elementary education 'for workmen and servants' in the nineteenth century not only reflected the need for the development of a literate working class, but also, in the emphasis of its curriculum on docility and pious acceptance of station, the power of the ruling classes; and the contemporary movement towards 'parity of prestige' for the different types of secondary school and towards the adoption of the comprehensive school, though it may be in part a response to changing economic needs, clearly also reflects political ideas.

Thirdly, the relationship between education and occupational structure must be seen in the context of the wider social structure. None of the relevant social institutions are alone and absolute in their effects. The influence through the school of the family, for example, will vary according to social class, according to its situation in town or country, according to its social, geographical, and occupational history, and according to the existence or non-existence of state social services supporting its functions.

Finally, account must be taken of the fact that special conditions may distort the relationship in peculiar ways at particular times. There may be large-scale unemployment, as in most countries in the nineteen-thirties, or full employment, as in England to-day; and obviously the general level of employment affects not only the freedom of choice open to the individual, but also the structure of the labour market itself.

However, we cannot in this essay do justice to the relationship by treating it historically in terms of the changing structure of the economy and the social class system. We must confine ourselves to illustrating the discussion by brief reference to one aspect only of the position in England to-day— namely, the influence of education on vocational choice and the supply of labour. We shall leave aside the less tangible question of the influence of twentieth-century changes in education on the skill of the working population;[4] and we shall not discuss the relation of education to the occupational and social mobility of adult workers.[5]

A Fluid Labour Supply

It is an economic truism that the distribution of labor among occupations cannot, as Professor Hicks has put it, "be left to be settled according to the preferences of producers alone; the desire of consumers must also be taken into account."[6] But the proposition applies with particular force to the economy of the Welfare State. The principle of 'citizenship' requires the greatest possible measure of freedom for every individual to develop his talents and to choose his vocation; but the needs of the economy for persons trained in appropriate numbers to fill posts at various levels of skill and responsibility must also be met. The provision of a basic equality of economic status among all citizens—of a minimum supply of essential goods and services—presupposes full employment and a high level of productivity and consequently an unavoidable degree of economic planning. Thus it is that although the 1944 Education Act embodies the maxim of extreme individualism, that each child shall receive an education suited to his aptitudes and abilities—with no mention of any obligation on the educational authorities to have regard to the needs of the economy for labour of particular kinds—there are, in fact, from time to time official attempts to estimate the need for teachers, doctors, nurses, scientists, or technicians and to stimulate the educational system to produce them in the required numbers.

In the long run, and theoretically, the apparent contradiction disappears: "Since every producer is also a consumer, it is to everyone's interest that (such) an adjustment should be made."[7] Even in the short run, the demands of the economy are less threatening to individual rights under the Education Act than appears at first sight. The intellectual requirements of occupations and the capacities of individuals cannot be directly equated, except possibly in the case of the relatively small number of occupations for which formal qualifications are required, and no economic system can be so organized as to allow everyone to use his full talents in his employment. Fortunately, however, the aptitudes and abilities of individuals are rarely specific, so that as long as there is freedom of vocational choice and of movement between occupations, they may be expected to find their way into positions which will stretch their capacities and enable them to make their maximum contribution to the needs of society.

Freedom of vocational choice and movement are both the citizen's right and the conditions of a fluid and economically distributed labour supply, which is, in turn, a prerequisite of the high level of economic prosperity on which the Welfare State depends. A high degree of vocational and social mobility (or, looked at in economic terms, the elimination of rigidities in the supply of labour) is, therefore, both a cardinal principle of policy and a condition of survival for the Welfare State.

The most useful general index of the extent to which mobility exists is some measure of the propensity of children to enter and remain in occupations of the same or similar grade as those of their fathers. If this propensity did not exist at all, i.e., if all new entrants were candidates for all posts in industry, there would be no rigidity of supply (though there might be a scarcity of individuals with particular potentialities). However, the hereditary element in ability and the different intellectual requirements of different grades of occupation introduce a basic rigidity. The only feasible principle of policy is to seek to minimize the influence of factors other than differences in capacity on the distribution of individuals between occupations.

There are a number of such factors, other than differences in capacity, making for an association between the occupational grades of fathers and sons. The demographic and occupational structures themselves are primary determinants of the association. Thus, for example, the proportion of skilled to unskilled workers in the population and the differential fertility of the various occupational groups define the opportunities for the sons of unskilled workers to enter skilled occupations.[8] The localization of industry, consequent regional differences in occupational structure, and the tendency of labour, especially juvenile labour, to be immobile[9] are also relevant.

Other rigidities in supply derive, however from the wider social structure—in particular, from the class structure as it finds expression in the relations between the family enviroments of individuals at different social levels and the educational system.

In any highly industrialized community the nature of the educational system has a special importance for the occupational structure. The influence of changes in the statutory length of school life on the supply of juvenile labour is obvious. More important is the fact that in an industrialized economy the educational system becomes the prime agency of occupational selection and mobility. The scale of enterprise limits the possibility of working up small concerns into large through the ploughing back of profits, and multiplies the number of 'black-coated' jobs; the significance of apprenticeship and long service as avenues of mobility declines, and formal educational qualifications, at least to the secondary level, are increasingly required of entrants to all but the lowest class of occupations. This may be differently expressed by saying that the greater the degree of industrialization the more are young people limited in their choice of employment by their educational attainments, and the more difficult it is for adults to move outside the range of occupations for which their formal educational attainments equip them.

The Welfare State, on grounds both of political principal and of economic expendiency, has made a renewed attack through its educational policy on the problem of securing a close relationship between ability and opportunity. The effect has met with a marked degree of success; but, as will be argued below, the organizational framework of English secondary education and the social assumptions which it reflects are such as to set arbitrary limits to the degree of vocational and social mobility which can be achieved.

Schooling and Vocational Choice in England

The English school system is heavily class-conditioned both historically and actually. In post-war years it has become the centre of fierce controversy as the outstanding support of old, and an important source of new, class differences. It exercises a remarkable influence on occupational recruitment, setting firm limits to the freedom of individual choice and to the possibilities of fluidity in the supply of labour. It is so organized as to demand that decisions which are critical for vocational choice are made at the age of 11 or 12, when they can reflect only the largely class-conditioned family enviroment of the child. At the secondary stage, children are not, except in the case of a small minority attending 'comprehensive' schools, allocated to various secondary courses within a common school, but are selected for one of the three types of secondary school (grammar, technical, or modern) each of which has more or less specialized relations with institutions of further education and the occupational structure.

The close association between type of secondary schooling, length of school life, further education, and vocational choice is illustrated in Table I below.

The majority of modern, technical, and comprehensive school pupils leave at 15, and in 1953 some three-fifths of boys under 16 entered unspecified semi-skilled and unskilled employment; about one-third entered apprenticeships or learnerships to skilled crafts, and about one in twenty

English Secondary Schools and the Supply of Labour

Table 1.

Boys Leaving School in Great Britain, 1953—4

BOYS LEAVING FOR	AGE ON LEAVING SCHOOL, OR ON FIRST ENTERING EMPLOYMENT				
	14, 15	16	17	18	19
			Percentages		
(1) Further full-time educa- cation[1] at:					
(a) Universities	—	0.1	10.0	55.0	64.2
(b) Other institutions	1.6	3.3	8.2	12.6	10.6
(2) Paid employment[2]:					
(a) Apprenticeships or learnerships to skilled craft	32.4	37.4	25.8		
(b) Employment leading to recognized pro- fessional qualifications	0.3	3.7	8.0	32.4[3]	25.2[3]
(c) Clerical employment	5.3	25.4	20.4		
(d) Other employment	60.4	30.1	27.6		
Total	100	100	100	100	100

1. Compiled from statistics of school-leavers in England and Wales for the educational year ending July 31st, 1953. Education in 1953 (Cmd. 9155).
2. Compiled from statistics of class of employment entered by boys in Great Britain below the age of 18 in 1953. Ministry of Labour Gazette, Vol. LXII, December 12th, 1954.
Note.—In order to take account of the difference in the form of the statistics from these two sources, appropriate corrections have been made to those derived from Education in 1953 (Cmd. 9155).
3. Percentage of boys leaving school "for paid employment and other reasons" (class of employment not specified). Education in 1953 (Cmd. 9155).

clerical employment. The 'superiority' of the occupational distribution of those leaving school at 16 or above is marked. The majority of grammar school pupils, and rather less than half of technical school pupils, leave at 16, and the proportion of boys at this age who entered apprenticeships was somewhat higher than among the under 16's, whilst the proportion going into clerical employment was much higher; a much higher proportion also went into employment or full-time further education leading to recognized professional qualifications (e.g., law, accountancy, surveying, etc.). The proportion going into the professional occupations, either directly or following further education, was considerably higher among those who entered employment at 17 or later, of whom most had attended grammar schools.

From the point of view of the national economy, the most serious shortage is in the supply of persons capable of following the more skilled and responsible occupations, and the educational system is the main source of rigidities here. It is true that, against the general background of full employment, shortages of juvenile labour have been created by the raising of the school-leaving age and the expansion of further education (both full-time in universities and other institutions, and part-time in county colleges and technical institutes) and the introduction of compulsory national service. The resultant over-all shortage has tended to upgrade the range of opportunities formerly available to school-leavers, and a special feature of recent years has been the multiplication of apprenticeship and learnership schemes in many branches of industry with the aim of improving the conditions and prospects, and therefore the attractiveness, of a wide range of industrial openings for the young wage-earner. However, the selective system of secondary education continues to set artificial limits to both the range of employment opportunities and the occupational aspirations of juveniles. Children are, in effect, graded 'superior,' 'mediocre,' or 'poor' in intelligence and attainments at the age of 11, educated accordingly for a few more years, and turned over for guidance into employment as manual or non-manual workers as their schooling dictates. Yet a knowledge of the real significance of the processes of educational selection and their relationship to the family environment of children and the occupational structure which confronts them on leaving school opens up the possibility of a longer-term educational and vocational guidance policy directed towards improving the supply of trained labour at all levels to meet the growing demand for it.

Some 20–25 per cent of the age-group of 11-year-olds is selected for education in grammar schools (though for particular districts the proportion may vary as little as 10 per cent to as much as 50 per cent, and the provision bears no necessary relation to the needs of the local occupational structure). It is sometimes suggested that this minority represents an intellectual *élite*—a broad-based aristocracy of brains. It is true that it probably contains the best brains of the social classes who do not send their children to independent schools, but it also represents virtually the entire reserve of potentially qualified manpower. Less than 10 per cent of the age-group is admitted at 11 to technical schools, and a still smaller fraction at 13. The remaining two-thirds of the age-group continue their education in the secondary modern schools, leaving for the most part at 15, to form the bulk of the supply of manual workers, very few of whom are destined to climb subsequently into posts of more than minor responsibility in industry or commerce.

Since 1945, when fees were abolished in all maintained secondary schools, the process of selection for secondary edcuation has been based almost solely on objective tests of intelligence and attainments in English and Arithmetic. This has had the effect of relating the distribution of grammar school places very closely indeed to the distribution of intelligence (as measured by the tests). Social-class inequalities of opportunity of proceeding to grammar schools are therefore almost entirely a function of social-class differences in measured intelligence, and there have been marked changes in the social composition of the grammar schools. Ten years ago more than 50 per cent of pupils in these schools paid fees, and the children of non-manual workers outnumbered those of manual workers. Since all places were opened to competition by examination in 1945, however, there has been a considerable influx of working-class children into the schools. This represents an important increase in mobility—a probable potential weakening of the present association of paternal and filial occupational status. For the more successful of these pupils there is entrance to the universities, and thence to administrative or professional occupations. For the middle group of those leaving at 16 or 17 there are careers in banks and insurance offices, the executive and higher clerical grades of the Civil Service and similar occupations. Even for those who do not complete the minimum grammar school course, some form of minor white-collar occupation is the typical expectation.[10]

But the selection process, though within its limits 'objective,' is nevertheless, as is widely recognized, very imprecise. It is difficult to know how much weight to attach to differences of ability between the selected and the rejected children in the middle ranges of the examination hierarchy. Within only a narrow range of differences in average I.Q., working-class children, divided according to certain features of their family enviroment,[11] show marked differences in success at the selection examination. The influence on children's educational performance and prospects of crude economic disabilities has been much reduced by social amelioration and post-war full employment; more subtle attributes tend to distinguish the home backgrounds of successful from those of unsuccessful children. Thus, the working-class child who secures a grammar school place tends to come from a small family, his father is more likely to have received some form of further education, his mother to have received something more than an elementary schooling, and, before marriage, to have followed an occupation 'superior' to that of his father. These factors are reflected in a complex of attitudes favourable to educational success and social mobility, and differences of this kind in home background presumably underlie differences in motivation which, in the absence of gross economic handicaps, are the key to differences in performance in a substantial border-line range of ability.

In so far as the Welfare State succeeds in providing a basic equality of economic status for all citizens, we may expect that increasing numbers of homes will provide the moral or cultural support which makes for success at school. The pressure on the grammar schools is then likely to increase from this cause, as well as from the increase in the birth-rates of the post-war years. It is unlikely that the number of places will be expanded sufficiently to maintain the provision at its present level—in which case the unselected reserve of educable talent in the modern schools (i.e., in effect, the number of 'border-line' children) will increase, the selection will become less effective than at present.

The selective influence of differences in cultural background continues to operate among the selected minority of grammar school entrants. Social class plays a very important part in determining the use that children admitted to the grammar schools can make of the course or, from the point of view of the occupational structure, the extent to which they in fact manage to equip themselves for, and enter, the grade of occupation for which their ability makes them eligible.

A recent official inquiry[12] has estimated that one-third of the grammar school boys who are capable of reaching a standard of at least two passes at Advanced Level in the General Certificate of Education leave school before doing so, and that the influence of home background is the major cause. The 15 per cent of all school children originating from the professional and managerial classes account for 25 per cent of the grammar school population and contribute 43.7 per cent of those reaching the Sixth form of the grammar school, whereas the 12 per cent from the homes of unskilled manual workers account for 5.6 per cent of grammar school pupils and contribute only 1.5 per cent of the Sixth formers. The Council's report confirms earlier inquiries which found that the child of the professional or business man admitted to a grammar school is likely to improve his academic status relative to others in his age-group, whilst the unskilled worker's child is likely to deteriorate. 'Wastage' from grammar schools, as the Central Advisory Council clearly recognized, is a social-class problem. The traditionally middle-class schools are evidently failing to assimilate large numbers of the able working-class children who win their way into them.

Selection is imprecise and is made at an arbitrary point in the scale of ability; yet it reinforces the differences both between and within social classes by fostering different levels of vocational aspiration among children attending different types of secondary school. Thus among a sample of lower-working-class boys in London grammar schools,[13] no fewer than two-thirds expected to rise considerably above their fathers in occupational status compared with 12 per cent of their comrades in secondary modern schools. Professor T. H. Marshall has commented on the results of this inquiry that "the boys from the humbler working-class homes may overrate their chances without fully realizing how ambitious their success has made them." Secondary modern school boys, on the other hand, are subjected to the inhibiting effects of rejection and their occupational aspirations are correspondingly lower. The limit of aspiration among these children seems to be the top of the manual working class from which, in the majority of cases, they originate. Powerful forces, grouped by Jahoda under the heading of "climate of opinion," appear to limit their horizon.[14] Jahoda reports that among secondary modern school-leavers in Lancashire, office or clerical work was the kind of job most frequently rejected and half of those who rejected it did so because they considered themselves unqualified for it. In her study of vocational choice in Ealing, Miss M. D. Wilson found that fewer than 5 per cent of the pupils in her sample of secondary modern pupils chose occupations unsuited to their educational standing.[15] She found the children "ambitious, but not excessively so," by which she meant that they tended, as had been noted of children in earlier inquiries, to aim at the highest levels available to the group to which they belong, showing, as she expressed it, "a healthy desire to climb to the top of the tree, but little yearning to move to another part of the forest where there are taller trees." she also produced evidence to show that selection at 11+ produced a marked modification of vocational aspirations, the children directing their interests soon after their admission to secondary schools to the general field of occupations available to them—the modern school boys, for instance, turning 'realistically' from occupational 'phantasies' to skilled manual work.

Yet if selection for secondary education is as faulty as the evidence suggests, the profound effect of the segregation of children into different types of secondary school on their attitude to vocations must be deplored.

Reorganization of the System

Selection at 11+ and segregation into separate schools is evidently a form of vocational as well as educational selection undesirable, because premature. It is sometimes defended in the post-war conditions of full competition for grammar school places as a promoter of social mobility and as a desirable method of selecting the best brains of all classes to form a much-needed democratic *élite*. In fact the post-war expansion of opportunity for working-class children to enter grammar schools directs attention away from the dysfunctional aspects of the system which we have been describing. What conclusions are we to draw from the discussion?

The most radical inference is that English secondary education should be reorganized along comprehensive lines. There is indeed something to be said for the view that the common secondary school is best suited to the needs of a technological society—least likely to stand in the way of free vocational choice and movement, most likely to produce the maximum supply of skilled and responsible individuals particularly in the middle ranges of the occupational structure. But these advantages could be reaped from such a reorganization only if the spirit as well as the form of English secondary education were changed. The emphasis on selection—on the sifting, grading, and sorting of ability—during the school years would need to be severely modified, and the relation of the schools to the occupational structure would need to be made much more flexible. The task of occupational selection which is at present performed by the secondary schools, with the adverse economic effects which we have noted, would need to be shifted to post-school educational institutions, and the intensive preparation of the *élite* now undertaken by the grammar schools postponed.

These are large questions, with profound social and educational, as well as economic, implications, into which we cannot enter here. The debate on the comprehensive school is still in progress. Meantime, however, within the traditional organizational framework of secondary education much can be done in the same spirit to loosen the bonds that tie occupation to schooling. More than lip-service must be paid to the arbitrary and imprecise nature of selection—every effort must be made to mitigate its effects on vocational choice. Thus, the increasing tendency to encourage children to stay in modern schools to take advanced courses after the age of compulsory attendance is a step in the right direction—as are also any measures which may be adopted to open up a new route to positions of industrial and technical responsibility by creating new technical qualifications accessible to ex-modern school pupils through a reorganized system of technical colleges. Such measures will be the more successful in that the unselected reserve of educable talent in the modern schools is likely to grow for the reasons mentioned above.

It is also desirable that the policy of vocational guidance should be reoriented in a deliberate attempt to increase the fluidity of the supply of labour. To be effective for this purpose guidance cannot afford to begin its work only at the end of the children's school days, concentrating on the end-products of the educational process. If boys and girls are to be candidates for the widest range of occupations for which their ability fits them, and if this involves overcoming obstacles to their educational progress arising out of their family environment, vocational guidance has to start much earlier in their careers and to be part and parcel of the school system rather than an offshoot of the Ministry of Labour. Vocational guidance in England has made impressive strides in the short period of its existence as a national service. But it is perhaps an indication of progress yet to be made that Logan and Goldberg are able to report that among the majority (of a sample of 18-year-old boys in a London suburb) the Youth Employment Service seemed to exert little influence on the choice of job, being mainly used as a convenient agency for the notification of vacancies in semi-skilled and unskilled work.[16]

The service has not merely to make contact with the heads of schools and with parents when the children leave school, but to extend the conception of its task to include counselling at all points in the school course and the building up for this purpose of a detailed knowledge of home circumstances. Traditionally, this work has been done by teachers in the schools, who frequently have very considerable knowledge, not merely of their pupils' abilities and aptitudes, but also of the sources and determinants in their home circumstances of their attitudes and interests, or apathy and ignorance. However, it is doubtful whether, with the greatly extended professional demands on teachers to-day, they can be expected to undertake in the course of their ordinary duties what may approximate, with a large number of pupils, to social case-work.

Vocational guidance, to be effective, must therefore extend back into the school, becoming in the first place educational guidance based on a full knowledge of home as well as school circumstances and also, if necessary, family guidance. This kind of social and educational case-work, directed towards popularizing unfamiliar educational objectives or occupation prospects amongst children and their families, can be extraordinarily effective, as may be seen by comparing the reactions of their grammar school course and the occupational destinies of working-class children in neighbouring schools distinguished only by the enthusiasm and competence in this direction of the head master. The question is whether a national guidance policy, aimed at stimulating the ambitions of the unselected school population and tackling the problem of social assimilation which underlies the wastage of able working-class children from the grammar schools, does not demand the appointment of counsellors or guidance officers to the staffs of all secondary schools who would undertake what teachers cannot ordinarily be expected to do as part of their daily work.

NOTES

1. Marx Engels, *Selected Works* (Moscow, 1951), Vol. II, p. 33.
2. O. Banks, *Parity and Prestige in English Secondary Education* (London, 1955), p. 239.
3. "Prospects of Labour," *Economica,* 1949, p. 4.
4. A less tangible question both because it has not been subject to investigation, so that present knowledge is limited, and because the effect of reforms is necessarily very gradual. Professor Hicks has caluculated that in 1924 not more than 40 per cent of the occupied male population are likely to have had any experience (in their school years) of the educational improvements which followed the Act of 1902, but by 1938 the proportion may have risen to 80 per cent; and that although the proportion of those who had experienced the effects of the 1918 Act will have been continually rising, it cannot have reached more than 40 per cent in 1938, and will take until about 1960 to work itself out fully. (*The Social Framework* (1952), p. 192.)
5. See D. V. Glass (ed.), *Social Mobility in Britain* (Kegan Paul, 1954), Chapter X, for an analysis of the relation between education and mobility based on a national sample inquiry in 1949.
6. *Op. cit.,* p. 60.
7. J. R. Hicks, *op. cit.,* p. 60.
8. It is possible to measure, for past periods, the extent to which occupational 'fluidity' has existed between generations. It is necessary to know the occupational distribution of fathers and sons. Then the actual distribution of the sons may be compared with the distribution which would have occurred if occupational recruitment had been made by a random process. This latter defines the conditions of 'perfect mobility,' and has been used as a model in a recent British study. (See D. V. Glass (ed.), *op. cit.*)
9. The extreme geographical immobility of juvenile labour was illustrated in an investigation (J. and S. Jewkes, *The Juvenile Labour Market* (London, 1938)) which showed that the unemployment rate in Warrington among juveniles was negligible in 1935, while, in St. Helens, *only ten miles away,* it was around 20 per cent. Since the Employment and Training Act of 1948, efforts have been made in the Youth Employment Service to foster mobility by maintenance grants, etc., to apprentices and learners who need to live away from home in order to train.
10. Although an increasing minority is now beginning to take up industrial apprenticeships. Hitherto the occupational ambitions of grammar school pupils have not been directed towards industry. It is difficult to decide how much this has

been due to the academic atmosphere and curriculum of the schools, the lack of co-operation of employers, the difficulties of apprenticeship regulations, or the prejudices of parents. But is beyond doubt that the field of acceptable choice for the grammar school-leaver has been and remains restricted. (See O. Banks, *op. cit.*)

11. E.g., family size, parents' attitudes towards education, etc. For fuller information on this and the following points concerning the relation of the home background to educational performance, see J. Floud, A. H. Halsey, and F. M. Martin, *Social Class and Educational Opportunity* (Heinemann, 1956).

12. Central Advisory Council for Education (England), *Early Leaving* (H.M.S.O., December 1954).

13. H. T. Himmelweit, A. H. Halsey, and A. N. Oppenheim, "The Views of Adolescents on Some Aspects of Social Class Structure," *British Journal of Sociology,* June 1952.

14. C. Jahoda, "Job Attitude and Job Choice among Secondary Modern School Leavers," *Occupational Psychology,* April and October, 1952.

15. M. D. Wilson, "The Vocational Preferences of Secondary Modern School Children," *The British Journal of Educational Psychology, June* and November, 1953.

16. R. and L. Logan and E. M. Goldberg, "Rising 18 in a London Suburb," *British Journal of Sociology,* December 1953, p. 327. See also L. T. Wilkins, *The Employment of the Adolescent* (Central Office of Information, 1951).

10   *Schools and Systems of Stratification**

HOWARD S. BECKER

IN MOST COMPLEX SOCIETIES, and particularly those organized in terms of the values and institutions of Western culture, schools tend to play an important role in the drama of social mobility. Education being at the same time a symbol of social position and a means by which higher position may be achieved, the amount of access to it is one of the keys to the amount of mobility possible in a society. Research on the American school system has alerted us to to some of the ways in which schools tend to aid or hinder mobility on the part of subordinate groups.[1] In this paper, I compare the American situation with what is known of the educational systems of colonial and underdeveloped areas, with an eye to tracing some of the more general dimensions of this relationship between schools and systems of social stratification.

It must be said immediately that in many areas of the world this whole question of mobility and education may be irrelevant. In the first place, education is not often sufficient in itself to make mobility possible. Other things are needed, and a person who acquires a schooling has only begun to move. How far he gets depends, among other things, on where there is to go. If there are no available positions in the upper strata, as there are not in many colonial societies, no way of earning a living in a properly prestigeful way, schooling does not produce mobility but only frustrates desire; it has no effect on the status system. In such a situation disappointment may be avoided by ignoring the mobility possibility.

This raises another qualification limiting the applicability of our analysis. The degree to which mobility is desired by members of subordinate groups cannot be taken for granted but must rather be regarded as problematic. To the degree that such groups consider mobility in fact impossible it will not be sought. Equally important, to the degree that a subordinate group maintains a self-sufficient culture and shares only a minimum of

Reprinted from Howard S. Becker, "Schools and Systems of Social Status," *Phylon*, Vol. XVI (1955), No. 2, with the permission of the author and the editor.

*Paper read at the seminar on Group Conflict held at the Institute of Social and Economic Research, University College of the West Indies, Jamaica, B.W.I., August 9–13, 1954. I would like to acknowledge the substantial debt this essay owes to the thinking of Everett C. Hughes, and thank David Riesman for his critical reading of an earlier version.

common understanding with those above it—to the degree that the society is what Dr. M. G. Smith has termed a "plural society"[2]—mobility will be sought only within the group; movement to the culturally alien superordinate group will be neither desired nor pursued. Under these circumstances the school has little effect on systems of status, since mobility between groups, however accomplished, is not an important feature of the society.

Within the limits suggested by these qualifications, i.e., insofar as mobility is considered worth attempting and is aided by exposure to schooling, it becomes pertinent to inquire into the ways in which schools affect mobility. In succeeding sections I consider a number of ways in which school organizations, through their institutional structure, act on the stratification system. (Systems in which openly discriminatory law and practice prevent subordinate groups from gaining access to schooling have not been dealt with, their workings being too obvious to require discussion, although perhaps of major importance in any assessment of the current situation.)

I

Societies vary in degree and kind of cultural heterogeneity, and in the way in which these various cultures are taken account of by the school system. In the United States there is, of course, tremendous cultural diversity: ethnic mixture, rural-urban differences, and, in the larger cities, particularly, well developed social-class subcultures, with characteristic emphases in language, thought, behavior, and values.[3]

Underdeveloped areas, while they do not often exhibit the ethnic variety of the metropolitan centers, tend toward a much more radical gap between the cultures of dominant and subordinate groups. Class cultures in European and American cities, greatly though they differ, are grown from the same root. Ethnic differences, while they may be considerable, tend for the most part to be variants of Western European culture. In colonies, established when Europeans migrated and set up governments incorporating the early inhabitants of the territory and perhaps other people brought from still elsewhere, the groups may come from two totally different civilizations, as when Europeans met Asians; or Europeans may come into contact with people still living a tribal life, as in Africa. The groups are fewer, the cultures more distinctive, and the distance between much greater.

Not all of these cultures are taken account of and made the basis of practice in the educational institutions that arise in either of these situations. And so the question arises, as Tax puts it,[4] "whose cultural tradition is to be transmitted?" In the cities of America and Europe there is ordinarily some basic ethnic tradition which, without argument, becomes the medium and content of educational activity. (There may occasionally be two, as in the case of the French and English in Quebec, or the Flemings and Walloons in Belgium.) Education in this culture is available and those wishing something else for their children must make their own provisions. Of the social-class cultures, that of the middle class (in which most educational personnel have their origin[5]) is usually made the standard.

In the colonies and underdeveloped areas, this issue is not so simple. Those at the top waver between wanting everyone else to learn their language and culture, and either of the two opposites of providing no education at all or education more or less within the framework of the native culture. It is easier to rule and to run economic enterprises where native cultures are abandoned for that of the ruling power, for the difficulties in operating Western legal systems and industrial organizations in the midst of an alien culture are tremendous.[6] This implies schools teaching the rulers' culture, in their tongue. On the other hand, the dominant group may take seriously the anthropologists warnings about the consequences of disrupting the subordinate group's culture in this way. They may feel a sympathy for, or be fascinated by, a primitive and exotic way of life. If it is felt that the value of maintaining the native culture ought to be combined with progress of some sort, vernacular schools may be set up; or, if no such combination is sought, the solution might be no schools at all for the subordinate group. This latter possibility is, in effect, what occurs in those places in which a small elite endeavors to retain its position through a monopoly of education, as in Haiti.

The subordinate group may take one of several attitudes toward this question, to the degree that it interests them at all. They may desire strongly education in the culture of the dominant group because of the status advantages with which they know it can equip them. As in Ireland, and more recently, Africa, they may be caught up in a developing nationalism and wish to reject the dominant culture, uniting the institution of the school with their own language and culture. Where the subject people have their own civilization with well-developed schools holding a ritually-sanctioned status in the society, as in India, resistance to Western education may be led by the teachers of these schools, whose jobs and social position would be lost in the change.[7] Because some knowledge of the culture and more especially the language of the ruling power has been essential if one was to better himself, the dominant attitude has usually been a desire for as much education in that area as could be obtained.

The educator faces a real dilemma in such situations, where subordinate groups require training in the dominant culture for social "success." If, on the one hand, teaching proceeds within the cultural and linguistic framework of the dominant group, members of the subordinate group, who have not had the preparation in daily experience presupposed by such an educational program, do not do well. It bears no relation to their daily life, is unfamiliar, difficult to understand, largely meaningless, and can be learned only by rote if at all. This seems to be one of the major problems in Africa,[8] where the African must attempt to acquire a British education, as it is in the cities of the United States, where the lower-class child must try to absorb the teaching of a school oriented to the quite different culture of the middle-class.[9] The problem of motivation is likewise important. As Davis point out, the urban American lower-class child is likely to believe that education will not do him much good, that it is not really worth trying and will not make the effort needed to surmount the obstacles of an unfamiliar culture.[10] (This, of course, is no problem in colonial areas, except to the extent that compulsory education becomes a reality and students are recruited who must be kept in school against their will.) In such situations the child of the subordinate group gets little education; the school may stick determinedly to the alien agenda, but it does not accomplish much. The students learns little that will help them better their social position.

On the other hand, if an attempt is made to adapt the curriculum to the language and/or culture of the subordinate group, in the hope of increasing the achievement of the school, they are likely to interpret the move as an attempt to prevent them from learning what they need to know and acquiring the diplomas they need to get ahead in the world. If, for example, a colonial school is taught in dialect rather than standard English, it may do more teaching; but the students and their families may feel, possibly with some justification, that this only prevents them from learning the language of the dominant group, precisely what they require for successful mobility. Attempts to introduce "native" subjects and dialects, to provide education different in any way from what would be given a child of the dominant group, are interpreted as an attempt to make sure that the man on the bottom stays there, and may in fact have this consequence, intended or not.[11] For such systems of dual education may easily turn into segregated deadends for the racial or otherwise subordinate groups they are intended to aid. It is for this reason that labor unions in the United States have traditionally opposed plans to build technical secondary schools for working class areas, interpreting this as a move to deny the sons of workers the education they need to rise out of the working class. This even where the ordinary secondary school proceeds in a manner that makes it difficult for the lower-class child to succeed.

In addition, teachers in such areas are likely themselves to be mobile from the subordinate group, one sign of their successful mobility being their ease in the language and cultural ways of the dominant group. They are likely to reject efforts to get them to teach in a language or dialect carrying less prestige.[12]

In short, educators in culturally differentiated societies are caught on the horns of this dilemma: to bring education "down" to the level of the subordinate group and thus give something, but not very much, to all, or to "maintain standards" and thus aid only the gifted few? In whichever direction they move, they are likely to end by perpetuating the cultural differences between groups, and slowing the mobility flow to the continuing disadvantage of those at the bottom.

(By focusing only on mobility, this kind of argument ignores the importance of the school's function as the transmitter of a valued cultural heritage. From a different perspective than the rather one-sided one of this paper, one might raise questions about the fate of this important function in school systems faced with these problems.)

II

Not all societies are organized so as easily to accommodate schools fashioned on the Western model. The question of whether a society can support such institutions involves not only the financial problems which are everywhere a concern of educational administrators, but also the questions of the degree to which the society's values mesh with the notion of formal education and the extent to which they can furnish personnel to man the schools.

Although there are many failures of modern Western societies to support fully formal education, these societies do accept the notion of education of all children up to some specific age and pattern social arrangements in such a way as to allow this to go on. In many of the world's underdeveloped areas, on the other hand, particularly those in which subordinate groups are still organized at the tribal level, the very notion of a school is foreign to the accepted way of life. In addition, the child is an economic asset on which the family depends. Schooling, because it ties up a potential worker in non-productive activity, is expensive for them even when it is free. Consequently, attendance is erratic, always at the mercy of family need.

One result of the lack of cultural support of the educational enterprise in either kind of area is that education cannot be really cumulative, cannot progress year by year to new and higher subjects and skills. The teacher can never count on his pupils having already mastered some set of facts or skills just because they have had so-and-so many years of schools, and each year tends to become a repetition of the last, devoted to attempting to make sure that everyone has at least mastered the basic skills of reading and writing. At each higher grade level the gap between what should be learned and what actually is learned becomes greater; teaching degenerates into a desperate attempt to instill some minimum amount of learning. Teachers are tempted in such a discouraging situation to take the easy way out, either giving up completely or devoting their efforts only to those few students who will accept them wholeheartedly and are comparatively easy to teach. The teachers' stereotypes about the subordinate group's lack of ability tend to be confirmed by their experience and leads to less effort being expended where more is in fact required, thus increasing the school's failure.

The question of financial support is of course important. Within the limits imposed by the extent of the society's resources—and these are immensely limiting in an area such as Africa where the money is simply not available to do the job—the problem is one of the allocation of funds. How much are people willing to pay to have children educated, particularly where schools are supported through taxation and the person who pays the largest taxes finds himself subsidizing the education of children of the subordinate group? Hughes has suggested that Canadian public education suffers from the reluctance of the smaller group of well-to-do English to so subsidize the education of the poorer and more numerous French Canadians.[13] The same political problems of the allocation of funds, rooted in the relations of status groups, are found in the segregated schools of the southern United States, and in those cities in which residential segregation makes possible selective spending for the education of racial and social-class minorities. Such financial dilemmas tend to be resolved to the disadvantage of subordinate groups.

Finally, there is the question of providing sufficient adequately trained personnel to keep the institution operating. What incentives are available to induce people of the desired kind to become teachers and are they sufficient to do the job? This may be put in terms of what might be called career potential. Starting as a teacher, where can one go, and are these prospects attractive enough to those who might enter the profession? In the United States, there are many people with appropriate education. From these, it appears that teachers are drawn largely from the ranks of those of limited ambition, who prefer the relative security of the school teacher's restricted occupational horizon to the risks of occupations which allow for more movement up and down. There are a great many people possessing this combination of limited ambition and higher education, and teachers are recruited in sizeable numbers.

In the underdeveloped areas, on the other hand, anyone who perseveres enough to get the education necessary for teaching wants a greater reward for his effort. And such rewards are often available. In Africa and India, better careers in industry and government were available to English speaking school graduates. Few received the basic education necessary for teacher training; they were ambitious, and passed up teaching for these alternative careers which carried more prestige, paid better, and tended to be nearer the centers of population.[14] This meant, in the first place, a shortage of teachers. Second, when coupled with the inevitable desire of educational authorities to get people with the highest educational qualifications, it meant that teachers tended to be those who had failed in a try for the bigger prizes. "There has been (in India) a tendency to prefer 'failed matriculates' ready for the sake of a living to face work and surroundings with which they are out of sympathy, to less advanced, but more appropriate candidates."[15] A system which thus almost deliberately selects disgruntled failures for its teachers is bound not to get the greatest amount of teaching enthusiasm, which may be more important than a degree.

It may be taken for granted that where teachers are difficult to recruit, those groups that they dislike teaching—the subordinate ones—will get something less than their share. Any system faced with a real shortage of teachers, therefore, will operate in such a way as to reduce the possibility of upward mobility for these groups, and it is only where an institutional system has been devised that will recruit successfully that this tendency is reversed. It is clear that different kinds of incentives and potential careers than those made available by the bureaucratic seniority systems of the older countries must be utilized in the underdeveloped areas if recruitment is to be successful.

III

Individual schools are linked, formally or otherwise, into systems, within whose boundaries teachers move from school to school in search of whatever satisfactions they happen to seek in their work. The teacher's career is made up of a series of such movements between schools in the system, each of these constituting a stage in the career.[16] Looking at such a system at any given moment, we see a distribution of teachers at various stages of their careers among the schools making up the system. Systems tend to breed distinctive career patterns and this distribution of teachers of various kinds is not random. The question can thus be raised: what kinds of teachers do schools of various types tend to get?

The first point to be noted is that all schools in such a system do not look alike to the teacher. They differ in the kind of children they have as pupils, in the salaries they pay, in location, and so on. Some schools are very attractive to the teacher, places at which she would like very much to teach, while others are thought of as places to be avoided if possible. It may be, as in Chicago, that lower-class and Negro children are considered hardest to teach and most difficult to handle, so that schools containing them are avoided.[17] It may be, as in many places in the United States, that the teacher attempts to work her way out of the poorer paying, socially constraining rural hinterland into the nearest big city; Kansas City exemplifies this.[18] In underdeveloped areas, generally, living conditions, salaries, prestige, and ease of teaching, all combine to draw teachers toward the centers of population and away from the "backwoods" areas. For any of the reasons suggested, it is typically the schools handling children of subordinate groups which are least desired, and teachers' careers tend to be structured in terms of movement away from such schools.

Career movements tend to take this pattern, no matter what the arrangements by which movement occurs. In Chicago, teachers may request transfers to other schools, and will be moved as soon as there is a vacancy for which their request is of longest standing; this is essentially an arrangement by which seniority gets one the desired job. The record of these requests, when mapped, shows a tremendous movement away from the slums toward the middle-class areas. The same pattern may be seen in those informal rural-urban systems, like that of Kansas City, in which movement is accomplished by acquiring experience and bargaining successfully for the more desired jobs. In general, those teachers who have what the system wants—experience, teaching ability, whatever it may be—have most choice of position, and this leads to the pattern described.

Such a pattern of movement means that the less desirable schools, those teachers want to avoid, get something less than an equal share of teaching talent. At the least, it typically means that they do not get the experienced teachers, for experience is almost always a ticket to a better job, whether through the workings of a seniority system or through the greater bargaining power it provides in bidding for jobs. In Chicago, many lower-class Negro schools are staffed almost entirely by teachers fresh from training school, the only ones who cannot choose their assignments; as soon as they build up enough seniority to move, they go, to be replaced by a new batch of beginners. More generally, it is probably true that, whatever the qualities a school system wishes to reward in its teachers, those qualities can be effectively rewarded only by assignment to the more desired schools, so that disadvantaged groups, who require the most skilled and experienced teaching, get the opposite and something less than an equal chance to an education.

There is very little information on problems of this order in underdeveloped areas. It seems likely that this picture holds for the West Indies, and for Africa—the poor, the rural folk, those most backward being taught by teachers who, through lack of experience or ability, cannot get positions in the cities. It would be most revealing to see studies made of the aspirations and careers of teachers in such societies, with special emphasis on the fate of enthusiasm and ability in these systems. Is it true here too that careers move in such a way that students of the dominant groups get the best teaching, and vice versa, with the obvious consequences for the mobility chances of the subordinate group?

Such tendencies get reinforced, after they have been operating for any length of time, in a way that makes them very difficult to change. The teachers who have been fortunate enough to locate in what are commonly considered the "more desirable" schools come to consider these positions to be their inalienable property. They feel that they have "served their time" (suggestive phrase!) and are now enjoying a well-earned reward. Others look forward to an equal reward when they too have served their time in the less desirable places; careers are built around this expectation. Any attempt to remove teachers from these schools and put them in places where their skills are more needed is looked on with great disfavor, as though the terms of contract were being broken; it may even be regarded as a species of punishment. (It is said that such transfers were used as disciplinary measures in the Chicago schools at one time, in much the same way that policemen are punished by being assigned a beat in the "sticks.") There are hints of this tendency in Africa. The group reporting on educational problems in East and Central Africa mentions a similar "uneasiness in the teaching profession at the arbitrariness with which teachers and especially heads of schools are transferred from one school to another. . . . Instances were encountered in which a head of a school was transferred to a backward school as soon as his energy had produced an obvious improvement in his present school."[19] A transfer is arbitrary only when it violates some established expectation, and it appears that such expectations have already begun to form.

IV

Institutions tend to try to become self-contained systems of power and to protect themselves against interference from the outside. Institutions are the means by which society delegates particular functions to specialized groups, always retaining the right to examine and pass judgment on that group's performance. Institutional functionaries feel that they understand the problems involved better than any layman and dislike any potential or actual interference, wanting to be left free to run things in their own way. Consequently, they erect defensive barriers designed to keep outsiders on the outside and prevent the surrounding society from directly affecting the institution's operation.

Schools share this tendency. Teachers and administrators find most satisfaction in their work, and feel that they do their best work, when there is no interference by the layman. They erect such barriers of secrecy and mutual defense. It is likely that the development of such defenses proceeds in relation to the perceived possibility of effective attack from the outside. The independence of the schools from such interference has an important, though by no means always the same, effect on the way the schools affect social mobility patterns.

Educational institutions differ greatly in the degree to which they are likely to be attacked, and in the success of their defense of their autonomy. The Chicago situation presents a fully developed case. These schools are very likely to be attacked at almost any time by the parents of their pupils, for not doing their job well enough or in the right way, for using improper disciplinary measures, and so on. They have developed, quite informally, an amazingly strong self-protective code. No principal or teacher ought ever to admit that anyone on the school staff has done anything wrong, even if this necessitates open lying, for to admit such a thing would be to admit the parents into the power structure of the school. The fact that anything has gone wrong is a closely kept secret. Parents and other outsiders are allowed to see the schools in action only when there is plenty of warning and a "show" of some kind has been prepared for them.[20] In systems oriented more toward examination systems of one kind or another, the possibility of attack may produce in addition an emphasis on demonstrable results—a high production of passes, for instance—even when this must be achieved by using rote learning methods in preference to more substantial kinds of education.

Such a system does not work equally well with all kinds of people. In Chicago, it works to perfection with lower-class parents who are easily intimidated by middle-class institutions. But it does not work well at all with the middle-class parent, who knows how to make trouble for the school and will do so without compunction if not satisfied.

Along with these two possibilities—that attacks will be successfully defended against, or that defense will fail—is a third: that there is no danger of attack and no need of defense. This may be the case in some of the newer colonies in which the parents are relatively unable to assess the school's work and deal with educational authorities. (It is always possible, however, that groups from outside the society whose opinion carries weight will play the role that parents do elsewhere). It is likely, in colonial situations, that such attacks as are made will be focused more on quantitative concerns—numbers of schools and teachers, etc.—and that the brunt of any attack will be borne not by the teacher but by those administrative officers in charge of running the whole system.

In any case, whether by protective arrangements or through freedom from attack, the schools may gain for themselves an almost free hand, so that the teachers can pursue their real purpose relatively unhampered. In a system like Chicago's, particularly in lower-class areas, the teacher's primary aim is just to get along and not have too much trouble; educational standards come second. It is only where the institutional defenses are breached, as they are in middle-class areas, that this can be avoided and educational standards maintained. One of the elements preventing the lower-class from receiving the full benefits of education in a class society is its lack of organization and effectiveness in pushing teachers to do better work. Where, on the other hand, public demand is for quantity rather than quality, as may be the case in Africa, a determined teaching group able to withstand attack may actually provide more lasting benefit to underprivileged groups.

Again, such a public may be effective in forcing the schools to give out symbols of achievement whether or not there has been any achievement in fact; this is probably particularly the case in status-conscious underdeveloped societies, where the certificate or degree is almost a passport to higher position; see, for example, Tugwell's description of the University of Puerto Rico where, at one time, students demanded and got, from a vulnerable faculty, degrees without accomplishment.[21] These can be hollow victories for the native group where, as in Africa and India, some real learning—at least, of a new language—must occur, where the symbols of accomplishment without the fact do no good.

The results of the educator's effort to run his enterprise in his own way, with no interference from outside, is thus quite important for the kind of education the child receives and the amount of social mobility made possible. The specific effect in any situation depends on three variables: the desires of parents and others who may possibly wish to have a voice in the school's operation; the desires of teachers and educational administrators; and the way in which the conflict over control of the schools is resolved, either in such a way as to make them more responsive to outside pressure or so as to preserve for them effective autonomy.

V

The schools, then, function importantly in the operation of the system of status and social class of the societies in which they exist. Where a society contains disadvantaged groups, education is one of the possible means of mobility for them just as it is one of the means by which members of the dominant group maintain their status. Education can provide a sizeable amount of opportunity for disadvantaged groups, if all groups have an equal chance to get an education.

It has been the concern of this paper to point out the ways in which the ordinary operation of educational institutions, quite apart from deliberately discriminatory measures, tends to cut down the amount of mobility opportunity the schools provide. Its major thesis is that in solving such problems as the recruitment and distribution of personnel, the defense of institutional autonomy, etc., the schools, organized in terms of one of the sub-cultures of a heterogeneous society, tend to operate in such a way that members of subordinate groups of differing culture do not get their fair share of educational opportunity, and thus of opportunity for social mobility.

If it is true that the schools tend to have this conservative effect in general, it is of great importance, both theoretically and practically, to search for and investigate systematically such situations as that which existed, for example, in various cities of the United States at various times, in which the schools functioned in the opposite direction, becoming great channels of mobility for large groups. More research is needed on cases of this kind in order to bring out more fully the basic forces at work in orienting educational institutions toward one or another of these modes of relation to status system.

NOTES

1. On the American situation in general, see W. L. Warner, R. J. Havighurst, and M. B. Loeb, *Who Shall Be Educated?* (New York: 1944). I have relied heavily on the studies of the Chicago school system done under the direction of Everett C.

Hughes, reported in a number of M.A. and Ph.D. theses at the University of Chicago, as well as in three papers by the present author: "The Career of the Chicago Public Schoolteacher," *American Journal of Sociology,* LVII (March, 1952), 336–43; "Social-Class Variations in the Teacher-Pupil Relationship," *Journal of Educational Sociology,* 25 (April, 1952), 451–65; and "The Teacher in the Authority System of the Public School," *ibid.,* 26 (November, 1953), 128–41.

2. See his "Social Structure in the British Caribbean about 1820," *Social and Economics Studies,* Vol. 1, no. 4 (August, 1953), 55–79; and "Slavery and Emancipation in Two Societies," *ibid.,* Vol. 3, nos. 3 and 4 (December, 1954), 239–90.

3. On the differences between lower and middle class behavior and values, see Allison Davis, "The Motivation of the Underprivileged Worker," in *Industry and Society,* ed. by William F. Whyte (New York, 1946), pp. 84–106. On the differences in language and thought, see Leonard Shatzman and Anselm Strauss, "Social Class and Modes of Communication," *American Journal of Sociology,* LX (January, 1955), 329–38.

4. Sol Tax, "The Education of Underprivileged Peoples in Dependent and Independent Territories," *Journal of Negro Education,* XV (Summer, 1946), 336–45.

5. Cf. Warner, Havighurst, and Loeb, *op. cit.*

6. On legal systems, see Rene Maunier, *The Sociology of Colonies,* ed. and trans. by E. O. Lorimer (London, 1949), Part III; on industrial systems, see Everett C. and Helen M. Hughes, *Where Peoples Meet* (Glencoe, 1952), Chapter 5.

7. See J. R. Cunningham, "Education," in L. S. S. O'Malley, *Modern India and the West* (London, 1941), pp. 142–3.

8. T. R. Batten, *Problems of African Development,* Part II (London, 1948), p. 66. See also J. M. van der Kroef's description of a classical case of the effect of this problem on the school's mobility function in Indonesia, both before and after independence from the Dutch had been achieved: "Educational Development and Social Change in Indonesia," *Harvard Educational Review,* 24 (Fall, 1954), 239–55.

9. Cf. Allison Davis, *Social-Class Influences upon Learning* (Cambridge, 1950), and Kenneth Eells, et al., *Intelligence and Cultural Differences* (Chicago, 1951).

10. Davis, "The Motivation of the Underprivileged Worker," *op. cit.*

11. Cf. Arthur Mayhew, *The Education of India* (London, 1926), p. 71.

12. Cf. J. G. Leyburn, *The Haitian People* (New Haven, 1941), p. 279.

13. Everett Cherrington Hughes, *French Canada in Transition* (Chicago, 1943), Chapter XI. Professor Hughes has made the same point more strongly in lectures at the University of Chicago.

14. Cunningham, *op. cit.,* pp. 150, 160; Batten, *op. cit.,* pp. 43–7; The Nuffield Foundation and the Colonial Office, *African Education: A Study of Educational Policy and Practice in British Tropical Africa* (Oxford, 1953), p. 37.

15. Mayhew, *op. cit.,* p. 250.

16. On careers, see Everett C. Hughes, "Institutional Office and the Person," *American Journal of Sociology,* XLIII (November, 1937), 404–13; and Oswald Hall, "The Stages of a Medical Career," *ibid.,* LIII (March, 1948), 327–36.

17. Becker, "The Career of the Chicago Public School Teacher," *op. cit.*

18. I draw here on an unpublished study of Kansas City teachers by Warren Peterson.

19. The Nuffield Foundation and the Colonial Office, *op. cit.,* p. 117.

20. Summarized from Becker, "The Teacher in the Authority System . . . ," *op. cit.,* and from material in the Ph.D. thesis of Harold MacDowell, "The Principal's Role in a Metropolitan School System," (University of Chicago, 1954).

21. Rexford G. Tugwell, *The Stricken Land* (New York, 1947), p. 109.

11   *Education and Social Mobility in Four Societies*

ROBERT J. HAVIGHURST

ONE of the most important aspects of social change in modern times is the vertical social mobility connected with it. This movement up or down on a scale of socio-economic status is related to education. The three variables—social mobility, social change, and education—are related to each other in ways which this paper will discuss.

The interrelations of social mobility, social change, and education can be seen better if they are viewed comparatively in several societies which are in different stages of economic development. In this way one may avoid over-hasty generalizations and secure a broader sweep for such conclusions as can be drawn. Therefore we have used data from the United States of America, Brazil, England, and Australia. The data are not altogether adequate, but much is gained by using data as are available from several countries.

Social Mobility in the Four Societies

For the purpose of this paper we must define individual socio-economic mobility as mobility in a scale of occupational prestige. This procedure is not an ideal one, but it can be defended in modern urban-industrial societies, where work has a central position and a person is evaluated socially by the work he performs unless he is in the uppermost class. No doubt mobility on an occupational scale is more easily achieved than mobility on a more general social scale, and there is quantitatively more of it, in modern societies; but the correlation between occupational status and general status is so high that we can use mobility on an occupational scale as a good index of general social mobility.

The facts about individual social mobility in the four countries are summarized in Table 1, which tells what proportions of the present adult population have been stable, or upward or downward mobile during their lives—that is, how their social status at age 30 to 70 compares with that of their fathers when the latter were in the same age range.

Reprinted from Robert J. Havighurst, "Education, Social Mobility and Social Change in Four Societies," *International Review of Education,* Vol. IV (1958), No. 2, with the permission of the author and the publisher.

The USA and Brazil show the greatest net upward mobility, while it appears that Great Britain and probably Australia have some net downward mobility during the present century.

These comparisons are crude, but they almost certainly show the rela-

Table 1.

Individual Social Mobility in the Four Societies

Crude Comparisons
PERCENTAGES OF ADULTS WHO HAVE BEEN:

Country	Stable	Upward Mobile	Downward Mobile
USA	55	33	12
England	40	27	33
Australia	45	20	35
Brazil	43	40	17
(São Paulo)			

Note: These comparisons are highly tentative. The Australian and Brazilian data are based on a sample in only one urban area. The number of classes used in the analysis was 4 in Australia, 5 in the USA and England, and 6 in Brazil.

tive differences between the four countries. They depend on studies made with different methods, but all using the same basic concept of socio-economic class, and using 4, 5 or 6 classes.

The British data are based on the best sample (6) but are limited by the fact that social status was determined entirely on the basis of occupation, whereas the American data employed a broader socio-economic criterion. The American data are based on a sample of adults aged 40–70 in the metropolitan area of Kansas City. (7) While they represent only one (but a typical) area, there are other studies which agree with this one in reporting a net upward mobility of about 15 to 20 percent. (10) The Brazilian data are based on a sample of men in the city of São Paulo (9) and certainly over-estimate the degree of mobility for the country as a whole, since São Paulo is the center of industrial development. The Australian data are the least adequate, being taken from a study of the fathers of sixth grade children in a suburb of Melbourne of "mixed socio-economic classes." (11)

GROUP MOBILITY

In addition to discussing *individual social mobility*, we shall consider *group mobility*. In this case a social group moves up or down on the socio-economic scale. For instance, the urban working class has moved up on the socio-economic scale in all four countries. Possibly Australia has seen the greatest working-class gains, relative to the lower-middle class. Since 1900 the Australian working class has much improved its group status, through a government wage control board, and through a liberal system of family allowances (based on number of children) together with a fairly generous system of old-age benefits.

The British working class has also increased its relative status, compared with the middle class, mainly through a system of health service, insurance against unemployment and retirement and disability, and through an extensive program of free public secondary education. Most of Britain's increased productivity since 1900 has gone to raise the standard of living of the working class, after subtracting the cost of two disastrous World Wars.

Brazil's urban working class has seen a substantial increase of economic status since 1900, enough to put a big distance between it and the rural working class. Furthermore, the inflation since 1930 has hurt the middle classes more than the working class and thus has reduced the distance between them.

The American working-class has been upward mobile as a group, perhaps as much as the Australian working class, and more than the working class of any of the other three countries if we consider only economic gains without making comparisons with the middle classes. This is evidenced by the increasing real income of the working-class group, and by its increasing possession of certain symbols of middle-class status, such as labor-saving devices in the home, vacation with pay, and secondary and higher education for the children.

CONDITIONS WHICH TEND TO PRODUCE NET UPWARD MOBILITY

If we identify social status with occupational position, in order to study social mobility, we have to ask ourselves what conditions increase the number of positions of middle and upper status in a society; and, what conditions create vacancies in these positions that permit upward mobility.

There are two general conditions which make for a net upward mobility.

1. A shift in occupational distribution so as to increase the proportion of middle and higher status occupational positions. This could result from:

a. Change in technology of production which increases the proportion of more technical and highly-skilled and better paid positions at the expense of semi-skilled and unskilled jobs. For instance, automation does this.

b. Change in type of industry from those with many unskilled jobs to those with more jobs requiring technical training. The change from agriculture to manufacturing industry usually does this; and so does a change from farming with human labor to farming with machinery.

c. Introduction of new industries which require a high proportion of technically-trained and well-paid workers.

d. Increase of industrial productivity with resultant increase in wages and salaries, which allows people to spend more of their income on services provided by professional people, thus increasing the proportion of such people.

e. Free or easy access to valuable natural resources, such as good land, gold, diamonds, oil, uranium. This creates people with wealth who take the status positions of owners of wealth.

2. Differential fertility, with upper and/or middle status people not

reproducing their numbers. They leave gaps in the upper and middle classes which are filled from below, provided the society maintains or increases the number of its middle and higher status positions.

CONDITIONS WHICH PROMOTE BALANCED MOBILITY,
BOTH UPWARD AND DOWNWARD

Another set of conditions promote both upward and downward mobility —the relative amounts of the two being determined by the factors already mentioned. They are:

1. Free and easy access to the kind of education that opens the way to middle and higher status occupations, combined with fairly rigorous standards. This condition tends to create an elite of talent rather than of birth.

2. Open competition for middle and higher status jobs, based on objective procedures for filling positions. Again, this condition tends to create an elite of talent rather than of birth.

3. Changing industrial procedures, creating new jobs and making old ones obsolete, thus preventing a man or his family from getting a vested interest in a particular position.

4. Upward group mobility of the lower classes, increasing their standard of living and thus enabling them to give advantages of better education and better health to their children, thus increasing their competitive ability.

Social Change in the Four Societies

The basic proposition of this paper is that industrialization leads to social change which produces social mobility (group and/or individual) and that education may effect the pace of social change and the degree of social mobility.

INDUSTRIALIZATION

Commencing with England in the beginning of the 19th century, the process of industrialization next became dominant in the USA, then Australia, and then Brazil. This involves a movement of population from rural areas to cities, a change in the occupational distribution of the population, a rise in economic productivity and in per capita income. England was mostly rural in the 18th century, but became urbanized in the 19th century. Agriculture was displaced as the principal occupation of the people with only 17 percent of the labor force in agriculture in 1871 and only 6 percent in 1931.

The United States followed the same course as Britain but about 50 years later. In the USA the proportion of the male labor force engaged in agriculture dropped from 65 to 13 percent in the century before 1950, while the proportion engaged in manufacturing and mining increased from 17 to 34 percent, the percentage in the professions increased from 2.5 to 6.3, and the percentage engaged in owning or managing a business increased from 4 to 13.

These social changes created and enlarged the "new middle class" of salaried and highly trained people—chemists, engineers, factory-managers, teachers, nurses, and office workers. Thus it was inevitable that there would be a movement of upward mobility into these new positions, unless the middle classes were producing many more than enough children to replace themselves.

Australia moved into a phase of industrialization during the present century, reducing her agricultural labor force to only 15 percent of the total. Output per worker in manufacturing and handicrafts in Australia was worth $3,600 in 1948, compared with $4,110 in the USA, $1,450 in Great Britain, and $520 in South America (13).

Australia differs somewhat from the USA in that the proportion of manual workers' jobs in the labor force seems not to have declined in the present century. Oeser and Hammond (11) comment on this fact as follows:

> In the period 1900–48 there has been a clear decline in the relative proportion of the employer and self-employed class and a corresponding increase in the other levels, particularly in that of white-collar workers; for example, in factory employment in Australia since 1900 the proportion of owners has been halved while that of white-collar employees has practically doubled; this is owing to the greater centralization of industry going along with the increasing size of factory units. In factory employment the proportion of skilled and semi-skilled together has remained fairly constant at about 70 percent.

In England, also, the proportion of manual workers' positions in the labor force seems not to have declined since 1900 (6). This is an important fact, and goes far toward explaining why England and Australia probably do not have net upward mobility. Increasing productivity in these countries has taken place without a decrease of the proportion of manual workers,

Table 2.

Comparisons of Labor Force

	% of Pop. in Labor Force	PRIMARY Agric. Min'g Frstry.	SECONDARY Mfg.	Const-ruct'n	Total	TERTIARY Com-merce	Transp. & Comm.	Serv-ices	Oth-ers
USA (1950)	39.8	13.8	28.2	6.2	51.8	18.5	7.0	23.7	2.6
Australia (1947)	42.2	17.0	27.1	7.3	48.6	15.1	8.0	18.0	7.5
Great Britain (1931)	43.0	12.1	40.0		48.0	15.8	6.9	24.4	0.9
Brazil (1950)	38.1	66.1	9.2	2.9	21.8	5.5	3.5	12.8	—

Source: United Nations Demographic Yearbook. 1955.

while in the USA there has been a substantial decrease in the proportion of manual workers.

Brazil's industrialization has only just commenced. As can be seen in the labor force data of Table 2, the agricultural labor force is still two-thirds of the total, and the proportion engaged in the tertiary occupations is less than half of what it is in the other three countries. Still, there has been a rapid trend toward industrialization and urbanization, especially since 1940. National production climbed at the rate of 6 percent from 1949 to 1955, while the population was increasing 2.5 percent a year. Brazilian agriculture and industry have a relatively low level of productivity which causes a low per capita income. Brazil is about at the place where the USA was in 1870, or Great Britain in 1840. The great change for Brazil lie ahead.

Productivity and Income. All of these countries have increased their productivity and therefore their per capital income as a result of industrialization. The USA is in the lead, as can be seen in Table 3. British per capita

Table 3.

Mean Annual Per Capita Income 1952–4.

Current Prices

United States of America	$ 1,870
Australia	950
Great Britain	850
Brazil	230

Source: Statistical Report of the United Nations.

Note: Comparisons of this sort may be misleading because no account is taken of differences in the cost of living in the several countries. Thus, if Britain had a lower cost of living than Australia, the per capita income in Britain would seem to be lower than its real value, as compared with Australia. The same criticism can be made of the comparisons of output per worker, made earlier. Colin Clark has made comparisons of "real income" per capital, using an "international unit," which still places the four countries in the same order, but reduces the differences between them.

income multiplied about four-fold from 1870 to 1950, while that of the USA multiplied five-fold. Output per man-hour is higher in the USA and Australia than in England. Brazilian per capita income approximately doubled in the last ten years.

Natural Resources. The availability of natural resources has a great deal of do with national productivity. In this respect the USA and Australia have profited most during the past century, with cheap and fertile land, gold, oil, and then uranium. Englishmen exploited the natural resources of the Empire in the 19th century, by taking up cheap land in Canada, Australia, or South Africa, or by finding gold, diamonds, and exotic agricultural products. Brazil's exploitable natural resources are not fully known, but it seems that with oil, iron ore, and probably much undeveloped fertile land, there may be a considerable addition to Brazil's income from these sources in the future.

DIFFERENTIAL BIRTH-RATES

The population growth of the four countries is shown in Table 4. Eng-

Table 4.

Population Growth

(Millions)

		COUNTRY		
Year	USA	Great Britain	Australia	Brazil
1800	5	9.5	—	3
1850	23	20	.43	7
1900	76	37	3.8	18
1940	132	46	7.0	42
1957	170	52	9.4	60

land's period of rapid growth ended with the 19th century. The United States and Australia probably have passed the peak of their growth rates but are still growing rapidly. Brazil's growth as been more rapid in the 20th than in the 19th century. All four countries show a differential birth-rate between the middle and the working classes. Britain probably has the greatest differential, but the USA has been quite similar to Britain during recent decades in this respect. In these two countries it has been some time since upper-middle and upper-class families have reproduced their numbers, and consequently they have left gaps in the social structure to be filled by children of working-class families. Some crude calculations made by the writer for the USA (7) indicate that the upward movement of youth from lower to higher status in order to make up for failure of the higher groups to reproduce themselves would create a net upward mobility of about 13 percent per generation, moving up one step on a five-step social class scale.

The failure of England to show a net upward mobility in spite of a differential birth-rate must be due to an actual decrease of middle and higher status positions in the past half-century.

Australia has a differential birth-rate, but a lesser one than that of the USA. At the same time, it appears that the proportion of upper-middle and upper-class positions in Australia may have decreased in the past half century.

Brazil certainly has a differential birth-rate, with differences between rural and urban people and between working-class and middle-class people (2). On the other hand, this differential is partly neutralized by a differential infant mortality rate which reduces the relative numbers of working-class infants who survive. But infant mortality is declining rapidly, and may permit the differential birth-rate to become an effective force for upward mobility, provided the birth-rate of upper and middle-class people declines below the replacement level, as it has in other countries with the coming of urbanization and industrialization. At present the Brazilian upper and middle classes are reproducing themselves, though not with as much surplus as the lower classes are. Therefore, the differential birth-rate, though it exists, is not at present a source of upward mobility.

SOCIAL STRUCTURE

The social structures of the four societies are basically similar, with a small upper class based on wealth acquired in the past, a growing middle class which can be divided into an upper-middle and a lower-middle segment, and a large working class which can also be divided into upper and lower segments, primarily depending on the possession of a trade or a technical skill and a steady job by the upper segment. Table 5 gives a rough estimate of the percentage distribution of the population in the five social

Table 5.

Comparative Data on Social Structure

Approximate Percentages of the Population in the Various Social Classes

Social Class	USA	Great Britain	Australia	Brazil
Upper	3	3	2	2
Upper Middle	10	7	6	3
Lower Middle	30	20	18	12
Upper Lower	40	50	54	33
Lower Lower	17	20	20	50

Note: These are very rough approximations, mainly because the social classes in the four countries are not strictly comparable. An attempt has been made to equate the other three countries as nearly as possible to the system of classes found in the USA.

classes. For England and the USA the estimates are fairly good. (6, 7). For Australia the estimate is hardly more than an intelligent guess. For Brazil, the writer has worked out the distribution after studying data on occupational distribution, land ownership and income (1, 3, 4, 9, 12). The relatively large middle classes of the USA and the relatively small middle classes of Brazil are the most important facts in the Table. This explains why the USA has had a net upward mobility in the past 50 years, and why Brazil may expect a net upward mobility for the next 50 years.

In the USA, the working-classes have grown smaller and the middle classes larger since 1900. This is due mainly to the development of the tertiary occupations in a highly productive economy capable of supporting the people who perform the characteristic services of these occupations.

In Great Britain and Australia, the middle classes have not grown larger. They may actually have decreased in relative size in Great Britain, due to loss of middle class positions in the Empire's service as the Dominions filled more and more of their higher status positions with their own natives. Furthermore, Britain's costly twentieth century wars have used up wealth which otherwise would have gone to maintain more people in hereditary upper and middle class statuses.

Brazil is in transition: from an agricultural aristocracy to an industrial democracy. It seems certain that in Brazil the agricultural workers will decrease, the urban industrial workers will increase, and the tertiary occupations of commerce, transport and social services will increase. The middle classes might double in a generation, which would require a great deal of upward mobility. In addition there certainly would be a great deal of mobility up from the agricultural lower-lower class to the urban upper-lower class.

The speed of social change in Brazil will depend on the relative strength of the two social structures which now exist—the aristocratic and rural social structure of the old Brazil and the incipient industrial democratic structure.

Education in Relation to Mobility and Social Change

In discussing education in relation to social mobility, it is useful to distinguish between the *functional* and the *symbolic* values of education. Education has a functional value when it is used *directly* to accomplish a purpose. For example, when a person takes an engineering course and becomes an engineer, his education has had a functional value for him. Education has a *symbolic* value when it is used as a *symbol* of status. For example when a person takes a doctor's degree in medicine and uses the degree as a symbol of status, but does not practice medicine, his education has a symbolic value. Or when an uneducated man earns a good deal of money in business and then sends his son to a selective private school before the son enters the family business, the son's education has a symbolic value.

Of all modern countries, the United States has gone the furthest in stressing the functional rather than the symbolic values of education, except perhaps the Soviet Union.

The great increase in American secondary school enrolment after 1900 came because parents thought their children could get better jobs through learning the skills and knowledge taught in school. In the United States there has been a great development of schools and courses of business administration in the universities, because boys and their parents believe that such courses will make successful business men. And the enormous technological development of the 20th century saw the multiplication of enrolments in schools of engineering, and of technical secondary school courses to train people directly for the new jobs in industry.

In Brazil education of a functional type is beginning to be used consciously and explicitly as an instrument of social change to increase productivity. The use of functional education for economic and industrial development is an aspect of Brazilian government policy, as is indicated in the 1957 Annual Message to Congress of President Kubitschek, who called for a new type of education which would teach the farmers to use machines and thus to increase their producitvity. At the same time he called for an expansion of the country's production of engineers and technicians. In effect President Kubitschek was asking Brazilians to give up their 19th century emphasis on the symbolic values of education in favor of a new kind of education with functional values. However, this change is only just beginning, and has not appreciably influenced the Brazilian secondary schools.

Great Britain and Australia have relied more on the symbolic values of education than has the USA. Secondary education has had a great symbolic value in the eyes of the English and Australians, though primary education has been recognized to possess functional values. Thus, after a man has had a primary education, he has been expected in England and Australia to learn "on the job," if he is a manual worker. If he is to go into business management, he has been expected to get a secondary education mainly for its symbolic value and then to learn "on the job."

Only since 1940 have Great Britain and Australia adopted a policy of using secondary education and higher education in a functional way for economic development of the society. Even as late as 1952, writing about "the Australian Way of Life," Mr. Frederic W. Eggleston could say (5) "The attitude of the ordinary Australian to education is not encouraging— so many people have succeeded in life without education, in politics, in business, and in the public service, that there is not the "magic" in education that exists in some countries. It is not regarded as a step to wealth or to a higher social grade."

EDUCATION FOR MOBILITY

A functional type of education serves both to promote individual upward mobility and group upward mobility, under certain conditions.

Individual Mobility. The major way in which education has fostered individual mobility is by training lower-status youth to take positions in the tertiary occupations and thus to enter the "new middle class." In the USA the new middle class has grown very rapidly. These people—engineers, chemists, accountants, teachers, nurses, etc., together with the older professions of law, medicine, and the clergy—increased from 6 percent of the labor force in 1870 to 25 percent in 1950. There were 7,000 engineers in 1870 and fifty times as many in 1950.

This group is now just beginning to grow rapidly in Brazil, and will require education to support its growth.

Individual upward mobility may be increased by a system of scholarship grants to poor but able youth, or by a system of free secondary and

Table 6.

Education of Youth in the Four Countries

Percentages of Young People in Primary and Secondary School and College, 1950–5.

	USA 1955	Great Britain 1950	Australia 1952	Brazil 1956
Primary School Age 7—13	98	98	98	62 (7—11 incl.)
Secondary School Age 14—17	81	38	60	12 (12—15 incl.) 4 (16—18 incl.)
University Age 18—21	31	2.5	6	1.5 (19—22 incl.)

Enrolment Figures from: UNESCO-Current School Enrolment Statistics. Jan. 1956, and James B. Conant, Education and Liberty. Cambridge, Mass., Harvary University Press, 1953.

higher education. Table 6 shows the proportions of youth attending secondary school and university in the four countries, and gives some indication of the role of education in promoting upward mobility.

Obviously the USA has made greater use of education for this purpose than the other countries. Australia has made a considerable use of it, and is intensifying this at present by increasing the enrolments of secondary schools and by moving toward a more functional type of secondary and higher education. Great Britain has also extended free secondary education, and has changed the system to permit poor but able youth to get into the universities by means of a new "comprehensive" secondary school. Even though the number of university attendants in Great Britain is low, compared with the USA and Australia, the British system of government scholarships has made university attendance possible for many poor but able youth. Glass' study indicated that 26 percent of university graduates came from working class families during the past 30 or 40 years (6).

In Brazil, Hutchinson's study of students at the University of São Paulo indicates that only 10 percent of entering students in 1954 were from working class families. This indicates that Brazil is not using the Universities to assist much individual mobility. The University of São Paulo probably draws more working class students than most other Brazilian universities.

Table 7 shows how the social class origins of students in various types of higher institutions in the USA compare with Brazil and England. It appears that there is a higher proportion of students of working class

Table 7.

Social Status of University Students

PERCENTAGE DISTRIBUTION OF STUDENTS

Social Status	São Paulo	University of Wiscon- sin, USA	USA in general	England (graduates)
Upper	38	15	10	15
Upper Middle	36	25	30	26
Lower Middle	16	30	30	32
Upper Working Class	8	25	25	21
Lower Working Class	2	5	5	6

Data on São Paulo students from Hutchinson.
Data on American University students adapted from Havighurst and Neugarten.
Data on English University graduates from Glass.

origin in American and British universities than in Brazil. Australia is more like Britain and the USA in this respect.

Group Mobility. Education of a functional type is generally used by a government as a means of upward group mobility for the working classes. It serves to increase their productivity, and the additional income they obtain thereby is used by them to raise their socio-economic level.

Primary education was used for this purpose in Great Britain, the USA and Australia in the latter half of the 19th century, and is being used for the same purpose now in Brazil.

Secondary education has also been used for the purpose of group mobility since 1900 in the USA, and since World War II in England and Australia. Functional secondary education not only increases productivity and makes possible an increase of income for the working classes; it also increases the extent to which people may enjoy life, through reading, taking part in musical and artistic activites, travel, etc., and is therefore a mark of higher social status in itself.

Brazil has not yet made use of secondary education for group mobility.

Conclusion About Mobility and Education

The purpose of this study was to find out how social mobility and education are related to each other in societies undergoing industrialization and urbanization. From the four societies we have studied, the following generalizations can be made.

A. *There is a great deal of social mobility in an industrial society.*

There are two types of social mobility, individual upward or downward mobility and group upward or downward mobility.

Individual upward mobility is made possible in a society by:

1. Technological development which increases productivity and changes the structure of the labor force so as to include higher proportions of middle class and of skilled worker positions.

2. Differential fertility, with the higher classes failing to reproduce themselves.

3. Individual talent and effort.

Group upward mobility is made possible by:

1. Technological development which increases productivity.

2. Distribution of the increased social income in such a manner that one or more groups get especially large shares.

3. Use by the mobile group of its income to purchase the symbols of higher status (home furnishings, education for children, clothing, etc.).

B. *Education has tended to foster mobility.*

Education affects all of these factors, directly or indirectly. Technological development depends upon the supply of technically-trained people, while the improvement of technology requires research-trained people. Individual talent is developed by education, and children with potential talent are often motivated by education to develop their abilities. Indirectly, education probably affects differential fertility, by making it easier for the better educated people to get information on contraception. Education also affects the consumption habits of lower class people, teaching them about middle class values and middle class material possessions. Even the differential economic gains of the working class can be ascribed partly to the fact that through workers' education and through the extension of primary and secondary education, working-class people have learned how to organize and assert their interests.

But education is one factor among several which affect the degree of upward mobility, including natural resources, the nature of organization and administration of industry, religious and social beliefs concerning fertility and contraception, and politico-economic factors such as the ways in which national income is allocated, and immigration policy.

C. *Different countries make different uses of education in relation to social mobility.*

Brazil. Brazil is just at the beginning of industrialization and urbanization. While large sections of the country retain a rural and aristocratic social structure, the industrial areas exhibit a high individual upward mobility rate together with upward group mobility for the working class.

Education has been involved in this process to only a limited degree. Foreign technologists have been imported to assist the process of industrialization, which otherwise would have waited upon the development and expansion of technical education in Brazil.

At present, however, education is becoming important in the current phase of industrial development. Primary education is increasing the productivity of factory workers. Secondary and higher education are beginning to supply people for the new middle class positions created by developing technology. Enrolments in engineering and the physical sciences are increasing rapidly. Thus the individual talent and effort factor is being influenced by education more now than in the past.

Probably education will have more influence on group mobility in Brazil during the coming two or three decades. The question of how the national income shall be allocated among the several economic groups will be settled through political contests and through bargaining between capital and labor, with education assisting the working classes to formulate and argue their case more effectively.

The United States. The USA is past the middle of its evolution toward industrialization. At this point education is involved with all of the factors affecting social mobility. Technological development is tied closely to the training of technicians and managers. There may be further net upward mobility due to automation, but probably not much of it. Further increase of productivity will result in further upward group mobility for the working classes, but this will depend increasingly on their educational level. Individual mobility, both upward and downward, will be increased by the extension of educational opportunity to working class youth through expanded scholarship aid.

Education will probably tend to decrease the amount of upward mobility through differential fertility, for the trend seems to be toward a roughly equal fertility rate among urban classes as the working classes get more education.

Great Britain. Great Britain is in a later phase of industrial development than the other countries. At this point education seems not to be productive of net upward mobility. Technological development is not increasing the productivity of the country at such a rapid rate as in the USA. Differential fertility is less than formerly, and less effective in producing mobility. But British education is becoming more functional at the secondary school and university levels, and therefore is likely to be more effective than formerly in promoting individual upward mobility through talent, together with an equal amount of downward mobility. If present political policies continue, most of the increased productivity of the country will go into group mobility of the working classes.

Australia. Australia is between the USA and Brazil in its stage of industrial evolution, but has adopted the English technology, which relies more on manual labor and less on mass production and automation than does the American technology. Consequently Australia has not had any increase of upward mobility due to technological change in the past 50 years. However, education is becoming more functional, and secondary and higher education are becoming more accessible to working-class youth, with the consequence that individual upward and downward mobility will be kept at a rather high level. In Australia, as in England, political policies will probably convert the increased productivity of the country into group mobility for the working class.

THE FUTURE OF SOCIAL MOBILITY IN RELATION TO EDUCATION

It is foolhardy to predict the course of future productivity based upon technology, with atomic energy almost ready for use but with petroleum resources becoming depleted and other natural resources being used up in the more industrial countries. However, it seems reasonable to suppose that productivity may reach something of a plateau in the technologically mature nations, while it increases rapidly in the less industrialized countries. If this happens, social mobility due to technological development will be great in the less industrialized countries, as it is now in Brazil, and will tend to disappear in the more developed countries. What increase of productivity does take place in the more developed countries, such as Great Britain and the USA, will depend more and more on research and on the technical and managerial skills of the population—that is, upon their education.

Social mobility due to differential fertility is likely to decrease or disappear in the more industrialized countries, because differential fertility will decrease in size and importance. In this, education will play a part, both in reducing families of the working classes and in enlarging families of the middle classes. This process can already be seen in Sweden.

The upward group mobility of the working classes may reduce the social distance between the working classes and the middle classes. If the difference in income between manual and non-manual workers becomes less, then the main differences between classes will be non-economic, and the nature of these differences will be largely determined by the uses they make of their money and of their leisure time. These uses will be considerably affected by their education.

Finally, it appears that the evolution of a modern industrial society tends toward a reduction of net upward individual mobility or perhaps toward its disappearance; but at the same time, this evolution tends toward increasing the amount of balanced upward and downward individual mobility. In this type of society there is likely to be increased opportunity for people with talent and ambition to get the education they need for "better" positions and to achieve these positions while those with less talent and ambition will tend to be downward mobile.

The industrial and democratic society of the year 2000 will be even more open and fluid than the most highly industrialized societies today, so that education will be the main instrument for upward mobility, and lack of education or failure to do well in one's education will be the principal cause of downward mobility.

Bibliography

1. Instituto Brasileiro de Geografia e Estatistica. *Annuario Estatistico do Brasil, 1955.* Rio de Janeiro 1955.
2. Alceu Vincente de Carvalho. "Alguns Aspectos da Natalidade No Brasil." *Revista Brasileira de Estatistica 15,* No. 59. pp. 117–185. July/Sept. 1954.
3. *Conjuntura Social,* "Evolucão da Mao-de-Obra Brasileira." *Conjuntura Economica 10,* Nos. 7, 8, 9, pp. 79–86; 49–56; 43–50. July, August, Sept. 1956.
4. *Conjuntura Social,* "Tipos de Trabalhadores Rurais No Brasil." *Conjuntura Economica 10,* No. 12, pp. 71–77. Dec. 1956.
5. EGGLESTON, FREDERIC W., "The Australian Nation." p. 17 in *The Australian Way of Life,* ed. by George Caiger. Wm. Heinemann, London 1953.
6. GLASS, D. V., et al. *Social Mobility in Britain.* Routledge & Kegan Paul London 1954.
7. HAVIGHURST, ROBERT J. and NEUGARTEN, BERNICE L., *Society and Education.* Ch. 2. Allyn and Bacon, Boston 1957.
8. HUTCHINSON, BERTRAM. "Origem Socio-economica dos Estudantes Universitarios de São Paulo," *Educaçao e Ciencias Sociais* 2, No. 3, Dec. 1956.
9. HUTCHINSON, BERTRAM, "*Social Mobility in the City of São Paulo,*" Unpublished paper, 1957.
10. National Opinion Research Center. "Jobs and Occupations: A Popular Evaluation." in *Class, Status, and Power.* Ed. by Reinhard Bendix and Seymour M. Lipset. *The Free Press,* Glencoe, Illinois 1953.
11. OESER, O. A. and HAMMOND, S. B., *Social Structure and Personality in a City* p. 239. Routledge and Kegan Paul, London 1954.
12. Américo Barbosa de Oliveria, "O Ensino, O Trabalho, A População e A Renda." CAPES; Série "*Estudos e Ensàios.*" No. 1 Dec. 1953, Ministério de Educação e Cultura. Rio de Janeiro.
13. W. S. WOYTINSKY and E. S. WOYTINSKY, *World Population and Productivity.* Twentieth Century Fund, New York 1953.

12 Modes of Social Ascent through Education: Sponsored and Contest Mobility[1]

RALPH H. TURNER

THE OBJECT of this paper is to suggest a framework for relating certain differences between American and English systems of education to the prevailing norms of upward mobility in each country. Others have noted the tendency for educational systems to support prevailing schemes of stratification, but this statement will dwell specifically on the manner in which the *accepted mode of upward mobility* shapes the school system directly and indirectly through its effects on the values that implement social control. The task will be carried out by describing two ideal-typical normative patterns of upward mobility and suggesting their logical ramifications in the general character of stratification and social control. In addition to showing relationships among a number of differences between American and English schooling, the ideal-types have broader implications than those developed in this paper. First, they suggest a major dimension of stratification, which might profitably be incorporated into a variety of studies on social class. Second, they can be readily applied in further comparisons, between countries other than the United States and England.

The Nature of Organizing Norms

Many investigators have concerned themselves with rates of upward mobility in specific countries or internationally,[2] and with the manner in which school systems facilitate or impede such mobility.[3] Preoccupation with *extent* of mobility has precluded equal attention to the predominant *mode* of mobility in each country. The central assumption underlying this paper is that within a formally open class system providing mass education the organizing folk norm that defines the accepted mode of upward mobility is a crucial factor in shaping the school system, and may be even more crucial than is the extent of upward mobility. In England and the United

Reprinted from Ralph H. Turner, "Sponsored and Contest Mobility and the School System," *American Sociological Review,* Vol. XXV (1960), No. 5, with the permission of the author and the publisher.

States there appear to be different organizing folk norms, which may be labelled *sponsored mobility* and *contest mobility* respectively. *Contest* mobility is a system in which elite[4] status is the prize in an open contest and is taken by the aspirants' own efforts. While the "contest" is governed by some rules of fair play, the contestants have wide latitude in the strategies they may employ. Since the "prize" of successful upward mobility is not in the hands of the established elite to give out, the latter are not in a position to determine who shall attain it and who shall not. Under *sponsored* mobility, elite recruits are chosen by the established elite or their agents, and elite status is *given* on the basis of some criterion of supposed merit and cannot be *taken* by any amount of effort or strategy. Upward mobility is like entry into a private club, where each candidate much be "sponsored" by one or more of the members. Ultimately, the members grant or deny upward mobility on the basis of whether they judge the candidate to have the qualities that they wish to see in fellow members.

Before elaborating this distinction, we must note that these systems of mobility are ideal types, designed to clarify observed differences in the predominantly similar English and American systems of stratification and education. As organizing norms, these principles are assumed to be present at least implicitly in people's thinking, guiding their judgments of what is appropriate and inappropriate on many specific matters. Such organizing norms do not correspond perfectly with the objective characteristics of the societies in which they exist, nor are they completely independent of them. Out of the complex interplay of social and economic conditions and ideologies, the people in a society come to develop a highly simplified conception of the way in which events take place. This conception of the "natural" as contrasted with the unnatural is translated into a norm—the "natural" becomes what "ought" to be—and in turn imposes a strain toward consistency upon relevant aspects of the society. Thus, the norm reacts upon the objective conditions to which it refers and has ramifying effects upon directly and indirectly related features of the society.[5]

Four statements will briefly outline the conception of an ideal-typical organizing norm. (1) The ideal types are not fully exemplified in practice since they are normative systems, and no normative system can be devised so as to cope with all empirical exigencies. (2) Predominant norms usually compete with less ascendant norms engendered by changes and inconsistencies in the underlying social structure. (3) Although not fully explicit, organizing folk norms are reflected in specific value judgments. Those judgments, regarded as having a convincing ring to them irrespective of the logic expressed, or seeming to require no extended argumentation, may be presumed to reflect the prevailing folk norms. (4) The predominant organizing norms in one segment of society will be functionally related to those in other segments.

Two final qualifications to the scope of this paper must be made. First, the organizing folk norm of upward mobility affects the school system because the school has as one of its functions the facilitation of mobility. Since fostering mobility is only one among several social functions of the school, and not the most important function in the societies under examination, we can give only a very partial accounting of the whole set of forces making for similarities and differences in the school systems of United States and England. Only those differences directly or indirectly reflecting the performance of the mobility function can be noted here. Second, the concern of this paper is with the current dynamics of the situation in the two countries rather than their historical development. No effort will be made to explain how the systems became what they are. The concern will be solely with what keeps them operating as they do.

Major Distinctions Between the Two Norms

Contest mobility is like a sporting event in which many compete for a few recognized prizes. The contest is judged to be fair only if all the players compete on an equal footing. Victory must be won solely by one's own efforts. The most satisfactory outcome is not necessarily a victory of the most able, but of the most deserving. The tortoise who defeats the hare is a folk prototype of the deserving sportsman. Enterprise, initiative, perseverance, and craft are admirable qualities if they allow the person initially at a disadvantage to triumph. Even clever manipulation of the rules may be admired if it helps the contestant who is smaller or less muscular or less rapid to win. Applied to mobility, the contest norm means that victory by a person of moderate intelligence accomplished through the use of common sense, craft, enterprise, daring, and successful risk-taking[6] is more appreciated than victory of the most intelligent or the best-educated.

Sponsored mobility, on the other hand, rejects the pattern of the contest and substitutes a controlled selection process. In this process the elite or their agents, who are best qualified to judge merit, *call* those individuals to elite status who have the appropriate qualities. Individuals do not win or seize elite status, but mobility is rather a process of sponsored induction into the elite following selection.

Pareto had this sort of mobility in mind when he suggested that a governing class might dispose of persons potentially dangerous to it by admitting them to elite membership, provided the recruits change character by adopting elite attitudes and interests.[7] Danger to the ruling class would seldom be the major criterion for choice of elite recruits. But Pareto's assumption was that the established elite would select whom they wished to enter their ranks and would train the recruits to the attitudes and interests of the established elite.

The governing objective of contest mobility is to give elite status to those who earn it, while the goal of sponsored mobility is to make the best use of the talents in society by sorting each person into his proper niche. In different societies the conditions of competitive struggle may reward quite different attributes, and sponsored mobility may select on the basis of such diverse qualities as intelligence or visionary capability, but the difference in principle remains the same.[8]

Under the contest system, society at large establishes and interprets the criteria of elite status. If one wishes to have his high status recognized he must display certain credentials that identify his class to those about him. The credentials must be highly visible and require no special skill for their assessment, since credentials are presented to the masses. Material possession and mass popularity are perfect credentials in this respect, and any special skill that produces a tangible product easily assessed by the untrained will do. The nature of sponsored mobility precludes this type of operation but assigns to credentials instead the function of identifying the elite to one another.[9] Accordingly, the ideal credentials are special skills requiring the trained discrimination of the elite for their recognition. Intellectual, literary, or artistic excellences, which can only be appraised by those trained to appreciate them, are perfect credentials in this respect. Concentration on such skills lessens the likelihood that an interloper will succeed in claiming the right to elite membership on grounds of the popular evaluation of his competence.

In the sporting event there is special admiration for the slow starter who makes a dramatic finish, and many of the rules are designed to insure that the game should not be declared over until it has run its full course. Contest mobility incorporates this fear of premature judgments and of anything that would give special advantage to those who are ahead at any point in the race. Under sponsored mobility, fairly early selection of only the number of persons necessary to fill the anticipated vacancies in the elite is desirable. Early selection allows time to prepare the recruits for their elite position. Aptitudes, inherent capacities, and spiritual gifts can be assessed fairly early in life, by techniques ranging from divination to the most sophisticated psychological test, and the more naive the subject at the time of selection, the less likely his talents are to be blurred by differential learning or conspiracy to defeat the test. Since the elite will take the initiative in training the recruit, they are more interested in his capabilities than in what he will do with them on his own, and they are concerned that no one else should first have an opportunity to train the recruit's talents in the wrong direction. Contest mobility tends to delay the final award as long as practicable, to permit a fair race; sponsored mobility tends to place the selection point as early in life as practicable, to insure control over selection and training.

A system of sponsored mobility develops most readily in a society with but a single elite or with a recognized elite hierarchy. When multiple elites compete among themselves, the mobility process tends to take the contest pattern, since no group is able to command control of recruitment. Sponsored mobility further depends upon a societal structure fostering monopoly of elite credentials. Lack of such monopoly undercuts sponsorship and control of the recruitment process. Monopoly of elite credentials is in turn typically a product of a society with a well-entrenched traditional aristocracy, employing such intrinsically monopolizable credentials as family line and bestowable title, or of a society organized along large-scale bureaucratic lines, permitting centralized control of movement up the hierarchy of success.

English society has been described as the juxtaposition of two systems of stratification, the urban-industrial class system and the surviving aristocratic system. While the sponsored-mobility pattern reflects the logic of the latter, our impression is that it pervades popular thinking rather than merely coexisting with the logic of industrial stratification. Students of cultural change note that patterns imported into an established culture tend to be reshaped into coherence with the established culture as they are assimilated. Thus, it may be that the changes in stratification attendant upon industrialization have led to many alterations in the rates, the specific means, and the rules of mobility, but that these changes have taken place within the unchallenged organizing norm of sponsored mobility.

Social Control and the Two Norms

Every society must cope with the problem of maintaining loyalty to its social system, and every society does so in part through norms and values, some of which vary by class position and some of which are relatively uniform through the social strata. Norms and values prevalent within each class must direct behavior into channels that support the total system, while the values that transcend strata must support the general class differential. The way in which upward mobility takes place determines in part the kinds of norms and values that will serve the indicated purposes of social control in each class and throughout the society.

The most conspicuous control problem is that of ensuring loyalty in the disadvantaged classes toward a system under which they receive less than a proportional share of society's goods. Under a system of contest mobility, this is accomplished by a combination of future orientation, the universal norm of ambition, and a general sense of fellow-feeling with the elite. Every individual in encouraged to think of himself as competing for an elite position, so that in preparation he cultivates loyalty to the system and conventional attitudes. It is essential that this future orientation be kept alive by delaying any sense of final irreparable failure to reach elite position until attitudes are well established. Likewise, by thinking of himself in the successful future, the elite aspirant forms considerable identification with the elite, and any evidence that they are just ordinary human beings like himself helps to reinforce this identification as well as to keep alive the conviction that he himself may someday succeed in like manner. To forestall rebellion among the disadvantaged majority, then, a contest system must avoid any absolute points of selection for mobility and immobility and must delay clear recognition of the realities of the situation until the individual is too committed to the system to change radically. The future orientation cannot, of course, be inculcated successfully in all members of lower strata, but sufficient training to a norm of ambition tends to leave the unambitious as individual deviants and forestalls their forming a genuine subcultural group able to offer collective threat to the established system. Where this kind of control system operates rather effectively, it is notable that such organized or gang deviancy as does develop is more likely to take the form of an attack upon the conventional or moral order rather than on the class system itself. Thus, the United States has its "beatniks,"[10] who repudiate ambition and worldly values altogether, and its delinquent and criminal gangs, who try to evade the limitations imposed by conventional means,[11] but very little in the way of active revolutionaries who challenge the class system itself.

The system of sponsorship makes the foregoing control system inappropriate, since the elite recruits are chosen from above. The principal threat to the system would lie in the existence of a strong group who sought to *take* elite positions themselves. Control under this system is by training the masses to regard themselves as relatively incompetent to manage society, by restricting access to the skills and manners of the elite, and by cultivating belief in the superior competence of the elite. The earlier that selection of the elite recruits can be made, the sooner the masses can be taught to accept their inferiority and to make "realistic" rather than phantasy plans. Early selection prevents raising the hopes of large numbers of people who might otherwise become the discontented leaders of a class challenging the sovereignty of the established elite. If we assume that the difference in competence between masses and elite is seldom so great as to support the usual differences in advantage accruing to each,[12] then the differences must be artificially augmented by discouraging acquisition of elite skills by the masses. Likewise, a sense of mystery about the elite is a common device for supporting in the masses an illusion of a much greater hiatus of competence than in fact exists.

While the elite are unlikely to reject a system that benefits them, they must still be restrained from taking such advantage of their favorable situation as to jeopardize the entire elite. Under the sponsorship system, the elite recruits, who are selected early, freed from the strain of competitive struggle, and kept under close elite supervision, may be thoroughly indoctrinated in elite culture. A norm of paternalism toward inferiors may be inculcated; a heightened sensitivity of the good opinions of fellow-elite and elite recruits may be cultivated; and the appreciation of the more complex forms of aesthetic, literary, intellectual, and sporting activities may be taught. A norm of courtesy and altruism can well be maintained under sponsorship, since the elite recruits are not required to compete for their standing and since the elite may deny high standing to any who strive for position by unseemly methods. The system of sponsorship provides an almost perfect setting for the development of an elite culture characterized by a sense of responsibility for inferiors and for preservation of the "finer things" of life.

Elite control under the contest system is more difficult since there is no controlled induction and apprenticeship. The principal control seems to lie in the insecurity of elite position. In a sense, there is no final arrival under contest mobility, since each person may be displaced by newcomers throughout his life. The limited control of high standing from above prevents the clear delimitation of levels in the class system, so that success itself becomes relative. Rather than constituting primarily an accomplishment, each success serves to qualify the participant for competition at the next higher level.[13] The restraints upon the behavior of a person of high standing, therefore, are principally those applicable to a contestant who must not risk having the other contestants "gang up" on him, and who must pay some attention to the masses, who are frequently in a position to impose penalties upon him. However, any special norm of paternalism is hard to establish, since there is no dependable procedure for examining the means by which a man achieves elite credentials. While mass esteem is an effective brake upon overexploitation of position, it does not so much reward scrupulously ethical and altruistic behavior as it rewards evidence of fellow-feeling with the masses.

Under both systems, unscrupulous or disreputable persons may become or remain members of the elite, but for different reasons. In contest mobility, popular tolerance of a little "craft" in the successful combined with the fact that the newcomer does not have to undergo the close scrutiny of the old elite leaves considerable leeway for unscrupulous success. In sponsored mobility, the unpromising recruit reflects unfavorably on the judgment of his sponsors and threatens the myth of elite omniscience. Consequently, he may be tolerated, and others may "cover up" for his deficiencies in order to protect the unified front of the elite to the outer world.

Certain of the general values and norms of any society incorporate emulation of elite values by the masses. Under sponsored mobility, a good deal of the protective attitudes and interest in classical subjects percolates to the masses. Under contest mobility, however, there is not the same apparent homogeneity of moral, aesthetic, and intellectual values to be emulated, so that the conspicuous attribute of the elite is their superior level of material consumption. Consequently, emulation follows this course.

There is neither effective incentive nor punishment for the elite individual who fails to interest himself in promoting the arts or literary excellence, or who continues to maintain the vulgar manners and mode of speech of his class origin. The elite have relatively less power and the masses relatively more power to punish or reward a man for his adoption or disregard of any special elite culture. The extreme importance of accent and of grammatical excellence to the attainment of high status in England, as contrasted with the "twangs" and "drawls" and grammatical ineptitude among American elites, is the most striking example of this difference. The strength of the class system is therefore not geared into support of the *quality* of aesthetic, literary, and intellectual activities in a contest system. Only those well versed in such activities are qualified to distinguish authentic products from cheap imitations. Unless those who claim superiority in these areas are forced to submit their credentials to the elite for evaluation, poor quality will often be honored equally with high quality, and class prestige will not serve to maintain an effective norm of high quality.

The foregoing is not to imply that there will be no groups in such a society devoted to protection and fostering of high standards in art, music, literature, and intellectual pursuits, but that such standards will lack the support of the class system, which is frequently found when sponsored mobility prevails. The selection, by official welcoming committees in California, of a torch singer to entertain a visiting king and queen and "can can" dancers to entertain Mr. Krushchev illustrates how little American elites suppose that high prestige and popular taste cannot go together.

Formal Education Under Contest and Sponsorship

Returning to our conception of an organizing ideal form, we assume that to the extent to which one such norm of upward mobility is prevalent in a society there will be a constant strain to shape the educational system into conformity with that norm. These strains will operate in two fashions: directly, through blinding people to alternatives and through coloring their judgments of what are successful and unsuccessful solutions to recurring educational problems; and indirectly, through the functional interrelationships between school systems and other aspects of the class structure, systems of social control, and many features of the social structure neglected in this paper.

The most obvious application of the distinction between sponsored and contest mobility norms is to afford a partial explanation for the different policies of student selection in the English and American secondary schools. Although American high-school students take different courses of study and sometimes even attend specialized high schools, a major preoccupation has been to avoid any sharp social separation between the superior and inferior students and to keep the channels of movement between courses of study as open as possible. Even recent criticisms of the way in which superior students may be thereby held back in their development usually are qualified by insistence that these students must not, however, be withdrawn from the mainstream of student life.[14] Any such segregation offends the sense of fairness implicit in the contest norm and also arouses the fear that the elite and future elite will lose their sense of fellow-feeling with the masses. Perhaps the most important point, however, is that schooling is presented as an opportunity, and the principal burden of making use of the opportunity depends on the student's own initiative and enterprise.

The English system has undergone a succession of liberalizing changes during this century, but all of them have remained within the pattern of attempting early in the educational program to sort out the promising from the unpromising, so that the former may be segregated and given a special form of training to fit them for higher standing in their adult years. Under the Education Act of 1944, a minority of students have been selected each year by means of a battery of examinations popularly known as "eleven plus," supplemented to varying degrees by grade-school record and personal interview impressions, for admission to grammar schools.[15] The remaining students attend secondary modern or technical schools, in which the opportunities to prepare for college or train for the better occupations are minimal. The grammar schools supply what, by comparative standards, is a high quality of college preparatory education. Such a scheme embodies well the logic of sponsorship, with early selection of those destined for middle-class and better occupations, and specialized training to suit each group for the class in which they are destined to hold membership. The plan facilitates considerable mobility, and recent research reveals surprisingly little bias against the child from a manual-laboring family in the selection for grammar school, when related to measured intelligence.[16] It is altogether possible that adequate comparative research would show a closer correlation of school success with measured intelligence and a lesser correlation between school success and family background in England than in the United States. While selection of superior students for mobility opportunity is probably more efficient under such a system, the obstacles to a person not so selected "making the grade" on the basis of his own initiative or enterprise are probably correspondingly greater.

That the contrasting effects of the two systems accord with the social-control pattern under the two mobility norms is indicated by research into student ambitions in the United States and England. Researches in the United States consistently show that the general level of occupational aspiration reported by high-school students is quite unrealistic in relation to the actual distribution of job opportunities. Comparative study in England shows much less in the way of "phantasy" aspiration, and, specifically, shows a reduction in aspiration among those not selected following the "eleven-plus" examination.[17] One of the by-products of the sponsorship system is the fact that students from middle-class families whose parents cannot afford to send them to a private school suffer severe personal adjustment problems when they are assigned to secondary modern schools on the basis of this selection.[18]

While this well-known difference between the early British sorting of students into grammar and modern schools and the American comprehensive high school and junior college is the clearest application of the distinction under discussion, the organizing norms penetrate more deeply into the school systems than is initially apparent. The most telling observation regarding the direct normative operation of these principles would be evidence to support the author's impression that major critics within each country do not usually transcend the logic of their respective mobility norms in their criticisms. Thus, British critics debate the best method for getting people sorted according to ability, without proposing that elite station should be opened to whoever can take it. Although fear of "sputnik" in the United States introduced a flurry of sponsored-mobility thinking, the long-standing concern of school critics has been the failure to motivate students adequately. Preoccupation with motivation appears to be an intellectual application of the folk idea that people should *win* their station in society by personal *enterprise*.

The functional operation of a strain toward consistency with the organizing norm of upward mobility may be illustrated by reference to several other features of the school systems in the two countries. First, the value placed upon education itself is different under the two organizing norms. Under sponsored mobility, schooling is valued for its cultivation of elite culture, and those forms of schooling directed toward such cultivation are more highly valued than those which are not. Education of the non-elite is difficult to justify clearly and tends to be half-hearted, while the maximum educational resources are concentrated on "those who can benefit most from them." In practice, the latter means those who can learn the elite culture. The secondary modern schools in England have regularly suffered from less adequate financial provision and a lower teacher-student ratio, from less-well-trained teachers, and from a general lack of prestige, in comparison with the grammar schools.[19]

Under contest mobility in the United States, education is valued as a means of getting ahead, but the contents of education are not highly valued in their own right. There is even a suspicion of the educated man as one who may have gotten ahead without really earning his position. Over a century ago, De Tocqueville had commented on the absence in the United States of an hereditary class "by which the labors of the intellect are held in honor." In consequence he remarked that, "A middling standard is fixed in America for human knowledge."[20] In spite of recent criticisms of lax standards in American schools, it is in keeping with the general mobility pattern that a Gallup Poll in April, 1958, showed that school principals were much more likely to make such criticisms than parents. While 90 per cent of principals thought that ". . . our schools today demand too little work from the students," only 51 per cent of parents thought so, with 33 per cent saying the work was about right, and 6 per cent that schools demanded too much work.[21]

Second, the logic of preparation for a contest prevails in United States schools, with emphasis on keeping everyone in the running until the final stages. In primary and secondary schools, the assumption tends to be made that those who are learning satisfactorily need little special attention, while the less successful require help to be sure that they remain in the contest and may compete for the final stakes. As recently as December, 1958, a nationwide Gallup Poll gave evidence that this attitude had not been radically altered by the international situation. When asked whether teachers should devote extra time to the bright students, 26 per cent said "yes," and 67 per cent answered "no." But the responses changed to 86 per cent "yes," and only 9 per cent "no," when the question was asked concerning the "slow students."[22]

In western states, the junior college offers many students "a second chance" to qualify for university, and all state universities have some provision for substandard high-school students to earn admission.

The university itself is run like the true contest, standards being set competitively, students being forced to pass a series of trials each semester, and only a minority of the entrants achieving the prize of graduation. Such a pattern contrasts sharply with the English system in which selection is supposed to have been relatively complete before entry into university, and students may be subject to no testing whatsoever for the first year or more of university study. Although university completion rates have not been estimated in either country, some figures are indicative. The ratio of bachelor's and first-professional degrees in American institutions of higher learning, in 1957–58, to the number of first-time degree-credit enrollments in the fall, four years earlier, was reported to be .610 for men and .488 for women.[23] The indicated 39 and 51 per cent drop-out rates are probably underestimates, because transfers from two-year junior colleges swell the number of degrees without being included in first-time enrollments. In England, a study following up the careers of individual students, found that in University College, London, 81.9 per cent of entering students, between 1948 and 1951, eventually graduated with a degree. A similar study a few years earlier at the University of Liverpool revealed a figure of 86.9 per cent.[24] Under contest mobility, the object is to train as many as possible to the skills necessary for elite status so as to give everyone a chance and to maintain competition at the highest pitch. Under sponsored mobility, the objective is to train in elite culture only those for whom the presumption is that they will enter the elite, lest there be a dangerous number of "angry young men" who have elite skills without elite station.

Third, systems of mobility precipitate different emphases regarding educational content. Induction into elite culture under sponsored mobility makes for emphasis on school *esprit de corps,* which can be employed to cultivate norms of intraclass loyalty and elite tastes and manners. Likewise, formal schooling built about highly specialized study in fields with entirely intellectual or aesthetic concern and no "practical" value serves the purpose of elite culture. Under contest mobility in the United States, in spite of faculty endorsement of "liberal education," schooling tends to be measured for its practical benefits and to become, beyond the elementary level, chiefly vocational. Education does not so much provide what is good in itself as it provides skills necessary to compete for the real prizes of life, and of these vocational skills are the most important.

An application of these points can be seen in the different national attitudes toward students being gainfully employed while in university. More students in the United States than in Britain have part-time employments, and in the United States relatively fewer of the students receive subsidies toward subsistence and living expenses. The most generous programs of state aid in the United States, apart from those applying to veterans and other special groups, do not normally cover expenses other than tuition and institutional fees. British maintenance grants are designed to cover full living expenses, taking into account parents' ability to pay.[25] Under sponsored mobility, gainful employment serves no apprentice or testing function, and is thought merely to prevent the student from gaining the full benefit of his schooling. L. J. Parry speaks of the general opposition to students working and asserts that English university authorities almost unanimously hold that ". . . if a person must work for financial reasons, he should never spend more than four weeks on such work during the whole year."[26]

Under contest mobility, success in school work is not a sufficient test of practical merit, but must be supplemented by a test in the world of practical affairs. Thus, in didactic folk tales, the professional engineer will also prove himself a superior mechanic, the business tycoon, a superior behind-the-counter salesman. Consequently, by "working his way through school" the enterprising student "earns" his education in the fullest sense, keeps in touch with the practical world, and has an apprenticeship into vocational life. Students are often urged to seek part-time employment, even when there is no financial need, and in extreme instances schools have incorporated paid employment as a requirement toward graduation. As R. H. Eckleberry states the typical American view, a student willing to work part-time is a "better bet" than "the equally bright student who receives all of his financial support from others."[27]

Finally, social-adjustment training is peculiar to the system of contest mobility. The reason for emphasis on adjustment training is clear when its nature is understood. Adjustment training is preparation to cope with situations in which there are no rules of intercourse or in which the rules are unknown, but in which the good opinions of others cannot be wholly ignored. Under sponsored mobility, the elite recruits are inducted into a homogeneous stratum in which there is consensus regarding the rules, and in which they succeed socially by mastering these rules. Under contest mobility, the elite aspirant must relate himself both to the established elite and to the masses, who follow different rules; and the elite themselves are not sufficiently homogeneous to evolve consensual rules of intercourse. Furthermore, in the contest the rules may vary according to the background of the competitor, so that each aspirant must deal successfully with persons playing the game with slightly different sets of rules. Consequently, adjustment training becomes one of the important skills imparted by the school system.[28] That the emphasis on adjustment training in the schools has had genuine popular support is indicated by a 1945 Fortune poll, in which a national sample were asked which one of two things would be very important for a son of theirs to get out of college. Over 87 per cent chose "Ability to get along with and understand people," in answer to the question.[29] This answer was the second most frequently chosen as being the very most important thing to get out of college. In the present connection, it is possible that British education is better preparation for participation in an orderly and controlled world, while American education prepares better for a less ordered situation. The reputedly superior ability of "Yanks" to get things done seems to apply to this ability to cope with a chaotic situation.

To this point discussion has centered on the tax-supported school systems in both countries, but the different place and emphasis of the privately supported secondary schools can also be related to the framework at hand. Since private secondary schools in both countries are principally vehicles for transmitting high family status to the children, the mobility function is quite tangential. Under contest mobility, the private schools should presumably have no mobility function. On the other hand, if there is to be mobility in a sponsored system, the privately controlled school, populated largely with the children of elite parents, would be the ideal device through which to induct selected children from lower levels into elite status. By means of a scholarship program, promising members of lesser classes could be chosen early for recruitment into the top classes. The English "public" schools have, in fact, incorporated into their charters provisions to insure that a few boys from lesser classes would enter each year. Getting one's child into a "public" school, or even into one of the lesser private schools, assumes an importance in England relatively unknown in the United States. If the children cannot win scholarships the parents often make extreme financial sacrifices in order to pay the cost of this relatively exclusive education.[30]

Just how much of a place private secondary schools have played in mobility in either country is difficult to determine exactly, since American studies of social mobility regularly omit information on private or tax-supported secondary school attendance, and English studies showing the advantage of "public" school attendance generally fail to separate the mobile from the non-mobile in this respect. However, it has been observed that during the nineteenth century the English "public" schools were largely used by the new-rich manufacturing classes to enable their sons to achieve an unqualified elite state.[31] In one sense, the rise of the manufacturing classes through free enterprise represent a genuine contest mobility that threatened to destroy the traditional sponsorship system. But by accepting the "public" schools in this fashion they bowed to the legitimacy of the traditional system—an implicit acknowledgment that upward mobility was not complete until the final sponsored induction had been carried out. Dennis Brogan speaks of the nineteenth-century public schools' task as "the job of marrying the old English social order to the new."[32]

It is of interest to note the parallel between the tax-supported grammar schools and the "public" schools in England. The former have been in important respects patterned after the latter, adopting the latter's view of mobility but making it a much larger part of their total function. In a general way, the grammar schools are the vehicle for sponsored mobility throughout the middle ranges of the class system, modelled after the pattern of the "public" schools, which are the agencies for sponsored mobility into the elite.

Effects of Mobility on Personality

Passing note should be taken of the importance of the distinction between sponsored and contest mobility for the supposed personality-shaping ing effects of the upward mobility experience. Not a great deal is yet known about the distinctiveness of the mobile personality nor about the specific features of importance in the mobility experience.[33] However, three facets of the mobility experience are most frequently stressed in discussions of the problem. First is the stress or tension involved in striving higher than others under more difficult conditions than they. Second is the complication of interpersonal relations introduced by the necessity to abandon lower-level friends in favor of an uncertain acceptance into higher-level circles. Third is the problem of working out an adequate personal value system in the face of movement between classes having somewhat variant or even contradictory value systems.[34] The impact of each of these three facets of mobility experience should be different depending upon whether the pattern is that of the contest or of sponsorship.

Under the sponsorship system, recruits to mobility are selected early, segregated from their class peers, grouped with other recruits and with youth from the class to which they are moving, and are trained specifically for the class that they are to enter. Since the selection is made early, the mobility experience should be relatively free from the strain that comes with the series of elimination tests and long-extended uncertainty of success. The school segregation and the integrated school community of the "public" school or grammar school should clarify the mobile person's social ties. It is to be noted that A. N. Oppenheim failed to discover clique formation along lines of social class in a sociometric study of a number of grammar schools.[35] The problem of a system of values should be well solved when the elite recruit is taken from his parents and peers to be placed in a boarding school, although it may be less well clarified for the grammar-school boy who returns each evening to his working-class family. Undoubtedly, this latter limitation has something to do with the observed failure of working-class boys to continue through the last years of grammar school and into the universities.[36] In general, then, the crucial factors that have been stressed as affecting personality formation among the upwardly mobile are rather specific to the contest system of mobility, such as is found in the United States, or the incompletely functioning sponsorship system.

It is often taken for granted that there is convincing evidence to show that the mobility oriented student in American secondary schools suffers from the tendency for cliques to form along lines predetermined by family background. However, these tendencies are statistically quite moderate, leaving much room for individual exception. Furthermore, the mobility oriented students have not generally been examined separately to see whether they might in fact be incorporated into higher-level cliques in contrast to the general rule. Nor is it adequately demonstrated whether the purported working-class value system, which is at odds with middle-class values, is as pervasive and constraining throughout the working class as it is conspicuous in delinquent gangs. Thus, while the model of contest mobility indicates that there should be more serious and continuing strain over the uncertainty of attaining mobility, more explicit and continued preoccupation with the problem of changing friendships to fit class position, and more contradictory learning to inhibit the acquisition of a value system appropriate to class of aspiration than should be found under sponsored mobility, the ramifications of these differences depend upon further understanding of the workings of the American class system. A search for personality-forming experiences specific to a sponsorship system has yet to be made.

Conclusion

In the foregoing statement, two ideal-typical organizing norms concerning the manner in which mobility should properly take place have been outlined. On the one hand, mobility may be viewed as most appropriately a *contest* in which many contestants strive, by whatever combinations of strategy, enterprise, perseverance, and ability they can marshal, restricted only by a minimum set of rules defining fair play and minimizing special advantage to those who get ahead early in the game, to take possession of a limited number of prizes. On the other hand, it may be thought best that the upwardly mobile person be *sponsored,* like one who joins a private club upon invitation of the membership, selected because the club members feel that he has qualities desirable in a club member, and then subjected to careful training and initiation into the guiding ethic and lore of the club before being accorded full membership.

Upward mobility actually takes place to a considerable degree by both the contest pattern and the sponsorship pattern in every society. But it has been suggested that in England the sponsorship norm is ascendant and has been so for a century or more, and that in the United States the contest norm has been ascendant for a comparable period. A norm is ascendant in the sense that there is a constant "strain" to bring the relevant features of the class system, the pattern of social control, and the educational system into consistency with the norm, and that patterns consistent with the ascendant norm seem more "natural" and "right" to the articulate segments of the population.

The statement has been broadly impressionistic and speculative, reflecting more the over-all impression of an observer of both countries than a systematic exploration of data. Relevant data of a variety of sorts have been cited, but their use has been more illustrative than demonstrative. Several lines of research are suggested by the statement. One of these is an exploration of different channels of mobility in both countries to discover the extent to which mobility corresponds to each of the types. Recruitment to the Catholic priesthood, for example, probably follows a strictly sponsorship norm regardless of the dominant contest norm in the United States.

The effect of changes in the major avenues of upward mobility upon the dominant norms requires investigation. The increasing importance of promotion through corporation hierarchies and the declining importance of the entrepreneurial path to upward mobility undoubtedly compromise the ideal pattern of contest mobility. The increasing insistence upon higher education as a prerequisite to a variety of employments is a similar modification. On the other hand, there is little evidence of a tendency to follow the logic of sponsorship beyond the bureaucratic selection process. The prospect of a surplus of college-educated persons in relation to jobs requiring college education tends to restore the contest situation at a higher level, and the further fact that completion of higher education may be more determined by motivational factors than by capacity suggests that the contest pattern continues within the school.

In England, on the other hand, two developments may dull the distinctive edge of the sponsorship system. One is response to popular demand to allow more children to secure the grammar-school type of training, particularly through including such a program in the secondary modern schools. The other is introduction of the comprehensive secondary school, relatively uncommon at present but a major plank in the Labour party's education platform. It remains to be determined whether the comprehensive school in England will take a distinctive form and serve a distinctive function that preserves the pattern of sponsorship or whether it will approximate the present American system.

Finally, the assertion that these types are embedded in genuine folk norms requires specific investigation. A combination of direct study of popular attitudes and content analysis of popular responses to crucial issues is necessary. Perhaps the most significant search would be for evidence showing what courses of action seem to require no special justification or explanation because they are altogether "natural" and "right," and which courses of action, whether approved or not, seem to require special justification and explanation. Such evidence, appropriately used, would permit study of the extent to which the patterns described are genuine folk norms rather than the mere by-product of particular structural factors in society. It would also permit determination of the extent to which acceptance of the ascendant folk norm is diffused among the varied segments of the population.

NOTES

1. This is an expanded version of a paper presented at the Fourth World Congress of Sociology, 1959, and abstracted in the *Transactions* of the Congress. A special indebtedness should be expressed to Jean Floud and Hilde Himmelweit for helping to acquaint the author with the English school system.

2. A comprehensive summary of such studies appears in Seymour M. Lipset and Reinhard Bendix, *Social Mobility in Industrial Society* (Berkeley and Los Angeles: University of California Press, 1959).

3. *Cf.* C. A. Anderson, "The Social Status of University Students in Relation to Type of Economy: An International Comparison," *Transactions of the Third World Congress of Sociology*, V, 51–63 [Chap. XXI in this volume (eds.)]; J. E. Floud, A. H. Halsey, and F. M. Martin, *Social Class and Educational Opportunity* (London: Heinemann, 1956); W. L. Warner, R. J. Havighurst, and M. B. Loeb, *Who Shall Be Educated?* (New York: Harper and Bros., 1944).

4. Reference will be made throughout the paper to "elite" and "masses." The generalizations presented are, however, intended to apply throughout the stratification continuum to relations between members of a given class or classes above it. Statements about mobility are intended in general to apply to mobility from manual to middle-class levels, lower-middle to upper-middle class, etc., as well as into the strictly elite groups. The simplified manner of expression avoids the repeated use of cumbersome and involved statements that might otherwise be required.

5. The normative element in an organizing norm goes beyond Max Weber's *ideal type*, conveying more of the sense of Emile Durkheim's *collective representation*. *Cf.* R. H. Turner, "The Normative Coherence of Folk Concepts," *Research Studies of the State College of Washington*, XXV (1957), 127–36. Charles Wagley has developed a similar concept, which he calls "ideal pattern" in his as yet unpublished

work on Brazilian kinship. *Cf.* also Howard Becker, "Constructive Typology in the Social Sciences," *American Sociological Review,* V (February, 1940), 40–55.

6. Geoffrey Gorer remarks on the favorable evaluation of the successful gamble in American culture. "Gambling is also a respected and important component in many business ventures. Conspicuous improvement in a man's financial position is generally attributed to a lucky combination of industry, skill, and gambling, though the successful gambler prefers to refer to his gambling as 'vision.'" *The American People* (New York: W. W. Norton, 1948), p. 178.

7. Vilfredo Pareto, *The Mind and Society* (New York: Harcourt, Brace & Co., 1935), IV, 1796.

8. Many writers have noted that different kinds of society facilitate the rise of different kinds of personalities, either in the stratification hierarchy or in other ways. *Cf.,* Jessie Bernard, *American Community Behavior* (New York: Dryden, 1949), p. 205. A particularly interesting statement in Martindale's exploration of "favored personality" types in sacred and secular societies. *Cf.,* Don Martindale and Elio Monachesi, *Elements of Sociology* (New York: Harper and Bros., 1951), pp. 312–78.

9. At one time in the United States, a good many owners of expensive British Jaguar automobiles carried large signs on the cars identifying the make. Such a display would have been unthinkable under a sponsored mobility system, since the Jaguar owner would not care for the esteem of the uninformed masses who could not tell a Jaguar from a less prestigious automobile.

10. Lawrence Lipton, *Holy Barbarians* (New York: Messner, 1959).

11. *Cf.,* Albert K. Cohen, *Delinquent Boys: The Culture of the Gang* (Glencoe, Ill.: Free Press, 1955).

12. D. V. Glass (ed.), *Social Mobility in Britain* (Glencoe, Ill.: Free Press, 1954), pp. 144–45, reports studies showing only small variations in intelligence between occupational levels.

13. Geoffrey Gorer, *op. cit.,* pp. 172–87.

14. *Los Angeles Times,* May 4, 1959, Part I, p. 24.

15. The nature and operation of the "eleven plus" selection system are fully reviewed in a recent report by a committee of the British Psychological Society and a report of extensive research into the adequacy of selection methods. *Cf.,* P. E. Vernon (ed.), *Secondary School Selection: A British Psychological Inquiry* (London: Methuen and Co., Ltd., 1957); and Alfred Yates and D. A. Pidgeon, *Admission to Grammar Schools* (London: Newnes Educational Publishing Co., 1957).

16. J. E. Floud, A. H. Halsey, and F. M. Martin, *op. cit.*

17. Mary D. Wilson documents the reduction in aspiration characterizing students in British Secondary Modern schools and points out the contrast with American studies revealing much more "unrealistic" aspiration. *Cf.,* "The Vocational Preferences of Secondary Modern School-children," *British Journal of Educational Psychology,* XXIII (1953), 97–113. *Cf.,* also, R. H. Turner, "The Changing Ideology of Success," *Transactions of the Third World Congress of Sociology, 1956,* V, esp. p. 37.

18. Pointed out by Hilde Himmelweit in private communication.

19. Less adequate financial provision and a lower teacher-student ratio are mentioned as obstacles to parity of secondary modern schools with grammar schools in *Times Educational Supplement,* Feb. 22, 1957, p. 241. On difficulties in achieving prestige comparable with grammar schools, see G. Baron, "Secondary Education in Britain: Some Present-Day Trends," *Teachers College Record,* LVII (1956) 211–21; and O. Banks, *Parity and Prestige in English Secondary Education* (London: Routledge and Kegan, Paul, 1955). *Cf.* also P. E. Vernon, *op. cit.,* pp. 19–22.

20. Alexis de Tocqueville, *Democracy in America* (New York: Alfred Knopf, 1945), I, 52.

21. An earlier Gallup Poll had disclosed that 62 per cent of parents opposed stiffened college entrance requirements, while only 27 per cent favored them. *Time,* April 14, 1958, p. 45.

22. *Los Angeles Times,* December 17, 1958, Part I, p. 16.

23. U.S. Department of Health, Education and Welfare, Office of Education, *Earned Degrees Conferred by Higher Education Institutions, 1957–58* (Washington: Government Printing Office, 1959), p. 3.

24. Nicolas Malleson, "Student Performance at University College, London 1948–51," *Universities Quarterly*, XII (May, 1958), 288–319.

25. See C. A. Quattlebaum, *Federal Aid to Students for Higher Education* (Washington: Government Printing Office, 1956); and "Grants to Students: University and Training Colleges," *The Times Educational Supplement*, May 6, 1955, p. 446.

26. "Students' Expenses," *The Times Educational Supplement*, May 6, 1955, 447.

27. "College Jobs for College Students," *Journal of Higher Education*, XXVII (1956), 174.

28. Adjustment training is not a necessary accompaniment of contest mobility. The shift during the last half-century toward the increased importance of social acceptability as an elite credential has brought social adjustment training into correspondingly greater prominence.

29. Hadley Cantril (ed.), *Public Opinion 1935–1946* (Princeton: Princeton University Press, 1951), p. 186.

30. For a popular account of the place of "public" schools in the English educational system, see Dennis Brogan, *The English People* (New York: Alfred Knopf, 1943), pp. 18–56.

31. A. H. Halsey of Birmingham University called my attention to the importance of this fact.

32. *Op. cit.*, pp. 24–25.

33. *Cf.* Lipset and Bendix, *op. cit.*, pp. 250 ff.

34. *Cf.* August B. Hollingshead and Frederick C. Redlich, *Social Class and Mental Illinois* (New York: Wiley and Sons, 1958); W. Lloyd Warner and James Abegglen, *Big Business Leaders in America* (New York: Harper and Bros., 1955); Warner *et al.*, *Who Shall be Educated?*

35. "Social Status and Clique Formation among Grammar School Boys," *British Journal of Sociology*, VI (1955), 288–45. Oppenheim's findings may be compared with A. B. Hollingshead, *Elmtown's Youth* (New York: Wiley and Sons, 1949), pp. 204–42. *Cf.* also Joseph Kahl, *The American Class Structure* (New York: Rinehart and Co., 1957), pp. 129–38.

36. J. E. Floud *et al.*, *op. cit.*, pp. 115 ff.

13   *American Public Schools and Equality of Opportunity*

NATALIE ROGOFF

ENTRANCE INTO COLLEGE is the problematic concern of the paper that follows. Once enrolled in college, students exhibit variation in classroom performances, interests, and orientations to the major institutions of society. However much of these divergences spring from experience on the campus itself, dissimilarities in provenience of America's college students—whether of place of residence, ethnic affiliation, or of social class—contribute their share as well.

From the point of view of learning more about higher education, it is well to know as much as possible about the *origins* of student recruits. But in fact it is at least as important to reverse the question, and to compare the *destinies* of young people—particularly, their chances of going to college—who come from unlike educational, familial, or community backgrounds. The following remarks will develop some reasons for claiming the significance of this field of inquiry.

Diversity stands out as the quality best describing the American educational scene. But clear though the signs of diversity may be the implications are not. What are we to make of all the variations we know to exist in our schools? As a touchstone, as a principle for organizing and evaluating the observations we make, the ancient but still unanalyzed idea of equality of opportunity has a great deal to recommend it. What do we mean by equality of opportunity? What social and educational arrangements make it easiest to realize? Does it ever conflict with other accepted social aims? These questions assert themselves as some of the keystones of social research on education.

First, to hallow and enrich the problem, one of the oldest, most beautiful and clearest expressions of the ideal will be cited—Plato's parable of the metals in *The Republic*. Plato proposes that the people be told a deliberate falsehood, an old Phoenician tale that all men were brought to maturity in the bowels of the earth, that the soil of their country is thus their mother and all their fellow citizens, brothers. Then they are to be told:

Reprinted from Natalie Rogoff, "Public Schools and Equality of Opportunity," *Journal of Educational Sociology*, Feb., 1960, pp. 252–59, with the permission of the author and the editor. This article may be identified as publication No. A-295 of the Bureau of Applied Social Research, Columbia University.

Citizens, . . . you are brothers, yet God has framed you differently. Some of you have the power of command, and in the composition of these he has mingled gold, wherefore also they have the greatest honour; others he has made of silver, to be auxiliaries; others again who are to be husbandmen and craftsmen he has composed of brass and iron; and the species will generally be preserved in the children. But as all are of the same original stock, a golden parent will sometimes have a silver son, or a silver parent a golden son. And God proclaims as a first principle to the rulers, and above all else, that there is nothing which they should so anxiously guard, or of which they are to be such good guardians, as of the purity of the race. They should observe what elements mingle in their offspring; for if the son of a golden or silver parent has an admixture of brass or iron, then nature orders a transposition of ranks, and the eye of the ruler must not be pitiful towards the child because he has to descend the scale and become a husbandman or artisan, just as there may be sons of artisans who having an admixture of gold or silver in them are raised to honour, and become guardians or auxiliaries. For an oracle says that when a man of brass or iron guards the State, it will be destroyed.[1]

Lifetimes of useful work could be devoted to searching out all the ways of applying modern social science theory, techniques and knowledge to Plato's ideas. Here are some of the elements to be made use of. There are rulers or guardians, who, for our purposes, observe the children of the Men of Gold and the Men of Brass and play a part in assigning them to whatever role they seem best capable of filling. Who are the guardians of modern American society, and how do they make assignments?

Let us confine our attention to the secondary schools in the United States today. Certainly one of the consequences of prolonging the years of compulsory education is to keep most of the children in the limelight, to increase their visibility to the "guardians" and to increase the number of guardians by whom they are observed—all of which conditions perhaps lead to more accurate and objective judgments of their worth. But the thousands of schools differ among themselves in bewildering fashion; do any of these differences lead to impairing the work of the guardians in their crucial role of seeing gold, silver, and brass wherever they are found?

How, for example, could the matter of a school's size, now more than ever under scrutiny since President Conant's emphasis on it, affect its capacity to observe and assign each student to his most appropriate role?

Are small schools in a better or a worse position than large ones to evaluate their students? Immediately a number of empirical questions come to mind: is the size of a school related to the frequency and objectivity of the performance tests its students take? Is size associated with the "clear-sightedness" of teachers, that is, their capacity to make sound judgments of students? Does a small school give a few teachers the opportunity to make many observations, while a large school gives many teachers the opportunity to make only a few observations of each student? If these are the most frequent patterns, which of them is the more effective?

Enlarging the problem, a school's size is not unrelated to other structural and institutional attributes. To consider only one, smaller schools are more isolated from the great centers of population and from the larger society as a whole. This may lead to less awareness of the standards of performance by the average American student, so that no matter if teachers at small schools see a great deal more of their students, their evaluations may be less correct because of their remoteness from national norms.

No indictment of small American high schools is intended by these remarks, which are incidental to and illustrative of a more basic idea—that the structure of our schools may, in a totally unplanned way, lead to inequalities in the opportunities students have for being evaluated and selected for the roles in society for which they are well suited.

For another example, a puzzle in Plato's statement provides the stimulus. Recall that he began with a preposterous myth and was in fact so ashamed of proposing to pass it off that he said to Glaucon, "I really know not how to look you in the face, or in what words to utter the audacious fiction." Devoted as he was to the search for truth, what impelled Plato to propose so extreme a departure from it? Let me suggest that the myth of autochthony is a brilliant, poetic solution to perhaps the greatest impediment to equality of opportunity. To persuade all the citizens of a state that they spring full grown from its soil, which bore and nurtured them all, is absurd precisely because it denies all the loyalties, ties, identifications, and memories linking each individual with his own family, clan, race, and religion. All these sources of separateness, of individual or group uniqueness, make of any society a collection of better or more poorly integrated subgroups, each of which presses its claims of superiority and none of which refrains from that sense of pity for its inferior offspring which Plato saw as a major deterrent to true equality.

To return to our own time and location, not only do we live in a more than usually heterogeneous society but the separate sub-groups in America have a noticeable impact on the schools and colleges here. On the one hand, the vast system of private schools, colleges, and universities has been spawned by this very sense of religious, ethnic, and regional separateness. On the other, the residential propinquity of sub-group members—Catholics, Jews, Negroes, lower class persons, or Swedes, for example, tending to live in settlements each with his own—gives to many public schools a membership of both students and teachers predominantly affiliated with one such social category, whether it be of a religious, ethnic, or class character. Not all public, nor indeed all private schools share this quality, which means that only some of our young people experience the pleasures and pains of attending schools that are socially heterogenous.

What influence does this quality of our schools have on the chances of each student to be seen for what he is and selected for an appropriate adult role? Does the evaluation of a lower class, or a Protestant, or a Japanese child, let us say, depend on whether he attends a school where lower class or Protestant or Japanese children predominate rather than a school where children from his background are mixed in equal or unequal parts with others? The current state of knowledge bearing on this question is such that we might be led to any one of the possible answers to it. That the problem is complex is undeniable; we need to know in detail, among many other things, how this structural attribute of schools is related to the behavior and the qualifications of teachers, how it affects informal relations among students, and how it bears on the interaction between students and teachers.

This only begins the program of studies that might be carried out, using equality of opportunity as an ethical, a theoretical, and a technical yardstick. To throw a few more coals on the fire, we need to distinguish between the role of schools in furnishing young people with equal chances of being *selected* for and of being *provided* with appropriate educational and other opportunities. We need to distinguish between our schools' performances in recognizing talent and in knowing how best to utilize it. And between deliberate and unanticipated barriers to equality of opportunity. And between those sources of inequality which are connected with other of the major institutions in society—the family, the church, and economic and political institutions—in contrast to those stemming primarily from schools and colleges themselves. The work will take us far outside the orbit of the classroom, as research in education always has done, but perhaps the connections with the outside world will be better apprehended and of more point if this compelling principle furnishes the motive power.

Specifying the Idea of Equality of Opportunity

To advocate such a program of research is gratifying; to initiate it is perilous and sobering. In the following remarks, the reader will find untested assumptions, oversimplifications, and arbitrary selection of problematic elements. Time, work, and help of others will, hopefully, reduce these.

Here are some of the things that have to be specified in order to apply the concept of equality of opportunity. First, between whom should there be equality of opportunity? Presumably, between those who "deserve" it equally, or those of equal capacity to take advantage of given opportunities. So we must have some way of classifying individuals according to their capacities—a task that psychologists, at least since the time of Binet, have taken as a serious and continuing responsibility.

Next, we have to have some ideas about the major sources of *inequality*. This is necessary because we must be able to compare the opportunities available to those equal in capacity but unequal in some respect that we believe affects their chances of getting such opportunities. Here we are in a fortunate position, because there is so vast an amount of previous research all of which shows the central role of *social class* as one of the leading sources of inequality.

Finally, we should specify the nature of the opportunities most crucial to the life chances of individuals. What are the rewards which should be equally available to those of equal capacity? Once again, we do not have to rely on our own efforts to find an answer. *Higher education,* to an increasing extent, is perhaps the major gateway to the personal and social rewards available to the members of modern industrial societies. While in the past it was only one of several alternatives, more and more higher education preempts the part formerly played by inherited wealth, personal daring and energy, or the slow climb from job to next higher job.

We already know a great deal about the empirical relations among ability, social class, and access to higher education, and even something about the processes underlying these relations. But we have not let looked at the facts in connection with various patterns and possibilities of equality of opportunity. Some of the patterns are sketched below.

A. THE "RADICAL" PATTERN

For centuries, men have dreamed of ideal societies wherein all persons of equal capacity would be treated alike, without respect to their social origins. A very crude translation into contemporary research language might be as follows:

Let R_{ij} be the rate of college-going among persons of ability level i and social class j.

Then, $R_{aa} = R_{ab} = R_{ac} = \ldots R_{an}$, and $R_{aa} > R_{ba} > R_{ca} > \ldots R_{na}$.

Equal ability would lead to equal rates of college-going, no matter what the social class background, and higher ability would always lead to higher rates, no matter what the social class.

B. THE "MODERATE" PATTERN

Although not as readily put into ideological form, a moderate set of views on equality of opportunity would go about as follows:

To strive for a set of selection processes that puts every person in a social class according to his ability may be not only impossible, but perhaps not even desirable. Native ability is modified continuously by myriad social mechanisms. To overcome their force might lead to such disruptions of the social structure that, had we the knowledge, we might actually prefer not to pay so high a price.[2] Therefore, not ability alone, but some combination of ability and its social "facilitators" and "detractors" (here represented by social class) should be taken into account to produce the following pattern of opportunity (college-going): $R_{aa} > R_{ba} > R_{ca} > \ldots R_{na}$, and $R_{ab} - > R_{ba}$; $R_{ij} - > R_{ji}$, but $R_{aa} > R_{ab} > R_{ac} > \ldots R_{an}$.

The first condition specified is certainly the simplest: within a given social class, the college-going rate is higher at higher levels of ability. The third condition states, however, that the rate is higher in more favored social classes at every ability level. In other words, social class facilitates college-going, independent of ability. Finally, the second condition attempts to say something about the *relative* weight of ability and social class in affecting the college-going rate, and specifies that ability should have an effect equal to or greater than that of social class position.

C.   THE "CONSERVATIVE" PATTERN

The stance of the conservative toward equality of opportunity is easily discerned from what has been said before. It is his position that, in the long run, we delude ourselves if we believe that talent and ability observed among the lowest social classes should be taken seriously and encouraged. What really counts is the character of the social class into which the youngster was born. Society will be better off if it allocates opportunities according to social class and does not try to tinker with the biological and socially reinforcing mechanisms that have worked well enough for centuries.

In our crude terms, the conservative pattern is described by the following conditions:

$$R_{aa}=R_{ba}=R_{ca}= \ldots R_{na}, \text{ and } R_{aa}> R_{ab}> R_{ac}> \ldots R_{an}.$$

The pattern of opportunity would show no sensitivity to ability but would decrease at successively less favorable social class positions.

Though stated here in the optative mode, the radical, moderate, and conservative patterns of equality of opportunity will serve equally well as a crude research tool. In fact they are nothing more than a way of evaluating the relative effect of two "independent variables," i.e., social class position and talent or ability, as such evaluations are ordinarily made in multivariate analysis. There is one difference, however. Must of the time, survey analysis deals with a single "population" and attempts to discern the underlying links among various attributes concerning that population. But here, we have in mind a way of comparing one population with another, describing each by its relative position between the radical and conservative extremes. A more adequate statement of this point must be deferred until a later occasion.

The criteria of equality of opportunity proposed here are unlike those generally invoked by others interested in the problem. It is customary, for example, for comparisons to be made of public expenditures for education, or of the training of teachers, the average size of classrooms, and so on, between different states or regions of the nation. Differences in such standards are then cited as evidence of "inequality of opportunity" between residents of the states or regions. But this seems to miss at least one aspect of the concept. Equality of opportunity refers to the way *individuals* are treated relative to one another; as T. H. Marshall has suggested, it stands for "the equal right to display and develop differences, or inequalities; the equal right to be recognized as unequal."[3] It is an empirical question as to whether one community or region with a high level of "opportunity," however we choose to indicate that term, allocates those chances more equitably, i.e., in closer correspondence to individual differences among its residents, than does a community or region with a low level of opportunity.

EMPIRICAL APPLICATION

The rather simple and crude patterns described above for evaluating equality of opportunity have already proved useful in organizing various sets of empirical data now under scrutiny at the Bureau of Applied Social Research. We were fortunate enough to gain access to information collected by the Educational Testing Service concerning the college-going and career plans of over 35,000 American high school seniors, who constituted the "Class of 1955" at over five hundred public secondary schools. Information concerning the schools (a fairly representative sample of the 20,000-odd senior public high schools in the United States) was collected from the principals at the time of the field work.[4] This has since been supplemented by consulting national and state school directories, other listings and surveys, and census material pertaining to the towns and counties where the schools are located.

The key element in the design of the survey is the inclusion of over five hundred schools, representing almost as many communities. This permits the close study of communities and neighborhoods, both in their own right, and as contexts which may affect the behavior and orientations of the young people located in them. Among other things, we are in a position to see whether some types of communities conform to the "conservative" pattern of equality of opportunity, others to the "moderate" or "radical" patterns. Although this work is still in a preliminary stage, it is possible to report that communities *do* vary in this respect. Some towns— perhaps the smaller and less well-to-do, if the tentative evidence is later confirmed—are relatively close to the conservative pattern, allocating opportunities more on the basis of a youngster's class position than of his ability; others—again tentatively, wealthier and larger communities—appear to come closer to the radical pattern, showing more sensibility to their students' talents than to their social origins.

It is not too early, however, to suggest that inquiries into the state of affairs concerning equality of opportunity is a desirable field of social investigation, with serious implications for understanding schools, communities, and the stratification hierarchy.

NOTES

1. Plato, *The Republic*, Book III, Modern Library edition, p. 125.
2. Michael Young, in his recent book, *The Rise of Meritocracy* prophesies, with grace and humor, the disastrous, unanticipated consequences for a society which

realizes the goal of equality of opportunity. Writing a "social history" of England from 1870 to 2033, Young foresees the doom of a social system wherein all persons with talent really do rise to the top, leaving nothing but mental dullards to carry out the humble manual work.

3. T. H. Marshall, *Citizenship and Social Class,* Cambridge University Press, 1950, pp. 65–66.

4. See the following mimeographed reports prepared by the Educational Testing Service: Glen Stice, W. G. Mollenkopf, and W. S. Torgerson, "Background Factors and College-Going Plans among High-Aptitude Public High School Seniors," 1956; and "Background Factors Relating to College Plans and College Enrollment among Public High School Students," 1957.

14   *Social Selection in the Welfare State*[1]

T. H. MARSHALL

THERE NEED BE little ambiguity about "social selection." I take it to refer to the processes by which individuals are sifted, sorted and distributed into the various positions in the social system which can be distinguished one from another by their function, status, or place in the social hierarchy. I shall be considering, in this lecture, social selection through the educational system.

The Principles of the Welfare State

The Welfare State is a tougher proposition, because it would be difficult to find any definition acceptable both to its friends and to its enemies —or even to all its friends. Fortunately I needn't try to define it; I have only to explain what are the characteristics of the Welfare State which seem to me to provide a distinctive setting to the problem of social selection. I take the most relevant aspect of the Welfare State, in this context, to be the following.

First, its intense individualism. The claim of the individual to wefare is sacred and irrefutable and partakes of the character of a natural right. It would, no doubt, figure in the new Declaration of the Rights of Man if the supporters of the Welfare State were minded to issue anything so pithily dramatic. It would replace property in those early French and American testaments which speak of life, liberty and property; this trinity now becomes life, liberty and welfare. It is to be found among the Four Freedoms in the guise of "Freedom from Want"—but that is too negative a version. The welfare of the Welfare State is more positive and has more substance. It was lurking in the Declaration of Independence, which listed the inalienable rights of man as "Life, Liberty and the Pursuit of Happiness." Happiness is a positive concept closely related to welfare, but the citizen of the Welfare State does not merely have the right to pursue welfare, he has the right to receive it, even if the pursuit has not been particularly hot.

Reprinted from T. H. Marshall, "Social Selection in the Welfare State," *Eugenics Review,* Vol. XLV (1953), No. 2, with the permission of the author and the publisher.

And so we promise to each child an education suited to its individual qualities, we try to make the punishment (or treatment) fit the individual
criminal rather than the crime, we hold that in all but the simplest of the
social services individual case study and family case work should precede
and accompany the giving of advice or assistance, and we uphold the
principle of equal opportunity, which is perhaps the most completely individualistic of all.

But if we put individualism first, we must put collectivism second. The
Welfare State is the responsible promoter and guardian of the welfare of
the whole community, which is something more complex than the sum
total of the welfare of all its individual members arrived at by simple
addition. The claims of the individual must always be defined and limited
so as to fit into the complex and balanced pattern of the welfare of the
community, and that is why the right to welfare can never have the full
stature of a natural right. The harmonizing of individual rights with the
common good is a problem which faces all human societies.

In trying to solve it, the Welfare State must choose means which are
in harmony with its principles. It believes in planning—not of everything
but over a wide area. It must therefore clearly formulate its objectives and
carefully select its methods with a full sense of its power and its responsibility. It believes in equality, and its plans must therefore start from the
assumption that every person is potentially a candidate for every position
in society. This complicates matters; it is easier to cope with things if
society is divided into a number of noncompeting social classes. It believes
in personal liberty because, as I choose to define it, it is a democratic form
of society. So although, of course, like all States, it uses some compulsion,
it must rely on individual choice and motivation for the fulfilment of its
purposes in all their details.

How do these principles apply to selection through the educational
system? The general social good, in this context, requires a balanced supply
of persons with different skills and aptitudes who have been so trained
as to maximize the contribution they can make to the common welfare.
We have, in recent years, seen the Welfare State estimating the need for
natural scientists, social scientists and technicians, for doctors, teachers
and nurses, and then trying to stimulate the educational system to produce what is required. It must also be careful to see that the national
resources are used economically and to the best advantage, that there is
no waste of individual capacities, by denying them the chance of development and use, and no waste of money and effort, by giving education and
training to those who cannot get enough out of them to justify the cost.

On the other side, the side of individualism, is the right of each child
to receive an education suited to its character and abilities. It is peculiar,
in that the child cannot exercise the right for itself, because it is not expected to know what its character and abilities are. Nor can its parents

wholly represent its interests, because they cannot be certain of knowing either. But they have a rather ambiguous right at least to have their wishes considered, and in some circumstances to have them granted. The status of parental rights in the English educational system is somewhat obscure at the moment. There is no reason to assume that the independent operation of the two principles, of individual rights and general social needs, would lead to the same results. The State has the responsibility of harmonizing the one with the other.

So far I have merely been trying to explain the general meaning which I have discovered in the title of this lecture. As I have already said, I shall first limit this broad field by concentrating on selection through the educational system. I shall then limit it further to the two following aspects of the problem. I shall look first at the selection of children for secondary education and try to see what is involved in bringing it into harmony with the principles of the Welfare State. I choose this particular point in the selection process partly because of its intrinsic and often decisive importance, and partly because so much has recently been written about it. I shall look in the second place rather at the social structure and consider how far it is possible to achieve the aims of the Welfare State in this field —particularly the aim of equal opportunity—in a society in which there still exists considerable inequality of wealth and social status. In doing this I shall be able to draw on some of the still unpublished results of researches carried out at the London School of Economics over the past four years, chiefly with the aid of a generous grant from the Nuffield Foundation.

Selection for Secondary Schools

We are all, I expect, aware that for some time past educationists (both teachers and administrators), and psychologists and statisticians (I sometimes find it hard to distinguish the one from the other) have been hurling themselves at the problem of selection for secondary schools with a determination and a ferocity of purpose which are positively terrifying. A good general survey of the campaign can, I think, be extracted from four sources. There is first the Report of the Scottish Council for Research in Education on *Selection for Secondary Education,* presented by William McClelland in 1942. This is an impressive document which might be described as a bold and challenging advance by the forces of pure science and exact measurement. It was met and held in check by a counterattack delivered by the National Union of Teachers in its Report on *Transfer from Primary to Secondary Schools,* published in 1949. Meanwhile there had opened, in June 1947, a friendly contest conducted under strict tournament rules in the *British Journal of Educational Psychology,* in the form of the "Symposium on the Selection of Pupils for Different Types of Secondary School," which continued until February 1950. It was richly informative, and contained a little bit of everything. Finally we have the two Interim Reports of the Committee of the National Foundation of Educational Research on *The Allocation of Primary School Leavers to Courses of Secondary Education,* published in 1950 and 1952. It is too soon to say exactly what position this new detachment will take up on the battlefield, but the wording of its title is highly significant when compared with that of the Symposium. "Selection" has been replaced by "allocation" and "types of secondary school" by "courses of secondary education."

The first point to note is that, in this matter of selection for secondary education, the State is in full command of the whole situation. It provides the primary schools which prepare children for the examination, it designs the secondary school system for which they are being selected, and therefore determines the catergories into which they are to be sorted, and it invents and administers the tests. Such power is dangerous. It is easy in these circumstances to make sure that one will find what one is looking for, and it is, no doubt, gratifying to discover that one's artistic masterpiece has been faithfully copied by Nature. I find it unfortunate that, just as there are three main types of secondary school, so there are three types of ability with which educational psychologists juggle—g or general, F or technical and k or spatial. I am afraid people may come to regard this as evidence of collusion, when in fact, of course, the two trinities do not correspond.

The second point to note is that the principles of the 1944 Act, which I take to be the principles of the Welfare State, have not yet been put into effect. The Act, according to the N.U.T. Report, "has given the problem of tranference from the primary to the secondary school an entirely new form," which necessitates a thorough reassessment of our old methods of selection (p. 16). The profound change referred to is that from competitive selection of a few for higher things to allocation of all to suitable schools, or as Kenneth Lindsay phrased it nearly twenty years before the Act, from "selection by elimination" to "selection by differentiation."[2] When allocation is working fully, says the N.U.T., "the situation ought not to arise in which it is impossible to send a child to the school most suited to his needs because there is no place available for him in a school of this kind" (p.20). We are still a long way from this, and "for the time being the sole certain indication for a modern school is unsuitability for a grammar or technical school" (p. 18).

I see danger lurking here too. If too long a time passes during which an ideal cannot be realized, it may become unrealizable—a myth, as it were, which has lost contact with the world of experience, and which has never been through the testing which must lie between the blueprint and the finished machine. There is a danger, too, that we may imagine we are preparing the instruments for use in the new operation when in fact we are only perfecting those which are suited for use in the old. In the first Interim Report of the National Foundation there occurs the sentence: "It is the procedure of competitive entry to grammar schools that has been responsible for the undue importance which has been attached to objective tests and to external examinations" (p. 62). Note "external examinations," for there is something pretty fundamental there.

But the principle of allocation is not a new idea. It was implicit in the Act of 1918, which stated that sufficient provision must be made to ensure that no children are "debarred from receiving the benefits of any form of education by which they are capable of profiting through inability to pay fees," and it has been steadily developing since that date. And the importance attached to objective tests and external examinations is not an old phenomenon which happens to have survived into the new age. It has grown side by side with the growth of the idea of allocation, and continued to grow after the passing of the 1944 Act.

The movement in the field of ideas towards allocation instead of selection, and the movement in the field of practice towards uniform general standardized testing have been contemporaneous. I think, too, that any reader of the Symposium must be struck by the intense interest shown in the possibility of devising objective tests accurate enough to be used for allocation on the basis of special aptitudes, as well as for selection on the basis of general ability. There are, of course, signs of movement in other directions among education authorities, such as the greater use made of cumulative school records and so on; and, as regards the Symposium, it must not be overlooked that Sir Cyril Burt opened boldly with the statement that the problem was "administrative rather than psychological."[3] This sounded very much like the old-fashioned rebuking the newfangled, and no doubt some psychologists thought that he was letting the side down.

In all this I seem to see evidence of a clash between what I earlier referred to as the collectivist and individualist elements in the Welfare State. Allocation, interpreted along N.U.T. lines, represents unqualified individualism. The right of each child to receive the education best suited to its unique individual needs should not be inhibited by reference to the cost of providing the necessary schools and teachers nor to the demand in society at large for particular numbers of persons educated and trained in particular ways. But to the collectivist principle these limiting factors arise from rights of the community as a whole, which the Welfare State cannot ignore. And they may favour a provision of grammar school places which is less than the provision needed to accommodate all who could benefit from a grammar school education. As long as this happens, competitive selection will remain with us. How long that will be, I do not propose to guess. But, when selection is competitive, the authorities must reach a decision somehow, using the best means at their disposal. And they must be able to enforce the decision negatively(that is to say, the decision not to admit) against the wishes of the parents. When faced with the necessity of filling the last five places in a grammar school from twenty applicants, all backed by ambitious and determined parents, you may feel that the best means of selection are either to follow the mark order or to toss up. The public may prefer you to follow the marks, even though you know that in this border zone the verdict of the marks has no real validity. So the use of imperfect selection methods can be justified by the inadequacy of the educational system, as judged by the ideal of allocation.

But in my view, if allocation replaced selection, then no amount of improvement would make the tests sufficiently exact to carry the weight of decision enforceable against parental wishes. For the question to be answered in each case would not be: "Is this child better suited to a grammar school than the other applicants? If so, we must tell the others we are full up." But: "What, as judged by absolute standards and without reference to competing claims, is the education best suited to this child's needs?" I feel convinced that, in the majority of cases, questions in this form will remain unanswerable by tests and examinations—unanswerable, that is, with the degree of assurance necessary before the answer can be made the basis of administrative action. So we should find, I think, that instead of allocation in the sense of the definitive assignment of each child to an appropriate school or course, we should have something more like an advisory service which left the responsibility of decision to the parents. And that, I understand, is what happens now in so far as the principle of allocation already enters into our system. And in support of the view that it *should* be so, I can quote, from the Symposium, Mr. Dempster of Southampton, who writes: "The wishes of the parents are possibly the best guide at present available to selectors in deciding between grammar and technical school education."[4]

This sounds in many ways a very attractive prospect, though we ought to know a little more about how parental wishes work before we acclaim it, and I shall have something to say on that later. But I fancy it conflicts with another aspect of the collectivist element in the Welfare State. The principle I have in mind is the one which says that all should be judged by the same procedure, as impartially and impersonally as possible, that favouritism and privilege must be eradicated, and also the effects of differing social environments on the critical turning-points in life. So far so good. The principle must be allowed to have full weight. There is one obvious point at which it favours objective tests. Because children come to their examination at 11+ from schools and neighbourhoods of very different quality, they cannot be judge by their attainments only; an attempt must be made to discover natural abilities which may have been frustrated by circumstances but may still be able to come to fruition if given a fair chance. But latent capacities are concealed, and something more scientific than a teacher's judgment or a school record is needed to reveal them.

But the collectivist principle goes farther, and sometimes assumes shapes which are more open to question. The doctrine of fair shares and equal opportunity sounds admirable, but it may become so distorted as to merit the cynical comment that fair shares means "if we can't all have it, nobody shall," and that equal opportunity means "we must all have an equal chance of showing that we are all equally clever." And the present situation may encourage this type of distortion, if it leads us to regard competitive selection as a necessary evil. If the Welfare State is to bring its two principles into harmony, it must conceive of the basic equality of all as human beings and fellow-citizens in a way which leaves room for the recognition that all are not equally gifted nor capable of rendering equally valuable services to the community, that equal opportunity means an equal chance to reveal differences some of which are superiorities, and that these differences need for their development different types of education, some of which may legitimately be regarded as higher than others. The notion, therefore, that selection, even competitive selection, can be eliminated from our educational system seems to me to be a pipe-dream and not even a Utopian one.

Obstacles to Equal Opportunity

I will defer making any general comment until I have considered my second question, to which I now turn. This relates to another dilemma or antithesis inherent in the principles and structure of the Welfare State. It is the problem of establishing equal opportunity without abolishing social and economic inequality. I say this is inherent in the nature of the Welfare State because it is my opinion—which I do not propose to argue here— that the Welfare State, as we know it, must necessarily preserve a measure of economic inequality. This problem, therefore, is a permanent and not a transitory one.

One of the most striking passages in Kenneth Lindsay's well-known and farsighted study of this question in the interwar period is the quotation from Lord Birkenhead which runs: "There is now a complete ladder from the elementary school to the university, and the number of scholarships from the elementary to the secondary school is not limited, awards being made to all children who show capacity to profit."[5] This fantastic illusion was blown skyhigh by Lindsay's book, and later studies showed that equality of educational opportunity was still a distant ideal at the outbreak of World War II. The research carried out at L.S.E. during the past four years, to which I have already referred, has drawn in more firmly the outlines of the picture and added some details. We can see pretty clearly what the situation was when the Welfare State took over and what were the obstacles it had to overcome.

This research included a 10,000 sample survey of persons aged 18 and over in Great Britain in 1949. Mobility was examined on the basis of the seven-point scale of occupational status, widely known as the Hall-Jones scale, which had been prepared for this study. Groups 1 and 2 included the professional and managerial occupations, and groups 3 and 4 the supervisory and clerical—to give a rough idea of their character. Together they comprised about 30 per cent of the sample, which can be called the middle-class section (the upper class is too small to appear in a sample of this size). Group 5, including routine non-manual and skilled manual jobs, was a very large one comprising 40 per cent, while group 6 and 7, semi-skilled and unskilled manual, provided approximately another 30 per cent. Of the general picture I will say little; I would rather wait for the papers to be published with full statistical tables. But one or two points may be noted. We find that the social forces holding a son to the occupational group of his father are significantly strongest in groups 1 and 2 and weakest in group 5. We can summarize crudely by saying that money and influence count for most at the top, and life's chances lie most widely open, for good or ill, in the melting-pot in the middle of the scale. This is interesting, because it is at this middle point in the scale that we might expect to find many families ambitious for their children's future and ready to forgo their earnings while they get secondary and further education, but not in a position to pay fees. It is precisely among such families that the building of an educational ladder is likely to have the greatest effect.

The second point of relevance in the general picture is that the returns show what to many may be a surprising amount of downward movement. There is a common saying, which in the United States has had the force of a political dogma, that "there is plenty of room at the top." And one re-members benevolent members of the upper layers of society who have strongly advocated the building of a social and educational ladder under the impression, apparently, that it could carry one-way traffic only, and that the ascent of the deserving from below would not have to be accompanied by a descent on the part of any of their own children to make room for the newcomers. But, if we take all the male subjects in the sample, we find that 35.2 per cent had the same occupational status as their father, 29.3 per cent had risen and 35.5 per cent had fallen. These figures probably exaggerate the falls because they include the young men in the sample who had not yet reached their final occupational level, and, of course, they tell us nothing of the distance risen or fallen, which is an important factor. The believers in one-way traffic thought that upper- and middle-class jobs were increasing faster than jobs in general, while upper- and middle-class families were producing fewer children than families in general. But it seems clear, and the 1951 census sample confirms this, that this was true, as regards middle-class jobs in general, only of women's employment. The proportion of occupied men in such jobs showed no significant increase from 1911 to 1951, while the proportion of occupied women in such jobs rose approximately from 24.5 per cent to 45.5 per cent.There was some increase in clerical jobs for men, but even here the spectacular advance was in the employment of women. In 1947, to quote one illustrative case, of those leaving secondary grammar schools at the age of 16 to go straight into jobs, just about 43 per cent of the boys went into the "clerical and professional" category and of the girls 68 per cent, or, if nursing is included, nearly 77 per cent. Since there was an expansion of grammar schools during this period, and since grammar schools were largely an avenue to middle-class jobs, these facts are interesting. There may have been many boys who hitched their wagon to a white collar without realizing that their most serious competitors were their own sisters.

The educational data in the survey confirm and extend the picture presented in 1926 by Kenneth Lindsay. The most interesting general lesson to be drawn is that it is harder than one might suppose to ensure that the new opportunities created go to the people for whom they are intended, provided the fundamental principles of a free democracy are preserved. The survey covered the period of the introduction and expansion of the Free Place system in secondary schools, and its successor, the Special Place system, and it is possible to compare the experience of the first wave of entrants following the Act of 1902 (those born from 1890 to 1899) with the last prewar wave (those born from 1920 to 1929). In the period covered by this comparison the percentage of boys in families belonging to the top three occupational groups who went to grammar schools rose from 38.4 to 45.7, and the corresponding figures for group 5 (the skilled manual and routine non-manual workers) are 4.1 and 10.7. The percentage increase for the working-class group is much greater than for the middle-class group, but the inequality that remains is enormous. And it is still greater if one includes boarding schools. The reason for this was not only that the total provision was insufficient, but also that a considerable part of the benefit went to the middle classes. It is true that the proportion of children in grammar schools who are occupying free places increases as you go down the social scale. But the proportion of the whole company of children of an occupational group who hold free places in grammar schools is highest at the top, 13.2 per cent in status groups 1 and 2 (upper middle class) and 5 per cent in group 5 (upper working class). I have picked these pieces of information from the analysis which Mrs. Floud has made of this part of the survey and which contains many more points of equal interest.

My point is this. It may look at first sight as if the bourgeoisie had, as usual, filched what should have gone to the workers. But, in the circumstances, that was bound to happen in a free democracy and is bound to go on happening in the Welfare State. For the Welfare State is not the dictatorship of the proletariat and is not pledged to liquidate the bourgeoisie. Of course more and more middle-class families made use of the public elementary schools as the quality of these improved, and of course more and more of them competed for admission to secondary schools through free and special places. And since the children were backed by a better educational tradition and stronger parental support, because more of their families could afford to forgo the earnings of the children, because they came from more comfortable homes, where it was easier to work, and from smaller families, they were certain to be more successful. And when it came to deciding as to remission of fees for Special Places, many of the middle-class families had a genuine claim. Today, with the 100 per cent free place system in maintained schools, there can be no question of discriminating against middle-class families, and the competitive advantages of social and economic status can operate without check. Other inquiries conducted at the L.S.E., either within or in close relation to the main project, have begun to throw some light on the nature and extent of these competitive advantages.[6]

That there is a greater preponderance of working-class children in the modern schools today and of middle-class children in the grammar schools is a fact which no one is likely to dispute. In an article in the March 1953 issue of the *British Journal of Sociology,* Messrs. Halsey and Gardner produce evidence to show that, in the London areas they studied, this uneven distribution could not be attributed solely to the intelligence of the children, but must be in large part the result of social forces. When, for instance, comparison was made of two groups with the same mean I.Q., one of which had been assigned to a grammar school and the other to a modern school, it was found that the middle classes were heavily over-represented and the working classes, especially the unskilled families, heavily under-represented in the grammar school group. It is also interesting that of working-class children in grammar schools in the areas studied 63 per cent came from small families with one or two children and 37 per cent from larger families with three or more. Among working-class children in modern schools the proportions were almost exactly the reverse, and among middle-class children there was no signficant relation between type of school and size of family. No known correlation between fertility and intelligence could possible explain this, and it is clear that powerful social influences are at work. And they show themselves in other ways. A similar, though less marked, correlation with size of family appears when we ask how much thought parents give to their children's school career, how much interest they show in their work and progess, and how ambitious they feel about their future. Here, then, is a social factor causing what might be called "unfairness" in social selection about which the Welfare State can do very little. Positive action, by improving the physical conditions in poorer families and by stimulating greater interest and ambition among apathetic parents, can only be a very slow process. Family differences will continue to have their influence as long as the family is the basic cell in the social structure.

Social Ambition and Educational Achievement

The interest of parents may be shown by their giving thought to the matter of secondary schooling for their children. In one county area parents of children about to sit for the examination for secondary schools were asked whether they had thought a lot, a little, or not at all about the matter. The proportion claiming to have thought a lot declined steadily as one moved down the social scale and was little over a third among the unskilled workers. But the preference for a grammar school education, though it showed the same trend, did not fall so low. The lowest proportion preferring the grammar school was 43.4 per cent and the highest preferring the modern school 23.9 per cent—these figures being those for unskilled workers. But over two-thirds of the unskilled worker parents preferring the grammar school did not want their child to stay there after the age of 16. Their ambitions were limited. And about half the professional and a quarter of the clerical families said that if their child did not get a grammar school place they would not send it to a modern school.

The picture is slightly distressing. It suggests that those who care about education, and some who do not care much, almost automatically aspire to a grammar school for their children; but the aspiration may vary from the desire of a steady job, with good prospects, to be entered at sixteen, to the hope of admission to a university and a professional career. There cannot be much homogeneity of purpose in a grammar school population. And, looking at the other side of the picture, we find a low opinion of the modern school which to many appears as a catastrophe and a disgrace. Talk of "parity of esteem" is a little premature.

Now these likes and dislikes owe something, no doubt, to real or supposed differences in the quality of education received in the different types of school. But I doubt whether most parents are following the advice of the N.U.T. to concentrate on the "present educational needs of the child" and not to think too much "what these needs may be at some later stage in his development."[7] They are thinking of what the school may lead to in the way of employment or further education, and perhaps of what it stands for in terms of social prestige. This last point is one on which it is extremely hard to get reliable information, since much of the mental process involved may be only semi-conscious. If social status is not offered by the questioner as a possible reason for aiming at a particular school or job, it is not likely to be put down spontaneously; if it is offered, it may score a fair number of votes, but less than job attributes as good prospects, security, and interesting work. Another cause of difficulty is the lack of uniformity in the use of class names. People differ widely in the way they classify themselves or typical occupations as middle or working class, and it is clear that the term "lower middle class" is becoming abhorrent. But, in spite of this, there is fairly close argeement as to the order in which jobs should be ranked, even though there is disagreement as to the social class to which they should be assigned.

The material dealing with job ambitions is too complicated to be briefly surveyed in an intelligible form. So I shall confine myself to two points. In a sample of adults in two urban areas who were asked what occupation they would like their son to enter, more than a fifth of the working-class subjects chose a profession and less than 8 per cent a clerical job; the commonest choice (about 36 per cent) was for a skilled trade. The figures are not complete, as a good many said their son must choose for himself. In the middle-class section of the sample, clerical jobs were even less popular, and the total vote for independent business was practically negligible. A similar dislike of the sound of clerical and office jobs was found by Dr. Jahoda among school leavers in Lancashire—that is to say, among the boys. The girls put office work at the top of the list. When boys were asked what jobs they most definitely rejected, office work was the one most often chosen, but half of those who named it did so because they did not think they were qualified for it.[8] It would be very rash to jump to conclusions from such fragmentary evidence, but it does seem possible that office work is losing its charm. It is often described as dull and monotonous, and perhaps the rise in wages for manual work and familiarity with conditions of full employment are robbing it of some of its other former attractions.

The second point of interest is the clear evidence, at present confined to one area, that working-class boys who get into grammar schools have very high expectations that they will rise in the world, while middle-class boys in modern schools are inclined to expect to fall below the position of their parents. No less than 63 per cent of the boys of lower working-class origin in grammar schools expected to rise at least two steps on a five-point status scale above their fathers; only 12 per cent of their comrades in the modern schools were equally ambitious. But, if we measure the rise by the boys' own estimate of it and not by objective standards, the percentage falls from 63 to 21. This inquiry was reported in Dr. Himmelweit's article in the *British Journal of Sociology,* June 1952. It suggests that the boys themselves feel that selection for secondary schooling has a decisive effect on future careers, and that boys from the humbler working-class families who get into grammar schools may overrate their chances without fully realizing how ambitious their success has made them. So long as this is the case, "parity of esteem" is hardly possible.

Effects of Social Distance

My last point relates to the possible effects of social distance on life in a grammar school. Grammar schools, one might say, have a tradition, an educational atmosphere, and contacts with the world outside which have for some time past belonged to the way of life of the middle classes. And the middle classes are over-represented in the school population, even though the skilled working-class families may supply the largest absolute numbers. If, then, we introduce boys and girls from outside this circle, can they fit in? Can they become sufficiently assimilated to enter into the life of the school and get out of it what is has to give, and yet retain enough of their identity to break down, in the course of time, any class barriers which exist, and thus make the way easier for their successors, and for the Welfare State? Much study is needed before this question can be fully answered. We have evidence to show that middle-class boys in grammar schools (in the area studied) do better on average in class examinations in pretty well all subjects than working-class boys, and that, when teachers are asked to rank the boys in their class in terms of such things as industry, responsibility, interest in school affairs, good behaviour, and popularity, the middle-class boys do definitely better than the rest. And working-class boys are inclined to care less about their marks and to take less part in general school activities, and yet, as we have seen, they expect great results from their grammar school status when the time comes for them to get a job. On the other hand may not a school have an assimilating influence and mould its members into a more homogeneous group than they were to start with, thus, producing in reality the category of children which until then existed only in the imagination of the selectors? That is a question which points the way to a fascinating piece of research which has hardly yet been begun.

The Americans have similar problems today, and there is much evidence of status-consciousness in the high schools of the United States. The Book *Who Shall Be Educated?* by Lloyd Warner, Havighurst and Loeb (1946) is a revelation on this point. We hear a junior high-school principal say: "You generally find the children from the best families do the best work. The children from the lower class seem to be not as capable as the others," and on this the authors comment that "this correlation holds true. There is a strong relationship between social status and rank in school." A teacher then says that there is a lot of class feeling in the school. "Sections [i.e. streams] are supposed to be made up just on the basis of records in school but it isn't [*sic*] and everybody knows it isn't. I know right in my own A section I have children who ought to be in B section, but they are little socialites and so they stay in A," and there is much more in the same strain (p. 73). But the problem there is allocation between streams or courses, rather than between schools.

It was on this general question that Sir Cyril Burt made one of his most challenging remarks. "A realistic policy," he wrote, "must take frankly into consideration the fact that a child coming from this or that type of home may as a result be quite unsuited for a type of education, occupation or profession, which lies at an excessive 'social distance' from those of his parents and friends."[9] Whereupon Dr. Alexander descended on him like a ton of bricks, saying that no Authority could act on the view "that the present social circumstances of a child should be a criterion limiting his future opportunity."[10] Undoubtedly he is right. No Authority can act on the principle that social circumstances must limit educational opportunity, but in fact they do, and the accepted methods of educational selection cannot wholly prevent this. The remedy lies in the reduction of "social distance."

Conclusions

I must now try to sum up. The Welfare State, as I see it, is in danger of tying itself in knots in an attempt to do things which are self-contradictory. One example, I submit, is the proposal to assign children to different schools, largely on the basis of general ability, and then to pretend that the schools are all of equal status. If this means that we shall take equal trouble to make all schools as good as possible, treat all the children with equal respect and try to make them all equally happy, I heartily endorse the idea. But the notion of parity of esteem does not always stop there; and I feel it really is necessary to assert that some children are more able than others, that some forms of education are higher than others, and that some occupations demand qualities that are rarer than others and need longer and more skilled training to come to full maturity, and that they will therefore probably continue to enjoy higher social prestige.

I conclude that competitive selection through the educational system must remain with us to a considerable extent. The Welfare State is bound to pick the children of high ability for higher education and for higher jobs, and to do this with the interests of the community as well as the rights of the children in mind. But the more use it can at the same time make of allocation to courses suited to special tastes and abilities the better. It further seems to me that, for the purpose of selection on grounds of general ability, the objective tests are already accurate enough to do all that we should ever ask them to do, while, so far as "allocation" is concerned, they will never be able to give a decisive verdict in more than a minority of cases, although they can be of great value in helping to decide what advice to give.

So I agree with Sir Cyril Burt that the problem which now faces us is more administrative than psychological. There is less to be gained by trying to perfect the tests and examinations than by thinking how to shape the structure of our educational and employment systems. It is better to minimize the effects of our decisions in doubtful cases than to imagine that, if we only try hard enough, we can ensure that all our decisions in such cases are correct. The word "correct" has no meaning in this context; it is a bureaucratic fiction borrowed from the office where there is a correct file for every document.

By "minimize the effects of our decisions" I mean refrain from adding unnecessary and artificial consequences to acts whose real meaning and necessary consquences I have been urging that we should frankly recognize. A system of direction into distinct "types of secondary school" rather than "courses of secondary education" (to use the titles I quoted earlier) must, I think, intensify rather than minimize the consequences. I am aware of the educational arguments on the other side, but do not intend to enter into a controversy for which I have no equipment. The other point at which artificial consequences may be added is the point of passage from education to employment. The snobbery of the educational label, certificate or degree when, as often, the prestige of the title bears little or no relation to the value of the content, is a pernicious thing against which I should like to wage a major war.

There is another matter on which the Welfare State can easily try to follow contradictory principles. It relates to occupational prestige, social class and the distribution of power in society. All I can do is to throw one or two raw ideas at your heads as a parting gift.

Although the Welfare State must, I believe, recognize some measure of economic inequality as legitimate and acceptable, its principles are opposed to rigid class divisions, and to anything which favours the preservation or formation of sharply distinguished culture patterns at different social levels. The segregation when at school of those destined for different social levels is bound to have some effect of this kind and is acceptable only if there are irrefutable arguments on the other side. Further, a system which sorts children by general ability and then passes them through appropriate schools to appropriate grades of employment will intensify the homogeneity within each occupational status group and the differences between groups. And, in so far as intelligence is hereditary and as educational chances are influenced by family background (and I have produced evidence to show that they are), the correlation between social class and type of school will become closer among the children.

Finally, the Welfare State, more than most forms of democracy, cannot tolerate a governing class. Leadership and power are exercised from many stations in life, by politicians, judges, ecclesiastics, business men, trade unionists, intellectuals and others. If these were all selected in childhood and groomed in the same stable, we should have what Raymond Aron calls the characteristic feature of a totalitarian society—a unified élite.[11] These leaders must really belong to and represent in a distinctive way the circles in and through which their power is exercised. We need politicians from all classes and occupational levels, and it is good that some captains of industry should have started life at the bench, and that trade unions should be led by genuine members, men of outstanding general ability who have climbed a ladder other than the educational one. It is important to preserve these other ladders, and it is fortunate that the selection net has some pretty big holes in it. It is fortunate too, perhaps, that human affairs cannot be handled with perfect mechanical precision, even in the Welfare State.

NOTES

1. The Galton Lecture delivered at a meeting of the *Eugenics Society on February* 18th, 1953.
2. *Social Progress and Educational Waste*, p. 28.
3. *Loc. cit.,* June 1947, p. 57.
4. *Loc. cit.,* November 1948, p. 130.
5. *Op. cit.,* p. 9.
6. The work has been done by Dr. Hilde Himmelweit, Mr. Martin and their associates. Since the information has been collected in intensive local studies it cannot be used for generalization of any kind as yet.
7. *Op. cit.,* p. 20.
8. *Occupational Psychology,* 26, pp. 132–4.
9. *Loc. cit.,* June 1947, p. 67.
10. *Ibid.,* November 1947, p. 123.
11. *British Journal of Sociology,* March 1950, p. 10.

15 *A Skeptical Note on Education and Mobility*

C. ARNOLD ANDERSON

SOCIOLOGISTS have been unable to reach a consensus about vertical mobility. A decade ago it was widely agreed among American sociologists that mobility was diminishing. Dissent by a few writers and many new studies have virtually reversed that conclusion. In turn, the firmly accepted view that mobility is distinctively frequent in the United States has been challenged. This article does not deal with either of these two controversies but instead examines a more widely shared conclusion: namely, that in complex societies vertical mobility is closely dependent upon formal education. This proposition is central in theories concerning education as well as in those concerning mobility. Though there are few data at hand suitable for testing this proposition, it is useful to see what those few data can tell us. Moreover, since the data come from three countries they may indicate something about varying functions of education.

A whole series of corollary relationships are related to this one proposition.

1. In order for schooling to change a status system, schooling must be a variable; i.e., its amount or quality must differ among the members of the society. If everyone received the same schooling, it could not be correlated with other individual attributes. The shape of this distribution of schooling also is important; the results are quite different when the mode is high from when it is low or when skewness is upward rather than downward.[1] As schools enroll progressively larger proportions of children and retain them longer, the correlation between schooling and later occupations can diminish over time.

2. Macro effects must be distinguished from micro effects. Even though all children receive identical schooling, the aggregate impact of education upon the society (in the form of productivity or citizenship) could be enormous without any individual receiving a differential benefit.[2]

3. The influence of schooling upon mobility depends partly upon changes in the number of "openings"; here we focus upon opening at the top.[3] If children born in upper strata are distinctively capable genetically or

---

American Journal of Sociology v.66(1), May, 1961. Reprinted by permission of author and editor.

receive superior training, there will be fewer vacated openings into which children of lower origins can penetrate. In dynamic economies, multiplication of tertiary and shrinkage of primary occupations plays a major part in alteration of opportunities.

4. It has been shown that those children born in lower strata who do receive an education comparable to that of upper class children experience greatly enhanced chances of upward mobility. It is probable, moreover, that for the most talented lower class children, even a more modest training beyond that of their fellows in the same class of origin suffices to equip them for mobility.

5. One must also scrutinize the nature of the education supplied. Considered from the viewpoint of its mobility implications, education can be divided into that for production and for consumption. That kind or part of schooling regarded as a good-in-itself, as preparation for leisure, or as mere display—when not taken account of in allocating individuals to adult roles—is irrelevant to occupational mobility. On the other hand, widespread use of school certificates with precise vocational implications or emphasis upon the "proper" training favors a close correlation. The existing moderate correlation of schooling and occupational level would presumably be higher if one could distinguish the part of training that is job or income oriented.

6. Schooling may inhibit elite status maintenance. Upper-class schooling may be dysfunctional in that respect; conceivably also upper-class children are not better endowed genetically. In such circumstances change in the shape of the structure is of less moment. Account must be taken also of the initial degree of heterogeneity of the strata. If parental intelligence is closely graded with stratus and has low variance within strata, and if children's ability is appreciably genetic in source and influences the schooling they receive, then education would have only a modest influence on mobility.[4] If mean parental ability does not differ greatly among strata while variance is large within each stratum, one would expect more mobility; however, the net effect of schooling after partialing out native ability might be slight if ability and schooling of children are highly correlated.

7. The mobility effects of schooling depend also upon the selective mechanisms at work within the schools and upon the character of the formal requirements for particular jobs. The latter may automatically insure that no one without the stated preparation will be admitted into favored positions, but they do not prevent men who meet the formal but not the underlying functional requirements from falling by the wayside. Reliability, validity, and suitability of the selective procedures within the schools are critical. Thus, if pupils are weeded out ruthlessly and "validly" at successive hurdles, education will show a higher correlation with later vocation than if routine promotion prevails. The consequences of strict selection

depend upon the extent to which the qualities determining occupational success are directly taken account of by the schools. If curricula are mainly "cognitive" while job selection is based on "personality," schooling and occupation would be only moderately correlated. A persisting strong influence of schooling upon mobility would imply that school performance is accurately assessed by teachers and examinations and that such performance closely reflects those capacities that determine vocational performance.

A satisfactory analysis of this problem presupposes data showing intelligence scores for fathers and for sons, social status of fathers and sons, and schooling of sons. No such data exist. However, we do have a few samples supplying status of father and son and education of son, and fortunately these samples represent three societies.

A few years ago Centers published a special tabulation from his national study of social class.[5] He related sons' schooling to occupational attainment, both stated relative to position of father. Among sons of fathers in white collar occupations whose schooling was superior to their fathers', 38 per cent achieved an occupation above the father's while 29 per cent were in a lower occupation. When the son's schooling was inferior to that of the father, only 11 per cent held a superior position and 68 per cent had a poorer one. For better-schooled sons of manual fathers 53 per cent achieved a position above the father's while only 14 per cent were in a poorer job; if the son had less schooling, 23 per cent had a superior and 18 per cent an inferior job. It was noteworthy that a considerable proportion of sons had received less schooling than their father (even with no correction for intergeneration changes in median schooling). The mobility effects of schooling seem to have been important.

Similar, though less striking results, are reported for Britain.[6] Among the sons of semi- and unskilled workers 38 per cent of those with more than a grammar-school education achieved positions in the top stratum; when such sons had not gone beyond elementary school, less than one in twenty rose to the top. Even among sons born in middle strata the effect of schooling was marked.

It would be possible to cite also considerable evidence from studies of lifetime (intrageneration) mobility testifying to the influence of schooling upon mobility. It has been shown for Sweden[7] that a fourth of the urban laborers with more than folkschool training had entered white-collar positions five years later; of those with only folkschool, one man in twenty did so.

We turn now to a more detailed analysis of data from three countries for the purpose of assessing the relative influence of schooling upon vertical mobility. In the more usual analyses, as above, it is demonstrated that a son is more likely to be mobile upward if his schooling is superior to that of other sons in the same class of origin (and conversely for downward mobility among the relatively poorly educated sons born in upper strata). The present article is less concerned with this problem, however, than with ascertaining the relative order of magnitude of other factors as against schooling in determining the total amount of mobility.

We examine the total flow of sons among strata, identifying the sons with respect to their origin, their final position, and their schooling. Intergeneration shifts in the number of positions at each status level (marginal totals) are taken into account only as constraints of an essentially static nature. On the other hand, the fact that the status structure is much smaller at the top than at the bottom is fundamental. Hence, while entrants into an upper stratum may form only a tiny proportion of all sons born into a

Table 1.

Distribution of Sons' Socio-economic Status and Education Relative to Fathers'

A. Actual Distribution

SON'S EDUCATION RELATIVE TO FATHER'S	SON'S STATUS RELATIVE TO FATHER'S			
	Higher	Same	Lower	Total
Higher	134	96	61	291
Same	23	33	24	80
Lower	7	16	22	45
Total	164	145	107	416

B. Random and Maximum Relative Education Association Distributions and Deviation of Actual Cases Therefrom

1. Random Distribution

	Higher	Same	Lower	Total
Higher	115	102	75	291
Same	31	28	20	80
Lower	18	16	12	45
Total	164	145	107	416

2. Maximum Relative Education Association Distribution

	Higher	Same	Lower	Total
Higher	164	127	—	291
Same	—	18	62	80
Lower	—	—	45	45
Total	164	145	107	416

3. Deviations of Actual from (1)

	Higher	Same	Lower
Higher	19	–6	–14
Same	–8	5	4
Lower	–11	1	10

4. Deviations of Actual from (2)

	Higher	Same	Lower
Higher	–30	–31	16
Same	23	15	–38
Lower	7	16	–23

lower stratum, those few upwardly mobile sons may supply a large fraction of the present top stratum. Likewise, the few sons sliding down into a lower class may be a sizeable fraction of the upper class in which they originated. It is of secondary importance, in the present context, whether inheritance of status exceeds "expectancy" or whether the share of manual workers' sons rising is a smaller number than "would be expected."

From Centers' data (Table 1.A) one can compute that 82 per cent (134/164) of the sons with a better occupation than the father had more schooling than the father, 14 per cent had the same schooling, and only 4 per cent had less. When the occupation level was the same for both generations the respective percentages were 66, 23, and 11; and where the son's occupation was lower the percentages were 57, 22, and 21. These data suggest that schooling exerts a strong influence upon mobility. However, let us look at the picture in another way. Table 1.B shows (1) the distributions that would prevail if the relations between relative education and relative status were random and (2) if these relations were maximal; deviations of actual from the random and from the maximum relative-education association are also given.[8] It is evident that the actual figures are considerably closer to the random than to the hypothetical distribution assuming education to dominate. The latter discrepance is especially great among sons whose status is lower than that of their fathers and among sons with an education above the father.

Boalt traced the 1925 cohort of Stockholm-born sons until the year 1949.[9] He used a status rather than an occupational classification, and we have designated sons passing the *realschool* examination or doing better as having a "high" education (Table 2). Of the sons with "high" schooling,

Table 2.

Distribution of Sons' Social Status by Education of Sons in Stockholm

| Son's Schooling | SON'S SOCIAL STATUS RELATIVE TO FATHER'S | | | |
	Higher	Same	Lower	Total
High	271	369	111	751
Low	465	794	181	1,440
Total	736	1,163	292	2,191

36 per cent (271/751) have risen to a status above the father; of the sons with poorer schooling, 32 per cent did so. On the other hand, of all sons with a present status superior to that of the father 37 per cent had received a "high" schooling, but so also did 40 per cent of those now having a status lower than the father. These sons are still young and some will make later moves, but Boalt's data do not reveal schooling to be a major factor in mobility.

Table 3.

Distribution of Sons' Status Relative to Fathers' by Education of Sons in Sweden

	SON'S EDUCATION RELATIVE TO FATHER'S†			
Education of Son*	Higher	Same	Lower	Total
Low	99	381	127	607
Medium	13	43	16	72
High	11	32	6	49
Total	123	456	149	728

* Low: elementary; medium: some or complete middle school; high: at least some gymnasium (including university attendants).
† In terms of three-class status scale.

To Gösta Carlsson must go the credit for the most explicit questioning of the conventional view that schooling is a powerful influence upon mobility, and the writer owes the impetus to reassess the data on this topic to a rereading of his discussion.[10] Carlsson concluded that in Sweden schooling is "hardly the decisive factor in the majority of cases where people have moved upwards on the social ladder."[11] His data (summarized in Table 3) relate to a national sample of men. Overall about four-fifths of the upward as well as the downward mobile sons had only an elementary schooling.

Since the data for Britain are more detailed, we make them the main object of analysis.[12] The percentages of sons moving from one stratum to another, classified by their education, appear in (Table 4).[13] Inheritance of status exceeds chance and mobility is definitely correlated with the sons' schooling; the exposition on these points can be found in the source.

When we view mobility from the sons' positions, we can trace the varying channels of recruitment. It is a striking fact that at each level the number of sons born into and remaining in a stratum is smaller than the number entering. Of the 257 sons now in the top stratum, for example, 124 inherited their position and 133 entered from below; 35 per cent of the latter came from the stratum immediately below, 23 per cent came up two levels, 35 per cent came up from the next to lowest and 7 per cent from the lowest level. In the lowest stratum there are now 1,010 sons, of whom 407 inherited their position and 603 came down from various higher strata.[14]

When we look at the educational composition of these ascending and descending streams we see that over nine-tenths of the sons moving into level 5 from below were in the two lowest educational categories. Given the relative sizes of these two strata and the preponderantly poor schooling of sons who grow up there, this is to be expected on a random basis, as it would be for sons moving into the lowest from the next higher level. At the top of the scale, sons circulating among the upper strata only tend to be

Table 4.

Percentage Distribution of Entrants into Each Status Category of Sons by Category of Origin and Education of Sons, Great Britain

	SONS' STATUS CATEGORY				
	1, 2	3	4	5	6, 7
Present Number of Sons	257	324	450	1,409	1,010
Number Born There and Staying	124	64	108	702	407
Number of Entrants	133	260	342	707	603
Sons Coming Up, Number	133	201	251	316	—
From (%): 3a	8				
b	6				
c	5				
d	16				
T	35				
4a	5	10			
b	5	12			
c	2	1			
d	11	5			
T	23	28			
5a	7	22	43		
b	16	25	25		
c	4	1	1		
d	8	7	3		
T	35	55	72		
6, 7a	1	8	18	74	
b	2	5	9	19	
c	—	1	—	4	
d	4	2	—	3	
T	7	16	27	100	
Percentage Distribution of All Upward Mobile Education					
a	20	41	61	74	
b	29	43	35	19	
c	11	2	1	4	
d	39	14	3	3	
Sons Coming Down, Number	—	59	91	391	603
From (%): 1, 2a		24	11	5	2
b		22	3	2	1
c		15	6	2	1
d		39	8	2	—
T		100	28	12	4
3a			25	19	6
b			29	7	1
c			12	2	—
d			7	3	—
T			73	31	7
4a				37	13
b				13	3
c				3	—
d				3	—
T				56	16
5a					63
b					8
c					2
d					1
T					74
Percentage Distribution of All Downward Moves by Education					
a		24	36	61	83
b		22	32	23	12
c		15	18	7	3
d		39	14	9	1

comparatively well educated, for such sons are more numerous among those growing up in those sets of families.

The fact that the numbers entering upper strata from below or the lower strata from above are fewer than "expected" does not contravene the importance of these observed patterns of recruitment. While few well-educated sons descended from upper to the lowest strata, a considerable number fell from the top into middle levels; over half of those moving down from the top to the second level have grammar school training—possessed by only one in seven of all sons, by a half of those born in the top, and by a quarter of those born in the second stratum. Much more impressive is the fact that half of the sons moving into the top stratum were in the two poorest categories of schooling. Moreover, half of these poorly educated sons moving into the top level originated in the two lowest strata. In total, two-fifths of the present top class originated in the two lowest classes, of whom three-fifths had less than a grammar school education.[15]

The proportions of sons with varying amounts of schooling who move upward or downward one step, two steps, etc. is shown in Table 5 ("actual" lines). The better educated sons were more likely to move up, while those with little schooling were more likely to descend. But, as the first section of Table 6 shows, the distribution of schooling among all sons moving upward was not greatly different from that among the downwardly mobile. No one could deny that, looked at from the class of origin, better schooling has a favorable influence upon mobility. But one may conclude also that a large proportion of the entrants to a higher class will be relatively poorly educated and will have been born in lower strata. While education certainly influences a man's chances to move upward or downward, only a relatively modest part of all mobility is linked to education.

In an effort to disentangle the influence of the educational from other factors, a hypothetical mobility table was constructed on the assumption that the sons' status is determined solely by schooling.[16] On this hypothesis ("schooling dominant" lines in Table 5 and appropriate section of Table 6) the correlation between schooling and degree of mobility would be somewhat closer than it is in the actual data. By a similar procedure, a second hypothetical table was constructed by assuming that mobility reflected paternal status only; on this assumption no sons moved upward and about a tenth went down.[17] Finally, the random distribution of sons was computed from the basic data.

It is of particular interest to identify the location of the discrepancies between the actual distribution of mobility and that expected under each of the three hypotheses. Part A of Table 7 summarizes those discrepancies as absolute differences, first unweighted and then weighted by number of steps of mobility involved.[18] (A positive difference indicates that the actual moves exceed the hypothetical.)

Table 5.
Comparison of Actual with Hypothetical Mobility Under Various Assumptions, and Son's Schooling (%'s)

Assumption	+4	+3	+2	+1	0	−1	−2	−3	−4	Total	Total Up	Total Down	Ratio's up/down
Son's schooling: not beyond elementary													
Actual	*	1	4	17	42	25	7	2	1	100	22	36	.63
Schooling dominant	—	—	—	17	39	28	10	5	1	100	16	45	.36
Status dominant	—	—	—	—	91	9	—	—	—	100	0	9	.00
Random	2	6	9	20	30	20	8	4	1	100	38	32	1.17
Son's schooling: senior elementary supplemented													
Actual	1	4	11	21	35	19	6	2	1	100	37	28	1.33
Schooling dominant	—	2	17	38	24	12	6	1	—	100	57	19	3.00
Status dominant	—	—	—	—	90	10	—	—	—	100	0	10	.00
Random	1	5	8	16	29	23	10	6	2	100	31	40	.78
Son's schooling: grammar but none further													
Actual	0	3	2	13	43	23	8	6	2	100	18	39	.47
Schooling dominant	—	10	22	15	22	31	—	—	—	100	47	31	1.51
Status dominant	—	—	—	—	90	10	—	—	—	100	0	10	.00
Random	*	3	4	11	19	18	17	19	9	100	18	63	.29
Son's schooling: grammar school plus													
Actual	2	5	10	16	41	16	7	3	*	100	33	26	1.23
Schooling dominant	6	20	20	17	32	5	—	—	—	100	63	5	12.60
Status dominant	—	—	—	—	89	11	—	—	—	100	0	11	.00
Random	—	2	4	9	18	21	17	19	10	100	16	66	.24
Total sons													
Actual	*	2	6	17	41	23	7	3	1	100	26	33	.80
Education dominant	*	3	7	21	33	23	8	4	1	100	31	36	.86
Status dominant	—	—	—	—	90	10	—	—	—	100	0	10	.00
Random	2	5	8	18	28	21	10	6	2	100	34	38	.85
Total sons: numbers													
Actual	9	80	212	600	1,405	789	243	93	19	3,450	901	1,144	—
Schooling dominant	17	94	228	715	1,173	788	275	127	33	3,450	1,054	1,223	—
Status dominant	0	0	0	0	3,120	330	0	0	0	3,450	0	330	—

Mobility, by steps

A Skeptical Note on Education and Mobility

Table 6.

Percentage Distribution of Son's Schooling Within Mobility Categories

| | TYPE OF SCHOOLING | | | | |
	a	b	c	d	Total
Actual Data					
All Cases	65	21	5	9	100
Upward mobile	55	30	4	11	100
Non-mobile	67	18	6	9	100
Downward mobile	69	18	6	7	100
Assuming Schooling alone to Dominate					
Upward	35	39	8	18	100
Non-mobile	73	15	4	8	100
Downward	82	12	5	1	100
Assuming Paternal Status alone to Dominate					
Upward	—	—	—	—	
Non-mobile	65	21	6	8	100
Downward	62	24	6	8	100
Random Distribution					
Upward	73	20	3	4	100
Non-mobile	69	22	4	5	100
Downward	54	22	9	15	100

There are two interesting features in this table. First, the actual moves are clearly much more deviant from the status-dominant hypothesis than from the two other hypothetical distributions for those sons lacking any grammar-school education but this is less true for those with such schooling. Second, and of greater importance, are the systematic reversals of direction in the deviations of the actual from the education-dominant and the random distributions between the lowest level of schooling and the other levels. (Incidentally, in each instance the negative deviation is of greater magnitude than the positive.)

Do these patterns hold when account is taken of the underlying numbers of cases and the constraints on up and down movements (implied in the limited number of status categories and in the initial position of sons with varying amounts of education)? A correction for these factors is provided in Part B of Table 7, where ratios of actual to hypothetical moves are shown.[19]

Expressed in ratio form, the greater deviation from the status-dominant hypothesis is most striking. The only ratios approximating the latter relate to the excess downward movement of the best-schooled sons, where ratios are much higher than in the intermediate schooling levels. Once more, there is no clear shift between the second and third educational levels even with respect to downward moves, nor is the best-schooled group distinctive from the intermediate ones in deviations of actual upward

Table 7.

Comparisons of Actual with Hypothetical Moves

A.   ABSOLUTE DEVIATIONS

| | | | UNWEIGHTED | | | WEIGHTED | |
| | Mobility | | Education- | Status- | | Education- | Status |
Schooling	Direction	Random	Dominant	Dominant	Random	Dominant	Dominant
a	Up	−342	134	498	−821	287	651
	Down	67	−221	586	−21	−479	890
b	Up	47	−142	273	35	−137	429
	Down	−89	64	128	−188	88	218
c	Up	0	−55	34	−8	−119	50
	Down	−47	14	54	−155	62	102
d	Up	50	−90	96	95	−242	170
	Down	−119	64	46	−329	108	90

B.   RATIOS OF ACTUAL TO HYPOTHETICAL MOVES

Schooling	Direction	Random	Education-Dominant	Status-Dominant	Random	Education-Dominant	Status Dominant
a	Up	.58	1.41	6.44	.44	1.79	8.63
	Down	1.12	.77		.98	.70	
b	Up	1.21	.66	6.21	1.09	.75	9.40
	Down	.70	1.45		.61	1.43	
c	Up	1.00	.38	5.63	.86	.30	9.00
	Down	.61	1.24		.44	2.10	
d	Up	2.06	.52	5.36	2.27	.41	9.13
	Down	.39	5.57		.27	8.71	

mobility from that presupposed by the education-dominant hypothesis. In relative as in absolute terms, the major break is between the lowest schooling category and all the others.

To sum up, sons with low education lose status far less often and those with intermediate or higher levels of education rise far less often than would be the case if education were the sole determinant. The "favorable" achievement of the least educated sons stands in contrast to their conspicuously large downward discrepance from the status-dominant hypothesis (Table 7.A). At the other extreme, by far the greatest relative deviation from the education-dominant hypothesis is manifested in the excess cases of status decline among the sons with the most education.

The least-educated sons made many more up and fewer down moves than would be expected on the basis of their schooling. But they did make fewer up and more down moves than chance ("random") would bring about. This situation is reversed for the best educated sons; they make fewer up and more down moves than education would bring about, but their upward moves are more frequent and their downward moves less frequent than chance would produce.

Adding algebraically the actual up and down moves of each educational group and then those to be expected on the education-dominant hypothesis, and expressing the former sums as a ratio to the latter pro-

Table 8.

Efficiency Index: Education as a Factor in Mobility

	UNWEIGHTED			WEIGHTED		
Education Group	Net Actual	Net Hypothetical	Index	Net Actual	Net Hypothetical	Index
a	−290	−635	.46	−441	−1,207	.37
b+c	29	304	.10	73	479	.13
d	18	172	.10	48	398	.12

vides a crude set of "efficiency indexes" with respect to schooling as a job allocation mechanism (Table 8). These indexes could range (for small segments of a population) from negative to positive infinity. Values of zero and +1 have special meaning; the latter would mean perfect correlation between actual and education-dominant mobility while zero would imply education played no role. Negative values imply that net mobility is in a direction contrary to that expected on the basis of education; if the negative index is large enough one would infer that schooling was actually dysfunctional or (and this appears to be true for those with grammar school only) that selection of students at a given educational level was markedly out of line with their underlying relative abilities and achievement motivations.

At the lowest educational level the positive indexes are much higher than at the other levels, though even for those with elementary school only the index is below .50. This might be interpreted to mean that less than half of the actual mobility (or lack thereof) among the least schooled can be "explained" by their schooling. How about the rest? Here there is a drag on the index limiting its possible range so that approximation to zero is virtually impossible; this is because group (a) forms the bulk of the population and is dominated by men whose fathers, like themselves, are in low-ranking occupations; failure to move is in accord with their educational backgrounds. This is the only group for whom net downward movement is theoretically required.

More surprising is the extremely low index for the men with the most education (d). Undoubtedly we see here a reflection of the fact that men in the top occupations try to give their sons the "best" of schooling regardless of their abilities and personalities. The well-schooled sons of high status fathers who are not suited to high status jobs lost status despite their training; thus among the best educated we get the previously noted high ratios of actual downward mobility to that predicted by the education-dominant hypothesis.[20] This interpretation is strengthened by the negative ratios noted for group (c), if one assumes that the downwardly mobile among these are sons of upper class fathers who were especially low in "ability" and hence did not go beyond grammar school. These ratios point to major defects in the selection of students for grammar school and higher education if the "ideal" criterion is taken to be the individual's potentialities. The situation is quite different from that indicated for sons with supplemented senior elementary training (without grammar school), the upwardly mobile group for whom education appears to have played the largest part, having a weighted index of .36.

In conclusion, education is but one of many factors influencing mobility, and it may be far from a dominant factor. To say that its efficiency is low in this respect measured on an absolute scale, however, is not necessarily to say it "should be" higher. Education has multiple functions and preparation for a vocation is only one of these. Moreover, qualifications not easily provided by formal schooling affect job success, status advantages or disadvantages aside. There are objections to setting up as a goal the maximization of correlations between education and occupation. There is no reason to disregard individual preferences concerning education as a consumer good or preferences among jobs. Moreover, there are many individual qualifications that are relatively independent of formal training.

In an earlier article on "intelligence and occupational mobility"[21] I suggested that "before we lament the disappearance of opportunity or herald the iron laws of status fixation, it may be prudent to estimate just how effectively the existing mechanism of selection operates in sorting persons out, not according to inherited status, but according to their capacities." In that study it was concluded that from two-thirds to three-fourths of the mobility in the United States was congruent with "intelligence" differentials. I would interpret the present findings as suggesting that ability (whether genetic or not)—and associated motivation—varying independently of schooling plays a powerful role in generating mobility.

It was concluded also that much of the mobility occurring served to compensate for "incorrect" placement among occupations of the fathers, combined with "regression" of intelligence. Hence, "when we talk of intergeneration mobility, we must think in terms not only of the actual occupational status of fathers and of sons but also of the occupations that the fathers 'should be' pursuing." The present analysis appears consistent with that conclusion.

In the three countries for which data exists, mobility independent of schooling occurs frequently. Because of the different classifications used in the three sets of data one cannot draw explicit comparisons, though one might infer that education has more influence in the United States. Even with more equal distribution of educational opportunities, the independent operation of "intelligence" will probably damp the impact of schooling upon individual careers.

Appendix

A. Part 2 of Table 1B was derived as follows. There were 164 sons with higher status and 291 with higher education. Taking all of the 164 higher-status sons from those with higher education leaves 127 (291–164) better-schooled sons; these are given the most favorable possible remaining status, "same," none going into "lower." Among "education same" sons, none can go into "status higher," and only 18 (145–127) can go into "status same," leaving 62 in "status lower." The remaining 45 go in the lowest diagonal cell.

B. The construction of hypothetical distribution on the British data is more intricate. Regardless of parental status, all possible sons with more than grammar school (d) were placed in status 1, 2. Since there were 296 sons with this schooling but only 257 places in 1, 2, the numbers from each parental status group were multiplied by the ratio of 257/296, which allocates the 257 by taking the same proportion from each parental category. Hence, some sons must go into status-level 3. This first step is summarized as follows:

Fathers' Status	Total Sons	Sons in 1, 2	Sons in 3
1, 2	103	89	14
3	51	44	7
4	59	51	8
5	64	56	8
6, 7	19	17	2
Total	296	257	39

There were 324 sons in status 3 of whom 39 are accounted for from group (d). There are already 189 (c) sons distributed as follows by paternal status: 59, 41, 28, 42, 19. Since 324— (39 + 189)=96, these remaining 96 places must be filled from the next lower education category in proportion to their distribution by paternal status.

Distribution of Sons with Senior Elementary Plus (b)

Father's Status	Total Sons	Sons in 3	Remainder	Sons in 4*	Sons in 5
1, 2	40	5	35	25	10
3	82	11	71	50	21
4	120	16	104	74	30
5	359	47	312	221	91
6, 7	131	17	114	80	34
Total	732	96	636	450	186

* In ratio 450/636.

The (b) sons in status 3 were computed by multiplying the total (b) sons from each parental stratum by the ratio of 96/732. Subtracting these from the total sons with (b) schooling leave 636. There were 450 sons in 4, so each remainder is multiplied by 450/636 and when the derived numbers are subtracted we have the sons with (b) schooling who must go into status 5. They provide 186 of the 1,409 sons in status 5. There remain 1,409–186 or 1,223 positions in 5. None had yet been put in 6, 7 which has 1,010 positions. 1,010 is 39 per cent of all (a) sons (2,233); multiplying the (a) sons in each parental category by .39 allocates these sons to 6, 7; the remainder go in status 5.

Distribution of Sons with Elementary Schooling Only (a)

Father's Status	Total Sons	Sons in 5	Sons in 6,7
1, 2	74	41	33
3	168	92	76
4	304	167	137
5	1,022	559	463
6, 7	665	364	301
Total	2,233	1,223	1,010

NOTES

1. See our "Educational Distribution and Attainment Norms," *1954 World Population Congress,* v. 4, Session 27.

2. T. W. Schultz, "Education and Economic Growth," *National Society for the Study of Education Yearbook,* v. 60 (forthcoming).

3. See our "Intelligence and Occupational Mobility," *Journal of Political Economy,* LX (June 1952), 218–39 in which a share of total mobility was allocated to such structural change.

4. *Ibid.*

5. R. Centers, "Education and Occupational Mobility," *American Sociological Review,* XIV (Feb., 1949), 143–4.

6. D. V. Glass (ed.), *Social Mobility in Britain* (London; Routledge and Kegan Paul, 1954), ch. 10 with J. R. Hall.

7. See our "Lifetime Inter-Occupational Mobility Patterns in Sweden," *Acta Sociologica,* I (1956), 168–201.

8. See appendix for method of computation.

9. G. Boalt, "Skolgang och Standcirkulation," *Tidens Kalendar,* XXXII (1953), 113–16.

10. G. Carlsson, *Social Mobility and Class Structure,* (Lund: Gleerup, 1958), Ch. 7.

11. *Ibid,* 137.

12. Glass, *Op. cit.* From the table on p. 296 the numbers in each cell were reconstructed.

13. The schooling categories are: a) senior elementary only; b) (a) plus some supplementary training; c) Grammar school but no further; d) (c) and more. The status categories are: 1, 2) professional and higher administration, managerial and executive; 3) supervisory and other higher non-manual; 4) supervisory and other non-manual of lower grade; 5) skilled manual and routine non-manual; 6, 7) unskilled and semiskilled.

14. The downward drift of net mobility in the sample is puzzling; it may arise from the mixed "occupational" and "status" categories used or there may be deficiencies in the sample or the scale of status.

15. If categories 1 and 2 were separate, recruitment from below to 1 would presumably be less.

16. See appendix for explanation.

17. See f.n. 14.

18. The weighted figures make the conventional assumption that distances between categories are equal.

19. Fortunately, direction is unimportant in comparing with the status-dominant assumption, which for these data involves small downward movements associated

with an over-all shift in the structure between generations; the problem of zero denominator for upward moves is thereby avoided by summing both directions for actual and hypothetical data.

20. There is also the restraint on upward mobility for well-educated sons of low status fathers, but, as the previous discussion shows, this is a lesser element in explaining their low-efficiency ratios.

21. See f.n. 3.

PART III

The Selection Process in Education

16 *Selection for Secondary Education in France*

A. GIRARD

Prefatory Note: This paper gives some of the results of a sample survey carried out on a national basis in France in the spring of 1954. The object of the inquiry was to find out what happened to children who left the elementary school before the end, and at the end, of their period of compulsory school attendance, at the age of about eleven or twelve in the one case, and at about fourteen in the other. The findings about these two groups of children are presented in relation to their home background, size of family, age, and scholastic achievement. They reveal the decisive influence of the last-named on the orientation of the children, but also the obstacles that sometimes stand between children of proven ability and the continuation of their studies.

All in all, the inquiry covered 18,331 children who left elementary school in July, 1953. Of this number 5,208 were below the school-leaving age and proceeding to other institutions of full-time education (pupils transferring to other elementary schools were eliminated from our sample.) Readers are referred to Population, 1954, No. 4, pp. 597–604, for particulars of the construction and geographical distribution of the sample, which was fully representative of all parts of France and excluded only the Département of the Seine, which was separately investigated on an earlier occasion (see Population, 1953, No. 4, pp. 649–722).

Selection for Secondary Courses

OUR INQUIRY enabled us to establish exactly how many children stay in elementary school until the end of their period of compulsory education— i.e., until they reach the age of fourteen, as was laid down in 1936—and how many, on the other hand, go on at about eleven years of age to other kinds of schools. It is in fact at that age, when a child starts on his first year in a secondary or higher-grade course of one kind or another, that his future begins to take shape. If a child stays on in the elementary school after eleven or twelve, it is a sign of lack of drive or decision on the part of his parents, which in itself would be enough to prevent his proceeding to secondary or higher education.

If we disregard the children in preparatory departments of grammar schools, not covered by the inquiry, the proportion of those who take a definite step towards their future career by leaving the elementary school at the age of eleven, can be estimated at 29 per cent for the whole of

Translated and abridged from A. Girard, "Enquête nationale sur l'orientation et la sélection des enfants d'âge scolaire," *Population,* Oct.–Dec., 1954, pp. 597–634, with the permission of the author and the publisher.

Table 1.

Distribution of Elementary Schools by Type of Locality; Average Number of Leavers at Ages 11 and 14 According to Locality and Type of School, in July, 1953.

Locality*	State Schools							Private Schools						
	Seine	1	1a	2	2a	3	4	Seine	1	1a	2	2a	3	4
No. of schools	57	97	22	120	24	501	1150	29	47	15	46	6	93	134

A. LEAVERS AT 11+: PERCENTAGE OF SCHOOLS IN EACH LOCALITY WITH NUMBERS LEAVING AS INDICATED:

No. of leavers	Seine	1	1a	2	2a	3	4	Seine	1	1a	2	2a	3	4
0	—	8	9	6	20	44	55	—	2	—	7	—	24	39
1–2	—	14	27	16	26	33	35	—	29	13	18	17	31	38
3–4	—	14	13	14	13	9	7	—	21	33	21	66	19	14
5–9	—	29	32	28	29	9	3	—	27	33	37	17	12	6
10–14	—	13	14	19	8	4	—	—	19	21	13	—	5	3
15–19	—	7	5	10	4	1	—	—	2	—	4	—	7	—
20–24	—	11	—	4	—	—	—	—	—	—	—	—	1	—
25–29	—	2	—	2	—	—	—	—	—	—	—	—	—	—
30–34	—	2	—	1	—	—	—	—	—	—	—	—	1	—
Total	—	100	100	100	100	100	100	—	100	100	100	100	100	100
Average no. of leavers at 11+, all schools	—	9.1	5.4	7.7	4.1	2.1	1.0	—	4.9	5.1	4.9	3.2	3.5	1.5

B. LEAVERS AT 14: PERCENTAGE OF SCHOOLS IN EACH LOCATITY WITH NUMBERS LEAVING AS INDICATED:

No. of leavers	Seine	1	1a	2	2a	3	4	Seine	1	1a	2	2a	3	4
0	—	1	—	2	20	9	14	10	8	7	9	17	10	7
1–2	—	3	—	3	26	29	37	14	9	26	16	17	16	22
3–4	2	4	10	14	13	22	24	7	25	—	18	17	18	17
5–9	9	18	27	15	29	23	21	53	32	46	25	32	34	29
10–14	10	18	15	18	8	6	4	3	10	14	22	—	15	21
15–19	12	11	15	17	4	5	—	7	6	7	6	17	2	3
20–24	12	21	18	13	—	3	—	3	—	—	4	—	4	—
25–29	25	12	10	6	—	2	—	3	6	—	—	—	—	1
30–34	16	7	—	8	—	1	—	—	—	—	—	—	—	—
35–39	2	—	—	2	—	—	—	—	2	—	—	—	1	—
40 & over	12	5	5	2	—	—	—	—	2	—	—	—	—	—
Total	100	100	100	100	100	100	100	100	100	100	100	100	100	100
Average no. of leavers at 14, all schools	25.0	17.7	15.1	14.7	10.8	5.7	3.4	7.3	8.9	6.5	7.2	5.7	6.7	5.9
Percentage of all leavers proceeding to secondary courses at 11+	—	36	28	37	30	29	24	—	38	46	43	38	37	22

*1–Towns of over 100,000
1a–Suburbs thereof
2–Towns of 20,000–100,000
2a–Suburbs thereof
3–Cantons having at least one town of 5,000–20,000
4–Other cantons

France, excluding Seine. This figure is obtained by relating the average number of children leaving school before the end of the period of compulsory attendance, to the average number of all leaving in July, 1953.

Table 1 shows how this figure varied, between state and private schools and according to the degree of urban density. In the towns, it is higher for private than for state schools; and apart from the rural areas where there is often no possibility of choice, it shows little variation for private schools, whatever the degree of urban density. In state schools, however, it rises regularly with increasing urban density. As far as the 14-year-old leavers are concerned, Table 1 suggests that they form, on the average, a relatively small group, even in the biggest towns—17.7 in towns of over 100,000 inhabitants; 25 in Seine. Only 12 per cent of schools in the former and 30 per cent in the latter have more than 30 leavers of this age. This need not surprise us, if we remember that the organization of the schools has the effect of scattering the age-group. It is only in the center of the biggest towns, and in Paris, that it will be found concentrated in homogeneous classes, with their own classrooms and teachers. Everywhere else, schools on the outskirts of towns are organized on the rural pattern as all-age community schools; that is to say, they have only one or two classrooms and one or two teachers for all the pupils of the locality.

Social Factors in Selection for Secondary Courses

A marked process of selection according to the children's home background takes place before the end of the period of compulsory education. Children's chances of access to secondary schools at the age of eleven, and consequently to higher education later on, vary very much, as is revealed by a comparison, set out in Table 2, between the social origins of those who do and those who do not stay on at the elementary school until the age of fourteen. Two-thirds of the classes at the top of the elementary school consist of children of agricultural laborers, farmers, and workmen; while only one-third of those who leave for a secondary school around eleven come from the same circles. For all the other social groups, the proportion of children who proceed to secondary courses before the age of fourteen is greater than the proportion of those who stay on at the elementary school until they are fourteen. In the top elementary class there are hardly any children from the highest social groups, e.g., administrators, industrialists, senior civil servants, and the professions. This is true for both boys and girls, so that the figures are presented for both sexes together, and in all degrees of urban concentration.

The same method of selection is used for state and private schools, but in fact certain social categories are less well represented in the private

Table 2.

Social Origins of Leavers (Boys and Girls) from Elementary Schools in July, 1953.

Father's occupation	Towns of more than 100,000	Sub- urbs thereof	Towns of 20,000 to 100,000	Sub- urbs thereof	Semiurban, semirural cantons	Rural cantons	All
A. PERCENTAGE OF LEAVERS AGED 11+							
Farmers	1	1	3	2	10	24	15
Agricultural laborers	—	1	2	3	3	3	2
Unskilled workers	14	24	19	26	19	15	17
Clerks, formen	33	33	23	28	21	14	20
Tradesmen, artisans	17	15	14	12	16	21	19
Lower-grade officials	14	8	15	14	11	10	11
Administrators, senior officials	10	7	10	7	8	4	6
Industrialists, professionals	3	1	3	3	4	4	4
Retired, occupation unknown	8	10	11	5	8	5	6
Total	100	100	100	100	100	100	100
No. of children	1,105	195	1,152	117	1,364	1,275	
B. PERCENTAGE OF LEAVERS AGED 14+							
Farmers	2	2	3	3	19	43	29
Agricultural laborers	1	1	4	5	5	10	8
Unskilled workers	29	41	35	38	37	19	27
Clerks, foremen	31	29	22	29	13	7	12
Tradesmen, artisans	13	9	11	10	8	9	9
Lower-grade officials	8	6	9	6	6	4	5
Administrators, senior officials, industrialists, professionals	2	1	1	1	1	1	1
Retired, occupation unknown	14	11	15	8	11	7	9
Total	100	100	100	100	100	100	100
No. of children	2,210	431	2,113	292	3,499	4,678	

schools—e.g., agricultural and urban laborers, and, to a less degree, clerks and lower-grade civil servants. The reverse is true in the case of the other occupational groups.

This social inequality seems even greater when one considers the differences in the proportions of children at each social level proceeding to secondary courses, as set out in Table 3. For all social groups, the proportion is 29 per cent; but it is 13 per cent for children of agricultural laborers; 16 per cent for children of farmers; and 21 per cent for children of workers and general laborers. The figure rises to between four and five out of ten among children of clerks, lower-grade civil servants, and tradesmen; and reaches seven, eight, or even nine out of ten in the other categories. There is little difference between the figures for boys and those for girls, although the former are slightly higher.

Table 3.

Percentage of Elementary Pupils from Each Social Category Who Proceed to Secondary Education

	Boys	Girls	Total
Agricultural laborers	13	14	13
Farmers	17	15	16
Unskilled workers	21	20	21
Clerks, foremen	45	42	43
Tradesmen, artisans	41	37	39
Lower-grade officials	46	48	47
Industrialists	61	75	68
Administrators	80	83	81
Senior officials	89	82	86
Professionals	89	85	87
All	30	28	29

The localities we have distinguished naturally vary in their social and occupational structure: differences in the proportions of children leaving elementary school for secondary courses before fourteen, are as follows:

	%
Towns of over 100,000 inhabitants	37
Suburbs of these towns	33
Towns of 20,000 to 100,000 inhabitants	38
Suburbs of these towns	31
Cantons with a town of 5,000 to 20,000 inhabitants	30
Other cantons	23

Size of Family

Table 4, which refers only to completed families,[1] shows clearly that in all but the most favored social classes the children left in the elementary school until the age of fourteen are drawn from larger families than those

Table 4.

Index of Size of (Completed) Families of Children Staying on at Elementary School Until the End of Compulsory Education, in Relation to Social Class

	Leavers at:	
	11 years	14 years
Agricultural laborers	100	106
Farmers	100	102
Unskilled workers	100	111
Clerks, foremen	100	103
Artisans, tradesmen	100	112
Lower grade officials	100	115
Other occupations	100	74
All	100	112

who proceed to secondary schools at eleven. It is very rare in any case for children of the more favored classes to stay on at elementary school. Hence, children who go on to secondary and higher education enjoy from the start a double advantage, social and demographic: they tend to have better home backgrounds and to come from smaller families.

The Orientation of Children Aged Eleven to Twelve Years

It is at about the age of eleven or twelve, then, that the pattern of a child's future begins to emerge: only those who leave the elementary school at that age have the opportunity of going on to secondary or higher education. Since their period of compulsory education is not completed at that age, the children start on other courses of study. More than half go on to secondary schools—"grammar" or "modern"; slightly more than one third go to senior elementary courses (*Cours complémentaires*); and 6 per cent to technical schools. Table 5 sets out the relevant figures.

Table 5.

Destinies of Leavers from Elementary Schools at Age 11–12 in Relation to Sex and Place of Residence

	Towns of more than 100,000	Sub- urbs	Towns of 20,000 to 100,000	Sub- urbs	Semiurban, semirural cantons	Rural cantons	All
Boys	%	%	%	%	%	%	%
Secondary schooling	59	50	57	54	55	53	54
grammar	12	11	14	16	22	16	17
modern	24	30	17	32	21	16	18
unspecified	22	5	25	2	11	20	18
preparatory classes	1	4	1	4	1	1	1
Senior elementary courses	16	31	23	20	33	32	30
Technical schools	17	6	12	6	6	7	8
Unclassified	8	13	8	20	6	8	8
All	100	100	100	100	100	100	100
Total Number	567	112	592	50	716	678	
Girls							
Secondary schooling	61	62	62	66	34	52	50
grammar	14	7	12	13	10	16	13
modern	25	35	32	44	13	22	22
unspecified	21	16	17	9	10	13	14
preparatory classes	1	4	1	—	1	1	1
Senior elementary courses	25	25	26	28	57	36	39
Technical schools	8	11	5	2	1	3	3
Unclassified	6	2	7	4	8	9	8
All	100	100	100	100	100	100	100
Total Number	538	83	560	67	648	597	

It appears that girls proceed to senior elementary courses more often than to secondary schools; if they do go to the latter, their preference is for the "modern" rather than for "grammar" schools. Very few girls go to technical schools—in fact, only one-third of the number of boys who go there.

There are variations according to the type of locality. In towns of over 20,000 inhabitants, the most popular choice, especially for girls, is a secondary school. This may be because the "grammar" and "modern" schools are situated in the towns; but the number of children who live in rural or semirural districts and nevertheless proceed to secondary schools is by no means negligible.

One apparent anomaly concerns the girls in cantons having one town of 5,000 to 20,000 inhabitants. Contrary to what happens elsewhere, and even to what happens to the boys in these same localities, the majority of the girls go to senior elementary courses rather than to grammar schools. This appears, however, to reflect local variations in the provision of secondary courses for boys and girls.[2]

Children from private elementary schools tend to choose differently from those attending state schools. They mostly go to secondary schools, and in particular to grammar schools with a classical tradition. This difference in orientation is connected with the fact that, as we have already seen, private-school children come chiefly from the more privileged social classes.

We give here only the national figures, but the same difference can be seen in the different localities, urban as well as rural.

| | PERCENTAGE OF PUPILS COMING FROM: | |
	State elementary schools	Private elementary schools
Pupils proceeding to:		
Secondary schooling:		
grammar	14	28
modern	22	22
unspecified	18	18
preparatory classes	1	3
	—	—
	55	71
Senior elementary courses	39	25
Technical schools	6	4
All	100	100
Unclassified	6	20

The Role of Ability

Although it is true that social and economic background and, to a lesser degree, size of family play an important part in deciding where a child is to finish his period of compulsory education, it must not be assumed that these are the only selective forces. Ability and aptitude, as measured by scholastic achievement, are the decisive factors, as can be seen from a comparison of the distribution of teachers' assessments in the two groups of leavers.

Teachers were asked to grade the children's school work on a five-point scale: excellent, good, average, fair, or poor. Grades for the fourteen-year-old leavers from the elementary schools present a normal distribution, with approximately equal proportions at the head and tail. It can be assumed that this normal curve holds for most classes of children, and in fact there were no deviations from it by locality in our sample.

If we take it that a class of eleven- to twelve-year-olds is made up in the same way before the departure of those who are going on to other schools at the end of the year, then the distribution of assessments among these two groups of children are strikingly different, especially among the most able of them. Twenty-nine per cent of the leavers are aged eleven to twelve, and their scholastic achievement may be compared with that of those aged fourteen who had stayed on in the elementary school:

Ability groups	Pupils leaving at 11–12 for secondary courses	Pupils staying on at the elementary school	All leavers
Teacher's assessment:	%	%	%
excellent	5	3	8
good	14	13	27
average	8	25	33
fair	2	19	21
poor		11	11
	—	—	—
	29	71	100

Thus, about one-third of the "excellent" children, representing 3 per cent of the over-all numbers, are not selected at eleven years of age and 6 per cent of those whose work is "fair" or "poor" (equal to 2 per cent of the total) are.

The shape of the distribution is much the same whatever the social origin of the children, as can be seen from Table 6; selection by scholastic achievement operates for all classes. However, since there are wide differences in the proportions proceeding to secondary education at each social level, the inference is that the social distribution of scholastic achievement is very uneven.

Table 6 also shows the scholastic achievement of leavers for secondary courses in relation to size of family and to the age of the children themselves. It confirms what we have just said: whatever the size of the family, whatever the children's age, the proportion of "excellent" and "good" pupils who go on to other schools is similar. External factors—social, economic, or personal—do have an influence on the children's potential

Table 6.

Scholastic Ability of Children Proceeding From Elementary to Secondary Schools at Age 11–12, in Relation to Their Social Origin, Size of Family, and Age

| | TEACHERS' ASSESSMENT | | | | | |
| | Excellent | Good | Average | Fair | Poor | Total |
	%	%	%	%	%	
Fathers' occupations:						
Farmers	21	46	24	7	2	100
Agricultural laborers	18	47	26	7	2	100
Unskilled workers	19	47	28	5	1	100
Clerks, foremen	16	50	27	6	1	100
Lower-grade officials	19	53	24	4	—	100
Artisans, tradesmen	17	47	30	5	1	100
Administrators, senior officials	24	50	21	4	1	100
Industrialists, professionals	24	42	29	4	1	100
Retired, occupation unknown	14	46	31	6	3	100
Number of children in family:						
1	18	48	27	6	1	100
2	18	48	29	4	1	100
3	19	50	26	4	1	100
4	20	48	24	6	2	100
5	15	48	29	6	2	100
6	20	46	27	7	—	100
7	19	51	22	8	—	100
8	14	44	31	11	—	100
9 or more	33	34	31	2	—	100
Age:						
Under 10 years	25	35	25	10	5	100
10 yrs. –10 yrs. 5 mths.	33	44	18	3	2	100
10 yrs. 6 mths.–10 yrs. 8 mths.	21	55	19	5	—	100
10 yrs. 9 mths.–10 yrs. 11 mths.	18	52	26	4	—	100
11 yrs. –11 yrs. 2 mths.	20	53	24	3	—	100
11 yrs. 3 mths.–11 yrs. 5 mths.	19	51	27	3	—	100
11 yrs. 6 mths.–11 yrs. 8 mths.	15	50	28	6	1	100
11 yrs. 9 mths.–11 yrs. 11 mths.	13	51	30	5	1	100
12 yrs. –12 yrs. 2 mths.	10	48	35	6	1	100
12 yrs. 3 mths.–12 yrs. 5 mths.	20	45	30	4	1	100
12 yrs. 6 mths.–12 yrs. 8 mths.	14	40	39	6	1	100
12 yrs. 9 mths.–12 yrs. 11 mths.	9	45	34	10	2	100
13 yrs. and over	18	50	22	8	2	100

achievement in that they reduce the number of outstanding scholars, but within each group, the great majority of able children are directed toward secondary, technical, or higher studies, for which their success at primary school has qualified them; while the less able children, for the most part find themselves excluded.

Table 7 shows the scholastic ability of the same children in relation to their sex and place of residence. The similarity of the figures in each sub-group reiterates the same story: that the ablest children are not left to stay on at the elementary school until they are fourteen.

The Selection Process in Education

Table 7.

Scholastic Achievement of Children Who Left
Elementary School in July, 1953

Teachers' Assessment	Towns of more than 100,000	Sub- urbs thereof	Towns of 20,000 to 100,000	Sub- urbs thereof	Semiurban, semirural cantons	Rural cantons	All
A. PERCENTAGE OF LEAVERS FOR SECONDARY COURSES AT 11+							
Boys							
Excellent	19	21	14	20	19	21	19
Good	48	42	50	42	50	49	49
Average	27	29	29	28	24	23	25
Fair	5	3	6	10	6	6	6
Poor	1	5	1	—	1	1	1
Total	100	100	100	100	100	100	100
Not classified	1	—	6	—	1	—	1
No. of children	567	112	592	50	716	678	
Girls							
Excellent	18	16	13	22	15	21	18
Good	44	45	47	47	49	52	50
Average	32	31	35	25	30	22	27
Fair	5	8	4	3	5	4	4
Poor	1	—	1	3	1	1	1
Total	100	100	100	100	100	100	100
Not classified	—	—	2	—	1	2	1
No. of children	538	83	560	67	648	597	
B. PERCENTAGE OF LEAVERS AT 14+							
Boys							
Excellent	9	8	4	9	6	7	7
Good	25	26	25	20	26	27	26
Average	35	34	36	43	37	30	33
Fair	22	14	22	19	20	24	22
Poor	9	18	13	9	11	12	12
Total	100	100	100	100	100	100	100
Not classified	5	—	—	—	2	2	2
No. of children	1,105	276	976	142	1,764	2,323	
Girls							
Excellent	7	6	7	9	8	10	9
Good	26	16	21	21	28	31	29
Average	36	40	36	28	33	31	32
Fair	18	23	21	18	20	20	20
Poor	13	15	15	24	11	8	10
Total	100	100	100	100	100	100	100
Not classified	5	3	1	—	3	3	3
No. of children	1,005	155	1,137	150	1,735	2,355	

Summary and Discussion

These figures relate to the school year, 1953–54, when our investigations were made. But developments are taking place constantly. In particular, there is a steady increase in the number of children desiring secondary education, in spite of the fact that less numerous age-groups, born since 1930 and especially between 1940 and 1944, are now reaching eleven and twelve years of age. The increase is therefore relatively all the greater.

If we take into account the children who have attended the preparatory departments of grammar schools from the age of six or seven, and reckon that all of these—7 per cent of the boys, 10 per cent of the girls—will go on to secondary schools, we find that in the year 1953–54, nearly one-quarter of the child-population aged eleven to twelve was in secondary schools; 10 per cent were in senior elementary courses; and 2 per cent were having technical education. Separating the figures for boys and girls, and relating them not to 100 per cent but to 93 per cent and 90 per cent respectively for those who go on from elementary to other schools at eleven or twelve, we arrive at the following proportions:

	Boys %	Girls %
Secondary schools	7 + 16 = 23	10 + 13 = 23
Senior Elementary courses	9	11
Technical schools	3	1

Since the figures were obtained by a sample survey, they can only be regarded as an indication of the relative size of the various groups. They are, however, borne out by other statistics of secondary school entrants in 1953–54.

Given that the situation in schools is fluid, it is impossible to foresee exactly what those children who stay on at the elementary schools will be doing three years hence, i.e., in October, 1960. But a survey in 1953–54 of such children shows that 15 per cent, or about one out of ten of all children in the same age-group, do continue their studies; a very small number—about 1 per cent—go to secondary schools; rather more—4 per cent—go to the senior elementary schools; and 5 per cent go to technical schools.

One can say, then, that for about nine out of ten children the question as to whether they will continue their education beyond the period of compulsory schooling is decided at the age of eleven or twelve, and that after that age there is little chance of their gaining admission to a secondary school, or, consequently, to higher education later.

The inquiry's findings confirm that children of varying home backgrounds do not have equal chances of selection at eleven or twelve, or, in particular, of gaining admission to secondary schools. For agricultural laborers' children, the chances are slightly more than one in ten; whereas children from more fortunate homes have eight or nine chances in ten.

Another disadvantage, of a demographic nature, is added to this social inequality. In the modest homes the children from small families have a better chance from the start than those from large families.

A further aspect of the matter is emphasized by the inquiry. It is that scholastic achievement appears to be the determining factor for all social categories in the orientation of children at eleven or twelve. On the whole, it is the children with the greatest ability who are selected. The number of brilliant children left at the elementary school is relatively small, and corresponds more or less to those who, after leaving school at fourteen, do continue with their studies. This is not to say, however, that parents should not be urged—or helped—to encourage their children up the educational ladder as far as they can go. But it does show that the increased numbers in the postprimary schools have not been achieved by lowering the standards for admission. It also bears witness to the fact that the schools are, to the best of their ability, carrying out their proper function, which is not merely to instruct, but also, with the support and help of the parents, to select and orientate their pupils.

It has already been observed many times, in France and elsewhere, that children from different socio-economic backgrounds do not achieve the same degree of scholastic success, any more than they obtain the same scores in tests of intelligence.[3] This phenomenon can be explained in various ways, and in the present state of knowledge the parts played by heredity and by environment in the development of the individual are difficult to estimate. It is, however, certain that in most cases, and where intelligence is equal, the children of the upper classes benefit from a material and psychological environment more favorable to their full development than that of children from less fortunate homes. Therefore, by raising the standard of living, and providing better facilities for the education of children of all classes, we could enable the talents of a greater number to be given their due measure of recognition.

NOTES

1. That is, families with one child, or those, of whatever size, whose last-born child was the one we studied—the second of two, the third of three, fourth of four, etc. In such cases it is very rare for another child to be born after an interval of 14, or even 11 years.

2. Readers are referred to *Population*, No. 4, 1954, p. 616, for particulars.

3. See especially *Le niveau intellectuel des enfants d'âge scolaire*, Vol. I and II (Parts No. 13 and 23 of *Travaux et Documents*, I.N.E.D., Paris: 1950 & 1954).

17   *Selection in Scottish Secondary Schools*

JOHN S. MACPHERSON

Prefatory Note: The following is an excerpt from the report of a seven-year follow-up of a representative sample of 1,208 children from the 1947 Scottish Mental Survey of all children born in 1936. A group test score, an IQ and a number of sociological data were recorded for each child in 1947; subsequently, information was obtained by written questionnaires from Head of Schools and home visitors.

WE HAVE SEEN that of the whole sample, 75 pupils (or 6.2 per cent) achieved a leaving certificate score[1] of eight or more points (referred to as LC 8+ in the text) which corresponds to three higher passes and two lower passes, the minimum requirement for entry to a Scottish university. This number comprised 49 boys (8.3 per cent) and 26 girls (4.2 per cent) so that almost twice as many boys as girls achieved this standard of success. Does this number represent all the pupils in the sample capable of attaining this level? How many able pupils leave school before attempting to obtain a good leaving certificate? This problem of the potential high ability in an age-group has become one of great urgency in recent years. The demand for highly trained man-power has increased enormously particularly in the technical field and in education. It is important to know the size of the potential pool supplying these vital needs. The word 'wastage' has become part of the terminology in this connection. If a very able pupil leaves school before completing a leaving certificate course he is included in the 'wastage.' It is unfortunate that this word should have a philosophical implication. Some of our great statesmen and successful businessmen would be included in the 'wastage' category, and on the other hand one would seldom meet with intelligent tradesmen in a world where there was no wastage. To what extent wastage is a good or a bad thing, then, we leave to the philosopher. If we apply the word to a pupil it will simply be in the more objective sense that he would probably have gained a good leaving certificate if he had entered and completed a five-year course.

The criteria to be adopted in assessing wastage are far from clear. Certain assumptions must be made, and the answer we obtain will depend on which are adopted. To some extent any assumption will envisage some ac-

Reprinted from John S. Macpherson, *Eleven-Year-Olds Grow Up* (London: Scottish Council for Research in Education, 1958), pp. 64–77, 126–29, with the permission of the publisher.

tion being taken to change the educational or social system, because in attempting to increase the percentage of good leaving certificates we will require to alter things as they are today. Thus we might say 'The number of good leaving certificates of a certain level would be increased if such-and-such were done or if such-and-such were the case.' It is immediately obvious that some assumptions are more realistic than others. For example, it would probably be correct but unrealistic, and even ridiculous, to estimate the probable increase in leaving certificates on the assumption that every child in the population was sent to a senior secondary language course and kept there for at least five years. There are other more plausible assumptions which would also lead to unrealistic estimates. For example, there is the danger of neglecting some important factors correlated with success. Suppose we have a group of 100 pupils all of the same IQ level and in five-year courses, 50 of whom leave before completing the course and 50 who proceed to a good leaving certificate. On the face of it, using the limited data, we would appear to have a wastage of 50. But suppose that in addition we know that, compared with the 50 who remained at school, most of those who left early were deficient in personal qualities such as industry, or had very difficult home circumstances, or did not find the course interesting or useful for the career they had in mind, or were known not to be succeeding in the course for other reasons known or unknown, then valid estimation becomes extremely difficult and many of the measures which would have to be adopted to realise the increased number of certificates become impracticable. In this example we should have to improve the characters of some so that they become industrious, remedy the social system so that home circumstances are not a handicap, revolutionise the secondary school system so that all pupils may be interested, take measures to ensure that they all complete the course, and even then it would be foolish to guarantee the desired result. It is clear that lack of data correlated with success will, in general, lead to an overestimate of the potential. On the other hand, the greater the number of factors taken into account the greater the number of conditions to be altered before the increased estimates can be realised in practice.

With these considerations in mind we proceed first of all to an examination of data showing the distribution of IQ remaining after each barrier of final success. The main assumption throughout is that all early leavers from five-year courses are persuaded to remain at school. We start by taking IQ only into account, then taking teacher's estimate of success into account. Later we shall discuss the effect of social factors. The present estimates then are probably exaggerated.

First of all we combine boys and girls in Table 1 below.

It is of some importance to estimate the probability of success at each IQ level. For example, one of the principles governing the pass-mark to senior secondary courses in most transfer examinations in Scotland is that

Table 1.

Boys and Girls in Five-Year Courses

IQ	Whole sample	All in 5-year courses	All completing 5-year courses	All attaining LC 8+
170+	3	3	3	3
165–9	4	4	3	1
160–4	3	3	3	2
155–9	6	6	6	5
150–4	9	9	9	6
145–9	11	11	8	4
140–4	23	20	12	9
135–9	20	19	11	7
130–4	43	36	19	13
125–9	47	37	22	9
120–4	67	47	18	7
115–9	76	41	16	6
110–4	86	36	6	1
105–9	111	31	6	1
100–4	129	23	6	1
95–9	132	18	2	
90–4	111	11		
<90	327	10		
Total	1,208	365	150	75

the pupil at the border-line should have a 50 per cent chance of success. This principle was intended to ensure that the number of 'misfits' would be a minimum. An estimate of the value of IQ associated with this 50 per cent chance can be made by noting the relation that the fourth column in the above table bears to the first, assuming in this case that our standard LC 8+ is taken as the criterion of success. A cursory examination yields a value around 145 IQ. Similar relations between other pairs of columns are also of interest.

The numbers of pupils within the five-point class-intervals of IQ are too small to give a smooth graduation of proportion. An attempt has been made to smooth the distributions and the proportions graphically to enable better estimates to be made but it must emphasised that although this gives results which are probably as accurate as the scope of the present data permits they can only be considered as very crude estimates if they are to be taken as a guide to educational policy.

Figure 1 shows the smoothed distribution of IQ for
    (i)   those who were in five-year courses before they left
    (ii) those who completed five-year courses
    (iii) those who attained the leaving certificate standard—LC 8+.

Also included in the same diagram is part of the distribution of IQ for the whole sample. The successive selection is evident. The ratio of ordinates gives an estimate of probability at any IQ level. For example, the ratio of the ordinates of the two lower curves gives the probability of success at any IQ level with respect to all the pupils who completed a five-year course.

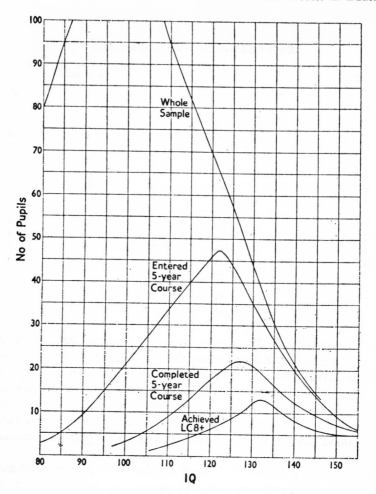

Figure 1. Smoothed distributions of IQ for those who entered five-year courses showing those who completed the course and those who achieved a leaving certificate score of 8+

Some of the more interesting probability relations are shown in Figure 2. These are not all independent. For example, pupils of IQ 127 have a 50 per cent chance of completing a five-year course when considered in relation to all those who were actually in five-year courses. If the same pupils (IQ 127) went on to complete the course they would again stand a 50 per cent chance of attaining the LC 8+ standard with respect to all those who actually complete a five-year course. The product of these two probabilities (25 per cent) is the probability that a pupil of IQ 127 who has entered a five-year course will attain a leaving certificate of the specified standard.

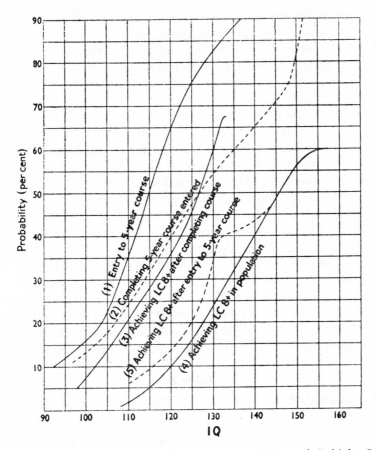

Figure 2. Terman-Merrill IQ (taken at 11 years—Boys and Girls) by Probability of achieving (1) Entry to a 5-year course (2) Completion of 5-year course once it has been entered (3) 8+ group in leaving certificate if (1) and (2) have been achieved (4) 8+ group in leaving certificate, based on whole 11-year-old population (5) 8+ group in leaving certificate, based on all in 5-year courses

Considered in relation to the whole population, however, the probability for this level of IQ is only about 19 per cent.

From the graphs we find that pupils of IQ 115 have a 50 per cent chance of following a five-year course, and that a pupil requires an IQ of 146 before he stands a 50 per cent chance of passing all the barriers and ending with the minimum leaving certificate passes required for University entrance.

The value of IQ for the 50 per cent points on these curves may seem much higher than expected. It should be remembered that the large standard deviation and the skewness of the distribution of Terman-Merrill IQs tend to exaggerate these figures in comparison with what they would have been if a test with the more generally accepted standard deviation of 15 and with normality of distribution had been used.

Using the smoothed probabilities, and knowing the numbers of early leavers at each IQ level, we can make estimates of wastage. These estimates will be too great if the early leavers are differentiated from those who completed the course by factors other than IQ (and we shall see later that such is the case). Thus if we had 10 pupils of IQ 127 who left early from five-year courses we should expect 5 of them to attain the standard if they had remained (other things being equal). With these conditions we find that approximately 66 more would probably achieve the criterion, which would increase the actual 75 to 141. We proceed to demonstrate that this is probably a great exaggeration of the true position and arises from the fact, already mentioned, that we have not made use of relevant data. The factor we shall now introduce is whether the pupils were making a success of the course in the head teacher's judgment.

Let us consider the boys first. Table 2 (A) below provides the data.

Out of the 85 boys who completed the course, 49 achieved LC 8+. If we ignore differences of IQ and teachers' estimates of success, then of the 78 early leavers we should expect about 45 to attain this level, if the proportion is the same. This would indicate that the numbers of good leaving certificates among boys could be almost doubled, a result which is clearly

Table 2.

A. Teacher's Estimate of Success in Five-Year Courses by IQ: Boys

IQ	Completed the course		Did not complete		Attaining LC 8 +		Completed but failed LC 8 +	
	Y	N	Y	N	Y	N	Y	N
170+	2				2			
165–9	3				1		2	
160–4	2				1		1	
155–9	3				3			
150–4	4				4			
145–9	3	1	2		3			1
140–4	7		1	1	5		2	
135–9	7		1	1	4		3	
130–4	9	2	3	2	9			2
125–9	14	2	5	2	8		6	2
120–4	6	1	8	6	4		2	1
115–9	5	2	5	5	2		3	2
110–4	5		8	3	1		4	
105–9	2		5	6	1		1	
100–4	2	1	4	1	1		1	1
95–9	1	1	3	1			1	1
90–4				3				
85–9				1				
80–4				1				
Total	75	10	45	33	49	—	26	10

Y = succeeding   N = not succeeding

Table 2.

B. Teacher's Estimate of Success in Five-Year Courses by IQ: Girls

IQ	Completed the course		Did not complete		Attaining LC 8 +		Completed but failed LC 8 +	
	Y	N	Y	N	Y	N	Y	N
170 +	1				1			
165–9			1					
160–4	1				1			
155–9	2	1			2			1
150–4	5				2		3	
145–9	3	1			1		2	1
140–4	5		3		4		1	
135–9	3	1	2	1	3			1
130–4	7	1	6	2	4		3	1
125–9	5	1	6	1	1		4	1
120–4	8	3	7	1	3		5	3
115–9	8	1	7	2	4		4	1
110–4		1	6	4				1
105–9	3	1	6	2			3	1
100–4	1	2	2	4			1	2
95–9			5	4				
90–4			6					
85–9			1	1				
< 85			1	1				
Total	52	13	59	23	26	–	26	13

Y = succeeding   N = not succeeding

much too great when the other data in the table are taken into account. First we note that among those who left early the proportion judged to be not succeeding is much greater than among those who stayed on, and in particular we note that not one of those who were not succeeding and carried on achieved the required standard, nor did any below 100 IQ. Eliminating these categories from the early leavers we are left with 42 pupils (the top ones in the successful early leavers column). If these had stayed on to complete the course and if they had attained the same overall proportion of success as those who actually stayed on, they would probably have attained 24 certificates of the specified standard. By taking these two facts into account we have reduced our first estimate of wastage from 45 to 24.

Next we take IQ into account. It is clear that those who did not complete the course were, as a class, of lower average IQ than those who did. If at each IQ level we take the crude proportion of those completing the course who achieved the required standard of success and apply this proportion of the 42 early leavers described above, the estimate obtained is probably a more accurate one as far as the data we have taken into account permit. The result of this operation is approximately 19. Thus if the early leavers had remained at school the boys' total of 49 might have been increased to about 68, an increase from 8.3 to 11.5 per cent of the boys in the sample. Since other correlated factors have not yet been taken into account even this estimate is probably higher than we should expect to obtain in practice if we managed to make the early leavers finish the course.

Since a greater proportion of girls than boys leave before completing the course we now turn hopefully to the girls' data. It might be expected that there is a considerable unrealised potential of untrained ability to be found in the early-leaving girls. The data for the girls are given in Table 2 (*B*) above.

Of the 65 girls who completed the course only 26 attained the specified standard. There were 82 early leavers. Once more ignoring IQ and teacher's estimates of success the same proportion would lead us to expect 33 more certificates if all stayed on at school. No girl below 115 IQ, and none of those judged to be not succeeding, achieved the criterion level, and if we omit similar cases in the non-completers column we are left with a group of 32 'possibles.' Once more using the crude success ratio at each IQ level we find that of these 32 some 14 would probably achieve the standard. These results are summarised in Table 3.

Table 3.

Crude Estimates of Additional Numbers Who Would Probably Have Attained LC 8+ if They Had Remained at School

	Boys	Girls	Total
Actual	49	26	75
Probable extra	19	14	33
Total	68	40	108

The increase is from 6.2 per cent to 9 per cent of the sample.

Once more it must be reiterated that even these estimates of wastage probably on the large side since other factors, particularly those of a social nature, have not yet been taken into account.

A Study of the Early Leavers

In the discussion of wastage we found that, so far as the average is concerned, those who left from five-year courses before completing them were lower in intelligence and less successful (in the teacher's judgment) than those who remained to complete the course. The average, however, hides a considerable number of individual cases where pupils of relatively high IQ and who appeared to be succeeding in their work left school early. It was from this group of 74 'possibles' that we estimated the wastage. It comprised 42 boys and 32 girls, and of these we estimated that some 19 boys and 14 girls would probably have succeeded if they had remained at school. This was a statistical estimate based on proportion, so the particular individuals who might have succeeded were not predicted.

On the fourth Home Visitor's Schedule all pupils were asked 'Why did you not stay on at school?' It was felt that a study of wastage would be incomplete without an examination of the motives and circumstances behind early leaving. The number of pupils involved is small. Nevertheless we have attempted to classify the reasons given and include typical case histories from each category.

Since the pupil's personality characteristics seem to have an important bearing on this question, use has been made of the teacher's ratings of the pupils on a five-point scale for each of six traits. It will be recalled that these ratings were made in 1950 when the pupils were about 14 years of age, an age when such characteristics might be expected to be very unstable. Nevertheless, it has been surprising how often later remarks of teacher or home visitor agreed with these earlier data. The characteristics rated (given on the first school schedule) were:

$$
\left.
\begin{array}{l}
\text{1 Self-confidence} \\
\text{2 Perseverance} \\
\text{3 Stability of moods} \\
\text{4 Conscientiousness} \\
\text{5 Originality} \\
\text{6 Desire to excel}
\end{array}
\right\}
\begin{array}{l}
\text{Scale A B C D E} \\
\text{for each} \\
\text{characteristic}
\end{array}
$$

As might have been expected, ratings for characteristics 2 and 4 were found to be very highly correlated, with number 6 quite closely related to both. Number 3, stability of moods, was not correlated highly with any of the others, and numbers 1 and 5 went together but were more or less distinct from the others. Thus, 2, 4 and 6 give a fair picture of the pupil's will to work hard, while 3 gives us some idea of his emotional stability at age 14.

For example, a pupil whose six ratings were BABABA would be exceptionally hard-working and ambitious to succeed, the type one would expect to succeed if he has the ability. One who had ratings CECDBA would be extremely lazy but nevertheless ambitious—one who wanted things the easy way, a typical 'spiv.'

It is interesting to see to what extent one could have predicted, from these personality ratings at the age of 14, the pupils who were likely to complete the five-year course, and those who were not. To what extent did the ratings differentiate those who stayed the course from those who did not?

In Table 4 below the distribution of the ratings in each characteristic is given for the boys who eventually completed the course, the early leavers from five-year courses and, for comparison, the boys in three-year no-language modified courses. Note how 2, 4, 6 differentiate between the early

Table 4.

Distribution of Personality Ratings by School Course to Compare Boys Who Eventually Completed the Course with Those Who Did Not

Characteristic 2—Perseverance

			CATEGORY			
	A	B	C	D	E	Total
5 yr completers	12	31	34	7	1	85
5 yr early leavers	1	17	56	20	3	97
3 yr modified		9	44	38	13	104

Characteristic 4—Conscientiousness

			CATEGORY			
	A	B	C	D	E	Total
5 yr completers	12	35	33	5		85
5 yr early leavers	6	21	48	20	2	97
3 yr modified	5	11	56	20	12	104

Characteristic 6—Desire to Excel

			CATEGORY			
	A	B	C	D	E	Total
5 yr completers	9	30	36	10		85
5 yr early leavers	3	12	61	16	5	97
3 yr modified	1	16	45	32	10	104

Characteristic 3—Stability of Moods

			CATEGORY			
	A	B	C	D	E	Total
5 yr completers	19	21	41	4		85
5 yr early leavers	10	19	63	3	2	97
3 yr modified	7	5	67	18	7	104

Characteristic 1—Self-Confidence

			CATEGORY			
	A	B	C	D	E	Total
5 yr completers	5	28	47	5		85
5 yr early leavers		27	51	19		97
3 yr modified	6	12	45	31	10	104

Characteristic 5—Originality

			CATEGORY			
	A	B	C	D	E	Total
5 yr completers		23	53	9		85
5 yr early leavers		15	55	24	3	97
3 yr modified	1	6	34	40	23	104

leavers and completers. The others 1, 3, 5 do not differentiate to any great extent.

In perseverance, for example, roughly 14 out of 20 pupils rated above average remained to complete the course while only 5 out of 20 rated below average did so.

In conscientiousness approximately 13 out of 20 rated above average remained, while only 4 out of 20 rated below average did so.

In desire to excel approximately 14 out of 20 rated above average remained, while only 6 out of 20 rated below average did so.

In the other characteristics the differences are not nearly so striking. In self-confidence and originality a below-average assessment seems to have more significance for prediction than an above-average one.

From these results it seems inescapable that character plays a most important rôle in determining whether a pupil stays the course or drops out. Perseverance, conscientiousness, and the will to do well are factors which count. Without these qualities a pupil is not likely to have much success in a five-year course. We must, nevertheless, not exaggerate the relationship between rating and whether or not pupils complete the course, since to some extent both are correlated with IQ. From a study of individual cases, however, the personality ratings are frequently found to be most illuminating, independently of IQ, as an indication of future progress.

For reasons explained in the previous section the estimate of wastage given above is more likely to be too large than too small, since we did not take industry into account and we now see that this is a factor correlated with success. Unless we are prepared to take measures to improve pupil's characters and attitudes, a most difficult task, it would seem that not all of the potential ability in an age-group could be realised in practice. . . .

Social Factors Related to Educational Career

We are particularly concerned with any sociological barriers to educational progress; for example, is the wastage in secondary schools related to the socio-economic status of the home?

For this examination most interest centres on the group which comprises those who entered a five-year course, sub-divided into those who completed (C) and those who did not complete (NC) the five years. In an attempt to hold IQ constant only those lying in the range 120 to 145 have been included in the first instance. For this group the distribution of occupancy rate[2] and father's occupational class are given in Table 5.

This band of IQ was chosen partly because, as Table 5 (*c*) shows, the distributions of IQ in the two groups (completed and not completed) are very similar, and partly because this is a range of particular interest when we consider success in leaving certificate examinations. With this in mind it is clear that the first two parts of Table 5 disclose a relationship between occupancy rate (or father's occupational class) and the chances of completing a five-year course which is practically independent of IQ.

A more detailed examination (Table 6 below) for IQ-range of 110 to 149 underlines that this relationship appears to hold even within very narrow bands of IQ.

Each row and the marginal totals at the foot tell the same tale—the pattern of occupancy rate is quite different and is considerably better for

Table 5.

Occupancy Rate, Occupational Class of Father and IQ for Boys Who Entered Five-Year Courses

(in the range 120–145 for IQ)

(a) BY OCCUPANCY RATE

OR	Completed	Not completed	Total
1	10	5	15
2	19	17	36
3	5	10	15
4		5	5
X		1	1
Total	34	38	72

(b) BY FATHER'S OCCUPATIONAL CLASS

FOC*	Completed	Not completed	Total
1	5	1	6
2	4	3	7
3	4		4
4	5	8	13
5	11	18	29
6	2	4	6
7	1	2	3
8	1	1	2
9	1		1
X		1	1
Total	34	38	72

(c) BY IQ

IQ	Completed	Not completed	Total
140–5	5	6	11
135–9	4	4	8
130–4	8	10	18
125–9	6	6	12
120–4	11	12	23
Total	34	38	72

*Father's Occupational Class

1. Professional and large employers
2. Small employers
3. Salaried employees
4. Non-manual wage-earners
5. Skilled manual wage-earners
6. Semi-skilled manual wage-earners
7. Unskilled manual wage-earners
8. Farmers
9. Agricultural workers
X. Unclassified or unknown

the group who completed five years—despite equality of IQ. Thus the barrier to completing a five-year course for those who surmount the first barrier (obtaining entrance to a five-year course) and have the requisite intelligence, does appear to be related to some extent to the degree of over-crowding in the home. The chance of completing the course does not ap-

Table 6.

Occupancy Rate for Boys in Five-Year Courses by IQ (110–149)

IQ	COMPLETED 5 YEARS				DID NOT COMPLETE 5 YEARS				AVERAGE OCCUPANCY RATE	
	1	2	3	4	1	2	3	4	Completed	Not completed
145–9	1	1	2			1	1	1	2.3	3.0
140–4	4	3				1	1		1.4	2.5
135–9	1	5	1		1	1	1	1	2.0	2.5
130–4	4	5	1			4	2	1	1.7	2.6
125–9	4	7	3			4	5		1.9	2.6
120–4	3	2		1	4	8	1	3	1.8	2.2
115–9	2	4	1			7	4	2	1.9	2.6
110–4	3	2				5	7	1	1.4	2.7
Total	22	29	8	1	5	31	22	9	1.8	2.5

pear, within this range of IQ, to vary with IQ and we may therefore sum up these chances as follows:

For boys who enter a five-year course and have IQ between 110 and 150 their chances of completing the course will be approximately,

4 in 5 if they come from occupancy rate 1,
1 in 2 if they come from occupancy rate 2,
1 in 4 if they come from occupancy rate 3,
1 in 10 if they come from occupancy rate 4.

Being based on extremely small numbers these figures, particularly the last one, should not be quoted as reliable, but the general trend seems to be beyond reasonable doubt. Again it may be pointed out that if the pupils who came from high occupancy rate homes could have been persuaded to stay on at school, there is no reason to suppose that they would have been successful.

In view of these results it is perhaps worth while to consider a wider group of five-year entrants divided into high and low IQ-bands, say 120 to

Table 7.

Distribution of Occupancy Rate and Occupational Class of Father for High and Low IQs Entering Five-Year Courses

Group I: IQ 120 to 149 ⎫ Boys
Group II: IQ 95 to 119 ⎭

(a) Occupancy Rate

	GROUP I			GROUP II		
OR	Completing	Not completing	Total	Completing	Not completing	Total
1	17	4	21	5	5	10
2	24	20	44	12	24	36
3	7	11	18	1	13	14
4	1	6	7	1	7	8
X	3	1	4	—	—	—
Total	52	42	94	19	49	68

(b) Fathers' Occupational Class

	GROUP I			GROUP II		
FOC	Completing	Not completing	Total	Completing	Not completing	Total
1	10	1	11	3		3
2	4	4	8	1	1	2
3	10	5	15	4	4	8
4	5	3	8	2	4	6
5	15	19	34	4	19	23
6	3	2	5	4	9	13
7	1	6	7	1	5	6
8	1		1		1	1
9	1	2	3		4	4
X	2		2		2	2
Total	52	42	94	19	49	68

145 and 95 to 119, and to compare the distributions of occupancy rate and occupational class of father for those completing and not completing the five-year course. Table 7 presents the results.

This table enables us to obtain a rough idea for most of the five-year entrants, of the relative importance of IQ and sociological factors. For example, for boys coming from occupational classes 1 to 4 their chances of completing are about 2 in 3 if over 120 IQ, and about 1 in 2 if below 120 IQ. Again, for boys coming from occupational classes 5 to 7 their chances of completing are about 2 in 5 if IQ is over 120, and about 1 in 5 if IQ is less than 120.

Once more we would point out that the estimates for wastage given earlier ignored sociological factors. We now see that these are of great importance in determining the probability that pupils will complete a five-year course. We cannot say, of course, that if they had remained at school they would have attained a good leaving certificate and it seems very likely in the light of these facts that our estimates of wastage in the secondary school are still too large.

NOTES

1. The Scottish Leaving Certificate examination is arranged and set on a national basis by the Scottish Education Department, and is taken by pupils who have pursued a course in a secondary school for at least five years. The pupils are therefore around 17 or 18 years of age. Each of the main school subjects may be attempted on a 'higher' or 'lower' grade. The Scottish Universities Preliminary or Entrance Examination is regarded as equivalent in standard.

2. An index relating the number of persons in the house to the number of rooms.

18   *Social Class, Intelligence Tests, and Selection for Secondary Schools*

JEAN FLOUD and A. H. HALSEY

IN 1953, a Local Education Authority in England abandoned the use of intelligence tests in selecting children for admission to grammar schools. An inquiry into social factors in educational selection was already under way in the South-Western Educational Division of the County[1] and with the co-operation of the Divisional Education Officer and the Heads of secondary schools, certain additional information was collected to enable the effect of this measure on the social distribution of opportunity of entering grammar schools to be examined.

In the inter-war years the use of intelligence tests was widely regarded as a guarantee of the objectivity of the selection procedure; the results of the tests were held to be as nearly as possible free of bias from environmental influences, so that by giving them an important place in the selecion procedure, social discrimination in the award of grammar school places could be reduced to a minimum. More recently, the reputation of the tests as an objective and administratively convenient instrument for the diagnosis of potential educability has been seriously undermined and the Hertfordshire example in abandoning them was widely welcomed and has since been followed by other Authorities. The campaign against the tests has been strongly supported, if not actually led, by egalitarian reformers in education, and although, admittedly, the case against them does not rest wholly on the demonstration of environmental influences biasing their results against children from working-class homes, it is relevant to the discussion, and of some interest, to see how in fact the use of intelligence tests in selection affects the social distribution of grammar school places.

The following analysis relates to the cohort of boys entering secondary schools in the Educational Division of the South-West Hertfordshire in 1952, 1953 and 1954. The occupations followed by the fathers of boys entering in 1952 were obtained by interview with their parents as part of the wider inquiry already referred to, and in the same connection the authority kindly supplied the I.Q. of the boys based on their performance

---

Reprinted from Jean Floud and A. H. Halsey, "Intelligence Tests, Social Class, and Selection for Secondary Schools," *British Journal of Sociology*, VIII (1957), 33–39, with the permission of the authors and the publisher, Routledge and Kegan Paul, London.

in the Moray House 37 intelligence test, administered under their auspices as part of the selection procedure. With the co-operation of the Heads concerned, the same test was administered under our auspices in the schools to entrants in 1953 and 1954 and a brief statement of his father's occupation was obtained from each boy, so that the social and intellectual composition of the entry could be compared for these three years. The information as to the father's occupation in 1953 and 1954 was necessarily less reliable than in 1952 and the proportion of unclassifiable cases was higher. To ensure that any error in the analysis would be in the right direction (i.e. that the opportunity of working-class children would not be underestimated) all doubtful or unclassifiable cases were added to the working-class group. The occupational classification used is a modification of that used by the Government Social Survey.

There are two questions to be answered: what was the *social distribution of opportunity* before and after the change in selection procedure? and was there, either before or after these changes, *equality of opportunity for children of equal ability* irrespective of their social origins?

In order to answer the first question, we may compare, for each age-group of boys, the proportions allocated to grammar schools from each social class (defined in terms of paternal occupation). These proportions we may call *class chances,* since they express the probability that a boy originating from a given social class will be allocated to a grammar school. Class chances depend upon three factors; the size of the age-group and its social composition, and the number of available grammar school places. For example, an increase in the numbers of children in a given social class will, *ceteris paribus,* reduce the chances of that class.

In order to answer the second question, we may compare, for each social class, the proportion of 'able' children (i.e. with I.Q.s above a given level) with the proportion allocated to grammar schools. The result of the comparison may be expressed as *ability/opportunity ratios,* equality of opportunity being represent by a ratio of 1. Ability/opportunity ratios will depend on the three factors already mentioned together with the intellectual composition of the social classes as measured by intelligence tests. Taking all four factors into account, the actual proportions from each social class allocated to grammar schools are compared with the hypothetical proportions which would have been allocated had selection been based solely on the results of intelligence tests, thereby measuring how far the actual results of selection approximate to the hypothetical conception of equality of opportunity. By repeating the analysis for a series of years, we can assess the effect of changes in selection procedure which may have intervened. For example, we may measure the impact of the abolition of fees in maintained secondary schools in 1945,[2] or as here, the effect of abandoning the use of intelligence tests in the selection procedure.

The Social Distribution of Opportunity

At first glance the abolition of intelligence tests and the associated changes in procedure[3] appear to have resulted in a marked diminution in the opportunity of working-class children. Thus (Table 1) the proportion of working-class boys in the grammar school entry has fallen from 51.4 per cent in 1952 to 47.8 per cent in 1953 and 39.3 per cent in 1954.

Table 1.

Social Origins of Boys Entering Maintained Secondary Schools in South-West Hertfordshire, 1952–4

Father's Occupation	1952 All	1952 Modern	1952 Grammar	1953 All	1953 Modern	1953 Grammar	1954 All	1954 Modern	1954 Grammar
	%	%	%	%	%	%	%	%	%
Professional and Managerial	7.0	5.2	14.4	7.4	3.9	20.2	8.7	3.7	24.4
Clerical	8.3	6.8	14.4	7.4	5.2	15.2	7.3	4.9	16.2
Supervisory, small shop-keepers, etc.	18.3	18.0	19.8	12.1	10.9	16.8	13.1	11.3	20.1
Manual workers, skilled and unskilled*	66.4	70.0	51.4	73.1	80.0	47.8	70.9	80.1	39.3
All	100.0	100.0	100.0	100.0	100.0	100.0	100.0	100.0	100.0
N	(756)	(610)	(146)	(947)	(744)	(203)	(1094)	(865)	(229)

* Including unclassified pupils.

CLASS CHANCES

In 1952, there were 146 places available for boys in grammar schools in the area, compared with 203 in 1953 and 229 in 1954. Meanwhile, the size of the relevant age-group of boys[4] rose from 756 in 1952 to 947 in 1953 and to 1,094 in 1954, so that the proportion of the age-group as a whole allocated to grammar schools has remained constant at about 21 per cent. However (Table 2), the social composition of the

Table 2.

The Proportion of Boys Aged 10–11 in Each Social Class Awarded Grammar School Places in South-West Hertfordshire, 1952–4

Father's Occupation	1952 %	1953 %	1954 %
Professional and Managerial	39.6	58.5	63.6
Clerical	34.9	44.2	46.2
Supervisory, small shopkeepers, etc.	20.8	29.5	31.9
Manual workers, skilled and unskilled*	14.9	14.0	11.5
All	19.3	21.4	20.9
(N)	(756)	(947)	(1094)

* Including unclassified pupils.

age-group has changed in the direction of an increased contribution from the families of manual workers, whereas as we have seen, the social composition of the grammar school entry changed markedly in the opposite direction. Consequently, as is shown in Table 2, class chances have deteriorated for working-class boys and improved for the sons of the professional and white-collar groups.

Equality of Opportunity for Children of Equal Ability

ABILITY/OPPORTUNITY RATIOS

Our information concerning the intellectual composition of the age-group shown in Table 3 accords with what is generally known about the social distribution of measured intelligence. Intelligence test scores rise with social level but the differences within occupational groups are greater than those between them. It is also clear from the table that the mean I.Q. of each group improved slightly over the period 1952–4.

Table 3.

Social Distribution of Intelligence in the Age-Group of Boys Entering Maintained Secondary Schools in South-West Hertfordshire, 1952–4

Father's Occupation	1952		1953		1954	
	Mean I.Q.	S.D.	Mean I.Q.	S.D.	Mean I.Q.	S.D.
Professional and Managerial	112.62	13.30	113.50	13.82	114.05	14.35
Clerical	110.95	13.46	111.36	15.02	111.49	14.81
Supervisory, small shopkeepers, etc.	103.48	12.76	107.58	14.84	109.72	13.45
Manual workers, skilled and	100.08	12.62	101.69	14.41	100.59	15.05
unskilled	95.92	14.10	96.00	14.25	98.06	15.38
All*	100.97	14.15	103.14	15.35	103.92	15.09

* Including unclassified pupils.

There are a number of possible methods of arriving at a definition of the minimum level of ability (I.Q.) at which a boy in any given year would qualify for admission to a grammar school. We have chosen to adopt as a hypothetical qualifying minimum the I.Q. at and above which there is a number of boys as nearly as possible equal to the number of grammar school places available.[5] The procedure is to compare the distribution of measured intelligence in the group allocated to grammar schools with that in the group allocated to modern schools, fixing the hypothetical qualifying I.Q. at the point where the number of grammar school boys below that level is equal to the number of modern school boys above it. On this basis, the hypothetical qualifying I.Q. was 114 in 1952,

117 in 1953, and 116 in 1954, and the number above this level in the modern schools and below it in the grammar schools was approximately 50 in each year.

For each year, the proportion of boys in the age-group qualified by I.Q. in each social class is compared in Table 4 with the proportion awarded grammar school places and the results are expressed in the form of ability/opportunity ratios in Table 5.

Table 4.

Proportion of Boys in Each Social Class Qualifying by I.Q. and Allocated to Grammar Schools in South-West Hertfordshire in 1952, 1953, and 1954

	1952		1953		1954	
Social Class	Proportion of 'Qualified' boys	Proportion of boys allocated to Grammar Schools	Proportion of 'Qualified' boys	Proportion of boys allocated to Grammar Schools	Proportion of 'Qualified' boys	Proportion of boys allocated to Grammar Schools
	%	%	%	%	%	%
Professional and Managerial	35.8	39.6	54.2	58.5	51.1	63.6
Clerical	38.0	34.9	47.1	44.2	46.2	46.2
Supervisory, small shopkeepers, etc.	20.1	20.8	32.2	29.5	31.9	31.9
Manual workers, skilled and unskilled	15.3	14.9	15.4	14.0	12.9	11.5

Table 5.

Ability/Opportunity Ratios

	1952	1953	1954
Professional and Managerial	1.10	1.08	1.23
Clerical	0.92	0.94	1.00
Supervisory, small shopkeepers, etc.	1.04	1.08	1.00
Manual workers, skilled and unskilled	0.97	0.92	0.89
All	1.00	1.00	1.00

Conclusions

1) It will be seen that, despite changes in procedure, ability and opportunity as defined for present purposes have remained in close relationship in South-West Hertfordshire since 1952. The decline in the proportion of working-class boys in the annual grammar school entry, shown in Table 1, and the deterioration in class chances for these boys, shown in Table 2, are accounted for by variations in all the four factors shown to affect the relation between social class and the opportunity of entering a grammar

school (viz. the size and the social and intellectual composition of the age-group, and the number of grammar school places available.)

The figures in Table 5, nevertheless, suggest that the changes in procedure have resulted, at any given level of ability, in a slight but presistent diminution of opportunity for working-class boys and a corresponding increase in opportunity for those at the higher social levels.

2) It is perhaps also worth emphasizing what this analysis makes very clear (although this is an issue separate from the relation between selection methods and the social distribution of opportunity with which we have been concerned in this Note), namely that quite small fluctuations in the size and social composition of the age-group, such as inevitably accompany changes in the birth rate and movements of population, can give rise to quite marked swings in the terms of competition for a fixed number, or even proportionate provision of grammar school places. Although 'class chances' of admission to grammar schools, as has been shown, may improve or deteriorate from year to year without serious lapses from the equilibrium of equality of opportunity for children of equal ability, it remains the case that a child may suffer for, or benefit from, its year of birth, as well as its place of residence, according as these demographic fluctuations impose a higher or lower qualifying minimum I.Q.[6] for admission to grammar schools in a particular year. Boys with an I.Q. of 114 were held in 1952 in South-West Hertfordshire to be capable of profiting from a grammar school education and were awarded places. There seems no reason to doubt that children of similar ability in subsequent years could have benefited also. Yet despite a considerable and successful effort to maintain the provision of grammar school places at 21 per cent of the age-group (Table 2) such boys were not admitted in 1953 and 1954 when the qualifying I.Q. rose to 117 and 116 respectively. This is social waste no less serious than that resulting from the social discrimination in selection which has been so successfully tackled since 1945. It must be admitted that it is difficult to avoid so long as grammar school provision takes the relatively inflexible form of places in separately organized and housed schools, entrants to which are selected by competitive examination.

NOTES

1. Cf. J. E. Floud (ed.), A. H. Halsey, and F. M. Martin, *Social Class and Educational Opportunity*, Heinemann, 1957.

2. Cf. J. E. Floud (ed.), A. H. Halsey, and F. M. Martin, *op. cit.* In this study we had complete information for only one year. For the purposes of historical reconstruction, we had therefore to assume constancy in the size of the age-group and its social and intellectual composition.

3. A paper in English composition has been introduced, and increased emphasis has been given to primary school records.

4. I.e. for present purposes, the number of boys actually entering maintained secondary schools in each year. Boys in the age-group attending independent schools are not included, with the result that both class-chances and ability/opportunity ratios are under-estimated for the higher social levels.

5. *Cf.* Gray and Moshinsky. Ability and Opportunity in English Secondary Education in Hogben (ed.) *Political Arithmetic,* where the point chosen was that level of I.Q. attained by 50 per cent of children in selective secondary schools.

6. Or some alternative measure of capacity. Though intelligence tests are precise and relatively objective, Professor Vernon points out to the authors that the strict argument from borderline I.Q.s has the disadvantage that the tests may not be completely comparable from year to year, and that greater familiarity with them (e.g. through coaching) may rise the qualifying minimum independently of the social factors analysed here.

19 *Educational Opportunity, Measured Intelligence, and Social Background*

DAEL WOLFLE

Who Goes to College

THE FACTORS WHICH determine who goes to college can be divided into two categories, those which are essentially related to school progress and those which are related, but not in any essential way. Mental ability illustrates the first category. If a student is not able to perform the intellectual tasks of a school program he is forced to turn to something else. Ethnic differences are an example of the second category. There is no evidence that members of one ethnic group are inherently better scholars than are members of another ethnic group, but social customs and educational ambitions are related to ethnic differences, with the result that the members of some groups are much more likely to continue to higher levels of education than are members of other groups.

In the essential category are four factors. One is possession of adequate ability of the type which is measured by standardized tests of academic aptitude. If a student is unable to score above a minimum level on such tests he is unlikely to be able to master the content of college courses.

A second essential factor is a record of satisfactory previous school work. If a student does not graduate from high school he is not likely to be admitted to college. Colleges occasionally accept the "equivalent" of a high school education and there have been several programs designed to bring bright students into college without waiting for completion of all four years of high school work. But by and large, the rule is: no high school diploma, no admission to college.

A third essential factor is money. The prospective student must be able to secure enough money to pay his college expenses.

The fourth essential is the student's own desire. He must want to go to college strongly enough to make him apply the time, the energy, and the money which college work requires.

Reprinted from Dael Wolfle (ed.), *America's Resources of Specialized Talent* (New York: Harper and Bros., 1954), with the permission of the publisher.

Among the variables which are in fact related to the question of who goes to college but for which the relationship is not an essential one are sex, cultural background, geographic location, and ethnic and religious background. Statistically these variables are sometimes useful in predicting which pupils will attend college and which will not. Yet no essential relationship is involved. Instead, the relationship is indirect. The social, cultural, ethnic, and religious background in which a person is reared may make him want to attend college or make him want to do something else. Some of these factors may make it easier or more difficult to secure a good elementary and secondary education, or may make it more or less likely that there will be money enough for college expenses.

In taking up the variables related to college attendance first attention will be given to intelligence and academic records. Both of these variables are of primary significance in determining whether or not a student is admitted to college and both are indications of how successful he is likely to be if he is admitted. Both, in the sense of the distinction given above, are essential for college attendance. After discussing intelligence and academic record separately, an analysis will be given of their joint contribution to the determination of which high school graduates enter college and which college entrants earn degrees. The other two essential variables, money and the desire to attend college, will next be considered. Finally, four other variables will be reviewed: cultural background, sex, geographic factors, and ethnic differences.

The fact that the variables are discussed separately does not mean that they work independently. Quite the contrary, their effects are always intertwined. Bright children usually earn better grades than do dull ones. Children from professional homes are more likely to be academically motivated than are children from laboring class homes, and more likely also to make high scores on intelligence tests. Even within an individual student the factors are interrelated. His grades depend upon his ability and his interest in school work. The score he makes on an aptitude test is influenced by his interests and by what he has learned. His educational aspirations are affected by his past academic successes and by the attitudes of his family. Furthermore, these factors are, to some extent, compensatory. An extremely bright student can earn creditable grades despite a degree of laziness that would spell failure in one of lesser ability. On the other hand, persistent application can overcome in part the handicap of mediocre ability. In general it is impossible to select a minimum point on any of the variables and to say: people above this point are potentially qualified; those below it are not. Neither in terms of earlier achievement, nor of intelligence test scores, nor for any other variable can such a division be made. All that can be done is to determine the probability or expectancy—to state the betting odds, as it were—that a person of a given level of intelligence, or with a given academic history, from one ethnic group or another, or from a particular socioeconomic background will achieve some designated educational level. That is what will be done.

INTELLIGENCE

The scores on any intelligence test scatter over a considerable range. In order to facilitate comparisons between the scores made by one group and those made by another, or between people given one test and those given another, it is convenient to have a standard scale on which to report all of the score distributions. The scale used during World War II in reporting the scores of Army enlisted men has been adopted for use in this report. The Army General Classification Test (AGCT) scale is centered about a score of 100, that being the score made by the average person in the total population. For the population as a whole, 34 per cent make scores between 80 and 100 and another 34 per cent between 100 and 120. Practically everyone scores somewhere between 40 and 160, although an occasional score falls outside of those limits. The Army General Classification Test itself was not used in any of the studies to be reported; other tests are more suitable for high school and college use. But in order to compare high school students with college students or to compare either with the total population, all test scores have been converted to AGCT terms.

The IQ, or Intelligence Quotient, is perhaps a more generally familiar term than is AGCT. The IQ was not used because it is not a suitable scale for expressing differences in the intelligence of adults or of the more intelligent adolescents. However, the IQ scale resembles the AGCT scale; the average score is 100 on both and the spread of scores is roughly the same for both scales. No great distortion will be involved if IQ is read wherever AGCT is printed, but the AGCT scale is preferable and will be used throughout.[1]

Figures 1 and 2 show the more and more rigorous intellectual selection which takes place as students move up the educational ladder. Within each of these two figures all the curves were drawn to the same size scale so that by its area each curve pictures the proportion of the total age group which reached the indicated educational level. The size scale differs in the two figures, however. In Figure 1, which includes the curve for the total age group, the scale is too small to show the differentiation among those who advance beyond college entrance. Figure 2 was drawn to a larger scale in order to separate those groups more clearly.

All the curves are based primarily upon studies made by the Commission, but none depends solely upon those studies. The curves were drawn to take account of the results of other studies and to take into consideration information from the Office of Education and the Bureau of the Census on the percentage of students reaching each level. The curves, therefore, are presented as the Commission's estimates of national totals—estimates

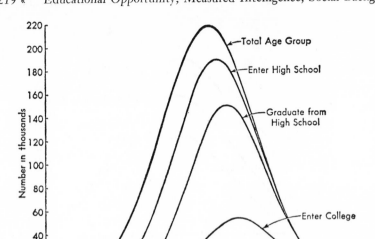

Figure 1. Distribution of Army General Classification Test scores of all members of an age group and of those reaching several educational levels

of the AGCT score distributions of all students in the United States at each of the indicated educational levels. In Figure 1 the upper curve is for an entire age group, for example all people reaching the age of 18 in 1954. The scale of relative numbers at the left indicates approximately how many are in each score interval. For example, nearly 220,000 of the people reaching age 18 in 1954 score within two points of 100.

About 80 per cent of all boys and girls enter high school. Most of those who do not enter high school come from the lower half of the ability distribution. Comparatively few high school pupils drop out during their first two years. But when they reach the end of the age of compulsory school attendance a large dropout occurs, mostly among students of mediocre or poor intellectual ability. About a fifth of the dropouts score 100 or higher and are thus above the national average. Above 100 the loss decreases rapidly; only about 1½ per cent of the dropouts score 120 or higher.

After high school there is a big drop, numerically the largest which occurs anywhere in the whole educational system. Unlike the earlier ones, that loss is not closely related to intelligence. Students who enter college average a little better than do all who finish high school, but the margin is only 5 points and other factors seem to be more important in determining which high school graduates do and which do not go on to college.

Some students drop out during college, but the next big break occurs

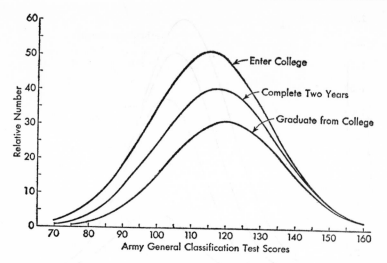

Figure 2. Distribution of Army General Classification Test scores of college students

after college graduation. Students who go on to graduate or professional schools average about 5 points higher on the AGCT scale than the totality of college graduates.

The amount of selection at successive levels can be shown by giving a series of average AGCT scores.

The average of the total population is 100.
The average of those who enter high school is 105.
The average of those who graduate from high school is 110.
The average of those who enter college is 115.
The average of those who graduate from college is 121.

College graduates are a select group. Ninety per cent of them score above 100 on the AGCT, which means that 90 per cent of college graduates come from the upper half of the total population. Half of the college graduates score 121 or higher on the AGCT; of the total population, only 15 per cent score that high. Twelve per cent of college graduates score 140 or higher; only 2 per cent of the total population do as well. As compared with the total population, college graduates are an intellectually superior group.

College gradutes are also a variable group. The geniuses among them are mixed up with many others of considerably lesser ability. In fact a few college graduates make scores below the average of the entire population. There is also variation from one school to another, for the students at some colleges are much more highly selected than are those at other colleges. For 41 colleges which were studied by the Commission a comparison is given in Figure 3. Each college is represented by a line which

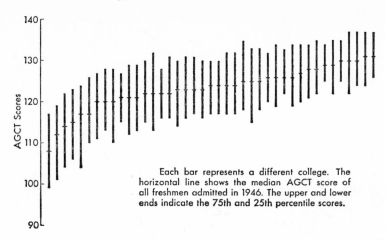

Each bar represents a different college. The horizontal line shows the median AGCT score of all freshmen admitted in 1946. The upper and lower ends indicate the 75th and 25th percentile scores.

Figure 3. Intelligence differences of students enrolled in different colleges

shows the spread of scores of the middle 50 per cent of the freshmen admitted in the fall of 1946. For the lowest school, half of the freshmen made scores between 99 and 117. The bottom quarter were below 99 and the top quarter above 117. The median score of all freshmen at that school was 108. Freshmen attending the school at the upper end of the distribution average 131 and half of them fell between 126 and 137. The other lines, representing other schools, are to be interpreted similarly.

The diversity is sufficiently great that it is worth while to emphasize that some colleges are so selective in admitting students that nearly all their graduates are above the average of all college graduates. On the other hand, some colleges get a comparatively mediocre group. While most of the graduates of these schools are above the average of the entire population, most of them are below the average of all college graduates. The highest and lowest schools pictured in Figure 3 are both private non-sectarian colleges. Both are accredited. They lie in adjoining southern states and both limit their enrollment to white students. These contrasting schools make it clear that the statements above concerning the intellectual ability of the average college graduate may badly misrepresent the graduates of some schools. Those statements were not intended to represent individual schools, but college graduates as a whole, the best and poorest and average together.

INTELLIGENCE AND THE PROBABILITY OF GRADUATING FROM COLLEGE

Another method of analyzing the relations between intelligence test scores and academic achievement is to determine how the probability that a student will progress to different educational levels shifts as one moves up the ability scale. That is done in Figure 4. A 14-year-old with an AGCT

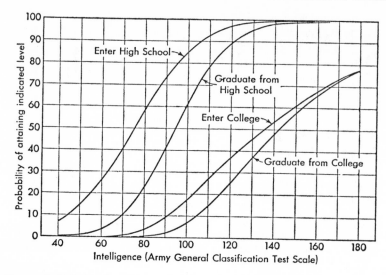

Figure 4. Relation between intelligence and educational level attained

score of 110 has 93 chances out of 100 of entering high school, and 78 chances out of 100 of graduating. His expectation of entering college is 27 out of 100 and of graduating from college 15 out of 100.

For people with scores below 110 all these expectations are lower and for those with higher scores all the expectations are greater. None of the curves, even the one which shows the probability of graduating from college, reaches zero until considerably below average intelligence. For high school entrance and graduation the probabilities approximate 100 at an intelligence level somewhat above the population average. But the probability of entering or of graduating from college does not get close to 100 even at the high intelligence level indicated by an AGCT score of 160 to 180. Table 1 amplifies this point; it shows, for 5 different levels of intelligence, the percentage graduating from college. Of the brightest 5 per cent of an entire age group, almost half finish college and slightly over half do not.

Table 1.

Percentage of Youth of High Intelligence Graduating from College

Ability Level	AGCT Score	Per Cent Graduating from College
Top 0.1%	160 and higher	69
Top 1%	147 and higher	59
Top 5%	133 and higher	49
Top 10%	126 and higher	42
Top 20%	117 and higher	34

Source: Commission estimates.

Even at the 1-in-1,000 level of the top 0.1 per cent only 2 out of 3 graduate from college. Obviously there are factors other than those measured by intelligence tests which differentiate college graduates from nongraduates.

HIGH SCHOOL GRADES

Pupils who earn good grades are more likely to become high school graduates, and high school graduates with good scholastic records are more likely to enter college than are their classmates with poorer records. But it is more difficult to express the relationships in quantitative form than was true for intelligence test scores, because high school grades are not so comparable from one school to another as are aptitude test scores and because not so much information is available about school grades. The figures in Table 2 are estimates which have been based upon some of the Commission's studies and upon comparable studies reported by others. Approximately 53 per cent of students who finish high school in the top 20 per cent of their classes enroll in college. As grades go down, so does the likelihood of entering college, until only 17 per cent of the lowest fifth enters college. The lowest group made good enough grades to graduate from high school, but their not very satisfactory grade records indicated a lack of ability or a lack of interest in academic matters which made them poor college risks.

Table 2.

Percentile Rank in High School Graduating Class and Probability of Entering and of Graduating from College

Percentile Rank in High School Graduating Class	Percentage of High School Graduates Who Enter College	Percentage of College Entrants Who Graduate	Percentage of High School Graduates Who Graduate from College
81–100	53	82	43
61–80	44	68	30
41–60	35	54	19
21–40	26	40	10
1–20	17	26	4

Source: Commission studies.

Students who finish high school at the top of their classes are likely to enter college. Harrell[2] found that 94 per cent of past valedictorians and salutatorians of one high school had entered college. An examination of the rank in high school graduating classes of the students who entered the 41 colleges which were studied by the Commission indicates that a similarly high percentage of the valedictorians and salutatorians of most high schools go to college. The percentage entering college falls off rapidly, however, as one comes down the class roll, indicating that many students who receive excellent grades in high school do not attend college.

Nevertheless, high school grades predict which pupils enter college better than do scores on tests of academic aptitude. The explanation can be looked at from two different points of view. From the standpoint of the college admissions officer, an applicant who received good grades in high school has already demonstrated that he can do acceptable academic work. He is a good prospect for admission to college.

When a high school student tries to size up his prospects for successful college work, school grades are an obvious guide for him to use. Ginzberg and his associates[3] found that an adolescent characteristically goes through a stage of appraising his potential success in fields which he is considering by thinking in terms of the caliber of work he has done in relevant school courses. He is usually vague about the concept of intelligence and frequently has no way of knowing his own score on a standardized intelligence test. But he does know his class standing, and it is likely to be the most important single variable in helping him to decide about his chances of doing successful college work.

As can also be seen from Table 2, the percentage who remain in college and earn degrees is considerably lower for entrants with poor high school grade records than it is for those who made good grades in high school. The final column of the table gives the percentages from each fifth of the high school graduating class who later receive college degrees. Students who stood low in their high school graduating classes have little chance of getting college degrees. Those who were near the top have about a 50-50 chance of getting through college.

The figures in the second column of Table 2 go up a little less steeply than do comparable figures for aptitude test scores. In both cases, however, there is a similarity: the biggest increase in probability of graduating comes near the bottom of the scale. Colleges weed out the lowest students—or those students withdraw voluntarily—but the rest have moderately good chances of receiving degrees.

RELATION OF INTELLIGENCE AND HIGH SCHOOL GRADES TO COLLEGE ENTRANCE

Since college freshmen are selected, or select themselves, partly in terms of the grades they make in high school and partly in terms of the scores they receive on academic aptitude tests, it is desirable to examine these two variables together to see how they contribute to the selection of college students. That is done in Table 3, which classifies all high school graduates into subgroups, each of which includes students who are similar both in terms of grades and intelligence test scores. The figures given in the table are the percentages of high school graduates from each subgroup who enter college.

Table 3.

Estimated Per Cent of High School Graduates Who Enter College, Classified by AGCT Score and High School Grades

	HIGH SCHOOL GRADES (PERCENTILE RANK IN GRADUATING CLASS)					
AGCT Score	1–20	21–40	41–60	61–80	81–100	Total
155 and above	38	45	52	59	66	66
145–154	34	41	47	54	61	61
135–144	30	37	43	50	57	54
125–134	26	33	40	47	54	48
115–124	24	30	37	44	51	42
105–114	21	28	35	42	48	35
95–104	19	26	32	39	46	29
85–94	16	23	30	36	43	22
75–84	12	19	26	33	40	16
65–74	8	15	22	29	36	10
Below 65	4	11	18	24	31	4
Total	17	26	35	44	53	35

Source: Commission studies.

The probability of entering college increases with an increase either in grades or in intelligence test scores, as, of course, is known from the separate analyses of these variables which have already been given. When grades and intelligence are studied together, the range of percentages of high school graduates who start to college runs from 4 per cent of those in the bottom group in both grades and intelligence up to 66 per cent of those in the top group in both grades and intelligence. There is in these figures evidence of greater selection of college entrants than showed up when the two variables were examined individually. Nevertheless, many well-qualified high school graduates do not enter college. In fact a third of those who rank in the top subgroup on both intelligence and high school grades fail to enter college.

Table 4 shows what happens to students, classified in the same way, after they enter college. The percentages in this table indicate that fairly rigorous selection takes place within the colleges. The few students who enter college despite the fact that they are in the bottom subgroup in both grades and intelligence are so handicapped in their efforts to do college work that few of them ever get degrees. At the upper extreme, 98 per cent of the entrants in the top subgroup on both variables remain in college and earn bachelors' or first professional degrees.

If college entrance and college graduation were determined entirely by ability, the percentages would rise from 0 to 100 per cent. For if entrance and graduation were solely determined by ability, the unqualified would not attempt college and the qualified would all get degrees. But neither entrance nor graduation is solely determined by ability. Consequently it

Table 4.

Estimated Percentage of College Entrants Who Graduate, Classified by High School Grades and Intelligence

	HIGH SCHOOL GRADES (PERCENTILE RANK IN GRADUTING CLASS)					
AGCT Score	1–20	21–40	41–60	61–80	81–100	Total
155 and above	71	78	84	91	98	98
145–154	69	76	83	90	97	96
135–144	66	72	79	86	93	92
125–134	59	66	73	79	86	84
115–124	50	56	63	70	77	72
105–114	38	45	52	59	65	57
95–104	27	34	41	48	55	42
85–94	17	24	30	37	44	27
75–84	8	16	22	29	36	15
65–74	4	11	18	24	31	7
Below 65	2	9	16	22	29	3
Total	26	40	54	68	82	61

Source: Commission studies.

is necessary to examine some of the other variables which influence students to enter college or to avoid it, and, if they do enter, to drop out or to remain and take degrees.

FINANCIAL SUPPORT FOR COLLEGE STUDENTS

It costs money to go to college, and ability to pay is undoubtedly one of the important determiners of who goes to college. John Millet of the Commission on Financing Higher Education summarized a study of attendance costs in the following paragraph.

> The total costs of attending a high-quality private college or university on a residential basis were at least $1,500 in 1951–52 and seem likely to be closer to $2,000 in 1952–53. There were private institutions where these total fee and residential costs fell as low as $1,000, and at a few they were as low as $800. At a state university the "in-state" student attending on a residential basis was likely to spend at least $1,000 in 1951–52, and might well spend more.[4]

Higher education can be inexpensive only if the student lives at home and attends an institution which receives enough income from other sources to enable it to maintain low tuition charges.

Millett also considered the question of how many families in the United States could afford to send a child to college. After giving the information which is contained in Table 5, he commented:

> Let us assume for purposes of comparison that $3,000 a year represented the minimum family income required in 1941 to support a young person in college. Then, allowing for changing price levels, we should have to say that as of 1950 at least $5,000 a year represented the minimum family income needed to finance a higher education for one young person.

When we compare the distribution of incomes in our society for the two years, we find that 30 per cent of all family units in 1950 had income of $5,000 a year or more, whereas in 1941 only 17 per cent of all families had incomes of $3,000 a year or more. In these terms we may say that the ability to pay for a college education was enjoyed by 76 per cent more American families in 1950 than in 1941.[5]

Table 5.

Percentage Distribution of Family Units by Money Income Before Taxes in 1942 and in 1950

ANNUAL MONEY INCOME	PERCENTAGE OF FAMILY UNITS 1941	1950
Less than $1,000	29	7
$1000–1999	31	14
$2000–2999	23	16
$3000–3999	8	19
$4000–4999	4	14
$5,000 and more	5	30
Total	100	100

Source: Commission on Financing Higher Education.

While a college education is too costly for many families, and while the income figures take no account of higher taxes and increased desires for automobiles, travel, household appliances, or other aspects of a high standard of living, Millett's figures indicate that in 1950 more families were able to bear the expense of sending a son or daughter to college than was true ten years earlier:

. . . the decade saw only a one-third increase in the percentage of youths going to college, while ability to pay for a college education as we have calculated it was three-fourths greater. This would suggest that our society has actually increased the capacity of families to pay for higher education more rapidly than young people have been motivated to go to college.[6]

THE DESIRE FOR COLLEGE TRAINING

The fourth essential for getting to college is the wish to attend. In some ways this is the most important variable of all, for it has no effective substitute. A poor boy can work his way through college or can be aided by a scholarship. One with a mediocre academic record can compensate by hard work. One of undistinguished ability can find a college in which the standards permit him to get along with fair success. But if he does not want to go to college neither money nor high ability nor an outstanding academic record is likely to get him there.

Berdie[7] asked all Minnesota high school seniors in the spring of 1950 whether or not they planned to go to college. Of those whose scores on the American Council on Education Psychological Examination placed them among the top 10 per cent of all graduates, but who were not planning on college, he asked whether they would attend if more money were available. Only half of these superior prospects answered yes. Despite their high ability, the other half had decided not to attend college and did not think that their decisions would be altered by additional funds.

Similar evidence was obtained by Barber[8] in a study of the graduating classes of the 5 high schools in Erie, Pennsylvania in June 1948. Of 763 graduates, 183 were recorded as having IQ's of 115 or higher. (An IQ of 115 is approximately equivalent to an AGCT score of 115.) Barber interviewed these 183 students to determine which had gone to college, which had not, and why. He found that 32 per cent went to college; 68 per cent did not. Of those who did not, over half had graduated in the upper third of their class and all but 15 per cent had been in the top two-thirds. Obviously neither low ability nor poor high school work had kept most of them from obtaining further education.

Economic barriers had undoubtedly prevented some from going on, but not all. Two-thirds of them lived in homes of average or higher rental value and some were from quite expensive homes.

The attitude of parents was an important variable. In a fourth of the cases the parents expected the child to go to work instead of to college. In another fourth the question of college attendance had never been discussed. Various other attitudes were taken by other parents. In general, the parents were opposed or indifferent, but one-fourth of the students did not go despite their parents' encouragement.

One-fourth of the group had never expected to attend college. Thirty per cent made up their minds during the ninth, tenth, or eleventh grade. Forty-three per cent did not decide until during the twelfth grade or after graduation. Three per cent were still hoping to attend.

One more illustration is provided by Havighurst and Rodgers. These authors studied all the children who were born in one midwestern community in 1926. The number of cases was small, but the fact that the entire age group was included and the detailed information which was available about each child gave added significance to the results. On the basis of information concerning each child's closest associates and the socioeconomic status of the homes from which they came, Havighurst and Rodgers derived an "Index of Peer Adjustment" (IPA) for each child. The IPA was developed as a measure of the child's motivation for higher education. Since this group was born in 1926 the young men in it were just the right age for service during World War II. The GI bill later provided an excellent opportunity for testing the predictive effectiveness of the IPA, for the GI bill made it financially possible for all the veterans to enroll in college if they wanted to. The following quotation summarizes what actually happened.

. . . some 75 per cent of the boys were eligible for scholarship aid under the GI Bill. All those with high IPA scores took advantages of the scholarship assistance. Only two boys with medium IPA scores went to college, although seven others finished high school and were eligible for GI scholarships. No boy with a low IPA score even graduated from high school, though two of them took trade training with GI assistance. The conclusion is inescapable that the offer of scholarship aid alone did not change the proportion of boys who went to college very much. From our knowledge of these boys we can discover only two out of twelve who we believe would not have gone to college if they had not had GI scholarships. In the 1926 group we see what scholarship aid alone, without any change in motivation over what now exists, can bring about in the way of college attendance among boys.[9]

All these studies contain evidence that unless a person wants to go to college the existence of other favorable circumstances is unlikely to get him there. The question of why some children grow up with the desire to go to college while others lack that desire has many answers. The final decision in each individual case is probably always the net result of many contributing factors. Some of those factors are considered in the following section.

Other Factors Related to College Entrance and Graduation

Among the factors which help to shape a growing child's educational plans are the general economic and cultural environment in which he is reared, his sex, his geographic location with all the variables which are related to geography, and his ethnic background. Of the various measures of socio-economic background, one of the most widely used is the occupation of the father.

FATHER'S OCCUPATION

The occupation of a high school student's father is a good predictor of whether or not he will enter college. The socioeconomic factors which are indicated by the father's occupation begin early to influence a child's educational progress and expectations. In some homes a child finds books, parents who value education, and many other things which point him toward college. He is expected and encouraged to do satisfactory school work and when the time for college arrives financial plans have frequently already been made. He "just naturally" goes to college.

At the other extreme a child grows up in an atmosphere which is little congenial to school matters and educational ambitions. Since he normally plays with children from similar homes, such academic ambitions as he may entertain receive less support than they would if his playmates were from families which expected their children to go to college. These environmental factors work together to discourage educational ambition. As the child gets old enough to consider leaving school, financial questions arise. Not only is there less money to pay for further education, there is also frequently positive pressure to get to work in order to add to the family income.

Granting that there are many exceptions to these contrasted conditions, the statistical fact has been demonstrated many times that the socioeconomic background of the child is related to school retardation, academic grades, age of leaving school, and percentage of youngsters who remain in school to any designated level.

Both intellectual selection—as evidenced earlier—and socioeconomic selection influence continuation through or dropping out of high school. Both factors continue to operate in determining which high school graduates enroll in college. The Commission's studies on the socioecenomic selection of college entrants were not extensive enough, by themselves, to justify a national estimate. But those studies plus a number of others on the same point—for example the extensive investigations of what happened to all Minnesota high school graduates of the years 1938 and 1950—justify the rough estimates given in the first column of Table 6.

It is true that school grades and scores on aptitude tests are both significantly related to the father's occupation, with the highest average grades and scores typically going to the children of professional men, but the relationship is not high enough to justify the differences summarized in Table 6. Over and above differences in ability, the financial, educational, and cultural differences which are indicated by the occupation of the father clearly play an important role in determining which high school graduates enter college.

Table 6.

The Relation Between Father's Occupation and Probability That A High School Graduate Will Enter College and That A College Entrant Will Graduate

Father's Occupation	Percentage of High School Graduates Who Enter College	Percentage of College Entrants Who Graduate from College	Percentage of High School Graduates Who Also Graduate from College
Professional and semiprofessional	67	60	40
Managerial	50	55	28
White collar (clerical, sales, service)	48	57	27
Farmer	24	44	11
Factory, craftsmen, unskilled, etc.	26	58	15

Source: Commission estimates.

After students get to college, however, there is a change. The influence of socioeconomic differences disappears almost entirely. When college entrants are classified by the occupations of their fathers the percentages getting degrees are fairly constant. For 5 occupational groups the percentages are as shown in the second column of Table 6.

The sons and daughters of farmers are the only important exception. Those who start to college are less likely to get degrees than are the sons and daughters of men in other types of work. The difference may be due to the handicap of poorer elementary and secondary education. Despite many improvements and much consolidation of rural schools, inadequate facilities and poorly prepared teachers are still too common in rural areas. While children of professional and semiprofessional men have a slight advantage over other groups, once a student has entered college, unless he be a farmer's child, his father's occupation apparently makes little difference in whether or not he receives a college degree.[10]

This lack of significant relationship remains substantially the same when college students are classified by level of ability. At all levels of intelligence and at all levels of high school grades, farmers' children who start to college are less likely to graduate than are the children of men in any of the other four occupational groups. This relationship was perfectly consistent and had no exceptions in the data analyzed by the Commission. Among the other four occupational groups, the influence of parental occupation was small. At the upper levels of ability the children of professional men had a slightly greater expectation of earning degrees than did the children of men in other occupational groups. At the lower end of the ability scale the margin was a little greater. The differences at all levels were small, however, and more important than the differences is the comparative unimportance of the father's occupation in indicating which college entrants will graduate.

Although there is comparatively little socioeconomic selection within college, the selection which occurs before entry determines the college population. Consequently, as shown in the third column of Table 6, college graduation is much more probable for some young people than for others. High school graduates with fathers in professional and semiprofessional fields are about four times as likely to become college graduates as are those whose fathers are farmers.

But there are more farmers' children than there are professional men's children and the disparity between the two groups is not so great when a college graduating class is divided according to the occupations of their fathers. That is done in Table 7, which divides 1,000 children according to the occupations of their fathers, shows the percentage of each group which can be expected to continue in school until the end of college, and then shows the result in terms of the distribution of a college graduating class. Approximately one-fifth of the graduates are the sons and daughters of professional and semi-professional men. Another fifth are the children of managers, and still another fifth of salesmen, clerks, and men in service occupations. One-tenth have farmers as fathers, and over a fourth are the sons

Table 7.

Estimated Distribution of College Graduates Classified
by Occupation of Father

FATHER'S OCCUPATION	DISTRIBU-TION OF 1,000 CHILDREN	PERCENTAGE OF EACH GROUP GRAD-UATING FROM COLLEGE	NUMBER AND PERCENTAGE AMONG COLLEGE GRADUATES	
			Number	Per Cent
Professional and semiprofessional	65	43	28	22
Managerial	128	19	24	19
Sales, clerical, and service	158	15	24	19
Farm	162	6	10	8
Skilled, unskilled, factory, etc.	487	8	39	31
Total	1,000		125	100

Source: The distribution of children was taken from Bureau of the Census report P-20, No. 32, December 4, 1950, Children and Youth: 1950, which gives the distribution of children under the age of 18 by occupation of the employed head of the household. The other figures are quite tentative Commission estimates.

and daughters of factory workers or men in the skilled and unskilled trades. The groups which send relatively small proportions of their children through college are so large that they account for relatively large fractions of college graduating classes.

In general summary of the influence of socioeconomic status, the situation seems to be this: economic and social factors play an important role in helping to determine which children graduate from high school and enter college. The differential is less marked, however, for children of superior ability than for those of lesser ability. The high school valedictorian is almost certain to enter college, regardless of who his parents are. (As a matter of fact, however, he is more likely to be the class valedictorian if he comes from a home of middle or higher socioeconomic level than if he comes from a home of low socioeconomic level.) To a lesser extent the socioeconomic barriers are minimized for other superior students. In other words, the probability of enrolling in college decreases more sharply as one goes down the ability scale for children from economically and socially less favored homes than it does for children from more favored homes. After entering college, the situation changes. The student who gets into college has already overcome most of whatever handicaps his home environment offered; once there, his chances of graduating are much more dependent upon his ability and much less upon his family background than were his chances of getting into college in the first place.

SEX

More girls than boys graduate from high school. Before World War II the ratio was usually around 45 boys to 55 girls. The proportion of boys dropped during the war, but has since come back to approximately the prewar level.

Of high school graduates, the percentage of boys entering college is larger than is the percentage of girls. But there seems to be a difference in the timing of their entry; more boys work a year or two between high school and college. The requirement of military service has brought an additional factor into the situation; some boys will enter college immediately after completion of their military service. Just how these decisions will work out in the next few years remains to be seen.

In the fall of 1952, 60 per cent of the students who were attending college for the first time were men and 40 per cent were women. There was a slight remaining influence of the wave of veterans from World War II and an unknown number of men students who were getting into college before being called for induction. Normally the male percentage could be expected to be a little smaller, but what is "normal" now is largely a guess. Of all students enrolled during the academic year 1952–1953, 65 per cent were men and 35 per cent women. These figures were influenced by the presence of 233,000 World War II veterans who were still in colleges and universities. Of the nonveteran population, 60 per cent were men and 40 per cent women. The same ratio obtained in 1941.

Among college graduates, the normal sex ratio can be estimated at 60 men to 40 women. During the years since 1942 there have been great departures from that ratio, and the ratio itself has been slowly changing over time. In 1900, 32 per cent of bachelors' and first professional degrees went to women; in 1920, 34 per cent; and in 1940, 40 per cent. Men are more likely to graduate from college than are women, but the difference is diminishing.

GEOGRAPHIC INEQUALITIES

Geographically, college students are spread all over the United States and its outlying possessions. They tend to congregate in those states which have many, or more famous, colleges and universities. But about 20 per cent of all college students cross state lines and if one wants to study the potential supply of people qualified for work in the specialized areas it is of more interest to know where college students come from than to know where they enroll. Story[11] has provided that information for the school year 1949–1950. The numbers of students from different states vary greatly, partly because the states differ in total population and partly because different proportions of the eligible youth attend college. The values in Figure 5 represent estimates of the percentage of 18- through 21-year-old nonveterans from each state who were enrolled in a college or university anywhere in the United States. Because 1949–1950 was the peak year of college enrollment, with more World War II veterans in attendance than

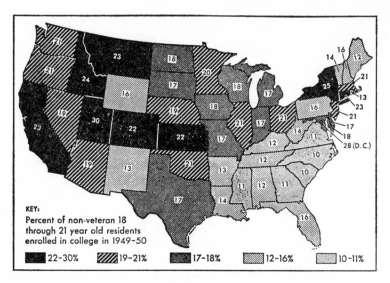

Figure 5. Geographic differences in college attendance

in any other year, the actual figures were adjusted to put them on a more normal, nonveteran, basis.

Utah was the leader, with 30 per cent of her college age youth actually in college. The District of Columbia with 28 and New York with 25 per cent came next in order. Of the states (treating the District of Columbia as a state) with 22 per cent or more in college, 3 were in the east, the District of Columbia, New York, and Connecticut, and 5 were in the west, Utah, Idaho, California, Montana, and Colorado. One, Kansas, was in the midwest.

Story compared the number of college students from each state with the total population of that state, instead of with the 18- through 21-year-old population as was done here. Using the college age population as a base gives more easily interpretable percentages, but does not greatly change the rank order of the states. Story's method, however, allowed direct comparisons with earlier studies of student migration:

> The 10 States having the highest proportion of their total population in college are: Utah, District of Columbia, New York, Idaho, Colorado, Kansas, Oklahoma, Washington, California, and Montana. In considering the geographical distribution of these States, it may be of interest to point out that in the three previous studies the top 10 States (exclusive of D.C.) were all west of the Mississippi. Thus, for the first time in many years an eastern State has gained a place among the upper 10.

Story also pointed out that the differences among the states have been decreasing. In 1950 Utah had 3 times as high a proportion of her college-age population in college as did the lowest states. In 1938 the top state had about 4 times, and in 1930 about 6 times as high a proportion as the bottom state.

The states with the smallest percentages in college were mostly concentrated in the south. A secondary concentration occurred in New England, where Maine, New Hampshire, Vermont, and Rhode Island were all low. The southern states would have had higher percentages in college if only white students and the white population had been considered, and New Mexico would have shown up more favorably if Mexicans had been omitted from the calculation.

How many young men and women from a state attend college is undoubtedly determined by many factors. Data on the elementary and secondary school systems of the several states suggest some of these factors. The number of students in a state who enter college is positively related both to the qualitative goodness of the elementary and secondary school systems and to the financial strength of the public schools. The American Association of School Administrators and the National Education Association have provided information on several measures of the quality of the public school systems of the individual states.[12] Their index of the non-financial aspects of the quality of a state's school system corresponded closely with the percentage of the youth of each state who attend college. So did a financial index based upon the average salary paid to schoolteachers, the value of school property per classroom unit, and the noninstructional expenditure per classroom unit. These relationships are to be expected. More college students would be expected to come from schools of high quality, strongly supported financially, and drawing upon populations in which the adults are above average in education and the children above average in ability. But there are some striking exceptions: Maine, Vermont and Rhode Island show up reasonably well on one or both of the non-financial and financial indexes of their public school systems, but all three send relatively small numbers of students to college. Maine, in fact, sends a smaller proportion than any other state which does not have a large Negro population.

At the other extreme, Utah spends no more money than do many other states and has a school system which is equalled or outranked by those of 8 other states. But Utah sends a higher percentage of its young men and women to college than does any other state in the union. Oklahoma, Idaho, Kansas, and Texas, while less spectacular than Utah, also send considerably more students to college than the statistics on their public school systems would lead one to expect. Clearly there are other differences among the states—differences which are not measured entirely by the dollars a state puts into its schools or by the quality rating of a state's school system which was used here. To find these differences will probably require an examination of more intangible factors such as the cultural characteristics and aspirations which predominate in each state.

STUDENTS FROM MINORITY GROUPS

Members of minority groups fairly generally experience some types of discrimination and that discrimination frequently affects educational opportunities and aspirations. Yet minority group membership, of itself, does not necessarily lead to lesser use of high-grade intellectual potential. Jews are a minority group. Yet the great esteem which Jewish culture gives to higher education has overcome quota barriers and other forms of discrimination, with the result that a Jewish boy is more likely to graduate from college than is a Gentile of equal ability. In contrast, Catholics, who are almost too many to be considered as a minority group, contribute relatively fewer people to science and scholarship than do Protestants.[13] The long tradition of Catholic preservation of scholarship and the existence of many Catholic colleges have not compensated for the fact that a large percentage of the Catholics in the United States come from cultural backgrounds which have not valued education highly.

While attitudes, economic status, and similar factors are primarily responsible for the ethnic group differences, minority groups as such are usually thought of as being less advantaged educationally. The comparison is usually correct, for Negroes, the French Canadians of parts of New England, Orientals, and the Spanish-speaking immigrants of the southwest all illustrate the lesser utilization of high intellectual potential of minority group members.

The problems of the bright Negro youth illustrates the differences. The factors which determine whether or not a bright Negro boy or girl will get to college are not different in kind from those discussed in the preceding sections. But they are more acute. Fewer Negroes have the money to pay for a college education. Fewer live near a college which will accept them. Fewer grow up in families which place a high value on college attendance. Fewer attend elementary and secondary schools which provide good preparation for college work and encouragement to attend college. If a Negro student does graduate from college he has greater difficulties in securing a position in many of the specialized fields than does a white student. Perhaps because of the discrimination, a Negro youth is likely to be less highly motivated to continue his education than is a white student.

The effects of these differences show up throughout the whole span of school years. Table 8 gives the census comparison of white and non-white youth enrolled in school in 1940 and in 1950. In both years and for all three age groups a higher percentage of whites was in school. But the differences were all smaller in 1950 than they were in 1940. The fact that a child is enrolled in school says nothing about the quality of the instruction he receives, which is frequently poorer for Negro than for white children. But in terms of percentages enrolled, the difference is growing smaller and it is not at all inconceivable that it will disappear entirely at the elementary and secondary school levels. Disappearance of the Negro-white differential in college will undoubtedly require a longer time, for qualitative equality of elementary and secondary school work, or other social changes of comparable magnitude, will be necessary before the percentage of Negro youth in college matches the percentage of white youth.

Table 8.

School Enrollment of White and Nonwhite Children in the United States in 1940 and 1950

| | Per Cent of Children in School | | | |
| | WHITE | | NONWHITE | |
AGE	1940	1950	1940	1950
6–13	92	92	87	90
14–17	81	85	68	77
18–24	14	19	9	14

Source: U.S. Census.

The topic of discrimination in education is too broad to be given detailed discussion here. But in addition to the facts given above it must also be pointed out that there is no evidence of a significant difference in ability between white and Negro children at early ages. As they grow older, white children tend to make higher scores on intelligence tests than do Negro children. But most of the evidence indicates that this difference can be explained by the differential schooling, opportunity, and social and cultural conditions which affect the two groups. A smaller percentage of Negro than of white children of the highest ability get the kinds of education, encouragement, and intellectual stimulation which permit them, as adults, to work at the level of their high potential. If America is wasting a portion of its intellectual potential in talented white youth, it is wasting an even larger percentage of the Negro potential.

A Further Note on Intelligence, High School Grades, and College Graduation

Prefatory Note: In addition to the foregoing essay extracted from his America's Resources of Specialized Talent, Dr. Wolfle has furnished unpublished tabulations for college students that take account of high-school record, along with intelligence and parental status, thus providing some evidence concerning the relationship of motivation to family background and ability.

The forty-one co-operating colleges in the original study supplied father's occupation, high-school rank in marks, and American Council on Education psychological examination scores for more than six thousand students enrolling in 1946.

It is well known that students scoring high on intelligence tests are more likely to enter college, as are those making high grades in secondary school. After students enter college, the same two factors predict a successful outcome of their studies. But these two variables are highly correlated, and other variables—cultural background, motivation, etc.—are associated also with continuation or withdrawal from college. Dr. Wolfle's data are unique in that they enable one to separate the effects of these factors.[14]

The table below provides an unusual penetration into some of the basic factors influencing accessibility to the stratum of college graduates. Among students from each type of home, whatever their level of measured intelligence, those who did better work in high school were more likely to

Percentage of College Entrants who Graduate from College, by Intelligence Rank in High School Graduating Class, and Father's Occupation

| Intelligence percentile | PERCENTILE IN HIGH SCHOOL GRADUATING CLASS | | | | |
	5th	25th	50th	75th	95th
A. Professional					
5th	29	34	41	48	54
25th	36	42	48	56	61
50th	45	50	57	64	70
75th	54	59	66	73	79
95th	61	66	73	80	86
B. Managerial					
5th	21	26	32	39	44
25th	31	36	42	48	53
50th	43	48	54	61	66
75th	56	61	67	73	78
95th	65	70	76	83	88
C. Service					
5th	9	18	30	41	50
25th	19	28	40	51	60
50th	32	41	53	64	74
75th	45	54	66	77	86
95th	56	65	76	88	97
D. Farm or Farm Labor					
5th	19	22	24	27	29
25th	30	32	35	37	39
50th	43	45	48	50	52
75th	56	58	61	63	65
95th	66	68	71	74	76
E. Manual Labor					
5th	27	34	44	54	61
25th	32	39	49	58	66
50th	38	45	55	64	72
75th	44	51	61	70	78
95th	48	56	65	75	83

finish college. Conversely, at each level of high-school performance the chances of graduation improved with test score. But (except for children of manual workers) intelligence scores were more closely associated with graduation than were high school marks. This relationship is the reverse of that found when predicting entrance to college; at that stage of education marks are usually the better predictor. Persistence within college appears to be predicted better by intelligence scores than by high-school record.

The slope of the plane from the low-low to the high-high corner of the table is almost identical for children of factory workers, farmers, and professional men; it is a little steeper for children of managers, and markedly steeper for children of men in service occupations.

Yet at each level of ability or marks, or of both together, the probability of completing college rises with social status. All in all, farmers' children display the lowest rate of graduation. But these status differentials are smaller for success within college than at prior points in the educational career. Although, in general, the children of professional men are most likely to graduate (being most likely to test high and to have high marks), when ability and previous school record are allowed for, this advantage tends to disappear.

NOTES

1. Theoretically, the standard deviation of the Stanford Binet Test on which the IQ is best determined is 16, while the standard deviation of the AGCT scale is 20. This difference would make an IQ of 116 equivalent to an AGCT score of 120, an IQ of 132 equivalent to an AGCT score of 140, etc. But the AGCT standard deviation was established on a cross section of the entire adult population, while the standard deviation of the Stanford Binet Test was established on school children. When the Commission had both tests administered to a group of high school juniors and seniors, the standard deviations of the two tests turned out to be practically identical. These data do not provide all the information desirable for a comparison of the two test scales, but justify the general statement that for much of the range no great distortion is involved in equating IQ scores with AGCT scores.

2. Ruth Harrell, *Observations of 118 First-Honor and Second-Honor High School Graduates,* unpublished study, 1952.

3. Eli Ginzberg and others, *Occupational Choice,* New York, Columbia University Press, 1951.

4. John D. Millett, *Financing Higher Education in the United States,* New York, Columbia University Press, 1952, p. 389.

5. *Ibid.,* p. 391.

6. *Ibid.,* p. 391.

7. Ralph F. Berdie, *After High School, What?,* Minneapolis, Minn., University of Minnesota Press, 1953.

8. Leroy E. Barber, *Why Some Able High School Graduates Do Not Go To College,* Ed.D. dissertation, University of Pittsburgh, unpublished, 1950.

9. Robert J. Havighurst and Robert R. Rodgers, "The Role of Motivation in Attendance at Post-High School Educational Institutions," in Byron S. Hollinshead, *Who Should Go to College?,* New York, Columbia University Press, 1952, pp. 153–154.

10. Socioeconomic factors are, however, involved in the selection of a college

to attend, are related to the choice of a curriculum or major field of study (See Chapter VII), and may be important in a number of aspects of college life.

11. Robert C. Story, *Residence and Migration of College Students, 1949–50,* Federal Security Agency, Office of Education, Misc. No. 14, 1951.

12. American Association of School Administrators and Research Division of the National Education Association. Educational Research Service Circular 7, October 1945.

13. Robert H. Knapp and Joseph J. Greenbaum, *The Younger American Scholar: His Collegiate Origins,* Chicago, University of Chicago Press, 1953.

14. The students from each status level were classified in a 10 x 10 table by deciles of intelligence score and high school marks, and for each cell the percentage graduating from college was computed. Dr. Toby Oxtoby of the Commission staff fitted a plane to each of the five tables by least squares. The summary included here gives the proportion of graduates (rounded to whole numbers) at five points on the distribution of each variable.

20   *Local Social Structure and Educational Selection*

NATALIE ROGOFF

THIS PAPER is concerned with the way young people are allocated to positions in the social-class structure and the part played by education in the allocating process.

Numerous studies in America, Britain, and western Europe document the fact that youngsters who start life in a given social class vary in the class status they achieve as adults in proportion to the amount of formal schooling they obtain. The more education, the more advantaged the class status. Depending on the starting point, education facilitates either upward social mobility or the maintenance of a favored class position; lack of education brings on downward social mobility, or stability in a disadvantaged class position.

But what are we to make of these facts? Particularly, what is it that sets some youngsters on a path leading ultimately to graduation from college, while others never even complete their secondary education? As usually stated, the facts convey little of a sense of social process, of one thing occurring before another in an identifiable social location, or of one event or status affecting a later event or status through the advent of specific social mechanisms. It is possible that any one or any combination of at least three disparate sets of happenings might bring about the observed relationships. Each of the three, to be proposed here, empahsizes a different key process—one stemming from the effect of schools on individual differences in ability, another from the effect of individual family differences in motivation, and the third from differences in community and school environments. In each case, the social process has a specified mechanism operating in a specified context. That these are extremely divergent interpretations of the observed correlation should be evident by the following discussion of each.

First, schools, like all formal organizations, develop a system of rewards and punishments as one way of implementing their goals. The acquisition of skills and knowledge by students is clearly one of the goals of schools. It is certainly not improbable that students who demonstrate

This paper was originally presented at the annual meeting of the American Sociological Society, September, 1959, Chicago, Illinois. It is published here for the first time.

the greatest success in acquiring skills and knowledge should most frequently receive the rewards that schools have at their disposal—promotion, high grades, prizes, and scholarships. Since the distribution of marked scholastic ability cuts across the social classes to at least some degree, the reward and punishment system of the schools would lead to a rearrangement of students with respect to their potential social achievement: the more able youngsters, motivated by scholastic rewards, would move further ahead in school, continue their education longer, and eventually move into more prestigeful occupational and social positions than the less able. Moreover, at the end of the school years, a certain amount of social mobility, upward and downward, could be attributed to the encouragement given by schools to the capable, no matter what their social origins, as well as to the discouragement given the less able of all social classes. The observed relationship between educational attainment and adult social-class position might, therefore, be due to the interaction between individual differences in ability and the reward systems of schools.

A second process that would lead to the observed results has its locus in the family, rather than the school, and hinges on attitudes rather than aptitude. Some families, valuing achievement, discipline, and social-economic success, encourage their children to do as well as possible in school; the youngster's ability, this interpretation runs, sets only the broadest of bounds on his school performance. More determining than ability is the family's attitude toward education—and the distribution of favorable attitudes toward education again cuts across the class structure to some degree. The education and, ultimately, the social-class achievement of youngsters represent family aspirations come true. Note that the school, in this process, plays essentially a passive role, or at least takes something of a secondary part. The school actually rewards, not necessarily those who merit it, but those who *want* to be rewarded, whether or not, in some abstract sense of equitable arrangements, they do merit it. The real locus of social mobility is the living room, not the classroom.

Finally, the possibility exists that educational attainment and adult class status are correlated because of processes arising from community and school structures. Because this idea is less familiar than the others and because the processes it highlights differ in certain formal ways from the others, it will be developed here at somewhat greater length. First, let it be granted that the various social classes are not randomly distributed among the diverse sizes and types of communities in the United States today. (We defer for the moment the evidence for this assertion.) It follows that each of the social classes will be more heavily concentrated in some kinds of community environments than in others, and that communities will vary in the predominant or average social-class affiliation of their residents. Such structural differences may set in motion both formal arrangements—such as school, library, and general cultural facilities in the community—and informal mechanisms, such as normative climates or modal levels of social aspiration, which are likely to affect *all* members of the community to some extent—parents and children, upper, middle, and working classes.

Many of the studies whose general findings are at issue here have, in fact, covered a wide variety of communities. By pooling the behavior of youngsters living in diverse communities, one of the sources of social mobility may be hidden from view, for it is possible that the formal arrangements and informal norms of the community set both a floor and a ceiling on the ultimate achievements in educational and social-class status of their young residents. For example, when we observe that youngsters from the more favored social origins end up on the average with greater educational attainment, we may in fact be observing the results of the greater concentration of such youngsters in communities that facilitate academic achievement through better schools and through prevailing climates of opinion that nurture and sustain high educational aspiration. Upward social mobility, under these conditions, would result for the lucky minority of working-class youngsters whose families live, by accident or design, in predominantly middle-class communities; and downward social mobility for the unlucky middle-class youngsters living in less favored environments; while stability of class position would be the typical outcome for the majority of youngsters living in towns, villages, or cities where their class status is not a deviant one.

One of the intriguing implications of this idea is that it proposes a continuing but ever-changing link between ecological processes that lead to spatial patterns of residence and work, on the one hand, and the processes through which persons are allocated to positions in the social-class structure, on the other. Socio-economic position influences the type of community or neighborhood where families will live; their ecological status then affects the life chances of their children, some of whom will maintain the social-class status of the parents, while others will shift in status. Both individual and net shifts of class status in the second generation lead to further changes in ecological patterns, and so on, possibly until some kind of equilibrium is reached.

In sum, three variant interpretations have been offered for a recurrent empirical observation: that young people from given social origins vary in their educational attainment; such variations eventually leading to differences in the social-class status achieved in adulthood. Educational attainment thereby leads to upward or downward social mobility, or to maintenance of parental class status. In effect, the three interpretations can be ordered with respect to the importance they attach to events transpiring in the classroom itself. According to the first, the classroom is the central stage, for it is there that youngsters are rewarded or punished for their scholastic ability and performance, and it is the rewards and punishments they experience that lead to their academic and social attainments. According to the second interpretation, youngsters are carriers of aspirations and attitudes acquired from their families, and it is these states of mind that prevail, although they may be reinforced (unwittingly?) by the reward-and-punishment system of the school. The last interpretation calls attention to the community setting of both schools and families, and suggests that the ecological environment leads to formal and informal arrangements within and outside of the schools, affecting the educational attainment of residents.

None of these interpretations excludes the others. It is not necessary to demonstrate that only one of the social processes can be observed, the others being absent. Instead, a research design is called for that permits us to see whether all three are operative and, if possible, to gauge their relative significance. An empirical study with such a design is currently in process at the Bureau of Applied Social Research of Columbia University. We were fortunate enough to be given access to information gathered by the Educational Testing Service, concerning the college-going and career plans of over thirty-five thousand American high-school seniors, who constituted the entire senior class of 1955 of over five hundred public secondary schools. Concerning the schools, which provide a fairly representative sample of the twenty thousand-odd senior public high schools in the United States, information was collected, at the time of the field work, from their principals. This has now been supplemented by consulting national and state school directories, other published surveys, and census sources describing the towns and counties where the schools are located.

What kinds of information are needed to provide empirical tests of the ideas advanced here? We need to know something about the social origins of the youngsters, something about their future orientations, and their scholastic ability. Finally, we need to introduce some principle for classifying the communities where they attend high school. Specifically, here are the indicators to be used in attempting to compare the proposed types of social processes with the factual evidence. First, we shall see how youngsters who vary in scholastic ability—indicated by their performance on a twenty-item test devised especially for this study by the Educational Testing Service—compare with respect to their plans for going on to college. This will provide the evidence for seeing whether or not the reward-and-punishment system of the schools helps to channel the more capable youngsters into the route of higher education. Moreover, we shall simultaneously trace the effect of the youngster's social background on his college-going orientation. Several criteria have been used to classify the families of orientation of the high-school seniors: their fathers' occupational status, fathers' educational attainment, and the college experience of their older siblings. Combining these three properties of the families with the average college-going propensities of the high-school seniors who be-

Local Social Structure and Educational Selection

longed to such family types permitted us to construct a set of ranked socio-educational classes, ranging from well-educated professional and managerial families, who clearly imbue their offspring with a desire to go to college, to poorly or uneducated unskilled manual and farm families who are far more indifferent to higher education as a desirable goal. Five such classes were finally discerned, each containing approximately 20 per cent of the thirty-five thousand high-school seniors, so that they may be referred to as the socio-educational status quintiles.

One further word about classifying the students according to their scholastic ability. At some of the high schools studied, the vast majority of seniors scored well above the mean, while at other schools, the bulk of the senior class did extremely poorly on the test. While this is in itself a significant result, it also has the following implication: if we were to classify individual seniors according to their absolute scholastic aptitude score, we should be comparing the behavior of youngsters who actually stood at just about all possible relative positions within their own school. Almost any given score represents the top, the middle, and the bottom relative position at one or more of the 518 high schools observed. Therefore, the scores were converted into school-specific quartiles for all those who were in a senior class of 15 or more. (This eliminates about 20 per cent of the schools, but less than 3 per cent of the 35,000 students.) Since we want to observe the effect of allocating rewards and punishments by school authorities, we clearly need to compare those who are at the top in their own school with those at the bottom, no matter what the absolute level of scholastic ability is at the school.

Finally, we have used the expressions "scholastic ability" and "scholastic performance" as though they were interchangeable, despite the fact that they are clearly disparate. Fortunately, the principals of about one hundred of the high schools were asked to check the school records of each of their seniors and indicate what his class standing was. The correlation between ability, as indicated by the short written test, and class standing, which summarizes the student's performance over a four-year period, is extremely high, although it does vary somewhat among the high schools. Table 1 presents the evidence—which we use as a justification for

Table 1.

Class Standing and Scholastic Ability

Scholastic-ability quartile*	Per cent who are in the top half of their senior class, by grade average	No. of cases
(Top) 4	75	1,558
3	56	1,614
2	40	1,689
(Bottom) 1	17	1,561

* Scores on the special aptitude test devised for this study were transformed into school-specific quartiles.

taking the student's performance on the aptitude test as a fairly good indicator of his behavior in the classroom.

Scholastic ability plays a decisive role in students' plans to continue with their education. Some 61 per cent of all high-school seniors in the top quarter of their class planned to go to college; in successive quartiles, the proportion drops to 44 per cent, 33 per cent and 24 per cent. The preliminary evidence suggests that the high school in effect *does* allocate rewards and punishments in such a way as to encourage the competent and discourage the incompetent. At the same time, there is a marked tendency for students' further educational plans to be influenced by the socio-educational status of their families. Seventy-two per cent of those from professional or managerial families plan to attend college; the proportion decreases to 47 per cent, 35 per cent, 26 per cent, and finally 24 per cent through the succeeding socio-educational status categories. And, as many other studies have shown, the two social processes reinforce one another. The full picture is given in Table 2, where the proportions planning to attend college are shown at every level of scholastic ability and from each of the five types of social origins simultaneously. College-going propensities vary greatly among the twenty categories of high-school seniors: 83 per cent of the brightest youngsters from the most advantaged families plan to attend college, but only 16 per cent of the least competent children of skilled and semiskilled workers (category 2) are college-oriented. Both the school and the family play a part in determining who is to gain education beyond high school. Among previous studies, the relative importance of the two has varied greatly; Kahl's study in the suburbs of Boston[1] shows the family to be almost twice as influential as the school, while Sewell's Wisconsin data[2] suggest the school to be almost three times as important as the family; our own nation-wide sample falls squarely between the two, with each of the sources playing about an equal role.

Table 2.

Per Cent of High-School Seniors Planning to Attend College, According to Scholastic Ability (in Quartiles) and Socio-Educational Status of the Family

Scholastic-ability quartile	FAMILY-STATUS QUINTILE					All quintiles	No. of cases
	(Top) 5	4	3	2	(Bottom) 1		
(Top) 4	83	66	53	44	43	61	(8,647)
3	70	53	37	29	29	44	(8,709)
2	65	41	31	20	21	33	(8,696)
(Bottom) 1	53	30	22	16	18	24	(8,509)
All quartiles	72	47	35	26	24	40	
No. of cases	(6,520)	(6,647)	(6,465)	(8,116)	(6,811)		(34,561)

Notes: Students are classified here according to their scholastic-aptitude quartile in their own high school. Family status position, however, is constant for all students coming from a given family background, no matter what the social composition of their high school.

The number of cases on which each of the percentages is based ranges from 963 to 2,505.

So much, then, for the first two social processes leading to the observed correlation between educational attainment and social mobility or stability. What of the third? With the first two, it was clear, both from the logic of the argument and from the guidelines provided by past research, just what indicators to use in order to test the validity of our ideas. The third set of social processes are, we suggested, generated by conditions in the community, which affect the type of educational and cultural facilities the town can provide and which presumably also shape the average social and education aspiration level of the residents. But what types of indicators would most accurately portray such environmental states? This is clearly a major sociological problem and one to which we can make only a limited contribution. Furthermore, we have only begun to probe the data in this study for tentative leads and therefore offer the following evidence with the appropriate reservations.

We start with a principle of classifying communities that derives from a set of frequently used descriptive terms, employed by laymen, educators, social scientists, and just about everyone who has ever given a moment's thought to the varieties of educational experience: the size and type of community—village or small town, suburban or metropolitan—where the schools are located. The temptation is strong to clothe this idea in polysyllabic sociological garb, but in fact the impulse to use such a classification scheme arose from the fact that it is one of the very few environmental properties used frequently enough and over a long enough period of time to warrant a systematic empirical test.

Nine types of communities were discerned, varying in population size and in their relationship to a metropolitan area. Table 3 identifies the types and presents the salient results concerning the college-going propensities of youngsters attending high school in each enviroment. It is up to the reader to decide whether or not the results confirm his expectations. For example, who would have predicted that the college-going propensities of youngsters attending high school in the very largest cities is almost as low as that of youngsters residing in the smallest towns and villages and is surpassed by that of youngsters from the larger towns and, of course, the suburbs? College-going is apparently affected by the size and type of community where the decision to attend college is made—but hardly in a simple, linear fashion. One note of caution. We were able to observe only those young people who remained in school until the twelfth grade, and the tendency to stay in school that long varies among the diverse type of communities. The college-going proportions need to be corrected, therefore, by taking into account those youngsters who will not attend college because they have not completed a secondary education. Community educational-retention rates are positively correlated both with urbanization and with community wealth (median family income), and much more markedly with the latter than the former. Therefore, the wealthy suburbs should

The Selection Process in Education

have their college-going proportions reduced the least, since most of their youngsters do stay in school through the twelfth grade, followed by the larger cities, and finally small towns and rural villages. This would keep the three main types of communities in the same rank order but would increase the gap between the smallest and largest placs.

Table 3.

College-Planning Rates and Social Composition of High-School Senior Classes in Diverse Community Contexts

Type of Community	Number of high schools	Number of seniors	Per cent planning to attend college	PER CENT OF SENIORS IN EACH FAMILY-STATUS QUINTILE (Top) 5	4	3	2	(Bottom) 1	Total
Small independent towns:									
Less than 2,500	270	6,991	33	9	17	12	20	42	100%
2,500–9,999	85	5,451	39	16	20	16	24	24	100%
10,000–49,999	42	5,591	48	21	20	19	24	16	100%
Suburbs:									
Less than 2,500	36	1,768	37	17	18	18	26	21	100%
2,500–9,999	15	1,085	46	30	18	19	23	10	100%
10,000–49,999	22	3,116	50	34	18	19	21	8	100%
Large towns and cities:									
50,000–99,999	10	2,176	45	22	20	22	23	13	100%
100,000–499,999	19	3,669	37	17	18	24	30	11	100%
500,000 or more	19	5,589	39	20	22	23	24	11	100%
All communities	518	35,436	40	19	19	19	23	20	100%

The second part of Table 3 describes the social composition of the student body attending high school in the various types of communities. Note the marked degree of social segregation implied by these distributions—the children of farmers (category 1) concentrated in the smallest villages and towns, the children of professionals and managers in the larger suburbs, and the children of industrial workers (category 2) most heavily concentrated in cities of 100,000–500,000. We cannot here mention more than a few of the major consequences of such ecological segregation.

One of the most interesting consequences concerns the scholastic aptitude of youngsters attending schools situated in diverse community contexts. Table 4 presents the trends, showing median aptitude scores of students coming from families of each of the five socio-educational status types and living in each type of community. Here, of course, we describe students according to their absolute scores on the aptitude test, since we want to evaluate the effect of the environment on scholastic ability. Test scores ranged from 0 to 20; the mean for all 35,000 seniors to whom it was given is 8.9; the standard deviation, 4.7.

Table 4.

Scholastic Ability and College-Planning Rates, by Social Origins and Community Context

A. Median Aptitude Scores

| | FAMILY–STATUS QUINTILE | | | | | |
Type of Community	(Top) 5	4	3	2	(Bottom) 1	Unweighted mean of all quintiles
Small independent towns:						
Less than 2,500	11.2	9.2	8.3	7.7	6.9	8.7
2,500–9,999	11.6	9.7	8.6	8.1	7.4	9.1
10,000–49,999	12.7	10.1	9.0	9.1	7.3	9.6
Suburbs:						
Less than 2,500	11.9	9.8	9.0	8.2	7.2	9.2
2,500–9,999	*13.0+	10.8	9.4	8.2	7.2	10.0
10,000–49,999	13.0	11.3	10.5	9.9	8.5	10.6
Large towns and cities:						
50,000–99,999	12.0	8.8	8.0	7.1	*5.0—	8.0
100,000–499,999	11.8	9.5	8.4	7.7	7.0	8.9
500,000 or more	11.7	9.6	8.8	8.6	7.2	9.2

* Medians were computed from grouped data, using four score intervals. In these two cases, the medians fell in one of the extreme intervals, and interpolation was not carried out.

B. Per Cent Planning to Attend College

| | FAMILY–STATUS QUINTILE | | | | | |
Type of Community	(Top) 5	4	3	2	(Bottom) 1	Unweighted mean of all quintiles
Small independent towns:						
Less than 2,500	66	45	35	25	25	39
2,500–9,999	73	50	33	25	27	42
10,000–49,999	78	55	42	32	32	48
Suburbs:						
Less than 2,500	69	50	35	25	15	39
2,500–9,999	74	51	38	22	29	43
10,000–49,999	77	51	40	26	22	43
Large towns and cities:						
50,000–99,999	67	44	36	35	37	44
100,000–499,999	69	45	32	22	20	37
500,000 or more	64	46	31	28	24	39

Again, the suburbs stand out as most conducive to pronounced scholastic achievement. For convenience, an unweighted average aptitude score is given for all students attending schools in each community context. This enables us to see the effect that schools exert on their student's academic capacity, without that effect's being obscured by the advantages or disadvantages individual students enjoy by virtue of their family background. It appears that all students, whether in the majority or the minority in the school they attend, enjoy the blessings or pay the price their school affords. From those at the top to those at the bottom of the social-class hierarchy, all students attending large suburban schools emerge from their educational experience relatively better equipped in academic skills, while youngsters who attend school in small villages or large industrial cities emerge from their educational environments less adequately prepared. Note how these trends account for some of the heterogeneity in scholastic aptitude *within* a given social class by the diversity in formal academic training received by the youngsters originating in that class.

The second part of Table 4 shows parallel trends for plans to attend college, according to young people's social origins and the type of community where they attend high school. On the face of it, small towns and suburbs appear to be at a par in producing college-oriented youngsters— but again, we should recall the difference between them in the school retention rates through the twelfth grade. After making the appropriate corrections, the suburbs will again rank first in productivity of college students.

The last word has hardly been said on the variety of ways young people may be affected by the community setting where they frame their career and educational goals. Quite the contrary—only after considerably more research effort has been expended will we be ready to make assertions with confidence on the whole matter of broad structural influences on individual behavior.

Specifically, when it comes to schools and social stratifications, the kind of analysis proposed here is carried out in the following spirit: heretofore, when sociologists have investigated the way education and social-class structure relate to one another, relatively scant attention has been accorded the fact that education is a long-term social process, occurring microscopically in the schoolroom and macroscopically in a definite and describable community context. Until now, the challenge of observing these processes has been evaded by the phrase: "Education is the high road to social mobility." No expression could more successfully divert us from the sociological point. The evasion has also directed sociologists to say that the heart of the matter is in the nuclear family, where all of the behavior and all of the attitudes and values are engendered that lead to scholastic achievement, and subsequent social-class achievement, by the members of each new generation. Nothing in our study belies the crucial role of the nuclear family, whose significance is so well recognized that we hardly feel the need to do any proselytizing in its behalf. But that this is all that counts in a bureaucratized, achievement-oriented society, where education is controlled by local communities each with its formally organized school system, is too much to believe. The more we turn in these other directions, the more will we learn about the social structure of our society.

NOTES

1. J. A. Kahl, "Education and Occupational Aspirations of 'Common Man' Boys," *Harvard Educational Review,* XXIII (1953), 186–203. [Chap. XXVI in this reader (eds.).]

2. W. H. Sewell, *et al.,* "Social Status and Educational and Occupational Aspiration," *American Sociological Review,* XXI (1956), 203–11.

21   *Access to Higher Education and Economic Development*

C. ARNOLD ANDERSON

IN RECENT DECADES the managerial, technical, and intellectual élites have come to be composed of individuals with higher education. Education, accordingly, has become increasingly necessary, though not sufficient, for high status positions even though other channels of upward mobility, or other means of status inheritance, remain. Higher education is not a sole qualification and one should not over-simplify the rôle of schooling in mobility.

Sociologists in recent years have begun to investigate the social composition of student bodies in higher schools as part of their renewed interest in social stratification. The import of the social system for the distribution of opportunities is indicated, in part, by the proportions of youth from various strata who attain university education.[1]

Within this setting, the present report has three aims. (1) The social composition of university student bodies is compared for two dozen countries.[2] (2) The degree of selectivity of university attendance is related to the type of economy and income level of the different societies. (3) The level of university attendance (in relation to population) is also used as a classification factor on the assumption that distinctive educational traditions may operate independently of economic factors, and in order to determine whether a higher attendance level itself alters selectivity.

Though the writer compares more countries than did the *Yearbook* editors, the same frustrations in procuring comparable data were experienced. Different sources use different numbers of occupational categories, often formed on quite dissimilar principles. The occupational categories for the base population often have little resemblance to those used for university statistics, even when prepared by the same agency.[3] The *Yearbook* comparisons reduced parental occupations to two groups: manual and nonmanual. Here more rubrics are retained.

The level of student enrollment was measured by the ratio of students to one hundred individuals aged 20–24. The index of type of economy was the percentage of employed male population engaged in primary produc-

---

Reprinted from C. Arnold Anderson, "The Social Status of University Students in Relation to Type of Economy: An International Comparison," *Transactions of the Third World Congress of Sociology,* V, 51–62, with the permission of the author and the International Sociological Association.

tion (agriculture, fishing, forestry, mining) or, alternatively, tertiary production (government, professions, transport, trade, etc.). (Secondary production is manufacturing and construction.) The income figures, expressed in "International Units," were taken from Clark[4] for the available year nearest that of the student data.

There are three basic methods for describing the social composition of students.[5] (1) One can compute the percentage of students coming from each social category; e.g., 10 per cent of students may be children of farmers, 20 per cent children of urban entrepreneurs, etc. This actual social profile of the student body is adequate for some purposes, such as comparative study of élites. (2) One can compute the number of students enrolled per thousand fathers in each social category; e.g., from a thousand professional homes come 30 students as contrasted with 5 from each thousand farm homes. (3) One can compare the percentage distribution of students by parental status with the distribution of families by status; e.g., professional families are 5 per cent of the total but furnish 20 per cent of students—the ratio of these percentages (here called the selectivity index) being 4.0. Either of the last two procedures (which are numerically interchangeable) measures selectivity, but the first does not. Principal reliance here is on the third procedure.[6]

Level of University Enrollment in Relation to Economic Factors

In Table 1 the populations here analyzed[7] are grouped by proportion of primary employment as a basis for examining variations in levels of enrollment. It is clear that using this index a nation's type of economy has only a limited relation to the rate of university attendance. On the average countries with less than 30 per cent in primary production have half again more students in relation to population aged 20–24 (even excluding the United States) than do the others; but intra-group variation is wide. Thus at both 2 per cent or less and at 4 per cent or more of attendance primary production ranges from under 20 per cent to about 70 per cent.

The correlation for male students alone is somewhat closer, but for level of female attendance there is virtually no association with type of economy. And the proportion of students who are women is quite unrelated to extent of primary or tertiary activity. Variations within each group are great. Thus at about 60 per cent primary and 20 per cent tertiary production the share of students who are women ranges from one in fifty to one in three; even among the post-war instances these percentages range from 14 to 38. Excluding the United States, in the most tertiary countries the average percentage of students who are women is in fact lower than in countries of intermediate tertiary level.

Table 1.

Rates of Attendance in Higher Schools, Arrayed by Proportion of the Working Male Population in Primary Employments

Country and Date	PERCENTAGE OF WORKING MALE POPULATION IN Primary Employment (1)	Tertiary Employment (2)	STUDENTS PER HUNDRED PERSONS AGED 20–40 All (3)	Male (4)	Female (5)	PERCENTAGE OF STUDENTS FEMALE (6)	INCOME; INTERNATIONAL UNITS PER MAN-YEAR IN EMPLOYMENT (7)
			Group I—Over 50% Primary Employment				
Yugoslavia, 1931	71	15	1.1	1.7	0.5	21.8	376
Yugoslavia, 1953	69	18	3.2	—	—	—	—
Latvia, 1939	69	16	4.0	5.7	2.4	29.8	530
Mexico, 1949	67	22	1.6	—	—	—	100
Greece, 1936	61	21	1.9	3.5	0.4	9.6	332
Finland, 1935	58	27	4.4	5.5	3.7	38.1	652
Hungary, 1913	54	24	0.9	1.9	—	2.3	427
Spain, 1945	53	24	2.5	4.6	0.7	14.0	825
Hungary, 1930	52	26	2.0	3.5	0.6	13.9	382
			Group II—30%–50% Primary Employment				
Italy, 1931	48	25	1.9	3.1	0.6	16.4	331
U.S. Negroes, 1940	47	34	3.6	3.4	3.6	55.2	(800)
U.S. Negroes, 1950[1]			5.8	6.7	5.1	47.0	
Denmark, 1880	42	31	0.1	—	—	—	—
Czechoslovakia, 1947	40	25	2.1	—	—	—	445
France, 1948	38	34	3.6	4.7	2.6	37.9	715
Sweden, 1930	36	34	1.8	3.1	0.5	12.9	818
Austria, 1953	33	26	4.2	6.5	1.8	20.7	825
			Group III—Less than 30% Primary Employment				
Denmark, 1921	29	35	—	—	—	—	964
Denmark, 1947	28	41	4.6	7.4	1.8	19.0	823
Sweden, 1945	26	38	2.8	4.3	1.3	22.2	980
Switzerland, 1945	21	36	3.7	6.4	0.9	11.8	696
Netherlands, 1948	21	47	3.4	5.7	1.1	15.8	1,070
U.S. Whites, 1940[1]			14.4	17.5	11.5	40.2	
U.S. Whites, 1950	21	50	20.9	28.5	13.4	33.0	2,566
Germany, 1928	19	37	1.7	2.9	0.5	14.5	795
West Germany, 1953	18	34	3.2	5.3	1.1	17.7	—
Indiana University 1946	12	48	—	—	—	—	—
			Group Means				
Group I	62	22	2.4	3.8	1.2	18.5	428
Group II[2]	40	29	2.3	4.4	1.4	22.0	627
Group III (1)[3]	22	40	5.6	8.6	2.9	19.1	1,128
Group III (2)[4]	23	38	3.2	5.3	1.1	16.8	888

1. The extra year is included to facilitate Negro-White comparisons in the face of the marked post-war changes in male attendance. The declines between 1940 and 1950 in proportions of females reflect the backlog of male students from the army and in part the impact of educational aid to veterans.

2. Excluding U.S. Negroes.

3. Including U.S. Whites for 1950 but not for 1940; including Indiana.

4. Excluding U.S. Whites and Indiana.

National income level (Table 1, column 7) shows a moderate positive association with level of enrollment. Of the countries for which income data were available, all with over 3 per cent attendance have incomes above 500 I.U.'s; but some countries with lower attendance (as Sweden) also have high income levels. For women students alone there is no association; the Netherlands and Sweden have female attendance rates similar to Greece or Italy. For males this association is considerably closer; yet pre-war Hungary had a higher rate than pre-war Germany, and pre-war Finland as high a rate as post-war Netherlands. As to the proportion of students who are women, the low income countries show great diversity—from 2 per cent in 1913 Hungary to 22 per cent in 1931 Yugoslavia and 38 per cent in Latvia. At intermediate income levels France and Finland have 38 per cent of students female while Switzerland has only 12 per cent. Among the more prosperous countries (excluding the United States) the range is less, from 13 per cent in pre-war to 22 per cent in post-war Sweden.

While there is some relation between date and attendance rates within the countries for which more than one sample was available, the variations among countries in the post-war period are marked. Excluding the United States, post-war rates of attendance ranged from 1.6 in Mexico to 4.6 in Denmark. Figures by sex are obtainable for fewer countries. For males alone the post-war range is 4.3 to 7.4 and for females 0.7 to 2.6. The post-war proportions of students who are women vary from 12 to 38 per cent. The phenomenal performance of the United States, and especially of the Negroes, deserves underlining. In deference to European opinion, which we believe to be only partially justified, one can eliminate a third or even a half of the white American students and still obtain a rate well above any other nation.

The data presented in Table 1 provide clear indications that rates of university attendance depend very little upon either the income level of a country or the extent to which its economy is of primary or tertiary type. Although an international upward trend over time seems probable, the underlying factors explaining national contrasts must be sought in values, customs, and public educational policies—each of which may be different in its effects on males and females.

Percentage Distribution of Students by Social Background

The relative size of the various strata-cadres among students gives no evidence about selectivity but does describe the composition of the student corps (Table 2). In all countries the majority of students come from non-manual (non-farm, non-labor) families, who of course are a distinct minority of the population. Among American Negroes only 44 per cent were from such homes. The other proportions range from nine-tenths down to

The Selection Process in Education

Table 2.

Percentage Distribution of Students by Paternal Occupations

Country and Date	AGRICULTURE AND LABOR (1)	NON-AGRICULTURE NON-LABOR[1] (2)	AGRICULTURE All (3)	AGRICULTURE Operators (4)	LABOR All (5)	LABOR Non-Farm (6)
Group I—Over 50% Primary Employment						
Yugoslavia, 1931	21.7	78.3	—	19.1	2.6	—
Yugoslavia, 1953	30.6	69.4	22.7	21.4	9.3	7.9
Latvia, 1939	—	—	33.6	—	—	—
Mexico, 1949	18.1	81.9	6.4	—	—	11.7
Greece, 1936	16.8	73.2	—	22.8	4.2	—
Finland, 1935	39.6	60.4	—	16.6	23.0	—
Hungary, 1913	21.8	78.2	18.4	15.7	6.2	5.2
Spain, 1945	9.4	90.6	7.0	—	—	2.4
Hungary, 1930	21.0	79.0	14.5	11.3	9.6	8.1
Group II—30%–50% Primary Employment						
Italy, 1931	8.8	91.2	6.6	5.9	2.9	2.6
U.S. Negroes, 1940	55.7	44.3	19.4	—	—	36.3
Denmark, 1880	—	—	—	8.2	—	—
Czechoslovakia, 1947	17.0	83.0	10.0	—	—	7.0
France, 1948	8.7	91.3	6.5	5.4	3.3	2.2
Sweden, 1930	23.1	76.9	9.5	—	—	13.6
Austria, 1953	14.3	85.7	—	5.6	8.7	—
Group III—Less than 30% Primary Employment						
Denmark, 1921	12.8	87.2	—	9.7	3.1	—
Denmark, 1947	17.6	82.4	—	9.9	7.7	—
Sweden, 1945	20.6	79.4	9.6	—	—	11.0
Switzerland, 1945	9.0	91.0	—	4.0	5.0	—
Netherlands, 1948	5.0	95.0	—	4.0	1.0	—
U.S. Whites, 1947	37.3	62.7	9.8	—	—	27.5
Germany, 1928	7.5	92.5	5.8	5.7	1.8	1.7
West Germany, 1953	9.6	90.4	4.9	4.8	4.8	4.7
Indiana University, 1946	42.2	57.8	—	9.9	32.2	—
Means by Primary Employment Groups						
Group I	22.4	76.3	17.1	17.8	9.2	7.1
Group II[2]	14.4	85.6	8.2	6.3	5.0	6.4
Group III (1)[3]	18.0	82.0	7.5	6.9	7.9	11.2
Group III (2)[4]	11.7	88.3	6.8	6.4	3.9	5.8
Means by Rate of Attendance Groups (as grouped in Table 3)						
Group A	18.2	78.9	9.3	12.9	3.5	7.0
Group B[2]	16.2	83.8	11.5	10.4	6.2	6.9
Group C (1)[3]	21.0	78.9	16.6	—	—	(14.9)
Group C (2)[4]	17.8	82.2	(20.1)	8.3	9.5	(2.2)

1. Including agricultural white collar, who are also included in "All Agriculture."
2. Excluding U.S. Negroes.
3. Including U.S. Whites, and for Group III (1) Indiana.
4. Excluding U.S.

three-fifths. The percentages coming from farm families vary from 5 to 34, and from farm operator families from 4 to 23. Over a third of the Negro students and almost a third of the white students in the United States were children of non-farm manual workers. Excluding the United States, for all laborer families the range is from 1 to 23 per cent and for non-farm labor alone from 2 to 14 per cent. As would be expected, the contribution from agriculture is larger in the primary production countries, but not uniformly so; it was only 6 per cent in Mexico as against 23 per cent in 1953 Yugoslavia and 33 per cent in Latvia. A similar situation prevails for farm operators alone. The proportions of students from laboring homes has little relation to the extent of primary production. (Grouping the countries by level of attendance shows no systematic pattern for any occupation.) These percentages must be interpreted in the light of the relative size of the occupational sectors; hence the discussion turns now to consideration of the selectivity indexes.

Social Selectivity of University Attendance

The selectivity indexes[8] in Table 3 are grouped by level of attendance rather than by type of economy since the former factor is more closely associated with selectivity. Averages for each set of countries (grouped alternatively by attendance and by economy type) appear at the foot of the table.

Though attendance is three times as high in Group C as in Group A, few of the selectivity ratios show a corresponding change. The trends for some ratios challenge accepted preconceptions, though plausible explanations can be offered. Thus the ratio of actual to expected share of students from manual families (labor plus farmers) remains unchanged if the United States is excluded. The drop in the favorable position of non-manual families is more definite, and does not depend on inclusion of the United States figures.[9] The ratio for all agriculture rises consistently from low to high attendance rates. The ratio for children of farm operators increases from Group A to B but not further, as is true also for non-farm labor (but Group C has only two cases). The representation from all labor homes doubles and becomes a fifth of expectancy in the countries with the highest general attendance rates. The excess in the contribution from professional homes is cut by three-fifths with expanded attendance, and urban entrepreneur families also show a decline in representation.

When the countries are grouped by type of economy the changes are more erratic. Here also it is between the two lowest levels that effects are largest, especially the sharp decline in the non-farm, non-labor ratio (column 2). In three countries (Mexico, Finland, Spain), all predominantly agricultural but with widely differing attendance rates, students from this category exceed five times their quota. Five quite diverse countries (Greece, Czechoslovakia, France, Austria, and 1947 Denmark) have about two and one half times their quota. And among whites in the United States the ratio is less than 2.0. This ratio for American Negroes is very high.

The decline in the labor group ratios from the most primary to the intermediate economies is presumably a transition phenomenon due to two causes. On the one hand, in the more primary production countries urban labor is relatively skilled while at the next stage it becomes diluted with less skilled industrial labor. Only at a later stage do industrial workers attain a level of living and of ideology leading to higher levels of university attendance, and few countries have yet reached this point. Related to this last feature is the second factor. The diffusion of ideologies favorable to less selective attendance takes time, quite apart from limited family incomes. In few countries has sufficient time elapsed for this assimilation. The fact that level of attendance has greater weight than type of economy suggests that distinctive educational policies and traditions play a major part in this process.

Among countries with unusually low indexes for manual labor are Italy, Spain, France, the Netherlands, and Germany. These range in income from 331 I.U.'s to 1,070 and from 18 to 53 per cent in primary and 34 to 25 per cent in tertiary employment. Rates of attendance are moderate: from 1.7 in pre-war Germany to 3.6 in France. The proportion of women among students is exceptionally high in France but somewhat below average in the other countries. The common factor underlying the low representation of manual worker's children appears to be the presence of aristocratic traditions of education and the absence of aggressive public policies breaking with those traditions.

At the other extreme are the United States—most strikingly the Negroes—together with post-war England, Yugoslavia (1953), Mexico, and Finland.[10] Incomes range from 100 I.U.'s (Mexico) to 2,500 (United States); primary production ranges from 67 to 21 per cent and rates of attendance from 1.6 to 20.9. These countries have in common an exceptional emphasis on "democratization" of education, expressed in both propaganda and public policies. The American tradition is "grass roots": free schooling through secondary level and public financial support for numerous higher schools—bolstered by generous educational stipends to war veterans. Finnish policies and traditions have stabilised worker representation at high levels. Emphasis on wider educational opportunity is more recent in Mexico, Yugoslavia, and England, and is associated with drastic changes in governmental policy.[11]

There is little relationship between the indexes of selectivity for labor and for agriculture. Italy, Spain and France have exceptionally low ratios for all agricultural and manual categories whereas the United States ratios are high. Though high in representation of urban labor, Mexico is lowest

Table 3.

Ratios of Percentages of Students to Percentages of Male Labor Force from Designated Occupational Categories, Arrayed by Rates of Attendance

Country and Date	STU-DENTS PER HUN-DRED PER-SONS AGED 20–24	AGRI-CUL-TURE AND LABOR (1)	NON-AGRI-CUL-TURE NON-LABOR (2)	AGRICULTURE All (3)	Opera-tors (4)	LABOR All (5)	Non-Agri-cultural (6)	PROFES-SIONAL (7)	PRI-VATE ENTRE-PREN-EURS (8)
Group A—Less than 2 students per hundred persons aged 20–24									
Denmark, 1880	0.1	—	—	—	0.26	—	—	5.5	1.4
Hungary, 1913	0.9	0.27[1]	4.4[2]	0.27	0.37	0.14	0.29[1]	14.0[3]	2.4
Yugoslavia, 1931	1.1	0.25	3.8	—	0.34	0.09	—	8.3	2.3
Mexico, 1949	1.6	0.20	7.7	0.10	—	—	0.46	9.8	12.5
Germany, 1928	1.7	0.11	2.8	0.32	0.60	0.03	0.04	17.2[4]	2.3
Sweden, 1930	1.8	0.29	2.8	0.29	—	—	0.30	25.6	2.1
Italy, 1931	1.9	0.09	3.2	0.11	0.13	0.05	0.07	24.8	—
Greece, 1936	1.9	0.39	2.4	—	0.52	0.16	—	8.6	—
Group B—2–3.5 students per hundred persons aged 20–24									
Hungary, 1930	2.0	0.24	3.4	0.25	0.37	0.15	0.24	9.3	1.6
Czechoslovakia, 1947	2.1	0.24	2.4	0.55	—	—	0.14	1.2[5]	3.8
U.S. Negroes, 1940	3.6	0.64	5.9	0.48	—	—	0.79	9.3	—
Spain, 1945	2.5	0.11	5.2	0.13	—	—	0.08	13.2	—
Sweden, 1945	2.8	0.27	3.2	0.32	—	—	0.24	10.9	2.7
Yugoslavia, 1953	3.2	0.33	4.0	0.29	0.29	0.46	0.53	27.0[5]	2.8
West Germany, 1953	3.2	0.15	2.7	0.38	0.64	0.08	0.09	16.3	1.7
Netherlands, 1948	3.4	0.07	2.8	—	0.50	0.02	—	—	1.8
Group C—Over 3.5 students per hundred persons aged 20–24									
France, 1948	3.6	0.12	2.5	0.24	0.25	0.07	0.05	4.6[6]	2.8
Switzerland, 1945	3.7	0.12	3.3	—	0.50	0.08	—	—	—
Latvia, 1938	4.0	—	—	0.54	—	—	—	5.0	—
Austria, 1953	4.2	0.22	2.4	—	0.43	0.17	—	3.4	2.0
Finland, 1935	4.4	0.44	5.6	—	0.34	0.57	—	—	—
Denmark, 1947	4.6	0.26	2.5	—	0.66	0.15	—	10.1	1.6
U.S. Whites, 1947	20.9	0.57	1.8	0.62	—	—	0.56	3.4[6]	3.0
Rates of attendance unknown or inapplicable									
Denmark, 1921	—	0.18	3.0	—	0.44	0.06	—	10.1	2.5
Indiana University, 1946	—	0.54	2.2	—	0.67	0.51	—	3.3	—
Means by Rate of Attendance Groups									
Group A	1.4	0.23	3.9	0.22	0.37	0.09	0.23	14.3	3.8
Group B[7]	2.7	0.26	3.7	0.34	0.45	0.18	0.30	12.5	2.4
Group C (1)[8]	5.3	0.29	3.0	0.47	—	—	(0.30)	5.3	2.4
Group C (2)[9]	4.1	0.23	3.3	(.039)	0.44	0.21	(0.05)	5.8	2.1
Means by Primary Employment Groups									
Group I	2.4	0.28	4.6	0.26	0.37	0.26	0.32	11.9	4.3
Group II[7]	2.3	0.19	2.7	0.30	0.27	0.10	0.14	10.9	2.4
Group III (1)[8]	4.6	0.30	2.7	0.41	—	—	0.23	11.6	2.2
Group III (2)[9]	3.2	0.25	2.9	0.34	0.58	0.07	0.12	13.6	2.0

1. Excludes some public labor.
2. Excludes some public labor.
3. Excludes minor professions in public service.
4. Includes upper white collar in public service.
5. Private only.
6. Computed from other sources.
7. Excluding U.S. Negroes.
8. Including U.S. Whites, and for Group III (1) Indiana.
9. Excluding U.S.

for farm people. In Germany representation of farm operators is very high but neither children of farm laborers nor of other workers often enter college doors. Only Denmark (1947) matches the German and American farm operator ratios. With the probable exception of Sweden (1945), the farm operator indexes are 0.50 or higher in all countries with less than 30 per cent primary production, whereas among the other countries only Greece, Latvia, and Czechoslovakia attained this level. The indexes for farm operators are of course consistently below those for non-farm entrepreneurs, reflecting tradition and place of residence as well as income. However, the frequent excess of farm operator over urban labor ratios suggests that the entrepreneur factor may be more important than the income factor, since non-farm workers live in cities (often with a university), have as much cash income and nearly as large families as the typical farmer.[12]

The index for business families is distinctively high in Czechoslovakia and phenomenally so in Mexico, but in most instances these ratios cluster around 2.0. Denmark, West Germany, and Netherlands show relatively low ratios today. Businessmen furnish comparatively more students in the primary economies and fewer in the tertiary ones; in fact these business ratios dropped more with the shift to tertiary economies than they did with expansion of enrollments.

The professional ratios are typically highest of all.[13] Except for Czechoslovakia (where the data concern "private" professionals only), the lowest ratios are in Austria, the United States, France, and Latvia. Very high ratios are found for pre-war Sweden and Italy and (paradoxically) present-day Yugoslavia. Attention should be called to the fact that there is no close parallel between the professional and the total non-manual ratios. Thus Sweden in 1930 had a high professional index but a moderate non-manual one whereas Mexico illustrates the opposite situation. The professional indexes show little relation to type of economy but do decline sharply as attendance levels rise. The relatively low ratio for professional families in the United States is the complement of the relatively high ratio for business men and may well reflect the strong "private enterprise" ideology. The professional ratios show more dispersion from country to country than those for business families.

For a few countries figures are available for separate professions. The ratios for all professions and for teachers were, respectively: Italy 24.8, 16.6; Yugoslavia (1931) 8.3, 15.3; West Germany 16.3, 14.2; Denmark (1880) 5.5, 4.5; and Denmark (1921) 10.1, 9.7. Clergy ratios were: Yugoslavia (1931) 6.7, West Germany 10.2, Denmark (1921) 21.0. The ratio for physicians in Yugoslavia (1931) was 12.0 and in West Germany 14.7; for lawyers in these two countries 5.2 and 10.9. These (and other) ratios shift from country to country or from time to time within the same country.

A few ratios for public employees are obtainable. For military and non-military public employees of all ranks the ratios are quite diverse; they were, respectively: Yugoslavia (1931) 1.8, 10.0; Hungary (1913) 3.4, 5.8; Hungary (1930) 1.1, 6.8; Spain 6.8, 2.0, Denmark (1921) 3.3, 2.3. Thus the public employee index was less than a fourth that of all professionals in Denmark (1921), nearly three-fourths of the professional index in 1930 Hungary, and a fourth larger than the professional index in Yugoslavia (1931). Non-farm entrepreneurs and public employees had about the same index in Denmark (1921); the public employee ratio was twice that of businessmen in Hungary (1913), and four times the business ratio in Hungary (1930) and Yugoslavia (1931).[14]

There are strong tendencies for professional indexes to be highest, for urban to exceed rural enterprisers, or for non-manual categories to exceed manual labor. But there are distinct factors determining the level of various vocations within one country or the ratio for the same group in different countries. In the absence of careful comparisons of relative incomes for all these categories one cannot do more than to suggest that non-economic factors appear to be of major importance in bringing about these variations.

Conclusions

The present study has compared several occupational groups in some two dozen populations with respect to the degree of inequality in opportunities for higher education enjoyed by their offspring. Despite many defects of indefiniteness and inaccuracy as judged by the standards of acceptable demographic research, the results complement other comparative studies of social structure.

A sufficient number and variety of societies were analyzed to establish a set of tentative "ranges" of inequality indexes for key occupational strata. A scale for judging general "educational inequality" definitely has not been established since the indexes for different strata are too loosely intercorrelated to permit combining them into an unambiguous single measure. No effort has been made to compare the degree of educational inequality for these populations with inequality in other features of the societies or with educational inequality in more remote decades.[15]

A major contribution of this study (and of the earlier report by the 1950 *Yearbook* Editors whose results were partially incorporated) is the establishment of definite norms by which to judge the comparative inequality of higher educational systems. In the light of the standing of the United States in the present data (which results were known approximately some years ago), it is evident that strictures on American education as "class bound" suffer from lack of perspective.

To be sure, none of the farm or manual labor groups attain much above half of parity attendance even in the United States. But in relation to the other populations studied here, those same American groups enjoy unusually favorable opportunities. The privileged sectors of American society, on the other hand, have retained less of their educationtal lead—on these criteria—than similar groups elsewhere. One recognizes that the higher schools attended by most Negroes are of too low quality. But even discounting heavily for these defects, the American Negroes show a degree of educational attainment and representation of manual workers that is distinctive in the set of peoples studied here. This is the other side of the American "Negro problem."

Even including the United States, however, the general picture emerging from these data is one of definite inequality in opportunities for higher education. The non-farm, non-labor sectors of society supply from three-fifths up to over nine-tenths of the students though this group is a small fraction of any society. Nowhere does the farm population furnish over a third of the students and in some cases less than one in ten; farm operator shares range from 4 to 23 per cent. Outside the United States, all laborers combined nowhere supply as many as a fourth and in some nations virtually none of the students; urban labor's share varies from 2 to 14 per cent (excluding the United States).

Rising levels of university attendance or the development of a tertiary type of economy bring little systematic expansion in the shares of farm or labor groups outside a few exceptional countries.

Judged by the more pertinent "inequality index" (a group's share of students in relation to its proportion of male population) some interesting patterns emerge, even excluding the United States.

1. The selectivity indexes for all farm plus labor categories combined range from 0.07 to 0.44 among countries. These indexes show little relation to either the proportions of primary and tertiary employment or attendance levels, though there is some indication that they may go through a declining and then a rising phase as primary employment decreases.

2. By contrast, the total non-agricultural, non-labor indexes (ranging from 7.7 to 2.4) drop with a shift to intermediate levels of primary production and decline more definitely and steadily as attendance expands. This index is more sensitive than the one for manual groups because of the smaller underlying populations that form its base.

3. The indexes for farm operators range from 0.13 to 0.66, rising between intermediate and tertiary economies. They rise between low and intermediate attendance levels.

4. The index for all agriculture ranges from 0.10 to 0.55 among countries; it rises continuously by a half with the growth of tertiary production and doubles with expanded attendance.

5. The index for non-farm labor ranges from 0.04 to 0.53; it declines

sharply between low and intermediate tertiary production but increases as attendance rises from low to intermediate levels.

6. The index for all labor ranges from 0.02 to 0.57; it drops with advancing tertiary production but doubles with rising attendance.

7. Professional indexes range from 27.0 to 3.4; they are unrelated to shift of economy but drop by three-fifths with the rise in attendance.

8. Entrepreneurial indexes range from 12.5 to 1.6; they drop with a shift from high to intermediate primary production and drop by a third with a rise in attendance from low to intermediate levels.

The complexity and looseness of the relations just summarized is evident. Part of the variation among inequality indexes or attendance levels is a correlation with time. To a limited extent and for certain types of change in selectivity patterns, a shift from primary toward tertiary types of economy may supply an explanation. Association of selectivity with attendance rates is a little closer. Advancing proportions of tertiary employment have a moderate though irregularly stimulating effect on attendance, especially of males. Rising levels of per capita income facilitate male attendance, but not female. The proportion of students who are women is unrelated to either of the foregoing economic factors. Expansion of university attendance appears not to depend basically on either economic factor but rather on "cultural" factors of educational ideology and policy.

The striking fact that emerges from these data is that as the economy becomes more tertiary (and even as university attendance expands) there is at most a sluggish tendency for the more disadvantaged sectors of the population to contribute an increasing relative proportion of students. Specific ideologies, traditions, and educational policies peculiar to each nation—and impinging uniquely on each sex and social stratum—appear to contain the principal explanations for the results found.

These findings raise a basic economic question. It is assumed usually that a productive economy requires high levels of education and a large, highly educated élite. Yet some of the countries studied here contradict this assumption. Is their less extensive schooling qualitatively superior? Do they provide equivalent training in schools not regarded as "higher education?" Do they combine the various types and qualities of human resources in different but equivalent ways?

The present results certainly demonstrate that inequality of opportunity for higher education is a widespread, and stubborn, characteristic of societies.[16] Many would therefore endorse the statement by the Editors of the 1950 *Yearbook* (p. 639) that "the best classification of student's parents would be their incomes and their ability to defray the costs of higher education." The writer interprets the data as demonstrating equally clearly the penchant for parents in certain groups in most nations to overlook existing opportunities well within their children's grasp, because of their own traditional preconceptions.[17]

NOTES

1. In most countries, however, the principal selection in fact occurs at the secondary level or earlier.

2. In this respect the present study extends and elaborates the comparison presented by the editors of the 1950 *Yearbook of Education* (London: Evans), pp. 639–44.

3. For example, farm operators are mixed with farm laborers; physicians in public health work are included with officials though teachers are given separately; private white collar workers may or may not be distinguished from publicly employed ones, etc. In the initial computations several dozen occupational rubrics were used to keep the fullest information; by successive regroupings the distributions given below were derived. Textual comments utilize fuller data for several countries.

4. C. Clark, *The Conditions of Economic Progress,* 2nd ed. 1951, London: Macmillan.

5. Compared in detail in an analysis of the 1897 Russian educational census (forthcoming in *Genus*).

6. Ideally one requires the occupations of fathers of potential students; but occupations for all men above, say, age 45 serve adequately. Unfortunately, one must use the distribution for all males since most countries furnish no other. This compromise unduly raises the selectivity indexes for higher status groups (and lowers those for manual workers) since men in higher occupations are older. Differential fertility has an opposite effect.

7. The data for the United States are from Havighurst's table in the 1950 *Yearbook* (p. 635) as are those for Czechoslovakia, France, Netherlands, Switzerland (pp. 639–44). For Sweden: S. Moberg and C-E. Quensel, *Studenternas Sociala Ursprung,* Statens Offentliga Utredningar, 1948: 48, p. 86. For Indiana University: R. A. Mulligan, "Socio-Economic Background and College Enrollment," *American Sociological Review* 16, 188–96, 1951. For Spain: M. F. Iribarne and J. T. Artigas, "Una Encuesta a los Estudiantes Universitarios de Madrid," *Revista Internacional de Sociologia 7,* 5–46, 1949. For Mexico: Universidad Nacional Autonoma, *Primer Censo Nacional Universitario,* 1949, 1950, p. 45. For Denmark: N. Bang, "Til Studentersporgsmaalet," *National-økonomisk Tidskrift,* 1901, 1–11; F. T. B. Friis, "De Studerende ved Kjobenhavns Universitet," *Ibid.,* 1919, 571–87. Other data were taken from documents. All higher schools, not merely "universities" are included.

8. Ratio of percentage of students from a group to the percentage of males employed in the same group.

9. Non-manual indexes can decrease markedly without manual indexes rising appreciably due to the large number of males employed in the latter groups.

10. To eliminate the first two college years from the United States data would reduce its ratio, but data not shown here suggest the effect would not be large. The *Yearbook* data give a non-farm labor ratio of 0.57; England was omitted due to non-comparability of the data on all other points.

11. The high levels of workers attendance in contemporary Yugoslavia may be partly factitious, reflecting guided recruitment and quotas. Judging from the course of Soviet policy and experience with "the reserve of talent" in the working class, regression from these high levels may be anticipated though the level may remain above most other countries shown here.

12. For three instances ratios are available for different groups of farmers. In 1913 Hungary the ratio for all farm operators was 0.37, for small farmers 0.25, but total for big plus middle farmers 12.4, and for farm labor 0.04. In 1930 Hungary the farm operator ratio was again 0.37, farm laborers 0.05, small farmers 0.27, middle farmers 8.3, and big farmers 16.0—the latter two ratios equalling professional families. In Denmark in 1921 the total farm ratio was 0.44, small and middle farmers .35, big farmers 10.0—again matching professionals. A similar sub-classification can be made between large and small businessmen for three countries, though the sources do not give the basis for grouping. The respective ratios in the United States were 4.3 and 1.6; in France 4.6 and 1.0; in the Netherlands 2.8 and 1.4. Since small en-

trepreneurs have very low incomes, attitudes appear as important as income in explaining their good showing.

13. These ratios are rather unreliable as a basis for comparisons, primarily because in some countries not all publicly employed professionals were identified.

14. This and other evidence suggests the urgent need for a study of the tendencies toward hereditary officialdom.

15. The formed topic is dealt with in a paper at the 1954 Rome Population Congress by M. J. Bowman and the writer, "Educational Distributions and Atttainment Norms in the United States," and material for comparison over longer time-spans can be found in the writer and M. Schnaper's "School and Society in England," *Annals of American Research,* 1952.

16. It is desirable perhaps to state that the author assumes that class inequalities in inherent intelligence are far less unequal than the differences here demonstrated.

17. D. Wolfle, *America's Resources of Specialized Talent,* New York: Harper, 1954. [Chap. XXIX in this volume (eds.).] See also the evidence for the equipotency of non-economic factors in R. F. Berdie, *After High School—What?,* Minneapolis: University of Minnesota Press, 1954.

PART IV

Social Factors in Educational Achievement

22 Social Factors in Academic Achievement: A Brief Review

PETER H. ROSSI

A BRIEF SUMMARY is presented below from the findings of a survey of researches on social factors affecting the achievement of students in American elementary and high schools. The summary concentrates on the findings of the literature, glossing over technical details; it is intended to indicate what is known about the determinants of achievement that are related to differences among students and teachers, among schools, and, finally, among communities.

I. Student Characteristics Related to Achievement

The major finding under this category is that a student's intelligence relates more strongly to his achievement level than any other characteristic. Surveying a large number of studies, we found that between 40 and 60 per cent of the variation among students could be accounted for by variations in I.Q. levels. Furthermore, holding I.Q. constant, the correlations between achievement and other characteristics are uniformly reduced in size. This finding holds for both the elementary and high-school levels.

Yet, despite the importance of intelligence, a considerable portion of the differences among individuals must be accounted for in other terms. Part of the remaining variation is taken up by socio-economic status: the higher the occupation of the breadwinner in the student's family, the greater his level of achievement. However, it should be pointed out that, while the studies under review uniformly find socio-economic status playing a role in achievement, it is not entirely clear how it does so. In fact, it is characteristic of past researches on individual differences that they have not gone much beyond measuring the association between characteristics of individual students and their achievement scores, to specify the processes by which these characteristics are translated into differences in achievement.

One line of research that holds some promise of specifying the relevant psychological processes is that which has been concerned with the "achieve-

The summary is published here for the first time. It was carried out at the National Opinion Research Center, University of Chicago, by the present writer in collaboration with James A. Davis and Miss Edna Raphael.

ment motive." Stemming from early attempts to specify the main forms of motivation in the individual, these researches have sought to discover what makes one person more motivated to achieve than another. Working mainly with children, these studies have defined achievement as accomplishment above and beyond what native capacities alone would provide. They have looked into the relationship between parents and children, between children and their peers, and the like; and while the studies are not yet in a form enabling one to say that the mechanisms have been clearly specified, their approach seems to be a very likely one.

Attitudes toward school and school work also have been found to play some role in achievement, but this role is considerably reduced when intelligence is taken into account. Thus, students who are more favorably inclined to school are more likely to get high achievement scores, but they are also more likely to be the abler students.

II.   Teacher's Characteristics and Student Achievement

A number of researches have tried to relate different characteristics of teachers to the achievement levels of their students. Because we can expect that the achievement of a student at any one point in time is not likely to be strongly affected by the teachers he happens to have at that time—being more a product of his total educational experience—we can anticipate that the findings of this sort of research will be very equivocal. In fact, such is the case: perhaps the strongest impression these researches make is that the teacher's contributions to his students' achievement, in the short run, are minimal. Thus, we find that indexes of teaching experience correlate with student achievement around $+ .2$ at the maximum and are often zero or slightly negative. Similar small correlations are obtained with measures of the quality and amount of teacher-training, some studies indicating that the more hours of college training a teacher has had, the higher his students' achievement levels. Some evidence was found that better teachers (in this sense) tend to come from private as opposed to state universities.

Most of the researches conducted on this topic have been rather poorly conceived. Only one study held constant the I.Q. levels of the students involved. This study found a number of rather surprising relationships between achievement and teacher characteristics: for example, the higher the teachers' rank positions in their own high-school training, the lower the achievement of their pupils!

In sum, no clear pattern of findings emerges from the researches on this topic. We may conclude that the teacher's contributions to his students' achievement do not arise directly out of his background, training, sex, or marital status.

III. Educational Practices and Student Achievement

Because a student spends a relatively long time within a particular school, we can anticipate that variables relating to the characterictics of schools and the activities within them would be more important to the achievement of students than characteristics of particular teachers. However, this literature also has the distressing characteristic of being contradictory in its results. By and large, no clear picture emerges from the research to indicate that a particular type of school, pursuing a particular type of educational policy, has a higher record of student achievement than other kinds of schools pursuing different educational policies.

Perhaps the reason why research in this area has been so barren lies in the crudeness of the measurements attempted. For example, schools have been characterized only by their grossest features, e.g., total size, classroom size, and the like, without much imagination being spent on devising measures that would catch more subtle distinctions in educational policy.

Researches on total school size indicate that the differences between school on this dimension are not very considerable. In general, very large schools and very small schools were disadvantaged when compared with schools in the middle range. However, it may be the case that these size differences mask community differences as well, indicating perhaps that the large urban school and the small rural school do not have as good students as middle-sized schools located perhaps in middle-sized cities or suburban areas.

Sizes of classes show a similar complicated relationship to achievement. Students in small classes do better in some subjects than students in larger classes, but there are subjects in which the difference accrues to the advantage of the larger classes.

Research on the auspices of high schools has fared somewhat better, perhaps because of their small number. Private secular schools do better than public schools, which, in turn, are better than denominational schools in achievement scores of students pursuing similar courses of study. It should be noted that the abilities of the students in the three types of schools have not been equated.

Finally, we may consider research bearing directly on the total educational experience within a school. Studies of "progressive" versus "conventional" types of schools, holding the abilities of students constant, have shown a slight but consistent advantage for students in "progressive" environments.

Researches on the relationships between educational practices and achievement have in the main failed to reveal that differences among schools and different educational practices contribute a great deal to the scores of students on achievement tests. To some unspecified degree, this failure may be due to the lack of ingenuity displayed by the researchers, who have measured only the grossest aspects of either schools or educational practices.

IV. Community Differences in Academic Achievement

While individual differences are perhaps the strongest differences to be encountered in a search of the literature on achievement, a close second are those differences to be found among regions and communities in the United States. The best and worst states in the Union are so far apart that they appear to have been drawn from separate although overlapping universes.

Two strong trends appear: first, students in states and communities in the South do not have achievement scores as high as students in the North. Second, the achievement levels of a state or community are highly correlated with indexes of economic well-being, e.g., telephone ownership, per capita income, proportion of professionals in the labor force, and the like. Several investigators have suggested that this regional difference has its source ultimately in the place accorded to intellectual matters in the culture of the region. Be that as it may, it is clear that students in Mississippi will fare poorly on achievement tests as compared with their fellows in New Jersey or Connecticut.

The strongest contrasts are provided by the regions of the United States. When individual communities within regions are examined, differences tend to be smaller and, furthermore, do not show as close a relationship to economic factors.

Although these studies have pointed to important sources of differences in achievement levels, it is only fair to point out that they have done little more than document their extent and nature. Thus, while one investigator suggests that attitudes toward education might account for the differences between the North and the South, this is pure speculation and has yet to be subjected to empirical proof. Furthermore, none of the studies holds the I.Q. levels of the schools constant. Thus, it may very well be the case that the mental abilities of southern students may be the cause of their low levels of achievement rather than influences of the schools which they attend. Of course, it must be remembered that I.Q. score is not an innate individual characteristic but is to some large degree affected by the environment of the individual.

*   *   *

Summing up this brief summary of the literature on achievement, it is apparent that there are variations in achievement among individuals, schools, and communities, which are related to factors as yet largely unspecified.

23 *Family Environment and Intelligence*

JOHN NISBET

ABERDEEN, as research workers in other fields have discovered, is a good district for population studies, for its position as the centre of a comparatively isolated region and its mixture of farming, fishing, industry, commerce and administration make it in many respects a representative urban population. Almost all the children under twelve in the city, in the Scottish tradition, attend local schools, and the Education Authority is progressive in authorizing and assisting research projects. The investigations described in this paper could not have been carried out without the generous facilities afforded by the Education Authority,[2] for it was possible in the administration of tests to achieve an almost complete coverage of age-groups of children, only two small primary departments of private schools being omitted.

In this paper a hypothesis is advanced which to some extent reconciles certain of the contradictory results which have emerged from recent studies of intelligence and family size. Investigations over the last thirty years—there have been at least thirty-three on this problem, among them particularly the Scottish Mental Survey with its 70,000 cases—have established that in any representative sample of the population there exists a negative correlation between the intelligence test scores of children and the size of the family to which they belong. In so far as intelligence is inherited this seems to imply a decline in the level of national intelligence; yet two recent studies[3] have not found any such decline. Those who have attempted to predict the amount of the possible decline in national intelligence are not unaware of the fact that environmental influences enter into intelligence test scores and affect the size of the negative correlation between intelligence test score and family size. They have attempted to allow for the influence of environment in two ways, both of which seem to have serious weaknesses. Some have tried to measure relevant environmental factors, such as parental occupation or overcrowding in the home, and then have observed the effect on the negative correlation when these environmental factors are held constant. Such a method, however, does not give accurate results if (as is suggested in this paper) one of the environmental

Reprinted from John Nisbet, "Family Environment and Intelligence," *Eugenics Review*, XLV (1953), 31–42, with the permission of the editor and the author.

factors is the size of family itself, the amount of contact between adult and child and the consequent stimulation of the child's verbal development. Again, other investigators have made allowance for environment by first estimating the future trend of intelligence as if intelligence test score were determined wholly by heredity, and then halving that estimate, since at least half the variance of intelligence is attributable to heredity. This, however, is not altogether a valid procedure: for it does not follow that if half the scatter of intelligence is due to heredity, then the negative correlation of family size and intelligence is half attributable to hereditary factors. If a variable X (e.g. intelligence test score) is determined by two factors A and B (e.g. hereditary and environmental factors), then the correlation of X with any other variable Y (e.g. family size) may be due to an association of Y with A or with B or with both A and B together.

The Hypothesis

The hypothesis which is advanced in this paper is that family size has a direct effect on the environmental aspect of mental development. This hypothesis derives from the view that language and words afford a system of symbols which greatly increase the efficiency of abstract thought. Limitation of opportunities for verbal development is therefore likely to exercise a depressive influence on ability to score in a test even of general mental ability. It has been established that the only child enjoys a much greater verbal development than the child from an orphanage, because of greater opportunities of contact with adults and of acquiring adult vocabulary. The large family is considered here as an environment midway between that of the only child and the orphanage. The mere fact of belonging to a large family implies restricted contact with adults and fewer opportunities of acquiring adult habits of speech and thought, a disadvantage which enters into the intelligence test performance of children from large families. If this hypothesis is correct, if this is a factor in the negative correlation of test score and family size—and it is not suggested that it is the only factor —then a reduction in the average size of families will mask any decline in national intelligence which may be occurring. From the point of view of future research one important conclusion would result if the present hypothesis were confirmed: in any comparison of the mean intelligence scores of two generations, such as is strongly urged in the *Report* of the Royal Commission on Population (1949), the advantage would tend to be with the generation with the smaller family units, and some allowance for this would have to be made.

This is the sense in which the phrase "family environment" is used in the title of this paper; it is not concerned with income or nutrition or the number of rooms in the house—though of course these may be important factors—but only with the contact between child and adult, which is on average proportionate to the size of the family, except that in a large family the first and the last perhaps have some advantage over the others. (And, in fact, a tendency towards slightly higher test scores among first- and last-born has been observed.)

A summary of investigations of the language development of children is given by McCarthy (1946), who concluded that language development is affected by age of associates, children who associate most with adults being superior to others: thus only children show a striking superiority in language development, and children from institutions a marked retardation. This finding was based on her own work (1930) on the subject, and was supported by a number of studies reported from Iowa University. A conclusion in accordance with these was that of Smith (1933), that pre-school children use longer sentences and ask more questions when alone with an adult than when in a group of children. Day (1932) and Davis (1937) found a retardation in verbal development among twins; since this retardation was less marked after school attendance began it was suggested that the inferiority of twins to non-twins was due not to any prenatal handicap but to their family environment, in which twins are at first inclined to communicate non-verbally with each other and to have less verbal association with adults. In the Scottish Mental Survey (Mehrotra and Maxwell, 1949), the average test score of twins was slightly below that of non-twins, a phenomenon which may have been associated with a verbal handicap. In view of all these findings, it seemed probable that children from small families would have better opportunities for language development than children from large families, who have relatively less contact with adults and would thus suffer a slight environmental handicap.

Such an influence of family environment on verbal development could reasonably be expected to affect scores in a verbal test of intelligence, merely through the words used in the test. However, the effect may be more direct than this: ability to manipulate verbal symbol seems to play an important part in the process of thinking, and particularly in problem-solving. This is the point of view of Terman (1937), who wrote:

> Language, essentially, is the shorthand of the higher thought processes, and the level at which this shorthand functions is one of the most important determinants of the level of the processes themselves. (p. 5.)

This is not by any means a new idea. It appears in the writings of Dewey (1909), Thomson (1924), Ballard (1934), Watts (1944) and others, even of widely different background: for example, Head (1926), writing on aphasia, noted that speech disturbances sometimes impaired ability to perform mental operations which required the use of symbols. The problem of the relation of language and intelligence is not an easy one to put to the test of experiment, since in most cases verbal ability and general mental ability develop normally side by side. However, in two situations, those of deaf children and bilinguals, an experimental design has been set up by nature and throws light on the problem.

Children who have been deaf from an early age afford one situation in which mental development must occur without the usual accompaniment of language growth. These deaf children who have not learned to use words show retardation in mental development and even in their performance in non-verbal tests of intelligence. This is the general finding: of twelve studies from 1915 onwards, summarized by Pintner, Eisenson and Stanton (1941), all except one found that deaf children were on average mentally retarded. A recent investigation by Blair Hood (1949), using Alexander's Performance Test as a measure of intelligence, did not support this view; but Watts and Slater (1950) have shown that the standardisation of this test is misleading. In Aberdeen, on a small sample, Smith (1952) reported that the mental retardation of deaf children appeared to become progressively more serious as age increased. Pintner and his colleagues also summarized five studies of the language development of the deaf, all of which confirmed the very severe retardation suffered by these children.

Other children whose language development is unusual are the bilinguals whose average performance in verbal intelligence tests is inferior to that of monoglots. Smith (1923), Saer (1923) and others have found this result in Wales, though Barke and Williams (1933, 1938) found no inferiority of bilinguals on a non-verbal test of intelligence. Smith (1948), using a non-verbal test among the Gaelic-speaking population of Lewis, found the average performance of the bilinguals to be below normal. Christophersen (1949) suggested that in the case of monoglots, "after early youth . . . a linguistic 'crystallization' sets in: their speech organs become fixed in certain grooves, and their thoughts become inseparably linked with the words of their mother tongue"; but in the case of a bilingual person his "mental processes are not immediately linked with either of his languages," a theory which "will account for that hesitancy of speech that one sometimes notices in bilinguals." A bilingual person, he suggested, may become as competent as a monoglot if he is prepared to concentrate on one of his languages, as for example Conrad did, until that language becomes the natural medium of his thought.

On the basis of these findings it is suggested that restriction of the normal language growth of children may depress the standard of their performance in an intelligence test.

The hypothesis to be tested then is that a portion of the observed negative correlation between family size and intelligence test score is due to the limiting influence on general mental development exerted by an environmentally restricted development of verbal ability. If this hypothesis were justified it might afford a clue to a partial resolution of the paradoxical results of the Scottish Mental Survey, in which a negative correlation was established but no decline in intelligence observed. If part of the negative correlation were due to the effect of family environment, then a general reduction in the size of families would result in an artificial rise in mean score which might be sufficient to mask a real decline: a genetical loss would nevertheless be occurring in proportion to the extent to which intelligence is inherited and the extent to which the negative correlation is due to the limiting of families by intelligent parents. Other explanations of the situation have, of course, been made—for example, the explaining of the observed rise in score in terms of the test-sophistication of the 1947 children—and such influences as this may well be operating to complicate the situation still further.

Evidence for or against the hypothesis was sought in three ways: firstly, by finding if the method of partial correlation showed a negative correlation between verbal ability and family size independent of any association with general intelligence; secondly, by finding if the correlation between test score and family size differed from test to test when several tests affected in varying degrees by verbal ability were applied to a single group of children; and thirdly, by checking the prediction from the hypothesis that, if verbal intelligence tests were applied to children at different ages, the negative correlation between family size and intelligence test score would be more marked at later ages when the cumulative effect of environment began to show itself.

Partial Correlation

The first test of the hypothesis, then, involved determining whether a negative correlation between verbal ability and family size existed independently of any association with intelligence. The method of partial correlation was applied to the test scores of two large groups each of about 2,500 children. These were children at the stage of transfer from primary to secondary education in Aberdeen. Such transfer groups are approximately equivalent to a cross-section of the child population of the city.

The first of these transfer groups, the 1949 group, numbered 2,709 in all, and for 2,561 of these it was possible to obtain data on size of family, position in the family, and scores in two intelligence tests (Moray House Tests 39 and 40) and a test of English attainment (Moray House English Test 18). This was a 94 per cent coverage of the group. Their ages ranged from 10.5 to 12.10, but more than 90 per cent of them lay between the ages of 11.1 and 12.3, the mean age being 11.7. The mean family size was 3.41.

The 1950 transfer group numbered 2,638 in all, and by giving a second opportunity of testing to those who were absent on the appointed date it was possible to obtain full information on 2,607, or 99 per cent of the total. Their ages ranged from 10.2 to 13.5, but again more than 90 per cent of them lay between 11.1 and 12.3, and the mean age was 11.7. The mean family size was 3.38. The tests used were Moray House Tests 41 and 42, and Moray House English Test 19. The possibility of excluding all those whose ages lay outside a twelve-month range (to make the groups more strictly comparable with the eleven-year-old group of the Scottish Mental Survey) was considered; but it was thought inadvisable because of the fact that test scores were expressed as quotients to eliminate the effect of age, and because such a course would have excluded the brightest and the dullest sections of the group instead of making it more representative.

The tests in this part of the investigation were those used by the Education Authority for its transfer procedure, and so were not altogether suitable for the present purpose. The tests of intelligence were verbal tests, so that to use these for the holding constant of intelligence made likely an under-estimate of the relation between verbal ability and family size. Tests of English attainment were used for the measure of verbal ability; though scores in such tests are corrupted by a schooling factor, they do have a considerable verbal loading. It was clear that a certain negative correlation between the English score and family size would be attributable merely to the dependence of English attainment on intelligence. But if the hypothesis were correct, if the largeness of certain families operated to limit the verbal development of their members, the holding constant of intelligence test score would still leave a negative partial correlation between family size and English score. If, on the other hand, the environmental influence of the size of family were negligible, and if the negative association of intelligence and family size were due only to the limiting of families by intelligent parents, then one would expect no association between family size and English score except such as was due to the correlation of English score and intelligence. In that case the partial correlation would be zero. It is maintained in this study that both causes are at work. If this were so, the result which might be predicted would be that the partial correlation of family size and English score, with intelligence test score held constant, would be substantially smaller than the zero-order coefficient

Table 1.

Means and Standard Deviations of Quotients

1949 TRANFER GROUP 2,561 CASES			1950 TRANSFER GROUP 2,607 CASES		
Test	Mean	S.D.	Test	Mean	S.D.
M.H.T.39 ...	101.37	13.8	M.H.T.41 ...	102.59	13.8
M.H.T.40 ...	106.30	14.8	M.H.T.42 ...	106.31	15.2
M.H.E.18 ...	105.33	15.3	M.H.E.19 ...	103.35	15.6

Figure 1. Mean Test Scores at Different Sizes of Family

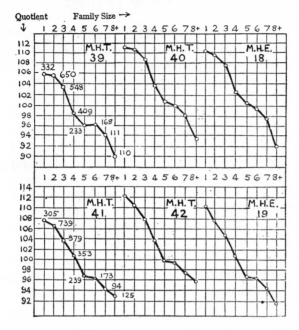

The figures give the number of cases for each group of tests

(due to the second of the causes mentioned above), but would still be negative and significantly different from zero (due to the first of the causes). This prediction was confirmed by the analysis of results.

The means and standard deviations given in Table 1 show that the groups are representative samples.

The mean scores in each test for each size of family were calculated, grouping together all sizes of eight and above because of the smallness of their numbers. The tendency for mean score to drop with increasing size of family can be seen in the results of all the tests, as is shown in Fig. 1.

The same results are expressed as correlation coefficient in Table 2.

Before applying the method of partial correlation a check on linearity of regression was made. The partial correlation coefficients are given in Table 3. All these partial correlations are negative and significantly different from zero. They are, however, substantially smaller than the zero-order coefficients.

Though this first prediction was confirmed there are too many sources of ambiguity in the method of partial correlation for it to be altogether satisfactory; and it was clearly desirable that alternative methods of approach to the problem should be tried to see if further support could be obtained for the hypothesis.

Different Verbal Loadings

In the second part of this investigation a number of tests, depending in varying degrees on verbal ability but otherwise as far as possible comparable with each other, were applied to a single group of children. The argument at this stage was that if the negative correlation of intelligence test score and family size was seriously affected by the family environment operating on verbal development in the manner suggested, the negative correlation would probably be greater with tests much dependent on verbal ability, and would tend to be less with tests more nearly independent of verbal ability, provided that the tests were comparable in other respects. Thus a test of vocabulary should show a relatively large negative correlation with family size; a verbal test of intelligence should show a certain negative correlation with family size; and a non-verbal test of intelligence, being only slightly influenced by family environment, may be expected to show a small negative correlation with family size. If, on the other hand, the negative correlation is relatively independent of this verbal environmental influence the variations in the verbal loadings of the different tests will not be accompanied by parallel variations in the size of the correlation.

Table 2.

Correlation of Family Size and Test Scores

Correlation of family size and:

Verbal intelligence test M.H.T.39 ...	...	...	...	...	—.320	1949
" " " M.H.T.40 ...	...	...	...	...	—.335	Transfer
M.H.T.39 and M.H.T.40 combined ...	...	...	...	...	—.333	Group
English attainment test M.H.E.18 ...	...	...	...	...	—.318	N=2,561
Verbal intelligence test M.H.T.41 ...	...	...	...	...	—.323	1950
" " " M.H.T.42 ...	...	...	...	...	—.334	Transfer
M.H.T.41 and M.H.T.42 combined ...	...	...	...	...	—.334	Group
English attainment test M.H.E.19 ...	...	...	...	...	—.342	N=2,607

Table 3.

Partial Correlation Coefficients

Partial correlation betweent family size and:

				Holding constant:			
M.H.E.18 (English)	...	...	...	M.H.T.39 (Intelligence)	...	...	—.081
" "	...	...	...	M.H.T.40 "	...	...	—.046
" "	...	...	...	M.H.T.39 and M.H.T.40	...	...	—.044
				Number of cases 2,561			
M.H.E.19 (English)	...	...	...	M.H.T.41 (Intelligence)	...	...	—.131
" "	...	...	...	M.H.T.42 "	...	...	—.091
" "	...	...	...	M.H.T.41 and M.H.T.42	...	...	—.109
				Number of cases 2,607			

With the limited facilities available, however, increasing the number of tests necessarily involved reducing the number of subjects tested. Consequently it was decided to apply as wide a variety of tests as possible to a small group which would be a random sample of the population, making sure that the sample was genuinely representative of the population and was fully located and covered by the testing.

The sample selected consisted of all the children in Aberdeen who were born in the month of April 1939—a total of 206. The choice of a single month avoided the necessity of age allowances and made possible the use of raw scores in calculation. The locating of the sample was done through the co-operation of the headmasters, and was checked during personal visits to the schools, against Education Authority records and by personal letters.

Test results were obtained for 198 of these children; and two others, in a special school for the mentally handicapped, whose intelligence quotients were below 50 (Stanford-Binet), were included in the lowest class interval of the distributions of scores, in accordance with the practice of the Scottish Mental Survey. This made the number for whom results were available exactly 200. The missing six were: three children from private schools, one deaf child, one invalid, and one with an irregular school history.

Among the twelve measures which were obtained for this sample of 200, there were four tests of intelligence, two non-verbal—Progressive Matrices (1938), untimed, and Jenkins' Scale of Non-Verbal Intelligence I—and two verbal—Moray House Tests 41 and 42. The vocabulary items of Moray House English Test 19 were scored separately to give an estimate of range of vocabulary; and the remaining measures were of various aspects of scholastic attainment.

The scores in the standardized tests were at first expressed as quotients in accordance with the published norms; but considerable differences emerged between the mean quotients in the four intelligence tests, in spite of the fact that the group was a random sample of the population and all the tests were applied in the same order at the same time, or at nearly the same time. Since correlational analysis of these results was proposed it seemed desirable to impose new normal distributions on the raw scores in all the tests, giving each a mean of 100 and a standard deviation of 15. Means and standard deviations are shown in Table 4: grouping of scores

Table 4.

Means and Standard Deviations of Quotients

Test			OLD QUOTIENTS		NEW QUOTIENTS	
			Mean	S.D.	Mean	S.D.
Progressive Matrices (1938) ...	...	...	102.50	13.0	99.98	14.6
Jenkins' Non-Verbal Scale I	...	...	107.95	14.3	100.05	14.6
Moray House Test 41	...	...	103.55	13.5	99.72	14.8
Moray House Test 42	...	...	108.30	15.4	99.90	14.9
Moray House English Test 19	...	...	104.28	15.5	99.80	14.6
Vocabulary	...	...	—	—	99.72	14.6

has introduced small deviations from the imposed statistics. The mean family size was 3.18 and the standard deviation of family size was 1.90.

Using the new quotients, correlations were calculated between family size and scores in these measures, and are given in Table 5.

Table 5.

Correlations of Family Size and Test Scores

Correlation of family size and:				
Progressive Matrices (1938)	...	...		−.197
Jenkins' Non-Verbal Scale I	...	...		−.249
Moray House Test 41	...	...	...	−.298
Moray House Test 42	...	...	...	−.303
Moray House English Test 19	...	...		−.289
Vocabulary	...	...	...	... |−.286

The main interest in these results lies in the difference in the correlation between family size and intelligence test score with a non-verbal test (Matrices —.197; Jenkins —.249) and that with a verbal test (M.H.T.41) —.298; M.H.T.42 —.303). The significance of these differences cannot be calculated exactly, for the family size measure is discrete; but it was tested by Cochran's formula[4] for a difference between two correlation coefficients based on the same random sample. The difference between the correlation involving the Matrices Test is significantly different at the .05 level from the correlations involving Moray House Tests 41 and 42. None of the other differences reaches the .05 significance level.

For the most part the results are in accordance with the prediction that the non-verbal tests would show a smaller negative correlation with family size than the verbal tests. The Jenkins Test is intermediate between the non-verbal Matrices and the verbal Moray House Tests, perhaps because the instructions in the Jenkins Test are printed in small type and difficult to interpret. This explanation is supported by the comparatively high correlation between the Jenkins Test and the Vocabulary Test of .73, compared with a correlation of .56 between Matrices and Vocabulary.

However, there are at least two alternative explanations of why the correlation involving the Matrices Test should be smaller than the others:

(i) It might be due to differences in reliability between the tests: unreliability of any of the tests would depress the correlation of that test with any other measure;

(ii) It might be due to differences in validity between the tests: it might be argued that the "intelligence" measured by the Matrices Test is a different type of ability from that involved in the Moray House Tests, and that the reason for the differences in the correlations is that the tests are measuring different abilities.

The first of these possibilities can be tested quite simply by means of correction for attentuation: such correction had virtually no effect on the difference between the correlations. The second is rather difficult to test, but a factor analysis of eight of the measures made possible a comparison of the "g" loadings of the various tests. From the results there seemed to be no basis for the suggestion that the differences between the correlations could be attributed to differences in the "g" loadings of the tests.

There remains the second part of the prediction, that the vocabulary test would show the highest negative correlation with family size. This was not supported by the results: all the correlations involving verbal tests, both verbal intelligence and English attainment, are of approximately the same magnitude. The vocabulary test, however, was shorter than any of the other tests. In case it might be thought that the test form of all these measures was introducing spurious results the correlation was calculated between family size and marks in a composition written by these children, and was —.253.

Different Ages

A third method of testing the hypothesis is to find if the age at which the intelligence test is administered affects the size of the correlation. A preliminary prediction may be made that the negative correlation, if it is subject to marked environmental influence, will tend to be greater at later ages when the cumulative effect of environment begins to show itself.

Ideally to test this prediction one should apply the same test to the same children at different ages. However, at different ages the children would score on different parts of a test and therefore would in effect be taking different tests, although these might be printed all in a single booklet. Consequently the need to use different tests at different ages is a weakness in the design of this part of the investigation. The performance of a small number of children was studied over a period of years; and the results from this small group were checked against the testing of large numbers at different ages.

Scores in verbal intelligence tests at ages seven, nine and eleven were obtained for 178 of the 200 children in the random sample described above. The test at age seven was Moray House Picture Test; at age nine, Schonell's Essential Intelligence Test. These were compared with the results of Moray House Test 41 at age eleven. The means and standard deviation given in Table 6 show that the group is representative of the population.

The intercorrelations of the tests were: between Moray House Picture Test and Schonell's Test, .738; between Schonell's Test and Moray House Test 41, .856; and between Moray House Picture Test and Moray House Test 41, .748.

The correlations of family size and intelligence test score at the different ages were: at age seven, —.209; at age nine, —.226; at age eleven,

Table 6.

Means and Standard Deviations

Small group:	N	Age	Mean	S.D.
Moray House Picture Test	178	7	99.22	14.5
Schonell's Essential Test		9	101.19	16.8
Moray House Test 41		11	102.79	13.8
Family size		7	3.00	1.93
" "		9	3.15	1.94
" "		11	3.28	1.94
Large age-groups:				
Moray House Picture Test	1,236	7	104.50	15.5
Schonell's Essential Test	1,270	9	104.63	17.1
Moray House Test 39 ... ... ⎱			101.37	13.8
Moray House Test 40 ... ... ⎰	2,561	11 ⎰	106.30	14.9
Moray House Test 41 ... ... ⎱			102.59	13.8
Moray House Test 42 ... ... ⎰	2,607	11 ⎰	106.31	15.2
Family size	1,236	7	2.77	1.54
" "	1,270	9	3.00	1.70
" "	2,561	11	3.41	1.87
" "	2,607	11	3.38	1.87

—.289. The correlation is smallest at age seven and increases as the children grow older. Because of the small number of cases the differences are not significant.

Significant differences emerged from the testing of large groups at different ages. In Aberdeen a representative group of about 1,200 children enter the primary schools every six months. Moray House Picture Test was applied to one such group of 1,236 children at age seven; and Schonell's Essential Intelligence Test to one group of 1,270 children at age nine. These two groups were compared with four groups tested at age eleven plus and described previously as the 1949 and 1950 Transfer Groups. This eleven-year-old group numbered 5,168 in all, 2,561 tested on Moray House Tests 39 and 40, and 2,607 on Moray House Tests 41 and 42. The means and standard deviations given in Table 6 show that all the groups are comparable and representative samples.

In the large age-groups the correlation of intelligence test score and family size was: at age seven, —.256; at age nine, —.287; and at age eleven, —.333. These coefficients are all larger than the corresponding coefficients in the small group, but they repeat the same pattern. The negative correlation is greater when the test is applied at a later age. The difference between the correlation at age seven and at age eleven is significant at the .01 level.

It is difficult to see why the coefficients from these large groups should be greater than the corresponding results from the small group. Vernon (1951) reported a correlation of —.34 between intelligence and family size in a group of 10,000 recruits aged 18: however, the tests in that investigation were both verbal and non-verbal tests, so that his results are not directly comparable with these.

The differences between the correlations at age seven and at age eleven may be due to any of three causes. They may be due to:

(i) Differences on the *size* side of the correlation, because the families are most nearly complete at age eleven;
(ii) Differences on the *test* side of the correlation, either (*a*) differences in test reliability, or (*b*) differences in validity;
(iii) Genuine differences in the degree of relationship, through the increasing effect of environmental influence.

It is only in the small group of 178 cases that the nature of the data allows a precise testing of these alternative explanations. The first alternative, attributing the result to differences in the completeness of families, may be tested easily. The family size at age eleven is the nearest available estimate of the completed size, and if the test scores at age seven and nine are measured against family size at age eleven, this will eliminate differences on the family-size side of the correlation.

The result of such a process was to raise the correlation at age seven from —.209 to —.225; to raise the correlation at age nine from —.226 to —.232; while the correlation at age eleven remained —.289. This brings the coefficients slightly closer, but the differences remain.

The second alternative explanation, attributing the results to differences in test reliability, may also be tested simply. Correction for attenuation, using the reliability coefficients given in the test manuals, was applied to the revised coefficients which have just been obtained. The result was to raise the coefficient at age seven to —.230, at age nine to —.242, and at age eleven to —.293. This has very little effect on the differences between the correlations.

The question of differences in validity is not so easy to handle. Moray House Test 41 was selected for this comparison because it appears to resemble the other tests more closely. It is certainly similar to Schonell's Essential Test; and it differs from Moray House Picture Test principally in that the latter does not require reading ability, although the oral instructions of the Picture Test are just as verbal as those of the other tests. It is clear from results mentioned earlier in this paper that if a non-verbal test had been chosen at age eleven for this comparison the correlation between test score and family size would have been much smaller. However, it is the verbal element that is of chief interest in this investigation.

It remains to be said that since all these calculations were based on the 178 cases of the small group the numbers are too small to yield significant differences at any point. Significant differences might be expected to emerge from numbers as large as those in the age-groups; but since these are separate samples of the population it is not possible to make an accurate calculation of the effect of incomplete families. A new but rather complicated method of estimating the degree of incompleteness of family among an age-group of children (which will be described elsewhere) suggests that the effect of incomplete families in the large age-groups is approximately the same as that found in the small group. If this assumption is valid, and corrections for incomplete families and unreliability of tests are applied to the correlation coefficients obtained from the large age-groups, the resulting corrected coefficients at age seven and at age eleven show a difference which is still significant at the .05 level.

The disposal of two of the alternative explanations suggests that the third explanation is the correct one, that the differences between the negative correlations of intelligence test score and family size at different ages are due to the cumulative effect of environmental influences.

Summary and Conclusions

A hypothesis has been advanced that the environment of the large family—the limited amount of contact between parent and child, and the consequent retardation of the child's verbal development—tended to depress the environmental component of a child's test score. This was based on previous work on the comparison of orphange children and only children, on studies of bilinguals, deaf children and twins. It was not suggested that this cause alone operated to produce the negative correlation of family size and intelligence test score, but only that it contributes to the correlation to an extent sufficient with other influences to mask any possible downward trend in national intelligence and to prevent the use of test scores of age-groups of children for predicting future intelligence levels in the nation.

Predictions from this hypothesis were tested by three methods: by partial correlation of family size and verbal ability with intelligence held constant; by correlation of family size and several tests with different verbal loadings; and by correlation of family size and intelligence at different ages. The fact that the hypothesis has survived these three tests does not, of course, mean that it is correct: there are still other possible explanations of the results. But it seems that part of (though not all) the negative correlation of family size and intelligence tets score may be attributed to an environmental influence of the size of family on verbal development and through it on general mental development. At the same time, at each stage of the investigation it seemed clear that the whole of the negative correlation could not be explained in terms of this environmental influence. Others who have worked on this problem on a nation-wide scale do not deny a certain amount of environmental influence, and would probably wish attention to be drawn to the substantial negative correlation which remains when the environmental influence is allowed for. Such remaining negative correlation, it would seem, must have the effect of depressing the trend of national intelligence, a tendency which may easily be masked by environmental influences.

NOTES

1. A paper read at a Members' Meeting of the *Eugenics Society* on January 21st, 1953.
2. The Education Authority is not in any way responsible for this investigation or its conclusions.
3. Scottish Mental Survey, 1949; Cattell, 1950.
4. Lindquist, 1940, p. 128.

REFERENCES

Ballard (1934), *Thought and Language*. University of London Press.
Barke (1933), *Brit. J. Educ. Psychol.*, 3, 237–50.
Barke and Williams (1938), *Brit. J. Educ. Psychol.*, 8, 63–77.
Cattell (1950), *Eug. Rev.*, 42, 136–48.
Christophersen (1949), *Bilingualism*. Methuen.
Davis (1937), *Inst. Child Welfare Monog. Series,* 14. University of Minnesota Press.
Day (1932), *Child Development*, 3, 179–99.
Dewey (1909), *How We Think*. Heath.
Head (1926), *Collected Papers on Aphasia and Kindred Affection*. Cambridge University Press.
Hood (1940), *Brit. J. Educ. Psychol.*, 19, 210–19.
Lindquist (1940), *Statistical Analysis in Educational Research*. Houghton Mifflin.
McCarthy (1930), *Inst. Child Welfare Monog. Series,* 4. University of Minnesota Press.
McCarthy (1946), Chapter X, *Manual of Child Psychology* (editor, Carmichael). Wiley.
Mehrotra and Maxwell (1949), *Poulation Studies,* 3, 295–302.
Pintner, Eisenson and Stanton (1941), *The Psychology of the Handicapped Child*. Crofts.
Royal Commission on Population (1949), *Report*. Cmd., 7695. H.M.S.O.
Saer (1923), *Brit. J. Psychol.*, 14, 25–38.
Scottish Mental Survey (1949), *The Trend of Scottish Intelligence*. University of London Press.
Smith, C. (1948), *Mental Testing of Hebridean Children in Gaelic and English*. University of London Press.
Smith, D. (1952), *Brit. J. Educ. Psychol.*, 22, 71–2.
Smith, F. (1923), *Brit. J. Psychol.*, 13, 271–82.
Terman and Merrill (1937), *Measuring Intelligence*. Harrap.
Thomson (1924), *Instinct, Intelligence and Character*. Allen & Unwin.
Vernon (1951), *Eug. Rev.*, 43, 125–37.
Watts (1944), *The Language and Mental Development of Children*. Harrap.
Watts and Slater (1950), *The Allocation of Primary School Leavers to Courses of Secondary Education*. Newnes.

24 Social Class and Linguistic Development: A Theory of Social Learning

BASIL BERNSTEIN

AN EXAMINATION of the literature of both sociology and psychology shows that socio-cultural factors can depress or raise the level of educational performance. It is clear that children from extreme social groups within societies are exposed from an early age to separate and distinct patterns of learning before their formal education begins. These patterns are progressively reinforced as the child develops. However, when one inquires through what process the growing child internalizes and synthesizes the various influences to which he has been exposed, the answer is no longer clear. It would seem that the social conditions that help to determine differential learning and orientation are so complex and interrelated that to ask what is the most significant variable is like asking which loose end will unravel a ball of knotted string. Those engaged in the practical business of education want an answer relevant to their day-to-day problems, and whilst the sociology of education is concerned with rather more than the vicissitudes of the teaching situation, the subject should be capable of showing the direct relevance of its theories and concepts to the abyss between the chalk-talk and pupil.

On a more formal level, the problem is this: How does a given social structure become part of individual experience, what is the *main* process through which this is achieved, and what are the educational implications? It is proposed that forms of spoken language in the process of their learning, elicit, reinforce, and generalize distinct types of relationships with the environment and thus create particular dimensions of significance. Speech marks out what is relevant—affectively, cognitively, and socially—and experience is transformed by that which is made relevant. A derivation from these propositions will be examined in some detail: that certain linguistic forms involve for the speaker a loss or an acquisition of skills—both cognitive and social—which are strategic for educational and occupational

Based on "Some Sociological Determinants of Perception," *British Journal of Sociology*, IX (June, 1958), 159–74, with the permission of the author and the publisher, Routledge and Kegan Paul, London.

success, and these forms of language use are culturally not individually determined.

It is of interest to begin with the effects of special environments on language skills. Studies of language development of institutionalized children, by Little and Williams (1937), Williams and McFarlane (1937), Fleming (1942), Goldfarb (1943ᵃ, 1943ᵇ, 1945), Brodbeck and Irwin (1946), Moore (1947), and Roudinesco and Appell (1950),[1] indicate that these children are often grossly retarded in vocabulary, complexity of sentence structure, and type and power of abstraction. Kellmer Pringle and Tanner (1958)[2] report that when two groups of preschool children were matched for age, sex, I.Q., and home/background the group who attended a day nursery school were found to be in advance, on all quantitative measures of language, of the group in a residential nursery. She further found (Kellmer Pringle and Tanner 1958ᵇ)[3] that in a group of institutionalized children the extent of the backwardness in language was greater than that found in any other aspect of development. A study of particular interest here is one by Dawe (1942),[4] who planned a training scheme with a group of orphaned children, matching eleven pairs of children for age, sex, I.Q., and school group. Gains in the trained group were reflected in an increase in average I.Q. from 80.6 points to 94.8 points. Although the relation between language ability and I.Q. is one of complex reciprocity, these studies indicate that the functional level of performance may be independent of the I.Q. in an environment detrimental to the development of language skills.

Linguistic differences—other than dialect—occur in the normal social environment, and status groups may be distinguished by their forms of language use. This difference is most marked where the gap between the socio-economic levels is very great. There have been many studies of children aimed at measuring this difference: Descoeudres (1921), Stern (1930), McCarthy (1930), Buhler (1931), Day (1932), Davis (1937), Schulman and Havighurst (1947), and Templin (1957).[5] Hurrell (1957)[6] did not find major differences in his study of oral and written language, but he found a small but significant correlation between the number of subordinate clauses and occupational status. The complexity of relationships symbolized were not adequate for the showing of differences between the status groups. Sampson (1956),[7] in a study of children between eighteen and thirty months, concluded that there was some indication of the contribution of the social environment to speech development. The important linguistic differences seem to be concentrated in the articulation of vowels, median and final consonants, the length of remarks verbalized, the degree of complexity of the verbalization, and vocabulary of recognition at the higher age ranges.

It has been found that there is little correlation between tests of early sensory-motor intelligence and intelligence as measured later by verbal symbolic tests. However, Catalano and McCarthy (1952)[8] found a correlation of 0.41 between consonant/vowel frequency ratio in infancy and later I.Q. scores; furthermore, consonant types in infancy correlated 0.45 with I.Q. at four years of age. It is of interest to place against this suggestive finding the work of Irwin (1948[a], 1948[b]),[9] who compared the effect of family occupational status on sound types and sound frequency in infants. Irwin found that the mastery of speech sounds for the low- and high-status groups proceeded at different rates. Significant differences in favor of the high-status group were found for the last year of infancy, and the infants of the high-status group had a greater sensitivity to phonome frequency after the first one and a half years. This seems to be a highly promising new field of research, perhaps elucidating the role of the social environment in very early learning.

Very interesting and highly stimulating work has been done by Nisbet (1953),[10] who investigated the effect of family size on the I.Q. on a sample of five thousand Aberdeen children. One of his conclusions was that the environment of a large family constitutes a handicap to verbal development and that this verbal retardation affects general mental development. It follows that part of the negative correlation between family size and I.Q. may be attributed to the depressing effect exerted by the environment on language ability. In a later study, Scott and Nisbet (1955)[11] reported that the negative correlation between size of a sibship and I.Q. was lower for non-verbal than for verbal tests, which confirms that the above environmental effects may affect test performance well into adulthood. It should be remembered that family size increases the lower the socio-economic level. These conclusions of Nisbet are reinforced by the work of Mitchell (1956)[12] in a very ingenious and important paper. Mitchell compared the factorial organization of mental abilities for a well-defined high- and low-status group. He found that the organization of mental abilities was much less differentiated for the low-status group. The roles played by verbal-meaning and word-fluency factors in the factor pattern suggested that this lack of differentiation was at least partly the result of the increased saturation of the general factor (g) with verbal components. This means that verbal skill for the low-status group is an extremely generalized function and permeates all mental tasks.

Bernstein (1958, 1960)[13] gave a group verbal–non-verbal intelligence test to over 370 working-class youth matched for education and occupation. The results showed that language scores were grossly depressed in relation to scores on the higher ranges of the non-verbal test. The second study included a comparison with a public-school group, and the relationship found between the verbal and non-verbal test for the working-class was not found in the public-school group. All language scores of the working-class group with the exception of a very few—fell with the *average* range of the verbal test. Educational performance as reflected in class work was related to the *verbal* score. Venables (1959)[14] compared the verbal and non-verbal intelligence test scores of a group of technical-college, day-release students (National Certificate and Craft) with those of university students. Only 8 per cent of the technical and 1.5 per cent of the craft students came up to the university standard in the verbal test. On the non-verbal test, 40 per cent of the technical and 12 per cent of the craft students were of equal intelligence to the university students.

The evidence from these language studies indicates that the level of linguistic skill may be independent of the potential I.Q., certainly independent of measured non-verbal I.Q., and that grossly different environments affect aspects of language structure and vocabulary. It is also clear that linguistic performance is basic to educational success. It is suggested that the measurable interstatus linguistic differences between the lower working-class and middle-class, rather than simply reflecting differences in potential capacity, result from entirely different modes of speech, which are dominant and typical of these strata. It is proposed that two distinct forms of language use arise because the organization of these two strata is such that different emphases are placed on language potential. Once the emphasis or stress is placed, then the resulting forms of speech progressively orient the speakers to distinct types of relationships of objects and persons. The role intelligence plays is to enable the speaker to exploit more successfully the possibilities symbolized by the socially conditioned linguistic forms. There are exceptions to this linguistic determinism, which arise under special limiting physiological and psychological conditions. It is suggested that the typical and dominant mode of speech of the middle class is one where speech becomes an object of special perceptual activity and one where a theoretical attitude is developed toward the structural possibilities of sentence organization. This speech mode is one where the structure and syntax are relatively difficult to predict for any one individual and where the formal possibilities of sentence organization are used to clarify meaning and make it explicit. This mode of speech will be called a *formal* language.

By contrast, the speech mode of the lower working class may be distinguished by the rigidity of the syntax and the limited and restricted use of structural possibilities for sentence organization. Thus, these speech elements are *highly* predictable for any one speaker. It is a form of relatively condensed speech in which certain meanings are restricted and the possibility of their elaboration is reduced. Although any one content of this speech is not predictable, the class of the content, the structural organization, and syntax are highly predictable. This use of speech will be called a *public* language. The individual, when he speaks a *public* language, operates within a speech mode in which individual selection and permutation are severely restricted; whilst in the case of a *formal* language, the speaker is able to make a highly individual selection and permutation. I am not arguing that a *formal* language speaker always does this. I am simply stating that the possibility exists. A *formal* language facilitates the verbal elaboration of subjective intent, sensitivity to the implications of separateness and difference, and points to the possibilities inherent in a complex conceptual hierarchy for the organization of experience. It is suggested that this is not so for members of the lower working class, *who are restricted to a public language,* which, although allowing for a vast range of possibilities, provides a speech form that discourages the speaker from verbally elaborating subjective intent, and progressively orients him to descriptive rather than analytic concepts. It limits the type of stimuli to which the speaker learns to respond.

Fundamental to this paper is the assertion that a middle-class child learns *both* these linguistic modes and uses them according to the social context, whereas a lower working-class child is restricted to a *public* language. A *public* language will occur in any social structure that maximizes identifications with others at the cost of the significance of individuated differences. Thus, approximations to a *public* language will be associated with the peer group of children and adolescents (irrespective of class), combat units in the armed services, criminal subcultures and rural groups.

The connections between the two modes of speech, social class, and educational performance will now be traced, although the major emphasis of the analysis will be given to the implications for a group *restricted* to a *public* language.

The child in the middle-class and associated levels is socialized within a formally articulated structure. Present decisions affecting the growing child are governed by their efficacy in attaining distant ends, affectually and cognitively regarded. Behavior is modified by, and oriented to, an explicit set of goals and values, which create a more stable system of rewards and punishments, although the psychological implications of this may vary from one family to another. The future is conceived in direct relation to the educational and emotional life of the child. Consequently, the child grows up in an ordered rational structure, in which his total experience is organized from an early age. Within middle-class and associative levels, direct expressions of feeling, in particular feelings of hostility, are discouraged. The word *mediates* between the expression of feeling and its approved social recognition, that is, a value is placed upon the verbalization of feeling. This is so in all societies, but the important determining factor here is the organization of the words and the type of language use; not necessarily the size of the vocabulary, but the degree to which the social emphasis on an aspect of the language structure mediates the relation between thought and feeling. Language exists in relation to a desire to express and communicate; consequently, the mode of a language structure—the way in which words and sentences are related—induces a particular form of the structuring of feeling and so the very means of interaction and response to the environment.

> From this standpoint language facilities and language barriers are of the utmost importance and must be studied in their inter-play with a host of other factors that make for ease or difficulty of transmission of ideas and patterns of behaviour. Furthermore the sociologist is necessarily interested in the symbolic significance in a social sense of the linguistic differences which appear in any large community (Sapir, 1946).[16]

Sapir goes on to say:

> Peculiar modes of pronunciation, characteristic turns of phrase, slangy forms of speech, occupational terminologies of all sorts—these are so many symbols of the manifold ways in which society arranges itself and are of crucial importance for the understanding of the development of individual and social attitudes.

Again: "Language is heuristic . . . in the much more far reaching sense that its forms pre-determine for us certain modes of observation and interpretation."[17]

When a middle-class mother says to her child, "I'd rather you made less noise, darling," the child will tend to obey because previous disobedience after this point has led to expression of disapproval or perhaps other punitive measures. The operative words in this sentence, which the middle-class child responds to, are "rather" and "less." The child has learned to become sensitive to this form of sentence and the many possible sentences in this universe of discourse. The words "rather" and "less" are understood, when used in this situation, as directly translatable cues for immediate response on the part of the middle-class child. However, if the same statement were made to a child from the family of an unskilled worker it would not be understood as containing the same imperative cues for response. "Shut up!" may contain a more appropriate set of cues.[18] Of course, the last statement is meaningful to a middle-class child, but what it is important to stress is the fact that the middle-class child, has learned to be able to respond to both statements, and both are differentially discriminated within a finely articulated world of meaning. We are discussing two modes of language; the working-class child has only learned to respond to one, and so although he may understand both, he will not differentiate effectively between the two. Further, if the first statement is made by a middle-class person to a working-class child, the child will translate it into "Shut up" and will relate the difference between the statements to the different social levels. What he will not have, and what he cannot respond to directly, is the different language structure of the first sentence. The working-class child has to translate and thus mediate middle-class language structure through the logically simpler language structure of his own class to make it personally meaningful. Where he cannot make this translation he fails to understand and is left puzzled.

The linguistic relationship between mother and child in the middle class is such that the personal qualification of the mother, the "I" of the mother, the way she reflects upon and organizes her responses to the environment (including herself) will primarily be through the verbal rather than the expressive aspect of the communication. Fine changes in word position and sentence structure signal important changes in states of feeling. The early linguistic relationship between mother and child is essentially one which maximizes cognitive and affective differentiation and discrimination, rather than affective inclusiveness and identity. The speech marks out a pattern of stimuli to which the child adapts, and in the learning of this pattern his perception is organized, structured, and reinforced. The adequacy of his socialization is revealed every time he speaks; in this way the vehicle of communication conditions his behavior to a wide variety of contexts. The child's responses are rewarded or punished until the child is able to regulate his own behavior independent of the adult model. The child learns his social structure and introjects it from the very beginnings of speech. This process of subordinating behavior to verbally elaborated meanings will progressively become the major instrument by which the growing child becomes self-regulating. (Luria and Yudovich 1959).[19] The *type of self-regulation achieved increasingly depends on the speech form.*

It is important to note that initially in the middle-class child's life it is not the type of word or range of vocabulary that is decisive, but the fact that he or she is sensitized to a particular *organization* of words and structural connections, which become the major medium for the expression of difference and separateness. It is the verbally differentiated "I" of the mother, to which the child progressively turns, and in so doing learns to respond to and emit distinctive linguistic signals that symbolize an individuated experience. In this process of language learning many elements of development are acquired. Affect is differentiated, made specific, and stabilized by being linked by language to a *wide* range of referents; and cognition is modified by the character of these referents. Such development inhibits the direct communication of affect, and so of impulse behavior. A way is open for the control of behavior through verbal means, which maximizes the possibility of rational ordering and manipulation. At the same time, sensitivity to a distinctive form of social relationship is engendered. Significant aspects of the social relationship will be primarily signalled by structural changes in the speech, in association with a particular form of expressive symbolism. Expressive symbolism will be such that finely graduated affect is employed to distinguish meanings within and between speech sequences. Simply, affect is transformed by the speech process, and the speech process offers the possibility of releasing individual differences through its structure. This process is reinforced every time the child speaks to an adult model. A tension is created between the child and his environment to induce speech that is designed to characterize relatively precisely that which initiated the utterance. Thus, the awareness of separateness and difference is intensified, and with this, the significance of objects is increased. A feed-back relationship between the effect of the mode of designation and that which is designated produces its own dynamic. An orientation to *seeking, exploring, and stabilizing* relationships is induced. The problem for the child, *from an early age,* progressively shifts from the word as referent (a matter of vocabulary) to *relationships* within and between referents. As Luria (1960)[20] has pointed out, speech does not merely indicate correspondencies in the environment, but it isolates, abstracts, and generalizes perceived signals and relates them to certain categories. This orientation is guided and regulated by a speech model that continuously makes available to the child a linguistic structure that facilitates this shift, *at an early age,* from substance to process. A dynamic interaction is set up: the pressure to verbalize affects in an individuated way and the implications of the speech structure combine to decide the nature of the cues to which the child responds and so progressively create an orientation to a particular order of learning.

The affective tension to verbalize intent and make it explicit, plus the means whereby this becomes possible, extends the system of relationships within which the child operates; it exposes him to a whole range of potential learning and so brings about an increase in cognitive and affective discrimination. When considerations of subjective intent are made relevant and are relatively well developed, the number of referents that condition the response of one individual to another is greatly increased. A heightened sensitivity to the motivation of self and others facilitates the development of a low guilt threshold. Thus, the rational control and manipulation of *induced* guilt will be a major means available to the middle-class mother for disciplining the child. These means reinforce the individuating process, and transfer attention from consequence, or result, to intent (Koln 1959[a] 1959[b]),[21] from the act, to the processes underlying the act. It is important to remember that all the behavior so far considered is triggered initially, and maintained primarily, through the developing linguistic relationship— before the child reaches the school, before the formal demands of the social structure are made.

One of the aims of the middle-class family is to produce a child oriented to certain values but individually differentiated within them. The child is born into an environment where he is seen and responded to as an individual with his own rights, that is, he has a specific social status. This early process of individuation is accomplished by two important factors: the scrupulous observation of the child by the parents so that the very fine stages of development and the emergence of new patterns of behavior are the object of attention and comment; together with recognition and communication in a language structure where personal qualifications are significantly used and which the child learns to use in response. The child's relation to the environment is such that his range and expression of discriminating verbal responses is fostered by the social structure from the beginning. A virtuous circle is set up which is continuously reinforced, for the mother will elaborate and expand the embryonic personal qualificatory statements that the child makes. It would follow that the greater the differentiation of the child's experience, the greater his ability to differentiate and conceptualize objects in his environment. This, of course, is part of the socializing process of any child, but it is the *mode of established relationships* that is of decisive importance, because the mode determines the levels of conceptualization possible. Different children will be able to benefit more from this environment as a result of other factors, e.g., specifically psychological factors, but the means of utilizing and exploiting formal educational facilities are provided.

The school is an institution where every item in the present is finely linked to a distant future, and in consequence there is no serious clash of expectations between the school and the middle-class child. The child's developed time-span of anticipation allows the present activity to be related to a future and this is meaningful. There is little conflict of values between the teacher and child, and even more importantly the child is predisposed to accept and respond to the language structure of communication. The school aims at assisting the development of consciousness of self and cognitive and emotional discrimination, and it develops and encourages mediate relationships. There is, in the child, a desire to use and manipulate words in a personal qualifying or modifying way, which together combine to reduce the problem of teaching of English—reading, spelling, writing. The middle-class child is predisposed toward the ordering of *symbolic* relationships and more importantly, *imposing order* and seeing new relationships. His level of curiosity is high. There is a conformity to authority and an acceptance of the role of the teacher, irrespective of psychological relationships to his personality. (This is not to say that at times feelings of rebellion will not appear.) The middle-class child is capable of manipulating the two languages—the language between social equals (peer groups), which approximates to a *public* language, and a *formal* language. This leads to appropriateness of behavior in a wide range of social circumstances. Finally, the school is an important and socially approved means whereby the developing child can enhance his self-respect. Thus, the social structure of the school, the means and ends of education, create a framework that the middle-class child is able to accept, respond to, and exploit.

*   *   *

The lower working-class family structure is less formally organized than that of the middle-class in relation to the development of the child. Although the authority within the family is explicit, the values that it expresses do not give rise to the carefully ordered universe—spatial and temporal—

of the middle-class child. The exercise of authority is not related to a stable system of rewards and punishments but may often appear arbitrary. The specific character of long-term goals tends to be replaced by more general notions of the future, in which chance, a friend, or a relative plays a greater part than the rigorous working out of connections. Thus, present, or near present, activities have greater value than the relation of the present activity to the attainment of a distant goal. The system of expectancies, or the time-span of anticipation, is shortened, and this creates different sets of preferences, goals, and dissatisfactions. This environment limits the perception of the developing child of and in time. Present gratifications or present deprivations become absolute gratifications or absolute deprivations, for there exists no developed time continuum upon which present activity can be ranged. Relative to the middle classes, the postponement of present pleasure for future gratification is found difficult. By implication, a more volatile patterning of affectual and expressive behavior will be found in the working classes.

In the lower working class, the linguistic relationship between mother and child is of a different order. It is essentially a verbal form, where, initially, personal qualifications are made through *expressive* symbolism; that is non-verbally, or through the possibilities of a limiting language structure. The child's relationship to the mother is of a direct, immediate nature. His strategic referent is not her language, for the personal qualification, the "I" of the working-class mother, will primarily be signalled by expressive symbolism that has no reference other than that to itself. Briefly, *subjective intent is not verbally explicit or elaborated.* The child early learns to respond to, and make responses to, cues that are immediately relevant. Thus, it is a form of communication that maximizes the direct experience of affective inclusiveness rather than verbally conditioned emotional and cognitive differentiation. The working-class child is sensitive to a form of language use quite distinct from the middle-class child's usage.[22] The characteristics of the language use are:

1) Short, grammatically simple, often unfinished sentences with a poor syntactical form.
2) Simple and repetitive use of conjunctions (so, then, and, because).
3) Little use of subordinate clauses used to break down the initial categories of the dominant subject.
4) Inability to hold a formal subject through a speech sequence, thus facilitating a dislocated informational content.
5) Rigid and limited use of adjectives and adverbs.
6) Infrequent use of impersonal pronouns as subjects of conditional clauses or sentences, e.g., "one."
7) Frequent use of statements where the reason and the conclusion are confounded to produce a categoric utterance.

8) A large number of statements and phrases that signal a requirement for the previous speech sequence to be reinforced— "Wouldn't it," "You see," "Just fancy." This process is termed "sympathetic circularity."

9) Individual selection from a group of idiomatic sequences will frequently occur.

10) *The individual qualification is implicit in the sentence organization: it is a language of implicit meaning.*

Some of these characteristics will occur at certain times in any form of language use, but the term *public* language is reserved for a form of communication in which all the characteristics are found. It is possible to speak of approximations to a *public* language to the extent that other characteristics do not occur (see *formal* language).[15] These characteristics interact cumulatively and developmentally reinforce each other; thus, the effect of any one depends on the presence of the others. This language use is not necessarily the result of a limited vocabulary but arises out of a sensitivity to a way of organizing and responding to experience. Thus, two children of four, one of whom comes from an unskilled or semiskilled home and the other from a middle-class home, might share a similar vocabulary but the way they relate the words they know will show differences.[23]

The short, grammatically simple, syntactically poor sentence, which is the typical unit of a *public* language, does not facilitate the communication of ideas and relationships requiring a precise formulation. This form of language use is continuously reinforced from the very beginnings of speech, and as the child learns no other possibility, subjectively, he has little or no experience of inadequate characterization. In fact, when a more appropriate formulation is pointed out to the user of a *public* language the latter may insist that this is precisely *what he meant*. The reformulation represents a second order characterization (that of a *formal language*), which is alien to the original speaker who will attempt to reduce the second order to the first. When this cannot be done, the second order will be considered unnecessary, irrelevant, perhaps silly, or the hearer will be bewildered.[24]

Because of a simple sentence construction, and the fact that a *public* language does not permit the use of conjunctions—which serve as important logical distributors of meaning and sequence—a *public* language will be one in which logical modification and stress can only be crudely rendered linguistically.[25] This necessarily affects the length and type of the completed thought.[26] Verbal planning functions are reduced. As there is a limited and rigid use of adjectives and adverbs, individual qualifications of objects (nouns) and individual modifications of processes (adverbs) will be severely reduced. Because the choice is restricted, the adjectives and adverbs function as *social counters,* through which the individual qualifications will be made. This drastically reduces the verbal elaboration of the qualification, which is given meaning by *expressive* symbolism (Miller and Swanson, 1960).[27]

Frequently, a statement of fact is used both as a reason and a conclusion; the reason is confounded with the conclusion to produce a categoric statement. The categoric statement would come at a different point in a behavioral sequence, if the categoric statement were part of a *formal* language. However, in a *public* language where this confounding feature frequently occurs, the authority or legitimacy for the statement will reside in the form of the social relationship which is non-verbally present (e.g., by a parent to a child; by a leader to a gang member), rather than in reasoned principles.[28] The categoric statement is used in order to bring about the immediate termination of behavior or the immediate initiating of new behavior. When this form of communication takes place between parent and child the reasons for the required change of behavior are rarely or only briefly given, and so a possible range of behavior, and, more importantly, learning will not occur. Equally as important as the cognitive implications are the social implications. For, if this categoric statement is to be challenged, as the reason *is* the authority conferred upon the person, the challenge immediately gives rise to another typical construction, "Because I tell you," "Because I'm your father." The challenger immediately attacks the authority or legitimacy, which is an attribute of the form of the relationship, and this brings the social relationship into one of an affective type. However, when a *formal* language is used, reasons tend to be separated from conclusions. The reasons can be challenged as inadequate or inappropriate, which may initiate a second set of reasons or a development of the original set. With a *formal* language, the relationship to authority is mediated by a rationality, and the final resort to the categoric statement will come at a different point in the behavioral sequence and possibility in a different situation, depending on the implicatons of the reasons given to support the conclusion. The frequency of, and dependency upon, the categoric statement in a *public* language, reinforces the personal at the expense of the logical, limits the range of behavior and learning, and conditions types of reaction and sensitivity toward authority.

A *public* language is one that contains a large number of idiomatic, traditional phrases, from which the individual chooses. Instead of an individual learning to create a language use, within which he can *select* to mediate his individual feelings, a *public*-language user tends to attach his feelings to social counters or tags that maximise the solidarity of the social relationships at the cost of the logical structure of the communication and the specificity of the feeling. For traditional phrases, idioms, etc., tend to operate on a low casual level of generality, in which descriptive, concrete, visual, and tactile symbols are employed aimed at maximizing the emotive rather than the logical impact. In a *public* language, the individual qualification creates a language of implicit meaning.[29] The individual qualification will be made primarily through expressive symbolism or through a selection from the possibilities inherent in a *public* language, which is tantamount to saying that it rarely occurs at all via the language; for the *public* language is primarily a means of making *social* not *individual* qualifications. If the characteristics are examined, the very means of communication do not permit, even discourage, individually differentiated cognitive and affective responses. This is not to say that speakers of this language interact in a completely uniform manner, for the potential of a public language allows a vast range of possibilities, but it provides a language use that discourages the speaker from verbalizing his relationships with the environment. The individual qualification is realized through a means offering an immediacy of communication; that is, by expressive symbolism, together with a linguistic form that orients the speaker to a relatively low casual order, to descriptive concepts rather than analytic ones. The result of this mediating process orients the child to a distinct relationship with objects in the environment and so to a different *order* of learning from that which accompanies a *formal* language. With a *formal* language, meaning is logically explicit and finely differentiated; whilst with a *public* language, meaning is implicit and crudely differentiated. By the term "differentiated" we mean not simply the range of objects that are elaborated or significant but the logical order of the elaboration or significance—that is, the matrix of relationships that arouse and condition responses.

In fact, when a child learns a *public* language, he *learns* to perceive the possibilities symbolized by language in a distinctive way. Language is perceived *not* as a set of possibilities, which can be fashioned subtly and sensitively to facilitate the development of a unique individual experience. Language is *not* a means to verbalize relatively precisely the experience of separateness and difference. Rather, with a *public* language, the child from an early age interacts with a linguistic form that maximizes the means of producing social rather than individual symbols; and of course the vehicle of communication powerfully reinforces the initial socially induced perference for this aspect of language use. It is a language use that encourages an immediacy of interaction, a preference for the descriptive rather than the analytic, a linguistic form such that what is *not* said is equally and often more important than what is said.[30]

It has been suggested that the number and type of new relationships available to an individual is limited as a result of a *learned* sensitivity to descriptive, global concepts; but equally as important is the fact that a particular cluster of relationships are not of great relevance to the speaker. These are relationships that are initiated by considerations of subjective intent. Subjective intent refers to the consideration of, and reflection upon, the motivations of self and others. Such statements will be made but they will be of a restricted and global nature. In information-theory terms, these relationships will not be adequately coded; not because the words are unavailable, but because of a lack of pressure to transform affect into verbally elaborated and explicit meaning. It has been suggested earlier that a heightened sensitivity to the motivation of self and others facilitates the development of a low guilt threshold, increases the number of referents that condition a social relationship, and opens the way to the control of behavior by inducing guilt. *Public* language use, which minimizes the verbal expression and elaboration of subjective intent, raises the guilt threshold.[31] This is *not* to say that punishment is unjust, but that feelings of guilt will tend to be divorced from the notion of wrongness. This would seem to make more likely the reoccurrence of the behavior and to create a particular attitude to the punishment. It is not suggested that if precise terms were used, they would, in themselves, inhibit the intended action, but that the action would be accompanied by psychological states that might not be present if the child spoke a *public* language. These psychological states may be of great importance in modifying both the form and content of punishment.[32]

A corollary of the fact that subjective intent is not adequately coded in a *public* language is the somewhat paradoxical result that, despite the warmth and vitality that so often goes with this mode of speech, the spoken language remains *impersonal* in the literal sense of that term. It is perfectly possible, despite a restricted vocabulary, to create individuated speech, but the *sensitivity* induced by a *public* language does not make such characterization appropriate. The factor of impersonality opens the way to a form of social behavior that is controlled by a rigid, explicit, authoritarian social structure, where status, role, age grade, and the customary relations between these elements, become strategic orientiating cues. This social structure channels and focuses the relatively diffuse affective potential that the use of the language, itself, helps to create. Conformity to symbols of solidarity will then be intense, and the level of activity may be reduced if they are not concretely there; these symbols *are absent* when the language is used in an inappropriate context. Such a situation will raise considerably the level of anxiety.

The impersonality allows for two almost contradictory types of responses. On the one hand, the mechanical solidarity that it facilitates creates loyalty to the group, its functions, and its aspirations; it creates a social relationship of a warm vital form; yet, it leads to a large measure of dependency on these symbols and so to an inherent *passivity*. On the other hand, the impersonality protects or insulates the speaker from responsibility, *personal* involvement and guilt for what he has said or done. A whole range of verbal behavior and action is made available, particularly forms of behavior often called "acting out." From the point of view of *formal* language speakers, the behavior may appear antisocial. This must *not* be understood to mean that such responses are necessarily frequent or dominant but, only, that this form of behavior is liable to be released, particularly if the level of tension is high. The speaker is more likely to blame the environment rather than himself, and this reinforces the development of the mechanisms of displacement and denial (Miller and Swanson, 1960).[27] The latter arise also because of the general rigidity of the cognitive system induced by the speaking of this language.

The psychological and sociological status quo of a speaker limited to a *public* language is accomplished by protective devices built into the linguistic medium. Perhaps the most important of these protective functions is that other forms of language use (i.e., *formal* language), can not be directly comprehended but will be mediated through a *public* language. In other words a *formal* language will be translated, and in this process an alternative orientation that would sensitize the speaker to a different dimension of significance is neutralized. Where a translation can not be made there is no communication and thus absolute protection. This linguistic form inhibits the verbal expression, and so limits the learning attendant on such expression, of those experiences of separateness and difference that would isolate the speaker from his group. It channels cognitive and affective states, which if expressed might constitute a potential threat to the equilibrium. For example, curiosity is limited and focused by the relatively low level of conceptualization. The primacy of mechanisms of displacement and denial act to preserve the status quo. A resistance to change or rigidity is partly related to the way authority is justified or legitimized. For the signals of authority will inhere in the *form* of the social relationship rather than in complex principles.

It may be helpful to summarize at this point some of the implications of a *public* language. The implications are logical, social, and psychological. It is suggested that a correlate of this linguistic form is a relatively low level of conceptualization, an orientation to a low order of causality, a disinterest in processes, a preference to be aroused by, and respond to, that which is immediately given, rather than to the implications of a matrix of relationships; and that this partly conditions the intensity and extent of curiosity as well as the mode of establishing relationships. These logical considerations affect what is learned and how it is learned, and so affect future learning. A preference for a particular form of social relationship is engendered; a form where individual qualifications are non-verbally communicated, or mediated through the limited possibilities of a *public* language; a preference for inclusive social relationship and a great sensitivity to the demands of solidarity with the group, which differs from the relationship to the group that is mediated through a *formal* language. There exists a socially induced conservatism and resistance to certain forms of change, which contrasts with an interest in novelty. There will be a tendency to accept and respond to an authority that inheres in the form of the social relationships, rather than in reasoned or logical principles. It fosters a form of social relationship where meaning is implicit, where *what* is not said, *when* it is not said and, paradoxically, *how* it is not said, form strategic orientating cues. It is a form of social relationship that maximizes identifications with the aims and principles of a local group, rather than with the complex differentiated aims of the major society. This correspondingly minimizes the expression of differences and individual distinctiveness in the sense of previous discussion.

A *public* language is a linguistic form that discourages the verbalization of tender feeling and consequently the *opportunities for learning* inherent in the verbal expression of such feelings. Again, it is important to add that this does not imply that tender feelings are not subjectively experienced, but that the form and implications of their expression are modified. Conversely, it is a linguistic form that will tend to elicit "tough" responses either through vocabulary or through expressive style or both. Further, it is probable that "tough" terms will be used to characterize situations or objects rather than the articulation of tender feelings in an individually discrete way. This in its turn modifies the individual's ready entertainment of such feeling. It is a linguistic form that will tend to minimize the experience of guilt in relation to particular classes of situations, so permitting a range of antisocial behavior (and learning) by divorcing individual responsibility and guilt from the evaluative judgments of the behavior involved. Finally, and most importantly, a situation calling for an explicit individual qualification may well be one that engenders critical psychological distress for the speaker of a *public* language. *A critical situation of this kind is one typically found in formal education.*

It is necessary to state at this point that the type of *public* language described and analyzed here will rarely be found in the pure state. Even if such an "ideal" language use were to be spoken, it would not be used in all situations within the local group. Modifications *within* the form would occur, most certainly, depending upon whether the situation is defined as social or personal. It is suggested that what is found empirically is an orientation to this form of language use, which is conditioned by socially induced preferences.

A linguistic environment limited to a *public* language is likely to produce (from a formal educational point of view) deleterious effects, both cognitive and affective, which are difficult but not, it is believed, impossible to modify. Verbal I.Q. tests may often yield a correct educational or occupational prediction for members of the unskilled or semiskilled social strata, not solely because of some general innate factor but because of the efficiency of early learning—specifically, the learning of a form of language use in a special environment.

There is an initial conflict between the need to make, and to be sensitive to, mediate responses, which formal learning requires, and the immediate responsiveness the child has learned from his social structure. This creates difficulties at many levels. The appropriate cues that enable a child to establish a personal relationship are absent; from the point of view of the lower working-class child, the teacher's feeling is impersonalized through the language he uses. The *public* language is, in fact, a language to be used between equals (from a middle-class point of view), for it contains little reference to social status; and the terms used to denote social status within the class environment are often judged unacceptable for use outside it. Thus, the use of this language in a superior-inferior situation (to a doctor, teacher, etc.) may often be interpreted by the superior as a hostile or aggressive (rude) response. Because the working-class child can only use—only know—a *public* language it is often used in inappropriate situations. The expressive behavior and immediacy of response that accompany the use of this language may again be wrongly interpreted by the teacher. This may well lead to a situation where pupil and teacher each disvalues each other's world, and communication becomes a means of asserting differences.

Fundamentally, it may lead to a breakdown of communications between teacher and child, for two different languages are in fact being used. If the teacher is conscious of a deficiency in his own status, this may exacerbate the existing difficulty of communication. In contrast to the middle-class child, who is brought up to respond to the distinction between an office and its content, the working-class child confounds the two, so that if there is no personal relationship with the teacher, his function and the subjects connected with it are together disvalued. Although the working-class child may have at the same time a sense of unease and a recognition of failure.

The fact that the working-class child attaches significance to a different aspect of language from that required by the learning situation is responsible for his resistance to extensions of vocabulary, the manipulation of words, and the construction of ordered sentence. Because he has previously learned to make personal qualifications through expressive symbolism and a *public* language, he has little desire to acquire new words or order his existing vocabulary in a way that expresses this qualification. There is, in fact, from his own standpoint, no *need* to do this. The "I" of the child is adequate, communicated by tone-volume-physical set, not in the language he uses. Unfortunately, within a formal learning situation, this means of communication is not recognized and must necessarily be disvalued. The attempt to substitute a different use of language and to change the order of communication creates critical problems for the lower working-class child, as it is an attempt to change his basic system of perception, fundamentally the very means by which he has been socialized. A new word, or a previously known word used differently, may not become a vehicle for future expression, for there exists no emotional and thus cognitive framework in which it can find a place *A situation is created of mechanical learning, with its implication of forgetting when the original stimuli are removed.* The working-class boy is often genuinely puzzled by the need to acquire vocabulary or use words in a way that is, for him, peculiar. It is important to realize that his difficulties in ordering a sentence and connecting sentences—problems of qualifying an object, quality, idea, sensitivity to time and its extensions and modifications, making sustained relationships—are alien to the way he perceives and reacts to his immediate environment. The total system of his perception, which results in a sensitivity to content rather than the structure of objects, applies equally to the structure of a sentence.

The mechanical understanding and manipulation of number, according to elementary rules of addition, subtraction, and multiplication, may not show a discrepancy between the two classes except in speed. Difficulties arise for the lower working-class child for he may be unable to generalize the principles and operations to different verbal contents. The principles and operations will tend to apply to discrete contents. The greatest disadvantage involved in the use of a *public* language is precisely a difficulty in formal generalization and an insensitivity to the means whereby this becomes possible. Verbal problems that require an initial *logical* ordering before arithmetic operations can be applied will create major difficulties. The understanding and application of *ratio,* transposition of simple formulae, is a critical step in the understanding of number and often indicates a point in the gradient of difficulty that the lower-working-class boy is unable to pass. Some children, irrespective of social class, have difficulty with number, but the point here, is the relative ease or difficulty of learning between the social strata.

These critical points of difficulty may not be directly the result of a deficiency of "intelligence," rather, because of the nature of an object and its symbolic relations (here the implication of number), much is lost to perception and not cognized. The lower working-class child will encounter difficulties with basic subjects that are of a different order from those encountered by the middle-class child, and these may inhibit learning, or the exploitation of what is learned, or both. Simply, what is learned by a middle-class child will have a different significance to him from that which it has to a working-class child, because of a differing perception of the items within a learning situation.

The very conditions of the classroom situation often makes effective education impossible. Large classes reduce the possibility of individual teaching, maximize impersonal authoritarian methods of class control, and increases the passivity of the lower-working-class pupil. A general rule should hold for the primary stage of education. The lower the status of the pupil, the smaller the number in the class. This is the basic condition for a *psychological* relationship (interpersonal rather than intergroup) between teacher and pupil. The social organization must enable the *person* as well as the function of the teacher to be felt and perceived. The teaching situation for the lower working-class child is often persecutory and exposes him to a persistent attack on his language and so his normal mode of orientation. *He is bewildered and defenseless in this situation of linguistic change.* The standardized reaction to the educational process is an unhappy defense against this change and its implications. In order for the pupil to participate actively and to learn to create appropriate speech, the relationship between teacher and pupil needs to be one of mutual respect and concern. This requires a sensitive understanding on the part of the teacher, an awareness of the emotional and cognitive difficulties for the child, and the ability to allay the pupil's anxiety and tension.

A major dilemma confounds the education of the lower working-class pupil. Unlike the middle-class pupil, he lacks the understanding of basic concepts; neither is he oriented to building his experience upon those concepts. Insightful generalization is difficult. His order of cognitive evaluation would indicate that drill methods are required, so that the elements for later conceptualization are gained. Although this is unfashionable, I suggest that where the culture induces a relatively low level of conceptualization, association rather than *gestalt* learning in children is more efficient.[33] This has important implications for teaching techniques, especially at the early stages of education. However, there is a possible conflict between such techniques and the need to encourage insightful generalization and to facilitate active exploration of relationships. The latter cannot be obtained until the rudimentary elements have been satisfactorily associated and reinforced. Simply, the lower working-class pupil does not possess basic *information*. The passivity of the pupil makes him peculiarly receptive to drill methods, but resistant to active participation and co-operation. The teacher requires techniques such that these elements are gained without prejudicing later generalization. Another aspect of this dilemma is related to the use of concrete as against logical or abstract presentation. Because formal relationships are difficult for the child to perceive (relative to the middle-class child), the tendency is to make the content of teaching very concrete. But this serves to reinforce the perceptual set of the child and the relevance of what he has learned to a discrete content. He must be exposed to the force of the formal relationship and *he must be able to verbalize this for himself.* Some of the experiments in Inhelder and Piaget (1958)[34] are highly relevant to this process. *The methods and problems of teaching need to be thought out almost as though middle-class children do not exist.* This does not imply that pupils of the two social strata need to be educated in different institutions.

This analysis has indicated the critical importance of the early stages of education; for that which is not efficiently learned and applied correctly will prejudice the pupil's success at the secondary level. The character of the educational process changes at the secondary level. It becomes increasingly analytic and relies on the progressive exploitation of what Piaget calls "formal operations," whereas the lower working-class child's linguistic history tends to restrict him to the *concrete* operational stage.[35] This shift of emphasis reveals the inadequacy of the lower working-class child's basic preparation. Although the primary stage is passed without an undue sense of failure or purposelessness, the discrepancy between what he can do and what he is called upon to do widens considerably at the secondary level. Society reinforces his perception of this discrepancy by often allocating him to what many people consider an inferior educational institution. Inadequate preparation causes him to lose ground rapidly. Failure, despite persistence, often ensues. Insulation from this failure is accomplished by denying the relevance of education and by the mechanical assertion of his own values. By fourteen years of age many lower-working-class children have become "unteachable."

Finally, there is no continuity between the expectancies of the school and those of the child. In the school, an activity or a series of activities are meaningful in relation to a distant goal, and the present has critical extensions in time and place. The working-class child is concerned mainly with the present; his social structure, unlike that of the middle-class child, provides little incentive or purposeful support to make the methods and ends of the school personally meaningful. The problems of discipline and classroom control result not from isolated points of resistance or conflict but from the attempt to reorient a whole pattern of perception with its emotional counterpart. This may create the disproportion between the intensity of any one response and the specific set of stimuli that occasion it. The school provides an important means by which the middle-class child enhances his self-respect; this is not so for the working-class child. His self-respect is in fact more often damaged. It is obtained elsewhere in the careful conformity to the symbols of his class.

Conclusions

It has been suggested that language use is the means by which the diverse influences of the socio-cultural environment are synthesised and reinforced. The child learns his social structure through its language, and this processing of learning begins when he can respond to, but not make, verbal signals. Language, spoken language, powerfully conditions what is learned and how it is learned, and so influences future learning.

Fundamental to the view presented is the fact that a middle-class child is capable of responding to, manipulating, and understanding a *public* language, as well as a language that is structured to mediate relatively explicit, individualized qualifications, as a result of his socio-cultural environment. It has been indicated that because of this a greater complexity of possible relationships are made available to him, which permits conceptualizing activity of a high order. Because of the different structuring of the lower working-class child's environment he is limited to a *public* language. This radically narrows the extent and type of his object relationships. Thus, the middle-class child and the lower working-class child are oriented to different orders of learning as a result of the implications of their forms of language use.[36]

It is thought that many aspects of the present controversy relating to the concept "intelligence" might be seen differently within this theoretical framework. Specifically, it might throw some light on the found discrepancies between potential ability and measured attainment of working-class pupils, by indicating how perception is patterned sociologically. The psychological causes of difficulties in the basic subjects is a different problem. What appears vital is the separating out of sociological and psychological factors in order that constructive methods may be worked out to prevent the wastage of working-class educational potential. If this theory is valid, it is thought that it is possible to systematize many disparate hypotheses and much established data relating to working-class and middle-class differences in attainment and behavior. Although the low mobility rate of the unskilled and semiskilled strata may imply educational waste, it is equally important to consider that as a result of the close relationship between education and occupation a situation may soon be reached when the educational institutions legitimize social inequality by individualizing failure. Democratization of the means of education, together with the internalizing of the achievement ethic by members of the working-class strata, may lead to an individualizing of failure, to a loss of self-respect, which in turn modifies an individual's attitude both to his group and to the demands made upon him by the society.

One major implication of the view held here, which is moral rather than sociological, is that the changing of a form of language use, in this case a *public* language, involves something more than might be thought at first sight. A *public* language contains its own aesthetic—a simplicity and directness of expression, emotionally virile, pithy, and powerful, with a metaphoric range of considerable force and appropriateness. It is a language which symbolizes a tradition and a form of social relationship in which the individual is treated as an end, not as a means to a further end. To simply substitute a *formal* language—which is not necessarily a logical, impersonal, emotionally eviscerated language—is to cut off the individual from his traditional relationships and perhaps alienate him from them. This is the old polarity of *Gemeinschaft* and *Gesellschaft* in another guise. The problem would seem to be to preserve *public*-language usage but to create for the individual the possibility of utilizing a *formal* language. This is no easy task for a society that distributes respect and significance according to occupational achievement. It would seem that a change in this mode of language use involves the whole personality of the individual, the very character of his social relationships, his points of emotional and logical reference, and his conception of himself.

There is some danger of creating the impression that a *public* language produces entirely standardized and uniform behavior in the speakers. This is not the case, for such a form of communication creates a vast potential of responses. All that is meant, is that the behavior that it releases will possess many significant and common features. It also follows that personality differences between speakers obviously occur and are significant in their effect upon behavior. It is of critical importance to separate sociologically relevant aspects of development. This is equally necessary for practical as well as theoretical reasons. If the theory of language behavior put forward here is substantiated, then the operation of sociological factors upon development is profound. Different social structures will emphasize or stress different aspects of language potential; this in turn will create for the individual particular dimensions of relevance. As the child learns his speech, so he will learn his social structure; and the latter will become the substrata of his innermost experience through the effect of linguistic processing. The major role of speech, from this point of view, is to sensitize the child progressively to the future demands that will be made upon him, by modifying his experience and stabilizing his perceptions. *This process is reinforced every time he speaks.* It does not make sense to talk of mechanical cause and effect; rather, what takes place is a progressive modification of learned responses, which become differentiated and stabilized by interrelated functional systems, initially created and later coordinated by speech.

This analysis has drawn attention to the relationship between linguistic processing, the type of self-regulation it induces, and the general level of social and educational competence. The linguistic coding and decoding systems discussed are highly resistant to change because of their psychological ramifications, and these systems are a direct function of a social structure. This suggests two means by which change may be introduced: by modification of the social structure, or by operating directly on the speech itself. The first is not within the province of the educational institutions and is essentially a political matter. The second, under suitable conditions and methods, could be undertaken by the schools, especially the nursery and primary schools working in intimate co-operation with the parents. However, an appreciation of the difficulties involved for the lower-class pupil in this process of linguistic change cannot be too strongly emphasized. Values are transmitted in any educational situation, but in this case of deliberate rational modification of experience we must be very sure that the new dimensions of relevance made available do not also involve that loss of self-respect engendered by measuring human worth on a scale of occupational achievement. The integration of the lower-working class into the wider society raises critical problems of the nature of society and the extent to which the school, by itself, can accelerate the process of assimilation.

NOTES

1. M. F. Little and H. M. Williams, "An Analytical Scale of Language Achievement," *University of Iowa, Stud. Child Welfare*, XIII (1937), 49–94.
H. M. Williams and M. L. McFarlane, "A Revision of the Smith Vocabulary Test for Pre-school Children. Part III," *Univ. Iowa Stud. Child Welfare*, XIII (1937), 35–46.
V. V. Fleming, "A Study of Stanford Binet and Growth in Children," *Journal of Genetic Psychology*, LX (1942), 359–73.
W. Goldfarb, "Infant Rearing and Problem Behavior," *American Journal of Orthopsychiatry*, XIII (1943), 249–65. "The Effects of Early Institutional Care on Adolescent Personality," *Journal of Experimental Education*, XII (1943), 106–29. "Effects of Psychological Deprivation during Infancy and Subsequent Stimulation," *American Journal of Psychiatry*, CII (1945), 18–33.
A. J. Brodbeck and O. C. Irwin, "The Speech Behavior of Infants without Families," *Child Development*, XVII (1946), 145–56.
J. J. Moore, "Speech Content of Selected Groups of Orphanage and Non-orphanage Pre-school Children," *Journal of Experimental Education*, XVI (1947), 122–33.
J. Roudinesco and G. Appell, "Les repercussions de la stabulation hospitalière sur le développement psychomoteur des jeunes enfants," *Sem. Hop.* (Paris), XXVI (1950), 2271–73.
2. M. L. Kellner Pringle and V. Bossio, "A Study of Deprived Children: Part II Language Development and Reading Attainment," *Vita Humana*, I (1958), 142–70.
3. M. L. Kellner Pringle and M. Tanner, "The Effects of Early Deprivation on Speech Development," *Language and Speech*, I (1958), 269–87.
4. H. C. Dawe, "A Study of the Effects of an Educational Programme upon Language Development and Related Mental Function in Young Children," *Journal of Experimental Education*, II (1942), 200–09.
5. A. Descoeudres, *Le developpement de l'enfant de deux à sept ans* (Neuchâtel et Paris: Delauchaux et Niestlé, 1921).
W. Stern, "Psychologie der frühen Kindheit bis zum sechsten Lebensjahre," 6 verb. Aufl. (Leipzig: Quelle und Meyer, 1930).
D. McCarthy, *The Language Development of the Pre-school Child*, (Inst. Child Welfare Monogr. Ser. No. 4; Minneapolis: University of Minnesota Press, 1930).
C. Bühler, "Kindheit and Jugend," 3 Aufl. (Leipzeg: Hirzel, 1931).
E. A. Davis, *The Development of Linguistic Skills in Twins, etc.* (Inst. Child Welfare Monogr. Ser. No. 14; Minneapolis: University of Minnesota Press, 1937).
M. J. Schulman and R. J. Havighurst, "Relations between Ability and Social Status in a Mid-western Community on Size of Vocabulary," *Journal of Educational Psychology*, 35 (1947), 437–42.
M. C. Templin, *Certain Language Skills in Children* (Inst. Child. Welfare Monogr. Ser. No. 26; University of Minnesota Press, 1957).
6. L. E. Hurrell, Jr., *A Comparison of the Development of Oral and Written Language in School Age Children* (Child Development Publication, XII, Ser. No. 66, No. 3; Lafayette, Ind.: Purdue University, 1956).
7. O. C. Sampson, "A Study of Speech Development in Children 18–30 Months," *British Journal of Educational Psychology*, XXVI (1956), 194–202.
8. F. Catalano and D. McCarthy, "Infant Vocalizations as Predictors of Intelligence," Unpub. study Fordham Univ. reported by D. McCarthy in *Manual of Child*

Psychology, ed. L. Carmichael (New York: John Wiley and Sons, Inc., 1954), p. 600.

9. O. C. Irwin, "Infant Speech: The Effects of Family Occupational Status and of Age on Sound Frequency," *Journal of Speech and Hearing Disorders*, XIII (1948), 320–23. "Infant Speech: The Effect of Family Occupational Status and of Age on the Use of Sound Types," *Journal of Speech and Hearing Disorders*, XIII (1948), 224–26.

10. J. D. Nisbet, *Family Environment* ("Occasional Papers on Eugenics," No. 8, London Eugenic Society, 1953). [See Chap. XXIII in this volume (eds.).]

11. E. M. Scott and J. D. Nisbet, "Intelligence and Family Size in an Adult Sample," *Eugenics Review*, XLVI (1955), 233–35.

12. J. V. Mitchell, Jr., "A Comparison of the Factorial Structure of Cognitive Functions for a High and Low Status Group," *Journal of Educational Research*, XLVII (1956), 397–414.

13. B. Bernstein, "Some Sociological Determinants of Perception," *British Journal of Sociology*, IX (1958), 159–74. "Language and Social Class," *British Journal of Sociology*, XI (1960), 271–76.

14. E. C. Venables, reported in *Fifteen to Eighteen* (*Report of the Central Advisory Council for Education in England*, I; London: H.M.S.O.), 394.

15. Some characteristics of a *formal* language are:
   1. Accurate grammatical order and syntax regulate what is said.
   2. Logical modifications and stress are mediated through a grammatically complex sentence construction, especially through the use of a range of conjunctions and subordinate clauses.
   3. Frequent use of prepositions that indicate logical relationships as well as prepositions that indicate temporal and spatial contiguity.
   4. Frequent use of impersonal pronouns, "it," "one."
   5. A discriminative selection from a range of adjectives and adverbs.
   6. Individual qualification is verbally mediated through the structure and relationships within and between sentences. That is, it is explicit.
   7. Expressive symbolism discriminates and distinguishes between meanings within speech sequences in fine graduations, rather than reinforcing specific dominant words and/or accompanying utterances in a generalized diffuse manner.
   8. A language use that points to the possibilities inherent in a complex conceptual hierarchy for the organizing of experience.

These characteristics must be considered to give a *direction* to the organization of thinking and feeling rather than to the *establishing* of complex modes of relationships. The characteristics are relative to those of a *public* language.

16. E. Sapir, "Linguistics as a Science," in *Culture, Language and Personality*, ed. D. G. Mandelbaum (Berkeley: University of California Press, 1956), pp. 70–71.

17. E. Sapir, "Language," in *Culture, Language and Personality*," ed. D. G. Mandelbaum (Berkeley: University of California Press, 1956), p. 7.

18. It is important to add that the command, "Shut up!" may be given at a different point in the behavioral sequence of a middle-class child than of a working-class child.

19. A. R. Luria and F. Ia. Yudovitch, *Speech and the Development of Mental Processes* (London: Staples Press, 1959).

20. A. R. Luria, *The Rôle of Speech in the Formation of Mental Processes* (London: Pergamon Press, 1960).

21. M. L. Kohn, "Social Class and Parental Authority," *American Sociological Review*, XXIV (1959) 352–66. "Social Class and Parental Values," *American Journal of Sociology*, LXIV (1959), 337–51.

22. It is relevant to quote here a finding of both G. Greenald (1954) and J. Floud (1956) that achievement in the grammar school was correlated with the social grading of the mother's occupation before marriage. This finding is of great importance as it indicates the order of the initial communication to the child.

23. Whilst it is obvious that certain aspects of children's speech development must necessarily hold irrespective of the social group, the structuring of the language used and responded to is of critical importance whatever the age of the child. The follow-

ing conversation took place in a middle-class nursery. Two little girls of four were arguing about their respective heights, e.g., "I'm bigger than *you*," "No, I'm bigger than *you*." When the dialogue suddenly took this turn; S: "Well, my sister's seven and a half"; K: "Well, but she's not you!" S: "No, everyone's theirselves."

24. This process of substitution also applies to nouns. A working-class mother's reply to her child on being asked the name of a particular building was, "It's a police station." The building was Scotland Yard. For ingenious experiments aimed at testing the relationships between linguistic codification, cognition, and recognition, see E. H. Lenneberg, "Cognition in Ethnolinguistics," *Language*, XXIX (1953), 463–71; R. W. Brown and E. H. Lenneberg, "A Study in Language and Cognition," *Journal of Abnormal and Social Psychology*, XLIX (1954), 454–62; R. W. Brown, Appendix on Language in *A Study of Thinking*, ed., J. C. Bruner *et al.* (New York: Wiley and Sons, Inc., 1957); R. W. Brown, "Linguistic Determinism and Parts of Speech," *Journal of Abnormal and Social Psychology*, LV (1957), 1–5; R. W. Brown and E. H. Lennenberg, *Studies in Linguistic Relativity;* also J. B. Carroll and J. B. Casagrande, "Language and Classification in Behavior"; both articles in *Readings in Social Psychology*, ed. E. E. Maccoby *et al.* (New York: Henry Holt, 1958).

25. See L. Schatzman and A. Strauss, "Social Class and Modes of Communication," *American Journal of Sociology*, Vol. LX (Jan., 1955). The authors describe the difficulty that poor rural respondents had in giving a sequential account of an Arkansas tornado. Examples of this difficulty are the following, given by messenger boys (17 years old) who attend a day-release college. "They have a novel idea where a gadget breaks (brakes) who on the road safety depends, then you press a button and you are looking at yourself in a mirror." "The aim of the motor show is to bring to the public and let them sit in where as they only saw them in the show rooms of car dealers before." "Only a few men there at one time owing to shift work and mainly waiting for the various brews." "A new design seen at the motor show was one big side window each side of the car instead of being broken up into two." "These cars have four doors but the front seat is in two pieces." "The gas also is for taking a certain place." "She ended with sea-cadets for training them about the sea." See also J. H. S. Bossard, "Family Modes of Expression," *American Sociological Review*, X (1945), 226–37: R. Mahmaud Khater, "The Influence of Social Class on the Language Patterns of Kindergarten Children," Unpub. Ph.D. thesis, University of Chicago, reported in J. J. De Boer, "Oral and Written Language," *Rev. Ed. Res.*, XXV (1955), 107–20.

26. See the work of Mildred C. Templin, *Certain Language Skills in Young Children* (Inst. of Child Welfare Monographs, Ser. No. 26; University of Minnesota Press: O.U.P., England, 1957). In a sample of 480 children between three years and eight years old, she found significant differences between upper socio-economic and lower socio-economic groups scattered throughout the entire age range. The greatest number of significant differences seem to be concentrated in the articulation of vowels, medial and final consonants, the length of remarks verbalized, the degree of complexity of verbalization, and in the vocabulary of recognition at the older ages.

27. D. R. Miller, and G. E. Swanson *Inner Conflict and Defense* (New York: Henry Holt and Co., 1960).

28. An example of this statement: Mother to child on bus: "Hold on tight." Child: "Why?" Mother: "Hold on *tight!*" Child: "Why?" Mother: "I told you to hold on tight, didn't I?" Father to Son: "You're not going out." Son: "Why?" Father: "You're always going out." Son: "Why can't I go?" Father: "I told you you're not going out. Now shut up!" See S. B. Sarason and T. Gladwin, *Psychological and Cultural Problems in Mental Subnormality: A Review of Research* (Genetic Psychol. Monogr., LVII, 1958), 3–290; especially chaps. iii, viii, xi, and on language, pp. 255–9; Also p. 157, "Of great importance . . . what happens when a child asks, 'Why?' Is he rewarded or punished, answered or not answered, in terms of *tradition* or *logic*, or is he told he is too young, or is he *encouraged* or *discouraged* to think about it himself?" (My italics.) Of course, this categoric statement will appear at times in any language use, but in a *public* language it not only is used more frequently,

it also becomes a *part* of a language pattern, which narrows the range of stimuli to which the child learns to respond. In a *formal* language, the categoric statement is simply an isolated statement with a specific and limited effect. The source of authority, if a *formal* language is being used, lies both in the status of the speaker *and* in the reasons given to support conclusions, whilst with a *public* language the reasons play a much smaller role in the establishment of authority. This, it is believed, is of great importance for the implication of early learning. See also M. L. Koln, "Social Class and Parental Authority," *American Sociological Review,* XXIV (1959), 352–66; "Social Class and Parental Values," *American Journal of Sociology,* LXIV (1959), 337–51.

29. The term "individual qualification" refers to the way an individual comments or reflects upon and verbally organizes his responses to the environment. In a *public* language, the qualification is limited to a global rather than a differentiated response. The verbal statement seems to arise out of an abstracting process without a prior differentiation, which leads to a condensation of experience to a word or to the use of a *portmanteau* term or phrase that blurs the nature of the experience. (I am grateful to Professor M. Ginsberg for clarification of this point.) The nature of the qualification tends to limit the verbal elaboration of subjective intent. It refers to concrete feeling experiences that have little concern with processes and generalizations except of a low causal order. Meanings are strung together like beads on a frame rather than following a logical sequence.

30. Of course, what is not said plays a great part in most communications. However, if a *formal* language were to be used, what is not said could in many cases be said. With a *public* language, this is not so, for verbal inarticulateness results from the language use, although a strongly uniting culture creates an affectual sympathy that fills the gaps. The latter becomes significant when a *formal* language speaker talks to a person limited to a *public* language and vice versa. See L. S. Vigotsky, "Thought and Speech," *Psychiatry,* II, 29–54 on condensed and abbreviated speech.

31. Koln (*ibid.*) has drawn attention to the fact that middle-class parents are more likely to respond in terms of their interpretation of the child's *intent* in acting as he does, whilst working-class parents are more likely to respond in terms of the immediate *consequences.* Thus, the working-class parent is responsive to ends directing to inhibiting disobedient or disreputable acts, while the middle-class parent is responsive to intent and acts with reference to individualized standards. Simply, there is little *talking through* of acts that require disciplinary measures in working-class homes, little *verbal* investigation of motive. It is suggested that behavior is subordinate to shame rather than guilt. Shame indicates a felt diminution of *respect* accorded to conduct by a group.

32. There is a tendency for this to be recognized. Punishment of a *public*-language user in a school will tend to be frequently corporal, either through threats or direct action, because it is difficult to elicit a sense of guilt or shame in the boy or a sense of personal involvement in the act. A mechanical relationship is set up between wrong-doing and punishment. Caning exists in public schools where a *formal* language is spoken; however, other methods are *also* used to modify behavior. With a *formal*-language user, punishment can involve a temporary rejection, or a talking through of the misdemeanour, with an aim to maximize the experience of guilt, shame, responsibility, and so personal involvement. The attempt to interchange the means of social control may lead at first to many difficulties. This is not to be taken to mean that corporal punishment is necessarily an effective means of social control. It is often used as a substitute for the real difficulty of making an interpersonal relationship and when it is so used it is rarely effective in the long run.

33. It is thought that teaching techniques derived from *gestalt* theory will be less successful with the lower-working-class child as the techniques rely on a basic generalizing act. *Phonic* methods of teaching reading, for example, may be more efficient than "look-say" methods.

34. B. Inhelder, and J. Piaget, *The Growth of Logical Thinking,* (London: Routledge and Kegan Paul, 1958).

35. The Piagetian developmental sequence from *concrete* to *formal* operations may not be inevitable for a child restricted to a *public* language. The child may well be limited to limited *concrete* operations (Inhelder and Piaget [1958], Bruner [1959]).

36. It is thought that the effects of linguistic processing operates negatively upon behavior. Below a level of linguistic skill certain responses are restricted. Raising the level creates only the necessary *condition* for expanding the range of responses. *Public* and *formal* languages, as discussed in this paper, are stages on a social continuum. It is thought that the transitional point will occur in a family where the father is more likely to have received grammar-school education, *or* some form of further education *or* certificated training for a skill; *or* one in which the mother is more likely to have received something more than elementary schooling, *or* before marriage to have followed an occupation superior to that of the father, *or* a non-manual occupation, e.g., domestic service.

25   *Family Integration, Values, and Achievement*

FRED L. STRODTBECK

Italian-Jewish Cultural Values

IT IS TO be assumed that successive generations of Italians and Jews in this country have progressively become more acculturated and thus more like one another. For guidance in the formulation of hypotheses about the way in which values differences between these cultures may have influenced their differential achievement, one needs to turn first to the original cultures from which they emigrated. For the Southern Italian background we found some nine substantive sources (4, 7, 21, 22, 23, 28, 29, 34, 35), all fairly consistent. For the Jews, the relevant literature was much larger. The present account was based primarily on Zborowski and Herzog's *Life is with People* (46). Their treatment of *shtetl* culture—perhaps idealized —is sympathetic but sharply focused on attitudes of great relevance to contrasts between Italians and Jews.

To begin with one of the most striking differences, Jews have traditionally placed a very high value upon *education and intellectual attainment.* The Jewish parent was expected to provide as much education as the sons showed themselves capable of absorbing, but not in a ritualistic manner. Learning in the *shtetl* society gave the individual prestige, respect, authority—and the chance for a better marriage. The Jews have a folk saying that "parents will bend the sky to educate their sons." Every first-generation Jewish parent can tell heroic stories of the sacrifices made by fellow parents, both in Eastern Europe and in this country, to educate their children.

The essential nature of education is further attested by the prestige associated with "brainwork," and the corresponding lack of prestige associated with physical accomplishments. This pattern of evaluation starts early in the child's career. Traditionally, a 3- or 4-year-old starting *kheyder* (elementary religious school) was regarded as a serious student; brilliant students, though youngsters, were treated with a deference ordinarily reserved for important adults. The weight of the opinion of the young scholar

Reprinted from David C. McClelland *et al., Talent and Society* (Princeton, N.J.: D. Van Nostrand Co., 1958) with permission of the authors and the publisher.

is reflected by the fact that a bearded man would not be ashamed to bring a difficult Talmudic question to a boy of thirteen.

Religious learning and the satisfactions of family life were not in this culture separated, as they were in monastic systems. It was the custom, indeed, to arrange the young scholar's marriage while he was still in his middle teens. In order that such scholars might give more attention to their studies, many of the economic repsonsibilities of the family were assumed by the wife.

In Southern Italian culture, on the other hand, the traditional attitude toward education was (and is) very different. School and book-learning were alien pursuits, remote from everyday experience. Priests were taken from their families and even their villages in order to be educated. To the typical Southern Italian peasant, school was an upper-class institution and potentially a threat to his desire to retain his family about him. Although education might well serve for some as a means of social advancement, the peasant was disposed to believe that this avenue was not open to his children—in their case, education was not functional. Family life, local political power, and other objectives were stressed as alternative goals to learning.

Even in this country, the attitude of the first-generation Southern Italian was, in part, negative to education. As an Italian educator reports, "Mother believed you would go mad if you read too many books, and Father was of the opinion that too much school makes children lazy and opens the mind for unhealthy dreams." Intellectualism, in itself, was not valued in Southern Italian communities. Learned men were of another class, or alternatively, they were men of the church. Status in the community changed slowly; property was in all cases more important than learning. Property could be accumulated faster by a trickster-trader than by a scholar (3). Scholars were like monks: good men, but not of the real world.

La famiglia in the Southern Italian culture was an inclusive social world. The basic mores of this society were primarily family mores; everyone outside the family was viewed with suspicion. Where the basic code was family solidarity, there was a strong feeling that the family should stay together —physically close together. The essence of the ethos has been most forcefully captured by Edward C. Banfield, who states the one premise from which the political orientation would seem to flow: "Choose so as to maximize the shortrun advantages of the family and assume others will do likewise."

Though the Jewish family was also traditionally a close-knit one, it was the entire Jewish *shtetl* community rather than the family which was considered the inclusive social unit and world. Relatives might be more important than friends, but all Jews were considered to be bound to each other. The primary unit, to be sure, was the family of procreation, but physical proximity was not so heavily stressed. Mandelbaum (20, pp. 28, 31) and Joffe (13) have both pointed out that the dynamics of benefice for the Jews was not in the nature of reciprocal exchange. Parents' gifts to their children were to be paralleled in the next generation. In the home, as in the community, giving must move in a descending spiral. Giving served not only to enrich the donor and succor the recipient, but also to maintain the constituency of fundamentally equal persons, and in this way, to enrich the community. The charitable contributions of American Jewish communities today owe much to this tradition.

For the Jewish parents, whose theme was so definitely *"Alles für die Kinder,"* there was an emphasis upon a better condition in the *future* which made them willing to let children leave the community for opportunities elsewhere. For the Italians, there was less of this emphasis upon the future. The external world for the world for the Jews was hostile, to be sure, but it was by nature solvable. For all goods there is a proper price, they say; for all labor there is a best way of doing something. For the Italians the equivalent phrasing is perhaps, "There is work which must be done." Perhaps he might go so far as to say that there are ways of doing the work which are more expeditious than others—but no matter how it is done, there is always the chance that fate will intervene. The unpredictable intervention of fate may be for good or evil, but *Destino* is omnipresent. If a man works all his life for something which *Destino* may deny him, well then, why should men look so far ahead? There is always the present, and the chance of a lucky break.

Zborowski, in his study in this country of the reactions of hospitalized Jews and Italians to pain, employs Florence Kluckhohn's well-known *time* orientation to differentiate the cultural responses (45). He finds that both Jews and Italians complain more about pain than do "old Americans." But, more important, sedation alone is enough to relieve the Italian; for the Jew, sedation is not enough. He continues pessimistic, concerned about the implication of the sedation for his eventual recovery. For the Italian there is a *present-oriented* apprehension of the sensation of pain; for the Jew there is a *future-oriented* anxiety concerning the symptomatic meaning of the pain. Neither group wishes to suffer alone; neither group believes it necessarily masculine to deny the existence of pain; neither group believes in suffering as an end in itself.

In the use of folk medicines and such things as a dread of the "evil eye," Jewish and Italian cultures shared many common elements of irrationality. Religious ritual was strong in both cultures. The behavior involved in an individual's participation in his own salvation, however, deserves separate attention.

In Italian folk theology, Catholic doctrine was popularly understood as requiring sheer obedience to arbitrary prescriptions for the sake of an arbitrary reward. Where the formula did not apply, the matter was of no real significance. Faith in the mystery of the Trinity and the timely inter-ventions of the priest were all that was required. For the Jews, religious improvement was always possible and perfection always denied. The scholar proceeded at his own rate after becoming a Rabbi. There were none to grant a learned and respected man a more advanced degree; his job was ever undone. During the middle years he might have to give more attention to business, but as he grew older he could spend his full time in discussion, study, and prayers.

In the East European *shtetl,* no man could occupy a position so humble that it could not in part be redeemed by his religious scholarship. Without that religious scholarship, a man of means alone could be *prost*—simple, common, vulgar. A diploma of any type which signified learning—even in non-religious fields—came to be accorded respect like that accorded reli-gious scholarship. It is important to stress that if Talmudic scholarship taught precision, juridic care, and dedication, it taught also attitudes to-ward learning which might, with a growth of heterodoxy, be transferred to other learning. As long as the ghetto confined the Jew's area of attainment, goals of religious scholarship were highly coveted. Upon release from the ghetto, the status and financial rewards available in such disciplines as law and medicine were also attainable by work of an intellectual character similar to Talmudic scholarship. Jewish mobility has in all probability been facilitated by the transformation of a complex of behavior which had not existed for the Italians.

A peasant's mistrust of books in contrast with veneration of learning does not exist in isolation from other attitudes. Zborowski and Herzog tell us that in the *shtetl* the hair line of babies would in some instances be shaved back so that the child would have a high forehead—hence, appear intelligent. Short, thick hands were thought to be inappropriate and ugly— *prost.* The Jewish attitude toward the body was not ascetic; the body was neither ugly nor inherently evil. Rather, it was looked upon as a vessel for containing the spirit. Rest, food, and procreation on the Sabbath were sanctioned, and keeping one's body at full efficiency was fully approved; but a specialized interest in physical development *per se* was improper. For the Jews the mind was the great tool—but ever under discipline and purposeful direction. In the early morning prayers, the mind is turned to sacred matters; on the Sabbath to non-business matters, etc. There is never a question of whether the mind can win over impulse.

It is perhaps true that the Italian emphasis on good food and proper relaxation is superficially similar to Jewish practice—and for that matter, to the practice in many cultures. The essential difference as we perceive it is that the Italian manual worker was never ashamed of his strength; to keep his body fit was a desirable end in itself, for it was never perceived to be in competition with other necessarily more important activities.

The contrast in child training in the old Italian and Jewish cultures may be further illustrated by data from one comparative American study which has come to our attention. Field workers from the Harvard University Laboratory of Human Development interviewed an area sample of families in greater Boston concerning methods of child-rearing. For second-generation Italians and Jews, the division of the families by social class was as follows:

	Italian	*Jewish*
Middle	7	64
Lower	36	15

As is consistent with the predicted differential status mobility, Jews are concentrated in the middle classes, Italians in the lower. Unfortunately, for purposes of comparison, this distribution does not provide many middle-class Italian or lower-class Jewish families, although the class distribution appears to be roughly "modal" for second-generation members of these two groups. In an unpublished report of this work, the following points are made:[1]

(a) In the amount of time spent in taking care of the child and in affectionate interaction with it, in the warmth of the mother-child relationship, and in the amount of enjoyment derived from child-care, there is no difference between the two groups. Both are relatively high in infant nurturance, save only for the greater severity of the Italian mothers in toilet training. With regard to sexual play with other children, masturbation or nudity in the home, Italians are markedly less permissive than Jews.

(b) Italians are less permissive also of aggression toward parents, and impose more restrictions on such things as table manners, conversations with adults, being a "nice" boy or girl, being careful of the furniture, and freedom to leave home. Jewish children admit deviant behavior more frequently than Italian children and, in addition, tend to require more attention from adults.

(c) At the five-year level, both groups of children are about equally dependent, but the Jewish mother is significantly more accepting of dependent behavior. In general, the emotional atmosphere of parent-child relations is somewhat warmer in Jewish than in Italian families, although at the same time Jewish families think more highly of the benefits to be gained by spanking.

(d) Jews expect much longer school attendance, but there is less insistence on the child's doing well in school. Perhaps there is implied a disposition to permit the child to set his own level of performance.

There were some marked differences between the 64 middle-class Jewish families and the 15 lower-class Jewish families. While this latter number is small, the lower-class families were significantly more severe in weaning and toilet training, took less pleasure in caring for their babies, and were less warm and nurturant when the child was an infant. Differences between Italians and Jews are greatly attenuated when class level is constant. Since class level was not controlled in the comparisons quoted above, the exact contribution of "class" in contrast with "culture" cannot be ascertained. So, too, the marked difference in "mastery expectations," reported previously from McClelland's work, is not confirmed by the Harvard study, but this may arise simply from differences in the categories of behavior considered.

From all this material, only briefly summarized here, we had now to choose those values which appeared most likely to have accounted for the differences in occupational achievement after these two groups came to the United States. This task entailed likewise a comparison of Italian-Jewish values, with the values we used earlier to describe the Protestant ethic of achievement. Finally the problem narrowed to a comparison at five points, as follows:

(1) *Man's sense of personal responsibility in relation to the external world.* The Calvinist's world was the work of God, its mysteries profound and not to be understood by the slacker. To work to understand and transform this world was the true Christian's personal responsibility. In such a scheme, misfortunes had a definite place; they were the tests which God sets before men. Although hard work was thus understood to be a prerequisite for all worldly accomplishment, there was still no guarantee that even a lifetime of hard work would necessarily be rewarded.

For the present-day achiever in the United States, rational mastery of the situation has taken the place of the "hard work" of the Calvinists, and the threat of almost continuous review of his record has been equated with anxiety over eventual salvation. There is no necessary personal deprivation which must be endured; indeed, one's accomplishment can be facilitated by "breaks." But the breaks are now of the individual's own making; it is a matter of being available with what is needed at the right place and at the right time. Just as the breaks are not doled out by a beneficent power, neither are failures. Whatever failure an individual has suffered could always have been foreseen and circumvented if the individual had been sufficiently alert. For the modern achiever there is no legitimate excuse for failure. His sense of personal responsibility for controlling his destiny is enormous.

Old-culture Jewish beliefs appear to be congruent in many, if not all, respects with such a belief in a rational mastery of the world. For the Jews, there was always the expectation that everything could be understood, if perhaps not controlled. Emphasis on learning as a means of control was strong. Neither religious nor secular learning, once attained (unlike the Protestant's salvation and the achiever's status), was in continual jeopardy. For men who were learned in trades but not religious scholars, the expectation of charity to others of the community who were less fortunate was a continuing goad to keep working; but if misfortune befell a former benefactor, the community understood. The sense of personal responsibility existed along with a responsibility of the community for the individual which eased somewhat the precariousness associated with "all or none" expectations of the individual.

For the Italian, there was no real logic in striving; the best-laid plans of man might twist awry. Misfortune originated "out there," out beyond the individual. *Destino* decreed whether a particular event would or would not come to pass. A sort of passive alertness was thus inculcated. Although no one knew when he might be slated for a lucky break, at the same time there was no motivation for any rational undertaking of heroic proportions; such an undertaking might be *destined* to fail.

(2) *Familism versus loyalty to a larger collectivity.* The essence of familism is an emphasis on filial obedience and parental authority. Familistic social organization tends to involve a particular locus of activity and a hierarchy of responsibility based upon age and kinship rather than upon impersonal technical requirements. Calvinism was almost anti-familistic in its emphasis upon a first obedience to one's own soul and to God. The achiever in the United States tends, like the Calvinist, to be anti-familistic. Otherwise, the desire to keep two or more generations together would compete with the job and with educational opportunities which require residential moves. On the basis of his technical qualifications alone, the present-day achiever is ready to move with his wife and children to whatever spot offers him maximum opportunities. At the early stages of his career he may even avoid a line of work in which his father could help him, so as to win for himself the privilege of being judged for his own competence.

The old Jewish pattern sanctioned separation from the family for purposes of business and education, and there was a distinct consciousness that a man's first responsibility was toward his children. That is, obligations were primarily from those who have more to those who have less—from which, practically speaking, it followed that children need not always stay to nurture parents who might be better off than they were. Although the Jews did not go so far as the present American achiever in weakening the ties to parents, the pattern contrasts sharply with that of the Southern Italians who put loyalty upward to the extended family first.

(3) *Perfectibility of man.* An aspect of Calvinism perhaps best captured for popular consumption in *Poor Richard's Almanac* by Benjamin Franklin is the insistence that at every moment of every day a man must work to improve himself. The old Jewish culture also, with its emphasis on religious scholarship and study, represented a similar belief in the responsibility for self-improvement. For the achiever in the United States, this perfectibility has, in one sense, been relaxed; but insofar as it remains, it has become even more stringent. Now, we are told, the improvement should be acquired in a relaxed manner, with no apparent effort; self-improvement is something to be "enjoyed" not "endured" as earlier. But in any case, an interest in education should be (and has been)

high because it is so obviously one of the ways in which man perfects himself.

For the Southern Italian there has always been considerable doubt as to whether man could perfect himself or, indeed, whether he need try. According to his interpretation of Catholicism, he must conscientiously fulfill his duties, but his "good works" do not form a rationalized system of life. Good works may be used to atone for particular sins, or, as Weber points out, stored up as a sort of insurance toward the end of one's life; but there is no need to live in every detail the ideal life, for there is always the sacrament of absolution. Furthermore, the Southern Italian sees man as living in an uneasy peace with his passions, which from time to time must be expected to break through. Man is really not perfectible—he is all too human. So he would do well not to drive himself or his mind too relentlessly in trying to reach that impossible goal, perfection.

(4) *Consciousness of the larger community.* The Calvinist's dictum that "each man is his brother's keeper" has given way in the United States to a less moralistic rationale based upon a recognition of the interdependencies in modern society. Just as the whole Jewish community could vicariously participate in the charities of its wealthiest members, there is a sense in which the strengthening of various aspects of American society is recognized as contributing to the common good.

The Jew from the older culture, enabled by his success to assume a responsibility for the community, had little choice in the matter. The social pressures were great, and they were ordinarily responded to with pride and rewarded by prominence in the community forum. The identification went beyond the extended family. The giver was not to be rewarded in kind; his reward came from community recognition. Such community identification—as contrasted with family identification—has not been highly developed among Southern Italians. Reduced sensitivity to community goals is believed to inhibit the near altruistic orientations which in adolescence and early maturity lead individuals to make prolonged personal sacrifices to enter such professions as medicine or the law.

(5) *Power relations.* Insofar as differences in status are perceived to be legitimate—because indeed the person involved *is* technically more competent—then the person in the subordinate position can still give his full commitment to organizational goals without feeling or acting as if he were being dominated by his superior. Early Calvinism laid the groundwork for such limited and specific relationships by insisting that each man had a post assigned him by God and that no one should feel inferior or superior. Today's bureaucracies create for modern achievers a greatly increased number of positions in our society where a person has a specific role to perform in a large impersonal system.

The old-culture Jew, on the other hand, did not see power in the context of some external system of pre-established impersonal relationships.

He tended, like the Calvinist, to translate power questions into other terms—to the equity of a particular bargain, for example; but unlike the Calvinist, he saw these relationships always as specific, both as to persons and content, and not part of a larger system. His primary concern was to make his relationships good with others with whom he was in close contact over a particular issue. The specificity of his relations with others, including his separation of business and family matters, is also like the functional specificity of modern bureaucratic society, but again unlike it in overlooking the *system* of such functional relationships.

The old-culture Italian tended to see power entirely in immediate interpersonal terms. Power was the direct expression of who can *control* the behavior of another rather than who knows more for a job in an impersonal system. "Who's boss?" was his constant inquiry. Every relationship he turned into a "for me-against me" or "over me-under me" polarity.

The New Haven Sample

In the process of developing the sampling frame in New Haven, further data were obtained which bear upon Italian-Jewish cultural differences. A questionnaire was administered to 1,151 boys between the ages of 14 and 17 (and a somewhat larger number of girls) in the New Haven public and parochial schools. Data obtained on this questionnaire were utilized primarily to identify a set of third-generation Italian and Jewish boys, who were in turn stratified by their school performance and socioeconomic status. The questionnaire touched generally upon values and more particularly upon materials relating to occupational choice, parental expectations, parental control, educational aspirations, and balance of power within the family.

Boys from Catholic families who reported one or more paternal and one or more maternal grandparent born in Italy were considered Italian. Boys who reported the religion of both their parents as Jewish were considered Jewish. Socio-economic status was determined from information provided by the son relating to his parents' education and his father's occupation. Classification was largely in terms of seven occupational groupings, with education an additional criterion for some categories. In terms of these two criteria the following frequencies were obtained:

Socio-economic Status	Italian	Jewish	Other
High (classes 1 and 2; owners of large businesses; major and minor professionals)	8	24	53
	80	66	213
Medium (classes 3 and 4; owners of small businesses; white-collar workers; supervisors)	182	17	455
	15	2	59
Low (classes 5, 6, and 7; skilled workers; laborers)	—	—	—
Unclassified	285	109	779

To demonstrate even more clearly the differential status distribution of the two groups, one may construct an index number using the distribution of "Others" as a base. For example, 52 out of the total 720 in column 3 (excluding the unclassified "Others") are of high socio-economic status. On a pro rata basis, 19.5 Italians of high status would be expected. Significantly fewer than this—only 8, or 41 per cent of the expected—turn up. For the Jews of high status, 310 per cent of the expected are observed. The full set of indices is as follows:

Percentage of Expectation

Socio-economic Status	Italian	Jewish
High	41	310
Middle	100	209
Low	107	25

We used the boy's achievement in school as a criterion of his own performance, just as the status of the family might be used as a criterion of the father's performance. Toward this end, each boy's performance on intelligence and achievement tests was inspected, and his grade performance in terms of the norms of the particular school predicted. When the boy's school grades exceeded the expected performance, he was considered an over-achiever; when his grades fell short, he was classified as an under-achiever. The different standards and testing systems of the various schools made it necessary to adjust slightly the degree to which the boy had to depart from expectation before he was considered an over- or under-achiever.

Being an over-achiever proved to be positively related to higher socio-economic status. This may be illustrated with the 674 "other" students for whom full information was available.

Socio-economic Status	Percentage of Over-achievers	
High	47%	(47)
Medium	35%	(201)
Low	27%	(426)

It thus becomes apparent that since socio-economic status is not an analytic element of central interest, provision must be made for controlling or removing its effect if other variables are to be understood. The standard procedure for making this correction is a factorial design. Forty-eight boys, according to our estimate, could be studied intensively, and they were selected from the larger frame of cases to be allocated as follows.[2]

Socio-economic Status	ITALIAN BOYS School Achievement		JEWISH BOYS School Achievement	
	"Over"	"Under"	"Over"	"Under"
High	4	4	4	4
Medium	4	4	4	4
Low	4	4	4	4

Total 48

This decision to work with a stratified sample both simplified and complicated our ensuing analysis. From the standpoint of the statistical analysis, it was possible to isolate with great precision the effects associated with each of the classificatory variables. From the standpoint of generalizing the findings to other Italians and Jews, or to other over- and under-achievers, major difficulties arose. Our sample had a disproportionately large number of higher-status Italians, and more lower-status achievers than would be expected in a probability sample, etc. In addition, the size of the sample was small—too small to enable us to weight and correct it. In short, the stratification served our theoretical curiosity about effects of combinations of classificatory factors rather than the straightforward descriptive objective of efficiently estimating parameters of incidence for particular populations. While in the present instance this decision is irrevocable, the reader should bear in mind that other investigators with different objectives might choose to select their samples in different ways. Certainly further study of some of the relationships revealed in this research would have to be examined with different types of samples.

To initiate our relations with the families, each of the 48 boys was first contacted in the school during his study period and told that he had been selected by a random process to assist with the development of a new kind of test. The "test" consisted of a set of six 8 x 10 pictures, similar in appearance to the TAT cards, designed to elicit *n* Achievement scores.[3] These pictures were presented to the boy one at a time, with instructions to make up a good story around the picture "about real people and real problems." The administration procedure adopted was comparable to what McClelland and his co-workers have described as "neutral" (24, pp. 100 ff.), and it was not assumed that the boy's achievement motivation was any more mobilized than it would ordinarily be in a school situation. The girl psychologist who administered the pictures was young and attractive; the atmosphere was casual and businesslike.

After the session, the boy's cooperation was sought in arranging a visit to his home at a time when it would be possible to talk with him and his parents. On that same day, a letter was sent from the principal explaining the investigation and stating a hope that the parents would cooperate. The experimenter then phoned the parents and completed arrangements to visit the home. The objective of the investigation was explained to the parents as an effort to illuminate ways in which parents and sons go about making occupational decisions.

The parents were almost unanimously cooperative (as soon as they were assured that we did not have anything to sell). Our only refusals came from two families—one where there was illness and one in which the father would not participate.

The Experimental Procedure

In addition to the questionnaire administered to the boy at school, questionnaires were given to the father, mother, and son in the home. Some questions were asked of the son both in school and at home so that instances of shift in response might be checked against other family information.

The team visiting each home consisted of an experimenter and an assistant, who carried portable sound equipment. As soon as the answer sheets had been completed, the assistant compiled a set of items for discussion. These he selected, if the distribution of original responses made it possible, with an eye to making three coalitions of the following type:

(a) Mother and son agree, father disagrees;
(b) Father and mother agree, son disagrees;
(c) Father and son agree, mother disagrees.

While this collation of responses was being carried out by the assistant, the experimenter gave the family other forms to fill out and subsequently moved them into position around the recorder. He than presented the first item to the family with the following instructions:

> We've looked over your responses to the first set of items and, in many cases, all three of you answered the items in the very same way. In some cases, two of you agreed, but the third person picked a different alternative. What we would like to do is ask the three of you as a group to consider again some of these items on which the agreement was not complete. We would like you to talk over the item until you understand clearly why each person marked the item as he did. We want you to try to agree on one choice which would best represent the opinion of the family, if this is possible.

The experimenter then read the item in question saying roughly:

> Mr. —— said, —— and Mrs. —— said, and (calling the son by his first name) said ——. Talk this over and see if it's possible to agree on one of the choices. When you are finished, call me.

As they began their discussion of the question, the experimenter handed the family a slip on which the item had been duplicated and their responses indicated. He then retired to an adjacent room where the controls for the equipment had been set up. He and the assistant did what they could to keep other children and in-laws from interrupting or overhearing the interaction of mother, father, and adolescent son. Between trials no interpretation was offered, and the experimenter tried not to engage in any very extensive discussion with members of the family.

The recorded interaction over the nine revealed differences took about forty minutes. The members of the experimental team spent, however, on the average, two and a half hours in each subject's home, and collected approximately a hundred attitudinal and informational responses from each family member in addition to the recorded sequence.

The details of the revealed-difference routine were evolved by a series of trial-and-error modifications which may be briefly described. If one contrasts conversations between husbands and wives obtained by concealed recording devices with those obtained by a recorder in full view, one finds no striking differences. Evidently (a) the importance of resolving a difference of opinion with a person with whom one had a solid relationship, and (b) the concurrent requirement of having each member act so that his behavior is consistent with the expectations developed in previous interaction, combine to give a measure which is not greatly influenced by the recording paraphernalia. At the heart of the process is the necessity for "revealing a difference," as has been most clearly demonstrated in a Cornell study by Arthur J. Vidich (42). Vidich attempted to have married couples discover and discuss whatever differences they might have about disposing of a legacy. In this he encountered great resistance, with a tendency for couples to be most interested in explaining their respective thinking to the experimenter instead of to one another. Vidich's experience suggests that the group cohesiveness which, when a difference is revealed, creates the motivation for interaction operates to conceal and resist differences when they arise under conditions which the group can control.

In the earlier research with married couples (39), we had had the subjects resolve their differences by interpretation of the behavior of three reference couples who were at all times unknown to the experimenter. The questions in the present experiment—involving father, mother, son—were less satisfactory for they dealt with abstract questions of value about which the family might reasonably believe the experimenter to have more authoritative opinions. It was for this reason, we emphasize again, that the experimenter always withdrew to another room and under no circumstances permitted himself to become engaged in the discussions.

To illustrate the experimental procedure concretely, we will quote from the discussion in one Italian home, along with scattered background information. Michael's father, a machinist who stopped attending school just before graduating from high school, conceived of himself as a strict disciplinarian.

> I probably should be ashamed to say it, but up to a few months ago I used to beat him, I really let him have it. I still believe that sparing the rod spoils the child. I still do let him have it every so often. I wore out a strap on that boy. You can't overlook badness. It's got to be nipped in the bud.

In his discussion with the interviewers, Michael's father gave this picture of his own discussions with Michael:

> Sometimes I feel he keeps quiet when I want him to put up an argument, especially when I look at things the wrong way; maybe I misunderstand the whole situation. I may be wrong, maybe I came home crabby, the kid may have an argument on his hands with me. He may be right; I may be wrong. Well, my tone of voice, my manner makes him keep

quiet. Maybe he had all the right in the world in his argument, and he keeps quiet about the whole situation, and then he gets heck from me for not putting up an argument.

Because Michael's father considered himself somewhat of a failure in his own occupation, he was concerned that his son be "not like his old man." He particularly wanted the boy not to have to "punch a clock and work for somebody else all of his life." To correct Michael's inclination to avoid spontaneous exchanges with him, the father deliberately engaged his son in arguments, so as to "sharpen him up." The protocol of their discussion of the first revealed difference question is as follows:

Michael's Family

Experimenter: Two fathers were discussing their boys, one of whom was a brilliant student and the other a promising athlete. Some people believe that one father was more fortunate than the other father. Do you think that the father with the athletic son or the father with the studious son was more fortunate? Michael said that the father with the athletic son was the more fortunate and (the father and mother) said that the father with the brilliant son was more fortunate. We would like you to discuss this.

Father: Why do you say the ah, ah, father of an athlete? (8)[4]

Michael: Because if the son is an athlete he must be getting good marks in order to play sports. (5) He must be getting good marks (6) and—

Father: Not necessarily. (10) Not necessarily. (10).

Mother: While he's out playing, he doesn't get his studies. (5)

Father: No! (10) No! (10) That's not it either. (10) Let's look at it this way. (6) Forget about the school part. (6) Don't attach the athletic life to the school life. (6) Don't make it— Don't make it that the boy in order to be an athlete has to have good marks. (6) We know that. (5) But take it as a kid's life; (6) as a guy's life. (6) Would you think that a guy who was a good athlete would get more out of life; (8) get ahead in life more than a kid who was smart in his studies and made every grade just like that? (5)

Michael: Well, the way you're asking the question, you're putting it a little different than the way it reads on the paper, I think. (10).

Father: No! (10) No! (10) I'm not. (10) It means the same thing. (10) It's just that I probably made it a little longer. (5)

Michael: Well, what is the last sentence on the paper exactly? (7)

Father: Look. Do you . . . (sternly) . . .? (12) I'll read the whole thing. (6)

Michael: (Attempts to protest that rereading is not necessary.) (11)

Father: Two fathers were discussing their boys; (6) one of whom was a brilliant student and the other an athlete of great promise. (6) (continues to read question given above.)

Michael: (inaudible remark) Athletic son . . . (11)

Father: Well. (6) I think if ah, ah, my son were studious and he pursued any vocation at all, (6) Michael (6), I wouldn't worry as much as I would even if I knew he were a brilliant football player. (5) What good is that? ah (8)

Michael: Well, it's like I said before. (10) If he's good in sports, he must be good in marks. (5)

Father: Yes, Michael. (3) What good is being a football player, ah, towards helping you to become something? (8) An engineer or draftsman or something? (6) Football and baseball, there a limit to it. (5) You've got to live with it and make something out of it. (5)

Michael: I don't know. (10) What do you think, Maw? (8)

Mother: I'd still say the studious type. (5)

Father: Try to make your son understand, Mother, that even if he were a great football or basketball player, after he's 35 or 40 he can't play any more. (4)

Mother: Play any more. (3) That's right, Michael. (5)

Father: What are you going to do then? (8) Live on your laurels? (12)

Michael: No! (3) No! (3) You'd have to quit by then (3) but I mean, I mean you'd have to have good marks before. (10)

Mother: Yes, but— (10)

Father: In other words you agree. (5) You agree you have to be studious first? (8)

All protocols were scored directly from the recordings and were not transcribed. The subsequent processing of the data may be illustrated with Michael's family's protocol. In Table 1 the number of acts by each family member is shown for each decision in each of the three coalition patterns. Previous research (36) leads one to expect that persons who talk most should have most power in the sense of winning the most decisions; and that an isolate role, necessitating an explanation of one's position to two others, should also increase participation.

Table 1.

Acts by Person by Decision for Michael's Family

		ORIGINATOR		
Type of Decision	Father	Mother	Son	Total
	47	16	28	91
Fa vs. Mo-So	65	19	37	121
	76	23	41	140
	188	58	106	352
	39	16	17	72
Mo vs. Fa-So	31	16	10	57
	52	39	43	134
	122	71	70	263
	52	6	17	75
So vs. Fa-Mo	23	4	21	48
	47	2	26	75
	122	12	64	198
Total	432	141	240	813

In Michael's family, the differentiation in participation is marked, with the father accounting for more than half of the total acts originated. Even in instances where others are the isolates, he continues to dominate. To anticipate the statistical analysis, the acts originated are converted to percentage values, then transformed to angular readings in this way:

	Father	Mother	Son
Original acts	432	141	240
Percentage	53%	17%	30%
Arc sine	47	24	33

Throughout the statistical analysis and in subsequent tables, arc sine values are used to stabilize the variance.

To form a power score based upon decisions won, it is convenient to assign arbitrary scores, so that winning, or holding one's position when in the minority, is weighted more heavily when one is an isolate than when one is a member of the larger coalition. The conventions are as follows:

Nature of Decision	Coalition Members		Minority Member
Coalition Wins	1	1	0
Minority Wins	0	0	2
No Decision	.5	.5	1

In Michael's family, the resultant measure of power is markedly differentiated:

	Father	Mother	Son
Original Score	9.5	5.0	3.5
Percentage	53%	28%	19%
Arc Sine	47	32	26

and it may be noted that Michael's father, who participated most heavily, also demonstrated the highest power. Michael had the second highest participation, but ranked third in power.

Beyond sheer participation, the use of Bales' interaction process categories enables one to create indices of certain qualitative aspects of the deliberation. For example, we utilize jointly the information concerning the originator and target of each act, as well as the category in which it is placed, to form an index which reflects the tendency of a particular actor, number 1, to give positive responses to the attempts at problem solution by another actor, number 2. To arrive at such an index of supportiveness, the sum of the negative acts from person 1 to person 2 is subtracted from the sum of the positive acts and the total dividend by the number of acts from person 2 to 1 in the problem-solving categories (4 to 9 in Bales' system). The resulting indices may be summarized in a matrix as follows:

To:			
	fa	mo	so
From:			
fa	—	−22	00
mo	03	—	07
so	−04	12	—

Inspection of the corresponding cells of the matrix provides a compressed reflection of role relations. The father balanced evenly his negative and positive remarks to the son (00), and the son was slightly more negative than positive to the father (—04). This contrasts with the mother-son relationship in which the highest positive ratios are observed (07 and 12). Between the father and mother there is an interesting asymmetry; the mother is preponderantly positive to the father (03), but the father is sharply negative to her (—22). Michael was quoted in the interviewer's notes as having made the statement, "In my family, it's my mother and I. My sister sides with my daddy." This fragment of information is in agreement with the relations reflected in the interaction process categories.[5]

The three measures, participation, power, and support, are available for each of the 48 families. Before proceeding with the analysis of these findings, however, we need to discuss how the value responses to the questionnaire were treated, so that subsequently we shall be prepared to compare values and interaction with the same family.

The V-Scale and Other Attitudinal Differences

Fifteen items were included in the original screening questionnaire. These items, adapted from research of the Harvard Seminar in Social Mobility,[6] dealt very generally with the types of value differences which have been previously described as characterizing older Italian-Jewish differences. Not all points in the value analysis were covered in the questionnaire. The analysis was completed late in the study, and the questionnaire had been the original device for selecting subjects for the study by the revealed difference technique.

In the first stage of the analysis, we were looking for items which would discriminate at the .05 level between over-achieving and under-achieving students (both Italians and Jews being excluded from this comparison). The original set of 15 items was reduced to 8 (see Table 2). Although in this process items of uneven coverage resulted, it was nonetheless apparent that these scores could be combined (1 for achievement-related responses, 0 for the alternate responses) to provide a moderately efficient discrimination of students receiving above average grades:

V-Score	Percentage above Average	Number
0	0	2
1	0	6
2	17	46
3	20	82
4	23	146
5	26	207
6	30	226
7	42	220
8	51	76

Since neither the Italians nor the Jews had been involved in the original computations, Italian-Jewish differences provide an independent check on

Table 2.

V-Scale Items, Factor Loadings and Italian-Jewish Response Levels

FACTOR	LOADING			
Factor I "Mastery"	Factor II "Independence of Family"	ITEMS	Jews	Italians
.64	.00	(1) Planning only makes a person unhappy since your plans hardly ever work out anyhow.	90	62
.49	.28	(2) When a man is born, the success he's going to have is already in the cards, so he might as well accept it and not fight against it.	98	85
.58	.15	(3) Nowadays, with world conditions the way they are, the wise person lives for today and lets tomorrow take care of itself.	(80)*	(79)
.04	.60	(4) Even when teen-agers get married, their main loyalty still belongs to their fathers and mothers.	64	46
.21	.60	(5) When the times comes for a boy to take a job, he should stay near his parents, even if it means giving up a good job opportunity.	91	82
.29	.68	(6) Nothing in life is worth the sacrifice of moving away from your parents.	82	59
−.02	.28	(7) The best kind of job to have is one where you are part of an organization all working together even if you don't get individual credit.	54	28
−.05	.00	(8) It's silly for a teen-ager to put money into a car when the money could be used to get started in business or for an education.**	(65)	(63)

The column header "PERCENTAGE WHO DISAGREE" applies over Jews and Italians columns.

* The difference is not significant at the .05 level for pairs of values in parentheses; for the remaining values the differences are signficant at the .05 level or greater.
** Per cent "Agree" reported for this item.

the distribution of one type of "achievement potential" in the two populations. From inferences made on the basis of status mobility, it was predicted that Jews would have higher achievement-related responses than Italians. Table 2 shows that this prediction was significantly confirmed for six of the eight items, with no differences observed in the other two cases.

A factor analysis reveals that the first three items, relating to a rejection of fate, have a high loading on Factor I (Mastery); and that the next three items, relating to independence of family, have a high loading on Factor II. Item 7, treating of organizational versus individual credit, discriminates between Italians and Jews but is not highly related to the other alternatives. Although Item 8, dealing with postponed gratification, had, like the other seven, discriminated between over- and under-achieving students, it did not

Family Integration, Values, and Achievement

discriminate between Italians and Jews, nor did it correlate significantly with other items in the set. The third of the mastery items, Item 3, also failed to discriminate between Italians and Jews. The items dealing with control of one's destiny, separation from the family, and working for a group differentiate between Italians and Jews as predicted in the introductory ethnographic contrasts.

Our practice of using a sum of achievement-related responses of the Likert type to form the V-score would be more clearly indicated if sets of items with common loading had been segregated. While in future studies the components of the scale may be reopened and new items developed, there was no practicable alternative in the present instance to the use of the combined scores since only eight items were available.

As to the validity of the scale so developed, three bits of evidence are relevant.

(1) The first is based upon the way the fathers responded to the V-items on the questionnaires administered in the home. One assumes that second-generation fathers of higher status have by their own work personally accounted for some appreciable part of their mobility. In terms of such an assumption, one might predict that fathers of higher status would have higher V-scores than those of lower status. These data, presented in Table 3, may be analyzed so that each effect associated with the factorial design (including status) is isolated. The form of the analysis is as follows:

Sources of Variation	Degrees of Freedom
Corrected Sum of Squares	47
Between Groups	11
1. Linear SES	1
2. Quadratic SES	1
3. Italian (I) v Jews (J)	1
4. (O) v (U) Achievers	1
5. I v J × O v U	1
6. I v J × Linear SES	1
7. I v J × Quadratic SES	1
8. O v U × Linear SES	1
9. O v U × Quadratic SES	1
10. I v J × O v U × Linear SES	1
11. I v J × O v U × Quadratic SES	1
Residual	36

It will be our practice throughout the analysis to examine the variance associated with each degree of freedom. In this instance three significant effects are observed:

Primary Sources of Variation for Father's V-Scores

Line 1.	Higher SES groups have higher values	$F =$	10.85
		$p =$	<0.01
Line 4.	Fathers of over-achievers are higher than fathers of under-achievers	$F =$	4.74
		$p =$	<0.05
Line 6.	There is a greater linear SES trend for Jews than for Italians	$F =$	4.16
		$p =$	<0.05

Of primary interest is the relation between the father's class position and the V-score. This effect is significant and in keeping with the hypothesis that persons who have achieved higher status have higher V-scores. We must not, of course, lean too heavily upon this finding, because we have not demonstrated that the higher V-scores preceded the attainment of higher status; the opposite might well be the case. But if there had been no relationship, or a reversed relationship, then there would have been less ground for believing that a high V-score in high school would necessarily be associated with status mobility. The observed finding leaves open the possibility that the higher V-scores of the higher-status fathers may have been continuously operative and contributed to the status attained.

From line 6 one learns that there is a greater difference between the V-score of high-status and low-status Jewish fathers than there is between high- and low-status Italian fathers. This finding, which in itself appears to

Table 3.

Father's V-Score by SES, Ethnicity, Over- and Under-Achievement

Socio-economic Status (SES)	ITALIANS		JEWS	
	Over-Achievers	Under-Achievers	Over-Achievers	Under-Achievers
High	6	6	8	7
	6	6	8	6
	8	5	8	7
	6	7	8	7
Medium	5	6	6	8
	7	2	7	6
	8	6	8	8
	7	5	7	6
Low	5	5	5	6
	6	8	6	3
	4	5	6	4
	7	6	6	6

be of little consequence, serves merely to draw our attention to the fact that, save for this exception, there were *no* Italian-Jewish differences. That is, the two items—stratification by class and educational achievement of son—remove the Italian-Jewish differences found originally in the school population.

(2) From line 4 one obtains a second, slightly different, validation of the significance of the V-score: fathers of over-achievers have higher V-scores than fathers of under-achievers.

Would the same effects be present for mothers, or is the pattern of their relationship different? To conserve space, the table of actual values for mothers' V-score is omitted, and the results of an analysis of variance examined directly.

Primary Sources of Variation for Mother's V-Scores

| Line 3. Jewish mothers are higher than Italian mothers | $F = 4.46$ |
| | $p = <0.05$ |

In this case, mother of higher socio-economic status are not differentiated from those of lower socio-economic status. As an after-the-fact speculation, one might say that the status of a family is primarily established by the husband's occupation; therefore there is less reason to believe that higher-status wives personally contributed by extra-familial efforts to the mobility. Hence the lack of SES effects would not controvert the finding in the case of the fathers. Equally interesting is the fact that the mothers of over-achieving boys do not show disproportionately higher V-scores. Again the mother's contribution to a highly achieving son might involve something other than parallel attitudes about the universe, family ties, work relations, and the like. The ethnic difference in the case of the mothers is not removed by the stratification; the expected cultural relationship persists: Jewish women have higher V-scores than Italian women. These data are provocative. Yet the one instance of V-score variation which goes toward validation—that is, the ethnic difference—is counterbalanced by the absence of higher V-scores for mothers of over-achievers.

(3) There remains, of course, the matter of particular interest—the son's' V-scores:

Primary Sources of Variation for Son's V-Scores

| Line. 4. Over-achievers have higher V-scores than under-achievers | $F = 5.17$ |
| | $p = <0.05$ |

For sons, as for fathers, there are, after stratification, no ethnic differences, but over-achieving boys are significantly higher than under-achieving boys. Insofar as both Italian and Jewish boys were excluded from the sample at the time the eight items were selected, this finding constitutes, on an independent sub-population, a third instance of validation of the V-scale as a measure of values which are associated with actual achievement. When both parents are in agreement on the positive alternative of the V-score item—or other attitudinal points, for that matter—then the son may be prevented from playing the parents against each other. It is notable that instances of joint V-score agreement in the positive direction are significantly more frequent among Jewish parents than Italian parents.

Primary Sources of Variation for Joint Parental "Achievement Positive"
Responses to V-Items

Line 1. Parents from higher SES groups agree more	$F = 9.78$
	$p = <0.01$
Line 3. Jewish parents agree more than Italians	$F = 13.43$
	$p = <0.01$

Choice of occupation for the son is another point at which the value structure of the family members is obviously apparent. Data on this point were obtained from the questionnaire. All the boys in our high-school sample, as well as the parents of the 48 boys in the intensive sample, were asked whether they would be pleased or disappointed if the sons chose the following occupations (listed by status rank):

1. Doctor, advertising executive
2. Druggist, jewelry store owner
3. Bank teller, bookkeeper
4. Carpenter, auto mechanic
5. Mail carrier, bus driver
6. Night watchman, furniture mover

The results have been reported in full elsewere (41). What is relevant here is that in the total sample, the slope of self-reported pleasure in the occupations by Jewish boys was significantly steeper ($p < .01$) than for Italian boys, meaning that the Jewish boys rejected the occupations of lower status more decidedly. The same result was obtained for the parents; Jewish parents rejected lower-status occupations for their sons more decidedly ($p < .05$) than Italian parents. Finally, there was more agreement among parents and sons ($p < .05$) in the Jewish than in the Italian families.

The difference in emphasis upon education also stands out. For example, the percentage of the respondents in the large sample who "want to" and "expect to" go to college is sharply differentiated between Italians and Jews; but, interestingly enough, Italians are not differentiated from "others."

SES	Italians	Jews	Others
High	(75%)*	83%	77%
Middle	45%	83%	51%
Low	38%	(71%)*	31%

* Values in parentheses are based on low frequencies.

Some of the same factors differentiate over- and under-achievers. In cases where boys differed from their parents, the over-achieving boys preferred the higher status occupations significantly more frequently than under-achieving boys ($p < .01$). Also there was more initial consensus among the three family members over all the "revealed differences" in the families of over-achievers. In short, these data support strongly the conclusion based on V-scale results: Jews have values more likely to promote high achievement than Italians do, and there is greater agreement among family members. The additional findings agree with the V-scale also in that they show higher occupational aspiration and greater family consensus among over-achievers than among under-achievers.

n Achievement Scores

A point of articulation between the V-scale and prior research arises in connection with the *n* Achievement scores. The scores for each boy in the sample, based on the presence or absence of achievement imagery in the stories written about the pictures shown him, have been analyzed in the manner illustrated with the V-scores.

Primary Sources of Variation for Son's n Achievement Scores

| Line 4. | Over-achievers have higher n Achievement | $F = 4.79$ |
| | than under-achievers | $p = < .05$ |

In view of previously reported differences between Italians and Jews as to "age of mastery," the absence of an Italian-Jewish difference is surprising, notwithstanding the stratification. The small difference present, an average of 3.2 stories with *n* Achievement imagery for Italians to 3.7 for Jews, is in the expected direction but *not* significant. The difference between over-achievers (3.9) and under-achievers (3.0) *is* significant at the 0.05 level and constitutes an additional confirmation of the relationship of *n* Achievement to high-school grades (31).

Family Interaction and Power

Examination of the family patterns of interaction in terms of Bales' interaction process categories showed no significant relationship to socioeconomic status, to ethnicity, to over- and under-achievement, to V-scores, or to *n* Achievement. Only two significant effects emerged for the supportiveness index. The first was a greater supportiveness toward their sons by Italian than by Jewish fathers. The interpretation seems to be that there was a tendency for the Italian fathers to look upon his son as a less mature person; hence it suggests a denial of near-adult status. Second, mothers were more supportive to fathers as the status of the fathers improved.

The point to be emphasized is the very great similarity of Italian and Jewish interaction patterns. If there has been differential achievement— and according to our data this is indeed the case—then one must conclude that ethnic differences in family interaction are not of great relevance in explaining it.

Because the use of power scores is so new, it may be useful to review a little how family discussions of revealed differences actually tended to proceed, what the resolution of such a difference means, and how we may expect Italians and Jews, or people in different status positions, to differ in this respect.

To begin with, what evidence do we have that the resolution of revealed differences is anything more than a chance phenomenon, depending on the particular turn of an argument? Can we assume that such decisions represent family characteristics? Actually, although power scores are assigned to individuals, they are more properly thought of as attributes of an individual's role in the particular group. This we see if we watch the way differences are typically resolved. The analysis is not in terms of what should be done, but rather in such cognitive terms as, "What kind of situation do we have here?" For example, we ask, "Should parents check a 14-year-old boy's homework?" The boy says, "No," and argues, "If a boy is going to college, he should know he has to do his homework." The parents say, "Yes." But it is soon apparent that they all are in agreement on the basic value: "homework must be done." Thus it becomes easy for the boy to shift his answer now that the issue is perceived differently, and there is no loss in family solidarity such as there would have been if the basic values of individual members had really differed.

There is a marked disinclination for families to recognize their differences in the abstract. The arguments soon take the form, "But son, if you were . . ." or "If mother and I . . ." For this reason it is particularly threatening to an experimenter and awkward to the family when disagreements are squarely joined. One lower-class Italian boy, for example, put the issue boldly: "I know what you want me to agree to, but I won't do it." There were several other instances when a father-son or mother-son coalition put pressure on the third member, and the third member adamantly refused to concur. In more than two-thirds of the families these "blocked" situations were avoided entirely; and in the other families they seemed to involve points of tension which had been previously under discussion within the family. The large majority of all the decisions have a quality which our formal analysis does not communicate; they seem to be brought to the conclusion that "we really never disagreed in the first place."

Obviously, then, the resolution of differences is carried out by families in a way to reflect their consensus on basic values. The outcome of the arguments is thus not a haphazard affair, but determined by stable family characteristics. So too, as in other small groups, particular members have styles of speech which are characterized by great stability of affective tone, burst length, and the like. These styles develop, as it were, in response to the need for communication when differences arise, and they seem not to change much from problem to problem—a fact which again suggests that individual reactions represent long-established roles and mutual expectations within the family.

A more formal way of checking on this matter of basic family characteristic versus chance resolution of arguments would be by test-retest reliability. Though the data are scanty, two types of evidence are available. A recording of one case in which the father had talked more than half of the time was played back to a family, and the heavy participation of the father was so conspicuous that he was moved to say, "Jesus, I talked all of the time." One week later, a repeat session with the same family revealed that, notwithstanding the father's previous insight, his high level of participation (60% of the total) was about the same. In addition to this dramatic instance, it has been shown that participation ranks determined on the first three decisions are consistently in agreement with ranks for the last three decisions (40).

If family interaction patterns do have the stability reported above, then why not just ask family members directly about their respective roles and eliminate field recordings and the like? Unfortunately such data turn out to be highly fallible. For example, sons who state that their parents "don't take a teen-ager's opinion seriously" (when asked on the questionnaire) have almost as high power scores in winning decisions as sons who believe their parents "regard a teen-ager's opinion almost as important as their own." Also, the son's observation as to whether the father's or mother's opinion is more important does not correspond closely with the experimental results, largely because the son tends to judge his parents as equal in influence, when in fact they are not.

The same tendency to consider parents equal is also present in the way boys in the total sample estimated the power distribution in their families. The results broken down for Italian-Jewish differences, are as follows:

Authority Pattern	Italians	Jews	Others
Fa > Mo	18%	12%	12%
Mo > Fa	13%	9%	6%
Equal	69%	79%	81%
	(n = 211)	(n = 80)	(n = 542)

Note that there is no very great tendency in any of the samples to mention the father more often as more powerful, despite theoretical expectations that he will be. On the contrary, the boys show a marked tendency to say both parents are of equal authority.

Although the differences between the reports of Italians and Jewish boys do not support the ethnographic evidence for the great power of the old-culture Italian father, they do show a smaller expectation of equality between Italian parents—a fact which also is found in ratings made of Italian and Jewish families in Greater Boston by field workers from the Laboratory of Human Development.

Finally, there is ample evidence from a number of the questionnaire items that sons from Italian homes and from homes of higher socio-economic status perceive parental power to be greater in controlling their behavior. An illustration is the item, "Is there a regular policy in your home for someone to check over your homework every day or almost every day?" The percentage answering "yes" is distributed as follows:

SES	Italians	Jews	Others
High	(29%)	17%	22%
Medium	23%	3%	19%
Low	16%	(0)	16%

Although the frequencies on which this table is based are small for the two values in parentheses, even for these cells the trend is unmistakable:

parental control is perceived to be greater in Italian and higher-status families.

Reassured that decision-winning in family arguments should reflect stable family characteristics, and primed as to which power differences to expect, let us look at the empirical findings, presented in full in Table 4. The scores of members of the same family must total 100 (that is, before the arc sine transformation). It is, therefore, to be expected that family members' scores will not be independent but will be negatively correlated. For this reason it is desirable to look at the effects associated with all three family members at the same time.

First it may be noted that in keeping with theoretical expectations (27) (if not with sons' perception of the situation), the power of fathers is considerably and significantly higher than the power of mothers. The power of mothers is somewhat, but not significantly, higher than that of sons.

Table 4.

Decision-Winning Power Score* for Fa-Mo-So in 48 Sample Families

| | Italians | | | | | | Jews | | | | | |
| | OVER-ACHIEVERS | | | UNDER-ACHIEVERS | | | OVER-ACHIEVERS | | | UNDER-ACHIEVERS | | |
SES	Fa	Mo	So	Fa	Mo	So	Fa	Mo	So	Fa	Mo	So
High	55	24	24	41	43	24	39	34	34	37	41	26
	39	39	28	35	30	40	43	33	28	45	35	24
	55	27	20	51	29	23	45	30	30	47	32	26
	48	28	28	48	30	27	46	36	22	32	37	35
Medium	33	22	48	39	28	39	33	43	28	34	46	24
	33	45	26	37	34	35	41	35	29	35	40	30
	55	16	30	43	30	32	35	35	35	31	39	36
	46	29	29	24	45	35	33	34	39	29	42	35
Low	33	39	33	48	33	22	37	41	26	35	40	30
	29	46	31	47	32	26	34	46	25	31	31	44
	27	25	51	45	30	30	45	28	32	40	30	35
	24	45	36	28	27	50	35	33	37	40	30	35

* We show the arc sine of the percentage throughout.

Family Role	Average Power Score p value
Father	38.85
	$<.05$
Mother	34.31
	n.s.
Son	31.54

Now let us break the scores down even further by ethnicity. In keeping with ethnographic expectations, Italian fathers are significantly higher than Italian mothers, but there is no significant difference between Jewish fathers and mothers. Jewish parents, however, are significantly higher than Jewish sons.

Family Role	Average Power Score			
	Italians		Jews	
		p value		p value
Father	40.1		37.6	
		<.05		n.s.
Mother	32.3		36.3	
		n.s.		<.05
Son	32.0		31.0	

The significant trends within the family are as follows:

Primary Sources of Variation in Family Power Scores

Fathers:	Line 1.	Fathers from higher SES groups have higher power scores	$F =$ 11.82	
			$p = <0.01$	
	Line 8.	There is a greater linear SES trend for fathers of over-achievers than for fathers of under-achievers	$F =$ 5.09	
			$p = <0.05$	
Mothers:	Line 3.	Jewish mothers have higher power scores than Italian mothers	$F =$ 4.19	
			$p = <0.05$	
Sons:	Line 1.	Sons from higher SES groups have lower power scores	$F =$ 6.47	
			$p = <0.05$	

The higher the status of the families, the less the power of the sons and the greater the power of the fathers (just as the sons had reported). The mothers' power scores do not seem to be influenced by status, but Jewish mothers have more power than Italian mothers. One significant interaction is found; namely, the trend over status is steeper for fathers of over-achievers than for fathers of under-achievers. There were no ethnic differences in fathers' and sons' power scores and no differences in the sons' power scores related to school achievement.

To test the assertions that there were more departures from equality among Italians than Jews, a coefficient was formed by squaring the mean deviations of the power scores within each family. Analysis of this measure by the standard techniques reveals:

Primary Sources of Variation for Coefficient of Dispersion of Family Power (Transformed to Rankits)

Line 3.	Power dispersion is greater in Italian than Jewish families	$F =$ 3.15	
		$p = <0.05$	

In short, our data show less equality among the family members in Italian than in Jewish families. This fact agrees with the ratings of power in Jewish-Italian families in the Greater Boston area reported earlier, as well as with the distribution of parental power as reported by Jewish and Italian boys in our own larger sample.

Although participation scores, like the other Bales categories, are not related to any of the variables in this study, they were significantly associated with power scores, as in the author's previous study of husband-wife interaction (39). The residual correlations (after effects of classificatory variables are removed) are for the father .57 ($p < .001$, for the mother .48 ($p < .01$), for the son .56 ($p < .001$). In short, he who talks most wins most.

Interrelationships among Power, n Achievement, and V-Scores

The easiest interrelationships to describe, the sons' *n* Achievement scores, are not significantly related to family power or participation, nor indeed are they very extensively related to V-scores. Note the following residual correlations: *

	Son's n Achievement Score
Father's V-score	.31 p ~ .06
Mother's V-score	−.27
Son's V-score	−.13

Very likely the father's interest in controlling his children's destiny and his willingness to have his son leave home have something to do with the son's *n* Achievement; but oddly enough, the mother's V-score is almost as highly correlated with the son's *n* Achievement in the *negative* direction. This apparent inconsistency with Winterbottom's finding (24) that mothers who favor early independence and mastery have sons with higher *n* Achievement is probably due to the fact that the V-scale, unlike Winterbottom's socialization schedule, contains items about leaving the family. These, if accepted by the mother, might well signify a certain coldness in her which, on other grounds, we would not expect to favor the development of *n* Achievement in her son.

Family unity also contributes to son's *n* achievement. Consensus on the revealed difference items was significantly related to son's *n* Achievement score ($r = .34$, $p < .05$) and also, not too surprisingly, with over- and under-achievement in school ($F = 10.6$, $p < .01$). The fact that the son's V-score and *n* Achievement score are not related is consistent with a large body of data showing that questionnaire measures of achievement values are unrelated to *n* Achievement scores based on fantasy (24). Since it was demonstrated in previous sections that both *n* Achievement and V-scores were related to over-achievement in school, their lack of interrelationship suggests that the joint use of these measures would provide a more efficient predictor of over-achievement. The matter will, of course, have to be investigated beyond the present set of data, but the distribution of over-achievers by a cross-tabulation of the measures suggests the possibility of increased prediction (see below), even though the number of cases is small and the results do not differ significantly from chance.

V-Scores	n Achievement	Percent Over-Achievers
Above Md.	Above Md.	77% (*n* = 13)
Above Md.	Below Md.	46% (*n* = 13)
Below Md.	Above Md.	36% (*n* = 11)
Below Md.	Below Md.	36% (*n* = 11)

---

* In these and the following residual correlations, the residual variances and covariances have been used to partial out effects associated with SES, ethnicity, and over- and under-achievement.

The residual correlations among family members' V-scores and power scores are as follows:

	V-Scores	Power Scores
Father, mother	.21	−.46
Father, son	.02	−.62
Mother, son	.35 p <.05	−.28

The intercorrelations of power scores are hard to interpret because the sum of the power scores must equal a constant. Under such conditions negative correlations are expected between pairs of values, and the usual significance levels cannot be used. With these cautions in mind, it is interesting to note that there seems to be a father vs. mother-and-son type of relationship; the correlation between mother and son is less negative than in the other two cases. This suggests either, as Simmel would have predicted, that the two members of the family system with less power more frequently act in unison, or perhaps, as Parsons would have predicted, that the mother more frequently attempts to help the son in an unequal contest. The same mother-son tie appears in the significant correlation between their V-scores ($r = .35$, $p < .05$) and in the pattern of residual correlations between power and V-scores as follows:

	Father's V-score	p	Mother's V-score	p	Son's V-score	p
Father's Power	0.18		−0.36	<.05	−0.44	<.01
Mother's Power	0.06		0.46	<.01	0.31	~.06
Son's Power	−0.36	<.05	0.07		0.17	

That is, the greater the father's power, the less the mother and son subscribe to ideas about controlling destiny and the son's leaving home, and vice versa; the greater the mother's power, the higher are both her V-score and her son's. Oddly enough, the more the father subscribes to achievement values, the less his son's power appears to be—perhaps because the father is himself so energetic that the son assumes a reciprocal passive role.

The relation between the son's own power and his V-score does not appear important; the correlation is a non-significant 0.17. Rather, it is the relation between the son's power and the balance of power between father and mother which appears to affect the son's V-score. When the mother's power and V-scores are high, the son's V-score is also high. Inspection of the data, however, suggests that an increase of the son's power over the mother while he is still subordinate to the father does not influence the V-score.

In short, the less the mother and son are dominated by the father in the power area, the greater the disposition of both to believe that the world can be rationally mastered and that a son should risk separation from his family. The son's V-score could be accounted for in two ways: by assuming he gets his ideas from his mother, since there is a positive correlation between their V-scores; by seeing in it a product of his power position. Lack of potency in the family might well lead him to infer that he could never control his destiny anywhere and that he had better stay near his parents; if he could not influence his family, how could he be sure that he could influence the larger community? Leaving the family under such conditions would be foolhardy.

These two explanations cannot be proved by the present data, but further light on the question is available from a study by M. L. Sangree (33), who, by the same methods used here, investigated n Achievement, V-scale, and power relations in eight middle-class and eight lower-class Japanese-American families in Chicago. She found a residual negative correlation between father's power and son's V-score ($r = -.60$, $p. <.01$) just as here; but the residual relationship between mother's and son's V-scores was *negative* ($r = -.63$, $p <.01$) instead of positive as here. Perhaps, in short, sons are more likely to get ideas about leaving the family and controlling their own destiny, not from their mothers' value system, but from a family situation in which the father has less power (whether because he is inadequate, or because the mother is stronger, or because he believes in democratic methods). The evidence is all the more impressive because the cross-check was carried out in a different language (Japanese). In addition, the strong cultural support for father dominance in Japan might have been expected to take some of the sting out of his power, leaving the son as likely to form one set of values as another. But such is not the case: father's power even here tends to make the son believe more in "fate" and less in leaving home.

Although it is difficult to fit together all the interrelationships noted in this section and unwise to generalize too much on the basis of one especially selected set of families, the best synthesis might run somewhat as follows. The son may be said to go through at least two stages of socialization critical for development of his latent potential. In the first (covering the ages of roughly 4–8) he is exposed to differing amounts of stress upon early mastery, independence, responsibility and the like. This stress, though strongly determined by the values of the mother, stems in part from the parents collectively. When the mother-child relationship is warm and the required acts of independence are slightly beyond the son's level of easy performance, then the child is exposed to the complicated system of rewards which requires him to withdraw from the intimate circle of his mother's activities in order to win the affection which is contingent upon his achievement. The strain of this relationship in which affection has become conditioned upon more mature performance has two effects. First, the more mature achievant behaviors which are rewarded are accepted into the response repertoire with a strength and resistance to extinction which may be likened to traumatic avoidance learning or, at least, the persistence of responses built by certain aperiodic conditioning schedules. Second, this substitute for direct interpersonal gratification creates a relatively greater sense of personal isolation. These tendencies combined result in be-havioral dispositions which are captured as expression of *n* Achievement in projective productions and as a disposition to substitute achievement grati-fications for interpersonal gratifications in later career crises.

In the second period (lasting from around 8 at least through ado-lescence) the son tests new limits in which the focus of socialization is not so much his within-home behavior, as it is his beyond-home behavior. Low decision-making power *in* the family, particularly when high V-score con-sensus of parents is not present, results in a generalization of this inade-quacy to matters *outside* the family.

Such a hypothesis must be regarded as circumscribed by cultural values and as highly tentative until confirmed by further research. It is offered merely to suggest directions which such research might take.

NOTES

1. Summarized from B. Tregoe, "An Analysis of Ethnic and Social Class Differ-ences," unpublished manuscript.

2. In making the final selection, it was necessary in scattered instances to use families with parents who were born elsewhere, but who had come to this country as very young children. The socio-economic status classification is in all cases based upon the interviewer's notes obtained in the interviews with the parents. One Italian family was obtained from a residential community adjacent to New Haven.

3. Briefly described, the pictures are as follows: (1) boy in classroom; (2) opera-tion in background, boy in foreground; (3) man and boy in foreground, horses in background; (4) young man in foreground, crossroads in background; (5) two male figures in workshop; and (6) boy with broom in foreground and several teen-agers in background.

4. The scores in parentheses are Bales' Interaction Process categories (2).

5. For a further use of the supportiveness index see Strodtbeck (40).

6. The assistance of Florence Kluckhohn, Talcott Parsons, and Samuel A. Stouffer, joint directors of this seminar, is gratefully acknowledged.

REFERENCES

1. Alexander, F. Our Age of Unreason. Philadelphia: Lippincott, 1942.
2. Bales, R. F. Interaction Process Analysis. Cambridge: Addison-Wesley Press, 1950.
3. Brown, N. O. Hermes the Thief. Madison: Univ. of Wisconsin Press, 1947.
4. D'Alesandre, J. J. Occupational trends of Italians in New York City. Italy American Monthly, 1935, 2, 11–12.
5. Dynes, R. R., Clarke, A. C., and Dinitz, S. Levels of occupational aspira-tion: some aspects of family experience as a variable. Amer. Sociol. Rev. 1956, 21, 212–215.
6. Eisenstadt, S. N. From Generation to Generation. Glencoe, Illinois: Free Press, 1956.
7. Guilds' Committee for Federal Writers Publications. The Italians of New York. New York: Random House, 1938.
8. Henry, W. E. The business executive: the psychodynamics of a social role. Amer. J. Sociol., 1949, 54, 286–291.
9. Hinkle, Gisela J. Review of Irvin G. Wyllie's The Self-Made Man in Amer-ica: The Myth of Rags to Riches. Social Forces, 1956, 34, 297.
10. Homans, G. C. The Human Group. New York: Harcourt, Brace, 1950.

11. Horwitz, M. Psychological needs as a function of social environments. In L. D. White (ed.) The State of Social Sciences, Chicago: Univ. of Chicago Press, 1956, 162–183.
12. Inkeles, A., and Levinson, D. J. National Character: the study of model personality and sociocultural systems. In G. Lindzey (ed.) Handbook of Social Psychology. Cambridge: Addison-Wesley Press, 1954, 977–1,020.
13. Joffe, N. F. The dynamics of benefice among East European Jews, Social Forces, 1949, 27, 239–247.
14. Kardiner, A. The Individual and His Society. New York: Columbia Univ. Press, 1939.
15. Kardiner, A., and others. The Psychological Frontiers of Society. New York: Columbia Univ. Press, 1939.
16. King, S. H., and Henry, A. F. Aggression and cardiovascular reactions related to parental control over behavior. J. Abnorm. Soc. Psychol., 1955, 50, 206–210.
17. Kohn, M. L., and Clausen, J. A. Parental authority behavior and schizophrenia. Amer. J. Orthopsychiatry, 1956.
18. Kluckhohn, C. Culture and Behavior. In G. Lindzey, (ed.) Handbook of Social Psychology. Cambridge: Addison-Wesley Press, 1954, 921–976.
19. Kluckhohn F., Strodtbeck, F. L., and Roberts, J. Variations in Value Orientations. New York: Roe, Petersen, to be published in 1958.
20. Mandelbaum, D. G. Change and Continuity in Jewish Life. Glencoe, Illinois: Oscar Hillel Plotkin Library, 1955.
21. Mangione, J. Mount Allegro. Boston: Houghton Mifflin, 1942.
22. Mangione, J. Reunion in Sicily. Boston: Houghton Mifflin, 1950.
23. Mariano, J. H. The Second Generation of Italians in New York City. New York: Christopher, 1921.
24. McClelland, D. C., Atkinson, J. W., Clark, R. A., and Lowell, E. L. The Achievement Motive. New York: Appleton-Century-Crofts, 1953.
25. McClelland, D. C., Rindlisbacher, A., and deCharms, R. Religious and other sources of parental attitudes toward independence training. In D. C. McClelland (ed.) Studies in Motivation. New York: Appleton-Century-Crofts, 1955, 389–397.
26. Parsons, T. The Structure of Social Action. Glencoe, Illinois: Free Press, 1949.
27. Parsons, R., and Bales, R. F. Family Socialization and Interacting Process. Glencoe, Illinois: Free Press, 1955.
28. Pellegrini, A. Immigrant's Return. New York: Macmillan, 1951.
29. Radin, P. The Italians of San Francisco: Their Adjustment and Acculturation. Monographs 1 and 2, S.E.R.A. Project, Cultural Anthropology. San Francisco: 1935.
30. Reissman, L. Levels of aspiration and social class. Amer. Sociol. Rev., 1953, 18, 233–242.
31. Ricciuti, H. N., and Sadacca, R. The prediction of academic grades with a projective test of achievement motivation: II Cross-Validation at the High School Level. Princeton, N.J.: Educational Testing Seervice, 1955.
32. Robinowitz, R. Attributes of pupils achieving beyond their level of expectancy. J. Personality, 1956, 24, 308–317.
33. Sangree, M. Lucinda. Expectations and interactions in Nisei families, unpublished Master's Thesis, University of Chicago, 1956.
34. Sangree, W., and Hybleum, M. A study of the people of Middletown of Sicilian extraction with special emphasis on the changes in their values re-

sulting from assimilation into the Middletown community, unpublished
Master's Thesis, Wesleyan Univ., 1952.
35. Sartorii, E. C. Social and Religious Life of Italians in America. New
York: Christopher, 1918.
36. Shannon, J. Early detachment and independence in a study of creativity,
unpublished manuscript, Univ. of Chicago, 1957.
37. Snyder, C. R. Culture and sobriety, Quart. J. Studies on Alcohol, 1955, 16,
101–177, 263–289, 504–532; 1956, 17, 124–143.
38. Stein, M. On the role of the industrial research chemist and its relationship
to the problem of creativity, unpublished manuscript, Univ. of Chicago,
1956.
39. Strodtbeck, F. L. Husband-wife interaction over revealed differences. Amer.
Sociol. Rev., 1951, 16, 468–473.
40. Strodtbeck, F. L. The family as a three-person group. Amer. Sociol. Rev.
1954, 11, 23–29.
41. Strodtbeck, F. L., McDonald, M. R., and Rosen, B. C. Evaluation of occupations: a step toward explaining Jewish-Italian mobility differences; Amer.
Sociol. Rev., to be published.
42. Vidich, A. J. Methodological problems in the observations of husband-wife
interaction. Unpublished manuscript, Cornell Univ., 1957.
43. Warner, W. L., and Abegglen, J. C. Big Business Leaders in America. New
York: Harper, 1953.
44. Weber, M. The Protestant Ethic and the Spirit of Capitalism (translated by
Talcott Parsons). New York: Scribner, 1948.
45. Zborowski, M. Cultural components in responses to pain. J. Social Issues,
1952, 8, 16–30.
46. Zborowski, M., and Herzog, E. Life Is With People. New York: International Univ. Press, 1952.

26 *"Common Man" Boys*

JOSEPH A. KAHL

THIS ARTICLE is concerned with the ambitions of high school boys. It reports an interview study of 24 boys of the "common man" or "working" class. They all had enough intelligence to go to college and thereby get a good start toward the higher levels of occupational life, yet one-half of the boys chose not to strive for such success. Instead, they planned little or no schooling beyond high school and said they would be content with the lesser jobs that would likely be open to them. The aim of the study was to explore the social influences which helped to explain the choices of these boys, with particular focus on the question: why were 12 boys striving to "better" themselves while 12 were not?

The study was part of a larger one called "The Mobility Project" underway at Harvard's Laboratory of Social Relations.[1] The sample of 24 for interview analysis was drawn from a larger sample of 3,971 boys on whom questionnaire data were available. A brief discussion of the questionnaire data is necessary in order to establish a framework for the interview material.

I.   The Questionnaire Study

It has long been known that occupational success is highly related to educational achievement. On the average, those with the most education get the best jobs (defined in terms of both income and prestige). Occupation, in turn, is at the center of the complex we call "social class." Thus if we learn more about the determinants of occupational placement, we learn more about social class placement. Yet the argument chases its tail, for we also know that social class of parents influences educational achievement of sons.

It seemed convenient to break into this circle of causation by studying large numbers of people who were readily available: boys in school. Their current educational plans would be predictors of their future occupational success. And their IQ scores plus their family class (status) backgrounds should divulge major determinants of their educational aspirations. There-

---

Reprinted from Joseph A. Kahl, "Educational and Occupational Aspirations of 'Common Man' Boys," *Harvard Educational Review*, Vol. XXIII, No. 3 (Summer, 1953), with the permission of the author and the editor.

fore a questionnaire was distributed to boys in public high schools in eight towns that are part of the Boston metropolitan area. (The omission of Catholic parochial schools was the major deficiency in the data). All the boys in the sophomore and junior classes of those schools filled out a form, regardless of their curriculum. If occupations of fathers are used as a guide to social class, then it can be said that the boys' families duplicated rather closely the class composition of the metropolitan area as disclosed by census figures. The distribution of fathers' occupations is shown in Table 1, along with the distribution of sons' aspirations. It is worth noting that if the job system remains constant, many boys will become dissatisfied, for more boys were aiming at high level jobs than can be absorbed by available openings.

Table 1.

Distribution of Father's Occupations and Son's Occupational Aspirations; 3,971 Cases

Occupational Level	Percentage of Fathers at this Level	Percentage of Sons who Aspire to this Level
Major White Collar		
(e.g. doctor, lawyer, dept. store executive)	4%	15%
Middle White Collar		
(e.g. office manager, school teacher, CPA)	14	29
Minor White Collar		
(e.g. small storeowner, bookkeeper, postal clerk)	20	10
Skilled Labor and Service		
(e.g. highly skilled trades, policeman)	32	23
Other Labor and Service		
(e.g. semi- and un-skilled factory workers, waiter)	21	5
Others:		
Indeterminate	9	7
Fantasy (Baseball, FBI)	—	8
Military Service Only	—	3
Total	100%	100%

The questionnaire showed that the boys who had fairly clear occupational aims also had plans for an education that would appropriately prepare them for the jobs of their choice. About one-fourth of the boys were in the college preparatory course *and* were definitely planning a college career (and a later follow-up disclosed that most of them actually did go on to college). The IQ scores of the boys and the occupations of their fathers turned out to be of practically equal utility as predictors of the boys' educational ambitions. Most boys with high intelligence or from high status homes planned a college career, whereas most boys with low intelligence or from low status homes did not aspire to higher education. But IQ scores and social class level are known to be related; consequently, the data were arranged in the form of Table 2 to show the independent operation of these two factors. It indicates the percentage of boys who aim toward college in various IQ and status categories. At the extremes, the prediction was very good: boys from "major white collar" families who were among the top quintile of their classmates in intelligence strove for college 89 per cent of the time, whereas boys from "other labor and service" families who were among the bottom quintile of their classmates in intelligence strove for college only 9 per cent of the time. (623 cases where father's occupation or son's IQ were unknown have been eliminated from Table 2.)

Although prediction was good at the extremes, it was not good in the middle of the distribution. Of particular interest was the fact that if a boy had high intelligence and came from the most populous part of the status range—its lower middle section—one could not well predict his aspiration. Thus a boy from the top quintile of intelligence whose father was a minor white collar worker or a skilled laborer had almost a fifty-fifty chance of aiming at a college career.

Table 2.

Percentage of Boys Who Expect to Go to College, by IQ and Father's Occupation; 3,348 Cases

| Father's Occupation | IQ QUINTILE (BOYS) | | | | | |
	(Low) 1	2	3	4	(High) 5	All Quintiles
Major White Collar	56%	72%	79%	82%	89%	80%
Middle White Collar	28	36	47	53	76	52
Minor White Collar	12	20	22	29	55	26
Skilled Labor and Service	4	15	19	22	40	19
Other Labor and Service	9	6	10	14	29	12
All Occupations	11	17	24	30	52	27

It was found that the predicting variables could be used, though less adequately, for grammar school as well as high school accomplishment. Boys with high IQ scores usually had good marks starting with the first grade, but more especially boys with low IQ scores had poor marks. Social status was not an important factor in the earliest grades; it began to take effect around the 4th grade and had increasing effect as each year passed. By the time they chose from among the separate curricula in the 9th grade, boys from low status families both performed at and aspired to much lower levels than high status boys of equal intelligence, even though they had been similar in early school accomplishment.

II. The Interviews

The answers to the questionnaires raised an important problem: *what influences the aspirations of the boys in the lower middle levels of the status range whose environment gives them a wide choice?* Many of these boys have sufficient intelligence to aim high. They will not necessarily be isolated if they look up, for some of their friends do, yet it is not taken for granted by their families and neighbors that *all* boys should go to college. Therefore these boys must make a conscious and pointed decision at some stage of their careers.

In order to explore the decision-making of such boys, 24 of them were chosen for interview analysis. They fell into two groups: 12 boys were in the college preparatory course, had marks in the top half of their class, and definitely planned to go to a regular academic college after high school. The other 12 were not in the college preparatory course and did not plan to go to college. All 24 had IQ scores in the top three deciles of their school; they had the intelligence to go to college if they chose to go. And all the boys had fathers who were petty white collar, skilled, or semi-skilled workers. The demographic variables of the larger study could not explain the difference in aspirations among these boys; the interviews were designed to begin where the statistics left off.

The interview material did disclose an additional factor which accounted for some of the remaining variation in aspiration: parental pressure, by which is meant a clear and overt attempt by either or both parents to influence their son to go to college. It was found that within a certain social class level to be defined and described below, namely the "common man" group, some parents were satisfied with their own lot in life and did not attempt to push their sons up the status ladder, whereas other parents clearly encouraged their sons to strive for a "better" life. When the parents were rated on this factor on the basis of their interviews, its strong relationship with aspiration was clear. The results are shown in Table 3.[2] These results fit the standard jibe that "sociologists spend a lot of money to prove the obvious." Everybody knows that parents influence their children. Yet the processes through which that influence is transmitted are perhaps worthy of study. The remainder of this article will summarize that part of the extensive case material which throws light on the relationship between parental pressure and son's aspiration.

Table 3.

Relation Between Parental Pressure and Son's Aspiration; 24 Boys*

	Parental Pressure Toward College	
Aspiration	NO	YES
College	4	8
No College	11	1

* Chi Square = 6.4; probability < .02

The boys who were interviewed came from two industrial-residential suburbs of Boston with populations between 50,000 and 100,000. Both towns have some wage earners who commute to work in central Boston, but the majority of them work in the industries of their own town. The boys were interviewed during school hours in repeated sessions which totalled about 5 hours per boys. The parents were interviewed for an hour or two in their homes. The interviews did not follow a fixed schedule, but were focused on attitudes toward school and work; many were mechanically recorded.

III. The Common Man Class

The cases were chosen from the minor white collar, skilled and semi-skilled occupational groups. Preliminary interviews indicated that most of these families thought of themselves as belonging to a status level which I shall call the "common man" class. A few families in the sample as it was first chosen fell outside the common man class and they were eliminated in picking the final 24 for analysis.[3]

Most parents spoke about a three class system with themselves in the middle. But they did not call themselves middle class; they used such phrases as "common man," "average sort," "ordinary folks," "working people." They saw a "lower class" beneath them—people who lived in slums, had rough manners and morals, and had tough kids who were a bad influence on their own children. And they saw a group of "rich people," "business class" or "professionals" above them; I shall call this the "middle" class. A few respondents detected a fourth level, "the very rich," but their understanding of this group was hazy, for, as many studies have indicated, people make subtle distinctions at levels close to themselves but merge people who are far from themselves into indistinct clusters.

The respondents used two main criteria for making status distinctions between people: prestige and consumption. The prestige ratings did not refer to personal reputation in the community, perhaps because these are big towns where people do not know many of their fellows by name. Instead, the ratings referred to the moral repute of people who lived a certain way. The respondents thought in terms of prestige categories which were based essentially on consumption behavior or general "style of life," and they recognized that consumption depends on occupation. But the ranking of occupations was derivative—a halo effect from the consumption privileges they bought.

No symbol better represents the common man in these communities (and of course it is a local symbol) than the two-family wooden frame house in good condition. These houses stretch out mile after mile all over the metropolitan area. They are crowded rather closely together; there is little lawn space except, perhaps, for a small yard in the rear. The houses have a living room, dining room, kitchen, two or three bedrooms and a bathroom. They are furnished for comfort, not for conspicuous style: furniture is not remodeled just to "bring it up to date." The furnishings are in the Sears-Roebuck tradition, usually 10 to 20 years old, and not necessarily conforming to any matched pattern. The walls are usually covered with flowered paper, and often the dining room has a linoleum rug. There is a small TV set, and in front is parked a secondhand Ford or Chevrolet. Most of the upkeep of the house is taken care of by father, who is "handy with tools."

The subjects thought themselves well off because nowadays father had a steady job, and they remembered well when jobs were scarce. But they faced a constant struggle with inflation, and often mother or older children worked part time to help balance the weekly budget. Savings accounts with more than a couple of hundred dollars were rare.

There were rather wide variations in income among these families, from differences in father's paycheck and from the number of family members who worked. But these variations are often matched by variations in the size of the family. A policeman who earned $3,600 a year and had two children lived approximately the same way as a milkman who earned $5,000 and had nine children, including an older daughter who contributed $5 a week from her secretarial earnings. The respondents recognized the variations in income, even to the extent of noting that some neighbors could afford a two week vacation in the country; yet they considered all people who lived about as they did, just getting by on a weekly paycheck, as similar to themselves. They readily distinguished themselves from people who could afford a large single family house with a yard, and from slumdwellers.

They did not make sharp distinctions between white and blue collar work. Often the fathers had had both types of jobs during their careers, and quite common was the family where one son worked in factory while another was a clerk. Prestige was based on income and style of life, not on the color of one's work collar.

About half of the parents had gone at least part way through high school; only one had attended a liberal arts college; and a few fathers had gone to a business college or technical trade school for a year or less after high school. Most of the parents were native born; they come predominantly from Yankee, Irish, Italian and French-Canadian stock.

This sample of common man families had a style of life, a set of value-attitudes about it, and a class-consciousness which distinguished people like themselves from others who lived differently. (The class-consciousness concerned a definition of social space and not an idea of joint action.) They felt that they were ordinary people who were respectable but unimportant; who were decent but powerless; who lived comfortably but without the flamboyance, the freedom and the fun of conspicuous consumption; who compared to the middle class, had inadequate income, inadequate education, inadequate understanding of the way things *really* worked, inadequate social and technical skills.[4]

The parents were articulate in varying degrees about these matters; a few seemed to live the daily routine without much awareness of their place in the social scheme of things, but most had at least some perceptions of social space and some way of placing themselves within it. Fifteen of the 24 families tended toward the view that the social scheme and their own place in it were morally proper and legitimate. They believed that people like themselves who were not overly bright or ambitious had, as a matter of course, a certain style of life which might be questioned in detail but not in substance. Some said this way of life was not only to be accepted but to be preferred, that the competitive game to rise higher was not worth the candle. These 15 families could be said to espouse the core value of "getting by."

Eight families felt that the general social scheme was not bad, but that they had not risen quite as high as they should have. And one man raised serious questions about the moral justice of the scheme itself—he had flirted with radicalism in his youth, but lacked the courage to stick to it in the face of social ostracism. These 9 families could be said to believe in the core value of "getting ahead."

The distinctions just made were based on the fathers' attitude toward their own success in life. In a few instances the fathers were considerably more satisfied with their achievement than were their wives, but usually both spouses told the same story.

Let us first examine the attitudes of those who accepted the scheme of things and their own place within it—who believed in just "getting by."[5] They were concerned with balancing the budget each week, with living for the moment in a smooth manner. They looked neither to the past nor the future. Father wanted a job which offered congenial workmates, an easy boss, a regular paycheck. Mother would work occasionally if current bills demanded it or if she enjoyed it—she generally had no strong principles for or against women working. The children were encouraged to enjoy themselves while they were young and before the burdens of life bound them to regular work—sometimes the school-age children were encouraged to work part-time to bring in a little extra money to the family purse, but the pressure was weak. The children were told to stay in high school because a diploma was pretty important in getting jobs nowadays, but they were allowed to pick their own curriculum according to taste. The value "doing what you like to do" was applied to schoolwork, to part-time jobs, and to career aspirations. Rarely was the possibility of a college education seriously considered: "we can't afford such things," or "we aren't very bright in school." Indeed, their perception of college and the kind of jobs college-trained people held were exceedingly vague; they understood that such people were professionals and made a lot of money, but they did not know any such people socially and had no concrete images of what such a life might be. In sum, they felt that common people like themselves were lucky to have a regular job, that the sons would be as the fathers, that such was life and why think about it.

By contrast, the parents who believed in "getting ahead" were more sensitive to social hierarchies and thought more about the subject than those who were satisfied with their lot. They used the middle class as a reference group that was close enough to have meaning, though far enough away to be different. They kept thinking: "there, but for a few small difficulties, go I." The difficulty they usually referred to was lack of education. These people spoke with monotonous regularity about their handicap of poor education. Sometimes they blamed themselves for not taking advantage of their opportunities when young; they said that they did not realize when they still had time how important it was to get advanced training. Other merely shrugged their shoulders with the comment that they came from large families without much money; everyone had to go to work.

Often fathers pointed to the men immediately above themselves in the work hierarchy: machinists to mechanical engineers, carpenters to architects, clerks to office managers. Comparing themselves to those from whom they took orders, the fathers would say: "those fellows are better trained than I and can do things I can't do." Rarely did they complain that the people who got ahead were the sons of the bosses or people with good connections. Instead, they saw an occupational world stratified according to the basic principle of education, and education was something you got when you were young. These people felt vaguely guilty: they accepted the middle class values of getting ahead, they knew they had not gotten ahead, and thus they felt they were to some degree inadequate. They rationalized that it may not have been their fault that they had not received a good education, but nevertheless they felt themselves at least partial failures. Yet if they were blocked, their sons were not. Consequently, they encouraged their sons to take school seriously and to aim for college. By way of contrast, it is interesting to observe that two middle class fathers though admitting that education was important, denied it was crucial. They pointed to "self-made" men who got up because they were smart and worked hard, and they pointed to educated men who were loafers or stuffed with useless book-learning and were not successful in business. Thus it seems that a sense of failure seeks to excuse itself by an external factor like education, whereas a sense of success seeks to glorify itself by an internal factor like brains or "push."

Here are some witnesses to support the general statements made above about the values of these common men:

> Case A: The father went to work as a machinist right after high school graduation. Two years later his parents talked him into going to Business College. After that training, he did very well as a sales manager but didn't like the work. He returned to the machine shop, and has been happy for 30 years. His wife points to the moral of his story: "I want my

boy to do what he likes. Now take my husband. He was very smart in school. He graduated a year young; he skipped a grade. Then his mother wanted him to go to the Business College and he did and he took a job selling, but he wasn't happy with it and so he went back to the machinist work that he had done. You know, he has been told several times that with all of that schooling he should have a better job but he likes what he is doing and I think if that makes him happy that is all that is important. I don't think a person should be made to do something he doesn't like. I I don't like housework, and I know I would just have hated it if I had had to do housework for somebody else; why, I would be the most unhappy woman in the world. . . . During the war my husband made a lot of money working overtime, but you had to work extra for it and I don't think it is good for them to have to work too hard. If you do you come home all tired out and it just doesn't seem worth it, so I'd just as soon have him work the regular day and get the regular day's pay."

Case B: The father is a bread salesman; he has five children. He is a high school graduate. "I was never a bright one myself, I must say. The one thing I've had in mind is making enough to live on from day to day; I've never had much hope of a lot of it piling up. However, I'd rather see my son make an improvement over what I'm doing and I'm peddling bread. . . . I think he's lazy. Maybe I am too, but I gotta get out and hustle. . . . I don't keep after him. I have five kiddos. When you have a flock like that it is quite a job to keep your finger on this and the other thing. . . . I really don't know what he would like to do. Of course, no matter what I would like him to do, it isn't my job to say so as he may not be qualified. I tried to tell him where he isn't going to be a doctor or lawyer or anything like that, I told him he should learn English and learn to meet people. Then he could go out and sell something worth while where a sale would amount to something for him. That is the only suggestion that I'd make to him. . . . I took typing, shorthand, bookkeeping and we had Latin, French, Geometry. We had everything. But anything I would know then I've forgotten now. . . . I suppose there are some kids who set their mind to some goal and plug at it, but the majority of kids I have talked to take what comes. Just get along. . . . I don't think a high school diploma is so important. I mean only in so far as you might apply for a job and if you can say, 'I have a diploma,' it might help get the job, but other than that I don't see that it ever did me any good."

Case C: The father is a baker; the mother works in a chainstore. Both parents have had some high school. They have eight children. She said: "I don't go to see the teachers. I figure the teachers know what they're doing. When I go up there I can't talk good enough. Some women go up there, and I don't know, they're so la-ti-ta. But I can't talk that way. Me, I'm just plain words of one syllable and that's all. And the teachers, they'd just as soon not have you get in their way, I figure. They know what they're doing. I figure he'll get his knocks later on, and he should do what he wants to now. . . . College would be out of the question. We figure we're lucky to be able to put them through high school. When they get out of school, I try to make them get a job as soon as they can. . . . I don't make them do homework or anything. I figure they're old enough to know what they want to do and they'll get their work done by and by. . . . If I didn't go to work, the boy would have had to leave school and go to work, and I didn't want that. It's better to have me working, so it all isn't on one kiddo. . . . They're not very friendly here. I don't really know the neighbors at all. It was different where we used to live. Of course, it wasn't as good a neighborhood as it is here, but I liked it better. Everybody was friendly. We'd all be in each other's hosse for tea all the time. And we were always having babies. There was about ten women always pregnant. And we'd always be sitting out on the steps talking to each other. . . . I'm not very deep-minded. We don't talk about things like that [the future]."

Case D: The father is a petty foreman in a factory with about 20 men under him. He had three years of high school, and is convinced he would have gotten further ahead if he had had more education. "Down at the shop we see a lot of men come in and try to make their way. The ones with the college education seem to succeed better. They seem better able to handle jobs of different sorts. They may not know any more than the other fellows but they know how to learn. Somehow they've learned how to learn more easily. Not only that, they know how to find out about things. If they don't know the answer to a question, they know how to find out about it. They know where to go to look it up. . . . If they get a job and see that they aren't going to get anywhere they know enough to get out of it or to switch. They know enough to quit. I don't blame them either. After they've sacrificed to go to college and had that training. So that's why I hope my boy will go to college. . . . The college men seem also better able to handle themselves socially. They seem smoother in getting along with people and more adaptable to new situations. I think that I would have gotten along a lot better myself if I had had that sort of an education."

IV. Boys' Attitudes Toward School and Work

School and the possibility of college were viewed by all the boys solely as steps to jobs. None was interested in learning for the subtle pleasures it can offer; none craved intellectual understanding for its own sake. The most common phrase in the entire body of interviews was "nowadays you need a high school diploma (or a college degree) to get a good job." Often a distinction was drawn between the diploma and the education it symbolized; the boys wanted the parchment, not the learning. In this pragmatic approach toward schooling, the boys reflected the views of their parents (and of most of their teachers).

All the boys who were convinced that a college degree was the basic essential for a job were seeking middle class jobs. Often they had a specific occupation in mind, such as engineering or accounting. Sometimes they just knew the level of job which they wanted, and talked more about the style of life that the income would buy than the details of the work itself. By contrast, the boys who were not aiming toward college occasionally had a specific common man job as their goal, but more often had no firm goal at all—they would "take anything that comes along."

It was not always clear which came first: the job ambition or the school performance. Sometimes the desire for the job did seem to be the base for the school motivation, yet sometimes a boy who did well in school became slowly convinced that he was good enough to think of a middle class job and sought for one that would be suitable without knowing in advance what it might be. Here are two contrasting examples: One boy had always wanted to be an architect. His hobby was drawing, and he proudly showed me the plans for many homes he had designed in his spare time. He wanted to go to the Massachusetts Institute of Technology, and was taking the technical college preparatory course. Another boy, who had always done very well in school, planned to be a high school teacher because everybody told him that a boy who did well with books would be a good teacher—but he had no special subject in mind and wasn't sure he would like teaching.

The attitudes of the boys toward schoolwork itself ranged from mild interest in a few courses that seemed to have the closest connection with future work, through tolerance for an activity that was simply a part of life to be taken for granted, through boredom, to active dislike of a dull and difficult task that distracted from more important activity. The mode was somewhere between taking it for granted and boredom. For example:

"I don't hate school, but I don't think there are many who are dying to go." (This boy get the best marks in his class.)

"Yes, I think school is important. If you don't know anything you won't be anything is the way I look at it. If you are going to make a name for yourself in the world you have to know something."

"I'd much rather be working and earning money than going to school and spending it. I'll be glad when I get through. . . . I'll stay until I graduate. . . . I might be trying to get a job sometime and they'd want to know how good I was. Then I could show them my high school diploma, and I might want to set up a small business, too. And then I'd want to know bookkeeping and how to type and how to spell."

"You do well in things you like."

"I don't see why you have to take English if you want to be a mechanic. I suppose it broadens your mind."

"I like school but not schoolwork."

"I think English is a lot of bunk. I don't mean it that way but I mean that we spend a lot of time reading books and poetry. I just don't see it. Then there's stuff like Trig. I can't see taking that unless you are going after a high position—like a doctor or scientist. If you've high ideals, have set high standards, it's O.K., but otherwise I can't see it's any help."

The boys, like the parents, can be divided into two groups: those who believe in "getting by" and those who believe in "getting ahead." This basic split was reflected in their more specific attitudes toward the details of schoolwork, after school recreation, and jobs. The boys who believed in just "getting by" generally were bored with school, anticipated some sort of common man job, and found peer group activity to be the most important thing in life. They were gayer than those who felt a driving ambition to do things and be successful. By contrast, the strivers who believed in "getting ahead" seemed to take schoolwork more seriously than recreational affairs. Each group noticed the difference in the behavior of the other. The nonstrivers "didn't know how to have any fun." The strivers said that the nonstrivers were "irresponsible; didn't know what was good for them."

It is interesting to speculate about the development of those attitudes in the future, using the fathers as indicators of how boys might feel when they are further along in the life cycle. The fathers all had common man jobs, and with the exception of a few skilled workers they found work a dull routine, not a creative activity. Their sons did not know from direct experience the monotony of work; instead many boys looked forward to a job in romantic terms. It symbolized to them an escape from childhood, an end to the school routine, a freedom from dependency on father's pocketbook, a chance to get money for cars and girls. But the boys who went into common man jobs would, if they repeated their father's experiences, suffer at least some disillusionment. Not only would they learn that work can be duller and more empty than school, but many would feel some pangs of failure, for even though they did not all embrace the middle class norm of getting ahead, they were aware that it existed and was to some degree the dominant norm of their society. They would feel just a little on the outside of things. Many fathers and sons who perceived this value conflict comforted themselves with the philosophy of just getting by—enjoy what you can and don't bother to worry or plan because there's nothing you can do about it. The irony of the situation lay in the fact that the sons looked forward to adulthood as their greatest chance to live according to this philosophy, while the fathers looked back on adolescence as their period of greatest glory. It may well be that the boys' gang is the one institution of our culture which best transforms the value of getting by into organized interaction and satisfying ceremony, yet the boys did not know it.

Those boys who were aiming at middle class jobs were sacrificing some adolescent freedom and fun in order to channel more energy into schoolwork; for some, the sacrifice would lead to professional careers that would have creative meaning. At any rate, while in school they felt that their books were tied in with important aspects of their future lives, even though the books were not very exciting in themselves. Both of these ways of life contained satisfactions and dissatisfactions; the important thing to notice is that they were different.

Let us turn to a consideration of the development through time of the boys' attitudes toward school and work. In many ways, the grammar school years were crucial in "defining the situation." From his experiences in those years, each boy gradually formed a conception of himself as a pupil based on his estimate of his intelligence and his interest in books.

Each boy's performance defined the situation for his parents as well as for himself. The parents in this sample had not studied Gesell; they had no scientific standards for estimating the intelligence of their children. Yet, intelligence is a basic value in American culture; people who are "smart" are expected to act differently from those who are "dumb." Parents used early school performance as their main criterion for placing their children. If a boy did well, his parents expected him to continue doing well; if he did poorly, they usually decided that he was just one of those who was not smart and good at books and often emphasized his other qualities, such as skill with his hands or ability to get on well with people. The boy who was defined as smart and then later began to slip seriously in his schoolwork often got into trouble with his parents: they would assume he had gotten lazy or had started to run around with bad companions who were ruining him.

These common man parents seemed to have more tolerance for individual differences than do middle class parents. Often they themselves had done poorly in school and felt that they could not expect all their children to be brilliant. Consequently, they paid much attention to their sons' demonstration of ability in grammar school. There was a feedback situation: the better a boy did in school, the better he was expected to do. Said a father of nine:

> "John and his sister are the only two that have talent—I think those are the only two that are college timber. One of the boys is going to work with his hands—he hasn't said anything about it, but I can watch him, I can see that he wants to do carpentry or mechanical work, machine work of some kind. Couple of the children have been held back in school— none of them are as good as John. You know, I try and keep him from being too much a model for them to follow. I think it's good, but I don't want them to feel that they have to do as well as he can because I know they can't—he's exceptional."

A boy from another family echoed the sentiments in the terse remark: "I suppose they figure: if ya got it, ya got it; if ya haven't, ya haven't."

The average marks for the first six years of school were significantly higher for the 12 boys who were college oriented than for the 12 who did not plan further education after high school. But the difference was not great; the first group averaged just above "B," the second group just below it. As has been remarked, the causal direction was not always the same; some boys had ambitions for college while in high school because they had done well in grammar school; some boys did well in grammar school in order to prepare themselves for college (probably more because their parents pushed them than because they understood the connection.)

By the time a boy entered junior high school in the 7th grade he had a conception of himself as a scholar: he knew how he *ought* to behave. But his behavior did not always match his own norms, for the situation contained cross-pressures. When homework first appeared (around 8th grade), it became a question of homework versus baseball, homework versus daydreaming, homework versus after school job that brought in precious money and independence from father's pocketbook. Before this time, it was easy for a bright boy to do well: spontaneous intellectual curiosity was all the teacher asked. Homework was a different matter.

Other difficulties arose about the same time. The boys had to choose their curricula and it was known to all that the four programs increased in difficulty as follows: trade, general, commercial, and college preparatory. The unanimity on this rank order was complete, even to those boys who admitted they were more interested in mechanical than verbal activity but wouldn't go to trade school because the trade diploma was not as "good" as the regular one. As one boy put it, and his words were repeated almost verbatim by many others:

> "I chose commercial because it was sort of in-between the general and the college course. I didn't want to take the general course, figuring, oh, you know, people would say, 'oh, he must be failing.' I didn't want to go to college; I don't have a brilliant mind."

There is another factor of importance that became important about the same time: peer group pressures. If a boy wanted to aim higher than his friends, he had to accept derision or isolation from those who thought it was stupid and sissified to join the "fruits" in the college course who carried books home at night. An occasional boy of exceptional social skill was able to stick with the old gang even though he followed a higher curriculum than they did; others gave up their aspirations; still others became isolates or managed to switch into a college-oriented peer group. This problem was of course more acute for ambitious boys from the common man than the middle class, for in the lower status neighborhoods the majority of boys were not oriented toward college, whereas the reverse was true in the upper status areas.

The questionnaire study discussed at the beginning of this article indicated that IQ was the one factor which best accounted for marks received in early grammar school, though the correlation was not very high. It also indicated that social status of family became an important explanatory variable *after* grammar school. For common man boys, the interviews seem to have given some of the reasons why status became important only in the later years. It was in junior high that school became a problem to the boys: homework, the increased difficulties of the work in the college preparatory curriculum (and the much greater competition therein which followed from the selection procedures for entering it), and peer group pressures all combined to make it harder for a bright common man boy to continue doing well in school—natural intelligence was no longer enough. In addition, he then began to worry about the availability of money for college—and college was the reason for doing well in high school. Some boys surmounted these difficulties and continued to do well. But this occurred because they had specific motivation that was strong enough to carry them over the hurdles—motivation which was more rare in the common man than the middle class. The interviews suggested that such motivation came from four directions:

1) If a boy had done well in the early years, *and* had built up a self-conception in which good school performance was vital, he would work hard to keep up his record. But an idea that school was vital occurred only when that early performance was truly exceptional, or if the importance of his standing to him was reinforced by one or more of the other factors listed below.

2) A boy would sacrifice other pleasures for homework when they weren't important to him. If a boy was not good at sports, if he did not have close and satisfying peer contacts, or if he had no hobby that was strongly rewarding as well as distracting, then the cost of homework was less and the balance more in its favor. In extreme cases frustrations in these alternative spheres motivated a boy to good school performance as compensation.

3) If a boy's family rewarded good school performance and punished poor performance, and the boy was not in rebellion against the family for emotional reasons, he was more likely to give up some play for homework.

4) If a boy had a rational conviction about the importance of schoolwork for his future career, he would strive to keep up his performance. But that conviction never appeared unless the parents emphasized it.

There were no cases in which the boy found in schoolwork sufficient intellectual satisfactions to supply its own motivation. And there were no cases where a sympathetic and encouraging teacher had successfully stimulated a boy to high aspirations.

As a result of the four motivational factors in combination, each boy chose his curriculum and reacted to homework in his own way. Sometimes the balance of factors shifted after the first decision. About one-fifth of the boys moved down from one curriculum to a lower one; one boy moved up a step. These adjustments resulted from a difference between a boy's anticipation of what the college preparatory work would be like and his discovery of the facts.

The argument so far is that an intelligent common man boy was not college oriented in high school unless he had a very special reason for so being. Behind all the reasons stood one pre-eminent force: parental pressure.

Parents who believed in the value of "getting ahead" started to apply pressure from the beginning of the school career. They encouraged high marks, they paid attention to what was happening at school, they stressed that good performance was necessary for occupational success, they suggested various occupations that would be good for their sons. Their boys reached high school with a markedly different outlook from those who were not pushed. The strivers tended to have more specific occupational goals, they had educational aims to match, they worked harder in school, they thought more of the future, they were more sensitive to status distinctions, and they believed they could somehow manage to pay their way through college and reach the middle class.

The reader is referred back to Table 3, above. In all the cases therein, except two, families who applied pressure were families who believed in "getting ahead." That usually meant that the father was dissatisfied with his own occupational success. In the two expectional cases where the father was satisfied, the pressure came from the mother, who was less content than her husband.

Two of the four boys who were aiming for college without pressure from home were instances of the "feed-back" phenomenon. They came from large families where the parents would support any aims of children without expecting them all to be alike. The boys had always done exceptionally well in school, and came to think of themselves as the kind of people who "ought" to go to college. The parents fully supported the high ambitions but did not initiate them. The other two boys who were aiming for college without pressure came from homes that were ambivalent: the father was more satisfied with his job than was the mother. The mother did not desire to repudiate her husband, so offered only the softest of suggestions that her son should try to do better.

The connection between parental pressure and sons' response was not just in the mind of the outsider who rated the cases; the boys were aware of it. One boy expressed clearly the relation between his views and those of his parents in these words:

> "I'd like to learn to specialize in college. My folks want me to go to college too. My father didn't get through high school, and he wishes he'd gone to college. He has a good job now but he says if he had just a little bit of college he could have gone much higher. He's got a good job but he's gone as high as he can without a college education. . . . My mother and father don't want me to be a hired man. They want me to be in the upper bracket. They want me to learn by going to school and college, to go ahead by getting a higher education."

A boy who was not being pushed by his parents took an entirely different approach:

"I'm not definite what I'd like to do. Any kind of job. Anything as long as I get a little cash. . . . My folks tell me to go out and get a job, anything, just as long as it's a job. They say I'm old enough to start turning in board. . . . I haven't got much brain for all that college stuff. . . . You know, nobody would believe me now, but I was an "A" student in grammar school. I dunno what happened; just started dropping gradually. . . . I guess the work just started getting harder. . . . I could do better work if I wanted to. As long as I pass I don't care. What the hell? I got nothin' to look forward to. . . . I was told to take the college course by the teachers. But I didn't want to. I wanted to take it easy."

The interviews indicated that the boys learned to an extraordinary degree to view the occupational system from their parents' perspective. They took over their parents' view of the opportunities available, the desirability and possibility of change of status, the techniques to be used if change was desired, and the appropriate goals for boys who performed as they did in school. The occasional boy who differed from his parents had gotten his ideas from a friend—never from an abstract medium of communication, such as books or movies.

V. *Summary and Conclusions*

This article began with a report of a questionnaire study which indicated that IQ and family status were useful predictors of the educational and occupational ambitions of high school boys. Yet those two variables left unexplained a considerable variance, which was particularly great for boys of high intelligence who came from homes of lower middle status. Consequently, a small sample was chosen from that group for interview analysis; half of the boys in the sample aspired to go to college and prepare for middle class occupations, and the other half of the boys did not desire to go to college and looked forward to common man occupations. The interviews disclosed that although there was a general way of life which identified the common man class, some members were content with that way of life while others were not. Parents who were discontented tended to train their sons from the earliest years of grammar school to take school seriously and use education as the means to climb into the middle class. Only sons who internalized such values were sufficiently motivated to overcome the obstacles which faced the common man boys in school; only they saw a reason for good school performance and college aspirations.

The American creed is supposed to teach everyone that he can become President—if not of the United States, then of United States Steel. Yet these interviews showed that the Creed is by no means universal. Some common man families do not think in such terms, and do not try to push their children up the ladder. The Horatio Alger myth is a middle class myth which percolates down to some, but not all, members of the common man class. If a common man family does accept the myth and has sons who show in their early school performance signs of talent, then they push him forward and encourage him to climb. The schools are more a means than an initiator of ascent.

If a boy does not take advantage of the schools to climb, his later chances will be slim. Many observers have noted that in recent decades the opportunities for getting ahead through owning independent business, or of ascending in the factory from apprentice to boss, are declining.[6] We seem to have approached a bureaucratized class system that has a fundamental split into two halves: the educated and the ignorant. The educated begin at a higher level than the ignorant ever reach. Ownership of property is far less significant than education as a dividing force for all except the very few at the top who own so much. In the early days of the Republic few men had a higher education but many owned productive property. Now the proportions are reversed; even most of the educated work for salaries. Therefore the fathers of the boys in this sample were realists; they were correct in teaching their sons that what they did in school would determine their whole lives. Some sons would not fully understand their fathers until they were out in the work world and could see for themselves. By then it would be too late to change.[7]

NOTES

1. The project is under the direction of Drs. Talcott Parsons, Samuel A. Stouffer, and Florence R. Kluckhohn. I am highly indebted to them and to Research Assistants Dr. Norman Boyan and Mr. Stuart Cleveland. The statistical computations are the work of Stouffer, Boyan and Cleveland; I merely summarize their results. Stouffer has prepared a detailed report on that data for early publication. The interviewing was under the supervision of Kluckhohn, with the cooperation of many graduate students. Of the total of approximately 160 hours of interviews with the 24 boys and their families, I conducted about 60. I alone am responsible for the interpretation of the interview data.

2. Some of the relationship between parental pressure and son's aspiration shown in Table 3 may be from contamination in the ratings: in most, though not all cases, I knew the aspiration of the son at the time I rated the pressure of his parents. The same problem occurred when Mr. Cleveland rated the cases. We disagreed on 4 out of the total 48 ratings; the association between pressure and aspiration in his ratings was higher than in mine. The Mobility Project is now working on a questionnaire for boys to measure their perceptions of pressure from their parents. Thus the interview study was not aimed at "proof"—it fulfilled its purpose of exploring a confusing questionnaire result and offering a new hypothesis which can be tested by further questionnaire data.

3. The scores of the 24 families on the Warner Index of Status Characteristics ranged from 43 to 71, with 57.5 as the median—right in the center of his "upper-lower" class. Warner writes that the upper-lower is the "least differentiated from the adjacent levels and hardest to distinguish in the hierarchy," and so he often combines it with the lower-middle and calls the combination the level of the "Common Man." See W. Lloyd Warner *et al., Social Class in America* (Chicago: Science Research Associates, 1949), Chap. 1. My data indicates that in the urban scene the line between lower-middle and upper-lower cannot usefully be distinguished. The overlap between the lower levels of the white collar world and the upper levels of the blue collar

world is pronounced and growing. For additional evidence see "Survey No. 244" (Chicago: National Opinion Research Center, March 1947).

4. For a vivid description of the attitudes of similar industrial workers, see Ely Chinoy, "The Tradition of Opportunity and the Aspirations of Automobile Workers," *Amer. J. Sociol.* 42 (March, 1952), 453–59.

5. For another way of phrasing the same observations, see Florence R. Kluckhohn, "Dominant and Substitute Profiles of Cultural Orientations: Their Significance for the Analysis of Social Stratification," *Social Forces,* 28 (May, 1950), 379–93. See also Clyde Kluckhohn and Florence R. Kluckhohn, "American Culture: Generalized Orientations and Class Patterns," in *Conflicts of Power in Modern Culture,* ed. by Lyman Bryson *et al.,* (New York: Harper, 1948).

6. See, for example, C. Wright Mills, *White Collar: The American Middle Classes* (New York: Oxford University Press, 1951), Chaps. 1, 2, 4, and 12.

7. For a contrasting description of the training of middle class children, see David F. Aberle and Kaspar D. Naegele, "Middle Class Fathers' Occupational Role and Attitudes Toward Children," *Amer. J. Orthopsychiatry,* 22 (April, 1952), 366–78.

27 Academic Achievement and the Structure of Competition

JAMES S. COLEMAN

IN SECONDARY EDUCATION (and to a lesser extent in lower grades), we are beset by a peculiar paradox: in our complex industrial society, there is increasingly more to learn, and formal education is ever more important in shaping one's life chances; at the same time, there is coming to be more and more an independent "society of adolescents," an adolescent culture which shows little interest in education and focuses the attention of teenagers on cars, dates, sports, popular music, and other matters just as unrelated to school. Thus while it is becoming more important that teenagers show a desire to learn, the developing adolescent cultures shifts their interest further and further away from learning.

Are these conflicting tendencies "natural" ones, irreversible processes resulting from changes in society? Is the nonchalance of the adolescent culture toward scholastic matters, its irresponsibility and hedonism, simply because "teenagers are that way"? Is it something which must be accepted? If so, then the hope of developing students truly interested in learning lies in "rescuing" from the adolescent culture a few students who accept adult values, set their sights on long-range goals, and pay little attention to the frivolous activities of their fellows. This approach is very nearly the one we take now, in our emphasis on special programs for "the gifted child," our concern with selecting the most intelligent and setting them apart with special tasks which will further separate them from their fellows.

This is one approach to the problem, but I think a too-simple one, which refuses to face the serious problem of raising the level of training of the less-than-gifted child, one which in effect says that we must accept the hedonism and lack of interest in learning of the adolescent culture, a hedonism which drains off the energies of the majority of high school students. And this is an approach which can fail even in its attempt to develop the potentialities of the gifted child, for it depends completely on the selection process, and at its best probably misses far more potential scientists and scholars than it finds.

Reprinted from James S. Coleman, "Academic Achievement and the Structure of Competition," *Harvard Education Review*, XXIX (Fall, 1959), 339–51, with the permission of the author and the editor.

If we answer the question differently, if we refuse to accept as inevitable the irresponsibility and educational unconcern of the adolescent culture, then this poses a serious challenge. For to change the norms, the very foci of attention, of a cultural system is a difficult task—far more complex than that of changing an individual's attitudes and interests. Yet if the challenge can be met, if the attention of the adolescent culture can be directed toward, rather than away from, those educational goals which adults hold for children, then this provides a far more fundamental and satisfactory solution to the problem of focusing teenagers' attention on learning.

Norms and Values in the Adolescent Culture

For the past two years, I have been conducting a study in nine public high schools of the "climate of values" which exists among the students in each school, and the effects of the different value climates upon achievement in school.[1] The schools, all located in the Midwest, include small-town schools, suburban schools (one—School F in Table 1—a working class school from which about 25 per cent of the graduates attend college, and one—School I—an especially well-equipped upper-middle-class school about 85 per cent of whose graduates attended college), and two schools (Schools G and H) in cities of about 100,000. Thus the range in social class, in size of school, in type of community, and in parental style is very great. Consequently, the schools, though far from constituting any cross-section or sample of American schools, cover a broad range of social contexts, a range which includes a large proportion of American schools.

Table 1.

Summary Data of General Characteristics of the Nine Schools

General Characteristic	SCHOOL								
	A	B	C	D	E	F	G	H	I
Number of students[a]	200	400	500	400	500	1100	1400	1900	1900
Location	town	town	town	town	town	suburb	city	city	suburb
Average family income[b]	6000	6400	6400	6400	5800	6200	5400	7200	11400

[a] Given to the nearest hundred of students.
[b] Given to the nearest hundred of dollars.

The interests of these teenagers, and the values of the adolescent culture itself, were studied in several ways, among them a questionnaire filled out by every student in each school.[2] To help get a picture of his general interests and activities, each student was asked:

What is your favorite way of spending your leisure time?

The responses went as follows:

Table 2.

**Percentage Distributions of the Favorite Leisure Time Activities
Mentioned by Boys and Girls**

Favorite Leisure Time Activity	Boys[a] (N=4,021)	Girls[a] (N=4,135)
1. Outdoor sports	36.7	18.2
2. Being with the group, riding around, going up town, etc.	17.2	32.5
3. Attending movies and spectator events (athletic games, etc.)	8.5	10.4
4. Dating or being out with opposite sex, or going dancing	13.6	23.6
5. Hobby (working on cars, bicycles, radio, musical instruments, etc.)	22.5	20.1
6. Indoor group activities (bowling, playing cards, roller skating, etc.)	8.0	8.1
7. Watching television	19.4	23.6
8. Listening to records or radio	11.2	31.7
9. Reading	13.7	35.5
10. Other	7.1	9.3
11. No answer	8.1	3.7

[a] Percentages add to more than 100 per cent because some students mentioned more than one activity as their "favorite."

NOTE: For all those readers who use statistical tests of significance to evaluate the results of such tables as this, it should be stated that all the differences discussed in the text from this and succeeding tables are significant at more than the .01 level. This does not imply, of course, that the inferred difference is an important one. It should also be recognized that the assumptions behind significance tests are not met in such survey statistics.

These responses indicate that boys like to spend a great deal of their time in fairly active outdoor pursuits, such as organized sports, boating, and just going around with the fellows. They spend it on hobbies, too (the most frequent of which is working on their car) and on such passive pursuits as movies, television, records, and the like. Being with girls does not, as adults sometimes think, occupy a large part of their time (though, to be sure, it comes to occupy more time as they go from the freshman year to the senior year).

The comparison with girls' leisure-time activities shows a sharp contrast in some categories. Girls spend far less time in active outdoor ways that boys enjoy themselves, more time "just being with their friends," and far more time in vicarious pleasures: reading, listening to records, watching television, movies, attending games.

The general pattern of these leisure pursuits, showing considerably more activity among the boys, is indicative of something which seems to be quite general in the adolescent community: boys have far more to *do* than girls have. Whether it is athletics or cars or hunting or model-building, our society seems to provide a much fuller set of activities to engage the interests of boys than of girls. Thus when girls are together they are much more often just "with the gang" than are boys (one of their frequent afternoon activities being simply "going up town" to window-shop and walk around).

There is a particular point of interest in these responses, thinking about their relation to the school. Few of these categories have any relation to things which go on in school. Some of the hobbies may, of course, have their genesis in school, and some sports are centered around the school, but, except for these, school activities are missing. No one responds that doing homework is his favorite way of spending his leisure time. To be sure, this is at least in part because homework is not viewed as leisure, but as work. Yet athletics manages to run over into leisure time, breaking the barrier that separates work from leisure. Perhaps it is not too much to expect that scholastic activities could also—if the right way were found to take them out of the category of pure work and allow them to spill over into leisure.

Table 3.

Percentage Distribution of the Criteria for Membership in the Leading Crowd Perceived by Boys and Girls

Criterion for Membership in the Leading Crowd[a]	Boys[b] (N=4,021)	Girls[b] (N=4,135)
Good personality, being friendly	26.6	48.7
Good looks, beauty	14.3	28.9
Having nice clothes	9.0	27.4
Good reputation	17.9	25.9
Having money	7.7	14.2
Good grades, being smart	11.9	11.6
Being an athlete (boys only)	16.3	——
Having a car (boys only)	10.7	——

[a] Only categories which were mentioned 10 per cent of the time or more are included.
[b] Percentages add to more than 100 per cent because some students responded with more than one criterion.

NOTE: In computing averages each of the nine schools was considered as a unit.

In a sense, we have spread out before us in Table 2 the activities which capture the energies and interests of teenagers, and the question we are asking is how schools can come to capture those energies and interests in a way that they presently fail to do.

The values of the adolescent subcultures in these schools were studied in several ways, including questions asked of each student. One question asked:

"What does it take to get to be a member of the leading crowd?"

The major categories of response are tabulated in Table 3, for boys and girls separately.

Consider first the girls' response, at the right of the table. Most striking in these responses is the great importance of "having a good personality" or "being friendly." Not only is this mentioned most often overall, but it is mentioned most often in seven of the nine schools. The importance of having a good personality or, what is a little different, "being friendly" or "being nice to the other kids," in these adolescent cultures is something which adults often fail to realize. Adults often forget how "person-oriented" children are: they have not yet moved into the world of cold impersonality in which many adults live. This is probably due to the limits on their range of contacts—for in the limited world of a grade school, a boy or girl *can* respond to his classmates as persons, with a sincerity which becomes impossible as one's range of contacts grows. One of the transitions for some children comes, in fact, as they enter high school and find that they move from classroom to classroom and have different class-mates in each class.

After "a good personality" comes a wide range of attributes and activities. A flavor of them is indicated by the collection of responses listed below—some hostile to the leading crowd (and in their hostility, often see-ing it as immoral), others friendly to it (and in their friendliness, attribut-ing positive virtues to it).

"Wear just the right things, nice hair, good grooming, and have a wholesome personality."

"Money, clothes, flashy appearance, date older boys, fairly good grades."

"Be a sex fiend—dress real sharp—have own car and money—smoke and drink—go steady with a popular boy."

"Have pleasant personality, good manners, dress nicely, be clean, don't swear, be loads of fun."

"A nice personality, dress nice without over-doing it."

"Hang out at ———'s. Don't be too smart. Flirt with boys. Be co-operative on dates."

Among these various attributes, the table shows some mention of "good looks" to be second to "personality" in frequency. Having nice clothes, or being well-dressed, is also important in most of the schools, as the re-sponses above suggest and as Table 2 indicates. What it means to be well-dressed differs sharply in a well-to-do suburb and in a working-class school, of course. Nevertheless, whether it is the number of cashmere sweaters a girl owns, or simply having neat, clean, pastel frocks, the matter of "having good clothes" is an important one in the value system to which these girls pay heed.

In part, the importance of having good clothes appears to derive from its use as a symbol of family status and general opulence. But in some part, it appears to derive from the same source that gives importance to "good looks": these items are crucial in making a girl attractive to boys. Thus in this respect the values of the girls' culture are molded by the presence of boys—and by the fact that success with boys is itself of overriding importance in these cultures.

Another element in the constellation of attributes required if one is to be in the leading crowd is indicated by the class of responses labelled "having a good reputation." In all these schools, this item was often mentioned (though in each school, a disgruntled minority saw the leading crowd as composed of girls with bad reputations and immoral habits). A girl's "reputation" is a crucial matter among adolescents. A girl is caught in a dilemma, a dilemma suggested by the importance of good looks on the one hand, and a good reputation on the other. A girl must be successful with the boys, says the culture, but in doing so she must maintain her reputation. In some schools, the limits defining a good reputation are stricter than others—but in all the schools, the limits are there, and they define what is "good" and what is "bad." The definitions are partly based on behavior with boys, but they also include drinking, smoking, and other less tangible matters—something about the way a girl handles herself, quite apart from what she actually *does*.

Another criterion by which a girl gets into the leading crowd or fails to get in is expressed by a girl who responded simply,

"Money, fancy clothes, good house, new cars, etc (the best)."

These qualities are all of a piece: they express the fact that being born into the right family is a great help to a girl in getting into the leading crowd. It is expressed differently in different schools and by different girls, sometimes as "parents having money," sometimes as "coming from the right neighborhood," sometimes as "expensive clothes."

These qualities differ sharply from some of those discussed above, for they are not something a girl can *change*.[3] Her position in the system is ascribed according to her parents' social position, and there is nothing she can do about it. If criteria like these dominate, then we would expect the system to have a very different effect on the people than if other criteria, which a girl or boy could hope to achieve, were the basis of social comparison—just as in the larger society, a caste system has quite different effects on individuals than does a system with a great deal of mobility between social classes.

It is evident that these family-background criteria play some part in these schools, but—at least, according to these girls—not the major part. (It is true that the girls who are *not* in the leading crowd more often see such criteria, which are glossed over or simply not seen by girls who are in the crowd.) Furthermore, these criteria differ sharply in their importance in different schools. In the working-class suburban school (F), for example, they are almost never mentioned. They are mentioned often in Schools B, D, and H—three schools in stable communities in which middle class families are somewhat more predominant (and more dominant) than in the other towns.

Another criterion for being in the leading crowd is scholastic success. According to these girls, good grades, or "being smart" or "intelligent," has something to do with membership in the leading crowd. Not much, to be sure—it is mentioned less than 12 per cent of the time, and far less often than the attributes of personality, good looks, clothes, and the like. Doing well in school apparently counts for something, though. It is surprising that it does not count for more, because in some situations, the "stars," "heroes," and objects of adulation are those who best achieve the goals of the institution. For example, in the movie industry the leading crowd is composed of those who have achieved the top roles—they are by consensus the "stars." Or in a graduate school, the "leading crowd" of students ordinarily consists of the bright students who excel in their studies. Not so for these high school girls. The leading crowd seems to be defined primarily in terms of *social* success: their personality, beauty, clothes—and in communities where social success is tied closely to family background, their money and family are important, too.

For the boys, a somewhat different set of attributes is important for membership in the leading crowd. The responses below give some idea of the things mentioned.

"A good athlete, pretty good looking, common sense, sense of humor."

"Money, cars, and the right connections and a good personality."

"Be a good athlete. Have a good personality. Be in everything you can. Don't drink or smoke. Don't go with bad girls."

"Athletic ability sure helps."

"Prove you rebel the police officers. Dress sharply. Go out with sharp Freshman girls. Ignore Senior girls."

"Good in athletics; 'wheel' type; not too intelligent."

By categories of response, Table 3 shows that "a good personality" is important for the boys, but of less prominence than it is for the girls. Being "good-looking," having good clothes, and having a good reputation are similarly of decreased importance. Good looks in particular are less important for the boys than for the girls. Similarly for the items which have to do with parents' social position—having money, coming from the right neighborhood, and the like.

What then are the criteria which are more important for boys than for girls? The most obvious is, as the table indicates, athletics. The role of athletics as an entree into the leading crowd appears to be extremely important. Of the things that a boy can *do*, of the things he can *achieve*, athletic success seems the clearest and most direct way to gain membership in the leading crowd. Having good grades, or doing well academically, appears to be a much less safe pass to the leading crowd than does athletics (and sometimes it is a path away, as the final quotation listed above suggests).

An item which is of considerable importance for the boys, as indicated in Table 3, is a *car*—just having a car, according to some boys, or having a *nice* car, according to others. But whichever it is, a car appears to be of considerable importance in being part of the "inner circle" in these schools. In four of the five small-town schools—but in none of the larger schools— a car was mentioned more often than academic achievement. When this is coupled with the fact that these responses include not only juniors and seniors, but also freshmen and sophomores, who are too young to drive, the place of cars in these adolescent cultures looms even larger.

Several other questions in the questionnaire present the same general picture that this "leading crowd" question reveals: social success with the opposite sex (to which good looks, a good reputation, good clothes, and a car contribute), athletic achievement for boys, a few school activities such as cheerleading for girls, being willing to "have a good time" for both boys and girls, are the attributes and activities which are highly valued among teenagers. Far less important to the adolescent community are the activities which school is obstensibly designed for: scholastic achievement, leadership of academic clubs, and the like. For example, the question:

> "If you could be remembered here at school for one of the three things below, which one would you want it to be: brilliant student, star athlete, or most popular?"

Boys responded star athlete over 40 per cent of the time, and brilliant student less than 30 per cent of the time. This despite the fact that the boy is asked how he would like to be remembered *in school,* an institution explicitly designed to train students, not athletes.

It is clear from all these data that the interests of teenagers are not focused around studies, and that scholastic achievement is at most of minor importance in giving status or prestige to an adolescent in the eyes of other adolescents. This is perhaps to be expected in some areas, where parents place little emphasis on education. Yet the most striking result from these questions was the fact that the values current in the well-to-do suburban school (I) were no more oriented to scholastic success than those in the small-town schools or the working-class school.

There were differences in the value climates, but not at all in expected directions. And the differences were dwarfed by the similarities. For example, in every school, more boys wanted to be remembered as a star athlete than as a brilliant student. And in six of the nine schools, "good looks" was first, second, or third in importance as a criterion for being in the leading crowd of girls. Having good grades almost always occupied roughly the same place for girls. It was seventh in seven schools, fifth in one (B), and eighth in one (F). That is, in eight schools, it ranked below some of the less-frequently mentioned items not included in Table 3. For boys, the average was higher, and the variation was the greater: it was fifth in three schools (F, G, & I), sixth in two (C & E), third in one (H), fourth in one (B), seventh in one (D), and eighth in one (A). In all schools athletic achievement held a high place for the boys (it was first, second, or third in six of the nine schools).

In short, despite differences in parental background, type of community, and type of school, there was little difference in the standards of prestige, the activities which confer status, and the values which focus attention and interest. In particular, good grades and academic achievement had relatively low status in all schools. If we add to this the fact that these responses were given in school classrooms, under adult (though not teacher) supervision, and to questions which referred explicitly to the school, then the true position of scholastic achievement in the adolescent culture appears even lower.

In fact, there is a good deal of evidence that special effort toward scholastic success is *negatively* valued in most teenage groups. Scholastic success may, in the minor way indicated by the data above, add to a student's status among his fellows; but the success must be gained without special efforts, without doing anything beyond the required work. For example, along with nine public schools, the research mentioned above included a private university laboratory school whose average IQ level is probably surpassed by few schools in the country. This school should be an extreme example of the academically-inclined school. It is, and many students individually pursue their studies with intensive effort. Yet student leaders of the school reported that the "thing to do" to be part of the crowd was to get reasonably good grades *without* expending special efforts in doing so. In other words, even at this extremely scholastically-oriented school, there are group norms in the direction of holding down effort. How effective they are at this high school is unimportant. The important point is that despite the academic inclinations and background of the students, there is a norm against working too hard on one's studies.

A pair of questions asked in the questionnaire gives some indication of the lack of encouragement teenagers give to scholastic effort. Boys were put in a pair of hypothetical situations, one having to do with an academic course, biology, and the other having to do with a non-academic course closely related to the adolescent culture, auto shop. (Some of the schools had no auto shop, but the hypothetical situation seemed to be understood well in all schools.)[4]

The situations, as posed in the questionnaire, were:

> Bill was doing well in biology class, because he had a hobby of collecting and identifying insects. One day his biology instructor asked Bill if he would act as the assistant in the class. Bill didn't know whether this was an honor to be proud of or whether he would be the "teacher's pet." How

would you feel—that it would be something to be proud of, or wouldn't it matter?

> something to be proud of
> something I wouldn't care for
> I'd have mixed feelings

Tom had always liked to fool around with cars and tear down engines and was very good at it. Because of this, the shop teacher singled him out to act as his special assistant. Tom didn't know what to do, since he had no use for boys who hung around the teacher. If you were in Tom's place what would you do?

> I would agree to be assistant.
> I wouldn't agree to be assistant.
> I am not sure.

After each of these questions, a second part was asked:

> Now suppose you decided to agree to be the assistant in biology. What would your friends think when they found out about it?
> They would envy me and look up to me.
> They would kid me about it, but would still envy me.
> They would look down on me.
> They wouldn't care one way or the other.

> If you did become the assistant in the auto-shop class, would your friends look up to you for it, or would they look down on you?
> They would envy me and look up to me.
> They would kid me about it, but would still envy me.
> They would look down on me.
> They wouldn't care one way or the other.

The distributions of responses on these two questions were as follows:

Table 4.

Percentage Distribution of Friend's Reactions to the Biology Assistantship and Auto Shop Assistantship Perceived by Boys

(N=3,830)[a]

Friend's Reaction	Biology Assistant	Auto Shop Assistant
Envy and look up to me	5.3	18.6
Kid me about it, but envy me	50.0	42.0
Look down on me	3.9	5.7
Wouldn't care	37.3	28.8
No answer	3.5	4.9
Total	100.0	100.0

[a] The number of cases is only 3,830 rather than 4,120 as in the previous tabulation because these questions were in a second questionnaire administered in the Spring of the school year (1957–58). The difference is due primarily to drop-outs.

Only 5.3 per cent of these boys felt that their friends would unambiguously look up to them for being biology assistant; over three times as many, 18.6 per cent felt that their friends would unambiguously look up to them for the non-scholastic activity, assisting in the auto shop.

Both these situations, however, involve special effort toward goals defined by the school. And in both these cases, the largest category of response (50 per cent for the biology assistant, 42 per cent for the shop assistant) is the ambivalent one: friends will kid him for becoming the teacher's assistant, but will nevertheless privately envy him. This ambivalent response illustrates the conflicting feelings of adolescents about scholastic success: privately wanting to succeed and be recognized themselves, but (in most adolescent groups) publicly making fun of the success of others, and disavowing interest in scholastic success. Thus it is not only that scholastic success counts for little in the adolescent culture; extra effort devoted to scholastic matters often counts negatively, and is discouraged.

It is true, as suggested above, that some students may be partially "immunized" to this culture, either by the attention of adults who have singled them out for special attention, or by their own concentration upon career aims. Yet in most schools, such a move is almost completely isolating, for the student must cut himself off from the activities of his friends, and in effect remove himself from the pursuits which would make him "part of the crowd." It is not a move easily made, and certainly not one frequently made in the schools I have been studying.

The question, then, is the one posed earlier: Is the nonchalance of the adolescent culture toward scholastic matters something which must be accepted? Or, on the contrary, is it possible for the school itself, or the community, to modify these values in such a way that they will reinforce, rather than conflict with, educational goals? The first step in answering these questions is to analyze the source of the existing norms of the adolescent culture—to refuse to explain away these values by asserting that "teenagers are that way," and instead to inquire how the social demands and constraints to which adolescents are subject may help generate these norms.

Institutional Demands and Group Response

There is a class of institutions which are essentially composed of an administrative corps and a larger group of persons subject to such administration. Schools are one such institution, the teachers of course being the "administrative corps" and the students subject to their ministrations.

The armed services are another example, the officers and enlisted men composing the two groups. Many factories, which have a great number of workers doing roughly similar tasks under the authority of management, are institutions of this sort. Jails are perhaps the most extreme example, for in jails the constraints placed upon the inmates by the guards are maximal, and there is no period of escape from the demands of the institution.

To be sure, these institutions have many differences. The demands placed upon prisoners by the warden, or the demands placed upon workers by management, are very different from those placed on teenagers by the school. Yet the fact remains that the school is an institution designed by the adult society to transmit adult values and skills to children. To transmit these values and skills, the school makes demands upon its students.

In all such institutions, the administrative corps makes certain demands upon, and places certain constraints upon, those under them. In some institutions, the demands and constraints are great; in others they are less so. A kind of continuum could be conceived, with jails at the one extreme of maximal demands and constraints, with the army somewhere in the middle, and schools and factories located further from the maximal extreme (though differences among schools and differences among factories are so great that both can vary almost from one extreme of the continuum to the other). The demands made by management upon workers are essentially that they work and produce, in return for which they receive pay. Similarly, in schools, the demands are that the students study and learn, in return for which they receive grades and are promoted.

The second characteristic of such institutions of importance to the present discussion is not part of the formal rules and regulations, and cannot be found in books of standard practice nor in the school principal's handbook of administration. Yet it is no less there. This is the collective response to the demands and constraints, the collective response made by the group upon which these demands and constraints are thrust. In jails, the codes and the norms to which the inmates hold each other, sharply divergent from the goals and aims of the prison, are well known. The fact that prisons do not rehabilitate, but largely confirm offenders in criminal ways, is almost solely attributable to the fact that each prisoner is subject to the society of the inmates, with its deviant norms and values, and cannot be reached by the professed goals of the prison.[5] A caveat must be entered at this point, however. Not *all* the prisoners adhere to the strong group values and norms of the body of prisoners; some isolates either go wholly their own way or go along with the administration.

The jail is an extreme case, of course. But it illustrates the kinds of processes which occur in other institutions. In factories, among groups of workers, the same process has been documented by much research.[6] Work groups develop norms about how much work is "appropriate," norms against working for employers who pay low rates, norms against taking the jobs of men protesting against an employer. The rules of unions against such practices are merely the formalization of these norms.

These norms are reinforced by all the means groups have at their disposal—ridicule, ostracism, loss of prestige, even physical violence. The "rate-buster" is only one of many epithets which serve to set apart the worker who refuses to reduce his pace to meet the norms.[7]

The defensiveness of these work groups of course varies quite radically from industry to industry and employer to employer. The organization of workers in response to employers' demands ranges from the most militant unions with their arsenal of defense weapons to non-unionized informal work groups which have no dispute with their employer and use only the mildest means to constrain their over-eager fellows. It is true also, as in the jail, that despite the strength of these informal norms among workers, some workers isolate themselves from the group constraints and set their own pace.

The same process which occurs among prisoners in a jail and among workers in a factory is found among students in a school. The institution is different, but the demands are there, and the students develop a collective response to these demands. This response takes a similar form to that of workers in industry—holding down effort to a level which can be maintained by all. The students' name for the rate-buster is the "curve-raiser" or the "D.A.R.—damned average raiser," and their methods of enforcing the work-restricting norms are similar to those of workers—ridicule, kidding, exclusion from the group.

Again it is true that not all the students give in to this group pressure. In particular, scholastically-oriented subgroups can form in large schools and insulate their members against the larger group. It is true also that many students, preparing for college, may work intensely in preparation for a competitive examination for college entrance. Nevertheless, the results of the research discussed above suggest that for most students such intense efforts remain within the framework laid down by the group, interfering little with social activities, sports, or dates.

Looking generally now at this class of institutions, it is characterized by demands on the one hand, and group norms resisting these demands on the other. What is the source of the group norms? Are they purely a social irrationality, a means by which workers foolishly reduce their own pay, as the employer would argue, a means by which teenagers impede their own development, as teachers would insist? Hardly so.

Such norms seem quite rational, given a goal of maximum rewards for minimum effort. If the employer sees what speed is possible, for one man at least, he is likely to revise the work standards upward, or more informally to expect more work from the others. Thus the majority is protecting itself from extra work by constraining the fast minority. Since work rates are necessarily relative, and cannot be judged except in relation to the rates of other men, then one man's gain is another's loss. Consequently such norms, holding down the faster men, act as a collective protection, to keep within reasonable bounds the effort each worker must expend on his job.

In a high school, the norms act to hold down the achievements of those who are above average, so that the school's demands will be at a level easily maintained by the majority. Grades are almost completely relative, in effect ranking students relative to others in their class. Thus extra achievement by one student not only raises his position, but in effect lowers the position of others.

Again the response of the group is purely rational. By holding down efforts and achievements of those who might excel, the general level of effort required to keep an average position is reduced. The group's effort can be seen as one of "combining to prevent excessive competition," and is precisely parallel to the trusts and combines of industries, which attempt by price-fixing and other means to prevent excessive competition. The structure of the situation is the same in both cases: the teacher (or the customer) is attempting to deal with each student (or manufacturer) independently, to obtain his best effort (or his lowest price). In response, the students (or manufacturers) combine, placing constraints on one another, so that the effort (or price) may be kept at a level which is comfortable for most members.[8]

The school creates, with its grading system, what an economist would call a "free-market" situation, with each student a competitor against all his classmates for scholastic position. This unlimited competition, to be sure, may operate without restraint in a few schools, and it is this "free-market" which has led some educators and laymen to attempt to reduce competition. In the large majority of schools, however, there is the collective protection, the defense against excessive effort by group norms which restrain efforts. The schools in which such norms do not exist are few indeed. My research included, as mentioned eearlier, one elite suburban school from which 85 per cent of the graduates attended college; even in this school, good grades were certainly *not* an important means of prestige, and extra effort devoted to scholastic matters brought on the usual kidding or ridicule. And the example of the university high school in which a norm of "good grades without extra effort" exists amid one of the most achievement-oriented student bodies in the country suggests that the school's demands seldom fail to create such a response from the adolescent society.

The result of these norms produces in students a conflict of motivation: put very simply, to be one of the fellows and not work too hard in school, or to work hard in school and ignore the group. Different teenagers resolve this conflict in different ways. Whichever way it is resolved, it sets an artificial dilemma. On the one hand are sociable average students (who could do far better); on the other hand are a few academically-oriented, highly competitive isolates. A boy or girl can be oriented to academic achievement *or* to being popular, but it is hard to be both. This is almost puzzling, because in certain activities (e.g., athletics), achievement generates popularity rather than scorn.

The question raised by this situation is whether such a conflict is necessary. Is it impossible to have the group's informal norms positively *reinforce* (or at least not conflict with) scholastic achievement? To answer this question it will be useful to go a roundabout way and to examine an experiment carried out by a social psychologist some years ago.

Deutsch's Experiment: "Competition vs. Cooperation"

Morton Deutsch carried out an experiment to show the effects of a "competitive situation" and a "cooperative situation" upon achievement, cohesion, and other matters.[9] The experiment went roughly as follows: Classes in industrial psychology were given hypothetical human relations problems to discuss and solve. There were two different reward structures: (a) In some classes, each member was told that he and his four fellow students would each be ranked from 1 to 5 according to the contribution of each to the discussion and to the problem's solution. At the end of the semester, each student's grade was based upon the average of his ranks through the semester. (b) In five other classes, each class was told that it would be ranked as a class from 1 to 5 on the basis of its solution to the problems. At the end of the semester, the ranks of the five classes were averaged, and the members of each class graded according to their class's average rank. Thus in condition (a), each student was being compared with his classmates. In condition (b), each class was being compared with other classes.

Deutsch found several things, all favoring condition (b). He found that the solutions to the problems were better among the classes in condition (b); the class members impeded one another in the discussion under condition (a), but aided one another under condition (b); the feeling of class members toward one another was more positive under condition (b) than (a).

The structure of rewards under conditions (a) and (b) is simple to state: in condition (a), individuals were compared with others in the same group and rewarded relative to these others. This produced competition between individuals. In condition (b), groups were compared with other groups and rewarded relative to the other groups. This produced competition between groups. But although there was competition in both cases, the second kind of competition produced very different consequences from the first: in achievement, in the group members' feelings toward one another, in the unity of the group. So long as the group was competing against other groups, one man's achievement benefited, rather than lowered, the position of other members of his group; consequently, the group's response to his achievement was positive rather than negative.

When the competition was between individuals, the fact that one individual's achievement lowered the position of other group members generated *interference* with one person's efforts by other members, though the interference was perhaps unconscious and subtle. When the competition was between groups, there was *support* of one person's efforts by others in the group. In effect, then, Deutsch's experiment answers the question raised earlier: whether it is possible for the group's informal rewards to reinforce the formal rewards from the outside. When competition was no longer between individuals, but instead between groups, this reinforcement occurred.

An excellent example of the group's norms reinforcing achievement rather than inhibiting it may be found within the high school itself. Athletics is the activity. In high school athletics, there is no epithet comparable to curve-raiser, there is no ostracism for too-intense effort or for outstanding achievement. Quite to the contrary, the outstanding athlete is the "star," extra effort is applauded by one's fellows, and the informal group rewards are for positive achievement, rather than for restraint of effort.

Why the difference between athletics and studies? The athletic team is competing as a team against another school. Thus any achievement by one person benefits those around him—who in turn encourage his efforts, rather than discourage them. His efforts benefit the team, and fellow-team members encourage his efforts. They bring prestige to the school, and other students encourage and look up to him. His achievements give a lift to the community as a whole, and the community encourages his efforts. The basketball player or aspirant who shoots baskets at lunch period in school is watched with interest and admiration, not with derision. This is in direct opposition to achievement in the classroom, which does not benefit the school and puts one's fellows at a disadvantage. A boy or girl who studies at lunch period is regarded as someone a little odd, or different, or queer.

A passage from a recent novel about a high school illustrates the general process:

> "In his home room Trent [a star halfback] received his schedule, made out for him while he was at football camp.
> "Are we going to have a good football team this year?" Miss Vereen asked, as she handed him his schedule slip.
> "Yes ma'am, I hope so."
> "Well, that's fine. That's certainly fine." Miss Vereen knew nothing about football and probably had never seen a game, but anything which increased the stature of Harrison [High School], to which she was fanatically devoted, had her loyal support.[10]

When I write to one of the principals in the schools I am studying and want to say something good or congratulatory about his school, what can I comment on? Nothing scholastic, for his school has little or no opportunity to do anything *as a school* in scholastic directions. I can congratulate him on the basketball team's success, for this is an achievement of the school. When I talk to a class of students and want to compliment their school, the same conditions hold—I can only congratulate them on what the school has done *as a school,* which is ordinarily some athletic success in interscholastic competition. Only when I am talking to one student, alone, can I congratulate him on his excellent grades.

Such congratulations and support of activities of the school as a whole, multiplied many times from persons inside and outside the school, persons inside and outside the community, encourage a school to do more and better in directions which bring on such encouragement. Thus in spite of itself the school's energies are channeled into these directions—the directions which generate support for the school, which make others look up to the school, and give the school a pride in itself for its achievements.

One finding from the research discussed earlier is relevant here. The students' school spirit or feeling of identification with the school was indicated by answers to several questions in the questionnaire. It was highest in those schools which had winning athletic teams, and lowest in schools whose teams had not been successful for several years. But lowest of all was the university high school mentioned earlier, which had a minimal athletic program and discouraged any sort of interscholastic competition. In this school there was seldom an activity which the students could "get behind" as a body.

The peculiar power of interscholastic competition to generate encouragement and support for achievement lies in two directions. First, competition with other groups has a magic ability to create a strong group goal. While some group projects succeed without the added incentive of competition, others would hopelessly flounder if it were not for the chance of winning. This has been the fate of many well-intentioned and well-planned group projects in high schools—projects which have failed to capture the energies of the group.

Secondly, interscholastic competition generates support at levels which intergroup competition within the school can never reach. Until now, I have discussed the social support given by other "group members," with no further differentiation. But consider the difference between interscholastic competition, on the one hand, and competition between two teams into which a school class has been divided, on the other. In the latter case, there will be support and encouragement only from fellow team members. In the former case, there will be support first from other team members, then from other non-participating students, and finally from persons in the community. That is, if the school's winning gives the community pride in itself and its school, they will encourage its efforts; if the team's winning gives the student body pride in their school, they will encourage its efforts.[11]

In other words, when competition is interscholastic, the social support and encouragement begins at the level of the school itself, thus permeating the whole social milieu surrounding the team members. When it is intramural, social support begins only at the level of the team, or the subgroup it represents, resulting in a much less supportive social environment for the team member.

An Alternative to Interpersonal Competition

The structure of competition in high schools—interpersonal competition in scholastic matters, interscholastic competition in athletics (and sometimes in music, and occasionally in a few fringe activities)—presents a curious picture. It undermines a student's efforts in scholastic directions (where he is working only for himself), and encourages his efforts in these other, tangential directions (where he is striving for team and school as well as himself). The interests of the adolescent community, emphasizing sports and ignoring studies, must be attributed in large part to this structure of competition—something for which adults, not adolescents, are wholly responsible.

One obvious solution is to substitute interscholastic (and intramural) competition in scholastic matters for the interpersonal competition for grades which presently exists. Such a substitution would require a revision of the notion that each student's achievement must be continually evaluated or "graded" in every subject. It would instead make such evaluations infrequent, and subsidiary to the group contests and games, both within the school and between schools.

Such a change from interpersonal to intergroup competition would also make it necessary to create, with considerable inventiveness, the vehicles for competition: intellectual games, problems, group and individual science projects, and other activities. Yet there are some examples which show that it can be done: debate teams, group discussion tournaments, drama contests, music contests, science fairs (though science fairs as now conducted lack one crucial element, for they are ordinarily competitions between individuals, and not competitions between schools, thus lacking the group reinforcement which would go along with "winning for the school"). There are, in one place and another, math tournaments, speaking contests, and other examples of interscholastic competition.

In other places, one can find the bases from which to develop new kinds of scholastic competition. For example, at Rand Corporation sociologists have developed "political gaming," in which teams represent policy-makers in various countries. An international situation is set up, the policy-making teams respond to it and to one another's moves (under the supervision of referees), and a game is pursued in earnest. It is not too difficult to see how this, and modifications of it to include legislative politics, union-management bargaining, and other such situations, could be brought to the high school level and used in interscholastic competition. (Rand reports that an experiment in political gaming at MIT induced such interest among the student players and spectators that for weeks afterwards they avidly followed international news events, to see how their moves corresponded with actual policies as they developed.)

As another example, business executives are now being trained in a few companies by "management games," in which hypothetical situations are set up requiring teams of executives to make decisions and observe the consequences. Electronic computers provide the hypothetical situation and the economic environment, so that the executive in a sense is playing against the computer. With effort and ingenuity, such games could be adapted to training in high school, not only in business economics, but in other areas.

There are many examples in high schools which show something about the effects such competitions might have. As an example, one of the schools I have been studying is too small to compete effectively in most sports, but participates with vigor each year in the state music contests. It nearly always wins a high place in the statewide contest. The striking result of this successful competition is the high status of music among the adolescents themselves. It is a thing of pride to be a trombone soloist in this school, and the leading boys in the school are also leading musicians—not, as in many schools, scornful of such an unmanly activity. This is despite the fact that the school serves a largely farming community.

It is true that many of the examples mentioned above have had far less effect in bringing informal social rewards, encouragement, and respect to participants than the present analysis would suggest. The reason is clear, however: such social rewards from the student body as a whole are only forthcoming in response to something the individual or team has done for *them,* such as bringing glory to the school by winning over another school. If the activity, whether it be debate or math competition or basketball, receives no publicity, no recognition in the newspapers and by the community generally, then its winning will have brought little glory to the school, and will bring little encouragement to the participants. (For example, basketball games at the University of Chicago have for years played to crowds of ten or twenty students.)

For this reason, sporadic and infrequent cases of interscholastic competition in non-athletic activities, with no attention to promotional activity, have little effect. However, if there were systematically organized competitions, tournaments, and meets in all activities ranging from mathematics and English through home economics and industrial arts to basketball and football, and if promotional skills were used, the resulting public interest and student interest in these activities would undoubtedly increase sharply. Suppose such a set of activities culminated in a "scholastic fair," which like a state fair included the most diverse exhibits, projects, competitions, and tournaments, not between individuals, but between *schools.* I suspect that the impact upon student motivation would be remarkably great—an impact due to the fact that the informal social rewards from community and fellow-students would reinforce rather than conflict with achievement.

These are simply examples of what might be done to change the structure of rewards in high school—to shift from interpersonal competition, with its conflict-producing effects, to intergroup competition, in which group rewards reinforce achievement. More important than these examples, however, is the general principle—that motivations may be sharply altered by altering the structure of rewards, and more particularly that among adolescents, it is crucial to use the informal group rewards to reinforce the aims of education rather than to impede them.

It is important, of course, that unintended consequences be taken into account in changing the reward structure in the ways that have been suggested. For example, in devising interscholastic games of an intellectual sort, it is important that they do in fact teach the skills desired. A carelessly-designed program of interscholastic games might result in nothing more than a series of quiz shows, which exercise no other mental activities than those of recall. It is for this reason that the recently-developed "political gaming" and "management games" which use electronic computers to simulate the market seem particularly interesting. Like debate, and unlike quiz shows, these games teach skills and impel the participants to learn how the economic, political, or other system operates.

Perhaps the most important problems in devising such games would be to insure a balanced system of rewards among the various activities and to insure a balanced participation among the various students. As many schools have found with extra-curricular activities, participation becomes narrowly confined to a few unless rules are set up to prevent such concentration. If interscholastic games were to replace the present within-school competition for grades, such rules to distribute participation would become even more important.

These problems indicate that such changes should be made with care. But the general point is clear: the present structure of rewards in high schools produces a response on the part of the adolescent social system which effectively impedes the process of education. Yet the structure of rewards could be so designed that the adolescent norms themselves would reinforce educational goals.

NOTES

1. This research was carried out under a grant from the U.S. Office of Education.

2. The problem of getting straightforward responses in such a questionnaire is extremely difficult. To help insure this, members of our staff administered the questionnaires in the absence of the teacher, and students were assured that no one in the school would see their responses. The responses we obtained were undoubtedly adult-oriented, but appeared, by all the criteria at our disposal, to give us as accurate a picture as adults are likely to obtain of the values current among the adolescents.

3. To be sure, she sometimes has a hard time changing her looks or her personality; yet these are her own personal attributes, which she can do something about, except in extreme situations.

4. Girls were asked a similar pair of questions, the first one the same biology question, and the second a question about sewing class. The results were essentially the same as those for the boys presented below, so that they are omitted for simplicity.

5. There are several interesting researches which show the values of the prisoners. A classic is Donald Clemmer's *The Prison Community* (Boston: Christopher, 1940). Richard Cloward, reporting upon intensive research in an army prison, shows well the norms which develop among prisoners in response to the demands of the prison. He shows also the different modes of response of different prisoners to the rehabilita-

tive aims of the prison. This is reported in *Social Control and Anomie: A Study of a Prison Community* (to be published by The Free Press).

6. The classic study is F. J. Roethlisberger and W. J. Dickson, *Management and the Worker* (Cambridge: Harvard University Press, 1930). A recent study of a number of work groups gives considerable insight into the conditions which generate norms of defensiveness among workers. See Leonard R. Sayles, *Behavior of Industrial Work Groups: Prediction and Control* (New York: John Wiley & Sons. Inc., 1958).

7. This is not to say that there are not sometimes pressures in the opposite direction—to work harder, faster. But these are pressures from the other workers as *individuals,* in the absence of group formation. Peter Blau shows this well in his *Dynamics of Bureaucracy* (Chicago: University of Chicago Press, 1955), in which he shows that one interviewing section in a welfare agency develops group norms which modify the demands upon them, while the other never develops such a group. Instead, each individual, in direct competition with the others, exerted a pressure for more and faster work.

8. The way in which a modification in the structure of institutional demands and rewards creates a modification in the group response is well illustrated by the following comment. It was written by a colleague (Jan Hajda) who had attended a Czechoslovakian gymnasium, upon reading a draft of this paper.

In the European gymnasium system, both the institutional demands and the group response to them are different. First, the levels of achievement are set by impersonal standards established by the Ministry of Education or a comparable distant supervisory body. Consequently, the standards themselves cannot be manipulated by students nor, for that matter, by their teachers. Theoretically, all students in a given class can pass a course on the highest level or fail to pass. Ideally, the performance of students is judged individually in terms of the set standards and not in comparison with the performance of his peers. This fact tends to minimize—although it does not eliminate—interpersonal competition.

Nobody benefits from holding down effort to a lower level and consequently there is no reason for protecting the collectivety from superior achievement of a few students. The group solution is not in "price-fixing" but in establishing a holding operation which benefits all participants—institutionalized cheating. The informal group norms demands that the top students help the mediocre ones by letting them copy their assignments or by circulating correct answers to a written class examination while the examination is in progress. In a way, the top student is giving up his chance to out-distance others without lowering his own performance. In return, he gets not only recognition for his cooperative behavior but also for his scholastic performance. The better his own performance, the higher the survival chance of his peers.

Thus it is in the interest of the collectivity that there be at least a few outstanding achievers. The top students become symbols of collective security. In turn, academic achievement becomes highly desirable, since it represents the safest way to informal leadership and prestige. The exception to this rule arises only in case the top students refuse to cooperate in cheating, i.e., refuse to share the product of their labors with their peers. In such instances the high achiever is ostracized, ridiculed, and stereotyped as teacher's pet, and his peers do their best to prevent him from making the grade he is aiming for.

9. Morton Deutsch, "The Effects of Cooperation and Competition upon Group Process," in D. Cartwright and A. Zander (eds.), *Group Dynamics* (Evanston: Row Peterson, 1953), pp. 319–53.

10. John Farris, *Harrison High* (New York: Rinehart, 1959), p. 5.

11. To be sure, there are interscholastic games between schools which are ignored by student body and community alike; but this is less true than is usually realized when such games are given attention and encouragement by the school administration.

PART V

The Changing
Social Functions of
Schools and
Universities

28   *Education and Social Change in Modern England*

DAVID V. GLASS

THOSE WHO have read Dicey's *Lectures* will remember that he has very little to say on the development of educational policy. He was concerned with the growth of collectivism—with that "combination of socialistic and democratic legislation" which, in his view, threatened "the gravest danger of the country."[1] Educational objectives as such, and their relation to the needs and structure of society, did not form part of his inquiry. Hence his brief comments on the then recent history of public elementary education were designed only to show that the new system was a "monument to the increasing predominance of collectivism."[2] In that respect the Education (Provision of Meals) Act of 1906 drew some of his sharpest criticism. "No one can deny," he said, "that a starving boy will hardly profit much from the attempt to teach him the rules of arithmetic. But it does not necessarily follow that a local authority must provide every hungry child at school with a meal; still less does it seem morally right that a father who first lets his child starve, and then fails to pay the price legally due from him for a meal given to the child at the expense of the ratepayers should . . . retain the right of voting for a Member of Parliament."[3] It would not be too difficult to envisage Dicey's attitude to present-day public expenditure of about £20 millions a year in subsidising school milk and meals.[4]

Whether or not it is appropriate to attach the label "collectivist" to the whole complex of educational change in England since the nineteenth century, the label itself provides no explanation of that change. Nor does the enunciation of the principle of the "Equalisation of Advantages among individuals possessed of unequal means for their attainment"[5]—a principle upon which Dicey calls in discussing the growth of State support of education—take us very much further. Educational policy, like all social policy, is rarely single-minded. To understand the final compromise of policy means tracing the main strands of ideas and influences which have been woven into it, and this, in a general way, is the aim of the present lecture. First, however, it is necessary to draw attention to the time-scale on which

---

Reprinted from M. Ginsberg (ed.), *Law and Opinion in England in the Twentieth Century* (London: Stevens and Sons, Ltd., 1959), with the permission of the author and the publisher.

educational change has taken place, for that has a bearing upon the present situation and upon future possibilities.

Education for the mass of children and young people, financed to the greatest extent by public money, has a short history in England. Though private philanthropy and governmental subventions joined together to support a considerable number of primary schools from the 1830s, it was not until 1870 that the law assured public primary education to children who did not have access to private schools. Compulsory attendance came afterwards—in 1880, up to the age of ten; in 1893, up to the age of eleven; and not until 1918 up to a minimum age of fourteen.[6] Substantial provision of secondary education began even later. The numbers of pupils in the boys' "public schools" had never been large, and by the early nineteenth century those schools had ceased to draw, to any appreciable extent, upon the general population. Nor did the endowed grammar schools cover more than a small fraction of children. Even after the work of the Endowed School Commissioners, by 1895, the total number of children in endowed and proprietary secondary schools was not, apparently, much above 100,000.[7] It was under the 1902 Act that responsibility for elementary education came to be laid on the local authorities, who were also given power to assist or provide secondary or other higher education. To the now subsidised endowed schools were added others maintained by the local education authorities. By the eve of the First World War the number of pupils in secondary schools recognised by the Board of Education was over 200,000, and by 1937 almost 560,000, of whom not far short of 90 per cent were in schools aided or maintained by public funds.[8] Secondary education for all was not, however, provided until the 1944 Act, under which the minimum school-leaving age was immediately raised to fifteen years. The numbers of children in local education authority secondary schools alone now exceed two million.[9]

Moving along a different route, central and local government support of university education has been equally recent. Public funds were first granted to the universities in 1882, but relatively large-scale financing dates only from 1920. Since that time British university income, which has grown more than eightfold, has become increasingly supplied from taxation. Today, the universities, autonomous institutions protected by the Treasury from parliamentary control, neither created nor maintained by the devices applied to primary or secondary education, receive about three-quarters of their income from parliamentary and local authority grants.[10] And in addition, aid from public funds is given to some 80 per cent of university students.[11] Since 1920, the numbers of full-time students have risen from 46,000 to nearly 90,000.[12] Thus, in less than forty years—that is, from the end of the First World War—secondary school populations have been multiplied by six and university populations have been doubled.

I have begun with this historical outline in order to emphasise two

points. First, that in the late nineteenth century England was still educationally a very underdeveloped society. It would, of course, be both incorrect and unjust to minimise the part which religious and philanthropic
bodies had already played in establishing schools. The incidence of illiteracy
could not have been as high as it is in some underdeveloped countries today. Even so, a third of the men marrying in 1840 in England and Wales,
and half of the women, signed the registers by a mark; the proportions in
1870 were still 20 per cent and 27 per cent.[13] The rate of change in the
provision of education since 1870 has been so rapid that it must be taken
into account when considering present-day educational deficiences.

Secondly, it must be equally clear that the phrase "the English tradition
of education," not infrequently used in arguing against further rapid change
in the character of secondary education, has a very limited validity. It can
scarcely apply to the public system which, even during its brief history, has
greatly altered in respect of objectives, structure and methods of selection.
Nor, in the sense of a centuries-old persistence of character, is the term
really applicable to the private sectors, whether secondary or university.
It is true that, as an institution, the grammar school "has a thousand years
of history behind it."[14] But the present character of grammar schools derives
from action taken during the nineteenth and twentieth centuries, action
originally taken because, however deeply rooted the grammar school idea
may have been, the schools themselves had ceased to be effective as educational institutions. In any case, most grammar schools today are not
private. They are maintained by the local education authorities; they are
thus part of the public system; and they have been exposed to powerful
pressures for change in the curriculum, in the universe from which pupils are
drawn, and in the qualifications of teachers. The public schools, too—the
schools belonging to the Headmasters' Conference and the most firmly
imbedded and "traditionalist" part of the private system—bear little resemblance to their original form. They were, on the contrary, the first
schools to be reconstructed in the nineteenth century. Indeed, it was the
reforms introduced by Arnold and others which, as G. M. Young has said,
"reconciled the serious classes to the public school,"[15] and which encouraged the establishment of additional schools; fifty-one out of the present
116 independent public boarding schools were founded in the nineteenth
century.[16] The curriculum has also changed, though more slowly, and half
the present public schools specialise in science and mathematics.[17] The
process of change has applied equally to the universities. The history of
university reform is too well known to need documenting here. But it is
evident that Trevelyan's description of Oxford and Cambridge in the days
of decay as "little more than comfortable monastic establishments for
clerical sinecurists with a tinge of letters"[18] would scarcely apply now.
Moreover, the larger part of the university complex is itself the creation of

the nineteenth century, and almost two-thirds of today's university students are studying in institutions established since the 1830s.[19]

Much of the present educational system is thus not traditional. Moreover, many of its characteristics are not particularly English. Even during the first half of the nineteenth century, once the memory of the French Revolution had become a little clouded, educational reformers in England drew markedly upon the experiments which were being conducted on the Continent.[20] And this was just as well, for the new influences helped to replace the more specifically British contributions of Lancaster's mutual system and Bell's "Madras" system, which appeared to require a school to be a combination of factory and of Bentham's Panopticon. Later in the century Matthew Arnold imported from France the term "secondary education" and with it the objective of a reorganised and comprehensive system. Technical education, too, especially in its shifting empasis from craftsmanship to general principles and their application, was influenced both by foreign competition and by foreign models. All this has clearly been to the good. But along with these innovations there has been one underlying continuity—the influence of the class structure on the images of education and its function. It is this continuity and its consequences which I should now like to discuss.

During the nineteenth century, educational developments reflected two fairly distinct sets of considerations, one relating to the mass of the population and the other to the middle classes. Public concern with elementary education was in large measure concern to meet certain minimum requirements in a changing society—the need to ensure discipline, and to obtain respect for private property and the social order, as well as to provide that kind of instruction which was indispensable in an expanding industrial and commercial nation. Though many individuals and groups showed a far broader vision, these minimal considerations are evident in the very limited objectives of the system which grew up at that time. In the earliest period, the Bible and the catechism were sufficient, Hannah More thought; she would "allow no writing for the poor." Later, the sights were set a little higher. Speaking of the working-class child, James Fraser, subsequently Bishop of Manchester, told the 1858 Newcastle Commission that: "we must make up our minds to see the last of him, as far as the day school is concerned, at ten or eleven . . . and I venture to maintain that it is quite possible to teach a child soundly and thoroughly, in a way that he shall not forget it, all that is necessary for him to possess in the shape of intellectual attainment, by the time that he is ten years old." The Commission accepted the fact that most children would go to work at the age of ten or eleven.[21] A similar assumption underlies the 1870 Act. It is not surprising that H. G. Wells referred to it as "an Act to educate the lower classes for employment on lower class lines, and with specially trained, inferior teachers. . . ."[22]

To gentle the masses was another explicit purpose. "A set of good schools civilises a whole neighbourhood," said the Newcastle Commission[23]; and Forster, when he introduced his 1870 bill in Parliament, spoke of "removing that ignorance which we are all aware is pregnant with crime and misery, with misfortune to individuals and danger to the community. . . ." And he continued, "I am one of those who would not wait until the people were educated before I would trust them with political power. If we had thus waited we might have waited long for education; but now that we have given them political power, we must not wait any longer to give them education."[24] Some of these notions were changed when the 1902 Act provided a framework for both elementary and secondary education. But the civilisation motive had a longer currency, and even in 1929 Sir Cyril Norwood argued that it was largely elementary education which had prevented "Bolshevism, Communism, and theories of revolt and destruction from obtaining any real hold upon the people of this country." "I hope," he added, "that those who attribute the scarcity of domestic servants to the unreasonable institution of elementary education, by which they are made to pay for the teaching of other people's children, will lay in the other scale this other service, which has made of Bolshevism only a bogy which sits by their pillows and frightens them in the night. . . ."[25]

Concern with secondary education sprang from different motives. The effectiveness of the public schools and the endowed grammar schools as educational institutions for those groups who could afford to make use of them was the main issue. In the early part of the century an attempt had been made to compel the public schools to give the local poor the rights to entry provided by the founders' statutes. But the attempt failed, and the place of the public schools in the national system of secondary education was not again discussed by a Government committee until 1942.[26] Instead, in 1861 a Royal Commission was appointed to study the quality of the education in what have ever since been known as the "Clarendon schools" —nine schools with 2,815 pupils. And the Clarendon Commission was immediately followed by the Taunton Commission, which inquired into the education given in the endowed grammar schools. Though expressing some disquiet at existing class distinction in education, the Taunton Commission in the main accepted the situation as they found it, and their recommendations were drawn up for the benefit of the middle classes by whom the schools were being used. What is particularly interesting is the emergence at this stage of a fresh criterion of the effectiveness of secondary education, the criterion of providing an avenue to the universities; and there were unfavourable references to the fact that 550 grammar schools sent no boys to universities, in sharp contrast to the large numbers now going from the nine Clarendon schools and from some of the recently founded proprietary schools.[27]

For university education, like secondary education, was coming to have a new meaning. The changing society needed individuals of greater educational maturity and tested qualifications. The old and the new middle classes needed avenues of employment which would provide both prestige and relatively high income for their sons. Considerations of both scientific and social status were causing the existing professions to raise their standards of entry, and additional professions, including the higher civil service, were beginning to develop, also demanding considerable educational attainments. In earlier days, when Fellows of the Royal College of Physicians were practising medicine in the intervals between their active social life rather than practising medicine in order to live, the College restricted its Fellowship to graduates of Oxford, Cambridge and Trinity College, Dublin. These were men of good breeding, and some of them earned substantial incomes. Their background and their style of living conferred prestige upon the profession. As one eighteenth-century pamphleteer wrote: "the very sight of a handsome dress is restorative and comes like a good prognostick . . . a sordid surface is not only unpromising, but prejudicial . . . ," and "poverty . . . in any profession is but a bad sign of qualification and ability."[28] The nineteenth-century objective went further: it was not simply to recruit members who would confer distinction upon the profession, but also to have a profession which would confer social prestige upon its members. And by the time the Taunton Commission was sitting, even Miss Marrable, Anthony Trollope's conservative old spinster, who entirely rejected the notion that wealth by itself might confer social distinction, was beginning to admit that medicine, surgery, the civil service and possibly civil engineering might offer suitable employment for the sons of gentlemen.[29]

Miss Marrable was in fact a little ahead of her time. It took State intervention to add the final touches to some of the professions and to intensify their social homogeneity. For the higher civil service, it was the application of the Northcote-Trevelyan reforms which, as the Permanent Secretary of the Board of Trade said at the time, involved the selection of individuals who had had "an expensive education in high subjects in early years, which only the rich can afford."[30] In medicine, as Professor Titmuss has suggested, it required the 1911 Health Act, which raised the income of the general practitioner; while the increasing spread of State medical aid also helped by narrowing the field of action of the unlicensed practitioner. Nevertheless, by the time of the Taunton Commission, secondary and university education were ceasing to be largely the concomitants of relatively high social status. They were becoming the means whereby, for the middle classes, status might be preserved or improved. The Commission clearly had this in mind in referring to the particular needs of "the great body of professional men, especially the clergy, medicine men and lawyers," who "have nothing to look to but education to keep their sons on a high social level."[31]

Though the grammar schools improved after the Taunton Commission, and though elementary education became far more widespread after the 1870 Act, in neither case was the rate of progress adequate. But change was in the air. Two further commissions were appointed, one of which, the Bryce Commission, not only laid the foundations of the 1902 Act, but also defined secondary education in terms not accepted until 1944. On the social and economic side there were stimuli equivalent to those which generated a more acute concern for public health. Foreign industrial competition was one such stimulus, and particularly competition by industries based upon the new chemical technology. The need for science teaching and for the training of technicians was acknowledged. Shortages of other kinds of trained manpower were also visible. The Boer War, which showed up physical defects in the working classes also revealed deficiences in the education of the officers. Comparable education deficiences lower in the social scale were such that, it was said, "city offices were forced to employ so many thousands of German clerks for want of a home-grown substitute."[32] When he was introducing the 1870 Bill, Forster spoke of the relation between education and national power, and he argued that "we must make up for the smallness of our numbers by increasing the intellectual force of the individual."[33] Now the slogan became "sea power and school power" as the essential basis of the Empire. The validity of assistance to the working classes was also being reviewed. Preston's pamphlet, *The Bitter Cry of Outcast London*—read and commented upon by Robert Morant when he was an undergraduate[34]—and Booth's encyclopedia of London poverty, had shown that, for a large proportion of urban workers, self-help was not a precept which could be followed. The total combination of influences made possible the 1902 Education Act, providing a national system in which public funds were to be used to assist secondary, in addition to providing elementary, education. Middle-class as well as working-class children were to benefit. The inclusion of the former perhaps helps to explain the otherwise curious fact that Dicey, though he criticises the granting of free school meals, makes no reference to the supply of subsidised secondary education.[35]

How did the national system work out in practice? The very great quantitative changes which occurred after 1902 Act have already been indicated, but it is equally important to emphasise the general improvement in the quality of the education given. In particular, the aims of elementary education were entirely redefined by Morant. To "make the best use of the school years available," was now the purpose, not to provide the "minimum mental equipment" required for the mass of the children, as Lowndes put it for the school board days.[36] With the educational objective thus changed, the middle classes, too, came increasingly to use the public elementary schools for their children—especially as the spread of suburbs lead to the building of new schools for populations which, socially, were relatively homogeneous.[37] Publicly aided and maintained secondary education experienced similar improvements, and the proportions of children going from an elementary to a secondary school more than doubled between the wars. Further, a new scholarship route was established between the elementary and the secondary school. So far as the middle classes were concerned, the Taunton Commission had already envisaged the need for a ladder, allowing able children to reach the higher grades of secondary school. The Bryce Commission extended the ladder to working-class children, and from 1907 onward increasing numbers of scholarships were provided out of public funds. To the surprise of some grammar school head teachers, who had envisaged the free-placer as a "fearsome wild beast," working-class scholarship winners behaved well, scholastically and socially, and one of the major pressures during the inter-war period was for more and more scholarships.[38] New links between school and university were also created by central and local government scholarships and the proportion of boys proceeding from secondary grammar schools to universities increased by about a third.

At the same time, it is clear from these percentages of growth in secondary and university education, that, though the situation was changed under the 1902 Act, it was by no means tranformed. In fact, speaking now not in terms of growth, but of the actual position of boys born between 1910 and 1929, less than a fifth of the generation (17.6 per cent) reached a secondary school; and of those reaching a secondary school, about a seventh (14.3 per cent) went on to university.[39] Moreover, the relative position of middle-class and working-class children remained substantially different. Again, taking the generation of boys born between 1910 and 1929, two-fifths (39 per cent) of those from the middle class, as compared with one-tenth of those from the working class, went to a secondary school, a ratio of 4:1; and for the universities the ratio was 6:1; the proportions being 8.5 and 1.4 per cent. There is no doubt, then, that the middle classes benefited greatly from the expansion of secondary and university education between the wars, and that they were aided in this by the more generous public provision after the 1902 Act. But why it is that the working classes profited so much less than might have been expected?

In part, of course, the explanation is an economic one. Thus, for example, the provision of scholarships did not catch up with the demand for them. Already in 1923, the President of the Board of Education was reporting so strong a pressure by parents for scholarships, that he doubted whether "even in normal times, with money easy, we could have been able adequately to cope with the demand."[41] But for most working-class parents, the scholarship road to the secondary school was the only one they could use. For middle-class parents, on the other hand, paying the relatively low, publicly subsidised fees at the grammar school was by no means impossible, and there were thus two access roads. Ability to pay became, relatively, still more important during the financial stringency of the 1930s, with the introduction of "special places" for which partial fees might be demanded on the basis of a means test. In 1938, children for whom full or partial fees were being paid were over half (53 per cent) of all the pupils in grant-earning secondary schools.[42] Ability to forgo the wages that a child might otherwise begin to earn at the age of fourteen years was another economic factor. When reference is made nowadays to the "deferred gratification pattern" of the middle classes, in contrast to the "live for the present" pattern of the working classes, it is important to remember that poverty and malnutrition—which were amply with us until the Second World War—are not the best bases for forethought or abstinence.

Measured intelligence, commonly referred to as I.Q., is also part of the explanation. But it is only one part, for even leaving aside the cultural components in intelligence tests, equal access to grammar schools between the wars would have produced a social class distribution, similar to, though not exactly the same as that found in, the grammar schools today, following the 1944 Act. That is, some 60 per cent of all the pupils would have been the children of skilled, semi-skilled and unskilled workers.[43]

A third factor, and one which I should like to emphasise, is the social class image of the secondary school and its purpose. The inter-war secondary school was a grammar school. The Bryce Commission, when it defined secondary education, took the revolutionary view that "secondary" and "technical" education were in large measure interchangeable concepts. They claimed that "no definition of technical instruction is possible that does not bring it under the head of Secondary Education, nor can Secondary Education be so defined as absolutely to exclude from it the idea of technical instruction. . . ."[44] The experiments which were being made by various school boards with higher grade schools—experiments possible because increasing numbers of parents were prepared to have their children continue at school beyond the minimum school-leaving age—certainly came under the category of secondary education as defined by the Bryce Commission. But with the 1902 Act, these schools were removed from the elementary sector, where they had been located, and absorbed in the new system of secondary schools. Technical education as such was henceforth put on a separate limb—in the central schools, which were higher elementary schools for purposes of administration; and in the junior technical schools. Though valuable work was done in both these types of school, and though the junior technical schools came to challenge more orthodox secondary education, the official view was that their status was, and should be, below that of a secondary school; that at best they were vocational schools, geared up with local employment possibilities.[45] In that sense a child had to choose a specific occupation when entering one of these schools at the age of thirteen.

Whether or not it was Morant who was responsible for imposing the pattern of the public school and of the grammar school upon the new system of secondary education, is not really important. The important point is that there was a powerful demand for just such a type of secondary school. For many middle-class parents, as well as for those working-class parents anxious to see their children rise in the social scale, a grammar school education was the kind which they wanted but to which they had not hitherto had access. It was the way to the black-coated job, respectable and secure. Conceivably, it might also be the way to the university and a profession, still more respectable and secure. And this impression must have been heightened by the emphasis which came to be laid on passing those external examinations—matriculation and the higher school certificate—which were the keys to higher education and higher social status. In many respects, the possibilities of social advance were rather limited. Sir George Kekewich was not entirely wrong when he said, as early as 1909, that the over-supply of clerks, depressing wages and conditions of work, was the result of that "national system of education that we are so abominably proud of. It is a bad system, directed at turning out a nation of clerks."[46] But for the lower middle class and aspiring working-class parents, a clerk's job was at least better than that of a manual worker —rightly so, if thought of in terms of the vista of security in a highly insecure world. In 1931 unemployment among male clerks amounted to less than half of that in the labour force as a whole (5.3 per cent as compared with 12.7 per cent). Among some groups of clerical workers there was hardly any unemployment and in general the higher ranks had the smallest proportions of dismissals.[47]

Since secondary education was focused upon black-coated employment, working-class parents who wished their sons to go to a grammar school had to accept the fact that they would move out of the parental "class." Some parents did accept this fact—indeed, they positively wished for it. But many did not. Today, some of the differences between the classes are less striking—differences in clothing and housing, for example; and the educational gap between the generations in working-class families is a little narrower. In the mid-thirties, it should be remembered, working-class fathers with children of secondary school age would themselves have ended their education at the age of twelve or thirteen in a not very greatly reformed schoolboard school. Even now, working-class fathers still do not show a strong drive towards black-coated employment for their sons.[48] In the thirties, moving out of one's class might well have involved a much sharper break between parents and children. And at the same time, clerical work, which constituted a large share of the available black-coated employment opportunities has not been held in very high regard by the working class as a whole.[49] If secondary education had led directly to supervisory or technical posts in industry, posts closely related to industrial production but nevertheless carrying social prestige, working-class attitudes to secondary education might have been somewhat different. But until the late thirties, apprenticeship regulations were not very helpful in that respect, for in general the age of entry was rather low. There were better opportunities for boys from the junior technical schools. Beginning as craftsmen, they were often promoted to technical or junior staff positions in factories. But there were not many of these schools, and this may help to account for their relative success.

Looking back over the inter-war years, it is obvious that "collectivism" is hardly the appropriate term for the kind of educational policy which was carried out, or for the results of that policy. Certainly the working classes benefited. But so far as secondary education was concerned, the middle classes benefited still more. Their wider use of publicly supported or provided secondary schools sprang from the same motives which, in the case of the working classes, acted in the contrary direction—from a desire to keep their sons in their own class, which in the case of the middle classes meant especially saving their sons from becoming manual workers. For such a purpose the new system worked fairly well, for the association between education and jobs carrying prestige became tighter during the period. University graduates, in particular, began to enter new fields, helped by the efforts made by university appointment boards to persuade industry to establish management traineeships. Recent studies have shown that, among managers, the proportions educated in a grammar or in a public school increased fairly steadily, and that the proportions with university degrees rose rather more steeply.[50] Those sections of the middle classes who sent their boys to boarding schools showed their realisation of this tighter operative relationship between university education and socially acceptable employment. Of their sons born between 1910 and 1929, almost a third went to universities, as against less than a fifth of the generation of boarding school boys born before 1910. A similar trend applied to the middle classes as a whole.[51] The university now began to be their target, perhaps made all the more attractive in that, with still relatively small numbers of students, Britain did not have an academic proletariat, as other countries did during the depression of the 1930s.[52] And in the late thirties the middle classes were being increasingly helped to reach their target by public expenditure on secondary and university education.

Finally, I should like to refer to the most recent changes—to the 1944 Education Act and its background, and to the way in which secondary and university education have developed since the Second World War. To those who believe that the demand for universal secondary education came from the Labour Party, the 1944 Act might appear the ultimate vindication of Dicey's forecast. But there were at least two sets of pressures working in the same direction, one political and the other specifically educational. It is true that the political pressures were very largely those of the Labour Party and its associated bodies. As Mrs. Banks has pointed out in her book, from at least the 1890s on, the Trade Union Movement was demanding equality of opportunity in secondary education; and from the end of the First World War, secondary education for all was the centre of Labour Party educational policy. The Conservative Party, though it acknowledged the need for additional free places, continued to regard secondary education as necessarily selective. Secondary education, said Lord Eustace Percy in 1933, should act as "a lift or stairway to the higher storeys of the social structure." His criticism of the existing system was that this function was not being adequately fulfilled.[53] But the educational pressures for universal secondary education were also strong. They came from teachers who saw their attempts to experiment in meeting the different needs of different children frustrated by the existing regulations; from educational associations; and from expert committees appointed by government. From 1926, when the Hadow Committee reported, the idea of primary education as a first stage, to be followed by secondary education as a second stage for all, became accepted educational currency. It was to be a differentiated system. The Hadow Committee proposed two kinds of school, grammar and modern.[54] Later, in 1939, the Spens Committee suggested three, adding the technical school. When in the atmosphere of the Second World War, the Government issued its proposals for educational reconstruction, they incorporated the Spens Committee's recommendations for grammar, modern and technical schools.[55] And shortly afterwards this idea of tripartism was supported by the Norwood Committee on the grounds of historical reality and on the basis of a typology of children which psychologists have not accepted.[56] Though tripartism was not specified in the 1944 Act itself, it was clearly intended by the Government, and this intention has been carried out in most subsequent practice. The link with the earlier conception of selective secondary education is evident. If the ladder between elementary and secondary education as a whole has been abandoned, it has been replaced by a ladder from the primary school to the grammar school. And the nineteenth-century social class homogeneity of the grammar school has been replaced by a homogeneity of measured intelligence, the upper 20 per cent on the I.Q. scale.[57]

Secondary education since the 1944 Act has become not only the subject of persistent wrangles between experts, but also one of the major topics of general conversation and general concern.[58] Parents promise their children costly gifts if they obtain grammar school places. Children's papers advertise textbooks designed to improve their chances. For middle-class parents, in particular, eleven-plus day is a day of national mourning. Like King Aegeus they sit on the cliffs, waiting to see if the returning sails are white or black. And if the incidence of neurosis among frustrated middle-class parents has not risen significantly, it is largely because the independent secondary schools, giving education of a grammar school variety, offer parents a possible alternative in the struggle to maintain or improve the social status of their children by the way of education. That is one of the reasons why the popularity of public schools has not diminished and why, as was said recently, "the average middle-class parent still regards a public school education as the best investment for his child's future."[59] Standing outside the general system, and protected by a cordon of preparatory schools, the public school has tightened its link with the university,[60] and in so doing it has helped to reinforce the widely held views that the ideal type of secondary school is the public school and that the main function of the university is to staff the professions and to supply the administrators. In my opinion, the social consequences of these views are even more important than the results of public school exclusiveness.[61]

So far as State-provided secondary education is concerned, the present situation has been aptly described in a governmental report. Speaking of the effect of examinations, the report argues that "there is nothing to be said in favour of a system which subjects children at the age of eleven to the strain of a competitive examination on which, not only their future schooling, but their future careers may depend." And referring to the grammar school, it adds, "too many of the nation's abler children are attracted into a type of education which prepares primarily for the university, and for the administrative and clerical professions; too few find their way into schools from which the design and craftsmanship sides of industry are recruited." I should explain, however, that the govermental report in question is the White Paper on educational reconstruction, and that the defects referred to are those which the 1944 Act was designed to remove.[62] It is sometimes a little difficult to distinguish the new cure from the old disease. But the present system is new, and it is neither completely uniform nor fixed throughout the country. In one important respect the situation today has no pre-war parallel. There is now a recognition that secondary education is a proper subject for discussion and for study. This is in striking contrast to the pre-war position, when attempts to investigate access to the various stages of education tended to be looked at by the Government as attacks on the class structure. And indeed they were, for, as I have indicated, secondary and higher education were in large measure tied to the middle classes. Since the 1944 Act, however, there has been a wealth of fresh inquiries into the working out of the new secondary education, one of the most illuminating having been sponsored by the Government itself.[63] The very acceptance of the principle of secondary education for all, however ambivalent the practice may be, is provoking a further review of the objectives of that education and of the kinds of institution in which it might best be obtained.

At the same time I do not see how a thorough review of the objectives and possibilities of secondary education can be undertaken unless the purposes of university education are also reviewed. And this is still largely to be done. There have, of course, been special studies of the needs for particular types of trained manpower, such as doctors, scientists and technologists. The further employment of Arts graduates in industry has been investigated. The anatomy of Redbrick has been displayed and the "crisis in the university" has been ventilated on the Third Programme. Less public consideration has, however, been given in recent years to the objectives of universities, to the way in which those objectives may be regarded by potential students, and to the kind of student population that may in consequence be recruited. But in a society in which universal secondary education has in principle become the accepted goal, these are questions of major importance.

Since 1938–39, the number of full-time university students have increased from 50,000 to over 85,000.[64] Most of the students are British—about 90 per cent of them—and about four-fifths of British students received financial assistance, much of it considerably more substantial than was the case in pre-war days. In addition, the universities themselves are heavily supported by public funds and are thereby enabled to pass on a further subsidy to students, in the sense that tuition fees probably do not cover more than one-seventh of the total cost of tuition. With this more solid basis of public financing, paralleling the more extensive financing of secondary education, how far does the composition of the student body reflect the statement of the White Paper on educational reconstruction, that "the aim of a national policy must be to ensure that high ability is not handicapped by the accidents of place of residence or lack of means in securing a university education."[65] Unfortunately, our knowledge of changes in the composition of the student body is quite inadequate, for the recent inquiry undertaken for the Vice-Chancellors' Committee was the first of its kind. But a comparison with our own, much smaller sample inquiries into education and social mobility does not suggest that there has been any basic change in recent years. It is very probable that there have been shifts within the middle classes, with a larger proportion of students coming from families of less wealthy black-coated workers. But of the undergraduates and diploma students admitted in October 1955, only a quarter were the sons and daughters of manual workers.[66] It is clear from the Vice-Chancellors' inquiry that this low proportion is not explained by a failure of working-class boys and girls to obtain university places when they apply for them, but by a failure to apply for places. So far it has been the middle classes who have made the most use of the increased public financing of university education.[67]

The Ministry of Education report on *Early Leaving* has shown how the school side of this situation works out. Within the grammar school, working-class children tend to perform less well than middle-class children as they pass through the school; they also leave earlier; and, when they leave, they go directly into employment rather than into further full-time education. In explaining these findings, the report emphasises the importance of the child's home background—both his physical and economic environment, and "the different social assumptions which affect not only a child's parents but the whole society in which he is brought up."[68] Of course, those assumptions include the views of society on the purposes of further education. And it is here that the dominant view of the vocational objectives of a university education may act as a constraint, as grammar school objectives acted as a constraint on the entry to secondary education between the wars.

Sir Alexander Carr-Saunders once said: "in England a university is just a place where by paying so much you prepare yourself for a certain career. . . ."[69] The careers contemplated are in the main the professions, and these do not as yet include employment for which higher technical education is required. On the contrary, the proposals of the recent White Paper would place higher technical education in about the same relationship to university education as junior technical schools were to grammar schools before the war—necessary and worthy, but of inferior status.[70] Most students who entered the universities in 1955 had in mind a professional occupation as their goal. Thus, in the eyes of the beholder, the university, whatever its intellectual function may be, is also to a great extent a device for achieving or maintaining social status.[71] That being so, for many working-class boys and girls the university route may mean a sharp break with their familiy and class environment, and one which neither they nor their parents can contemplate with unalloyed approval.

It is unlikely that the status aspect of university education could be entirely removed. But it is neither necessary nor desirable that undergraduate education should be as dominated as it is now by the expectations of employment with relatively high social status. The present dominance is a reflection of that continuity of attitude which associates secondary and university education with the middle classes, and which imposes middle-class needs and aspirations upon the education pattern.[72] Whatever may have been the position a century ago, when the professions were seeking to provide objective criteria of ability and training, it is no longer in the social or economic interest of the country for the image of undergraduate education in the university to be that of education for the small proportion of men and women who will enter professional or quasi-professional occupations. The wider needs of industry and of citizenship must be considered, and the range of undergraduate possibilities and objectives extended. Changing the objectives of undergraduate studies would not necessarily mean a lowering of standards; and at the same time, to postpone to the graduate stage those kinds of studies more closely connected with employment in the professions would raise professional standards and might well expand professional employment.[73] To effect the changes suggested would involve a reappraisal of both secondary and university education as a whole. But it is just such a reappraisal which is needed if we are to give real meaning to the aims of the 1943 White Paper on educational reconstruction: to combine diversity of educational provision with equality of educational opportunity; but so to combine them as to attain greater social unity within the educational system, and thereby to help in the creation of a more closely knit society.[74]

NOTES

1. A. V. Dicey, *Lectures on the Relation between Law and Public Opinion . . . ,* 2nd ed., reprint (London, 1926), p. xc.

2. *Ibid.,* p. 279.

3. p. 1.

4. England and Wales, 1954–55, after deducting parents' contributions. See J. Vaizey, *The Costs of Education* (London, 1957), Table XXI, p. 192. Total expenditure at current prices was about £44.5 millions and parental contributions about £24.2 millions. It is not clear whether the total figure includes expenditure by the Ministry of Food on milk supplied to independent and direct grant schools.

5. *Op. cit.,* pp. 260 and 275–279.

6. For the history of primary and secondary education in England and Wales since the early nineteenth century, I have drawn mainly upon J. W. Adamson, *English Education 1789–1902* (Cambridge, 1930); R. L. Archer, *Secondary Education in the Nineteenth Century* (Cambridge, 1921); G. A. N. Lowndes, *The Silent Social Revolution* (Oxford, 1937); and H. C. Dent, *Secondary Education for All* (London, 1949).

7. Lowndes, *op. cit.,* pp. 45–50.

8. Board of Education, *Report of the Consultative Committee on Secondary Education* (Spens Committee) (London, 1938), pp. 81–92. The number of grant-aided schools in 1937 was 1,397 of which 765 were council-maintained schools, 393 aided by L.E.A.s, and 235 in receipt of direct grants from the Board of Education (some of them also receiving L.E.A. assistance). There were also 397 schools recognised as efficient but not grant-anded. The school populations cited cover both grant-aided and recognised-schools.

9. Provision was made for raising the school-leaving age to sixteen years, but this has not yet (1958) been done. The figure of 2 million (2.057 millions) excludes a further 160,000 children aged twelve years and over in all-age schools. To complete the picture, 75,000 should be added for the upper-school pupils of direct-grant grammar schools, and about 130,000 pupils aged twelve years and over in recognised independent schools (excluding primary schools). See Ministry of Education, *Education in 1956,* Cmd. 223 (London, 1957), pp. 94–95, 111 and 119.

10. In 1955–56, 73.3 per cent of the published income came from parliamentary and local authority grants. Fees (forming 11.2 per cent of income) also include local and central authority payments in respect of students, and the figures suggest that such payments must represent a very substantial part of the total. Overall public aid must therefore amount to considerably more than 73 per cent of published income. But the published totals do not include Oxford and Cambridge college income used for specifically college purposes.

11. *Education in 1956,* p. 56, compares some 17,000 central and local government awards in England and Wales for 1956–57 with a university intake of about 20,000 full-time British students. The inquiry which we organised at the London School of Economics for the Committee of Vice-Chancellors and Principals shows that about 80 per cent of all British first degree and first diploma students admitted in October 1955 were in receipt of some kind of assistance, but does not record the proportion receiving public grants. See R. K. Kelsall, *Applications for Admission to Universities* (London, 1957), Tables 16a and 16b and p. 11.

12. Autumn 1956—includes graduates and overseas students. See U.G.C., *University Development: Interim Report on the Years 1952 to 1956,* Cmd. 79 (London, 1957), p. 8. The estimate of 46,000 is that given by Vaizey, *op. cit.,* p. 159, for 1921.

13. *Eighth Annual Report . . . of the Registrar-General* (London, 1848), p. lvii; *Thirty-third Annual Report* (London, 1872), p. vii. On working-class literacy in the nineteenth century, see R. K. Webb, "The Victorian reading public," in B. Ford (ed.), *From Dickens to Hardy* (Pelican), London, 1958, pp. 205–226.

14. W. O. Lester Smith, *Education: An Introductory Survey* (London, 1957), p. 105. According to Adamson, *op. cit.,* p. 43, legally a grammar school was a school for teaching Latin and Greek and nothing else, though Hebrew might be added. Thus, in 1805 it was ruled that Leeds Grammar School was not entitled to use its endowment for teaching arithmetic, writing and modern languages.

15. G. M. Young, *Victorian England* (Oxford, 1936), p. 97.

16. See G. C. Leybourne and K. White, *Education and the Birth-rate* (London, 1940), p. 45, n. 1, citing E. L. Clarke; and R. Williams, *Whose Public Schools?* (London, 1957), p. 7 (Bow Group publication). The Fleming Committee (Board of Education, *The Public Schools and the General Educational System* (London, 1944), p. 20) stated that fifty-four out of the eighty-nine independent public schools in England and Wales were founded after the beginning of the nineteenth century. The fifty-four here would include day schools. (The numbers of public schools at any time are the numbers belonging to the Headmasters' Conference at that time.)

17. R. Williams, *op. cit.,* p. 61.

18. G. M. Trevelyan, *British History in the Nineteenth Century,* cited by Leybourne and White, *op. cit.,* p. 40.

19. Autumn 1956.

20. H. M. Pollard, *Pioneers of Popular Education 1760–1850* (Cambridge, Mass., 1957), Chap. 22.

21. Adamson, *op. cit.,* pp. 209 and 221. The intellectual attainment in question was, according to Adamson, "to spell the words the boy will have to use, read a common narrative or newspaper paragraph, write a legible and intelligible letter, make out or test a bill, have 'some notion' where foreign countries lie on the habitable globe, be sufficiently acquainted with the Bible to follow 'a plain Saxon sermon,' remember enough of the Catechism to know his duty to God and man."

22. Lowndes, *op. cit.,* p. 5.

23. Adamson, *op. cit.,* p. 210.

24. National Education Union, *A Verbatim Report . . . of the Debate in Parliament during the Progress of the Elementary Education Bill, 1870 . . .* (Manchester, n.d.), pp. 5 and 18.

25. C. Norwood, *The English Tradition of Education* (London, 1929), pp. 171–172.

26. See E. C. Mack, *Public Schools and British Public Opinion 1780 to 1860* (London, 1938), pp. 132–137.

27. Archer, *op. cit.,* p. 167.

28. B. Holt-Smith, *Some Aspects of the Medical Profession in Eighteenth-Century England,* Ph.D. Thesis, University of London (1952), p. 176. The transition in medicine in the late eighteenth century is perhaps indicated in Heberden's attack on theoretical medicine—associated with the learned, gentlemanly physicians—and by his claim that more had been done by "illiterate, but enterprising quacks" to further medicine than by the theories of the learned. (Holt-Smith, *op. cit.,* p. 178.)

29. *The Vicar of Bullhampton,* which began to appear in parts in July 1869. (The reference is to the World's Classics edition, pp. 60–61.) G. M. Young *op. cit.,* p. 93, says that the foundation of the University of London "marks the entry of a new idea; the conception of a university as training for a specific profession, for medicine, law, engineering, or teaching, was in England a novelty to which the examples of Germany and Scotland both contributed."

30. Thomas Farrer. See J. D. Kingsley, *Representative Bureaucracy* (Yellow Springs, Ohio, 1944), pp. 76–77.

31. O. Banks, *Parity and Prestige in English Secondary Education* (London, 1955), pp. 2–3. The role of the State in relation to the position of the medical practitioner is discussed by Professor Titmuss in his chapter in this volume. See also A. M. Carr-Saunders and P. A. Wilson, *The Professions* (Oxford, 1933), pp. 88–89.

32. Lowndes, *op. cit.*, pp. 89–90.

33. *Op. cit.*, p. 18.

34. B. M. Allen, *Sir Robert Morant* (London, 1934), p. 25.

35. The 1902 Act was passed at one of the major crossroads of policy making. Theoretically, secondary education might have been provided for all children—in effect, in line with the Bryce Commission views on the nature of secondary education. That it was not, and that, instead, existing endowed schools were subsidised, are explicable in terms of the dominant middle-class views on the nature and purpose of secondary education.

36. *Op. cit.*, p. 141.

37. See Tables 3 and 4, pp. 126–127, in J. Floud, "The Educational Experience of the Adult Population of England and Wales as at July 1949," in D. V. Glass, ed., *Social Mobility in Britain* (London, 1954).

38. There were, of course, scholarships before 1907. On the impact of these in London, and on the judgment of head teachers as regards the scholarship winners, see F. Campbell, *Eleven-plus and All That* (London, 1956), pp. 70–76. See also O. Banks, *op. cit.*, p. 67.

39. All the statistics given here on inter-war changes in educational opportunity are, unless otherwise specified, from J. Floud, *op. cit.* Her chapter, based upon the sample inquiry carried out in connection with our studies, at the London School of Economics, of social mobility, is indeed one of the very few sources of such information.

41. O. Banks, *op. cit.*, p. 69.

42. J. Floud, *op. cit.*, p. 140, Appendix Table 1.

43. The proportion of working-class children in maintained and direct-grant grammar schools in England in the Ministry of Education sample inquiry, carried out in 1953, was 64.6 per cent (including shop assistants in the manual category—in our own inquiries we should classify them as non-manual wage earners. Judging from the guide list given to schools taking part in the Ministry's inquiry, it is not clear whether own-account workers or small employers in a number of occupations—*e.g.*, market gardening, tailoring, carpentry—were excluded from the "skilled manual" category. If not, the size of the working-class parent population would be unduly large.) But since I.Q. distributions are not identical for the different social classes, the proportion of working-class children actually found, assuming that selection is based primarily on I.Q. tests, will depend upon the proportion of the total universe of children covered by grammar schools. Thus, if grammar schools are to cover the top 23 per cent of children, 60.1 per cent would be of working class background; if, however, only the top 6.3 per cent are to be selected, then 48.6 per cent of the children would be of working-class background. These percentages are derived from the Scottish Mental Survey, assuming that I.Q. distributions by social class are the same in England and Scotland. See Scottish Council for Research in Education (J. Maxwell), *Social Implication of the 1947 Scottish Mental Survey* (London, 1953), pp. 45 and 328. The figure of 64.6 per cent for present grammar schools is from Ministry of Education, *Early Leaving* (London, 1954), p. 17, Table J. It should be also noted that, in recent years, the use of I.Q. tests for selection has been increasingly queried by educational psychologists and so, too, has selection at the age of eleven years in general. In view of the acknowledged cultural components in the tests, an I.Q. test, in addition to other defects, acts in some degree as a self-fulfilling prophecy.

44. H. C. Dent, *op. cit.*, pp. 32–33.

45. O. Banks, *op. cit.*, Chap. 8.

46. Cited in D. Lockwood, *The Black Coated Worker* (London, 1958), p. 117.

47. D. Lockwood, *op. cit.*, p. 55.

48. See F. M. Martin, in Glass, *Social Mobility*, pp. 68–69. On educational preferences, see also J. E. Floud, A. H. Halsey and F. M. Martin, *Social Class and Educational Opportunity* (London, 1956), pp. 75–86.

49. In our studies of occupational prestige, routine clerks were ranked about halfway down the scale of status. The attraction of clerical work to the lower middle class and aspiring working class was its combination of security and "respectability."

Further, like teaching, it appeared to provide a springboard for additional social ascent in the next generation.

50. Acton Society Trust (Rosemary Stewart), *Management Succession* (London, 1956), pp. 13–18.

51. The figures for boarding-school boys are 30.6 per cent and 19.0 per cent, respectively. For boys who went to secondary grammar schools the corresponding figures are 11.4 and 9.0 per cent. See J. Floud, *op. cit.,* p. 119. In 1938–39, according to U.G.C. returns, ex-public elementary school pupils constituted 46 per cent of the U.K. degree and diploma students entering British universities. When these figures were first published, there was some tendency to regard them as indicating the extent of working-class entry to the universities. Subsequent research—the inquiry carried out for the Vice-Chancellors' Committee—has shown that this is by no means the case. Of the male and female entrants in October 1955, only 23.4 per cent had *not* been to an L.E.A. primary school, and for 64.6 per cent this had been the only type of primary school attended. (See R. K. Kelsall, *op. cit.,* Table 9.) Nevertheless, entrants of working-class origin amounted to only 25 per cent of all entrants. Our social mobility inquiry suggested a similar proportion for pre-war years. But the definition of working class in that inquiry included routine grades of non-manual workers as a whole. It is likely, therefore, that taking the same basis of definition for pre-war and post-war entrants, the pre-war figure would be below 25 per cent.

52. See W. M. Kotschnig, *Unemployment in the Learned Professions* (London, 1937), pp. 121–125.

53. O. Banks, *op. cit.,* p. 124, citing *Hansard.*

54. This was, however, only the broad classification. The Committee distinguished, under the category of modern schools, between selective and non-selective (equivalent to the existing central schools) and the "senior classes" of public elementary schools, "providing post-primary education for children who do not go to any of the three previous types of schools . . ." See Board of Education, *The Education of the Adolescent* (London, 1926), pp. 172–175. The location of the junior technical school was left undecided.

55. Board of Education, *Educational Reconstruction,* Cmd. 6458 (London, 1943), p. 10, para. 31. The Spens Committee's recommendations are given in Board of Education, *Secondary Education* (London, 1938), pp. xvii–xviii and xxvi–xxxiii. The Spens Committee recommended the creation of technical high schools, fully equivalent in status to the grammar schools. As regards grammar schools, the Committee suggested as a "working standard," that these might cover 15 per cent of the ten to eleven year age group in public elementary schools, with the addition of 3 per cent of that group in other schools.

56. Board of Education, *Curriculum and Examinations in Secondary Schools* (London, 1943), pp. 2–4.

57. Secondary school selection procedures are now widely based on I.Q. tests. The proportion of 20 per cent in grammar schools is that given in the Ministry of Education report, *Early Leaving,* p. 14, as applying to England as a whole (excluding Wales), though there is considerable local variation. Criticism of the use of I.Q. tests for selection—and such criticism is now widespread, covering educational psychologists as well as teachers and parents—is sometimes met with the argument that, ofter all, I.Q. tests were suggested before the war as a means of combating the unequal access to secondary education at that time. But this is quite unsound. First, I.Q. analysis was used before the war—for example, by J. L. Gray and P. Moshinsky, in *Political Arithmetic,* ed. L. T. Hogben (London, 1938)—primarily to show how much ability was unused in a system in which capacity to pay fees was a basic determinant of access to secondary education. Secondly, whatever might be the justification for using such tests when secondary education is available to only a small proportion of children, the position is entirely different when such education is made available to all. The point is that the grammar school—which was in large measure a comprehensive school before the war—is now being invested with the rather different function of grooming an "intellectual élite." Why that function should

involve the separation of children in different schools has not, in my view, been demonstrated. On the contrary, the evidence suggests that the present situation is largely a derivative (with I.Q. tests thrown in) from the Hadow Report, which in turn was derived from, and grounded in, the then existing situation. Similarly, the idea that comprehensive secondary education must inevitably involve very large schools, with the disadvantages of bigness, derives from the Spens Committee Report (*op. cit.,* pp. 291–292), which in turn appeared to assume that the U.S. type of comprehensive high school was necessarily the kind of institution in which comprehensive education would be carried out. In general, though there has evidently been much thought about the problems entailed by universal secondary education, it has not been very fresh thought. This is particularly unfortunate in that the change from a limited to a universal system of secondary education involves socio-educational problems which cannot be met unless there is a fundamental review of the nature of the institutions in which that education is given. As a contribution to such a review, R. Pedley, *Comprehensive Education* (London, 1956) is very welcome indeed.

58. See, for example, R. Pedley, *op. cit.,* Chap. 2.

59. This was the comment of the chartered surveyor who carried out the recent valuation (for rating purposes) of the buildings of Uppingham School. See *The Times,* October 29, 1927. There is no point in summarising once again the evidence on the advantages of a public school background in respect of subsequent careers. They are well known and are now, to some extent, acknowledged by those who wish to reform the system—for example, by Sir Robin Williams, in his pamphlet, *Whose Public Schools?* He agrees (p. 18) that "a public school boy does still possess an intangible advantage in certain walks of life," but claims (p. 61) that "the demand for ability is such that the lack of an Old School tie does not debar the reasonably able from rising in virtually any career."

60. According to R. Williams, *op. cit.,* p. 39 (citing the Public Schools Appointments Bureau), 42.4 per cent of the public school leavers in 1954–55 were going to a university. This may seem a little high, unless the reference is to boarding school leavers. But there is no doubt that the proportion is higher than for direct grant or maintained grammar schools. The Ministry of Education, *Education in 1956,* pp. 98 and 112, records the proportion of school leavers in England and Wales proceeding to a university at 28.4 per cent for boys from direct-grant schools and 17.4 per cent for boys from L.E.A. grammar schools in the year ending July 31, 1956. The point is, of course, that nowadays both family and school pressures orient public school boys towards the university as a necessary stage in career preparation. This is quite apart from such other questions as the intellectual calibre of the boys and the quality of the education given. It is also clear that public school boys are oriented towards particular universities, namely, Oxford and Cambridge. Of the public school boys entering British universities in October 1955 (2,079 boarders and 1,045 day pupils), 64 per cent of the boarders and 42 per cent of the day pupils went to either Oxford or Cambridge. On a random distribution, the proportion for Oxford and Cambridge together would 23.9 per cent. The ratio of actual to expected is therefore 2.7 to 1 for boarders and 1.8 to 1 for day pupils. (Direct-grant schools are excluded from these calculations.) See R. K. Kelsall, *op. cit.,* Table 11. Public school boys formed 21 per cent of all male entrants to British universities in October 1955.

61. And, in addition, the view not infrequently expressed that the public school type of education is the best preparation for the university.

62. *Educational Reconstruction,* pp. 6 and 9.

63. The report on *Early Leaving,* referred to previously.

64. In Autumn 1956, 88,701 students. See U.G.C., *University Development: Interim Report on the Years 1952 to 1956,* Cmd. 79 (London, 1957), p. 22.

65. *Op. cit.,* p. 25.

66. Kelsall, *op. cit.,* pp. 9–10, and Tables 14, 16a and 16b. Since the data refer to full-time university students, they exclude registered students (at London University) who are studying in recognised institutions (*not* Schools of the university) as well as external students. The numbers involved are considerable. Thus, as regards external

students, in 1957 the University of London awarded 1,975 external, as compared with 3,725 internal first degrees. (See *University of London: Report by the Principal, 1957–58*, pp. 9, 10 and 31.) At present far too little is known about such students. Recent sample studies in two polytechnics suggest that among full-time students those of working-class background comprise about 12 per cent. Among evening course students taking G.C.E. or university courses, the proportion was about 29 per cent. (See S. F. Cotgrove, *Technical Education and Social Change* (London, 1958), Chap. 8.)

67. Students of all major categories of social origin are receiving assistance. Among the 1955 entrants, the proportions of male students receiving financial assistance were 73 per cent for those whose fathers were in the Registrar-General's classes 1 and 2 (professional, employers, managers, executives and similar occupations), and over 90 per cent for the students with routine clerical or manual backgrounds. (Kelsall, Table 16a.) It has been argued recently that entry to some of the professions has changed considerably with the increase in financial assistance to university studies. Thus a representative of the Royal College of Surgeons suggested that this was happening in medicine, and that students whose fathers were doctors were "a diminishing number." (*Manchester Guardian,* April 25, 1958.) Similarly, the President of the R.C.O.G. argued that many doctors "are dissuading their sons from entering the Profession" because of the now greater "uncertainty of a good living." (*The Times,* April 26, 1958.) But of the doctors' sons who became university students in October 1955, 50.6 per cent were proposing to become doctors, and such medical undergraduates constituted 16.4 per cent of all men proposing to study medicine. (Kelsall, Table 18a.)

68. See pp. 56 and 34–41. Among other factors mentioned in the report as associated with early leaving (especially of working-class pupils) are the restlessness and irritation felt by boys and girls at the age of fiteeen and sixteen, and the desire to "assert their independence and grown-up status," and it is surmised that "more than a third of the leavers are influenced at least in part by feelings of this kind." But this, too, is to a considerable extent a reaction against the institutional pattern which reflects English middle-class habits of treating boys and girls as children as long as they are at school. Such a pattern might have been acceptable as long as those working-class pupils in grammar schools were the children of aspiring parents, strongly oriented towards middle-class values. But with grammar school populations containing 60 per cent or more of working-class children, the position is quite different. Moreover, in some ways the pressures of outside society are now working much more strongly in a counter direction—for example, the marked increase in the proportions of young marriages. Earlier physical maturation is perhaps an additional factor. In spite of the criticisms—often justified—of American high schools (many coming from Americans themselves), we still have something to learn from the U.S. as regards the treatment of adolescents in school. See also Pedley, *op. cit.,* Chap. 3. The provision of a more adult atmosphere in the upper forms of secondary schools might also ease the transition from school to university.

69. In Kotschnig, *op. cit.,* p. 124.

70. See *Technical Education,* Cmd. 9703 (London, 1956). Though there has been much emphasis since the Second World War on the need for a larger supply of skilled manpower for industry, needs have still been looked at in traditional ways. This applies not only to the White Paper referred to above, but also to the more recent report on apprenticeship—The Carr Committee Report, Ministry of Labour, *Training for Skill* (London, 1958). The enthusiasm with which the Committee refers to the way in which the apprenticeship system has changed over the last hundred years to meet the changing requirements of industry (p. 4) is hardly in keeping with the conclusions of Lady Williams' study—G. Williams, *Recruitment to Skilled Trades* (London, 1957). There is still far too much emphasis on training in craftsmanship for particular types of employment, when general industrial change may well need a marked shift towards a more generalised technical education. Thus Professor D. G. Christopherson (*District Bank Review* (December, 1953)) draws attention to the greater emphasis in the U.S.A. on workers with a background of technology, able more easily to handle fairly rapid changes in industrial techniques. It is the large

numbers of men with first degrees in engineering and with a background of a general, academic education, who—according to Professor Christopherson—provide the basis for "the astounding achievements of American industry on the technological side . . ."

71. Of the male entrants to British universities in October 1955, 23 per cent had no classifiable occupation in mind—usually because they did not answer the question or because they had no particular occupation in view. But of the rest, over 90 per cent contemplated a professional occupation including teaching, research and the civil service, and only 10 per cent envisaged industrial or commercial occupations. For men of manual origin, industry and commerce were even less in view. (See Kelsall, *op. cit.,* Table 17g.)

72. Consider, for example, the statement of a former Chairman of the University Grants Committee, Sir Walter Moberly, in 1939: "If the chief object of going to the university was to secure a satisfactory niche in professional life, the universities could not afford greatly to increase their present intake, and the present social distribution of students could not with advantage be fundamentally modified. On a purely vocational basis something like saturation point had been reached." Moberly was replying to Professor Major Greenwood's argument that university education should be regarded as a preparation for life and leisure, not as a training for better jobs, and it is only fair to note that Moberly continued: "On the other hand, if university education was regarded as primarily an education for life rather than for livelihood, quite a different conclusion was indicated, though time did not permit him to develop it." (*J.R.S.S.,* Vol. CII, Part 3 (1939), p. 381.) But the latter view has scarcely been taken up, and it is the former, with successive modifications, which in large measure continues to apply. The point of saturation has been pushed forward, especially since the Second World War, and recent Treasury proposals for building anticipate a student population of some 140,000 by 1970 (*The Economist,* March 1, 1958, p. 734). Nevertheless, even the new targets envisage little more than the combined effort of the birth-rate boom and of the reduction of wastage in the grammar schools. Thus the present Chairman of the U.G.C., Sir Keith Murray, said in May 1958, in considering the possible national need to increase the number of graduates: "There seems to be a reservoir of potential students, though a relatively small one, in those who leave school before eighteen." (*J.R.S.S.* Part IV (1958).) A similar view may be seen in the study by the Association of University Teachers, *Report on a Policy for University Expansion* (n.d.). Perhaps the sharpest version of this attitude is that expressed by Sir Charles Grant Robertson, formerly Vice-Chancellor of Birmingham University (*The British Universities* (revised ed., London, 1944), p. 74): "It is more than questionable whether, dredge or subsidise as you will, there is, as is often suggested but not proved, a larger untapped reservoir of brains which ought to get to the universities, but owing to defects in the university ladder do not do so—to their loss and that of the whole community." Underlying these statements is a double assumption: that the "best" students are already reaching the universities; and that to admit lesser mortals will lower standards and perhaps even defeat the purpose of achieving the highest level of scholarship. As to the untapped reservoir, its size will depend upon our definition of the scope of the universities; but some indication has already been given in the report on *Early Leaving,* while evidence for Scotland can be seen in J. S. Macpherson, *Eleven-Year-Olds Grow Up* (London, 1958), especially pp. 78–88 and 126–129. As to the second assumption, our society needs not only intellectually outstanding individuals, but also large numbers of well-educated and trained men and women of less intellectual distinction. With our present system we may—though I doubt it—be fully successful in producing the first type, but we are certainly not producing sufficient of the second. The provision of a variety of first degree and diploma courses might stimulate the second without impeding the first category of students. (See, for example, the Principal of the University of London, with reference to general degrees, *op. cit.,* pp. 46–48; C. F. Carter, "How Britain Can Get More Scientists," *The New Scientist,* December 3, 1957, pp.14–15; and *The Economist,* March 1, 1958, pp. 734–735.) It does not at all follow that in expanding our university system to cover substantially more than the 3–4 per cent of the population at present covered by it, we should necessarily run up against the heterogeneity of standards found in the

U.S.A. Nor, at the same time and even allowing for this heterogeneity, should we underestimate the importance of the fact that, in the U.S.A., about 14–15 per cent of men and women aged twenty-two years obtain a bachelor's or a first professional degree. (See E. C. Hughes and P. E. Breer, "Educational Selection in the United States of America," paper prepared for the International Sociological Association, December 1957.)

73. With our present system, students tend either to have had so general a course that they are not professional in the sense of being able to show specific competence; or else to have concentrated upon a limited range of subjects in a professional or near professional course which cannot be broadened because there is not sufficient time. In preparing for professional work there is much to be said for a combination of a first degree and a more intensive graduate course, involving systematic, advanced training and, where appropriate, evidence of capacity to undertake research. In the social sciences, my own experience suggests that it is this systematic, advanced training which is particularly necessary if there is to be a rise in standards and an increase in the use of social scientists in professional employment.

74. In order to simplify the references and the citation of statistics, most of the discussion in this paper has been restricted to boys. The general argument and conclusions apply equally to girls, though there have been important qualitative and quantitative differences in their effective access to secondary and higher education, reflecting the different emphasis in our society on the education and careers of girls. This is particularly the case as regards university education. Though active interest in secondary education began rather later for girls than for boys (and there was nothing comparable to the early nineteenth-century concern with the public schools), access to secondary education was very similar for both sexes between the wars. But the proportions going to universities were more than twice as high for boys as for girls, and this is still the case. The combination of personal incentive and family pressure results in a higher incidence of early leaving from school among girls than among boys. Since the Second World War, there has been both wider discussion of these discrepancies, and a stronger emphasis on the possibility of drawing girls into technological and technical education and occupations. The White Paper on technical education (*op. cit.,* p. 21) refers to the need for a change of outlook on the part of employers and of girls themselves. Since, says the White Paper, "ambition to marry will very rightly continue to be uppermost in the thoughts of girls, progress in recruiting more girls and women for courses in technical colleges depends on their recognition that further education will help and not hinder the prospects of a happy married life." And the Carr Committee notes (*op. cit.,* p. 28) that "for women, marriage no longer means the immediate termination of employment. There is also an increasing tendency for women to go back to work, on either a full- or part-time basis, after they have brought up a family." But more than exhortation is needed. Opportunities, like justice, must be shown to exist. At present, career possibilities are far more limited for women than for men, and society makes little provision either for the continued employment of married women with young children or, if re-entry to employment is postponed until the children are less dependent, for the difficulties of bridging the gap in knowledge and experience resulting from the break in employment. Yet these questions must be considered, for to make more effective use of women as members of the labour force means to employ married women—especially as the age at marriage has been and is falling. Associated with the decline in family size and with the continuation of full employment, there has been a very considerable increase since the 1930s in the proportions of married women at work. But the range of employment is still limited and it will require a substantial expansion of career opportunities for women to convince them that employment can be regarded from a long-term point of view and not primarily as a fill-in between leaving school and marrying or as a means of achieving a somewhat higher level of living once the children are at school.

29 Family and School in Modern Society

H. SCHELSKY

The Role of School in a Class Society

IN A CLASS SOCIETY, the school system served as a stabilizer; the social status of parents determined the kind of school they chose for their children. The stratification of the school system reflected the stratification of society at large.

The social standing of the family in class society depended on a series of factors—inherited property or income; vested or inherited interests and rights; long-standing membership of a particular group; etc. School and vocational training represented but one status-conferring factor among others. The static character of a class society, with its caste-like subgroupings, still largely exemplified the traditional features of caste society—young people growing up, belonging in principle to the same social stratum as their parents.

The school system under these conditions merely reflected the existing pattern of social stratification: members of the upper class entered college or university; members of the lower class attended elementary school only. The manufacturing middle class kept apart from the rural and the new urban-industrial lower classes. As a result of this, and of the emergence of the new industrial and bureaucratic middle classes, the "middle school" was erected to satisfy the vocational as well as status needs of the middle classes. The hierarchy of teachers corresponded to the stratification of the schools in which they served, and parents chose their children's schooling according to the dictates of their social status. Attending a certain school confirmed social status, but did not serve to procure higher status.

The same rule applied to social mobility within the class society. Social demotion resulting from the intellectual incapacities of an upper-class child was rare under these conditions. School could not down-grade, for the indispensable minimum of educational requirements could be acquired by patience and other means—stupid children were for ever dragged along, sent to boarding schools or drilled by private teachers. Essentially, school had no effect on the preservation or loss of social status.

Abridged and translated from H. Schelsky, *Schule und Erziehung in der Industriellen Gesellschaft.* Würzburg: Werkbund Verlag, 1957, with the permission of the author and the publisher.

Education was, then, much less a means of upward social mobility than it is today. Lower and middle civil servants, for instance, acquired their status by military service. Social mobility on the basis of higher education required so many sacrifices from parents that only the exceptionally gifted, belonging to families obsessed with the idea of climbing, chose this way. Since they were the exception, their success had hardly any effect on the structure or function of schooling in class society. The establishment of "middle" and professional schools absorbed the first big wave of middle-class mobility; later, secondary schools were differentiated according to areas of knowledge—grammar, "modern," etc. Again, these types corresponded to the prevailing pattern of social stratification, so that mobility through education, although increasing, still reflected the social structure; there were more cases of mobility through certain types of "modern" secondary schools than through the grammar schools.

In short, in class society, school reflected the class structure, and therefore neither determined nor changed social status; it presupposed and confirmed it. School was not supposed to satisfy social demands and claims, and remained dedicated to educational and cultural tasks.

The Role of School Today

The present situation reflects a number of changes in the system of stratification. Class differences have to some extent been levelled off, on the one hand through the collective upward mobility of industrial workers and of the workers in the technical and administrative occupations (the new middle class); and, on the other, through the downward mobility of former upper strata, especially the professional classes.

These opposing tendencies have created a large, relatively undifferentiated, lower-middle class that today represents the main stratum of society. In comparison, the remaining social groups play little part in social structuring.

This newly emerged lower-middle-class society is characterized by its dependence—for the disposition of its everyday activities as well as for its security—on the large, impersonal bureaucratic organization. This dependence is accompanied by aversion and hostility to the bureaucratization of work and public life, and a marked feeling for intimacy and privacy.

The levelling of the social hierarchy is attributable less to the redistribution of incomes than to the uniformity of cultural life, resulting in the main from the dissemination of former luxury and upper-class goods through mass production. Equal participation in the material and intellectual culture of society not only characterizes the middle-class way of life but is accepted as a natural right of all.

These processes of destratification, of interchange between the social classes during and after the war (the result of geographical displacement, prohibitions on exercising one's profession, the death of the father, etc.), have created a high mobility among individual families, which has weakened class solidarity and given rise to a kind of family or small-group egotism typical of present-day society. The high rate of mobility is responsible for a strong desire for security, despite higher standards of living and organized welfare provision. Since this highly mobile society is characterized by widespread anxieties and a craving for security, it tends to degenerate into an eternal wanting-to-have-more and wanting-to-be-more; everyone wants to "climb" and everyone wants to live better.

However, people's notions of the social process and of the social implications of their own position in society have not been adjusted to the novel pattern of stratification and universal mobility. On the contrary, *old models and the prestige symbols of class society are preserved;* since a wholly mobile society cannot convey stable notions or feelings of social belonging, people cling to old ideas of rank and status. Furthermore, ideas typical of the old class society must serve to legitimize present social claims—status ideologies of the working class, the middle class, etc. In particular, upward mobility and pretensions as to standard of living are characterized by old prestige notions (for instance in the choice of occupation) that—in spite of their irrationality—mobilize strong private energies. These obsolete social models will remain valid for some time to come, since they are supported by the dissemination of former upper-class goods and rights in the political and economic structure—quite apart from the reactionary and restorative tendencies natural in a society that has been forced to endure an unusually rapid rate of social change.

Education today is thus confronted by a social situation of which the following are the principal features:

1. Universal striving for social mobility based on a craving for social security, rooted in the family.

2. Occupation as the only avenue of advance; hence a further striving for an education and professional training that will offer a wide range of opportunities.

3. Mobility largely determined by outmoded prestige symbols and ideas, behind which lies hidden the basic need for security.

4. Greatly enhanced demands for consumption of material and psychological goods; in particular, a generalized claim for social consumption in the name of "culture" (*Bildung*).

Implications for the Role of the School

School is thus confronted by a relatively undifferentiated and highly mobile society; differences in social status have been reduced to differences in income—hence the lack of criteria in educational selection. Every individual family is for ever on the verge of upward or downward social mobility. Social opportunities are offered exclusively by occupational qualifications, hence social mobility by way of professional training in order to get security; education is expected to offer all kinds of opportunities for social mobility and early guarantees of later professional achievement.

In such a society, school easily becomes a kind of distributive agency conferring future social security, status, and consumption possibilities. This becomes the more apparent when the assignment of young people to certain schools definitely excludes certain possibilities of social mobility. Given this distributive function, school is no longer dealing primarily with the child or adolescent and his future, but with the social claims of the family. Moreover, because more and more training and educational qualifications are necessary for almost all occupations, this distributive function of school is buttressed from the side of the economy.

School has thus become a decisive agency managing the status and life-chances of the individual; and this seems to be the core of the school problem from which derive the discords and tensions between school, teachers, pupils, and parents. Any attempt at school reform will have to take account of this state of affairs and the social and political implications.[1]

We should like to mention only two consequences of the tensions surrounding the role of school today as a bureaucratic mechanism assigning life-chances. School decides on the main social claims of the family. Teachers, or examining bodies who select or reject children for certain schools, play a key function in society—a function that parents (and sociologically speaking they are right) *cannot* appraise exclusively or primarily from an educational point of view. They tend rather to see in it a mechanism of social planning exercising jurisdiction over their private claims and playing the role of a kind of assignment office for social chances. School and teachers provoke the same aversion as the bureaucrat who apparently meddles with private affairs that do not concern him; nevertheless, bureaucracy is as indispensable as it is disliked. For school, however, this situation is far more dangerous. In the struggle of public versus private life, school—in the eyes of parents—seems to side more and more with public life, and parents react accordingly: they make claims and demands opposing their private interests to those of organizations, and they rarely co-operate.

From the point of view of school, this means—since social mobility and higher education have become generalized and since social determinants outside school, such as class and status, have ceased to exert any major effect on the chances of admission to certain occupations or schools —that the main social function of school is no longer the selection of gifted children and the clearing away of social obstacles to their education as it sometimes was in class society, but the rejection of social claims considered by the parents as justified. School not only promotes but assigns; it not only offers opportunities to gifted young people, but refuses opportunities to children it considers not gifted.

This function of school has to be emphasized because educators are often unaware of it. School, today, is an important agency of social demotion. This is all the more important since welfare provision and social-security schemes have closed almost all other structural channels of downward mobility, except of course for the possibility of social catastrophes. Owing to its selective function, school confronts parents early with the threat of downward social mobility and thus thwarts one of the strongest of family drives—the urge to secure social continuity through the generations. The family, therefore, comes to consider school as one of the main agencies of distributive justice in a planned society, a relationship that is reinforced by other connections between family and school working in the same direction.

All this involves almost intolerable strain for school and teachers. They are unable, as they could in class society, to ignore the rank and status claims of parents, taking them for granted or as relating to the world outside the school. They cannot, therefore, dedicate themselves exclusively to educational tasks. The fact that school and teachers, nevertheless, try to separate educational tasks and models from these social claims, throws into relief their shortcomings with respect to the distributive function imposed on them by the modern social structure. For my part, I think that this function is, indeed, too much of a burden for the school and teachers, and that any future reform should try to liberate teachers from it.

School is subjected to still further strain from a social process that I should like to call the *transformation of formal claims for freedom into material social claims*. As an example, I may mention one of the findings of an investigation into unemployment and occupational difficulties among working-class youth.[2] The general claim of all working-class people that their sons, and to some extent their daughters also, should have access to training for skilled work is based on the political guarantee of "freedom of occupational choice." The claim for educational opportunities as a social due is addressed to the state as a distributive agency of material and social chances. Thus, at least in the eyes of parents and young people, "the right to a free choice of occupation" loses its formal significance as the right to a free decision, i.e., the rejection of official direction, and is transformed into a material claim to the effect that everybody must be given the opportunity to exercise the profession he chooses. Thus, the "free choice of occupation" is turned into a claim addressed to the state to assign functions according to private choice. Our investigation showed that ability and talent took second place to social aims and demands. It is possible that the economic situation and outlook exercised an even more determining and restrictive influence; in any case, it was clear that material and social claims played a greater part in occupational choice than did considerations of individual aptitudes and abilities.

This dilemma becomes apparent already at the end of elementary school. The aspirations of parents for their children are determined by considerations of social security and mobility, rather than by an objective assessment of their capacities. This cannot be dismissed as unreasonableness on their part, but must be accepted as an understandable social claim, deriving from the fact that future status is determined by education, by professional achievement, and qualification. As Geiger maintained, vocational qualifications have, indeed, become the decisive "means of production" in modern society; therefore, the striving for social security is centered on them. Here too, the task of reform would consist in liberating the school from these extraneous social functions in order that it may dedicate itself more fully to teaching.

In order to achieve this release, it would be necessary to restore the original meaning of the formula "education according to talent," a meaning that implies a "formal demand for freedom," rather than a distributive principle. This formula arose in the context of class society as it was reflected in the inequality of educational opportunity and was directed against the tendency—inherent in this kind of society—toward sectional monopolization of important social positions and key occupations. The claim for "education according to talent" modified these tendencies at the school level, but it did nothing to contravene the given social order. In addition, there was another principle, "social position according to achievement," also implying that education was only one among several avenues of approach to such achievement, the final outcome of the struggle for success being left to the free play of forces in adult society. The modification of the class structure, and the rising educational threshold of employment in many occupations gradually transformed what had been an educational into a distributive principle. Today, the assignment of a social position depends on talent; school thus becomes the supreme manager, since it is school that decides who is "gifted" and who is not. As a principle of social distribution, the formula "social position according to talent" presupposes, however, that people become aware of their capacities in a realistic way, and that they regulate their social claims accordingly.

Yet, sociologically speaking, nothing is more illusory than this assumption. If this principle is accepted, all will claim education on the ground of presumed talent in themselves or in their children. Teachers and examining bodies will have to decide the relative merits of rival claims in an effort to secure the victory of the principle over the unrealistic demands of parents and children. But this is to ask too much of school and parents alike, and relationships between them are bound to deteriorate still further. The decision of the school as to a child's talents cannot be allowed to become the only criterion of reality, against which are smashed the social illusions of parents. The social reality that must apply the sanctions to illusory claims needs a broader basis.

The principle "education according to talent" is, moreover, limited by the economic structure of society. Pushed to its conclusion, it presupposes the equilibrium of demand and supply in the labor market—between the distribution of openings, on the one hand, and of the abilities of individual, on the other. Accordingly, the assignments to low, medium, and higher training would have roughly to correspond to the demands of the labor market at any given moment.

Rigidities are already apparent, however; for instance, in the prevailing shortage of technicians and the oversupply of certain categories of professional people.

NOTES

1. As to Great Britain, see T. H. Marshall, "Social Selection and the Welfare State." [Chap. XIV in this volume, (eds.).]

2. *Arbeitslosigkeit und Berufsnot der Jugend* (2 vols.; Cologne, 1952). See especially II, 288 and 292.

30 *The School in American Culture*

MARGARET MEAD

WHEN WE TURN from the teacher to the school, we again have a series of images. From this series three may be selected as useful, the little red schoolhouse, the academy, and the city school with its narrow cement schoolyard in which the children of immigrants mill about in a space too small for play. The little red schoolhouse, which exists today only in backward and forgotten areas of the country, is still the symbol of a stable, democratic, slowly changing, real American world. Here the teacher, herself often a mere slip of a girl, a young teacher, wrestles with her slightly younger contemporaries, boards with members of the school board, is chaperoned by the entire community of whom she is really one, and finally marries a member of that community—or goes on teaching forever with, happily, at least one attributed romance to give her dignity and pathos. For the teacher in the little red schoolhouse is not an old maid whom no man wishes to marry; she is a girl who is a little more intelligent, a little better educated, and more alert than the others, who will herself be very selective in marriage, and who may therefore in the end remain unwed. But she belongs within the community in which she teaches, a community which in the image is stylized, being without class structure, but made up of people who are more or less worthy and substantial, thrifty or shiftless, with large farms and well-kept fences, or small farms overrun by blackberry vines. She teaches the children pretty much what their parents learned; new teaching is viewed with suspicion, and the school board of the little red schoolhouse are traditionally regarded as the enemies of all change. Some schooling is conceded to be necessary, parents do not have time to do it, so one of their number is hired to teach what the parents know, or at least once learned for a little while, to the children. Parents and teacher are thoroughly in league as far as the child is concerned, standards of school and home are the same, and a "licking at home meant a licking at school." The school is a one-room school, the big pupils help the little ones, and the brighter little ones listen while the older pupils recite. In such a school, the gifted twelve-year old immigrant boy learns enough in a year to be an American. In such a school, mischief is innocent and sacred, the pranks against the teacher are as traditional as her reprisals,

Reprinted from Margaret Mead, *The School in American Culture* (Cambridge, Mass.: Harvard University Press, 1951), with the permission of the author and the publisher.

the struggle between the young teacher and the overgrown boy who is tired of book learning represents the victory of common sense and adulthood over the school room.

This image, the beloved image of the school, crops up in the minds of those who have never in fact seen such a school, so firmly is it rooted in our literature and tradition. Like so many of the symbols of the American dream, it stands both for a desirable state never attained and for a past golden age which has been lost—the school in a world which did not change, a world of rural images, where "blackberry vines are running" and goodness was literally symbolized by a "clean slate."

Beside this image, we must place two other schools. There is the academy, at which the children of the privileged were initiated into the mysteries of our heritage from Europe, Latin, Greek, music; the school to which the parents who could afford it sent their children, so that their children would remain part of the past to which they owed, or wished to owe, allegiance. Where the perspective of the little red schoolhouse was limited to the childhood of the parents themselves, with its folk statement, "What was good enough for me is good enough for my child," the perspective of the academy stretched back to the culture of the grandparents and great grandparents who had been judges and governors. Here the aspiration of the parent who wished to give his child not "what was enough for me," but "the advantages of a fine education" which was customary in his family, mingled with the aspiration of the parent who wished to give his child something better than he himself had had. Both aspirations sought to structure the future in terms of the past, to guarantee the child's future position by the degree to which he participated in the heritage of the past. Teachers in academies were more likely to be men than women, thus again symbolizing the relationship to Europe, rather than the new America where men were so busy building a new world that the "finer things of life" had to be left to women.

The third image is that of the city school, on the built-up street, a school so lacking in architectural personality that it would be almost impossible to represent one without the presence of the mass of children, crowded on the sidewalk, milling in the narrow playground. These children are the children of immigrants. They are not only poor, but they are foreign; they have unpronounceable names and eat strange things for breakfast; their mothers come with shawls over their heads to weep and argue and threaten a teacher who is overworked, whose nerves are frayed by the constant battle with the polygot youngsters who surge through her classroom. The classroom is crowded; through the windows nothing can be seen except another wall. Around the blackboard there is a pitiful row of cut-out bunnies, or on the blackboard a devoted but overworked teacher has traced Santa Claus and his reindeer. The children's speech is a babble of broken American; they must be taught to spell words they have never heard, to read about fairytale heroines and historical figures whose very names are strange to their parents. They must be taught to wash, to brush their teeth, to drink milk, to value time, to write a letter. They must be taught, not the constancies of their parents' immediate past, as in the little red schoolhouse, or the precious values of a long ancestral past, as in the academy, but they must be taught to reject, and usually to despise, their parents' values. They must learn those things which, to the extent that they make them Americans, will alienate them forever from their parents, making them ancestorless, children of the future, cut off from the past.

In any discussion of American schools, of "the American school system," of "the public school," if you listen carefully, you can see these images come and go, the loved and longed-for image of the little red schoolhouse, the deprecated and worried-over image of the city school, and the image of the private academy, which contains all of America's ambivalence about England, about tradition, about class. The affectionate note with which the little red schoolhouse is invoked is a statement of our sense of conflict between the academy that perpetuates the past—which in American terms means limiting the future, tying us to the old world and its caste lines and age-old solutions—and the city school which belongs only to the future, which turns out pupils who, because they cannot look back, have, in a sense, no perspective at all, but only the dreadful urgency of moving on, moving away from, knowing only that what was once theirs by birthright is bad and un-American, that what is NOT that, what is new and up to the minute, must therefore be American and good.

All three of these themes have become interwoven in our contemporary American culture so that a tenth-generation American,[1] educated in private schools, will have difficulty persuading his child, who has learned to speak Spanish from an upper-class but foreign mother, that it is not something shameful and disgraceful to be heard speaking a foreign tongue on the street. And the contrast between the mischief of the country boy and the delinquency of the immigrant slum boy has vanished too, so that the select suburb in which tenth-generation Americans and successful third-generation Americans live side by side has its juvenile delinquents also. It has its quarrels among the parent taxpayers as to whether foreign languages are to be taught in the schools, its conflicts as to whether the teacher is to be treated as an equal, as the emissary of a strange outside world, or as the poorly paid custodian of the gateway to "culture."

If we turn from images to look formally at the history of American education, of its theory and its practice, the conflict between the school oriented toward the past and the school oriented toward the future, with the seldom obtainable dream of a school which would hold the world steady, will be found to be a prevailing theme. This theme is expressed in many forms: in the struggle between the classics and modern languages; in the struggle between "at least one foreign language" and none at all; in the struggle between academic studies and vocational preparation; in the arguments about required courses versus electives, in which shared conformity to a common past is opposed to selectivity which is a preparation for an unshared future.

Before I go on to discuss the part which this threefold picture of the school has played and is playing in American educational theory and practice, I should like to turn for a moment to the contrasts and comparisons provided by primitive societies on the relationships between the generations. Primitive societies are our models for slowly changing homogenous societies[2] in which the children's lives faithfully repeat, gesture for gesture, and experience by experience, the lives of their parents and grandparents. Through the investigation of such slowly changing societies, we can form a picture of type relationships between the old generation and the new, against which such relationships, when they occur in an age of rapid change like our own, take on additional meaning. In these slowly changing primitive societies we find great variation as to which age group inducts the young child into his society; the baby may spend most of its time with its mother or father, or in the arms of an older sister or brother, or by the side of a grandmother or grandfather. Each is a possible way to learn the intricate, beautifully patterned way of perceiving the world and acting within that set of perceptions which a culture offers each child born within it.

But if we examine in detail some of the implications of the parent-child, sibling-child, and grandparent-child rearing situations, we find certain systematic differences. Those societies in which young children are reared by grandparents[3]—of which certain North American Plains Indian tribes are typical—have an enormous degree of conservatism. The culture survives, even as the buffalo disappear; the land is taken away by the advancing white peoples, and the tepee is displaced by the shack. Still the language, the way of thought, of the past endures. Sometimes we find only one or two survivors of a whole language group, two toothless, half-deaf old women, who will, however, have clung to their language and their memories, and are still able to dictate long texts to the patient ethnographer. This conservatism, this cherishing clinging to the old, can be related to the role which the grandparent played in the lives of Indian children, to the way in which the child, even as it struggled and wriggled in an ecstacy of beginning movement, apprehended in the tonus of the grandparents arms the sort of pact which its lively little body would someday make with death. As old hands and old voices, speaking with the gentleness and resignation of a people who saw human lives as like grass which grew up in the morning and at night was mown down, informed the child of the way that men and animals, the sun and the moon and the stars, seeking and power, vision and practicality, life and death were to be viewed, so the child was able to incorporate in early childhood all that his culture had to offer him. In such a rounded understanding, nothing was left unexplained, uncontemplated, which later would challenge or threaten. And the Indian has remained as one of our chief examples of the tenacity of a people who, robbed of every condition of their lives, still clung to the forms, to the pattern, meeting night after night to gamble for buffalo nickels where once the stake was a war horse.

At the opposite extreme, we find the cultures in which it is the child nurse—the elder sister or less frequently the elder brother—who carries the younger child about on a hip almost too slight to bear the burden.[4] Instead of the tremor of old age, there is the tenseness of the hands which can hardly lift, the hands which are almost unable to readjust the carrying sling, or shift the baby from one hip to another. These child nurses, far from having learned the nature of the whole life cycle from their old grand-mothers, are just out of babyhood themselves, and were reared by other children. The child on the hip is not something infinitely young and re-mote, waiting at the end of memory, but the child whom one was yesterday, with all the fears and urgencies which have just been partially mastered in the self. These are the cultures in which the growing child is kept close to infancy, sometimes only by way of keeping a great awareness of the rhythms of its own body, so that later dancing and love-making will be equally easy and graceful, as in Samoa.[5] Sometimes also the child is kept close to the images of infancy, so that the ritual resolutions of its early terrors are expressed in the theater by conflicts between witch and dragon, who reënact on a stage the conflicts which the child experiences in its relationship to father and mother, as in Bali.[6] Or the child nurse may help the child retain its passivity, in a world where every adult is egging it on to continuous unremitting displays of energy and anger, as among the Iatmul.[7] Among this head-hunting tribe of the Sepik River, where adult relationships are violent and assertive, the theater is a series of tableaux in which all movement is frozen and static, in contrast to the theater of Bali where a people whose daily life is ordered and gentle are able to express the most violent emotions. In the spontaneous drawings[8] and in the play of the children of the child-nurse age we can find the links which permit their child charges to retain the feeling that makes the adult theatrical presenta-tion both possible and meaningful, as the Balinese child keeps alive the capacity for plastic expression of feeling and the Iatmul child, who in his adult life must be stormy and noisy, keeps his capacity for stillness.

The child nurse may be seen not as the guardian and ally of any particular aspect of early childhood, but rather as a way in which the child's response within its culture is kept intact in spite of the pressures which will later fall upon the adolescent and the adult. From the child nurse there passes to the native child a kind of license to be itself, from one who has not yet departed far enough from that closeness to the experience of early childhood to be able to withdraw the license. And so we have a second model, the society in which the resources of early childhood, whether in directness of bodily expression or richness of phantastic elaboration or denial of the adult structuring of the world, are preserved for children, and therefore for adults also, because the child learns not from someone who has traversed the whole round of life, but from someone still very close to its beginning.

The two models of child and grandparent upbringing are brought together again when we consider the aristocratic society in which the upperclass child has a nurse drawn from the peasantry and in which the child of the peasant class is cared for by its grandmother, while the mother works in the fields. Here, the peasant child, like the Plains Indian child, is exposed to the whole of the culture which will be its for life, caught tightly in a mesh that it cannot break, born a peasant to die a peasant. In the same society the same type of peasant woman, not always so old, is performing quite a different function for the child of the aristocrat, keeping alive in it impulses and dreams which its more educated, differently controlled parents would, if they were its mentors, disallow.[9] So the peasant nurse keeps alive in the aristocratic child his sense of his own body and himself, which can then tolerate the rigors of court etiquette, rigid demands for posture and gesture, for honor and conformity to the demands of caste; while, as a peasant she communicates to her own grandchild a way of life in which body and self play a different part, upon a simpler stage.

The third model, the model which echoes the little red schoolhouse image, is that in which children are reared not by grandparents who represent the whole traditional definition of life, or by children whose own eager little mouths have hardly left the breast, or by nurses whose own peasant standards of eating and drinking perpetuate the pleasures of the breast with a frank enjoyment which is banished from ballroom and audience chamber, but by parents, by people of early maturity, the present possessors and inheritors of the adult world. This is the typical middleclass position: a family economically well enough off so that the mother is not burdened down with field or farm duties—or overwhelmed with more children than she can feed and care for, in which the father is making his way, actively, in a world of change and commerce, a world of entrepreneurship and profit. In such a rapidly changing world, grandparents are likely to be out of date, behind the times, and also to a degree rejected, as it was they who reared the present parents, and reared them purposefully and determinedly to become responsible, time-bound, goal-oriented adults. In such a world also elder siblings are busy themselves learning to outstrip their parents. They have too much to do to be efficient baby tenders; they must learn the skills and arts which will be necessary for success. Furthermore, the middle-class parent will distrust the child nurse, as also the servant girl is distrusted. The child who is to be inducted into a world where life is real and life is earnest must be exposed from the beginning to the model parent, who must herself, and himself, punish and reward the growing child. This middle-class picture is not only true of our own American middle-class life, but also can be found in primitive societies like that of the Manus of the Admiralities,[10] a tribe of stone-age fishermen. The Manus are efficient, profit-seeking, earnest, moral people, concerned to rear their children to follow the same pattern—not so much of life, as of goal seeking. And among the Manus the older children practice in play the arts of adult life, and the parents care for the children, who learn to think of adults as persons who are completely masters of their environment.

The child who is reared according to this third model—reared by parents who are at the height of their careers, far from childhood, and facing an old age about which they know little and expect little—grows up, far from its infant awareness of its body, far from the memory of the childhood fantasies which fed eagerly and hungrily on the very meagre set of symbols which such a culture possesses, but alert and ready to face a relatively new and uncharted world, in a thoroughly learned and thoroughly charted way. Close contact with the grandparent leaves little room for welcoming change or sailing strange seas. Close contact with child nurse or peasant nurse keeps the child so *en rapport* with its body and the arts and rituals whose meanings it is able to retain that it also will be, on the whole, uninterested in change and conquest. But parent-rearing produces a child who faces toward a partial future, who can conceive life as an unwritten chapter of a book that is unfinished.

But these three models which I have been discussing are models drawn from slowly changing homogeneous societies; I have been able to speak of a life in which those who rear were similarly reared, in which all the lullabies one sings to children are the lullabies one heard as a child. If such models are to be of any use in considering the problem of the teacher in the American school today, we must add to them from the actual situation in our own society, the condition of rapid change. We must add to them both the reflection in the adults, whether of the parent or of the grandparent generation, the changes through which they have passed, the fact that they were reared by parents whose hands were already fumbling before unfamiliar doors, or with hands which lay flaccid with despair in a world they had not dreamed of and could not cope with.[11] We must picture the adult who has been reared in a dozen tones of voice, reprimanded, rewarded, cajoled, and teased and appeased according to half a hundred systems, who has learned to move about somehow, in a series of rooms in which the very arrangement of the furniture either diagrams the lack of harmony in the tastes which gradually assembled it or in its perfection of harmony will give him a pattern which he is not likely to repeat. And to this picture of an adult who in personality is the expression of the great heterogeneity and rapid changes in our current society, we must add the picture of children who differ from the children who came ten years before them, and differ also from the children who will follow them, as children reared on schedules are followed by children rocked to sleep, to be in turn succeeded by children reared according to some new one of the prescriptions through which a newly selfconscious society is attempting to meet newly realized needs. The condition in our society today is dramatized by the late-born child, whose mother finds that nothing that she learned ten years ago about how to treat children or of what to expect from them, can be applied to this newcomer, who seems even to have learned to cry with a new note in its voice, who will have to have different clothes, will display different tastes, and will weep for quite different reasons. Where, in slowly changing societies, the adults are confronted by children whom they know—for were they not such children themselves, just such children with the same fears, the same joys, the same bits of mischief and rebellion—the adults in the modern world face children who are not only unlike their own past childhood, but who are actually unlike any children who have ever been in the world before.

How then does the teacher—the teacher who may stand at the door of the academy, or its successor the academic high school, ready to induct these unknown children into the tradition of the past, and the teacher who stands at the door of the crowded slum school, ready to prepare her pupils to enter the future by leaving their past—how does this teacher fit into the changing world in which she is called upon to play so sensitive and significant a role?

We may consider for a moment the way in which the teacher can approximate to each of the three generation positions: the grandparent who has seen the whole of life, the parent who is living it day by day, and the child or nurse who is the custodian not of the child's future so much as of the child's immediate past.

The type teacher who comes closest to the grandparental role is the teacher of the classics, or the teacher who treats mathematics and science as if they were classics, fixed and immutable, as unchanged and unchanging as the figures on Keats' Grecian urn. The gifted teacher of the classics conveys to the child a sense of the roundedness and relatedness of life, of the way in which each period repeats in its own way an old story that has already been written in a more gracious and finished way in the past. Any budding desire to explore the new, to make new conquests, can be gently, benignly reduced to the expected, by a reference to Diogenes or to Alexander. As man has been, man will be; one can learn to write different but not better sonnets in a world which has dignity and form. The teacher in the academy was typically such a teacher laying the groundwork for an orderly acceptance of a world which, however different today's version seemed, was mercifully never new.

The teacher in the overcrowded city school—where there were too few seats and too few books in a room filled with strange smells from foreign eating habits and foreign sleeping habits—is closest to the parent model, as she struggles to get her pupils to face away from the past and toward the future. She teaches her pupils to acquire habits of hygiene and of industry, to apply themselves diligently to prepare to succeed, and to make the sacrifices necessary to success, to turn a deaf ear to the immediate impulse, to shatter any tradition which seems to block the path to the goal, but to shatter it in a way and with the sanctions of the entrepreneur. This teacher is closest to the model in which the parents rear the child to a kind of behavior rather than to fit within a tradition. When she imitates the teacher of the academy and teaches her pupils to learn memory gems, she will find she faces confusion, because she is teaching them the past of older Americans in order to give them a future, and this contains contradictions. How will these children born in hospitals, treated at clinics, who celebrate a holiday in the biggest movie theater, use such memory gems as "I remember, I remember the house where I was born," or "over the river and through the wood to grandfather's house we go; the horse knows the way to carry the sleigh through the white and drifting snow"? She will be happiest when she teaches modern history, with the next pages still to be written, in a "current events" class; or when she teaches science as a way of looking at life which is constantly changing, constantly discarding what has been the best hypothesis for a better one. She—like the middle-class parent—faces forward into a future[12] that is only partially charted, and so she must furnish her children with a kind of behavior, a method of exploration, rather than with the parchment map, with its lines drawn in lovely fading colors, that is available to the teacher in the academy classroom.

The third model, the child nurse or the peasant nurse, the teacher whose task is to stay close to the young child's bodily impulses and exuberant imaginative attempts to take in the world around him, is a new type of teacher. She has come into being as one gifted thinker after another— Froebel, Montessori, Anna Freud—rebelled against the price which modern, urbanized, industrialized Europeans and Americans were paying for their new kind of civilization. From Germany, from Italy, from Vienna, from England, and from the United States there came a demand for some form of education which would fit the little child—a chair and table to fit his body, materials with which he could work out his groping attempts to relate inner and outer world,[13] and teachers who would kneel beside him, give him a shoulder to cry on or a body which could be turned into a steed, who would be allies of his infancy, rather than surrogates either of the finished world of tradition or of the fluid world-in-the-making of the entrepreneur. First in the kindergarten, and later and much more articulately in the nursery school, we have developed an educational pattern which contains some of the values of the child nurse, or the peasant nurse, in which sensitive teachers, who must almost always be young because of the

strenuous physical demands of working with little children who are permitted to move about freely, are taught how to ally themselves with the
immediacies of the world of the little child.

But in all three parallels which I have drawn, parallels which, like all
figures of speech, impose an extra degree of order and so distort the reality
—for in the teaming schoolrooms of America we find all three types of
teacher and every possible blend, in every sort of situation—I have still
ignored the changing children and have spoken as if the children who face
these different kinds of teaching were themselves all of the same stuff as
the teachers from whom they learn. If the children to be taught were of
the same stuff as the teachers, we would still have a problem in initially
training teachers for any one or any combination of the roles which I have
outlined. The teacher who is adequately to represent the order of the past,
the dignity and beauty of tradition, must, in the course of her training come
to terms with her own past. The Latin lines she wrote so unwillingly, the
theorems in geometry which were resented, the parents and teachers who
were responsible for making her learn her lessons, must all be reëxamined,
the rebellion exorcised or transformed, so that she can become the whole-
hearted and resigned exponent of traditional learning.

The teacher who is to help a generation go away from and beyond their
parents, who is to be forever exhorting her pupils to be up and doing, has
a different task; she must relive her childhood and exchange the specificity
of the demands which her parents and teacher made upon her for a new
set of demands, which she will make, in the same tone of voice, upon her
pupils. Where the teacher who represents the past and tradition must accept directly and finally both what she herself has been taught and those
who stood for the past, the teacher who must urge her pupils to desert or
surpass their parents has to abandon the matter but, in a way, keep the
manner. She comes to terms during her training, if that training is to
succeed, not with her own parents as they themselves were with all their
weaknesses and strengths, but with the demands which parents and teachers
in the abstract have a right and a duty to make on children. She must give
up any overfaithful clinging to the particulars of her own past, if she is to
face a roomful of children for whom it is her duty to wish a future very
different from that which their own parents' lives offer them.

Congruently, the type teacher of our city and town schools today is a
girl who is—in the words of the contemporary class analysis—mobile upward, moving from lower class to lower middle class, or from lower middle
class to a better middle-class position. She is someone who must transcend
her own past and so in a sense is the better prepared to help her pupils
repudiate theirs and become mobile also. The type teacher of the academy
or the academic subjects in a modern high school is, on the other hand,
mobile downwards, clinging to a past she is in danger of losing, as a family

that has fallen on hard days clings to the family portrait and the grand-father's clock.

The type nursery-school teacher is the girl from an upper middle-class background, who finds herself desperately out of sympathy with the verbal facility and concern with things rather than with people that seems to her a predominant characteristic of her world. Very often inarticulate and academically "slow," better able to communicate with a touch of the hand or the slant of a painted line than with words, she can become a nursery-school teacher only if she can come to sufficient terms with her own rebelliousness against adult standards—against, indeed, the whole adult world—so that while she acts as the little child's ally, she does not hold the child back. Very often the nursery-school teacher, and also the child therapist, is not a special kind of adult who has kept a closeness to his or her own childhood, which however is completely reorganized and made anew, but rather a young adult who is continuing to live out an unrealized childhood, and who, after a few years, wearies of the repetitive game and becomes a supervisor, or teaches teachers, or decides it is more rewarding to deal with adults than with children. The teacher who within the school fulfills one of these roles which have a formal relationship to the child-rearing practice of the grandparent, parent, or child-nurse patterns seems to be the more successful the less she is acting out some unresolved and overdetermined past, and the more she has reassimilated and revised her past to fit into the teaching role which she has chosen.

But what then, when the teacher, of whatever type, in whatever type of school, has come to terms with her own past, has clearly seen her own role and is well equipped and ready to carry it out, year after year, as one class succeeds another in her school room—what then, when she meets, year after year, different children? In a more slowly changing society, the good teacher, the *guru* of India, for instance, is typically old, wise, patient, grown mellow with teaching the young about whom he has learned more and more each year. When the pupils remain the same, the teacher has only to keep alive her capacity for lively observation and response, and each year will add to her wisdom, her understanding, and her gentleness. But the world that the modern teacher confronts is a world in which each year serves, not to reinforce and amplify what she is slowly learning about the nature of ten-year-old boys or ten-year-old girls, or about the differences between ten-year-old boys, or ten-year-old girls—constancies which will give her something firm on which to base her methods—but serves rather to dis-orient her. What seemed to be true as she observed the fifth grade five years ago is no longer true; the children's behavior becomes not more pre-dictable—as it should as she grows more experienced—but less predictable. Ten years ago older teachers expressed their bewilderment and resentment in the circumstances that years of teaching were crowned not with wisdom and the gentleness that comes with wisdom, but with increasing ignorance and an accompanying shrillness of voice and manner; they complained that children hadn't any manners any more, were badly brought up and undisciplined, had no respect. A dozen other familiar complaints come readily to mind. Today, in 1950, the phrasing is altered and teachers now complain of the number of "disturbed children" who complicate their teaching problems. But the terms "lack of manners," "lack of respect," "unwillingness to work," which reflect the more moralistic tone of the past, or the words "disturbed children," which reflect the psychiatrically oriented thinking of the present, refer substantially to the same condition. If the words used today sound more frightening, perhaps it is because the teachers of today are even more appalled at the unpredictableness of their mysterious charges. For all these phrases are ways in which the teacher says that each year she understands her children, not more, as she might reasonably expect, but less. A kind of nightmare reversal has been introduced into life, like an escalator which insists on running backwards; age and experience become not orienting factors but disorienting ones, so that the teacher of twenty years' experience may face her class less confidently than the teacher with only two.

This is, of course, no more than the normal accompaniment of the fantastic rate of change of the world in which we live, where children of five have already incorporated into their everyday thinking ideas that most of the elders will never fully assimilate. Within the lifetime of ten-year-olds the world has entered a new age, and already, before they enter the sixth grade, the atomic age has been followed by the age of the hydrogen bomb, differentiated from the atomic age in that many of those failed to understand the dangers of the atom bomb are painfully beginning to take in the significance of the hydrogen bomb. Teachers who never heard a radio until they were grown up have to cope with children who have never known a world without television. Teachers who struggled in their childhood with a buttonhook find it difficult to describe a buttonhook to a child bred up among zippers, to whom fastnesses are to be breached by zipping them open, rather than fumblingly feeling for mysterious buttons. From the most all-embracing world image to the smallest detail of daily life the world has changed at a rate which makes the five-year-old generations further apart than world generations or even scores of generations were in our recent past, than people separated by several centuries were in the remote past. The children whom we bear and rear and teach are not only unknown to us and unlike any children there have been in the world before, but also their degree of unlikeness itself alters from year to year.

NOTES

1. See Chapter III, "We Are All Third Generation," in Margaret Mead, *And Keep Your Powder Dry* (New York: Morrow, 1943). David Riesman, *The Lonely Crowd* (New Haven: Yale University Press, 1950).

2. "Educative Effects of Social Environment as Disclosed by Studies of Primitive Societies," *Environment and Education* (Chicago: University of Chicago) 1942, pp. 48–61.

3. Margaret Mead, "The Implications of Culture Change for Personality Development," *American Journal of Orthopsychiatry,* XVII (October 1947), 633–646.

4. For a discussion of the child nurse in family structure and relation to imagination see Margaret Mead, "The Family in the Future," in *Beyond Victory,* edited by Ruth Nanda Anshen (New York: Harcourt Brace, 1943). See also Margaret Mead, "Age Patterning in Personality Development," *American Journal of Orthopsychiatry,* XVII (April 1947) 231–240.

5. Margaret Mead, *Coming of Age in Samoa* (New York: Morrow, 1928). Reprinted by New American Library, 1949.

6. Gregory Bateson and Margaret Mead, *Balinese Character,* New York Academy of Sciences. Special Publications, 1942. Margaret Mead, "The Arts in Bali," *Yale Review,* XXX, 335–347.

7. Gregory Bateson, *Naven* (Cambridge: University Press, 1936) and Mead, *Male and Female.* See also Gregory Bateson, "Bali: The Value System of a Steady State," in *Social Structure: Studies Presented to A. R. Radcliffe-Brown,* edited by Meyer Fortes (Oxford: Clarendon Press, 1949).

8. Margaret Mead, "Research on Primitive Children," in *Manual of Child Psychology,* edited by Leonard Carmichael (New York: John Wiley, 1946), pp. 667–706.

9. The *babushka* and *nyanya* of prewar Russia is an excellent example of this dual role. See Geoffrey Gorer and John Rickman, *The People of Great Russia: A Psychological Study* (London: Cresset Press, 1949).

10. Margaret Mead, *Growing Up in New Guinea* (New York: Morrow, 1930). Collected in omnibus edition *From the South Seas* (New York: Morrow, 1939). Erik H. Erikson, *Childhood and Society* (New York: Norton, 1950). [For a follow-up on the Manus people see Margaret Mead, *New Lives For Old* (New York: William Morrow and Company, 1956 (eds.).]

11. Mead, "Implications of Cultural Changes for Personality Development," *American Journal of Orthopsychiatry,* XVII, 633–646. Margaret Mead, "Character Formation and Diachronic Theory," in *Social Structure,* ed. Fortes, pp. 18–35.

12. Margaret Mead, "An Anthropologist Looks at the Teacher's Role," *Educational Method,* XXI (1942), 210–223.

13. Muriel Rukeyser, *The Life of Poetry* (New York: A. A. Wyn, 1949). Miss Rukeyser has suggested the word "*invironment*" as a literal translation of Claud Bernard's *milieu interieur* for this inner world in contrast to the environment. See also Edith Cobb, *The Therapeutic Function of the Creative Fantasy in Childhood during Latency Period: A Study of the Psycho-biological Basis of Semantics* (New York: Survey Social Work, 1947).

31 *The School Class as a Social System: Some of Its Functions in American Society*

TALCOTT PARSONS

THIS ESSAY WILL ATTEMPT to outline, if only sketchily, an analysis of the elementary and secondary school class as a social system, and the relation of its structure to its primary functions in the society as an agency of socialization and allocation. While it is important that the school class is normally part of the larger organization of a school, the class rather than the whole school will be the unit of analysis here, for it is recognized both by the school system and by the individual pupil as the place where the "business" of formal education actually takes place. In elementary schools, pupils of one grade are typically placed in a single "class" under one main teacher, but in the secondary school, and sometimes in the upper elementary grades, the pupil works on different subjects under different teachers; here the complex of classes participated in by the same pupil is the significant unit for our purposes.

The Problem: Socialization and Selection

Our main interest, then, is in a dual problem: first of how the school class functions to internalize in its pupils both the commitments and capacities for successful performance of their future adult roles, and second of how it functions to allocate these human resources within the role-structure of the adult society. The primary ways in which these two problems are interrelated will provide our main points of reference.

First, from the functional point of view the school class can be treated as an agency of socialization. That is to say, it is an agency through which individual personalities are trained to be motivationally and technically adequate to the performance of adult roles. It is not the sole such agency; the family, informal "peer group," churches, and sundry voluntary organizations all play a part, as does actual on-the-job training. But, in the period

Reprinted from Talcott Parsons, "The School Class as a Social System: Some of Its Functions in American Society," *Harvard Educational Review,* XXIX (Fall, 1959), 297–318, with the permission of the author and the editor.

extending from entry into first grade until entry into the labor force or marriage, the school class may be regarded as the focal socializing agency.

The socialization functions may be summed up as the development in individuals of the commitments and capacities which are essential prerequisites of their future role-performance. Commitments may be broken down in turn into two components: commitment to the implementation of the broad *values* of society, and commitment to the performance of a specific type of role within the *structure* of society. Thus a person in a relatively humble occupation may be a "solid citizen" in the sense of commitment to honest work in that occupation, without an intensive and sophisticated concern with the implementation of society's higher-level values. Or conversely, someone else might object to the anchorage of the feminine role in marriage and the family on the grounds that such anchorage keeps society's total talent resources from being distributed equitably to business, government, and so on. Capacities can also be broken down into two components, the first being competence or the skill to perform the tasks involved in the individual's roles, and the second being "role-responsibility" or the capacity to live up to other people's expectations of the interpersonal behavior appropriate to these roles. Thus a mechanic as well as a doctor needs to have not only the basic "skills of his trade," but also the ability to behave responsibly toward those people with whom he is brought into contact in his work.

While on the one hand, the school class may be regarded as a primary agency by which these different components of commitments and capacities are generated, on the other hand, it is, from the point of view of the society, an agency of "manpower" allocation. It is well known that in American society there is a very high, and probably increasing, correlation between one's status level in the society and one's level of educational attainment. Both social status and educational level are obviously related to the occupational status which is attained. Now, as a result of the general process of both educational and occupational upgrading, completion of high school is increasingly coming to be the norm for minimum satisfactory educational attainment, and the most significant line for future occupational status has come to be drawn between members of an age-cohort who do and do not go to college.

We are interested, then, in what it is about the school class in our society that determines the distinction between the contingents of the age-cohort which do and do not go to college. Because of a tradition of localism and a rather pragmatic pluralism, there is apparently considerable variety among school systems of various cities and states. Although the situation in metropolitan Boston probably represents a more highly structured pattern than in many other parts of the country, it is probably not so extreme as to be misleading in its main features. There, though of course actual entry into college does not come until after graduation from high school, the main dividing line is between those who are and are not enrolled in the college preparatory course in high school; there is only a small amount of shifting either way after about the ninth grade when the decision is normally made. Furthermore, the evidence seems to be that by far the most important criterion of selection is the record of school performance in elementary school. These records are evaluated by teachers and principals, and there are few cases of entering the college preparatory course against their advice. It is therefore not stretching the evidence too far to say broadly that the primary selective process occurs through differential school performance in elementary school, and that the "seal" is put on it in junior high school.[1]

The evidence also is that the selective process is genuinely assortative. As in virtually all comparable processes, ascriptive as well as achieved factors influence the outcome. In this case, the ascriptive factor is the socioeconomic status of the child's family, and the factor underlying his opportunity for achievement is his individual ability. In the study of 3,348 Boston high school boys on which these generalizations are based, each of these factors was quite highly correlated with planning college. For example, the percentages planning college, by father's occupation, were: 12 per cent for semi-skilled and unskilled, 19 per cent for skilled, 26 per cent for minor white collar, 52 per cent for middle white collar, and 80 per cent for major white collar. Likewise, intentions varied by ability (as measured by IQ), namely, 11 per cent for the lowest quintile, 17 per cent for the next, 24 per cent for the middle, 30 per cent for the next to the top, and 52 per cent for the highest. It should be noted also that within any ability quintile, the relationship of plans to father's occupation is seen. For example, within the very important top quintile in ability as measured, the range in college intentions was from 29 per cent for sons of laborers to 89 per cent for sons of major white collar persons.[2]

The essential points here seem to be that there is a relatively uniform criterion of selection operating to differentiate between the college and the non-college contingents, and that for a very important part of the cohort the operation of this criterion is not a "put-up job"—it is not simply a way of affirming a previously determined ascriptive status. To be sure, the high-status, high-ability boy is very likely indeed to go to college, and the low-status, low-ability boy is very unlikely to go. But the "cross-pressured" group for whom these two factors do not coincide[3] is of considerable importance.

Considerations like these lead me to conclude that the main process of differentiation (which from another point of view is selection) that occurs during elementary school takes place on a single main axis of *achievement*. Broadly, moreover, the differentiation leads up through high school to a bifurcation into college-goers and non-college-goers.

To assess the significance of this pattern, let us look at its place in the socialization of the individual. Entering the system of formal education is the child's first major step out of primary involvement in his family of orientation. Within the family certain foundations of his motivational system have been laid down. But the only characteristic fundamental to later roles which has clearly been "determined" and psychologically stamped in by that time is sex role. The postoedipal child enters the system of formal education clearly categorized as boy or girl, but beyond that his *role* is not yet differentiated. The process of selection, by which persons will select and be selected for categories of roles, is yet to take place.

On grounds which cannot be gone into here, it may be said that the most important single predispositional factor with which the child enters the school is his level of *independence*. By this is meant his level of self-sufficiency relative to guidance by adults, his capacity to take responsibility and to make his own decisions in coping with new and varying situations. This, like his sex role, he has as a function of his experience in the family.

The family is a collectivity within which the basic status-structure is ascribed in terms of biological position, that is, by generation, sex, and age. There are inevitably differences of performance relative to these, and they are rewarded and punished in ways that contribute to differential character formation. But these differences are not given the sanction of institutionalized social status. The school is the first socializing agency in the child's experience which institutionalizes a differentiation of status on nonbiological bases. Moreover, this is not an ascribed but an achieved status; it is the status "earned" by differential performance of the tasks set by the teacher, who is acting as an agent of the community's school system. Let us look at the structure of this situation.

The Structure of the Elementary School Class

In accord with the generally wide variability of American institutions, and of course the basically local control of school systems, there is considerable variability of school situations, but broadly they have a single relatively well-marked framework.[4] Particularly in the primary part of the elementary grades, i.e., the first three grades, the basic pattern includes one main teacher for the class, who teaches all subjects and who is in charge of the class generally. Sometimes this early, and frequently in later grades, other teachers are brought in for a few special subjects, particularly gym, music, and art, but this does not alter the central position of the main teacher. This teacher is usually a woman.[5] The class is with this one teacher for the school year, but usually no longer.

The class, then, is composed of about 25 age-peers of both sexes drawn from a relatively small geographical area—the neighborhood. Except for sex in certain respects, there is initially no formal basis for differentiation of status within the school class. The main structural differentiation develops gradually, on the single main axis indicated above as achievement. That the differentiation should occur on a single main axis is insured by four primary features of the situation. The first is the initial equalization of the "contestants' " status by age and by "family background," the neighborhood being typically much more homogeneous than is the whole society. The second circumstance is the imposition of a common set of tasks which is, compared to most other task-areas, strikingly undifferentiated. The school situation is far more like a race in this respect than most role-performance situations. Third, there is the sharp polarization between the pupils in their initial equality and the *single* teacher who is an adult and "represents" the adult world. And fourth, there is a relatively systematic process of evaluation of the pupils' performances. From the point of view of a pupil, this evaluation, particularly (though not exclusively) in the form of report card marks, constitutes reward and/or punishment for past performance; from the viewpoint of the school system acting as an allocating agency, it is a basis of *selection* for future status in society.

Two important sets of qualifications need to be kept in mind in interpreting this structural pattern, but I think these do not destroy the significance of its main outline. The first qualification is for variations in the formal organization and procedures of the school class itself. Here the most important kind of variation is that between relatively "traditional" schools and relatively "progressive" schools. The more traditional schools put more emphasis on discrete units of subject-matter, whereas the progressive type allows more "indirect" teaching through "projects" and broader topical interests where more than one bird can be killed with a stone. In progressive schools there is more emphasis on groups of pupils working together, compared to the traditional direct relation of the individual pupil to the teacher. This is related to the progressive emphasis on co-operation among the pupils rather than direct competition, to greater permissiveness as opposed to strictness of discipline, and to a de-emphasis on formal marking.[6] In some schools one of these components will be more prominent, and in others, another. That it is, however, an important range of variation is clear. It has to do, I think, very largely with the independence-dependence training which is so important to early socialization in the family. My broad interpretation is that those people who emphasize independence training will tend to be those who favor relatively progressive education. The relation of support for progressive education to relatively high socioeconomic status and to "intellectual" interests and the like is well known. There is no contradiction between these emphases both on independence and on co-operation and group solidarity among pupils. In the first instance this is because the main focus of the independence problem at these ages is vis-à-vis adults. However, it can also be said that the peer group, which here is built into the school class, is an indirect field of expression of dependency needs, displaced from adults.

The second set of qualifications concerns the "informal" aspects of the school class, which are always somewhat at variance with the formal expectations. For instance, the formal pattern of nondifferentiation between the sexes may be modified informally, for the very salience of the one-sex peer group at this age period means that there is bound to be considerable implicit recognition of it—for example, in the form of teachers' encouraging group competition between boys and girls. Still, the fact of coeducation and the attempt to treat both sexes alike in all the crucial formal respects remain the most important. Another problem raised by informal organization is the question of how far teachers can and do treat pupils particularistically in violation of the universalistic expectations of the school. When compared with other types of formal organizations, however, I think the extent of this discrepancy in elementary schools is seen to be not unusual. The school class is structured so that opportunity for particularistic treatment is severely limited. Because there are so many more children in a school class than in a family and they are concentrated in a much narrower age range, the teacher has much less chance than does a parent to grant particularistic favors.

Bearing in mind these two sets of qualifications, it is still fair, I think, to conclude that the major characteristics of the elementary school class in this country are such as have been outlined. It should be especially emphasized that more or less progressive schools, even with their relative lack of emphasis on formal marking, do not constitute a separate pattern, but rather a variant tendency within the same pattern. A progressive teacher, like any other, will form opinions about the different merits of her pupils relative to the values and goals of the class and will communicate these evaluations to them, informally if not formally. It is my impression that the extremer cases of playing down relative evaluation are confined to those upper-status schools where going to a "good" college is so fully taken for granted that for practical purposes it is an ascribed status. In other words, in interpreting these facts the selective function of the school class should be kept continually in the forefront of attention. Quite clearly its importance has not been decreasing; rather the contrary.

The Nature of School Achievement

What, now, of the content of the "achievement" expected of elementary school children? Perhaps the best broad characterization which can be given is that it involves the types of performance which are, on the one hand, appropriate to the school situation and, on the other hand, are felt by adults to be important in themselves. This vague and somewhat circular characterization may, as was mentioned earlier, be broken down into two main components. One of these is the more purely "cognitive" learning of information, skills, and frames of reference associated with empirical knowledge and technological mastery. The *written* language and the early phases of mathematical thinking are clearly vital; they involve cognitive skills at altogether new levels of generality and abstraction compared to those commanded by the pre-school child. With these basic skills goes assimilation of much factual information about the world.

The second main component is what may broadly be called a "moral" one. In earlier generations of schooling this was known as "deportment." Somewhat more generally it might be called responsible citizenship in the school community. Such things as respect for the teacher, consideration and co-operativeness in relation to fellow-pupils and good "work-habits" are the fundamentals, leading on to capacity for "leadership" and "initiative."

The striking fact about this achievement content is that in the elementary grades these two primary components are not clearly differentiated from each other. Rather, the pupil is evaluated in diffusely general terms; a *good* pupil is defined in terms of a fusion of the cognitive and the moral components, in which varying weight is given to one or the other. Broadly speaking, then, we may say that the "high achievers" of the elementary school are both the "bright" pupils, who catch on easily to their more strictly intellectual tasks, and the more "responsible" pupils, who "behave well" and on whom the teacher can "count" in her difficult problems of managing the class. One indication that this is the case is the fact that in elementary school the purely intellectual tasks are relatively easy for the pupil of high intellectual ability. In many such cases, it can be presumed that the primary challenge of the pupil is not to his intellectual, but to his "moral," capacities. On the whole, the progressive movement seems to have leaned in the direction of giving enhanced emphasis to this component, suggesting that of the two, it has tended to become the more problematical.[7]

The essential point, then, seems to be that the elementary school, regarded in the light of its socialization function, is an agency which differentiates the school class broadly along a single continuum of achievement, the content of which is relative excellence in living up to the expectations imposed by the teacher as an agent of the adult society. The criteria of this achievement are, generally speaking, undifferentiated into the cognitive or technical component and the moral or "social" component. But with respect to its bearing on societal values, it is broadly a differentiation of *levels* of capacity to act in accord with these values. Though the relation is far from nearly uniform, this differentiation underlies the processes of selection for levels of status and role in the adult society.

Next, a few words should be said about the out-of-school context in which this process goes on. Besides the school class, there are clearly two primary social structures in which the child participates: the family and the child's informal "peer group."

Family and Peer Group in Relation to the School Class

The school age child, of course, continues to live in the parental household and to be highly dependent, emotionally as well as instrumentally, on his parents. But he is now spending several hours a day away from home, subject to a discipline and a reward system which are essentially independent of that administered by the parents. Moreover, the range of this independence gradually increases. As he grows older, he is permitted to range further territorially with neither parental nor school supervision, and to do an increasing range of things. He often gets an allowance for personal spending and begins to earn some money of his own. Generally, however, the emotional problem of dependence-independence continues to be a very salient one through this period, frequently with manifestations by the child of compulsive independence.

Concomitantly with this, the area for association with age-peers without detailed adult supervision expands. These associations are tied to the family, on the one hand, in that the home and yards of children who are neighbors and the adjacent streets serve as locations for their activities; and to the school, on the other hand, in that play periods and going to and from school provide occasions for informal association, even though organized extracurricular activities are introduced only later. Ways of bringing some of this activity under another sort of adult supervision are found in such organizations as the boy and girl scouts.

Two sociological characteristics of peer groups at this age are particularly striking. One is the fluidity of their boundaries, with individual children drifting into and out of associations. This element of "voluntary association" contrasts strikingly with the child's ascribed membership in the family and the school class, over which he has no control. The second characteristic is the peer group's sharp segregation by sex. To a striking degree this is enforced by the children themselves rather than by adults.

The psychological functions of peer association are suggested by these two characteristics. On the one hand, the peer group may be regarded as a field for the exercise of independence from adult control; hence it is not surprising that it is often focus of behavior which goes beyond independence from adults to the range of adult-*disapproved* behavior; when this happens, it is the seed bed from which the extremists go over into delinquency. But another very important function is to provide the child a source of non-adult approval and acceptance. These depend on "technical" and "moral" criteria as diffuse as those required in the school situation. On the one hand, the peer group is a field for acquiring and displaying various types of "prowess"; for boys this is especially the physical prowess which may later ripen into athletic achievement. On the other hand, it is a matter of gaining acceptance from desirable peers as "belonging" in the group, which later ripens into the conception of the popular teen-ager, the "right guy." Thus the adult parents are augmented by age-peers as a source of rewards for performance and of security in acceptance.

The importance of the peer group for socialization in our type of society should be clear. The motivational foundations of character are inevitably first laid down through identification with parents, who are generation-superiors, and the generation difference is a type example of a hierarchical status difference. But an immense part of the individual's adult role performance will have to be in association with status-equals or near-equals. In this situation it is important to have a reorganization of the motivational structure so that the original dominance of the hierarchical axis is modified to strengthen the egalitarian components. The peer group plays a prominent part in this process.

Sex segregation of latency period peer groups may be regarded as a process of reinforcement of sex-role identification. Through intensive association with sex-peers and involvement in sex-typed activities, they strongly reinforce belongingness with other members of the same sex and contrast with the opposite sex. This is the more important because in the coeducational school a set of forces operates which specifically plays down sex-role differentiation.

It is notable that the latency period sex-role pattern, instead of institutionalizing relations to members of the opposite sex, is characterized by an avoidance of such relations, which only in adolescence gives way to dating. This avoidance is clearly associated with the process of reorganization of the erotic components of motivational structure. The pre-oedipal objects of erotic attachment were both intro-familial and generation-superior. In both respects there must be a fundamental shift by the time the child reaches adulthood. I would suggest that one of the main functions of the avoidance pattern is to help cope with the psychological difficulty of overcoming the earlier incestuous attachments, and hence to prepare the child for assuming an attachment to an age-mate of opposite sex later.

Seen in this perspective, the socialization function of the school class assumes a particular significance. The socialization functions of the family by this time are relatively residual, though their importance should not be underestimated. But the school remains adult-controlled and, moreover, induces basically the same kind of identification as was induced by the family in the child's pre-oedipal stage. This is to say that the learning of achievement-motivation is, psychologically speaking, a process of identification with the teacher, of doing well in school in order to please the teacher (often backed by the parents) in the same sense in which a pre-oedipal child learns new skills in order to please his mother.

In this connection I maintain that what is internalized through the process of identification is a reciprocal pattern of role-relationships.[8] Unless there is a drastic failure of internalization altogether, not just one, but both sides of the interaction will be internalized. There will, however, be an emphasis on one or the other, so that some children will more nearly identify with the socializing agent, and others will more nearly identify with the opposite role. Thus, in the pre-oedipal stage, the "independent" child has identified more with the parent, and the "dependent" one with the child-role vis-à-vis the parent.

In school the teacher is institutionally defined as superior to any pupil in knowledge of curriculum subject-matter and in responsibility as a good citizen of the school. In so far as the school class tends to be bifurcated (and of course the dichotomization is far from absolute), it will broadly be on the basis, on the one hand, of identification with the teacher, or acceptance of her role as a model; and, on the other hand, of identification with the pupil peer group. This bifurcation of the class on the basis of identification with teacher or with peer group so strikingly corresponds with the bifurcation into college-goers and non-college-goers that it would be hard to avoid the hypothesis that this structural dichotomization in the school system is the primary source of the selective dichotomization. Of course in detail the relationship is blurred, but certainly not more so than in a great many other fields of comparable analytical complexity.

These considerations suggest an interpretation of some features of the elementary teacher role in American society. The first major step in socialization, beyond that in the family, takes place in the elementary school, so it seems reasonable to expect that the teacher-figure should be characterized by a combination of similarities to and differences from parental figures. The teacher, then, is an adult, characterized by the generalized superiority, which a parent also has, of adult status relative to children. She is not, however, ascriptively related to her pupils, but is performing an occupational role—a role, however, in which the recipients of her services are tightly bound in solidarity to her and to each other. Furthermore, compared to a parent's, her responsibility to them is much more universalistic, this being reinforced, as we saw, by the size of the class; it is also much more oriented to performance rather than to solicitude for the emotional "needs" of the children. She is not entitled to suppress the distinction between high and low achievers; just because not being able to be included among the high group would be too hard on little Johnny—however much tendencies in this direction appear as deviant patterns. A mother, on the other hand, must give *first* priority to the needs of her child, regardless of his capacities to achieve.

It is also significant for the parallel of the elementary school class with the family that the teacher is normally a woman. As background it should be noted that in most European systems until recently, and often today in our private parochial and non-sectarian schools, the sexes have been segregated and each sex group has been taught by teachers of their own sex. Given coeducation, however, the woman teacher represents continuity with the role of the mother. Precisely the lack of differentiation in the elementary school "curriculum" between the components of subject-matter competence and social responsibility fits in with the greater diffuseness of the feminine role.

But at the same time, it is essential that the teacher is not a mother to her pupils, but must insist on universalistic norms and the differential reward of achievement. Above all she must be the agent of bringing about and legitimizing a differentiation of the school class on an achievement axis. This aspect of her role is furthered by the fact that in American society the feminine role is less confined to the familial context than in most other societies, but joins the masculine in occupational and associational concerns, though still with a greater relative emphasis on the family. Through identification with their teacher, children of both sexes learn that the category "woman" is not co-extensive with "mother" (and future wife), but that the feminine role-personality is more complex than that.

In this connection it may well be that there is a relation to the once-controversial issue of the marriage of women teachers. If the differentiation between what may be called the maternal and the occupational components of the feminine role is incomplete and insecure, confusion between them may be avoided by insuring that both are not performed by the same persons. The "old maid" teacher of American tradition may thus be thought of as having renounced the maternal role in favor of the occupational.[9] Recently, however, the highly effective concern over the issue of married women's teaching has conspicuously abated, and their actual participation has greatly increased. It may be suggested that this change is associated with a change in the feminine role, the most conspicuous feature of which is the general social sanctioning of participation of women in the labor force, not only prior to marriage, but also after marriage. This I should interpret as a process of structural differentiation in that the same category of persons is permitted and even expected to engage in a more complex set of role-functions than before.

The process of identification with the teacher which has been postulated here is furthered by the fact that in the elementary grades the child typically has one teacher, just as in the pre-oedipal period he had one parent, the mother, who was the focus of his object-relations. The continuity between the two phases is also favored by the fact that the teacher, like the mother, is a woman. But, if she acted only like a mother, there would be no genuine reorganization of the pupil's personality system. This reorganization is furthered by the features of the teacher role which differentiate it from the maternal. One further point is that while a child has one main teacher in each grade, he will usually have a new teacher when he progresses to the next higher grade. He is thus accustomed to the fact that teachers are, unlike mothers, "interchangeable" in a certain sense. The school year is long enough to form an important relationship to a particular teacher, but not long enough for a highly particularistic attachment to crystallize. More than in the parent-child relationship, in school the child must internalize his relation to the teacher's *role* rather than her particular personality; this is a major step in the internalization of universalistic patterns.

Socialization and Selection in the Elementary School

To conclude this discussion of the elementary school class, something should be said about the fundamental conditions underlying the process which is, as we have seen, simultaneously (1) an emancipation of the child from primary emotional attachment to his family, (2) an internalization of a level of societal values and norms that is a step higher than those he can learn in his family alone, (3) a differentiation of the school class in terms both of actual achievement and of differential *valuation* of achievement, and (4) from society's point of view, a selection and allocation of its human resources relative to the adult role system.[10]

Probably the most fundamental condition underlying this process is the sharing of common values by the two adult agencies involved—the family and the school, in this case the core of the shared valuation of *achievement*. It includes, above all, recognition that it is fair to give differential rewards for different levels of achievement, so long as there has been fair access to opportunity, and fair that these rewards lead on to higher-order opportunities for the successful. There is thus a basic sense in which the elementary school class is an embodiment of the fundamental American value of equality of opportunity, in that it places value *both* on initial equality and on differential achievement.

As a second condition, however, the rigor of this valuational pattern must be tempered by allowance for the difficulties and needs of the young child. Here the quasi-motherliness of the woman teacher plays an important part. Through her the school system, assisted by other agencies, attempts to minimize the insecurity resulting from the pressures to learn, by providing a certain amount of emotional support defined in terms of what is due to a child of a given age level. In this respect, however, the role of the school is relatively small. The underlying foundation of support is given in the home, and as we have seen, an important supplement to it can be provided by the informal peer associations of the child. It may be suggested that the development of extreme patterns of alienation from the school is often related to inadequate support in these respects.

Third, there must be a process of selective rewarding of valued perform-ance. Here the teacher is clearly the primary agent, though the more pro-gressive modes of education attempt to enlist classmates more systemati-cally than in the traditional pattern. This is the process that is the direct source of intra-class differentiation along the achievement axis.

The final condition is that this initial differentiation tends to bring about a status system in the class, in which not only the immediate results of school work, but a whole series of influences, converge to consolidate different expectations which may be thought of as the children's "levels of aspiration." Generally some differentiation of friendship groups along this line occurs, though it is important that it is by no means complete, and that children are sensitive to the attitudes not only of their own friends, but of others.

Within this general discussion of processes and conditions, it is impor-tant to distinguish, as I have attempted to do all along, the socialization of the individual from the selective allocation of contingents to future roles. For the individual, the old familial identification is broken up (the family of orientation becomes, in Freudian terms, a "lost object") and a new identification is gradually built up, providing the first-order structure of the child's identity apart from his originally ascribed identity as son or daughter of the "Joneses." He both transcends his familial identification in favor of a more independent one and comes to occupy a differentiated status within the new system. His personal status is inevitably a direct function of the position he achieves, primarily in the formal school class and secondarily in the informal peer group structure. In spite of the sense in which achieve-ment-ranking takes place along a continuum, I have put forward reasons to suggest that, with respect to this status, there is an important differentiation into two broad, relatively distinct levels, and that his position on one or the other enters into the individual's definition of his own identity. To an important degree this process of differentiation is independent of the socio-economic status of his family in the community, which to the child is a prior ascribed status.

When we look at the same system as a selective mechanism from the societal point of view, some further considerations become important. First, it may be noted that the valuation of achievement and its sharing by family and school not only provides the appropriate values for inter-nalization by individuals, but also performs a crucial integrative function for the system. Differentiation of the class along the achievement axis is inevitably a source of strain, because it confers higher rewards and priv-ileges on one contingent than on another within the same system. This com-mon valuation helps make possible the acceptance of the crucial differentia-tion, especially by the losers in the competition. Here it is an essential point that this *common* value on achievement is shared by units with different

statuses in the system. It cuts across the differentiation of families by socio-
economic status. It is necessary that there be realistic opportunity and that
the teacher can be relied on to implement it by being "fair" and rewarding achievement by whoever shows capacity for it. The fact is crucial that
the distribution of abilities, though correlated with family status, clearly
does not coincide with it. There can then be a genuine selective process
within a set of "rules of the game."

This commitment to common values is not, however, the sole integrative
mechanism counteracting the strain imposed by differentiation. Not only
does the individual pupil enjoy familial support, but teachers also like and
indeed "respect" pupils on bases independent of achievement-status, and
peer-group friendship lines, though correlated with position on the achievement scale, again by no means coincide with it, but cross-cut it. Thus there
are cross-cutting lines of solidarity which mitigate the strains generated by
rewarding achievement differentially.[11]

It is only *within* this framework of institutionalized solidarity that the
crucial selective process goes on through selective rewarding and the consolidation of its results into a status-differentiation within the school class.
We have called special attention to the impact of the selective process on
the children of relatively high ability but low family status. Precisely in
this group, but pervading school classes generally, is another parallel to
what was found in the studies of voting behavior.[12] In the voting studies it
was found that the "shifters"—those voters who were transferring their
allegiance from one major party to the other—tended, on the one hand, to
be the "cross-pressured" people, who had multiple status characteristics
and group allegiances which predisposed them simultaneously to vote in
opposite directions. The analogy in the school class is clearly to the children
for whom ability and family status do not coincide. On the other hand, it
was precisely in this group of cross-pressured voters that political "indifference" was most conspicuous. Non-voting was particularly prevalent in
this group, as was a generally cool emotional tone toward a campaign. The
suggestion is that some of the pupil "indifference" to school performance
may have a similar origin. This is clearly a complex phenomenon and cannot
be further analyzed here. But rather than suggesting, as is usual on common
sense grounds, that indifference to school work represents an "alienation"
from cultural and intellectual values, I would suggest exactly the opposite:
that an important component of such indifference, including in extreme
cases overt revolt against school discipline, is connected with the fact that
the stakes, as in politics, are very high indeed. Those pupils who are exposed to contradictory pressures are likely to be ambivalent; at the same
time, the personal stakes for them are higher than for the others, because
what happens in school may make much more of a difference for their
futures than for the others, in whom ability and family status point to the

same expectations for the future. In particular for the upwardly mobile pupils, too much emphasis on school success would pointedly suggest "burning their bridges" of association with their families and status peers. This phenomenon seems to operate even in elementary school, although it grows somewhat more conspicuous later. In general I think that an important part of the anti-intellectualism in American youth culture stems from the *importance* of the selective process through the educational system rather than the opposite.

One further major point should be made in this analysis. As we have noted, the general trend of American society has been toward a rapid upgrading in the educational status of the population. This means that, relative to past expectations, with each generation there is increased pressure to educational achievement, often associated with parents' occupational ambitions for their children.[13] To a sociologist this is a more or less classical situation of anomic strain, and the youth-culture ideology which plays down intellectual interests and school performance seems to fit in this context. The orientation of the youth culture is, in the nature of the case, ambivalent, but for the reasons suggested, the anti-intellectual side of the ambivalence tends to be overtly stressed. One of the reasons for the dominance of the anti-school side of the ideology is that it provides a means of protest against adults, who are at the opposite pole in the socialization situation. In certain respects one would expect that the trend toward greater emphasis on independence, which we have associated with progressive education, would accentuate the strain in this area and hence the tendency to decry adult expectations. The whole problem should be subjected to a thorough analysis in the light of what we know about ideologies more generally.

The same general considerations are revelant to the much-discussed problem of juvenile delinquency. Both the general upgrading process and the pressure to enhanced independence should be expected to increase strain on the lower, most marginal groups. The analysis of this paper has been concerned with the line between college and non-college contingents; there is, however, another line between those who achieve solid non-college educational status and those for whom adaptation to educational expectations at *any* level is difficult. As the acceptable minimum of educational qualification rises, persons near and below the margin will tend to be pushed into an attitude of repudiation of these expectations. Truancy and delinquency are ways of expressing this repudiation. Thus the very *improvement* of educational standards in the society at large may well be a major factor in the failure of the educational process for a growing number at the lower end of the status and ability distribution. It should therefore not be too easily assumed that delinquency is a symptom of a *general* failure of the educational process.

Differentiation and Selection in the Secondary School

It will not be possible to discuss the secondary school phase of education in nearly as much detail as has been done for the elementary school
phase, but it is worthwhile to sketch its main outline in order to place the
above analysis in a wider context. Very broadly we may say that the elementary school phase is concerned with the internalization in children of
motivation to achievement, and the selection of persons on the basis of
differential capacity for achievement. The focus is on the *level* of capacity.
In the secondary school phase, on the other hand, the focus is on the differentiation of *qualitative types* of achievement. As in the elementary
school, this differentiation cross-cuts sex roles. I should also maintain that
it cross-cuts the levels of achievement which have been differentiated out
in the elementary phase.

In approaching the question of the types of capacity differentiated, it
should be kept in mind that secondary school is the principal springboard
from which lower-status persons will enter the labor force, whereas those
achieving higher status will continue their formal education in college, and
some of them beyond. Hence for the lower-status pupils the important
line of differentiation should be the one which will lead into broadly
different categories of jobs; for the higher-status pupils the differentiation
will lead to broadly different roles in college.

My suggestion is that this differentiation separates those two components of achievement which we labelled "cognitive" and "moral" in discussing the elementary phase. Those relatively high in "cognitive" achievement will fit better in specific-function, more or less technical roles; those
relatively high in "moral" achievement will tend toward diffuser, more
"socially" or "humanly" oriented roles. In jobs not requiring college
training, the one category may be thought of as comprising the more impersonal and technical occupations, such as "operative," mechanics, or
clerical workers; the other, as occupations where "human relations" are
prominent, such as salesmen and agents of various sorts. At the college
level, the differentiation certainly relates to concern, on the one hand, with
the specifically intellectual curricular work of college and, on the other
hand, with various types of diffuser responsibility in human relations,
such as leadership roles in student government and extracurricular activities. Again, candidates for post-graduate professional training will probably
be drawn mainly from the first of these two groups.

In the structure of the school, there appears to be a gradual transition
from the earliest grade through high school, with the changes timed
differently in different school systems. The structure emphasized in the
first part of this discussion is most clearly marked in the first three "primary" grades. With progression to the higher grades, there is greater fre-

quency of plural teachers, though very generally still a single main teacher. In the sixth grade and sometimes in the fifth, a man as main teacher, though uncommon is by no means unheard of. With junior high school, however, the shift of pattern becomes more marked, and still more in senior high.

By that time the pupil has several different teachers of both sexes[14] teaching him different subjects, which are more or less formally organized into different courses—college preparatory and others. Furthermore, with the choice of "elective" subjects, the members of the class in one subject no longer need be exactly the same as in another, so the pupil is much more systematically exposed to association with different people, both adults and age-peers, in different contexts. Moreover, the school he attends is likely to be substantially larger than was his elementary school, and to draw from a wider geographical area. Hence the child is exposed to a wider range of statuses than before, being thrown in with more age-peers whom he does not encounter in his neighborhood; it is less likely that his parents will know the parents of any given child with whom he associates. It is thus my impression that the transitions to junior high and senior high school are apt to mean a considerable reshuffling of friendships. Another conspicuous difference between the elementary and secondary levels is the great increase in high school of organized extracurricular activities. Now, for the first time, organized athletics become important, as do a variety of clubs and associations which are school-sponsored and supervised to varying degrees.

Two particularly important shifts in the patterning of youth culture occur in this period. One, of course, is the emergence of more positive cross-sex relationships outside the classroom, through dances, dating, and the like. The other is the much sharper prestige-stratification of informal peer groupings, with indeed an element of snobbery which oftens exceeds that of the adult community in which the school exists.[15] Here it is important that though there is a broad correspondence between the prestige of friendship groups and the family status of their members, this, like the achievement order of the elementary school, is by no means a simple "mirroring" of the community stratification scale, for a considerable number of lower-status children get accepted into groups including members with higher family status than themselves. This stratified youth system operates as a genuine assortative mechanism; it does not simply reinforce ascribed status.

The prominence of this youth culture in the American secondary school is, in comparison with other societies, one of the hallmarks of the American educational system; it is much less prominent in most European systems. It may be said to constitute a kind of structural fusion between the school class and the peer-group structure of the elementary period. It seems clear that what I have called the "human relations" oriented contingent of the secondary school pupils are more active and prominent in extracurricular activities, and that this is one of the main foci of their differentiation from the more impersonally- and technically-oriented contingent. The personal qualities figuring most prominently in the human relations contingent can perhaps be summed up as the qualities that make for "popularity." I suggest that, from the point of view of the secondary school's selective function, the youth culture helps to differentiate between types of personalities which will, by and large, play different kinds of roles as adults.

The stratification of youth groups has, as noted, a selective function; it is a bridge between the achievement order and the adult stratification system of the community. But it also has another function. It is a focus of prestige which exists along side of, and is to a degree independent of, the achievement order focussing on school work as such. The attainment of prestige in the informal youth group is itself a form of valued achievement. Hence, among those individuals destined for higher status in society, one can discern two broad types: those whose school work is more or less outstanding and whose informal prestige is relatively satisfactory; and vice versa, those whose informal prestige is outstanding, and school performance satisfactory. Falling below certain minima in either respect would jeopardize the child's claim to belong in the upper group.[16] It is an important point here that those clearly headed for college belong to peer groups which, while often depreciative of intensive concern with studies, also take for granted and reinforce a level of scholastic attainment which is necessary for admission to a good college. Pressure will be put on the individual who tends to fall below such a standard.

In discussing the elementary school level it will be remembered that we emphasized that the peer group served as an object of emotional dependency displaced from the family. In relation to the pressure for school achievement, therefore, it served at least partially as an expression of the lower-order motivational system *out* of which the child was in process of being socialized. On its own level, similar things can be said of the adolescent youth culture; it is in part an expression of regressive motivations. This is true of the emphasis on athletics despite its lack of relevance to adult roles, of the "homosexual" undertones of much intensive same-sex friendships, and of a certain "irresponsibility" in attitudes toward the opposite sex—e.g., the exploitative element in the attitudes of boys toward girls. This, however, is by no means the whole story. The youth culture is also a field for practicing the assumption of higher-order responsibilities, for conducting delicate human relations without immediate supervision and learning to accept the consequences. In this connection it is clearly of particular importance to the contingent we have spoken of as specializing in "human relations."

We can, perhaps distinguish three different levels of crystallization of these youth-culture patterns. The middle one is that which may be considered age-appropriate without clear status-differentiation. The two keynotes here seem to be "being a good fellow" in the sense of general friendliness and being ready to take responsibility in informal social situations where something needs to be done. Above this, we may speak of the higher level of "outstanding" popularity and qualities of "leadership" of the person who is turned to where unusual responsibilities are required. And below the middle level are the youth patterns bordering on delinquency, withdrawal, and generally unacceptable behavior. Only this last level is clearly "regressive" relative to expectations of appropriate behavior for the age-grade. In judging these three levels, however, allowances should be made for a good many nuances. Most adolescents do a certain amount of experimenting with the borderline of the unacceptable patterns; that they should do so is to be expected in view of the pressure toward independence from adults, and of the "collusion" which can be expected in the reciprocal stimulation of age-peers. The question is whether this regressive behavior comes to be confirmed into a major pattern for the personality as a whole. Seen in this perspective, it seem legitimate to maintain that the middle and the higher patterns indicated are the major ones, and that only a minority of adolescents come to be confirmed in a truly unacceptable pattern of living. This minority may well be a relatively constant proportion of the age cohort, but apart from situations of special social disorganization, the available evidence does not suggest that it has been a progressively growing one in recent years.

The patterning of cross-sex relations in the youth culture clearly foreshadows future marriage and family formation. That it figures so prominently in school is related to the fact that in our society the element of ascription, including direct parental influence, in the choice of a marriage partner is strongly minimized. For the girl, it has the very important significance of reminding her that her adult status is going to be very much concerned with marriage and a family. This basic expectation for the girl stands in a certain tension to the school's curricular coeducation with its relative lack of differentiation by sex. But the extent to which the feminine role in American society continues to be anchored in marriage and the family should not be allowed to obscure the importance of coeducation. In the first place, the contribution of women in various extra-familial occupations and in community affairs has been rapidly increasing, and certainly higher levels of education have served as a prerequisite to this contribution. At the same time, it is highly important that the woman's familial role should not be regarded as drastically segregated from the cultural concerns of the society as a whole. The educated woman has important functions *as wife and mother,* particularly as an influence on her children in backing the schools and impressing on them the importance of education. It is, I think, broadly true that the immediate responsibility of women for family management has been increasing, though I am very skeptical of the alleged "abdication" of the American male. But precisely in the context of women's increased family responsibility, the influence of the mother both as agent of socialization and as role model is a crucial one. This influence should be evaluated in the light of the general upgrading process. It is very doubtful whether, apart from any other considerations, the motivational prerequisites of the general process could be sustained without sufficiently high education of the women, who, as mothers, influence their children.

Conclusion

With the general cultural upgrading process in American society which has been going on for more than a century, the educational system has come to play an increasingly vital role. That this should be the case is, in my opinion, a consequence of the general trend to structural differentiation in the society. Relatively speaking, the school is a specialized agency. That it should increasingly have become the principal channel of selection as well as agency of socialization is in line with what one would expect in an increasingly differentiated and progressively more upgraded society. The legend of the "self-made man" has an element of nostalgic romanticism and is destined to become increasingly mythical, if by it is meant not just mobility from humble origins to high status, which does indeed continue to occur, but that the high status was attained through the "school of hard knocks" without the aid of formal education.

The structure of the public school system and the analysis of the ways in which it contributes both to the socialization of individuals and to their allocation of roles in society is, I feel, of vital concern to all students of American society. Notwithstanding the variegated elements in the situation, I think it has been possible to sketch out a few major structural patterns of the public school system and at least to suggest some ways in which they serve these important functions. What could be presented in this paper is the merest outline of such an analysis. It is, however, hoped that it has been carried far enough to suggest a field of vital mutual interest for social scientists on the one hand and those concerned with the actual operation of the schools on the other.

NOTES

1. The principal source for these statements is a study of social mobility among boys in ten public high schools in the Boston metropolitan area, conducted by Samuel A. Stouffer, Florence R. Kluckhohn, and the present author. Unfortunately the material is not available in published form.

2. See table from this study in J. A. Kahl, *The American Class Structure* (New York: Rinehart & Co., 1953), p. 283. Data from a nationwide sample of high school students, published by the Educational Testing Service, show similar patterns of relationships. For example, the ETS study shows variation, by father's occupation, in proportion of high school seniors planning college, of from 35 per cent to 80 per cent for boys and 27 per cent to 79 per cent for girls. (From *Background Factors Re-*

lated to College Plans and College Enrollment among High School Students [Princeton, N.J.: Educational Testing Service, 1957]).

3. There seem to be two main reasons why the high-status, low-ability group is not so important as its obverse. The first is that in a society of expanding educational and occupational opportunity the general trend is one of upgrading, and the social pressures to downward mobility are not as great as they would otherwise be. The second is that there are cushioning mechanisms which tend to protect the high status boy who has difficulty "making the grade." He may be sent to a college with low academic standards, he may go to schools where the line between ability levels is not rigorously drawn, etc.

4. This discussion refers to public schools. Only about 13 per cent of all elementary and secondary school pupils attend non-public schools, with this proportion ranging from about 22 per cent in the Northeast to about 6 per cent in the South. U.S. Office of Education, *Biennial Survey of Education in the United States, 1954–56* (Washington: U.S. Government Printing Office, 1959), chap. ii, "Statistics of State School Systems, 1955–56," Table 44, p. 114.

5. In 1955–56, 13 per cent of the public elementary school instructional staff in the United States were men. *Ibid.*, p. 7.

6. This summary of some contrasts between traditional and progressive patterns is derived from general reading in the literature rather than any single authoritative account.

7. This account of the two components of elementary school achievement and their relation summarizes impressions gained from the literature, rather than being based on the opinions of particular authorities. I have the impression that achievement in this sense corresponds closely to what is meant by the term as used by McClelland and his associates. Cf. D. C. McClelland *et al., The Achievement Motive* (New York: Appleton-Century-Crofts, Inc., 1953).

8. On the identification process in the family see my paper, "Social Structure and the Development of Personality," *Psychiatry*, XXI (November, 1958), pp. 321–40.

9. It is worth noting that the Catholic parochial school system is in line with the more general older American tradition, in that the typical teacher is a nun. The only difference in this respect is the sharp religious symbolization of the difference between mother and teacher.

10. The following summary is adapted from T. Parsons, R. F. Bales *et al., Family, Socialization and Interaction Process* (Glencoe, Ill.: The Free Press, 1955), esp. chap. iv.

11. In this, as in several other respects, there is a parallel to other important allocative processes in the society. A striking example is the voting process by which political support is allocated between party candidates. Here, the strain arises from the fact that one candidate and his party will come to enjoy all the perquisites—above all the power—of office, while the other will be excluded for the time being from these. This strain is mitigated, on the one hand, by the common commitment to constitutional procedure, and, on the other hand, by the fact that the nonpolitical bases of social solidarity, which figure so prominently as determinants of voting behavior, still cut across party lines. The average person is, in various of his roles, associated with people whose political preference is different from his own; he therefore could not regard the opposite party as composed of unmitigated scoundrels without introducing a rift within the groups to which he is attached. This feature of the electorate's structure is brought out strongly in B. R. Berelson, P. F. Lazarsfeld and W. N. McPhee, *Voting* (Chicago: University of Chicago Press, 1954). The conceptual analysis of it is developed in my own paper " 'Voting' and the Equilibrium of the American Political System" in E. Burdick and A. J. Brodbeck (eds.) *American Voting Behavior* (Glencoe, Ill.: The Free Press, 1959).

12. *Ibid.*

13. J. A. Kahl, "Educational and Occupational Aspirations of 'Common Man' Boys," *Harvard Educational Review*, XXIII (Summer, 1953), pp. 186–203. [Chap. xxvi in this volume (eds.).]

14. Men make up about half (49 per cent) of the public secondary school in-

structional staff. *Biennial Survey of Education in the United States, 1954–56, op. cit.,* chap. ii, p. 7.

15. See, for instance C. W. Gordon, *The Social System of the High School: A Study in the Sociology of Adolescence* (Glencoe, Ill.: The Free Press, 1957).

16. J. Riley, M. Riley, and M. Moore, "Adolescent Values and the Riesman Typology" in S. M. Lipset and L. Lowenthal (eds.) *The Sociology of Culture and the Analysis of Social Character* (Glencoe, Ill.: The Free Press, to be published in 1960).

32 *The Changing Functions of Universities*

A. H. HALSEY

Introduction

THE MAIN THESIS of this essay concerns the relations of higher education to social structure and involves the notion of a type of society—the technological society[1]—towards which Western industrial countries are more or less rapidly moving. The mark of the educational institutions of a technological society is that they are in a special sense crucial to its maintenance and, through the institutionalisation of technological research, to its further development.

In the mediaeval and industrial periods the history of the universities in relation to the economy is one of imperfect and usually belated adaptation to the occupational demands of a culture gradually increasing in its complexity. In the technological society the system of higher education no longer plays a passive role: it becomes a determinant of economic development and hence of stratification and other aspects towards the technological society as conditioned by the strength of the earlier traditions of higher learning in any given industrial country.

Universities and Social Structure

The basic function of education is the preservation and transmission of culture. In this broad sense all societies are educative. Sociologists of education, however, confine their studies largely to those societies in which there is a sufficiently complex culture to require its preservation and transmission by specialized agencies. Higher education is such a specialized agency charged with the conservation of the most highly prized beliefs and intellectual skills in the cultural heritage.

Accordingly organisations of higher education must be seen as partially independent of, but functioning in relation to, such other aspects of social structure as government, the economy and religious and military organ-

Reprinted from A. H. Halsey, "The Changing Functions of Universities in Advanced Industrial Societies," *Harvard Educational Review,* XXX (Spring, 1960), 119–27, with the permission of the author and the editor.

isations. The existence of the higher learning pre-supposes certain social conditions, notably a level of economic and political development that affords the possibility of "idleness" for a scholarly class.[2] Indeed universities always play a role in stratification because, controlling access to highly valued cultural elements, they are intrinisically inegalitarian. As Durkheim pointed out, "to find an absolutely homogeneous and egalitarian education, it would be necessary to go back to pre-historic societies in the structure of which there is no differentiation."[3]

   An adequate analysis of contemporary university developments therefore requires a theory of change involving multiple causes, conditions and consequences. But the crucial connection, in this context, is with the economy. This is basically because development of knowledge is always likely to issue from its conservation and, in fact, has done so intermittently throughout the history of higher learning. More particularly it is so because, in response to the demands set up by modern industrialism and scientific warfare, research has become institutionalised in universities. The universities have therefore become an established source of instability to the technology and hence to the economy. And at the same time they are the training institutions for the skilled manpower required by a complex technology.

Universities and the Emergence of Industrialism

   The present linkage of the university to the economy in industrial society is direct and obvious through the market for professional manpower and through research activities in the applied sciences. It was not always so. Richard Hofstadter has contrasted the present situation with the period before the American Civil War: "In the middle of the 20th century, the American student of the history of higher education will find it hard to understand why college teaching responded so slowly to social change unless he realises that the old-time colleges were not organically knit into the fabric of economic life."[4] The European universities were, in their mediaeval origins, an organic part of religious rather than economic life and this was true even of the much later American foundations where, until the early years of the 18th century, the majority of graduates became clergymen.[5] The subsequent development of new economic functions for the universities with the rise of industrialism is only one aspect, though an important one, of the broader process of secularisation of learning which spread with the Renaissance and which, through the teaching of Wyclif, Ockham and Duns Scotus, had already disrupted Oxford in the 14th century.[6] A negligible proportion of the alumni of modern western universities enters the ministry.[7]

   However, the typical transition of universities from their earlier functional emphasis was not a simple story of extension in provision for secular professional training as a response to the demands of developing industrialism. On the contrary there was an overlapping and, in England at least, still observable phase in which the universities were dominated by their function as preserves of the aristocratic and gentry classes. Indeed the history of European and American universities in the age of coal and steam industrialism is one of successful resistance, by ideological and other elements in the "superstructure," to the pressures set up by economic change.[8] Max Weber's view of education as a differentiating agency, socialising individuals into the total style of life of the strata for which they are destined, has to be used as if in application to an aristocratic "structure of domination" up to the Second World War. In this sense higher education has been essentially a phenomenon of status rather than class; a process directed "against the market."[9]

Traditionally the university has rightly been seen as primarily devoted to the education, moral and physical as well as intellectual, of the "cultivated man"[10] with its emphasis on "character," "service," poised and rounded personality and an easy amateur command of the nonspecialist skill appropriate to a ruling class in a world of steam navigation, gunpowder and manuscript.[11] For the lower strata the educational equivalent in Europe has been a simple literacy heavily imbued with ideas of docility, piety and nationalism.

Vocationalism was resisted in the European universities long after the religious domination of curricula had been overcome and long after secular universities had been founded on the basis of state and industrial patronage. Thus the creation of the University of Berlin in the early years of the 19th century, which set the tone for much of the subsequent modernisation of universities in Europe and America, "was intended primarily to develop knowledge, secondarily and perhaps as a concession, to train the professional and the official classes."[12] In America the land grant colleges created after the Morrill Act of 1862 failed, despite the lead given by Wisconsin[13] to create a comprehensive link between higher education and agriculture, through either research or teaching, until after the First World War. In England the great champion of the modern universities, T. H. Huxley, asserted before the Cowper Commission of 1892 that "the primary business of the universities is with pure knowledge and pure art—independent of all application to practice; with progress in culture not with increase in wealth."[14]

The emergence of the modern British universities as undergraduate professional schools, though it begins with the foundation of the University of London, is largely a 20th century phenomenon and even then is explicable primarily in terms of the continued command held by Oxford and Cambridge over the avenues of entry into the national elites. Even in America where the absence of an indigenous aristocracy made professional and technological training more acceptable, it was absorbed into the universities more by their extension into graduate schools than by revision of undergraduate curricula.[15]

The aristocratic domination of universities which was typical of Europe in the 18th century, with its American equivalent in the education of ministers and lawyers as community leaders, continued despite the shifting class basis of power in the 19th and early 20th century. However, this did not preclude the more limited function of higher education as an agent of social mobility, of assimilation into elite groups, of "resocialisation" for a selected minority of able boys from the lower strata. The 19th century American colleges and the German universities both recruited from the middle and lower classes. And in England with the beginning of expansion of professional and administrative employment in the second half of the century, "the old and the new middle classes needed avenues of employment which would provide both prestige and relatively high income for their sons."[16] But the working classes were scarcely touched by these developments.[17]

In any case, as Hofstadter says of the American college, "Education was for gentlemen, it was designed to create among them a core of central knowledge that would make of them a community of the educated."[18] And even Veblen's bitter classic, though directed against "the conduct of universities by businessmen" and the perversion of scholarly values by the predatory ethics of business, describes an example of the ideal university man as one striving for "lifelike, imitation of a country gentleman."[19]

Universities and Technological Society

A new relationship is now discernible. In general, whereas both Weber and Veblen saw the university as a corporate structure in process of adaptation (Veblen thought betrayal) to industrial society,[20] W. H. Whyte,[21] writing forty years later had to see it as an integral part of the organisation of a technological society. Development in this direction has its origins in the 19th century application of science to industrial processes, "the invention of invention," and the slow subsequent development of technological professions in agriculture, chemistry, metallurgy, mechanical and electrical engineering, etc. However it begins to become clear as a direct relationship of economic organisation to the higher learning only with escape from the economic depressions of the 1930s and the search for high productivity of the war and post war years. Both as research organisations and as training establishments, the institutions of higher education in this period have been drawn more closely into the economy either directly or through the state. The exchange of ideas, people, and contracts between university departments and research institutes and their counterparts in private industry and government agencies is such as to merge these organisations and to assimilate the life styles of their staff.

Basically, the new functions reflect a new stage in the development of the means of production in which, as Drucker puts it, "the highly educated man has become the central resource of today's society, the supply of such men the true measure of its economic, military and even its political potential."[22] The class formation appropriate to the new means of production is one in which educational institutions play a crucial role. The search for talent to man the economy implies democratisation of access to education and the development of selective processes. Schools, colleges and universities become the agencies through which "achievement" in the occupational role is largely determined and in which the forces of "ascription" and "achievement" contend to determine the life chances of individuals.

The educational characteristics of a technological society are clearest where they are most advanced—in America. The explosive expansion which has taken place there in the demand for high scientific manpower has not only created conditions of chronic shortage of supply; it has also transformed the universities. In 1900 the percentage of American 18–21 year olds enrolled in institutions of higher education was 4.0. It doubled in the next twenty years and again in the following twenty years to 15.6 in 1940. Since then expansion has been even more rapid until, in 1956 the figure was about one third.[23] Under these circumstances the function of universities as nurseries for elite groups is overlaid by their new function as a mass higher education service in an emergent technological society. The "community of the educated" similarly tends to disappear.[24] Meanwhile it should be noticed that the structure of higher education had adapted itself to the new conditions by forming itself into status hierarchy or "academic procession"[25] with graded access to "achievement" and power in the stratification system.[26]

Russia is the same kind of society in the sense that higher education is geared closely to the economy which, in this case, is controlled centrally in the interests of maximising economic growth. At first glance the USSR appears to be educationally under-developed. It has proportionately only half as many secondary school graduates as the U.S.A. and only 16 per 1,000 of its people have had higher education compared with the American figure of 44.[27] But the essential feature of the Russian case is that the sharp break with earlier social traditions which was made possible by the Revolution resulted in the development of a system of higher education adjusted directly to the demand for technological manpower. Thus in the supply of professional and scientific workers to agriculture, medicine, engineering, etc., the Russian system is as far advanced as the American.

For example, in engineering and science the number of graduates per 1,000 of the population is 9 in USSR and 10 in the U.S.A.

The different points reached by these two countries in their advance towards the technological society is indicated by the fact that in Russia the percentage of science and engineering graduates to all graduates is 55 whereas in America it is 21. This certainly does not mean that in America the higher learning either already is or is becoming less closely geared to the economy. On the contrary there is a strong tendency for business to increase its influence over the content of American higher education as is indicated by the decline of the fundamental disciplines and the rise of applied subjects, especially those connected with business administration and commerce.[28] The "extra" output of American graduates in the humanities and social sciences mainly reflects the professionalisation of the tertiary sector of American industry and may be viewed as an adornment of the affluent society, which Russia has yet to become.

The British case is instructive as one in which the mediaeval and aristocratic traditions of the universities have hitherto acted as a powerful brake against movement towards the technological society. British university life has been dominated by Oxford and Cambridge since the defeat of the migration to Stamford in 1334.[29] In the 14th century Oxford and Cambridge, backed by royal power, established themselves as national institutions with a monopoly over the higher learning. The monopoly was challenged frequently but unsuccessfully until the rise of the universities in the great industrial cities of the 19th century, and even then monopoly only gave way to pre-eminence.[30] The challenge of industrialism and nonconformity was met partly by reform and expansion of the ancient foundations, partly by assimilation of the sons of successful business men through the colleges and the "public schools" which supply them, and partly by sending staff to the newly created universities.

As a result a two tier structure emerged in the early 20th century. Oxford and Cambridge were national universities connected with the national elites of politics, administration, business and the liberal professions. The rest were provincial, all of them, including London, taking most of their students from their own region[31] and training them in undergraduate professional schools for the newer technological and professional occupations created by industrialism such as chemistry, electrical engineering, state grammar school teaching and the scientific civil service.

Since the war, as may be see from Table 1, a new wave of expansion, with some emphasis on science and the technologies, has been taking place. But the pace of expansion is much slower than in the U.S.A. or the USSR. The elite conception of the university continues to dominate development plans. Oxford and Cambridge are again expanding to assimilate the rising technological elite through the Cavendish Laboratories and Churchill College. A scrimmage for precedence on the second tier is taking place among

Table 1.

Percentage Distribution of Full-Time University Students by Faculties in the United Kingdom in 1938–39 and 1956–57

Faculty	1938–39 (N=50,002)	1956–57 (N=89,866)
Arts	44.7	43.1
Pure Science	15.3	22.2
Medicine, Dentistry	26.8	17.4
Technology, Agriculture	13.2	17.3
Total	100.0	100.0

Source: *University Development 1952–1957*, H.M.S.O. Cmd. 534.

the modern universities and the newly emancipated university colleges; and, in the process, the provincial universities are being nationalised. An indication of this trend may be had from the proportion of students drawn from within 30 miles of the university. In Table 2 some examples have been calculated from the Returns from Universities and University Colleges to the University Grants Committee.

Table 2.

Geographical Origins of University Students in English Universities, 1908–56

University	Per cent students drawn from within 30 miles 1908–09	1948–49	1955–56
Birmingham	—	56	38
Bristol	87	39	26
Leeds	78	60	40
Liverpool	75	62	55
Manchester	73	59	48
University College, London	66	53	43

For the United Kingdom as a whole, including Oxford and Cambridge, the proportion of university students living at home fell from 41.7 per cent in 1938/39 to 34.6 per cent in 1951/52 and further to 26.6 per cent in 1956/57. (*University Development 1952/57*, H.M.S.O. Cmd. 534, Table VII.)

Meanwhile a third tier in the structure of higher education is being formed by Colleges of Advanced Technology and Teacher Training Colleges offering courses of three years duration. The creation of this new level in the hierarchy is to the emerging technological economy what the provincial universities were to large-scale industrialism.

Conclusion

Throughout the period of emerging industrialism in Europe and America the principal social function of the universities has been that of status differentiation of elites with some assimilation of students from the lower strata. But the progressive secularisation of higher learning since mediaeval times has increased the potential of the universities as sources of technological and therefore of social change until now they are beginning to occupy a place as part of the economic foundation of a new type of society. In this new technological society educational institutions are expanded not only to exercise research functions but also to play a central role in the economy and the system of stratification as agencies for selection, training and occupational placement of individuals.

Movement towards this state of affairs is uneven among the Western Industrial countries. A comparison of America, Russia and Britain shows that it is furthest advanced in America where professionalisation has entered the tertiary sectors of industry and has resulted in far-reaching modifications of the content of university studies. It is fastest in Russia where the supply of graduates is closely attuned to the needs of a fast developing economy. It is slowest in Britain where the legacy of the traditional status differentiating function of Oxford and Cambridge persists and where the response to technological change is most strongly contained within an educational hierarchy corresponding to the power and prestige pyramid of the wider society.

NOTES

1. Cf. J. E. Floud and A. H. Halsey, "The Sociology of Education—A Trend Report and Bibliography," *Current Sociology*, VII, (No. 3, 1958).

2. More strictly, in the incipient phase of the development of higher learning, a "vicarious leisure class." Cf. T. Veblen, *The Theory of the Leisure Class* (London: Allen and Unwin, Ltd., 1924), p. 367.

3. E. Durkheim, *Education and Sociology*, trans. S. D. Fox (Glencoe, Ill.: The Free Press, 1956), p. 69.

4. R. Hofstadter and C. P. Hardy, *The Development and Scope of Higher Education in the United States* (New York: Columbia University Press, 1952), p. 21.

5. 70% of the first few years of Harvard graduates (in the 1640's) became clergymen and nearly 73% of Yale graduates between 1701–19. c.f. Hofstadter, *op. cit.*, pp. 6–9.

6. Cf. A. R. Myers, *England in the Late Middle Ages (1307–1536)* (London: Penguin Books, 1952), pp. 72–77.

7. At Yale it was reduced to 6% by 1900. In 1955 2% of those admitted to Oxford and Cambridge went to read theology, the figure for the modern British universities being 0.4%. R. K. Kelsall, *Applications for Admission to Universities* (London: Association of Universities of British Commonwealth, 1957), Table 1.

8. An excellent brief analysis of the impact of technology and science on the higher learning in Britain is given in Sir Eric Ashby, *Technology and the Academics* (London: The Macmillan Company, 1958). [Essay No. 39 in this volume (eds.).]

9. Though access to it, in accordance with Weber's general definition of status, is in the long run determined by access to market opportunities.

10. Weber points out that, " 'the cultivated man,' rather than the 'specialist' has been the end sought by education and has formed the basis of social esteem in such various systems as the feudal theocratic and patrimonial structures of domination: in the English notable administration, in the old Chinese patrimonial bureaucracy as well as under the rule of demagogues in the so-called Hellenic democracy." H. Gerth & C. Mills, *From Max Weber* (London: Kegan Paul, 1948), p. 242.

11. "In the 18th century while the gentry ruled, the country [England] had practically no officials; the Church and the Law were allied powers. . . . The Universities accordingly developed on lines convenient to the ruling caste, as seats in

which the youth of the country could acquire a modicum of classical learning; they gave an intellectual sanction to the domination of the gentry and brought up the young men to be gentlemen, accepting and exemplifying the ideals of a class. And such, despite the far-reaching reforms of the 19th century, Oxford and Cambridge remain to this day to a very large extent." W. Dibelius, *England*, trans. M. A. Hamilton (London: Jonathan Cape Ltd. 1929), p. 409.

12. A. Flexner, *Universities: American, English, German* (New York: Oxford University Press, 1930), p. 312.

13. Cf. C. McCarty, *The Wisconsin Idea* (New York: Macmillan Company, 1912).

14. Quoted in C. Bibby, "T. H. Huxley's Idea of a University," *Universities Quarterly*, X (August, 1956).

15. It is noteworthy that only very recently have investigations of socialisation into specialised professional groups such as the medical profession become a significant part of the sociological study of university life, e.g., R. K. Merton *et al.*, *The Student Physician: Introductory Studies in the Sociology of Medical Education* (Cambridge, Mass.: Harvard University Press, 1957). H. Becker and B. Greer "Student Culture in Medical School," *Harvard Educational Review*, XXVIII, (Winter, 1958), pp. 70–80.

16. D. V. Glass, "Education" in M. Ginsberg (ed.), *Law and Opinion in the Twentieth Century* (London: Stevens, 1959), p. 326. [Chap. 28 of this volume (eds.).]

17. Cf. D. V. Glass, *ibid.* Of the generation of working class boys born between 1910 and 1929 only 1.4% went to a university. For the best available statistical description see J. E. Floud, "The Educational Experience of the Adult Population of England and Wales as at July, 1949," in D. V. Glass (ed.), *Social Mobility in Britain* (London: Free Press, 1954). Writing of the German universities in 1929, Flexner (*op. cit.*, p. 337) states, "It has been estimated that at this moment not exceeding three per cent of the university students come from the working classes, and the number was formerly even smaller." In the American system of higher education initial access has traditionally been more open but selection *within* the system ("dropout") has been more severe and along class lines. This basic contrast between American and English education is discussed in an interesting fashion by Ralph Turner in his "Sponsored and Contest Mobility and the School System," [Chap. 12 in this volume.]

18. Hofstadter, *op. cit.*, p. 11.

19. T. Veblen, *The Higher Learning in America* (New York: B. W. Huebsch, 1918), p. 164. He goes on "the incumbent had no distinguishing marks either as a teacher or a scholar, and neither science nor letters will be found in his debt."

20. Cf. J. E. Floud and A. H. Halsey, *loc. cit.*

21. W. H. Whyte, *The Organisation Man* (London: Cape Ltd., 1957).

22. P. F. Drucker, *The Landmarks of Tomorrow,* (London: Heinemann, 1959), p. 87. [Ch. ★★★ of this volume (eds.).]

23. Cf. N. DeWitt, "Basic Comparative Data on Soviet and American Education," *Comparative Education Review,* II (June, 1958), p. 9.

24. It was once maintained in part by the role of two or three major universities as training institutions for all university faculty. But with expansion this integrating factor operates less and less. The minor universities are focused to become self-recruiting. Thus the status exclusiveness of the high prestige universities is preserved though the distribution of academic talent may be widening. c.f. T. Caplow and R. J. McGee. *The Academic Market-Place* (New York: Basic Books, 1958), p. 221, *et. seq.*

25. D. Riesman, *Constraint and Variety in American Education* (New York: Doubleday Anchor Books, 1958), Ch. 1. [Ch. xxxiv in this volume (eds.).]

26. E. Haveman and P. S. West, in their *They Went to College*, The College Graduate in America Today, (New York: Harcourt Brace, 1952), show that marked differences in earning increment are to be gained from attendance at the high prestige universities like Princeton as compared with the ordinary run of state universities.

27. For this and the following figures, c.f. De Witt, *loc. cit.*, also his *Soviet*

Professional Manpower (Washington: National Science Foundation, 1955), especially pp. 254–258 where a comparison is made of the supply of professional manpower in U.S.S.R. and U.S.A.

28. Cf. W. H. Whyte, *op. cit.,* pp. 80–82.

29. H. Rashdall, *The Universities of Europe in the Middle Ages* (Oxford: The Clarendon Press, 1936) III, 89–90.

30. Cf. E. A. Shils, "The Intellectuals. Great Britain," *Encounter,* VI (April, 1955), and A. Halsey, "British Universities and Intellectual Life," *Universities Quarterly,* XII (February, 1958), pp. 141–152. [Essay No. 41 of this volume (eds.).]

31. See below, Table 2.

33 On Universities and the Scientific Revolution

SIR ERIC ASHBY

I

THE INDUSTRIAL REVOLUTION was accomplished by hard heads and clever fingers. Men like Bramah and Maudslay, Arkwright and Crompton, the Darbys of Coalbrookdale and Neilson of Glasglow, had no systematic education in science or technology. Britain's industrial strength lay in its amateurs and self-made men: the craftsman-inventor, the mill-owner, the iron-master. It was no accident that the Crystal Palace, that sparkling symbol of the supremacy of British technology, was designed by an amateur. In this rise of British industry the English universities played no part whatever, and the Scottish universities only a very small part; indeed formal education of any sort was a negligible factor in its success. The schools attended by the prosperous classes followed a curriculum which had scarcely changed since the schooldays of John Milton two centuries earlier. For the working classes there was no systematic schooling. Illiteracy was widespread: even as late as 1841 a third of the men and nearly half the women who were married in England and Wales signed the register with a mark. There were a few 'cultivators of science' (as they were called) engaged in research, but their work was not regarded as having much bearing on education and still less on technology. There was practically no exchange of ideas between the scientists and the designers of industrial processes. The very stratification of English society helped to keep science isolated from its applications: it was admitted that the study of science for its useful applications might be appropriate for the labouring classes, but managers were not attracted to the study of science except as an agreeable occupation for their leisure.

So it came about that the first technological education in Britain was provided, not for the sons of managers in industry, but for that small minority of the working classes who could read and write: the craftsman, the foreman, the mechanic. The mechanics' institutes—one of the great educational movements in British history—had their origin in the 'anti-toga' lectures

Reprinted from Sir Eric Ashby, *Technology and the Academics* (London: Macmillan and Co.; New York: St. Martin's Press, 1958) chap. iii, with the permission of the author and the publishers.

(open to the public) given by a professor of natural philosophy in Glasgow, the querulous and eccentric John Anderson, known to his students as 'Jolly Jack Phosphorus.' He occupied the chair from 1757 until 1796, and he records that in 1791 he had nearly 200 students at his classes. He is known[1] to have given free tickets for his lectures to 'gardeners, painters, shopmen, porters, founders, bookbinders, barbers, tailors, potters, glassblowers, gunsmiths, engravers, brewers, and turners.' He quarrelled persistently with his academic colleagues. One outcome of his animosity toward the University was his will, endowing (quite inadequately) a second university for the people of Glasgow, 'for the Improvement of Human Nature, of Science, and of the country where they live.' In 1700 George Birkbeck was appointed professor in this strange establishment. His principal duty was to give courses of lectures and scientific demonstrations to a middle-class clientele prepared to pay a fee of some two guineas. In addition to this duty Birkbeck imposed on himself another one, namely to hold on Saturday evenings a course of lectures, without any fee, for working men. Five years later Birkbeck migrated to London and there, on the strength of his experience in Glasgow, he founded the London Mechanics' Institution. The movement spread. In 1841 there were some 50,000 members in more than 200 institutions, scattered the length and breadth of Britain. After the Great Exhibition the institutes in Yorkshire banded themselves together into a Union, with 20,000 members in 100 affiliated branches. In 1853 the secretary of the Yorkshire Union, James Hole, published an essay[2] in which he suggested that the mechanics' institutes should combine to become the constituent parts of a national industrial university. The Society of Arts, which had for many years been a pioneer in the applications of science to technology, encouraged the movement by arranging conferences on technical education, establishing examinations and awarding diplomas, and by trying to organise a nation-wide union of mechanics' institutes.[3] It is interesting to speculate on the way technological education might have developed in Britain if a national industrial university had emerged from these proposals. In his evidence before a committee of the Society of Arts in 1853 the Secretary of the Royal Institution said:

> As to the mechanics' institutes . . . they might become to such schools as I have contemplated what the *école des arts et métiers* is to the schools in France. . . . Each mechanics' institute, if appreciated, would be a self-governed and self-supporting academy for the particular speciality which the wants of the neighourhood indicated, whether agricultural chemistry, manufacturing chemistry, mechanics, metallurgy, etc.

But the soil of general education was at that time too thin to carry a system of technical education. The mechanics' institutes failed to make any impression on contemporary technology, partly because they catered for a class which was too illiterate, and too overworked, to absorb scientific education in the evenings; partly because industry offered no inducements to the few students who did survive the Society of Arts examinations and emerge with diplomas; and partly because many of the institutes, in order to retain their membership, dropped systematic instruction in the scientific principles of various trades in favour of popular science, entertainment, and the amenities of a working-men's club. This is not to say that the mechanics' institutes were a negligible influence in the history of British education: on the contrary, they lie at the foundation of such great institutions as the Royal College of Science and Technology in Glasgow, the Heriot-Watt College in Edinburgh, and the Manchester College of Technology. But in their own generation they did not bring technology within the pale of the formal educational system.

To the general public the 1851 Exhibition was a reassurance of Britain's industrial supremacy. There were a hundred categories of manufacturers, and in most of these categories the international jury awarded prizes to British manufacturers. Nevertheless, discerning observers detected alarming evidence of competition from abroad, and foresaw Britain's need for technological education if her industrial supremacy was to be maintained. 'Raw material' (wrote Lyon Playfair, one of the organisers of the Exhibition[4]), 'formerly our capital advantage over other nations, is gradually being equalised in price, and made available to all by improvements in locomotion, and Industry must in future be supported, not by a competition of local advantages, but by a competition of intellects.' The Society of Arts, encouraged by the Prince Consort, launched a campaign to persuade the Government to take some responsibility for technological education. The outcome was the establishment of the Department of Science and Art. The Department stimulated the teaching of science in schools—particularly in schools attended by the lower middle class—through a system of payment-by-results. Schools which conducted classes in mathematics or science received subsidies. Teachers received remuneration according to the number of their pupils who passed examinations. Pupils were encouraged through prizes and scholarships. For fourteen years this mercenary traffic in scientific education continued. It was criticised because it led to the mere cramming of examinees, to the teaching of the right things for the wrong reasons. But the examinations of the Department of Science and Art did inject science-teaching into some schools. In 1872, fourteen years after the scheme started, there were 948 schools in the country in receipt of grants for science teaching, and 36,783 pupils were receiving instruction in science.[5] In this same year a Royal Commission was set up under the Duke of Devonshire to inquire into scientific instruction and the advancement of science. The Commission made recommendations which would have been unthinkable ten years earlier (when the Clarendon Commission reported on schools) and which, alas, would not be acceptable to many headmasters even in the 1950's. The recommendations were:[6]

(1) That in all Public and Endowed Schools a substantial portion of

time allotted to study, should, throughout the School Course . . . be devoted to Natural Science; and we are of opinion that not less than Six hours a week on the average should be appropriated for the purpose.

(2) That in all General School Examinations, not less than one sixth of the marks be allotted to Natural Science.

(3) That in any Leaving Examination, the same proportion should be maintained.

Thus, by the 1870's, the schools of England were beginning to produce a flow of pupils who had passed examinations in science and who were accordingly both prepared and predisposed for the study of science and technology at universities.[7]

II

The expansion of undergraduate courses in science and technology had to await this supply of recruits from the schools. We have already discussed how British universities under the influence of German *Wissenschaft* adapted themselves to the teaching of experimental science. It now remains to discuss how higher technology found a place in British universities.

It was doubtless the propinquity of industrialisation which persuaded the University of Glasgow to establish a chair of engineering in 1840. It is said to be the first chair of engineering in any British university, though the Jacksonian professor of natural philosophy in Cambridge was lecturing on the principles of engineering as long ago as 1796; however, Cambridge had no chair of engineering until 1875.[8] The Glasgow chair was set up by royal warrant and was evidently not welcomed by the academics in the University: for the Senate refused to supply the first professor with a classroom until the Lord Advocate intervened on his behalf, and even as late as 1861 engineering was not 'considered a proper department in which a degree should be conferred,' and the subject remained for years in the Faculty of Arts. University College, London, too, has had a chair of engineering since 1841; and the University of Edinburgh in 1855 created a part-time chair of technology, which was occupied by George Wilson, regius director of the Industrial Museum of Scotland. Wilson's chair was not endowed. His classes were not part of the academic course and were not included in the curriculum. Such were the facilities for technological higher education provided by a nation which was at that time leading the world in commerce and industry. Before the 1870's there was neither an adequate supply of pupils trained in science from schools nor an adequate demand from industrialists for graduates. Training in technology was through apprenticeship, on the job; and any formal training in colleges was regarded with suspicion, as likely to lead to the disclosure of 'know how' and trade secrets. There was no lack of warning against the inadequacy of this provision. Even the circumspect royal commissioners of the University of Cambridge suggested that the basic principles of engineering should be taught there. But warnings were not enough; a much more powerful impact was needed to overcome public inertia toward technological education.

That impact was provided by the International Exhibition held in Paris in 1867. In 1851 British products had carried away most of the prizes. In 1867 British products received a bare dozen awards. No longer was there the reassurance of easy industrial supremacy. Instead there was alarming evidence that Britain had made little progress in the peaceful arts of industry since 1851 and that continental countries had become very serious competitors. For example, a building was being put up at Glasgow with iron girders from Belgium, and it was asserted by Lyon Playfair that Belgian girders were cheaper because the Belgians had introduced economies depending on chemical analysis of the ore and limestone and fuel.[9] Playfair had served on the international juries of both the 1851 and 1867 exhibitions. He was—as an ex-professor of chemistry, an influential member of Parliament, and a personal friend of the late Prince Consort—able to command a respectful hearing for his opinions. He summarised his anxieties in an open letter to Lord Taunton (who was at that time chairman of the Schools Enquiry Commission); it was this letter which goaded Parliament to inquire seriously into the need for some State support for technological education. After reporting the widespread opinion that Britain had fallen behind her competitors in industrial progress Playfair went on to say: 'The one cause upon which there was most unanimity of conviction' (at the Exhibition) 'is that France, Prussia, Austria, Belgium, and Switzerland possess good systems of industrial education for the masters and managers of factories and workshops, and that England possesses none.'[10]

The publication of Playfair's letter was followed by a broadside from the Society of Arts, in the form of a report on technical education which followed a conference held in 1868.[11] Correspondence, public comment, and deputations to Whitehall followed, and finally the massive inertia of Parliament was overcome. The Government set up a Select Committee[10] 'to inquire into the Provisions for giving Instruction in Theoretical and Applied Science to the Industrial Classes.' The Committee's report is a classic in educational history. It constitutes the blueprint for technological training which led ultimately to twentieth-century industrial Britain; for it was this Committee which produced overwhelming evidence that it was not the artisans who needed education in applied science, but the managers. On one hand 'there is a preponderance of evidence' (the Committee said) 'that so far as the workmen, as distinguished from the managers, are concerned it [the acquisition of scientific knowledge] can be considered an essential element only in certain trades, or, generally, as enlarging the area from which the foremen and managers may be drawn.' On the other hand 'all the witnesses . . . are convinced that a knowledge of the principles of science on the part of those who occupy the higher industrial ranks . . . would tend to promote industrial progress.' The Committee's recommendations are remarkable for their prescience and sanity: elementary instruction within reach of every child, elementary science as an ingredient of all schooling, the reorganisation of some secondary schools as science schools, State support for 'superior colleges of science' to be established in centres of industry, the encouragement of education for higher science teachers 'by the granting of degrees in science at Oxford and Cambridge . . . and by the opening of a greater number of fellowships to distinction in natural science.'

Gradually, and with reluctant and inadequate State support, technology took its place in the curricula of the colleges and universities of Britain. As with science, so with technology: it was fear of industrial competition (reinforced in the twentieth century by fear of war) which pushed British government into State support for higher technological education, and it was to the Continent that Britain turned for models of how technology should be taught. Also, as with science, the continental models for technological education were not simply copied: they were profoundly modified and adapted to suit British conditions. The chief adaptation is a fundamental one and it lies at the root of a major problem which faces British universities today. On the Continent higher technological education is not a primary responsibility of universities: it is conducted in institutions *sui generis*, called polytechnics or *Technische Hochschulen*. Thus in Western Germany higher technological education is concentrated in eight *Technische Hochschulen* which have the status and dignity of universities. With minor exceptions, the seventeen universities in Western Germany do not offer courses in technological subjects. In Britain higher technological education is a primary responsibility of universities. Colleges of Advanced Technology share this responsibility, but it is now evident that they are not going to replace universities as centres for research and teaching in higher technology. Eighteen out of twenty-two British universities include technology in the curriculum, and the great colleges of technology which do bear some resemblance to the continental polytechnics (for example, the Imperial College of Science and Technology in London, the College of Technology in Manchester, and the Royal College of Science and Technology in Glasgow) are either integral parts of universities or are affiliated to one or other of them.

III

This inclusion of technology in the curriculum of most British universities, and its exclusion from the curriculum of most continental universities, can be understood in the light of history. While the countries of continental Europe were being harassed and impoverished by wars and revolutions, England was exploiting her mineral resources and her work people and building up a supremacy in manufacture and trade. When peace finally came to the Continent, the countries of Europe were able to turn their attention to making up leeway in the industrial revolution. Naturally England did not encourage them in these endeavours. Until 1825 it was a penal offence to enlist English artisans for employment abroad. When Queen Victoria came to the throne the export of English spinning machinery (for example) was still prohibited. Foreign industrialists had no access to the 'know how' of English industry. Accordingly the countries of the Continent had to discover the new technology for themselves. Their response to this challenge was to produce a new species of professional man: the manager-technologist.

The universities of Europe were not at that time appropriate places for this essentially empirical education. French universities had lost their initiative under the centralisation imposed by Napoleon. German universities were too pre-occupied with the philosophical ferment nurtured by Hegel and Schelling, and in any event the training of techologists was not consistent with ideas of *Lernfreiheit*. And so the production of manager-technologists was entrusted to polytechnics which in the course of the century acquired the rank and prestige of universities. In France there was already the famous École Polytechnique which became the prototype of all colleges of higher technology. In Germany some technical schools were raised to the status of *Technische Hochschulen,* and others were founded on the model of the École Polytechnique. In Switzerland one of the first activities under the new federal constitution was to found (after much acrimonious discussion) a central polytechnic in Zürich. In Holland a polytechnic school was opened in Delft in 1864, to train works managers, civil engineers, naval architects, and science teachers for schools. The response spread even to the United States: the Massachusetts Institute of Technology was founded in 1865, to become a place 'intended for those who seek administrative positions in business . . . where a systematic study of political and social relations and familiarity with scientific methods and processes are alike essential.'

The prime purpose of this widespread system of technological education was not humanitarian: it was to enable continental countries to catch up and to overtake British industry. Accordingly the polytechnics laid emphasis upon a combination of science, technology, and general knowledge, suitable for men who would direct policy in industry or State enterprises. Already by 1867 this new educational system was producing gratifying results. From the *Technische Hochschulen* Germany drew her manager-technologists; from the universities she drew her industrial chemists. There was both a demand for applied scientists and an adequate supply. Meanwhile in Britain Owens College (sixteen years after its foundation) had only 116 students; the Royal School of Mines in London had fewer than 20 matriculated students; there were 40 students in the laboratory of the Royal College of Chemistry; no technology (except the fortuitous course at

Cambridge) was being taught in Oxford or Cambridge; and the efforts of the Prince Consort and his advisers to establish an industrial university in London had failed. It was under these circumstances that the British public reluctantly awoke to the need for manager-technologists in Britain. This awakening coincided in time with pressure from big centres of population to have their own facilities for higher education, not solely to provide vocational training but also to give the lower middle classes opportunities for a liberal education. So it happened that seven new colleges for higher education[12] were founded at the confluence of two currents of opinions: the one local and indigenous, generated by the University Extension Movement, in favour of regional centres for liberal education to compensate for the inaccessibility of Oxford and Cambridge; the other national and imported, in favour of institutions which would do for British industry what the great polytechnics were doing for industry on the Continent. The leaders of educational thought in Britain were under the spell of Newman's lectures and Pattison's essays and Jowett's teaching. It is not surprising, therefore, that they opposed the segregation of technological education into separate institutions. The manager-technologist must receive not only a vocational training: he must enjoy also the benefits of a liberal education; or at least he must rub shoulders with students who are studying the humanities. And so, through pamphlets, speeches, resolutions at conferences, and memoranda to committees, it became accepted policy that higher technology should be incorporated, as it already had been in Scotland and London) into the new university colleges. Moreover, those were the days when neither governments nor benefactors could easily be convinced that the lower middle classes needed the cultural benefits of higher education; and so the most powerful argument for the new university colleges was one based on their utilitarian value.[13] It was natural, therefore, that technology should be one of the subjects taught at the outset in the civic colleges. From Scotland, London, and the industrial cities the teaching of higher technology spread to the older English universities, and ultimately became an integral part of the university curriculum.

Technology entered the British universities partly through a chance encounter of history and partly through the deep conviction among leaders of educational thought that scientific and technological education should not be separated from liberal studies. On the Continent the phase of founding new universities was over before the need for higher technological education arose; in Britain the phase of founding new universities (by way of university colleges teaching for degrees of the University of London) coincided with the need for higher technological education. On the Continent, universities were not sympathetic to the constraints of vocational education, except in the traditional professions already established in universities; in Britain there was a strong utilitarian bias among the founders of university colleges, mellowed by a respect and attachment to the ideals for which Oxford and Cambridge stood.

IV

It is, therefore, more than three generations since the decision was made to include technology in the university curriculum and not to create polytechnics on the continental model. But State support for higher technology in universities lagged far behind this decision. In 1865 the total parliamentary vote for science and technology 'for the Middle and Upper Classes, exclusive of the cost of the Queen's Colleges, Ireland,' was £4812:8:8, distributed among the four Scottish universities and the University of London.[14] In 1889–90 the State accepted financial responsibility for technical education, local authorities were empowered to set up and to finance technical colleges, and the Science and Art Department was made the central authority for technical instruction. But this legislation worked mainly for the benefit of technical education at sub-university level; it did not confer much benefit on higher technological education. It has required more than sixty years of pamphleteering and propaganda, reinforced by the anxieties of two world wars and the fear of foreign economic competition, to persuade British parliaments to take full financial responsibility for teaching and research in higher technology. The first block grants to civic university colleges were made in 1889 (the total sum distributed was £15,000). Since then—within the lifetime of one man—parliamentary grants to British universities have increased two thousandfold. Although these vastly increased grants have been administered by the University Grants Committee (and its forerunners) with exemplary enlightenment, it cannot be said that Parliament has increased the grants solely from enlightenment. Often the spur to action has been fear, beginning with the alarm expressed as long ago as 1887, that educated Germans were penetrating Britain's oriental markets, and still continuing at the time of the 'Sputnik-hysteria' of 1957. Some German educationists (Paulsen, for example[15]) have regretted that the *Technische Hochshulen* were not integrated with the universities of Germany, and perhaps in the long run it will be to the advantage of British higher education that the patterns of Zürich and Charlottenburg and Delft were not followed in London and Glasglow and Manchester. But the British pattern sets its problems too. It was difficult enough for British universities to adapt themselves to scientific thought; it is proving much more difficult for them to adapt themselves to technological thought. For pure scientific research is akin to other kinds of scholarship: it is disinterested, pursued for its own sake, undeterred by practical considerations or popular opinion. There is no great divergence between the attitude of the physicist toward the concept of entropy and the attitude of the philosopher toward the concept of virtue. But teaching and research in technology are unashamedly tendentious, and their tendentiousness has not been mellowed (as it has for medicine and law) by centuries of tradition. Technology is of the earth, earthy; it is susceptible to pressure from industry and government departments; it is under an obligation to deliver the goods. And so the crude engineer, the mere technologist (the very adjectives are symptoms of the attitude) are tolerated in universities because the State and industry are willing to finance them. Tolerated, but not assimilated; for the traditional don is not yet willing to admit that technologists may have anything intrinsic to contribute to academic life. It is not yet taken for granted that a faculty of technology enriches a university intellectually as well as materially. The attitude of universities toward technology is still ambiguous; until the ambiguity is resolved the universities will not have adapted themselves to one of the major consequences of the scientific revolution.

NOTES

1. Kelly, Thomas, "George Birkbeck: Pioneer of Adult Education." Liverpool University Press, 1957. This book is an authoritative account of the history of the mechanics' institutes.

2. Hole, James, "An Essay on the History and Management of Literary, Scientific and Mechanics' Institutions." Society of Arts, London, 1853.

3. Cardwell, D. S. L., "The Organisation of Science in England." Heinemann, London, 1957. This book has a useful summary of the influence of examinations on technical education in England and a collection of references to nineteenth-century writing on scientific and technological education.

4. Playfair, Lyon, "Lectures on the Results of the Great Exhibition of 1851." London, 1852.

5. Balfour, G., "The Educational Systems of Great Britain and Ireland." (2nd edn.). Clarendon Press, Oxford, 1903.

6. Reports of the Royal Commission on Scientific Instruction and the Advancement of Science. Sixth Report, p. 10, 1875.

7. If this eighty-year-old practice had continued, every pupil who qualified to enter a university through the G.C.E. would have been able (if he had wished to do so) to enter faculties of science or technology. As matters stand, thousands of pupils are called upon to make a decision at the age of about 15 which restricts their choice to arts faculties on the one hand or faculties of science and technology on the other. No other European country tolerates such premature specialisation. The retreat from the recommendations of the Devonshire Commission is due to three main causes: (*a*) the transfer of the 'Science and Arts schools' to the grammar-school system when State-aided secondary education was established in 1902; (*b*) the staffing of the new grammar schools with men from public schools and a consequent imitation by the new grammar schools of public school education; and (*c*) the narrow scope and high specialisation demanded for open scholarships by the Universities of Oxford and Cambridge.

8. Baker, J. F., "Engineering Education at Cambridge." Paper read before the Institution of Mechanical Engineers, July 1957.

9. Report of the Select Committee on Scientific Instruction. London, 1868.

10. Published in the *Journal of the Society of Arts*, XV, p. 477, 1867. In its spirit of urgency the letter is very similar to contemporary pamphleteering on the need to expand technological education in Britain.

11. Journal of the Society of Arts, XVI, p. 183, 1868.

12. Birmingham (1880), Bristol (1876), Newcastle (1871), Leeds (1874), Liverpool (1881), Nottingham (1881), and Sheffield (1879). The circumstances

of their origin are well described by W. H. G. Armytage in *Civic Universities*. Benn, London, 1953. This book contains the best account there is on the origin of modern British universities.

13. This argument was less persuasive in Wales. In Aberystwyth and Bangor it was the idea of a university as a place for liberal education which aroused public support. See Evans, B. E., *The University of Wales: a historical sketch*. Cardiff, 1953.

14. Reference 37, Appendix, p. 462.

15. Paulsen, F., "The German Universities and University Study." Trans. F. Thill. Longmans, London, 1906.

34 *The Academic Procession*

DAVID RIESMAN

Orthodoxy and Emancipation in the Nineteenth-Century College

I WAS READING not long ago, in *Grandmother Brown's Hundred Years,* about the founding of Ohio University at Athens, Ohio, in the 1820s. The New Englanders who had come out there in the first decades of the last century included some who were passionately concerned lest their culture become attenuated in the new setting; they were willing to endure physical but not intellectual or religious poverty. Clergymen ordinarily took the lead in founding academies and colleges, partly to keep the young in the fold and out of secular temptations, and partly to train aspirants for the ministry. Many of the colleges, however, were no sooner founded than the founding fathers were accusing them of deviation from orthodoxy—of Arianism, Unitarianism, godlessness; indeed, such developments often gave rise to new, schismatic colleges which in turn developed their own orthodoxies.[1] As Richard Hofstadter and Walter Metzger have observed in their fine book on the history of academic freedom, these theological controversies antic- ipate the form, though seldom the content, of later conflicts over academic freedom—both those of the last several generations between business and education and those of today between politics and education. The ministers discovered, as businessmen and legislators were later to do, that by calling something a college, one could hardly help giving it some leeway for self- definition, transcending its partisan or pious origins. The situation re- sembles that of a parent who wants his son to be mobile socially, to rise to a higher station than his own, while yet fuming at the way he has taken to drink or divorce or voting Republican or whatever else goes in the community with an elevated social-class position.

If this dialectic between the parish and the world is endemic in Ameri- can education, what has definitely changed is the degree of investment in education as a messianic movement. The struggle both to found and to attend college in the last century sprang often from booster and commercial motives, but there remained in the idea of a college a certain visionary element, whether religious or secularized, which linked education with more than training for professional success—linked it with the promise of

Reprinted from David Riesman, *Constraint and Variety in American Education* (New York: Doubleday Anchor Books, 1958), with the permission of the author and the publisher. (Copyright 1956 by the University of Nebraska Press.)

a nobler, less demeaning life. Education still has something of this aura in the "underdeveloped" areas of the world, where poor communities establish colleges as if life itself depended on them, or the glory that makes life worth living.

"PIONEER'S PROGRESS"

Any number of autobiographies of distinguished Americans of earlier generations testify to what the struggle for education meant in a day when going to college was something uncommon, and when for a community to possess a college was hardly less a sign of progress than for it to get a railway or canal to wind its way there. For example, Alvin Johnson in *Pioneer's Progress* vividly describes his experience in the 1890s at the then newly founded University of Nebraska: of the classical training he had there which opened up before him what Lionel Trilling, in *The Opposing Self,* eloquently describes as that "other culture" of Greece and Rome. Johnson grew up among the sod huts, but he was no barbarian pioneer, no sabra of the American plain. Likewise, Thorstein Veblen, when he entered Carleton College, was able in some measure to emancipate himself from the constricted world of Norskie farmers and Yankee traders; languages were important to him also as a means of contact with other patterns of culture. For such men, an education meant rescue from a life in a harsh environment—harsh not only physically but emotionally; it was a way out of class and ethnic oppression, a way out of the poverty of horizon in the family, on the farm, and in the small-town community. Of course, we seldom hear from the men who were not stimulated by their college attendance; we know they endured much dreariness and rote learning—but even the trappings of education were then often lent significance by hope and enthusiasm.

We must not forget that, in the nineteenth century and after, many men went to college to roister and so to become gentlemen. Hofstadter and Metzger remind us that before the days of organized sport, the teachers were frequently proctors and patrolmen, barely able to control their charges. Those expelled from college today on disciplinary grounds are a tiny fraction of the minatory discharges of an earlier day—despite panty raids, students are less rowdy than they used to be. Nevertheless, the creed of the Enlightenment was strong enough to give many educators the sense of participating not so much in a scientific and scholarly as in a missionary movement.

THE FAILURE OF SUCCESS

Today, as I have indicated, one is not likely to find this spirit inside the U.S.A. One might look for it among some of the depressed Delta Negroes whom the Army taught to read; and here and there—in a remote

Idaho valley or Chicago's Back of the Yards or in a small Vermont village —one can find colleges struggling for survival and proud of keeping a beacon alight. But on the whole American higher education is dizzy from success; in spite of all complaints, it is rich, fabulously well attended, and generally taken for granted. Among our sophisticated people, in fact, a great disillusionment has spread.

To be sure, we must not equate the loss of enthusiasm among the professionals in education with the experience of the students themselves, who may appear more sophisticated than they in fact are—and for whom the exploration of self in the college setting can be an ever-renewed source of wonder. As Lyman Bryson has written me, "The most lackadaisical priest may be droning what is heavenly music to someone in the pews and the dullest teacher—even he!—may, by no virtue of his own, be handing out manna to healthy, even if fashionably disavowed, young appetites." But if we concentrate now, not on the students, but on the educators, we realize that most of them no longer see their work as an "Operation Bootstrap" by which a whole society can be made over, and only a few repeat the early chiliastic claims for higher education. As a big business in its own right— whatever its immediate and prospective financial crises—it can no longer afford the irresponsibility of the marginal institution. In its relation to the other major powers in contemporary society, it has experienced what Harold D. Lasswell terms "restriction by partial incorporation"; that is, the "movement" aspects of higher education have had limits set to their progress by partial acceptance on the part of what was once the enemy: the influential Americans who, especially in the post-Civil War period, worshiped the plainly practical, the self-made, the ruggedly unscholarly. Today, a modus vivendi appears in sight between education and business, if not quite yet between education and the politics of the discontented classes.[2]

Lasswell's concept is perhaps less pessimistic than Michels' "iron law of oligarchy," which assumes that every reform movement must become bureaucratized and hierarchical, or Troeltsch's "law" that every sect with success becomes a church, bound to repress and stultify those spontaneous feelings which led to its birth. For Lasswell assumes that the reform movement does have an impact, and that it is precisely this which leads to its becoming incorporated in a new equilibrium at a higher level. Along this line we can see that education, whether in the colleges and universities or through the mass media, has generally moved to liberate Americans from regional and parochial attachments; it has been a way of escape from village pressures, whether of gossip or of vigilantism. Indeed, Samuel Stouffer's *Communism, Conformity, and Civil Liberties* shows how decisively college education today introduces people into a "natural" culture, so that, for example, Southerners who have graduated from colleges are closer to college-educated Northerners in their views than to Southerners with a high-school education.[3] But, as a result of the same development, the big universities, which operate on the national scene, lack the protective encapsulation of the parish: they are bigger game, harder to attack but offering more glory to the attacker, than any local college or county weekly ever could be. Thus we face the paradox that higher education in this country is better in general level of performance than it has ever been, yet we hope for less from it as a means of radical cultural renovation.

FROM CAPTAINS TO STAFF SERGEANTS OF ERUDITION

In a way, of course, this is true of other aspects of our national prosperity. The businessman who takes a local industry and makes a national combine of it is brother under the skin to the educational reformer who parlays a small denominational college into a national university. But entrepreneurs in business today only crop out along the edges, in marginal companies, or die unsung, their accomplishments buried, in plant or division of a big corporation. And tycoons or reformers are presently found in higher education primarily in small women's colleges or other marginal outposts, or as unsung deans in major institutions. Let us remind ourselves that, even a generation ago, there were many exciting figures on the American collegiate scene. Most of us have forgotten the fight Woodrow Wilson waged against the eating clubs of Princeton; we are perhaps more likely to associate Princeton with F. Scott Fitzgerald than with Wilson. How many of us remember Alexander Meiklejohn and his campaigns at Amherst and Wisconsin; Clarence Cook Little and what he tried at Michigan; Arthur E. Morgan and the remaking of Antioch; Glenn Frank's lively Wisconsin; as well as such less embattled captains of erudition as Edmund Ezra Day of Cornell and George Edgar Vincent of Minnesota? The founding of Bennington and Sarah Lawrence and the rise of Reed date from the end of this epoch, and Hutchins at Chicago represented a kind of Indian summer of this rebellious and experimental outlook. (Not believing it could have passed, he blamed the universities themselves as if, had they only a clearer mind and a stronger will, they could have made over the world.)[4]

However, innovation is by no means completely dead; rather, just as big corporations have left innovations to research and development departments and confined the work of their top executive to that of chief public relations officer, so at the big universities what innovation there is seems to have been shifted out of the president's hands into those of the deans. Some of these anonymous men, if more ingratiating than Hutchins or the earlier generations of reformers, have quietly promoted quite far-reaching changes. (It takes modesty and courage in a university president to run interference for a dean more imaginative than he; to be sure, some deans, when things appear quiet, know how to benefit from a lazy or limelight-loving man at the top.) General education at Harvard, humanistic education at MIT, the

General College of Minnesota, and a host of smaller and less spectacular notions owe much to the handiwork of such deans. Thus, in a sense, innovation has, in our greatest institutions of learning, become institutionalized and no great revolutionary figure is likely to appear.

The Loss of Obvious Models

Summing all this up, it would seem that education in its topmost reaches, and at the secondary school level as much as in the universities, has lost its excitement and enthusiasm for a large part of its professional cadre. As I have already implied, much the same thing has happened to the United States as a whole. We can no longer look abroad for inspiration for our models of cultural and educational advance—nor even react against foreign models which, in so many cases, are busy imitating us. In 1850 Tappan was fighting to make Michigan like Harvard, and in 1900 Gilman was fighting to made Hopkins like Göttingen or Berlin—while Eliot was fighting against the German model, to make Harvard an American university, indigenously relevant (Ernest Earnest gives a lively account of all this in *Academic Procession*). But in 1950? Europeans and Japanese, West Africans and Burmese, now come here to look for models or invite American professors to visit and bring with them the "American Way" in higher education. This is understandable, for at least at the graduate level, our universities—and many, many more of them than simply Harvard, Columbia, Chicago—are in their energy and accomplishments as good as any the planet offers.

As I have remarked, this stalemate of success has overtaken many other aspects of our national life. Save in the South, we are not an underdeveloped country any more (and the South, of course, is rapidly being jerked out of colonialism). Whereas a generation ago American expatriates who went to Europe were quicker to seize on what was avant-garde there than most Europeans themselves, complacent as the latter could often be about their cultural superiority, today the American in Paris or Rome can wryly observe the spread of American fashions in design, fiction, music, and film. The time for maturation of an idea or a style which is possible for creative workers in an outpost or a marginal group is not easily available to those in the centers from which diffusion occurs; and, in part because higher education has made such spectacular advances in this country, diffusion of our cultural models occurs with unprecedented speed. Like a mobile man who has shot to the top so fast as to arrive there with undissipated energies and time to look around, American intellectual and educational leadership often seems haunted by the question where to go from here.

SEARCH FOR A SCALE OF JUDGMENT

Of course the problem of where to go next which besets the richest and most advanced institutions, a problem they often manage to postpone by keeping an eye mainly on each other, as do the Big Three in the design of automobiles, does not beset those schools whose goal can simply be to overtake the leaders. But in education it is perhaps not as easy as in manufacturing to say who is the leader, who is at the top, or which way is up: there is no World Series or All-American team. Harvard once assumed that it could call to its faculty anyone from anywhere in the country, but this is no longer quite so. Along with all the "nationalizing" tendencies mentioned a moment ago has come a growth of complexity so that no single prestige system can dominate the great variety of subsystems, any more than the first families of one city can dominate the whole country. The president of a land-grant college is not likely to feel that any Ivy League college is really relevant for his problems, which include how to get his institution's name changed from Morrill State College to Morrill State University while not losing his agricultural economists or professors of forestry.

To be sure, there has been one very interesting effort to rank institutions by other than the plainly irrelevant criteria of size or endowment or age, and that is by the series of studies carried out at Connecticut Wesleyan of the collegiate origins of American scholars. In their volume on *The Younger American Scholar: His Collegiate Origins,* Knapp and Greenbaum rank colleges in terms of their proportionate production of recognized scholars. Most of those at the top are small liberal arts colleges such as Reed, Swarthmore, Oberlin, Carleton, Chicago, and Antioch. Yet I wonder how many administrators have pondered this list with an eye to improving their home institutions, or how many faculties could accurately guess the leaders in this league! And of course students are even less likely to know these batting averages, though eventually the news does get around.[5] Thus, the flow of influence, from institutions which serve as models to others in academia, is one not easily marked out, and one cannot say that there is a single recognizable system of prestige. College public relations departments seldom vaunt curricular developments, unless they can be claimed as unique, but rather such more easily demonstrable matters as new buildings and equipment, number of students, and alumni gifts.

The Snake-Like Procession

Despite these difficulties, I am going to present a concededly oversimplified picture in order to try to capture certain large trends in the movement and rhythm of American academic development. It may be illuminating to see the avant-garde, both educational and more generally cultural, as the head of a snake-like procession—the head of which is often turning back upon itself, as at present, while the middle part seeks to catch up with where the head once was. When the middle part becomes aware, as doesn't always happen, that the position of the head has shifted, it may try to turn in two directions at once.

We might begin by asking in what direction is such a university as that of Nebraska turning, i.e., what are the models to which it and others like it look for possible direction? There is no doubt that colleges and universities in this country do model themselves upon each other, and the question remains: which other? All one has to do is read catalogues to realize the extent of this isomorphism. Once one enters, let us say, the state university league, this involves the full line of departments. People who come into the league to teach, having done graduate work elsewhere, bring with them an image of what a proper university should look like—and this image consists truly of castles in the air, not located on a particular, carefully studied terrain. The image may have been formed in England or Germany, in Berkeley or Cal Tech, in Chicago or Columbia or Michigan or the University of Iowa. But of course, it need not have so specific a location: isomorphism in this area as in others depends not only on direct imitation but on general social patterns which are refracted in specific institutional forms. The tendency to add rather than to integrate is, according to John Kouwenhoven, a peculiarly American one; he observes it in city and rural-section layout, skyscraper architecture, jazz improvisation, the assembly line, comic strips, and so on.[6] The one or two thousand courses given in a large college or university likewise reflect this willingness to add, this omnipresent university extension. Moreover, as my colleague Richard J. Storr has pointed out to me, to bring a few professors from one place and to set them up in business in another is a relatively inexpensive operation (notably so in the humanities); to add a new department often costs less than to add a new dormitory or a hockey rink.

"LOCALS" VERSUS "COSMOPOLITANS"

Such a new department, then, oriented to the places where its members were trained, may try to set new sights for the university to which it has been moved. But understandably, these new outsiders or "cosmopolitans"[7] do not always have an easy time of it. The drive which brought them there may have spent itself in that very act, and the home-guard, the "locals," of the university may resent and frustrate any efforts at further departure from its locally approved ways. It is a rare institution where some departments do not carefully staff themselves with home-brew talent and thus avoid disagreement comparisons; the locals or "nativists" will insist complacently that what is done at Harvard or Oxford, Ann Arbor or Princeton, is quite meaningless in Fayetteville, Lincoln, Parkville, Missouri, or at Doane College or Peru State Teachers. Home-brew is easier to take in some flavors than in others: if one wants a good physics department, it will hardly do, but in agronomy or English one could make a go of it. At the University of Illinois, as I understand it, the home-guard was able to defeat itinerants from so near a place as Iowa State College—economists who had the bad luck not to have done their graduate work at Urbana.

THE HOME GUARD AS A "FRONT," FACING BOTH WAYS

The home guard is, by its nature, likely to be integrated into the local community; its members play golf with the local realtors, car dealers, and doctors in the small towns, and are active in civic associations in the larger ones. Where they are intellectual fellow-travelers of the cosmopolitans, they can help integrate them also into the community, or at least defend them against local pressure; where they are not, they can be extremely effective antagonists of the cosmopolitans by "explaining" locally just how bad, how radical, they are—a reaction which, in times of general fear of radicalism, has helped to erode academic freedom at a number of institutions. Moreover, the home-guard are typically concerned with the university's service functions to students and to the locale, rather than with research and with participation in the national intellectual life; they have no objection to growth, much as this may lead to departure from tradition; if it involves larger numbers of students, more popular courses, and athletic prowess, whereas the itinerant cosmopolitans bring with them, as already implied, a more elitist conception of academia which emphasizes a small but select student body and a research-oriented curriculum, and deprecates athletics. (Naturally, as with all such typologies, there are individuals who fit neither category, or combine elements from both.)

Veblen saw the university president as the very archetype of home-guarder, so mixed in with the local business community as to be indistinguishable from it, save in possessing the promotional gifts of a Captain of Erudition. In my own observation, and that of other present-day observers, the president is as likely to be fighting home-guardism, with elements in his faculty—and especially perhaps in the lower administration, including many department heads—sitting tight. Yet if he alienates the home guard too much, he will have only the cosmopolitans to fall back upon—mobile men who will in many cases be moving up and out; they cannot help him much with the legislature or the local Legion post or the Grange.[8]

The president has less chance to move (rarely can he move back to his old league, into a professorship), and he can certainly not count on moving; whatever mobility drive he has must go into the institution itself. And here is where the prestige of other institutions is apt to be used as a debating point for adding new fields and departments and new men from elsewhere to staff them. "If Chicago has a sociology department, why can't we have one?"—this must have been asked for several generations, as this new field spread throughout the country until only in the Ivy League do there remain significant colleges, such as Hopkins or Wesleyan, which take a certain wry pride in resisting this newcomer among the disciplines. And our medical schools have been under the same kind of scrutiny and pressure. "How can you call yourselves a medical school without a pathologist?"—the Flexnerites asked such questions in eliminating virtually all the Class C medical schools. Medical schools of course have been "nationalized" as colleges have not and many among the latter neither die nor rise but hang grimly on because some-one sometime gave them a plant, a president, and a push. But I am not talking now, as I briefly shall later, about those institutions so far below the level of current discourse as not to be faced with pressures for improvement, but about those near enough the top in one league or another to be influenced. And as I have indicated, this influence leads to a tug of war between the home-guard locals who make a fortress of local traditions, no matter how happenstance these are, and the cosmopolitan itinerants who bring the prestige of other institutions, often without making too much of an effort to adopt their models to the local potentialities.

REGIONAL VERSUS NATIONAL MODELS

Let me illustrate this characteristic conflict by reference to the experience I had when I went as a young graduate of Harvard Law School to teach at the University of Buffalo Law School. At least half the faculty and all but one of its younger men were Harvard trained, for at that time Harvard dominated legal education, the world of the nationally oriented law schools, as no university now dominates legal, medical, or graduate education. Most of these Harvard-trained people wanted to teach those courses which, as students, they had learned were the subjects of greatest intellectual excite-ment—and there were then mainly oriented around the federal government, including such topics as labor law, constitutional law, administrative law, and so on. (Moreover, the contacts of these Harvard cosmopolitans were in Washington, and they could try to place their best students there.) As against this, several faculty members thought Buffalo should develop a cur-riculum that was not merely a minor league (though excellent) version of the Eastern Seaboard schools but rather one which was designed with ref-erence to the particular problems of Western New York. But such a change —to a more region-oriented outlook—would have been defined as an in-tellectual defeat, as having become provincial under the impact of local pressures, as a discredited vocationalism concerned with the State bar exams and the local job market. For a variety of reasons, the experiment was never made. In any event, as it turned out, the good students were in only a few cases interested in preparing themselves for careers confined to Upper New York State; for most of them, their models were their itinerant teachers and their eyes were on what the Supreme Court was up to, or the S.E.C., and not on Buffalo's City Planning Commission or Erie County's school consolidation program. In contrast, the home-guard faculty had on the whole little to offer in the way of a vision of a specialized but distinguished small school; they were apt to recall how it had been in their day, but failed to see (as Everett Hughes likes to put it) in what ways an institution has to change in order to remain the same.

IDENTIFICATION WITH TRENDS, WITH SCIENCE, OR WITH SIWASH

In this example we can glimpse another factor at work in academic isomorphism. If we assume that there is such a thing as a true scholar, he would not be swayed by trends (or even by the countering of trends)—by discovering that students had their eye on Washington, or that the Supreme Court got more headlines than the municipal bench; each would be relevant for him, not in terms of professional or student fashion—that is, in terms of power, but in terms of its intrinsic significance in his own transcending preoccupations. I think we have all met such men, in medieval history or the classics, for instance, who profess utter unconcern with the current market quotation on their disciplines and are ever prepared to see them sink lower on the national exchange. Some, understandably enough, wring a small "secondary gain" from their position by means of a Pharisaical pride vis-à-vis more worldly colleagues, especially social scientists. But most professors are not so independent of general cultural values and imperatives. As already mentioned, Veblen argued, as did Upton Sinclair, that scholars were subverted by businessmen in the guise of administrators; but I think most of us would today grant that professors are themselves apt to apply business standards to their work—just as I think it also to be the case that businessmen have increasingly adopted non-commercial values as they have become more sophisticated. More precisely, we academic people tend to judge ourselves as would a firm: does our university offer a full line; is it properly diversified; what is our Dun and Bradstreet rating in the proper accreditation association; how many students do we have, in absolute numbers and relative to those colleagues who, in sociological lingo, comprise our reference group? In fact, a state university, living on biennial appropriations, needs a very pertinacious president to do any long-term planning. Whereas Veblen thought professors ought to despise and reject administrators as displaced businessmen who should be sent back to their predatory trades, it may be that professors today look down on deans and college presidents for different reasons, and with some envy, because they think: "There but for the grace of non-promotion go I."

In the course of my work on behalf of the inquiry into teachers' apprehensions, I had occasion to talk to a number of college professors concerning academic freedom; and I was struck by the extent to which many identified themselves with their college rather than with their subject-matter or with the professorate as a whole. This often led them, not to criticize "their" institution for poor behavior in some *cause célèbre* or quiet firing, but rather to explain and apologize: they would say, "Sure, our President let So-and-so go after the Velde Committee got after him, but you must realize that he has to go before the legislature for a new medical research building this year; and anyway, So-and-so handled himself ineptly and was, for a state school like this, most indiscreet. . . ." Indeed, this tendency to turn on the victim and criticize him—and doubtless most victims in cases of academic freedom are tactless, or disingenuous, or too ingenuous—would seem to be part of the same public relations orientation in which the faculty understands the plight of the administration almost too well. Men who would not inhibit their frankness of speaking out for the sake of their own careers or peace of mind are often willing to do so for the sake of their college, lest they embarrass it in its relation to parents, alumni, the community, or other relevant constituencies outside the world of scholarship. There is in this a selfless and in many ways admirable loyalty to the institution and to the group of colleagues who momentarily compose it. And the professors who do this are not only the home guard who have few wider loyalties anyhow but the cosmopolitans who also try to maintain their loyalty to science. Understandably, the professors, in return for identifying themselves with the college and even on occasion sacrificing for it their wider identity with the cosmos of scholarship, require of their institution that it rate, that people know of it and think well of it.

Thus, a good deal of academic expansion and isomorphism is the result of administrators responding not only to their own drives but to those of their faculties, though the latter put the onus on the administrators and blame them for carrying out their half-secret wishes. What on the student and alumni level may take the form of wanting a winning football team, at the very least in order to explain one's choice of college to one's gang, may on the professional level appear in a comparable assumption. The assumption is that every decent university will offer courses in archaeology, in Tudor history, or in the sociology of small groups, whether or not there exist top-flight people to fill these lines, and even if to get them filled means sacrificing the possibility of building up a uniquely exhilarating department out of offerings not currently regarded as among the blue chips of academia.

THE MOBILE MIDDLE OF THE PROCESSION

Now there is no doubt that this process, this dialectic between parochial and cosmopolitan models, has resulted in giving the snake-like procession a great deal of momentum at its middle levels. Take, for example, what seems to have happened at a border state university during the regime of a politician-president who cared mightily for good football teams and, according to report, not a whit for scholarly distinction. It seems that strong department chairmen could go to him and say, "Look, Columbia has a good man in colonial history; I believe we should . . ."—and the president would happily agree, nothing was too good for his school (much as nothing was too good—for example, the first-rate *Southern Review*—for Huey Long's pet Louisiana

State University). These professors knew that, should they get into the papers, they would not be protected by the administration; but as long as things were quiet, the president would back them with money and enthusiasm. The shrewd men of his faculty, in other words, treated him much as Victorian wives eager for culture treated their tycoon spouses: the wives conspired with each other to drag their men to the opera, to tap them for the symphony, and otherwise to play on their desire to be well thought of in the new domains their money opened up to them. It is in part such phenomena that I have in mind when I say that, if professors have fallen prey to business values, so businessmen and some politicians have likewise been infiltrated by academic values.

HOW TO HANDLE TRUSTEES

Indeed, so much is the latter the case that many university administrators are mistaken in supposing that their businessmen trustees want what they pretend often to want, namely a "businesslike" administration of the university. Some of them would not have become trustees if they wanted a life composed of entirely homogeneous activities and evaluations; they may express a belief in such a life—a life free of contradictions and tensions—but their actions belie them. Especially the more complex and sophisticated businessmen would not appreciate a world populated wholly by people like themselves; it would not be interesting; they want their minister, their physician, their university president (and on occasion their personnel director) to tell them that they are miserable materialistic sinners, and make them pay for the privilege, and for their privileges. I recall once attending a luncheon of the Citizens Board of the University of Chicago. The board was then composed of Chicago businessmen who might someday, if they behaved themselves graduate into becoming trustees; most of them, however, had not had much cultivation as potential buttresses for academic freedom and vitality. At the table where I sat, rather reactionary talk flowed, led by a red-faced public relations executive who thought the University was badly managed, had too many Communists, and all the rest of it. Then Mr. Hutchins got up to talk. His first words were that he had two regrets as he looked forward to surrendering his stewardship of the University: first, that there wasn't enough red in the University budget; and, second, that there weren't enough Reds on the faculty! He went on in that vein, and when he ended was cheered to the echo, and by no one more than my tablemate who couldn't say enough about what a wonderful man Hutchins was. Magnetic leadership, such as Hutchins had, can get away with more than usually appears on the surface; one of the things it discovers, by taking chances, is that we do not always unequivocally want what we say we want. Or, to put it another way, we have wants of which, amid the noise and rhetoric of our talk, we are unaware, until someone comes along with the courage to brush aside our manifest claims and desires. And certainly when we consider the relations between Harper of Chicago and the elder Rockefeller, or Andrew White and Ezra Cornell, or Gilman and the trustees of Johns Hopkins' estate, we can see that many businessmen, who may fear to think themselves sentimental, can be grateful when someone gives them a good hard-headed reason to do something decent and unconventional.[9]

Turns and Twists at the Head of the Procession

THE HIGHBROW-LOWBROW ALLIANCE

Hutchins assumed in these remarks that the way for a university to advance was by attaining financial and intellectual irreverence and exuberance (the latter mistakenly, or perhaps only paradoxically and in order to shock, linked to the Communists and thus falling in with their own image of themselves as true rebels). However, this is a mood rather than a program, and the programs that have emanated from leading institutions in recent years have been of a less spectacular sort. They include a renewed emphasis on undergraduate teaching, on interdisciplinary courses and general education, including a spate of programs in American civilization, a revived interest in the humanities, in theology and in values generally. The avant-garde has added other pre-occupations. For example, at some Ivy League schools and at Chicago, there has developed a strong highbrow fondness for lowbrow or popular culture, and a knowledge of comic strips, jazz baseball, Westerns, and soap opera is occasionally *de rigueur* if one is to be up to date. In some quarters, this is part of a kind of late love affair with the United States, accompanied by a rejection of Europe (witness some of the contributions, including my own, to the *Partisan Review* symposium on "America and the Intellectuals"). Likewise, much of the so-called "New Conservatism" has developed as an avant-garde rejection of middlebrow liberalism—there would be no fun in being a new conservative if all one's colleagues shared the views of Senator Bricker or the late Senator Wherry.

In fact, the shifts of opinion that go on among the avant-garde, even when these include a belief in a closer attention to the American scene, are quite generally based on a desire to put oneself at a distance from the world of the academic middlebrow. Usually, this is the only part of the procession of American academia of which the intellectual leaders at the head are aware, for it is easy to forget the enormous contrasts that can still be found among people all of whom bear the title "Professor."

THE STRAGGLERS IN THE PROCESSION

There are plenty of colleges where the professors read nothing heavier than *Life* or the *Saturday Evening Post* or the local paper. The avant-garde, in looking back at the middle ranks of the procession, has ordinarily no idea how far these have traveled away from the bottom ranks: we see here a general phenomenon of hierarchy, that to the rich the poor may look more alike than they do to themselves, and to the poor, the rich. By the same token, the head of the procession cannot "see" the tail end, because the middle obscures its view, and the tail end moves so far behind the avant-garde turns and twists that it ordinarily fails to learn, for instance, that liberalism is out of date, or anti-clericalism, at many leading places.[10]

THE ACADEMIC TASTEMAKERS

But the middlebrow is not similarly defended against shifts in high-brow fashions of thought. He will often have staked a great deal of his drive and hope on imitating at his college some plank in a program developed at one of the pace-setters for his league. For him to learn that the pace-setter has changed course may completely dishearten him. Let me illustrate what I have in mind by reference to a conversation with a group of indisputably highbrow professors at Columbia. I was speaking of my visit several years ago to the University of Arkansas, where I had never been before, and of how much I admired the work being done there in the arts and theatre, and especially the modern theatre. The work, I remarked, seemed to me less outstanding than that at wealthier state universities like Wisconsin or Illinois, but it was pleasant to see boys from the Arkansas Ozarks doing modern dance. My friends interrupted to say how awful they thought this was; one of them quoted Santayana or someone to the effect that football was America's great contribution to the ballet, and said it would be better if the boys weren't corrupted by their University's efforts at uplift. I was grateful that no Arkansas professor or state legislator who had struggled to bring high culture to Fayetteville was there to hear this.

THE APPEAL OF HERESY

I trust that in these remarks, which aim to be descriptive, I am not patronizing either Arkansas or Columbia. At both places, many of the more alert faculty members are looking for a way up in the intellectual world, but at each the trail markers point in different directions. At both, the professors and administrators pride themselves on being ahead of the game, on being forward-looking—even if among some it is now forward to look backward. And unquestionably culture advances, and so does education, as the result of such not entirely saintly motives; many of us need to feel we are being a bit heretical, a bit out of step. We look askance and with some reason, at the TV comic who feels he is going great if his Hooper rating holds up, while we look with more sympathy on the author who wonders if he is slipping because the Book-of-the-Month Club took his last novel (even if there is evidence that the BOMC is rising).

Erich Fromm has suggested to me that our need to feel heretical is perhaps stronger when we have made compromises in other aspects of our lives (though in some instances having made a compromise leads to a rigid need to defend compromise as such), so that what I am saying now is only superficially contradictory to the point made earlier about the business and public relations values shared by many academic people. That is, we need aspects of heresy in order to reassure ourselves that we have not sold out, that we have not become mere conformists. We might even view this, by extension, as a kind of "countervailing power" (in Kenneth Galbraith's phrase) inside the individual, reflecting the division of values in the academic and the general culture.

Such tendencies must be one factor in a phenomenon which turned up in the Teacher Apprehension Study; Paul F. Lazarsfeld found that, at many avant-garde and middle-level institutions, the respondents described themselves as not only more liberal than the administration, the alumni, and the community wherein the college is located, but also as more liberal than each other, so that almost everybody is more liberal than everybody else. To some extent this reflects the fact that in a period of political reaction people may declare themselves as slightly less left than they feel, while assuming that everyone else is more candid than they, thus coming to think themselves more isolated among colleagues than would be warranted if what sociologists term their "pluralistic ignorance" could be dissipated. To some extent, this finding, as Professor Lazarsfeld has pointed out, also reflects the fact that the truly more liberal professors at the leading institutions are generally the more active-minded and productive ones, and thus set the tone to which the others seek to conform. Moreover, just as in a suburb or housing project of marginal status or in a mental hospital one can find people who will tell the interviewer that *they* don't really belong there and will soon move on, so in a college community many professors understandably want to think of themselves as different from the rest, thus having a motive to misperceive actual similarities. Indeed, in visting colleges in the summer of 1955 in connection with this study, Mark Benney and I talked to quite a few crusty self-styled reactionaries on liberal campuses who enjoyed their roles as rebels but would hardly qualify as stalwarts for reaction in one of the more benighted colleges.

To readers who are not academic people, it may perhaps come as a dismaying discovery that professors, like other people, engage in marginal differentiation and sometimes overrate the importance of distinctions which, to the outsider, seem negligible. In part, I would argue that the outsider often blurs differences which really do matter in the life of the mind and eventually, I would hope, in the life of the body politic. But even when the differences are less than vital, knowledge does advance when professors act as sounding boards for each other and critics for each other; in this way a great many positions are differentiated and new combinations sometimes found. Scholarship, like other human activities, proceeds through the mixed motives of its devotees, and the professional desire to be different (though, as we have seen, not different enough) is one source of the critical temper; indeed, an enormous amount of work goes on, which often leads to new findings, simply to prove that some other professor is wrong or crazy or has missed something. Freedom of speech and of investigation would, I fear, soon die out if they could only be claimed by the pure in heart, though I also fear that in many important areas they are dying because we lack the saving remnant of a few who are pure in heart.

Everett Hughes likes to point out that no college can exist solely for students seeking enlightenment, without also catering to students seeking marriage, useful contacts, or four more years on the old man's payroll. More generally, minority intellectual activities could hardly exist without harnessing against the general majority culture some of the same motives, such as fear to be alone, malice, or the wish for prestige, which along with sunnier and nobler drives support the culture. If this is not understood, people, including academicians, will despise academicians too readily for not in general being more heroic than they are. In fact, once one leaves the intellectual avant-garde and ventures into the middle range of colleges which have suffered much from public attack during the years of the Cold War, one can find (as the Teacher Apprehension Study did) a heartening number of defiant men who are at once apprehensive and unbowed; and there are such men holding exposed positions in the avant-garde too.

THE AMBIGUITIES OF EXCELLENCE

My concern in this lecture is, however, more with colleges as models for each other than with men as models for each other. I have no very clear idea as to how many pace-setter or avant-garde institutions there are which today influence wide collegiate orbits. A generation ago, as I remarked earlier, there were centers of ferment both in the Ivy League and in some of the big state universities like Wisconsin and Minnesota, as well as in some small liberal arts colleges throughout the country. At present there are undoubtedly a great many more places where some school or department is in the forefront of research, even though the major training of research men is still done at a handful of major universities.[11] There has been in general a tremendous advance in the level of instruction for what I would guess to be the first third of the academic procession. Undergraduates are now given books to read which professors a generation ago often had not read, or would have considered too difficult; and not only has there been a movement away from textbooks but the textbooks themselves have gotten on the whole much better.[12]

So far has this development gone at a few avant-garde places that I have had to consider the paradoxical possibility that teachers can be too erudite for the full development of their students: the latter are easily led to feel that there is little left for them to discover. When I was in college, we considered—to take an instance—most of our English and modern language professors as rather stuffy if learned worthies, who had read or liked nothing more recent than Thackeray or possibly Thomas Hardy. Joyce, T. S. Eliot, Proust were hardly mentioned, let alone American writers of any sort—Melville, perhaps, but not Faulkner, Gertrude Stein, Glenway Wescott, Dos Passos or Ring Lardner. This left the initiative to the students, and certainly many of us did not seize it and remained in ignorance of much that is valuable; but for others professorial pedantry and somnolence were countered by student vitality. Today, of course, Joyce, Eliot, Kafka, Proust, Faulkner are standard fare in many humanities programs—occasionally even in the better secondary schools. To be sure, as Lionel Trilling points out in *Freud and the Crisis of Our Culture,* these writers are still avant-garde; no new, greatly creative movement has replaced them as rallying points. Moreover, some professors of English, like Trilling or Leslie Fiedler, today write novels and stories themselves and show that they are not only scholars but lively and worldly men; in addition, these men read the *Kenyon Review,* the *Hudson Review,* the *Partisan Review,* the *Sewanee Review,* the *Pacific Spectator,* and all the rest, sometimes even write and edit them. Thus, the students readily learn that there is hardly any room left in which they can outflank their teachers and win the feeling of independence which comes in this way. Some of what appears as comformism among the young may be due to this.

But that the students so readily conclude this is also a result of their conformity, else they might be less impressed by the learning of their teachers and more aware of the latter's lack of concern with personal growth for themselves and for students. A teacher devoted at once to his subject and to his students' growth through that subject will not inhibit independence no matter how wide and up-to-date his knowledge. The very concept of the avant-garde may lead us astray here, for while education to be meaningful must make contact with the contemporary concerns students have, it must also communicate freshness of perception, new ways of seeing, rather than mere novelty of method or topic. It is thus not the truly creative teachers who tend to turn their students into somewhat apathetic, unadventurous captives but rather the academic gamesmen whom our graduate schools of arts and sciences tend to select and foster, at least in the humanities and the social sciences.

This tends to happen, I am suggesting, in our graduate schools and in the more high-power colleges which are dominated by overshadowing graduate schools. But I have very little idea how widespread this phenomenon is. Certainly it is not at all frequent in comparison with the many institutions where the students are still ahead of the faculty, and out of boredom or impatience are occasionally venturesome.

Movement in the Middle Ranks

Many colleges which twenty years ago were in the trough of complacency have been redecorated, as it were. This includes, I would suppose, some of the already famous like Yale, Brown, and Pennsylvania, and some of the less well known like Wooster and the University of Kansas. Hardly any of the state universities has been without some major effort in the liberal arts, and no part of the country is exempt. It is thus my over-all judgment that the differences which once separated the distinguished from the run-of-the-mill institutions have been greatly reduced. And this is one reason why the salience of the centers of decisive influence (I am speaking now of the undergraduate, not the graduate, level) has also been reduced: rather than having a few experimental pioneers, we have now something on the order of a hundred quite good schools moving along at fairly fast clip in pursuit of the ever-turning head of the procession.

So far, I have spoken as if the colleges in the middle ranks, those not quite in the avant-garde, looked only toward the front, either to where the avant-garde once was and is still thought to be, or occasionally, through the short circuits of mass communication, to where it is now. But not all these colleges, let alone all the faculties in them, are on the move, or keep their eyes focused toward the front. Some are focused on where they have just come from, or on the tail end of the procession, and they are so impressed with how far they have come that they do not try to go further. As we have already seen, many teachers colleges and small denominational schools are engaged in upgrading themselves into liberal arts colleges or universities. When this happens, some of the faculty may hark back to earlier, more limited aims, while others, brought in as part of the upgrading process, may think in terms of the liberal arts orbits in which they have themselves been trained. In some denominational schools, this transition might be symbolized in forms of conflict long since outdated among the middle and upper ranks of academia: thus, an argument over social dancing or over the teaching of evolution might represent an effort of the traditional constituency of a church-dominated college to call a halt to change.

When social scientists at such colleges were interviewed in the Teacher Apprehension Study, they were frequently ignorant of *causes célèbres* of academic freedom that were staple conversational topics at avant-garde institutions; they did not follow civil-liberties cases on the national scene—or, indeed, much of anything on the national scene—even though a few of the older men might belong to the American Association of University Professors. The visitor would occasionally be told at such places: "We've all the academic freedom we want here"—a pretty sure sign that they could not have had the faintest notion of what academic freedom embraces, save perhaps that it is something college professors are supposed to possess and therefore something that they, as bearers of that estate, ought to respond to.

PROBLEMS OF THE CATHOLIC COLLEGES

Although Catholic colleges were of course included in the sample of this Study, I was unable to visit more than a handful, and I know much less about the range of Catholic institutions than about the Protestant-controlled schools (and as to the latter, I don't feel cognizant of all the many variations either). In talking with several thoughtful priests concerning the survey, I found them understandably concerned to know how the Catholic colleges compared with the Protestant and the secular ones—matters as to which Paul F. Lazarsfeld's and Wagner Thielens' forthcoming *The Academic Man in a Time of Crisis* will contain some fascinating indications; in general, it seems fair to say that the major Catholic universities move in much the same intellectual world as their secular counterparts, while the small Catholic colleges, like their small Protestant counterparts (and like many of the teachers colleges), move in the great majority of cases in a very different, more traditional world.

Yet the Catholics, as late-comers to America, have not been able, even where they might have so desired, to maintain a system of higher education unaffected by Protestant norms; indeed (as I have learned from Everett Hughes and from the work of such Catholic sociologists as Father Joseph Fichter), Protestant models have influenced in subtle ways even liturgical behavior and parish organization. Nevertheless, in part as a reaction to such influences, there are tendencies among Catholic educators—stronger, of course, in some regions and some teaching orders than in others—to try to develop a total educational plant which is self-contained and sealed off from Protestant models, whether these are looked to in terms of excellence alone or also in terms of interfaith public relations. Thus, in the Teacher Apprehension Study one could find Catholic professors whose identifications were with the Church or their order or even diocese rather than with their intellectual discipline or with the academic fraternity at large. Such men would occasionally express satisfaction that proponents of "intemperate" academic freedom, of "license," were now on the defensive and that teachers were becoming more cautious and "responsible." As already indicated, such comments were more likely to be made by respondents at the smaller Catholic colleges, whereas at the large universities one would find much the usual smörgåsbord of courses and of viewpoints—sometimes imported by laymen (by no means always Catholic) teaching architecture or economic theory or physical chemistry.

Isomorphism combined with autarchy means that there will eventually be priest accountants and Notre Dame-trained physicists, but during the transition the full complement will be maintained by allowing teachers to come in who are not trained in ethics and dogmatics. In a way, as one

Catholic lay teacher informed me, this policy is safer for the Catholic schools than for their fundamentalist Protestant counterparts, for in the former one can count on students who have usually had a parochial high school education and a faculty most of whom are true believers, while in the Protestant school one must fight a constant battle for orthodoxy and hence can less afford a deviant faculty member. (He did not add, as I would have, that Protestant fundamentalism can be far more dogmatic than the Pope.) It is also true that the cleric, by virtue of his robe, has a certain protection in matters outside his faith—though of course what is "outside" is always open to question and redefinition; in the field of economics, for example, a liberal priest can stand on the Papal Encycylicals against a business community that demands obedience to its credo of free enterprise.

In similar fashion, the Catholic colleges have often held out for a version of liberal education—that is, an emphasis on the classics, on philosophy and ethics—against community pressures towards vocationalism and specialization. They have done so because they have sometimes had little choice, lacking sufficient priests and lay brothers trained in the sciences; because they have of course a tradition renewed by visits of American clerics to Louvain or Rome; and because the Catholic college, whether run by the diocese or by an order, is less susceptible to direct pressure from lay trustees than comparable Protestant or public colleges. But such insulation is far from complete. The Catholic colleges, expanding to try to cope with the growing multitude of Catholics attending college, desperately need money and often look to wealthy laymen for it. At the same time, in order to keep the best young Catholics within the fold, the colleges must offer them a technical training and chance for general alertness not much inferior to what they could get for less money at the nearest state university; paradoxically, there is some pressure on the Catholic colleges to reduce the diet of the humanities at the same time that the avant-garde nondenominational schools are re-emphasizing the liberal arts. Some Catholic educators have observed, as the result of a number of studies, that even the great Catholic universities such as Notre Dame, Fordham, Catholic University, St. Louis University produce few distinguished scientists (other than physicians), while the record of Catholic scholars in many fields of knowledge remains, in terms of population, relatively meager. Thus, to repair such lacunae of training and of place on the American intellectual map, vigorous priest-educators have inevitably used the model of the leading state and private secular institutions to shame the complacent in their own ranks.

Torpor in the Tail of the Procession

On the other hand, as just indicated, the smaller Catholic colleges have remained, with a few exceptions, relatively unemancipated and eagerly attentive neither to secular nor to European Catholic models. The more liberal-minded on their faculties cannot always count on hierarchical protection against lay anti-intellectualism, and they follow the cosmopolitan Catholicism of *America* or, even less ultra-American, *The Commonweal,* with some apprehensiveness. This is perhaps especially true of some of the small women's colleges where timid Sisters administer for parochially sheltered girls a curriculum ample in dogmatics (and often vocationally oriented towards white-collar jobs like nursing and teaching) but impoverished in many social-science and natural-science areas.[13] While Sisters of cultivation and animation of course exist in such colleges, the contemporary battles over academic freedom have largely passed them by (where they have not stood on the sidelines cheering the congressional committees).

As I have already implied, one can find in the tail of the procession Protestant denominational schools, perhaps particularly in the South, which are no less constricting—indeed, which lack the amplitude at least theoretically available to the Catholic teacher. Quite a few of these colleges, relics of earlier denominational zeal, have not been able to obtain accreditation and barely manage to keep alive on small enrollments of children of the faithful; indeed, when the children misbehave, the administration may face financial peril if it fires them.[14] But there are of course enormous differences both within and among the Protestant denominations in terms of the degree and severity of church control, and an imperceptibly diminishing distance separates a college like St. Olaf's, pride of Minnesota's Norwegian Lutherans, or Ohio Wesleyan or Drew (Methodist) from Southern fundamentalist colleges with an enrollment of two or three hundred students from nearby—students whose morals are more actively monitored than their minds.

I have spoken so far mainly of places where there is some life, some movement, even though it may take forms we cannot easily recognize at first glance. But there remain denominational schools which have not sought to become liberal arts colleges, and technical schools and teachers colleges which likewise seem little above the level of the average high school and indeed much inferior to the best high schools. And undoubtedly, as the colleges "above" them and the high schools "below" them improve, they must also change or perish, though for a time they can hang on by catering to ever lower intellectual levels and aspirations. In such institutions, the teachers are but hired hands, and their institutions are colleges only by grace of semantic generosity.[15]

Such grace, however, has a double aspect. On the one side, by being called a college, an institution may better claim the airs of academic freedom—much as a patent of nobility, however earned, may give the grantee a certain right to be eccentric. If a group of clerics or businessmen call what they create a "college," they give it at least a potential for upsetting them. But on the other side, by squatting on the title "college," the value of the label is diminished, and higher education becomes to that extent diluted and attenuated. While college education undoubtedly serves on the whole to raise the cultural level of America, there is also a counter-tendency in which the unprecedented millions who have demanded a college degree have not so much risen as pulled the colleges down.[16] To be sure, the big state and private institutions have discovered an appropriate metabolism for minimizing this: among the former, inadequately prepared or motivated freshmen are often flunked out in great numbers, and the majority of Good-time Charlies are digested without much pain on either side, the enzyme being a liberal sprinkling of what was once the gentleman's "C"—while the more scholarly professors concentrate on those students who are conscientious or seriously interested in their studies. But, despite the general growth in student seriousness in the period since the end of the Second World War, at the tail end of the procession there aren't enough good students to keep their professors alive (the climate remains "collegiate" in the derogatory sense). For the instructors whose community is limited to the local business and professional people in the locality, this presents no problem, for only peripherally would they define themselves as intellectuals. But some of the most bitter and pathetic men I know are those who, trained in a good graduate school, find themselves marooned at such places without the hope or energy of changing their school or their situation. Unless they have enormous self-reliance or the saintliness of the priest whom Georges Bernanos describes in his book, *The Diary of a Country Priest,* all they can do is to go to pot.

American higher education seems to me directionless at the head of the procession as far as major innovations are concerned, in rapid if sometimes contradictory motion in the middle, and lacking in much if any aliveness at the end. The idea of education has successfully infiltrated our national culture nevertheless and taken its place among the accepted powers. Our colleges and universities, however, may be in the situation of the churches today: better attended than ever, bigger and handling more gate receipts, while thoughtful theologians wonder whether religiosity doesn't actually provide an antibody against religion rather than a channel towards it. Education succeeds in emancipating a large proportion of its graduates from provincial roots, only to tie them the more firmly to the big and more subtly constricting orbits of corporate, academic, suburban, and military organizations. With other graduates, higher education lowers its sights in order to avoid despair, and hoping that some culture will rub off on the denizens in four years, often finds that these are only rubbed the wrong way and come out more anti-intellectual than they went in, and better able to throw their weight around. Yet, if I must make an over-all judgment, I am somewhat more impressed with the self-renewing tendencies in academia than depressed by complacent success and mindless stagnation. The spark-producing friction between American life and American universities visibly continues but the sparks, if more reliably produced, are less spectacular.

NOTES

1. Even fundamentalist sects, suspicious of intellect and opposed to formal theology, have been forced to found their own colleges in order to keep their mobile young within the fold and out of the hands of secularists. (Thomas Le Duc in his interesting study, *Piety and Intellect at Amherst College*, makes clear that in a struggle between piety and learning, one resolution could be for a college to emphasize "character"—a virtue on which classicists and the devout could agree.)

2. See my essay (written in collaboration with Nathan Glazer), "The Intellectuals and the Discontented Classes," in Daniel Bell, ed., *The New American Right* (New York: Criterion Books, 1955) pp. 56–91.

3. Cf. my article, "Orbits of Tolerance, Interview, and Elites," *Public Opinion Quarterly,* vol. 20 (1956), pp. 49–73; and see also Ernest Havemann and Patricia Salter West, *They Went to College* (New York: Harcourt, Brace and Co., 1952).

4. I might add that another kind of Indian summer has been given some of our leading colleges by the attacks of McCarthy and other intellectual commissars. These attacks have come at the time when it could least be said that anything experimental, let alone subversive, was going on at most of these colleges, and when in fact arthritis had often set in, with the wide acceptance among educated people of the fundamental tenets of liberalism. But the attacks, which of course had to be fought, brought exhilaration as well as anxiety and terror to many campuses—much as an elderly man, doubtful of his attractiveness, might reap a certain comfort from a false accusation that he is having an affair with a pretty girl. To be sure, academic heresy and political heresy are not the same thing, but their proponents and opponents are sometimes the same people, and many of the colleges under strong political attack—I think of Sarah Lawrence, Harvard, Antioch, Reed, Chicago—have also been among the most experimental educationally.

5. It seems possible that the news spreads a good deal faster today than it once did, thanks in part to more energetic recruitment by the colleges and more energetic guidance by high school counselors. The rate of change in fashion has accelerated in this as in so many other areas. Witness the boom in applications for Oberlin, Reed, Radcliffe, Swarthmore.

6. See "What's American about America?", *Colorado Quarterly,* vol. 3, Winter, 1955.

7. Sociologists will recognize here Robert K. Merton's distinction between locals and cosmopolitans in his article, "Patterns of Influence: A Study of Interpersonal Influence and of Communications Behavior in a Local Community," in Paul F. Lazarsfeld and Frank Stanton, eds., *Communications Research 1948–1949* (New York: Harper & Bros., 1949), pp. 180–219.

8. The president seems secure in his job at colleges located in the very head of the procession, where he is protected by traditions of civility and of faculty democracy, and in the lower reaches, where he protects himself by autocratic control—in the middle he is vulnerable much in the way a union leader often is, and must bring home the bacon from the legislature or rich alumni to prevent replacement by a more aggressive leader.

9. On several occasions when I have happened to see professors in conference together with trustees, I have noticed a tendency for the former to appear worldly-wise, practical, and even cynical, whereas the trustees have been the high-minded and "academic" ones. Likewise, when the Bell Telephone Company set up its remarkable program in humanistic education at the University of Pennsylvania—a program which required a small number of middle-level phone executives drawn from all parts of the country to spend a year in a liberal arts curriculum (including James Joyce, Bartok, Mies van der Rohe, Lewis Mumford, et al.), it was hard for

some of the professors who addressed the group to believe there was no need for an immediate vocational pay-off and that they could be as highbrow as they knew how to be; the Telephone executives who set the program up had to emphasize many times that they were not looking for industrial-relations gimmicks. I know that such encounters are not typical of trustee-faculty relations throughout the length of the academic procession, but I also know that higher education, like other cultural institutions, no longer is regarded as an affair only for culture-hungry women and for men, such as ministers and teachers, who are widely viewed as not quite manly.

Where trustees and regents are less enlightened than at a few leading institutions, I have sometimes speculated concerning the job-description of an appropriate university president. I have said that he should preferably be a man so arrogant and unapproachable that no parent, unacculturated trustee, or potential donor could possibly tell him what might be termed an off-color academic freedom story of the type: "Wouldn't it be a good idea, Jim, if our friend, Professor Contrarius, were not to be given that raise—might take the hint and go somewhere else, huh?" Perhaps he could even be a little bit stuffy, so that no one could dream of regaling him with an off-color story of any sort, let alone calling him by his first name. After a bit of casting about the American scene, it occurred to me that some haughty but charming Englishman would perhaps best fit my job-description.

10. This statement has to be qualified in the light of the many short-circuits in our politics and culture which diffuse avant-garde developments to all but the most deprived—precisely through such post-Chatauqua agencies as *Life, the Post, CBS,* and some big-budget movies.

11. In an unpublished paper, "Developments in the Behavioral Sciences during the Past 20 Years," Bernard Berelson shows that the men who have made important contributions to the social sciences, as judged by their colleagues, were trained principally, and now are connected with, what he calls "the Big Five": Harvard, Chicago, Columbia, Yale, California. The same paper, however, indicates a certain provincialism in the selection of contributions (very few European scholars are within the purview of the judges, for instance), thus supporting my argument later in these lectures on the new nationalism of American scholarship.

12. It is fascinating, in the leaflets put out by textbook publishers giving the names of colleges that have adopted a particular book, to trace the spread of highbrow thinking into the academic hinterland: there are many books which are in use virtually throughout the snake-like procession. To be sure, some of these books have, like Shakespeare, something for everybody; others, of course, are read in different places with very different understandings and overtones; still others may represent a young instructor's effort to deny the facts of local limitation (it often takes such a person several years to learn the local customs and taboos). Many publishers take very seriously their responsibility for the level of higher education (while others refuse books that will not sell in carload lots); and their agents on the road—like the detail men of the drug houses—bring the news of new academic formulae to the isolated and the unenterprising.

13. Intense efforts at upgrading are being made in this area: cf. Sister Ritamary, C.H.M., ed., *The Mind of the Church in the Formation of Sisters* (New York: Fordham University Press, 1956). And there are of course colleges for women of high academic standing, e.g., Manhattanville and New Rochelle.

14. This is not a new theme; Andrew White observed it in the last century. See *Autobiography of Andrew D. White* (New York: D. Appleton-Century, 1905); see also Ernest Earnest, *Academic Procession* (Indianapolis: Bobbs-Merrill, 1953), pp. 118–119.

15. Even today, of course, the terms "college" and "university" are not fixed. As we have seen, normal schools are becoming colleges; and colleges, universities, without much control of labelling by the FTC (while established colleges, e.g., Dartmouth, have often felt above the need for upgrading). Still, the levels are much better clarified now than in earlier generations when the nationalization of prestige and semantic fashion had not yet set in. On this topic Bernard Bailyn has written me as follows: "First-rate scholars like Osgood at the end of the 19th century spent

large parts of their careers teaching in high schools as a matter of course [I would like to add that in the days before lavish fellowships many scholars taught school to earn money for further study]. By present standards the institutional levels were simply not articulated. . . . Here are a few lines from Neal's *History of New England* (1747 ed.), reporting on a visit to Cambridge and Harvard (italics by me): "There are several fine streets and good houses in it, besides a flourishing *Academy*, consisting of two spacious *colleges* built of brick, called by the names of Harvard *College* and Stoughton-*Hall*, which are under the government of one president, five fellows, and a treasurer (who) are the immediate governors of the *college*. The learned and ingenious Mr. John Leverett is now president of this *Seminary* . . . the *Academy* is this year in a very flourishing condition. . . I have given a particular account of the foundation of this *university*."

16. Here again one is struck by the similarity of this development with the problems of the plight of high culture in the face of middlebrow advance (as discussed by Clement Greenberg, Ortega y Gassett, Q. D. Leavis, and Dwight Macdonald, *inter alia*). There is perhaps no inherent reason why mass participation in the culture (e.g., the extraordinary sales of LP records and paperback classics, or the rapid spread of avant-garde ideas through the mass circulation magazines) should threaten high culture with other than the loss of irrelevant snobbish complacencies based on coterie prejudices. But the fact is that many producers of avant-garde work do feel pursued by vulgarization and simplification, in which all that is difficult, opaque, and intractable in life and thought is strained out—a process in which what they consider most important in their work is (to recur to Lasswell's phrase) restricted by partial incorporation. I have myself come to feel that it is not only snobbery that leads people to have misgiving about the easy accessibility of higher education and higher artistic and intellectual attainment but something of a genuine concern lest, in our reaction against Puritanism, we throw out in our cultural life —as we are doing in our occupational life—whatever is effortful and challenging. Obviously, I cannot in a footnote begin to deal adequately with issues of such moment, which I have examined in another perspective in my Founders Day address at Antioch, *The Oral Tradition, the Printed Word, and the Screen Image* (Yellow Springs, Ohio: Antioch College Press, 1955).

35 British Universities and Intellectual Life

A. H. HALSEY

IT IS ONE feature of industrial society that the universities have never held a more central place in the structure of intellectual life than they do today. As the Vice-Chancellor of the University of Southampton has recently pointed out, 'it was London and not Christ Church which was midwife to Locke's *Essay Concerning Human Understanding.* Oxford and Cambridge could hardly claim the Royal Society as their child and Newton found London more congenial than Cambridge . . . But all this was changed as the nineteenth century drew on; increasingly the great names in science, philosophy and history were university names.'[1] Today the universities lead, if they do not monopolize, all branches of science and the arts except perhaps for the fine arts and poetry.

Yet superficial acquaintance with the great volume of recent discussion of liberal studies in the modern world quickly conveys an impression of pessimism, amounting almost to despair, on the part of the humanists. It is as if they accepted a general notion of historical development which postulates two extreme types of society, the aristocratic/feudal and the industrial/technological and which conceives of intellectual life as geared by irremovable chains to the technological base of society in its movements from the former to the latter. But leaving aside the simple minded monocausal nature of this notion, I would suggest that liberal studies are by no means necessarily in decline.

Of course, the crude historical theory underlying current pessimism has within it some truth concerning the intellectual balance of contemporary universities. It is true that the humanities are wedded historically to an aristocratic tradition. Their expression in the institutions of formal education originated in the vocational needs of aristrocracy and its religious and secular administrations. Accordingly, as vested interests in the universities, the humanities remain most strong in the European universities of ancient foundation and least confident, most defensive, in American communities founded on modern industrialism. On the other hand technology has, in the universities, all the characteristics of the parvenu; a brash con-

Reprinted from A. H. Halsey, "British Universities and Intellectual Life," *Universities Quarterly,* Vol. XII (Feb., 1958), with the permission of the author and the publisher, Turnstile Press Ltd., London.

fidence in a successful future based on the conspicuous achievements of modern applied science and on financial support from the new industrial sources of patronage as well as from governments concerned with national defence and increased standards of material life; but also frustration, irritation and feelings of inferiority towards the entrenched and apparently obstructive power of the old disciplines.

Present conditions in the British universities are of special interest in this connection since Britain has seniority in age both in its membership of Western civilization and in its industrialism. Moreover, it has, in the post war period, been passing through a period of relatively rapid social change in which educational reconstruction has held an honoured, or at least a much publicized place. These changes, and especially the changes in relations between social classes, offer a challenge to the universities which will test their adaptive capacities to the utmost limit and which involves the place of the liberal arts within them.

The extent to which humanistic traditions pervade British as contrasted with American university life was impressed upon me during a year at the Centre for the Advanced Study of the Behavioral Sciences in California, where I was naturally led to reflect on the position of the social sciences in the two countries.

Two differences seemed to me to be most noticeable. First the American social scientists are sufficiently numerous to form large and specialized occupational groups. There are, for example, some 2,000 teachers of sociology in American universities whereas the comparable figure for the United Kingdom is no more than 40. And yet, though it is the case in Britain that sociologists as such are scarcely recognized, sociological writing under other names holds an honourable place as part of an ancient tradition of humanistic writing. Second, the academic gods are different. In the United States natural science holds almost monotheistic sway over the social scientist whereas in Britain there is a polytheistic worship of diverse deities such as history, Karl Marx, positivism and the institution of the Royal Commission, and especially the humanistic aspect of each.

The training, research interests and writing of social scientists in the two countries are consonant with these differences. In American universities, the disciplines with the social sciences are more specialized and isolated one from another. Thus it is difficult in Britain to acquire a degree in sociology and yet remain innocent of economics, anthropology, philosophy and politics. The word inter-disciplinary is characteristically American and the problem which it denotes is scarcely recognized in England.

On the side of research interests, the Americans seem to be much more anxious than the British about their scientific status. Social science in post war Britain is still largely focused on problems of social policy. In the United States, by contrast, policy problems are usually subordinate to the search for rigorous scientific methods—albeit too often and too cheerfully applied to the more trivial aspects of social life. Professor R. K. Merton once aptly described American work on the sociology of knowledge by ascribing to it the motto, 'We don't know that what we say is particularly significant, but it is at least true.' Moreover, where there is reaction among American social scientists against what I would call the school of frantic empiricism, it often takes the form of a no less controversial, because too ambitious, theorizing. The more humanistic, less scientific English sociologist would be less inclined to equate truth with precision or significance with theory.

Again it follows from the differences in numbers that the American social scientists are able to write for each other, whereas when the English sociologist takes pen to paper he has before him a wider and more heterogeneous audience—an audience of 'intellectual laymen' which is not nearly so apparent on the American scene. This partly accounts for the very obvious differences in terminology and the flavour of the language used by social scientists in the two countries. It also explains the howls of exasperation so frequently emitted by the review columns of that part of the British press which reviews American sociological books on behalf of the 'intelligent laymen.'

Thus a glance at this small sector of intellectual life immediately reveals contrasts which reflect fundamental differences in the educational philosophy and institutions of these two countries. But now let us turn to look more closely at the British universities.

The British system of university education is highly selective in the sense that only between 3–4 per cent of the population passes through it, and also in the sense that the distribution of opportunity of entering a university is very unequally distributed between the various social classes. In fact England has probably less university students per thousand of the population than any other industrial country. The figure is double in Scotland but treble in Australia and Canada, four times as great in Russia and nine times as great in the United States.[2] In England, Scotland and Wales with a population of 50 million, there are now 21 universities, an independent university college and two colleges of technology of university rank attended by some 89,000 full-time students. Apart from the mammoth University of London with its 19,403 full-time students and the Universities of Oxford and Cambridge with 7,740 and 8,295 respectively, each of these institutions has less than 5,000 students and 13 of them have less than 3,000.[3] Accordingly the British undergraduate remains a member of a tiny privileged minority attending a university in which it is still possible to have personal contact with a significant proporton of his fellows.

The ancient universities of Oxford and Cambridge have always occupied a special and dominating position in the structure of British university life. Both in their self image and in the public mind they are clearly differentiated from all other institutions of higher learning. So enormous is their prestige that, to take two trivial examples, members of one can still refer unambiguously to the other as 'the other place' and *The Times* or the *Manchester Guardian* can entitle a sport column 'The University Football Match' with the confident assumption that the reader will know that the game is not soccer but Rugby Football and the universities Oxford and Cambridge. Professor Shils, in his brilliant essay on the British intellectuals, is only too accurate when he writes that 'if a young man talking to an educated stranger refers to his university, he is asked "Oxford or Cambridge?". And if he says Aberystwyth or Nottingham, there is disappointment on the one side and embarrassment on the other.'[4]

The generalization concerning historical development which I mentioned earlier might lead us to expect a quite different situation. The ancient universities are of feudal origin. They were well established before the development of the natural sciences made possible the present day demand for highly trained technologists and they reached something like their present size and structure before the demand for equality of educational opportunity became sufficiently powerful to be taken seriously. Yet the ancient universities are far from being in process of eclipse by institutions more closely and directly linked to the dominant trends of economic and social life in Britain. On the contrary, it is possible to argue against the view that the Redbrick university is 'the university of the future' that Oxbridge has never had a firmer grasp onto its position at the apex of British educational and intellectual life. Indeed, Shils has described the successful post-war resurgence of the aristocratic-gentry culture on the basis of what he calls 'the London-Oxford-Cambridge axis' and its 'restoration to pre-eminence among the guiding stars of the intellectuals' after nearly a century of retreat and, paradoxically in a period when political and economic ascendancy has clearly been passing to those classes of society which were formerly excluded from participation in its way of life.

What is the explanation of Oxbridge pre-eminence? What are the consequences, for the aims and characteristics of the modern universities and for the place of the liberal arts within them?

The ancient universities have been the champions of two related causes, one social and the other educational. Socially they have been the preserves of aristocracy and, more recently, the assimilating institutions for young entrants to the country's political, business and professional elites. Educationally they have stood for a broad humanism against a narrow professionalism, for 'education' as opposed to 'training,' Oxford more so than Cambridge, which was always more scientific and protestant. They are, of course, also scholarly institutions devoted to the advancement and preservation of knowledge. But undergraduate life in the colleges has traditionally maintained a nice balance between the intellectuals and the 'hearties.' The education of a gentleman involves attention to character and physique as well as to brains and if the claims of scholarship might not have been fully met by supply from within the ranks of the well-to-do classes then standards have been maintained and concessions at the same time made to popular demand by the provision of a proportion of competitive scholarship places for undergraduates. At the same time, a qualified support of intellectualism has fitted easily into the temper of widespread attitudes among the British—a respect for the grasp of matter-of-fact realities and a distrust of ideological cleverness or passion.

In the long history of the ancient universities the greatest challenge to their pre-eminence came with the beginnings of industrialism and the educational aspirations of Dissent. Subsequently during the last century and a half the educational needs of an increasingly technological age and the demands of educational opportunity for the plebs have resulted in the establishment of the modern universities first in London and later in the great provincial centres of modern industry and commerce, notably Manchester, Birmingham, Leeds and Liverpool. From the outset these universities have been devoted more to science than to the arts, more to the training of the specialist than the cultivation of the 'educated man' (even in the arts their main product has been school teachers), more to research at the frontiers of knowledge than to the preservation and transmission of accumulated scholarship. Their standards of scholarship are seldom equalled and probably not excelled either in Oxbridge or in the world. Yet their challenge to the social dominance of the ancient foundations has so far been completely without success. The reason for this will take us into the peculiarities of the history of English class structure.

The modern universities of nineteenth and twentieth century foundation are associated with bourgeois rather than aristocratic-gentry culture— the culture of the non-conformist provincial business classes. Shils described how, in the nineteenth century, 'living to itself, puritanical, pharisaical, proud and excessively sensitive to the slights and denials of the traditional society, the bourgeoisie of the big provincial towns, partly from local patriotism, partly from resentment, partly from love of learning created . . . a genuine civilization—earnest searching and profound'—and with the modern universities as it chief monument. This culture, he adds, 'has now been routed': 'The aristocratic gentry culture has come back into the saddle, and with little to dispute its dominion.'

Perhaps the most outstanding characteristic of the English class structure historically has been the remarkable absorptive capacity, the judicious and un-Marxist Fabianism of the upper classes. The culture of the gentry and of higher officialdom never quite lost control of the rising provincial centres. If the successful northern businessmen were themselves excluded from entry into 'the establishment,' their sons could cross the social barrier by southward movement through the public schools and Oxford by movement of religious adherence from Chapel to Church and by occupational movement from trade to profession or from a northern works to a London central office. To take but one of innumerable examples, I recently had occasion to explore the family biography of a leading firm of steel manufacturers. The first generation in the early nineteenth century—a northern non-conformist artisan nail maker. The second generation—a successful steel master who received a technical education at Owens College (later Manchester University). The third generation—public school and Church of England and including a knight, a barrister, a Conservative M.P. and the Chairman of the now large public steel corporation.

In discussing the present state of university education in the underdeveloped territories of the British Commonwealth, Mr. Balogh has argued that education ought to be in closest harmony with the technical and administrative requirements of the country and goes on to criticize the influence of Oxbridge and 'the desperately ill-fitting educational precepts of the Whig bureau-aristocracy of the last century.'[5] Whatever assessment we make of the value of its present influences, it is certain that the adaptation of Oxford and Cambridge to rising demands in the nineteenth century for administrators both at home and abroad and for entrants to the liberal profession was markedly successful at the time and has been a powerful factor in their continued prestige. In alliance with a public school system expanding on the model of Dr. Arnold's Rugby, they were able to take the rising elements of the middle classes into their orbit and to educate them with minimal modification to traditional ideas concerning the upbringing of a gentleman.

The firm possession thus gained of the avenues of entry to the most prestigeful occupations has never been lost. The success of Britain as an imperial power in the nineteenth century and especially the quiet and incorruptible efficiency of its high ranking civil servants and colonial administrators commanded universal esteem and at the same time a powerful validation of its educational institutions and the high values placed within them on classical studies and the liberal arts. In consequence, the humanities have been able to fight with more success in Britain than in America against the inroads of the social sciences (often referred to as the quasi-scientific studies) into the education of would-be entrants to the modern administrative professions. The education of Mr. W. H. Whyte's 'Organization Man'[6] is different in England. The English businessman will not look for a training in psychology or industrial sociology in his managerial recruits but rather for the vaguely defined qualities of the Oxbridge man. Another example is to be found in the journalistic professions. Mr. Dwight Macdonald has recently eulogized the essentially amateur tradition of writing in the British press in contrast with America. Oxbridge and the liberal arts lie behind this difference. In fact wherever the qualities required for a profession are not unambiguously capable of formulation in terms of natural science or its applications, the superiority of an Oxbridge type of education for entry is as yet scarcely challenged.

Just as the aristocratic-gentry culture was never quite routed from the industrial provinces, so Oxbridge had a secure foothold in the modern universities from their inception. Especially in the early stages of their development the staff of the civic universities was heavily recruited by migration from the Oxford and Cambridge colleges. And with the migrants came the Oxbridge ideals. There was no alternative idea of a university which was not at least partially informed by traditional notions. Certainly the modern universities set out to foster the natural sciences and in large urban centres residential collegiate life was impracticable. But even the greatest exponent of the scientific university for an industrial civilization, T. H. Huxley, could assert (before the Cowper Commission in 1892) that 'the primary business of the universities is with pure knowledge and pure art —independent of all application to practice; with progress in cluture, not with increase in wealth.'[7]

Of course, in the social conflicts of the inter-war period, traditional institutions came under heavy attack and the London School of Economics enjoyed its great days as a centre of intellectual radicalism. But again as Shils points out, the widespread alienation of intellectuals from established society did more damage to bourgeois than to aristocratic-gentry culture. English radicalism of the left had always some aristocratic colouring and re-integration in the war and post-war years has only served to strengthen the hold on intellectual life of the London-Oxford-Cambridge axis.

The traditions of the ancient universities have bequeathed to the British universities two distinctive characteristics. First and foremost they provide basically for a training of élites, the Trade Union leader being the only notable exception, and secondly the humanities and pure sciences are more highly valued in them than the technologies and the fine arts. These two characteristics in turn give rise to two urgent current problems—a problem of assimilation of new aspirants to university education and a problem of developing technological studies within the existing framework of university organization. The universities adapted successfully to the modest educational expansion of the nineteenth and twentieth centuries. They learnt to live with the scientist and to mould new generations of undergraduates from more diverse social origin. They must now face the problem of preserving their traditional ideals while incorporating an expansion of technological studies and while assimilating vastly increased numbers from all classes of society.

Between the two World Wars there were about 35,000 students in the universities of England and Wales and even this low figure represented an expansion of 75 per cent over the 20,000 in attendance before the 1914–18 War. The student body was overwhelmingly upper and middle class. It included only a minute proportion of young people of working class origin who had managed to win their way by scholarships through the grammar schools—a highly selected and intellectually able minority capable of easy assimilation into what were dominantly middle class institutions. In 1944 the Barlow Report, echoing the widespread demand for educational reform generated during the Second World War, demanded an 80 per cent expansion of university places and stated that 'only about 1 in 5 of the ablest boys and girls actually reach the universities . . . There is clearly an ample reserve of intelligence in the country to allow both a doubling of university numbers and a raising of standards.' In the event the demands of the Barlow Report were easily met. By 1950 the number of students was 68,000 and within the next 10 years a further expansion to at least 100,000 is expected.

These increases and expectations of further increases are, of course, partly a reflection of the main efforts to post war reconstruction which was directed at the secondary schools under the terms of the great Education Act of 1944. A recent study of English Education[8] has shown that the Act has resulted in a major advance towards equality of opportunity in education. Expansion in grammar school provision and the substitution of competitive entry for fee paying in state grammar schools has opened new opportunities for the mass of the population. In effect, the grammar schools, and therefore the highway to the universities, have been opened to large numbers of children from the homes of manual workers who have themselves received only the doubtful benefits of the older system of elementary education. At the same time many of these parents have revolutionized their attitudes towards education. The age to which they are willing to keep their children at school has increased dramatically in the post war period with the result that each year an increasing proportion of children enters the grammar school sixth forms which prepare entrants for the universities.

Of course we must not exaggerate the extent to which the revolution has already gone. There remains a severe class-linked process of selection operating from the bottom to the top of the British educational system. Its severity may be judged by the fact that though the unskilled labouring class contributes each year about 12 per cent of the nation's births it accounts for only 5.6 per cent of grammar school entrants, only 1.5 per cent of those entering the sixth forms[9] and only 0.9 per cent of the boys (0.6 per cent of the girls) going on to the universities.[10]

Nevertheless, as the universities expand and as the full effect on the schools of the 1944 Education Act emerges, the proportion of working class undergraduates may be expected to grow. Such a development can only be applauded. But there can be no doubt that it sets a pedagogical problem, especially perhaps for the teacher of the liberal arts. The problem in essence is one of bridging a cultural gap which is often not recognized for what it is. It is a problem with which the grammar schools have struggled painfully in the post war years. The following expression of it by a grammar school headmaster is typical. 'The grammar school now includes among its pupils a much higher proportion of children from poor homes. Some of these children come from homes which are barely literate and where a book is an unusual phenomenon . . . Others have very low standards of cleanliness and appearance, some seem to have had very little training in social behaviour; even table manners may leave much to be desired. Children like these have very little to give to the social or cultural life of the school; the school itself has to provide much which, before the war, would have been regarded as the normal contribution of the home.'[11]

It is hardly surprising that the master in the grammar school common room is perplexed by the paradox of post war children who are able but ineducable. It is all too easy for him to dismiss them as uncultured louts. It is far less easy to communicate his own learning to the children of a population with the barest and most recently acquired literacy and that largely through a popular press of impressive vulgarity. For the English university don the problem is virtually a new one and he now finds himself 'having to provide much which before the war would been been regarded as the normal contribution of the *school*.'

The difficulties are exacerbated by the fact that Oxbridge has, for the most part, sloughed them off onto the modern universities. In a recent article on Cambridge, Mr. D. Mack Smith claims that "the social basis of the community has also quite changed . . . the gilded youth have retreated, the have-a-good-timers with their champagne breakfasts and parties at Newmarket are swamped and the university again fulfils its old function of promoting an osmotic assimilation between the classes.'[12] This is Victorian thinking at latest. Mr. Mack Smith's classes clearly do not include that three quarters of the population which follow manual occupations *and which contributed only 9 per cent of the men admitted to his university in 1955–56.* The comparable figure for the University of Wales was 40, for the English provincial universities 31 and for London 21.

We are thus faced with a paradoxical situation. Current developments in the schools and expansion in the universities bid fair to amount to a revolutionary democratization of opportunities for university education. Yet, given the background of dominance by the London-Oxford-Cambridge axis, there is graver danger that this revolution will leave the British universities more socially stratified than ever before.

Similarly with the problem of developing technological studies, it may be true as Mr. Mack Smith suggests that 'During the last twenty years the older universities have both of them moved towards Redbrick, a direction symbolized by unexciting and efficient laboratory architecture.' Yet the main burden of technological expansion is being borne elsewhere, at Imperial College, London, at Glasglow, Manchester, Birmingham and

Leeds. The urgency of the need to expand is undisputed: both Russia and the U.S.A. produce about twice as many graduates in science and technology per thousand of the population as we do. But those who care for the liberal arts may be forgiven their anxiety in face of the fact that the solution of the problem is for the most part to be thrust onto those universities which are least firmly attached to the humanistic traditions of the ancient universities. The fact that the two problems are related makes the task doubly difficult. It is no accident that the technologies take in proportionately more young people of working class origin than any of the other faculties. If the proportion for Arts is also high this is because of the function of arts faculties in the modern universities as professional schools for would-be grammar school teachers.

In consequence, the position of the arts don in a modern English university is beset with difficulty. He will often have a sense of failure through the very fact of being there rather than in an Oxbridge college. And an anxious hovering on the outside of the literary élite will not be conducive to the solution of the very real problems facing him in a university increasingly devoted to technological studies. He may easily yield to discouragement in the face of a student body which he sees as uncultured in its background and materialistically vocational in its aspirations: and of colleagues in the senior common room who talk cheerfully in north-country tones of the technicalities of turbo-jets and electronic computing machines. Yet he must learn to live with and communicate with both if the great traditions of scholarship which he represents are to survive into the technological age.

NOTES

1. D. G. James, "University Commentary," *Universities Quarterly,* 10, no. 2, 1956, p. 117, and on p. 118. It is a matter of historical interest that Wittgenstein, who disliked universities (including Cambridge), judged it necessary that he should reside in one from time to time, whatever anguish it caused him.

2. cf. Lord Simon of Wythenshawe, "Student Numbers," *Universities Quarterly,* 10, no. 2, 1956.

3. Figures return from University Grants Committee Report on *University Development, 1952–1956,* Cmd. 79, H.M.S.O., March, 1957.

4. E. A. Shils, "The Intellectuals. I. Great Britain," *Encounter,* April, 1955.

5. T. Balogh, "Oxbridge Rampant," *Universities Quarterly,* 9, no. 3, 1955.

6. W. H. Whyte, Jr., *The Organization Man,* N.Y., 1956, Chapters 6–10.

7. Quoted in C. Bibby, "T. H. Huxley's Idea of a University," *Universities Quarterly,* 10, no. 4, 1956.

8. J. E. Floud, A. H. Halsey and F. M. Martin, *Social Class and Educational Opportunity,* 1956.

9. Central Advisory Council for Education (England) *Early Leaving,* H.M.S.O., 1954.

10. R. K. Kelsall, *Applications for Admission to Universities.* Report on an enquiry commissioned by the Committee of Vice-Chancellors and Principals of the Universities of the United Kingdom, 1957, p. 10, Table F. The report refers to admission in the session 1955–56. It points out that although, according to the 1951 Census, 72 per cent of the adult males followed manual occupations only 26 per

cent of the boys and 19 per cent of the girls admitted to universities originated in these classes.

11. Davies, H., "The Social Effects of the 1944 Act on the Grammar School." *The Bulletin of Education,* No. 23, Nov. 1950, p. 5.

12. D. Mack Smith, "The Changing University. A Report on Cambridge Today" *Encounter,* May, 1956, p. 54.

36   *The "Cooling-out" Function in Higher Education*[1]

BURTON R. CLARK

A MAJOR PROBLEM of democratic society is inconsistency between encouragement to achieve and the realities of limited opportunity. Democracy asks individuals to act as if social mobility were universally possible; status is to be won by individual effort, and rewards are to accrue to those who try. But democratic societies also need selective training institutions, and hierarchical work organizations permit increasingly fewer persons to succeed at ascending levels. Situations of opportunity are also situations of denial and failure. Thus democratic societies need not only to motivate achievement but also to mollify those denied it in order to sustain motivation in the face of disappointment and to deflect resentment. In the modern mass democracy, with its large-scale organization, elaborated ideologies of equal access and participation, and minimal commitment to social origin as basis for status, the task becomes critical.

The problem of blocked opportunity has been approached sociologically through means-ends analysis. Merton and others have called attention to the phenomenon of dissociation between culturally instilled goals and institutionally provided means of realization; discrepancy between ends and means is seen as a basic social source of individual frustration and recalcitrance.[2] We shall here extend means-ends analysis in another direction, to the responses of organized groups to means-ends disparities, in particular focusing attention on ameliorative processes that lessen the strains of dissociation. We shall do so by analyzing the most prevalent type of dissociation between aspirations and avenues in American education, specifying the structure and processes that reduce the stress of structural disparity and individual denial. Certain components of American higher education perform what may be called the cooling-out function,[3] and it is to these that attention will be drawn.

The Ends-Means Disjuncture

In American higher education the aspirations of the multitude are encouraged by "open-door" admission to public-supported colleges. The

Reprinted from Burton R. Clark, "The 'Cooling-out' Function in Higher Education," *American Journal of Sociology*, LXV (May, 1960), 569–76, with the permission of the author and the editor.

means of moving upward in status and of maintaining high status now include some years in college, and a college education is a prerequisite of the better positions in business and the professions. The trend is toward an ever tighter connection between higher education and higher occupations, as increased specialization and professionalization insure that more persons will need more preparation. The high-school graduate, seeing college as essential to success, will seek to enter some college, regardless of his record in high school.

A second and allied source of public interest in unlimited entry into college is the ideology of equal opportunity.[4] Strictly interpreted, equality of opportunity means selection according to ability, without regard to extraneous considerations. Popularly interpreted, however, equal opportunity in obtaining a college education is widely taken to mean unlimited access to some form of college: in California, for example, state educational authorities maintain that high-school graduates who cannot qualify for the state university or state college should still have the "opportunity of attending a publicly supported institution of higher education," this being "an essential part of the state's goal of guaranteeing equal educational opportunities to all its citizens."[5] To deny access to college is then to deny equal opportunity. Higher education should make a seat available without judgment on past performance.

Many other features of current American life encourage college-going. School officials are reluctant to establish early critical hurdles for the young, as is done in Europe. With little enforced screening in the pre-college years, vocational choice and educational selection are postponed to the college years or later. In addition, the United States, a wealthy country, is readily supporting a large complex of colleges, and its expanding economy requires more specialists. Recently, a national concern that manpower be fully utilized has encouraged the extending of college training to more and different kinds of students. Going to college is also in some segments of society the thing to do; as a last resort, it is more attractive than the army or a job. Thus ethical and practical urges together encourage the high-school graduate to believe that college is both a necessity and a right; similarly, parents and elected officials incline toward legislation and admission practices that insure entry for large numbers; and educational authorities find the need and justification for easy admission.

Even where pressures have been decisive in widening admission policy, however, the system of higher education has continued to be shaped partly by other interests. The practices of public colleges are influenced by the academic personnel, the organizational requirements of colleges, and external pressures other than those behind the open door. Standards of performance and graduation are maintained. A commitment to standards is encouraged by a set of values in which the status of a college, as defined by academicians and a large body of educated laymen, is closely linked to the perceived quality of faculty, student body, and curriculum. The raising of standards is supported by the faculty's desire to work with promising students and to enjoy membership in an enterprise of reputed quality—college authorities find low standards and poor students a handicap in competing with other colleges for such resources as able faculty as well as for academic status. The wish is widespread that college education be of the highest quality for the preparation of leaders in public affairs, business, and the professions. In brief, the institutional means of the students' progress toward college graduation and subsequent goals are shaped in large part by a commitment to quality embodied in college staffs, traditions, and images.

The conflict between open-door admission and performance of high quality often means a wide discrepancy between the hopes of entering students and the means of their realization. Students who pursue ends for which a college education is required but who have little academic ability gain admission into colleges only to encounter standards of performance they cannot meet. As a result, while some students of low promise are successful, for large numbers failure is inevitable and *structured*. The denial is delayed, taking place within the college instead of at the edge of the system. It requires that many colleges handle the student who intends to complete college and has been allowed to become involved but whose destiny is to fail.

Responses to Disjuncture

What is done with the student whose destiny will normally be early termination? One answer is unequivocal dismissal. This "hard" response is found in the state university that bows to pressure for broad admission but then protects standards by heavy drop-out. In the first year it weeds out many of the incompetent, who may number a third or more of the entering class.[6] The response of the college is hard in that failure is clearly defined as such. Failure is public; the student often returns home. This abrupt change in status and in access of the means of achievement may occur simultaneously in a large college or university for hundreds, and sometimes thousands, of students after the first semester and at the end of the freshman year. The delayed denial is often viewed on the outside as heartless, a slaughter of the innocents.[7] This excites public pressure and anxiety, and apparently the practice cannot be extended indefinitely as the demand for admission to college increases.

A second answer is to sidetrack unpromising students rather than have them fail. This is the "soft" response: never to dismiss a student but to provide him with an alternative. One form of it in some state universities is the detour to an extension division or a general college, which has the advantage of appearing not very different from the main road. Sometimes "easy" fields of study, such as education, business administration, and social science, are used as alternatives to dismissal.[8] The major form of the soft response is not found in the four-year college or university, however, but in the college that specializes in handling students who will soon be leaving—typically, the two-year public junior college.

In most states where the two-year college is a part of higher education, the students likely to be caught in the means-ends disjuncture are assigned to it in large numbers. In California, where there are over sixty public two-year colleges in a diversified system that includes the state university and numerous four-year state colleges, the junior college is unselective in admissions and by law, custom, and self-conception accepts all who wish to enter.[9] It is tuition-free, local, and under local control. Most of its entering students want to try for the baccalaureate degree, transferring to a "senior" college after one or two years. About two-thirds of the students in the junior colleges of the state are in programs that permit transferring; but, of these, only about one-third actually transfer to a four-year college.[10] The remainder, or two out of three of the professed transfer students, are "latent terminal students": their announced intention and program of study entails four years of college, but in reality their work terminates in the junior college. Constituting about half of all the students in the California junior colleges, and somewhere between one-third and one-half of junior college students nationally,[11] these students cannot be ignored by the colleges. Understanding their careers is important to understanding modern higher education.

The Reorienting Process

This type of student in the junior college is handled by being moved out of a transfer major to a one- or two-year program of vocational, business, or semiprofessional training. This calls for the relinquishing of his original intention, and he is induced to accept a substitute that has lower status in both the college and society in general.

In one junior college[12] the initial move in a cooling-out process is pre-entrance testing: low scores on achievement tests lead poorly qualified students into remedial classes. Assignment to remedial work casts doubt and slows the student's movement into bona fide transfer courses. The remedial courses are, in effect, a subcollege. The student's achievement scores are made part of a counseling folder that will become increasingly significant to him. An objective record of ability and performance begins to accumulate.

A second step is a counseling interview before the beginning of the first semester, and before all subsequent semesters for returning students. "At this interview the counselor assists the student to choose the proper courses in light of his objective, his test scores, the high school record and test records from his previous schools."[13] Assistance in choosing "the proper courses" is gentle at first. Of the common case of the student who wants to be an engineer but who is not a promising candidate, a counselor said: "I never openly countermand his choice, but edge him toward a terminal program by gradually laying out the facts of life." Counselors may become more severe later when grades provide a talking point and when the student knows that he is in trouble. In the earlier counseling the desire of the student has much weight; the counselor limits himself to giving advice and stating the probability of success. The advice is entered in the counseling record that shadows the student.

A third and major step in reorienting the latent terminal student is a special course entitled "Orientation to College," mandatory for entering students. All sections of it are taught by teacher-counselors who comprise the counseling staff, and one of its purposes is "to assist students in evaluating their own abilities, interests, and aptitudes; in assaying their vocational choices in light of this evaluation; and in making educational plans to implement their choices." A major section of it takes up vocational planning; vocational tests are given at a time when opportunities and requirements in various fields of work are discussed. The tests include the "Lee Thorpe Interest Inventory" ("given to all students for motivating a self-appraisal of vocational choice") and the "Strong Interest Inventory" ("for all who are undecided about choice or who show disparity between accomplishment and vocational choice"). Mechanical and clerical aptitude tests are taken by all. The aptitudes are directly related to the college's terminal programs, with special tests, such as a pre-engineering ability test, being given according to need. Then an "occupational paper is required of all students for their chosen occupation"; in it the student writes on the required training and education and makes a "self-appraisal of fitness."

Tests and papers are then used in class discussion and counseling interviews, in which the students themselves arrange and work with a counselor's folder and a student test profile and, in so doing, are repeatedly confronted by the accumulating evidence—the test scores, course grades, recommendations of teachers and counselors. This procedure is intended to heighten self-awareness of capacity in relation to choice and hence to strike particularly at the latent terminal student. The teacher-counselors are urged constantly to "be alert to the problem of unrealistic vocational goals" and to "help students to accept their limitations and strive for success in other worthwhile objectives that are within their grasp." The orientation class was considered a good place "to talk tough," to explain in an *impersonal* way the facts of life for the overambitious student. Talking tough to a whole group is part of a soft treatment of the individual.

Following the vocational counseling, the orientation course turns to "building an educational program," to study of the requirements for graduation of the college in transfer and terminal curriculum, and to planning of a four-semester program. The students also become acquainted with the requirements of the colleges to which they hope to transfer, here contemplating additional hurdles such as the entrance examinations of other colleges. Again, the hard facts of the road ahead are brought to bear on self-appraisal.

If he wishes, the latent terminal student may ignore the counselor's advice and the test scores. While in the counseling class, he is also in other courses, and he can wait to see what happens. Adverse counseling advice and poor test scores may not shut off his hope of completing college; when this is the case, the deterrent will be encountered in the regular classes. Here the student is divested of expectations, lingering from high school, that he will automatically pass and, hopefully, automatically be transferred. Then, receiving low grades, he is thrown back into the counseling orbit, a fourth step in his reorientation and a move justified by his actual accomplishment. The following indicates the nature of the referral system:

> *Need for Improvement Notices* are issued by instructors to students who are doing unsatisfactory work. The carbon copy of the notice is given to the counselor who will be available for conference with the student. The responsibility lies with the student to see his counselor. However, experience shows that some counselees are unable to be sufficiently self-directive to seek aid. The counselor should, in such cases, send for the student, using the Request for Conference blank. If the student fails to respond to the Request for Conference slip, this may become a disciplinary matter and should be referred to the deans
>
> After a conference has been held, the Need of Improvement notices are filed in the student's folder. *This may be important* in case of a complaint concerning the fairness of a final grade.[14]

This directs the student to more advice and self-assessment, as soon and as often as he has classroom difficulty. The carbon-copy routine makes it certain that, if he does not seek advice, advice will seek him. The paper work and bureaucratic procedure have the purpose of recording referral and advice in black and white, where they may later be appealed to impersonally. As put in an unpublished report of the college, the overaspiring student and the one who seems to be in the wrong program require "skillful and delicate handling. An accumulation of pertinent factual information may serve to fortify the objectivity of the student-counselor relationship." While the counselor advises delicately and patiently, but persistently, the student is confronted with the record with increasing frequency.

A fifth step, one necessary for many in the throes of discouragement, is probation: "Students [whose] grade point averages fall below 2.0 [C] in any semester will, upon recommendation by the Scholarship Committee, be placed on probationary standing." A second failure places the student on second probation, and a third may mean that he will be advised to withdraw from the college altogether. The procedure is not designed to rid the college of a large number of students, for they may continue on probation for three consecutive semesters; its purpose is not to provide a status halfway out of the college but to "assist the student to seek an objective (major field) at a level on which he can succeed."[15] An important effect of probation is its slow killing-off of the lingering hopes of the most stubborn latent terminal students. A "transfer student" must have a C average to receive the Associate in Arts (a two-year degree) offered by the junior college, but no minimum average is set for terminal students. More important, four-year colleges require a C average or higher for the transfer student. Thus probationary status is the final blow to hopes of transferring and, indeed, even to graduating from the junior college under a transfer-student label. The point is reached where the student must permit himself to be reclassified or else drop out. In this college, 30 per cent of the students enrolled at the end of the spring semester, 1955–56, who returned the following fall were on probation; three out of four of these were transfer students in name.[16]

This sequence of procedures is a specific process of cooling-out;[17] its effect, at the best, is to let down hopes gently and unexplosively. Through it students who are failing or barely passing find their occupational and academic future being redefined. Along the way, teacher-counselors urge the latent terminal student to give up his plan of transferring and stand ready to console him in accepting a terminal curriculum. The drawn-out denial when it is effective is in place of a personal, hard "No"; instead, the student is brought to realize, finally, that it is best to ease himself out of the competition to transfer.

Cooling-Out Features

In the cooling-out process in the junior college are several features which are likely to be found in other settings where failure or denial is the effect of a structured discrepancy between ends and means, the responsible operatives or "coolers" cannot leave the scene or hide their identities, and the disappointment is threatening in some way to those responsible for it. At work and in training institutions this is common. The features are:

1. *Alternative achievement.*—Substitute avenues may be made to appear not too different from what is given up, particularly as to status. The person destined to be denied or who fails is invited to interpret the second effort as more appropriate to his particular talent and is made to see that it will be the less frustrating. Here one does not fail but rectifies a mistake. The substitute status reflects less unfavorably on personal capacity than does being dismissed and forced to leave the scene. The terminal student in

the junior college may appear not very different from the transfer student—an "engineering aide," for example, instead of an "engineer"—and to be proceeding to something with a status of its own. Failure in college can be treated as if it did not happen; so, too, can poor performance in industry.[18]

2. *Gradual disengagement.*—By a gradual series of steps, movement to a goal may be stalled, self-assessment encouraged, and evidence produced of performance. This leads toward the available alternatives at little cost. It also keeps the person in a counseling milieu in which advice is furnished, whether actively sought or not. Compared with the original hopes, however, it is a deteriorating situation. If the individual does not give up peacefully, he will be in trouble.

3. *Objective denial.*—Reorientation is, finally, confrontation by the facts. A record of poor performance helps to detach the organization and its agents from the emotional aspects of the cooling-out work. In a sense, the overaspiring student in the junior college confronts himself, as he lives with the accumulating evidence, instead of the organization. The college offers opportunity; it is the record that forces denial. Record-keeping and other bureaucratic procedures appeal to universal criteria and reduce the influence of personal ties, and the personnel are thereby protected. Modern personnel record-keeping, in general, has the function of documenting denial.

4. *Agents of consolation.*—Counselors are available who are patient with the overambitious and who work to change their intentions. They believe in the value of the alternative careers, though of lower social status, and are practiced in consoling. In college and in other settings counseling is to reduce aspiration as well as to define and to help fulfil it. The teacher-counselor in the "soft" junior college is in contrast to the scholar in the "hard" college who simply gives a low grade to the failing student.

5. *Avoidance of standards.*—A cooling-out process avoids appealing to standards that are ambiguous to begin with. While a "hard" attitude toward failure generally allows a single set of criteria, a "soft" treatment assumes that many kinds of ability are valuable, each in its place. Proper classification and placement are then paramount, while standards become relative.

Importance of Concealment

For an organization and its agents one dilemma of a cooling-out role is that it must be kept reasonably away from public scrutiny and not clearly perceived or understood by prospective clientele. Should it become obvious, the organization's ability to perform it would be impaired. If high-school seniors and their families were to define the junior college as a place which diverts college-bound students, a probable consequence would be a turning-away from the junior college and increased pressure for admission to the four-year colleges and universities that are otherwise protected to some degree. This would, of course, render superfluous the part now played by the junior college in the division of labor among colleges.

The cooling-out function of the junior college is kept hidden, for one thing, as other functions are highlighted. The junior college stresses "the transfer function," "the terminal function," etc., not that of transforming transfer into terminal students; indeed, it is widely identified as principally a transfer station. The other side of cooling-out is the successful performance in junior college of students who did poorly in high school or who have overcome socioeconomic handicaps, for they are drawn into higher education rather than taken out of it. Advocates of the junior college point to this salvaging of talented manpower, otherwise lost to the community and nation. It is indeed a function of the open door to let hidden talent be uncovered.

Then, too, cooling-out itself is reinterpreted so as to appeal widely. The junior college may be viewed as a place where all high-school graduates have the opportunity to explore possible careers and find the type of education appropriate to their individual ability; in short, as a place where everyone is admitted and everyone succeeds. As described by the former president of the University of California:

> A prime virtue to the junior college, I think, is that most of its students succeed in what they set out to accomplish, and cross the finish line before they grow weary of the race. After two years in a course that they have chosen, they can go out prepared for activities that satisfy them, instead of being branded as failures. Thus the broadest possible opportunity may be provided for the largest number to make an honest try at further education with some possibility of success and with no route to a desired goal completely barred to them.[19]

The students themselves help to keep this function concealed by wishful unawareness. Those who cannot enter other colleges but still hope to complete four years will be motivated at first not to admit the cooling-out process to consciousness. Once exposed to it, they again will be led not to acknowledge it, and so they are saved insult to their self-image.

In summary, the cooling-out process in higher education is one whereby systematic discrepancy between aspiration and avenue is covered over and stress for the individual and the system is minimized. The provision of readily available alternative achievements in itself is an important device for alleviating the stress consequent on failure and so preventing anomic and deviant behavior. The general result of cooling-out processes is that society can continue to encourage maximum effort without major disturbance from unfulfilled promises and expectations.

NOTES

1. Revised and extended version of paper read at the Fifty-fourth Annual Meeting of the American Sociological Association, Chicago, September 3–5, 1959. I am indebted to Erving Goffman and Martin A. Trow for criticism and to Sheldon Messinger for extended conceptual and editorial comment.

2. "Aberrant behavior may be regarded sociologically as a symptom of dissociation between culturally prescribed aspirations and socially structured avenues for realizing these aspirations" (Robert K. Merton, "Social Structure and Anomie," in *Social Theory and Social Structure* [rev. ed.; Glencoe, Ill.: Free Press, 1957], p. 134). See also Herbert H. Hyman, "The Value Systems of Different Classes: A Social Psychological Contribution to the Analysis of Stratification," in Reinhard Bendix and Seymour M. Lipset (eds.), *Class, Status and Power: A Reader in Social Stratification* (Glencoe, Ill.: Free Press, 1953), pp. 426–42; and the papers by Robert Dubin, Richard A. Cloward, Robert K. Merton, and Dorothy L. Meier, and Wendell Bell, in *American Sociological Review*, Vol. XXIV, (April, 1959).

3. I am indebted to Erving Goffman's original statement of the cooling-out conception. See his "Cooling the Mark Out: Some Aspects of Adaptation to Failure," *Psychiatry*, XV (November, 1952), 451–63. Sheldon Messinger called the relevance of this concept to my attention.

4. Seymour Martin Lipset and Reinhard Bendix, *Social Mobility in Industrial Society* (Berkeley: University of California Press, 1959), pp. 78–101.

5. *A Study of the Need for Additional Centers of Public Higher Education in California* (Sacramento: California State Department of Education, 1957), p. 128. For somewhat similar interpretations by educators and laymen nationally see Francis J. Brown (ed.), *Approaching Equality of Opportunity in Higher Education* (Washington, D.C.: American Council on Education, 1955), and the President's Committee on Education beyond the High School, *Second Report to the President* (Washington, D.C.: Government Printing Office, 1957).

6. One national report showed that one out of eight entering students (12.5 per cent) in publicly controlled colleges does not remain beyond the first term or semester; one out of three (31 per cent) is out by the end of the first year; and about one out of two (46.6 per cent) leaves within the first two years. In state universities alone, about one out of four withdraws in the first year and 40 per cent in two years (Robert E. Iffert, *Retention and Withdrawal of College Students* [Washington, D.C.: Department of Health, Education and Welfare, 1958], pp. 15–20). Students withdraw for many reasons, but scholastic aptitude is related to their staying power: "A sizeable number of students of medium ability enter college, but . . . few if any of them remain longer than two years" (*A Restudy of the Needs of California in Higher Education* [Sacramento: California State Department of Education, 1955], p. 120).

7. Robert L. Kelly, *The American Colleges and the Social Order* (New York: Macmillan Co., 1940), pp. 220–21.

8. One study has noted that on many campuses the business school serves "as a dumping ground for students who cannot make the grade in engineering or some branch of the liberal arts," this being a consequence of lower promotion standards than are found in most other branches of the university (Frank C. Pierson, *The Education of American Businessmen* [New York: McGraw-Hill Book Co., 1959], p. 63). Pierson also summarizes data on intelligence of students by field of study which indicate that education, business, and social science rank near the bottom in quality of students (*ibid.*, pp. 65–72).

9. Burton R. Clark, *The Open Door College: A Case Study* (New York: McGraw-Hill Book Co., 1960), pp. 44–45.

10. *Ibid.*, p. 116.

11. Leland L. Medsker, *The Junior College: Progress and Prospect* (New York: McGraw-Hill Book Co., 1960), chap. iv.

12. San Jose City College, San Jose, Calif. For the larger study see Clark, *op. cit.*

13. San Jose Junior College, Handbook for Counselors, 1957–58, p. 2. Statements in quotation marks in the next few paragraphs are cited from this.

14. *Ibid.,* p. 20.

15. Statement taken from unpublished material.

16. San Jose Junior College, "Digest of Analysis of the Records of 468 Students Placed on Probation for the Fall Semester, 1956," September 3, 1956.

17. Goffman's original statement of the concept of cooling-out referred to how the disappointing of expectations is handled by the disappointed person and especially by those responsible for the disappointment. Although his main illustration was the confidence game, where facts and potential achievement are deliberately misrepresented to the "mark" (the victim) by operators of the game, Goffman also applied the concept to failure in which those responsible act in good faith (*op. cit., passim*). "Cooling-out" is a widely useful idea when used to refer to a function that may vary in deliberateness.

18. *Ibid.,* p. 457; cf. Perrin Stryker, "How To Fire an Executive," *Fortune,* L (October, 1954), 116–17 and 178–92.

19. Robert Gordon Sproul, "Many Millions More," *Educational Record,* XXXIX (April, 1958), 102.

PART VI

Teachers in Schools and Universities

37 Recruitment to Teaching in England and Wales

JEAN FLOUD and W. SCOTT

THE HISTORY of the modern teaching profession in England and Wales is dominated by the rapidity of its growth; in particular, its principal social characteristics—the social origins and academic quality of its members and its changing social status—are to a large extent the outcome of the remarkable rate at which it has expanded and of the economic and political conditions under which this expansion has taken place. The three great periods of growth have each been initiated by the passing of education acts —in 1870, 1902, and 1944. How was the increase in each period met? Where did the new teachers come from?

Information has been collected from a large representative sample of teachers serving in all types of publicly maintained or assisted schools in England and Wales,[1] on the basis of which an attempt can be made to answer this and other related questions about the profession. Since the teachers in this sample were asked to describe the occupations followed by their paternal grandfathers as well as by their fathers, we can analyse movement into the profession over three generations. The grandfathers of our teachers were born, on the average, well before 1869 and were of the same generation as the early recruits to the new profession of "elementary" teachers after 1870. The fathers of our teachers were born some thirty years later, on the average, and made their contribution to the growing profession after the passing of the 1902 Education Act. Half of the teachers serving in 1955 had entered the profession after 1945. We are thus in a position to say something about the changing social basis of the profession in the nineteenth and early twentieth centuries and, in a rather rough and ready way, to isolate the movement into teaching from general movements in the occupational structure over the same period. For the next thirty-five years or so up to the year of our inquiry, 1955, we can make a rather more precise analysis of a different kind, assessing the attraction of teaching by estimating the changing proportion of eligible boys and girls, forthcoming at different periods from middle-class and working-class families respectively, who enter the profession.

An expanded version of a paper submitted to the Third World Congress of Sociology, summarised as "The Social Origins of Teachers in England and Wales." *Transactions of the Third World Congress of Sociology* (London: I.S.A., 1956), VIII, 255–57.

Movement into Teaching over Three Generations

We may begin by looking at the movement into teaching in the days of its first expansion in the late nineteenth and early twentieth centuries. Our schedule included a question concerning the occupation of the teacher's paternal grandfather. Although, as was to be expected, the information obtained in response to this question was relatively incomplete, it seems likely that those replying are reasonably representative of the sample as a whole and that we may legitimately compare the distribution of occupations among teachers' fathers and grandfathers respectively—asking, for instance, what proportion of today's teachers from middle- or lower-middle-class families have grandfathers who were manual workers; or what proportion of those of working-class origin have emerged from families that have been working-class for it least two generations? We shall also want, if possible, to compare teachers' families with the rest of the population to see whether they have been more socially mobile than the average run of families—more mobile than could be accounted for by the push and pull of general changes in the occupational structure over the past two generations.

Table 1.

The Social Origins of Teachers over Two Generations*

Occupations of Paternal Grandfathers	Occupations of Fathers†					
	MEN TEACHERS			WOMEN TEACHERS		
	1	2	3	1	2	3
1. Major Professions, Higher Administrative, Substantial Business	34.6	5.3	2.9	26.7	3.7	26.8
2. Intermediate (Other Non-manual)	36.4	56.7	33.0	50.2	67.2	39.6
3. Manual	29.0	38.0	64.1	23.1	29.2	57.7
	100.0	100.0	100.0	100.0	100.0	100.0

† Classification as for grandfathers.

* The occupational classification used in this and subsequent tables is based on the socio-economic categories used by the Registrar General in the 1951 census of Great Britain:
A. *Professional and Administrative*
1. Upper professional—doctors, clergymen, solicitors, architects, University teachers etc.
2. Upper administrative and substantial business—administrative branch of the civil service, bankers, stock brokers, company secretaries, employers and directors in firms employing at least 10 persons, commissioned officers, etc.
B. *Intermediate*
3. Farming—farmers, farm managers, etc.
4. Teaching—teachers, both head and assistant, school and private.
5. Lesser professions, administrative and managerial—pharmacists, nurses, chiropodists, draughtsmen, executive branch of civil service, managers in mining, etc.
6. Lesser Business and Own Account—employers in firms employing fewer than 10 persons, working on own account.
7. Clerical work—clerks, secretaries, stenographers, commercial salesmen, insurance agents, etc.
8. Personal service—shop assistants, stewards, domestic servants, hotel porters, waiters, barmen, game keepers, etc.
C. *Manual*
9. Skilled manual, foremen.
10. Semi- and unskilled manual, agricultural workers, armed forces—other ranks.

Table 1 shows that of today's men teachers drawn from working-class families, almost two-thirds (64 per cent) are moving out of families that have been working-class for two generations past; whilst one-third are retrieving the family fortunes by rising once again, through teaching, into the non-manual occupational class from which their grandfathers came. Some 57 per cent of today's lower-middle-class teachers come from established lower-middle-class families at least two generations old; whilst nearly two-fifths (38 per cent) are maintaining an upward move in the occupational hierarchy begun by their fathers who were the sons of manual workers. The picture is similar in the case of women teachers, except that the proportion of the two-generation established lower-middle-class families is higher, and the figures for the other groups correspondingly lower.

To make the comparison with the national population, we need first to examine the distribution of the occupations of teachers' grandfathers and fathers set out in Table 2.

An asterisk indicates in each column those percentages that are significantly greater than the corresponding percentage in the companion column. We can see from the figures relating to both men and women that among teachers' grandfathers, as compared with their fathers, there were significantly more farmers, more small employers and workers on own account, and more semi- and unskilled manual workers; and among their

Table 2.

The Occupations of Teachers' Fathers Compared with Those of Their Paternal Grandfathers

	MEN		WOMEN	
	Fathers	Grand-fathers	Fathers	Grand-fathers
	%	%	%	%
Major Professions	4.7	2.9	6.6*	3.5
" Administrative	3.2	3.8	3.9	2.4
Farming	2.7	11.2*	5.5	14.6*
Teaching	5.8	1.6	4.6	2.0
Managerial and Minor Professions	11.4*	7.3	15.2*	10.9
Small Business	14.8	18.7*	14.6	22.1*
Clerical	11.5*	3.7	12.0*	4.4
Personal Service	2.9	2.4	2.2	1.7
Manual Skilled	31.9*	29.7	27.6	25.7
All	100.0	100.0	100.0	100.0
N (Weighted totals)	5138	4080	4951	4006

fathers, as compared with their grandfathers, more members of the professions, including teaching itself, more business managers and executives, more clerks and more skilled manual workers. The most striking differences between the generations are in respect of farming and clerical work—the former showing a sharp fall and the latter an almost equally sharp rise in the second generation.

Table 3 sets out for comparison with these figures a summary account of changes in the occupational distribution of the national population since 1901, compiled from Census data. A more detailed statement is hardly possible in view of the changes that have been made from time to time in the occupational classification used by the Registrar General. The table in-

Table 3.

Changes in the Occupational Distribution of the Male Population of England and Wales, 1901–51*

Occupational Group	1901	1911	1921	1931	1951
	%	%	%	%	%
Major Professions	1.12	1.25	1.23	1.40	2.36
Teaching	.30	.40	.37	.42	.57
Lesser Professions	.50	.49	1.13	1.19	2.23
Government and Defense	1.22	1.59	2.11	.94	1.51
Clerical Workers	3.46	3.58	4.25	5.30	6.01
Farmers	2.00	1.82	2.09	1.77	1.81
Shops Owners and Assistants	7.68	6.55	6.34	7.84	5.86
Other Non-Manual workers	3.99	4.76	4.11	4.58	6.66
Manual Workers	79.73	79.56	73.38	76.56	72.99
All Occupied	100.00	100.00	100.00	100.00	100.00

* Compiled from the occupational volumes of the Registrar General's Reports on the Censuses of Population, 1901, 1911, 1921, 1931, and 1951.

Changes in the classification of occupations, especially in 1921, make it desirable to confine comparisons to the two periods 1901–11 and 1921–51, except in the case of the figures for clerical workers, which are comparable for the period 1901–21 and 1931–51. (In 1931 clerks in government service were removed from the "government and defense" to the "Clerical" category.)

In 1951, the composition of the "manual" category was slightly changed. A small number of employers and persons working on their own account in industry (1.5 per cent) were included in it, and managers in industry (1.86 per cent) were transferred to the "other non-manual" category.

evitably conceals a number of important minor movements (in particular, the growth in the relative strength within the manual group of skilled as against the semi- and unskilled grades); but it brings out clearly the marked growth over the past half-century of the professional, clerical, and civil-service occupations; the increase in other non-manual occupations, such as business management, entertainment, transport, and communications; and the virtually unchanged proportion of farmers and of shopkeepers and shop assistants in the occupied population. In Table 4, these movements are expressed as index numbers and set against the changes described above (Table 2) in the occupational distribution of teachers' fathers and grandfathers.

It seems clear that the major changes between the generations in the case of teachers' families—the marked decline in farming in the first, and the rise of clerking and teaching in the second—are in excess of the corresponding movements in the national population and are peculiar to teachers' families. The smaller movements, into the professions and out of the manual group as a whole, seem to be more or less accounted for by changes in the national structure.

Table 4.

Changes in the Occupational Distribution of the National Population, Compared with Changes over Two Generations in Teachers' Families*

	OCCUPIED POPULATION (MALE) ENGLAND AND WALES		TEACHERS' FAMILIES Father/Paternal Grandfathers	
Occupation	1911/1901	1951/1921	Men Teachers	Women Teachers
Major Professions	112	192	162	189
Teachers	133	154	415	265
Clerks	123	113	312	273
Farmers	91	87	24	38
Manual Workers	100	93	74	92

*The distributions set out in Tables 2 and 3 are expressed as index numbers summarising the changes over time in each case; i.e., the earlier figure = 100.

However, it is possible to make a closer analysis of the manual group, distinguishing semi- and unskilled from skilled workers, by making use of information concerning the occupations followed by the fathers of a random sample of the national population, which was collected in the course of the inquiry into social mobility in Britain, undertaken at the London School of Economics in 1949.[2] The men in this national sample who were born before 1899, and who in 1933 were therefore on average 42 years old, although somewhat younger than the fathers of teachers in our sample, form a reasonably comparable group; and the occupations followed by their fathers may fairly be compared, as representative of the national population, with those followed by our teachers' grandfathers. Although the classification into status categories used in the survey of social mobility does not in general compare closely with our own occupational classification, a direct comparison is possible in respect of skilled workers on the one hand, and semi- and unskilled workers on the other. It is set out in Table 5, from which it will be seen that the movement of teachers' fathers out of these manual grades was in fact very much more marked than at the national level.

Of teachers' fathers coming from the families of skilled workers, only 7–8 per cent had failed to maintain their fathers' occupational grading—becoming semi- or unskilled manual workers—as compared with 32 per cent in the population as a whole at this social level. Rather more than in the national population had remained at their fathers' occupational level—42–47 per cent as compared with 39 per cent; and far more had bettered themselves—46–50 per cent took up non-manual occupations, as compared with only 29 per cent of the general population of skilled workers' sons. The same pattern holds for teachers' fathers who came from the families of

Table 5.

Changes in Occupational Status Between Generations: Teachers' Fathers Compared with a Random Sample of the National Population

A MEN TEACHERS

Occupations of Paternal Grandfathers	Fathers' Occupations				
	Non-manual	Skilled Manual	Semi- and Unskilled Manual	All	N
	%	%	%	%	
Non-manual	71	22	7	100	2219
Skilled manual	46	47	7	100	1181
Semi- and unskilled manual	40	30	30	100	630

B WOMEN TEACHERS

	Non-manual	Skilled Manual	Semi- and Unskilled Manual	All	N
	%	%	%	%	
Non-manual	76	21	3	100	2637
Skilled manual	50	42	8	100	972
Semi- and unskilled manual	42	33	26	100	397

C MEN BORN BEFORE 1899*

Fathers' Occupations	Occupations in 1949				
	Non-manual	Skilled Manual	Semi- and Unskilled Manual	All	N
	%	%	%	%	
Non-manual	60	23	17	100	458
Skilled manual	29	39	32	100	450
Semi- and unskilled manual	16	29	55	100	270

* Random sample of the national population, June, 1949. Occupational classification on the "Hall-Jones" scale for the social grading of occupations. See Glass, op. cit.

semi- or unskilled workers. A far smaller proportion than in the relevant national population—30–33 per cent as compared with 55 per cent—had failed to improve on their fathers' status and remained semi- or unskilled workers; and a far higher proportion—40–42 per cent as compared with 16 per cent—had made the considerable jump over the skilled manual grade into non-manual occupations of one kind or another.

Recruitment to teaching must always be selective, and not at random from the population at large, since a minimum educational qualification is always a condition of entry. We turn next to describe the social basis of recruitment since 1920, taking the educational factor fully into account. Evidently, however, selection has its roots farther back in the history of teachers' families, which, already two generations ago, were in process of social mobility to a greater extent than the rest of the population affected only by general changes in the occupational structure. Almost half of the present-day teachers are descended from working-class grandfathers whose sons showed a far more marked propensity to move upward in the social scale than the rest of their class. And far more than would be expected—some six or seven times as many—having regard to the strength of the farming community in the national population at the time, are descended from grandfather farmers.

Recent Changes in the Social Basis of Recruitment to Teaching

Teaching undoubtedly served as an important avenue of social mobility in the late nineteenth century and the early twentieth century. We have seen it exercise a very strong pull on the sons of working-class families, both between and across the generations. We cannot, unfortunately, be more precise about these earlier movements; we cannot say just how great the attraction of teaching was, or compare it in this respect with, for instance, clerical work. For the more recent period, however, we can attempt a fuller picture. We can show what changes there have been in the social origins of recruits to teaching since 1920, and we can relate these changes to the demand for, and supply of, teachers—to the growth of the profession and the increased supply of potential teachers created by the increase of secondary schooling and the lengthening of school life.

By dividing our sample according to the date at which teachers entered the profession, we can examine changes in the social origins of recruits at various periods.[3] Table 6 sets out the social origins of entrants by decades. As it seemed likely that the effect of the special postwar schemes of recruitment would be to distort the picture we need to form of trends in recruitment through the normal channels of training colleges and university departments of education, alternative figures are provided for the post-1945 entry, showing the distribution when emergency-trained teachers[4] are excluded from the calculations.

The proportion of working-class *men* in the entry through normal channels (i.e., excluding emergency-trained recruits) has been 40 per cent, or just under, for all periods except 1930–9, when it was 45 per cent. Since 1945, the entry through these channels from families in the intermediate (broadly speaking, lower-middle class) group has risen markedly—from 47.6 per cent prewar to 51.8 per cent postwar. But the immediate effect of this change on the social composition of the profession as a whole is less than might be supposed, since more than half the men teachers serving in 1955 had been recruited under the postwar emergency-training scheme and included a much higher proportion of working-class men than did the entry through normal channels.

The case of *women* is different. In the period 1930–39, the proportion of lower-middle-class girls in the entry was at its highest—58.1 per cent;

Table 6.
Social Origins of Teachers Entering the Profession
at Various Periods

Period of Entry to Teaching	FATHER'S OCCUPATION WHEN TEACHER LEFT SCHOOL				
	Professional & Administrative	Inter- mediate	Manual	All	(N)*
a) MEN	%	%	%	%	
Before 1919	11.3	49.5	39.2	100.0	218
1920–29	11.5	49.1	39.4	100.0	896
1930–39	7.0	47.6	45.4	100.0	1120
1940–44	10.3	49.1	40.6	100.0	124
After 1945					
(a) Total postwar entry	7.0	49.8	43.2	100.0	2733
(b) Emergency-trained teachers excluded	8.0	51.8	40.2	100.0	1942
All	8.3	49.5	42.2	100.0	7033
b) WOMEN					
Before 1919	10.9	56.2	32.8	100.0	352
1920–29	10.2	51.3	38.5	100.0	948
1930–39	9.0	58.1	32.9	100.0	970
1940–44	10.0	56.3	33.8	100.0	451
After 1945					
(a) Total postwar entry	11.2	52.6	36.2	100.0	2147
(b) Emergency-trained teachers excluded	10.6	54.0	35.4	100.0	1973
All	11.2	54.2	34.6	100.0	6841

* Weighted totals.

and the proportions of girls from both working-class and middle-class (professional and managerial) families were at their lowest—32.9 and 9 per cent respectively. Since 1945, the lower-middle-class entry through normal channels has fallen sharply—to 53.6 per cent; and the proportions of both working-class and middle-class recruits have risen. The influence of these immediate postwar changes on the social composition of the profession as a whole is greater than might appear, since some 45 per cent of women teachers serving in 1955 had entered teaching after the war, but very few through the emergency-training scheme.

These changes in the social composition of recruits to teaching bear no simple relation to the growth of the profession. Expansion has not necessarily been effected by means of an increased proportion of working-class recruits. In the case of women, it is true, the proportion of working-class recruits appears to be related to the expansion and contraction of numbers generally. But whereas the number of men teachers was growing in the period 1930–39, when there was a sharp increase in the proportion of working-class recruits, it was growing at an even greater rate in the postwar period, when the proportion of working-class recruits through normal channels fell. Nor do changes in the social composition of the entry necessarily imply changes in the social basis of recruitment. They may merely reflect fluctuations, arising out of changes in birth rates and in the distribution of educational opportunity, in the volume of available recruits at each social level. To get an accurate picture, we need to be able, for any period, to express the number of entrants to teaching from families at a given social level as a proportion of the total number of eligible candidates at that level —as a proportion, that is, not merely of all the available persons, but of those possessing the minimum educational qualification for entry, which we may take to be secondary schooling up to at least the age of seventeen.[5]

This can be done for the periods 1920–29, 1930–38, and 1950–54. Official sources provide adequate information, which is continuous from about 1920 (except for the period 1939–46, when no annual reports were issued by the Board of Education) concerning the numbers of school-leavers and of entrants to teaching. Our own enquiry provides a fairly reliable picture of the social origins of entrants to teaching over the same period, but the difficulty is in discovering the social distribution of school-leavers and university graduates. As will be seen below, we have made the estimates that seemed best in the light of the available information, but our results are necessarily tentative.

Table 7 shows the intake of school-leavers to teaching for three periods, allowing in each case for an interval of three years between the date of leaving school and entering teaching, representing the average length of time taken to obtain the necessary qualifications. For the majority of teachers, training

Table 7.

The Supply of Teachers, England and Wales, 1919–54*

	1			2			3		
	ESTIMATED ANNUAL AVERAGE NOS. OF SCHOOL-LEAVERS AGED 17 OR OVER			ESTIMATED ANNUAL AVERAGE NOS. ENTERING TEACHING THROUGH "NORMAL" CHANNELS †			ENTRANTS TO TEACHING AS A PROPORTION OF SCHOOL-LEAVERS AGED 17 OR OVER (COL. 2 AS % OF COL. 1)		
	Boys	Girls	Total	Boys	Girls	Total	Boys	Girls	Total
1. School-leavers, 1917–26; entrants to teaching, 1920–29	8,095	11,374	19,469	2,403	8,197	10,600	29.7	72.1	54.4
2. School-leavers, 1927–35; entrants to teaching, 1930–38	14,803	13,945	28,748	2,965	6,423	9,388	20.0	46.1	32.7
3. School-leavers, 1947–51; entrants to teaching 1950–54	21,808	21,145	42,953	4,569	10,014	14,583	21.0	47.4	33.9

* Calculated on the basis of figures taken from the annual reports of the Board and Ministry of Education, 1919–54.
† I.e., including "emergency-trained" teachers.

would consist of a two-year course in a training college, although a few would stay for a third year, and the substantial minority of graduates would take four years to qualify—three to obtain their first degree, and one to obtain a postgraduate certificate of education in a university department of education.

Although since the 1930's only one-third of the eligible school-leavers have taken up teaching, as compared with more than half in the 1920's (Table 7, Column 3), the expansion of the profession has kept pace in a remarkable manner since 1945 with the growth in the output of the secondary schools, the proportion taking up teaching rising slightly in the latest period despite a 50 per cent increase over the prewar figure in the average annual number leaving school at seventeen or over.

However, not only has the output of the secondary schools grown since 1945, but their social composition has changed. A far greater number of children from working-class families are passing through the grammar schools and, despite the problem of wastage through early leaving, increasing numbers of them are staying on to seventeen or over, swelling the numbers and changing the social distribution of eligible candidates for teaching. In the past, teaching recruited on favorable terms from working-class families. The absolute number of recruits from other families was of course, larger, but the proportion of eligible working-class boys and girls who entered the profession was greater than the proportion of those from other families, to whom alternative occupations of comparable prestige were more accessible. We may suppose the position to have changed since 1945 with the expansion of educational and vocational opportunities. Does teaching now compete with other occupations on equal terms for school-leavers, regardless of their social origin, or does it still exert a special pull on those from working-class families?

The answer to this question depends, as has already been explained, on our being able to establish the social distribution of school-leavers of seventeen or over at various periods. This can only be done with some difficulty.[6] Table 8 sets out the estimates arrived at of the proportion at different periods of school-leavers, aged seventeen or over, who were the children of fathers following manual occupations.

These proportions have been applied to the estimates already given in Table 7 (Col. 1) of the average total numbers of school-leavers aged seventeen or over coming forward at various periods. Table 9 (Col. 3) shows the resulting estimates for each period of the proportionate entry to teaching from eligible children drawn from working-class and other families respectively.

There are, unfortunately, no figures relating to girls in the earliest period; it proved impossible to relate the output of the schools to the entry to teaching, since, in the heyday of the uncertificated teacher, the latter tended to exceed the former in any given period. However, for the im-

Table 8.

**Social Origins of Boys and Girls Leaving School Aged
17 or Over, England and Wales, 1917–51**

Period	ESTIMATED PERCENTAGE FROM WORKING-CLASS FAMILIES	
	Boys	Girls
1917–26	16.9	17.7
1927–36	20.9	20.7
1947–51	42.3	38.3

mediately pre- and postwar periods—1930–8 and 1950–54—the figures are complete for boys and girls. It is clear, first, that there has been a very sharp fall in the proportionate entry of working-class boys and girls to teaching (a 50 per cent fall in the case of boys and almost a 40 per cent fall in the case of girls), and a much smaller but significant rise in the entry of boys and girls from other families; and second, that the traditional difference between the proportionate entry of middle-class and working-class children has virtually disappeared since the war, such difference as persists resulting from the slightly stronger pull of teaching today on middle-class rather than on working-class children.

The changing basis of recruitment does not exercise a direct effect on the social composition of the annual entry. The proportionate increase since the war in the annual output of school-leavers of 17+ has been far greater in the case of working-class than of middle-class children (Table 9, Column 1), so that the full effect of a fall in the proportionate entry of working-class children is masked by the growth in the absolute numbers of eligible candidates. Further, middle-class considerably out-numbered working-class recruits to teaching in the prewar as in the postwar period (Table 9, Column 2), and a substantial rise or fall in their numbers represents only a small change in their proportionate strength in the entry as a whole. In the event, therefore, despite a reduction of just over a quarter in the proportionate working-class entry to teaching, the postwar entry (through normal channels) shows a small but significant increase in the proportion of working-class women and a smaller fall than might have been expected in the proportion of working-class men.

We can examine the basis of recruitment in the postwar period in more detail by distinguishing school-leavers who proceed to a university from those who do not, as in Table 10.

Table 10 shows, first, that proportionately more non-graduates than graduates of both sexes take up teaching, but that whereas the pull of teaching is greater in the case of graduates on those of working-class origins, the reverse is true of non-graduates, among whom the propensity to teach is stronger for boys and girls from other families.

Broadly speaking then, teaching now has to compete on equal terms

Table 9.
The Supply of Teachers from Working Class and Other Families, 1917–54

| | 1 Estimated Annual Average No. of school leavers aged 17+ | | | | 2 Estimated Annual Average Nos. entering teaching through "normal" channels * | | | | 3 Entrants to teaching as a proportion of all leavers aged 17+ (Col. 2 as % of Col. 1) | | | |
| | BOYS | | GIRLS | | BOYS | | GIRLS | | BOYS | | GIRLS | |
	Working Class	Other	Working Class	Other	Working Class	Other	Working Class	Other	Working Class	Other	Working Class	Other
1. School-leavers, 1917–26; Entrants to Teaching, 1920–29	1,368	6,727	—	—	940	1,463	—	—	68.7	21.7	—	—
2. School-leavers, 1927–36; Entrants to Teaching, 1930–38	3,094	11,709	2,886	11,059	1,355	1,610	2,100	4,323	43.8	13.8	72.8	39.1
3. School-leavers, 1947–51; Entrants to Teaching, 1950–54	9,415	12,393	8,394	12,751	1,837	2,732	3,545	6,469	19.5	22.0	42.2	50.7

* I.e., including "emergency-trained" teachers

Table 10.

School Leavers Aged 17 or Over, 1947–51†: Per Cent Taking up Teaching on Leaving School and After Graduating

	Boys		Girls	
	After graduating	On leaving school	After graduating	On leaving school
Working-Class	18.5	20.0	39.9	42.4
Other	15.5	37.4	35.4	55.2
All	16.3*	26.5	36.3	49.6

* The P.E.P. report on Graduate Employment (Allen & Unwin, 1955), gives the proportion of men graduates entering teaching as 23 per cent, which is considerably above our figure of 16 per cent. A number of reasons may contribute to this discrepancy: (1) the P.E.P. figure relates only to men graduates from the arts, science and technical faculties which together comprise only 80 per cent of all graduates. Our own figure is not calculated on this restricted base, and since few teachers are likely to be drawn from other faculties, would probably be rather larger if brought into line; (2) the P.E.P. report includes Scottish graduates, and shows that the proportion taking up teaching (37 per cent) is well above that of English graduates (23 per cent). Our figure excludes Scottish graduates; (3) the P.E.P. figure relates only to graduates who obtain their degrees through a university or university college. Our figure includes all graduates regardless of the manner in which they obtained their degree.

† Numbers as in Table 9.

with other comparable professions for recruits from the sixth forms of the grammar schools. The traditional pull of the profession on working-class children is no longer effective. If anything, the attraction of teaching is slightly weaker today for working-class than for other children, despite the fact that, if the figures for graduates are examined separately it appears that the propensity to teach is still somewhat stronger for those with a working-class background. Since there are some 50 per cent more "middle-class" than "working-class" school-leavers of seventeen or over, this shift in the social basis of recruitment will, if it is perpetuated, mean a gradual transformation of the background of the profession.

The Social Origins of Teachers in Different Types of Schools

So much for the social history of recruitment to the profession as a whole. At the time of our enquiry, in 1955, as can be seen from Table 1, some 50 per cent of both men and women teachers had come from families that might be described as "lower-middle-class"—i.e., the father, at the time when the teacher left school, was neither a manual worker nor a professional or businessman, but a clerk, a small businessman or employee, or a member of one of the lesser professions.

However, there are quite striking differences in the social origins of the teachers serving in the different types of school. As Table 11 makes clear, this is true of both men and women teachers, although the general "superiority" of the social origins of women teachers indicated in the table holds in every case.

Table 11.

Social Origin of Teachers in Grant-Earning Schools, England and Wales, 1955

(A) MEN

Father's Occupation when Teacher Left School	Type of School				
	Primary	Modern	Technical	Maintained Grammar	Direct Grant Grammar
	%	%	%	%	%
Professional and Administrative	6.0	7.5	6.0	12.5	19.8
Major professions	3.2	4.2	3.0	8.4	13.7
Higher administrative and substantial business	2.8	3.3	3.0	4.1	6.1
Intermediate	48.3	45.9	51.0	55.1	61.5
Farming	3.2	2.1	2.3	2.6	2.5
Teaching	5.3	6.1	6.1	6.2	12.5
Lesser professions, administrative and business	11.2	10.8	12.1	13.5	16.2
Small enterprise and own account	15.0	12.8	16.0	17.0	12.8
Clerical work	10.6	10.3	12.8	14.1	13.9
Personal service	3.0	3.8	1.7	1.7	3.6
Manual	45.7	46.6	43.0	32.4	18.6
Skilled	32.5	36.5	36.1	25.3	14.6
Semi- and unskilled	13.2	10.1	6.9	7.1	4.0
All	100.0	100.0	100.0	100.0	100.0
(N)	1251	1178	897	1209	554

(B) WOMEN

Father's Occupation when Teacher Left School	Type of School				
	Primary	Modern	Technical	Maintained Grammar	Direct Grant Grammar
	%	%	%	%	%
Professional and Administrative	8.8	11.4	17.4	17.8	30.4
Major professions	6.0	5.2	11.8	11.4	18.7
Higher administrative and substantial business	2.8	6.2	5.6	6.4	11.7
Intermediate	52.2	54.8	58.1	63.1	57.4
Farming	6.3	3.7	3.2	4.4	2.3
Teaching	3.2	6.2	3.9	9.7	7.8
Lesser professions, administration and business	14.5	12.8	19.7	22.7	20.2
Small enterprise and own account	14.4	16.6	15.2	11.8	10.8
Clerical work	11.5	13.2	13.3	12.8	15.8
Personal service	2.3	2.3	2.8	1.7	.5
Manual	38.9	33.8	24.5	19.1	12.2
Skilled	29.6	28.1	21.9	16.4	10.4
Semi- and unskilled	9.3	5.7	2.6	2.7	1.8
All	100.0	100.0	100.0	100.0	100.0
(N)	1449	1083	534	1100	733

Only a very small minority of men teachers in primary, modern, and technical schools (6, 7.5 and 6 per cent respectively) come from the middle-class families of substantial professional and business men, but the proportion in the maintained grammar schools is 12.5 per cent; and in the direct-grant grammar schools, 20 per cent. At the other end of the occupational scale, we find well over 40 per cent of the men in the primary, modern, and technical schools coming from working-class families, as compared with approximately one-third in the maintained grammar schools and less than one fifth in the direct-grant grammar schools. Only in primary and modern schools do semi- and unskilled workers account for more than 10 per cent of teachers' fathers; substantial professional and business men account for more than 10 per cent only in the grammar schools.

The pattern is similar for women teachers. The proportion of working-class fathers declines as we move from left to right in Table 11, along what can only be described as the line of the social hierarchy of schools, whilst that of middle-class fathers—major professions, higher administration and substantial business—increases.

The social composition of the staff (men and women) of the grammar schools differs from that of the staff of the primary, modern, and technical schools. But the direct-grant grammar school in turn is distinct in this respect from the maintained grammar school. On the staffs of the primary and modern and technical schools, the sons and daughters of skilled manual workers largely predominate over those of professional people of any kind —business managers or employees or clerks—and the children of even semi- or unskilled manual workers form a sizeable group of 10 per cent or more; in the maintained grammar schools, skilled workers still contribute the largest single group of teachers, but they predominate by a much smaller margin; and semi- and unskilled workers contribute a tiny group of less than 3 per cent. In the direct-grant grammar schools; teachers from the families of lesser professional and business people predominate; only one in ten of the teachers in these schools (men or women) is the son or daughter of a skilled manual worker, and still fewer come from the families of semi- or unskilled workers.[7]

Table 12 sets out the changes in the social composition of the entry to the three main types of school that have taken place since the turn of the century. Although possible, it would be unrealistic in an historical account, to maintain the distinction observed in Table 11 between primary and modern schools on the one hand, and maintained and direct-grant grammar schools on the other. Before 1944, the modern school existed only as the senior department of the "public elementary" school; the profession of "elementary teacher," brought into being by the 1870 Education Act, was distinct from the older profession of "school master" (or mistress), teaching in the grammar schools. The maintained grammar school came into being after the 1902 Education Act, and although movement between the two "systems" of elementary and secondary education was not impossible, it was rare and is still limited. On the other hand, movement within each system was, and remains, common. Table 12, therefore, distinguishes only between "elementary" (i.e. primary and modern schools), technical, and "grammar" schools (i.e., maintained or direct grant) schools.

As far as concerns men teachers, the table is mainly of interest in showing a revival of interest in "elementary" teaching among those from middle-class (professional and managerial) families and a predominance in the recent entry of both "elementary" and grammar schools of men coming from families in the "intermediate" or lower-middle-class group.

In the period 1920–29, men from professional and administrative and substantial business families accounted for 9.7 per cent of the entry to the elementary schools; this proportion fell to 3.9 per cent in the 1930's, since when it has been rising, so that of the "normal" (non-emergency trained) post-1945 entry to the "elementary" (primary and modern) schools, 7.9 per cent were from professional and administrative families. At the same time, the proportion of recruits to these schools from working-class families has declined since it reached its peak in the 1930's, and the

Table 12.

Social Origins of Teachers in Three Types of Schools, Entering the Profession at Various Times

(A)   MEN

| | Type of School | | | | | | | | | | |
| | "ELEMENTARY" * | | | | TECHNICAL | | | | GRAMMAR | | |
Period of Entry to Teaching	Profes- sional & Adminis- trative	Inter- mediate	Manual	All	Prof.	Inter.	Man.	All	Prof.	Inter.	Man.	All
Before 1920	7.7	49.3	43.0	100.0	4.3	64.9	30.9	100.0	22.7	48.2	29.1	100.0
1920–29	9.7	47.0	43.4	100.0	4.9	60.0	35.1	100.0	19.1	53.9	26.9	100.0
1930–39	3.9	45.9	50.2	100.0	5.8	49.8	44.5	100.0	14.8	50.6	34.6	100.0
1940–44	8.7	38.5	52.9	100.0	32.4	35.1	32.4	100.0	9.0	72.4	18.5	100.0
Since 1945	6.6	47.8	45.6	100.0	4.9	48.4	46.6	100.0	9.0	59.4	31.5	100.0
Since 1945 (excl. emergency trained)	7.9	48.7	43.3	100.0	4.6	50.5	45.0	100.0	9.1	59.2	31.7	100.0

(B)   WOMEN

| | Type of School | | | | | | | | | | |
| | "ELEMENTARY" * | | | | TECHNICAL | | | | GRAMMAR | | |
Period of Entry to Teaching	Profes- sional & Adminis- trative	Inter- mediate	Manual	All	Prof.	Inter.	Man.	All	Prof.	Inter.	Man.	All
Before 1920	10.1	54.9	35.0	100.0	21.2	45.6	33.3	100.0	21.5	68.2	10.3	100.0
1920–29	8.5	50.2	41.3	100.0	22.2	67.0	10.8	100.0	26.5	61.8	11.7	100.0
1930–39	6.7	58.3	35.0	100.0	17.9	50.3	31.8	100.0	23.1	59.3	17.6	100.0
1940–44	7.7	56.2	36.0	100.0	3.8	69.2	26.9	100.0	19.9	55.9	24.2	100.0
Since 1945	10.7	50.9	38.4	100.0	16.9	57.5	25.4	100.0	15.0	64.7	20.2	100.0
Since 1945 (excl. emergency trained)	9.9	52.3	37.8	100.0	18.2	57.5	24.3	100.0	16.6	63.5	19.9	100.0

* Since 1944, primary and secondary modern schools.

proportion from families in the "intermediate" lower-middle-class group has been increasing over the same period.

In the case of the grammar schools, the table shows that the proportion of men coming from professional and managerial families has declined continuously since the earliest period and has done so very markedly since the end of the last war. At the same time, the proportion of recruits from working-class families, after rising to a peak in the 1930's has since declined, with the result that men from the "intermediate" or lower-middle-class group now predominate, forming 60 per cent of the entry to the grammar schools.

The origins of men entering technical schools do not appear to have changed to any extent worth noting since the 1930's, when the proportion of men from working-class families began to increase.

The case of women is, as may be expected, slightly different. There is the same tendency for the proportion of girls entering the "elementary" schools from professional and managerial families to increase in the recent entries, though the proportion has never risen as high, nor fallen as low, as in the case of the men. The proportion of working-class girls entering the grammar schools has risen steadily but undramatically since the earliest period, but has never been as large as in the case of the men, whereas the proportion of girls from professional and managerial families has fallen after reaching its peak in the 1920's, but again, has never been as small as in the case of the men.

This picture of the changes in the pattern of recruitment to the various types of school lends some support to the view that there is a breaking down of "caste" lines between the different types of school and more resemblance than hitherto in the social background of the teachers in them. In all types of school, the largest group of teachers entering is now drawn from non-manual families. This has always been the case for the grammar schools, but is a more recent development for other schools. In the grammar schools, furthermore, the trend is away from the middle-class background of a sizeable minority of the recruits in the earliest period, toward the predominantly lower-middle-class background of other non-manual families in the period since 1939.

NOTES

1. A randomly selected sample of 12,500 teachers, stratified by sex and type of school, were approached in May, 1955, by means of a postal questionnaire. A subsample of non-respondents was subsequently interviewed and the final total of 8,516 completed schedules was established as representative of the total population of teachers from which the sample had been drawn. In addition to the questions concerning the social origins, and the educational and occupational history of teachers and members of their families, the schedule contained questions on the present conditions of teachers—salaries and income from other sources; family circumstances— marital status, number and status of dependants; motives for joining the profession; and teachers' satisfactions and dissatisfactions with various aspects of their professional life.

2. See D. V. Glass (ed.), *Social Mobility in Britain* (London: Routledge and Kegan Paul, 1954).

3. It should be made clear, however, that the sample of teachers serving in 1955, on which the survey is based, represents only a remnant of all those who at any time in the past entered the profession—it represents those who remained teachers and neither retired, left on getting married, nor took up other occupations. We have no means of discovering how far it is properly representative of entrants at various periods, and we are obliged to work on the not unreasonable assumption that the likelihood that a teacher will leave teaching, get married, or retire, is not affected by his or her social class.

4. Special training courses were created immediately after World War II to alleviate the acute shortage of teachers in Britain. Suitable recruits were given teacher training in one year (eds.).

5. It is evident that very few boys and girls leaving school below this age enter teaching, unless after a period in some other occupation, or by special schemes of recruitment.

6. The overwhelming majority of school-leavers of 17 or over come from the grammar schools (i.e. prewar aided secondary schools, and postwar maintained and direct grant grammar schools.) A rough reconstruction of the social composition of these schools up to 1939 can be derived from the information provided by the inquiry into social mobility, undertaken from the London School of Economics in 1949, concerning individuals in a national sample of the adult population at that date claiming to have attended a secondary grammar school or its equivalent. The picture can be checked for 1913, 1921, and 1926 from the figures published in the annual reports of the Board of Education for these years, concerning the occupations followed by the fathers of pupils attending aided secondary schools in England and Wales. A picture of the postwar situation in a random sample of 10 per cent of all maintained and Direct Grant grammar schools in England is provided by the report on Early Leaving from Grammar Schools, H.M.S.O., 1954, which relates to the year 1953.

However, length of school life is related to social origins, and working-class children tend to be better represented in the school as a whole than in the group of leavers aged 17 or over. Information about the social composition of the school population therefore does not provide us directly with the picture we want of the social origins of leavers of 17 or over at various periods, and must be corrected on the basis of the only figures we have that indicate the magnitude of the discrepancy between the social composition of the school population and that of the late-leaving group. For the postwar period this correction is provided by the national figures of the Early Leaving report; but for the prewar period we have to rely on information provided by surveys of two localities only.

7. In considering the implications of these differences, it is worth remembering, however, that they are mediated through, and to some extent mitigated by, the influence of the educational background common to the overwhelming majority of teachers today. Over 90 per cent of men teachers and 80 per cent of women teachers, other than the emergency-trained, received their secondary education in the grammar schools. Some 10 per cent of the men and 20 per cent of the women attended independent secondary schools of one sort or another, including a small number who had a "public-school" education properly speaking. But less than 5 per cent (excluding the postwar "emergency-trained" recruits mentioned above) made their way into teaching without a selective secondary education.

38 *Teachers in England and America*

GEORGE BARON and ASHER TROPP

THE PURPOSE OF this study is to examine schoolteachers in England and America, in relation to the social contexts within which they are placed in their respective countries. Such an analysis presents certain difficulties, the most important being the incomplete nature of the available data. The majority of the research work in both countries has concentrated on the social origins of teachers,[1] the attitudes toward the teaching profession of potential students and their parents, criteria of success in teaching, and the activities of professional associations.[2] In America, although not in England, a great deal of work has been carried out on the position of the teacher in the local community and more recently on teacher-administrator relationships. The American work in these latter fields has been more substantial, partly because there are more sociologists interested in the sociology of education in America, but mainly because the whole field of teacher-community relationships represents a social problem in America affecting the whole success of the educational enterprise.[3] Education in America is a function of the local community, whereas in England, as we shall see later, there is a more widely diffused national responsibility. This crucial fact by itself does a great deal to explain the different position of the teacher in the two countries.

Ideally, comparison should await the results of similar research carried out with similar methods in the two countries. However, we hope in this paper to reveal gaps in the material and stimulate further thought and work. Our focus is on one dimension of the position of the teacher, which we consider decisive—the nature of the *authority* with which the teacher is vested in the two countries.[4]

This approach is adopted for two reasons: first, because the authority an occupation possesses determines the role it can play within the society of which it is a part and its adaptability when faced by new pressures and demands; second, because the understanding of American and English society largely depends upon an appreciation of how authority is distributed throughout the social structure of both countries.

Our approach to the topic is threefold: We begin by discussing the relationship of the school in both countries to two other major social groupings—community and family. Second, we describe the main relevant differences between the English and American educational structure and their consequences for teachers in the two countries. We then turn to the

---

Published for the first time in this volume.

distribution of authority within the distinctively professional organizational and occupational groupings of English and American teachers and their relation to national and local interest groups.

School and Community in England and America

In England, as in Europe generally, the teaching profession has a dual origin. On the one hand, it stems from the needs of what are traditionally ranked as the "learned professions," that is, the church, the law, and medicine; on the other, it has grown out of the increasingly elaborate provision, by national governments, of universal schooling. In both cases, the teacher has always been linked with sources of authority external to his immediate environment. At all times in England, behind the local grammar school have stood the universities of Oxford and Cambridge; behind the elementary school, the great religious voluntary societies in the nineteenth century and, from the 1830's, a central government department (now the Ministry of Education). In America, the situation has been quite different. National consciousness is at least as strong as in England and often more overtly expressed, but the necessity for each pioneering community to organize its own affairs made education a local responsibility in a way in which it has never been in England.[5]

Compare the following statements by American and English educators. First, George S. Counts:

> That system [of common schools] was not imposed from above by a strong central government or an influential intellectual class. Rather were its foundations laid by relatively untutored farmers who established one-room district schools in rural neighbourhoods as they moved across the continent.[6]

Second, Sir Fred Clarke:

> ... the mass of the English people have never yet evolved genuine schools of their own. Schools have always been provided for them from above, in a form and with a content of studies that suited the ruling interests.[7]

The essential difference is perhaps to be summed up as follows: whereas in England it is the teacher who represents to the community in which he works "nationally" accepted values, in America it is the community that interprets to the teacher the task he is to perform.[8] This difference is of supreme importance, because if it can be accepted it explains fundamental differences in the behavior of teachers as a professional body in each country. It explains, at least in England, why the *content* of what is taught in the schools is virtually never discussed save in professional gatherings of educators, whereas in America constant efforts are made, through citizen committees and parent-teacher associations, to insure that what is done in the schools is done with the "authority" of lay opinion.

The distinction suggested is, of course, expressed in formal governmental structures. In England, whilst education and hence teachers are the concern of local education authorities, the powers of the latter are exercised under the close supervision and control of the Minister of Education. For example, local education authorities have virtually no control over what they pay their teachers, since nationwide salary scales are settled by statutory negotiating bodies, superannuation is a matter for parliamentary legislation, and conditions of service (tenure, sick benefit) are nationally agreed. There can be no question in England, therefore, of local campaigns to improve or reduce salaries. In America, on the other hand, the conditions of service enjoyed by a teacher can vary very considerably from state to state and from district to district. One consequence is that there is, unlike England, a very considerable literature dealing with the internal comparison of conditions of service in different regions produced by teachers associations in America.[9]

Further differences emerge in the field of national and local politics. As already indicated, education in England is very much a national concern and, as such is a matter for debate between and within the major political parties and within parliament itself. At the local level, education is not administered by "school boards" but by "local authorities," which, besides being concerned with education, are responsible for the whole range of country and city administration.[10] Borough and county council elections are generally fought on party lines, councillors are looked upon as representing national political parties, and party "discipline" is strictly maintained. Citizens or groups with grievances or suggestions about educational matters can of course use normal pressure techniques on their local councillors, but they face men and women whose outlook is not limited to education alone, but who are firmly anchored within political parties. To vote against a particular member of the education committee means a change in basic political allegiance and, in England as in America, such a step is not taken lightly.[11] This involvement with political as well as with national- and local-government agencies contributes, paradoxically enough, to the *insulation* of the school system from direct social pressures. This insulation is not a matter of accident. From 1870 to 1902, in England and Wales, each area had its own school board, providing elementary schools and schooling according to the regulations of a central Education Department but with a considerable amount of freedom. The Education Act of 1902 abolished these school boards, which numbered several thousands, and brought education within the scope of the all-purpose local government bodies that have since served as local education authorities. There was a whole complex of reasons for abolishing the school boards— educational, administrative, and legal—but one pronounced motive was the desire to "insulate" the schools from popular pressure at the local level.[12]

Conservative, Labour, and Liberal parties alike have consistently held to the view that the content of education and methods of instruction are not matters for popular debate and decision, but should be left in the hands of teachers themselves and of other professional educators. This being so, individuals or groups seeking to "use" the schools for their own purposes are confronted, not by the hastily constructed defenses of the teacher or of a single school or school board, as in America, but by the massive disregard of experienced politicians and administrators.[13] This willing delegation of educational issues to educators is possible because the latter form a coherent and predictable element in the authority structure that moulds English society.

It is not only the size and relative insulation of the educational authority that is important, but also the nature of the community itself. Teacher-community relations in large urban areas in both England and America are different from similar relations in small towns. But not only is England a more highly urbanized country, with 40 per cent of the population living in six great conurbations, but there is no real equivalent to the American small-town life described so often by sociologists and novelists. The teacher is not under such close and continuous scrutiny.[14] What is more, while there are constant complaints by American educators that teachers play little part in voluntary associations and while they are often debarred from engaging in political life,[15] in England teachers play an extremely important part in all forms of voluntary associations, including political parties.[16] Thus, teachers are in a key position to ward off local attacks on the schools and are indeed, as we shall see later, the most powerful interest group acting in the educational field on both the local and the national level.

The relation between the school and the family also differs in the two countries. In America, for the most part, the parents hand over their child to the school system but maintain a continuous scrutiny over his progress. In England, "interference" by the parents in the school is resisted both by teachers and by educational administrators. Parents' associations and parent-teacher associations are becoming increasingly common, but they limit their activities to social functions and to meetings at which school policy is explained but not debated. As H. S. Becker has shown, there is a fundamental difference between American and English practice. In the lower-class schools he studied in Chicago, there had developed, quite informally, an amazingly strong self-protective code.

> No principal or teacher ought ever to admit that anyone on the school staff has done anything wrong . . . for to admit such a thing would be to admit the parents into the power structure of the school . . . parents and other outsiders are allowed to see the schools in action only when there is plenty of warning and a "show" of some kind has been prepared for them.[17]

Becker sees this system of defense as growing up only in schools that are "very likely to be attacked at almost any time by the parents of their pupils, for not doing their job well enough or in the right way, for using improper disciplinary measures, and so on." It should be noted that Becker works on the assumption that schools normally accept parents' criticisms and informal inspection. It is for this reason that lower-class schools have to develop special defensive mechanisms. In England, no such constructed and conscious mechanisms are necessary, because the school is already so *insulated* by the nature of the total institutional structure of which it is a part.

Bolstering the authority of the teacher in England is his own intellectual separation from the majority of the parents. Throughout his school life and subsequent training, the English teacher lives in a world that progressively removes him from the non-selected mass, that places him first in a grammar school in which he receives a grounding in "liberal" subjects and later in a college or university with essentially intellectual purposes. He feels, therefore, in a way not felt by the American teacher, that he has been linked, although remotely, with a world of scholarship, both literary and scientific, which gives him authority in dealing with parents, businessmen, and others, and with their possible criticisms or suggestions relating to his work. In large measure he is right in his assumption since, in England, where education for the larger part of the population ceases at the age of fifteen, the teacher will have had more education than all except a minority of parents.[18] In America, he faces a large number of graduate parents with their own expertise. Howard Becker and David Riesman have shown that in America it is the more highly educated and upper-class parents who are most ready to challenge the teacher's authority.[19] There are two other points to bear in mind in connection with this argument. The first is the different attitude toward the intellectual and the scholar in England and America. The teacher in England shares in the higher esteem of the intellectual. In America, the periodic attacks on intellectuals have involved the teacher as well. Second, the attachment of teachers in England to the world of scholarship and their removal from the "masses" have been a deliberate aim of powerful education administrators.[20]

English and American Teachers in the Educational Structures of the Two Countries

Let us now turn aside from these general considerations of the English and American teacher in relation to the societies in which they live and examine the specific positions they respectively occupy within the *educational* structures of the two countries.

The task of the American teacher is to provide for each child an education in no sense inferior to that provided for any other; differentiation in the quality of the service offered is unacceptable in a social situation in which schools are traditionally maintained by the equal contributions of each member of the community. The role of the teacher, therefore, is not concerned with selection; it is limited to the giving of guidance and advice, and even this tends to become a specialized function supported by administrative techniques. In short, decision-making is assumed to lie, not with the teacher, but with parents, students, or community; and it is for the teacher to meet the needs thus made evident.

Much of what has been said accords also with the overt purposes of the English educational system. Here, however, the basis for determining what provision shall be made for any individual child is not his simple status as a junior citizen, equal to all other junior citizens, but his qualities as an individual. Indeed, the 1944 Act stresses the age, ability, and aptitude of each individual child as the touchstone for deciding upon the educational provision to be made for him. From this it is clear that the assessment of ability and aptitude, and selection based upon performance, is implicit in the English approach. Moreover, selection and decision is placed, not with the community or the family, but with the educational system itself.[21] Hence, it is the teacher within the educational system, and not the parent within the community, who is in touch with the sources of authority. It is for him to judge whether or not a child can tackle work of a certain kind or level, to place him in an appropriate group for teaching purposes and, as he moves from primary to secondary education, to add his judgment to the results of standardized and other tests of performance. Within the secondary school, whether it be selective or not, the teacher is able, by reason of the typical structure of an English school, to determine educational opportunities more finally than is the American teacher by the typical structure of the American school.

A further distinction between the educational structures in which American and the English teachers work lies in the differing concepts of the "educational administrator." By and large, the American school superintendent is responsibile to his school board for all aspects of the education given in the schools of a city or district; school principals are his subordinates, and he is expected to give leadership, whether autocratic or democratic in nature, in purely educational topics, such as curriculum-building and the evolution of appropriate teaching methods.[22] In England, the domains of the teacher and the administrator are much more distinct. The functions of the latter are to provide the conditions under which education can take place, to insure that schools are built and equipped, that teachers are appointed, and that public money made available for education is properly accounted for. As an educator, his functions are to advise his committee on the large-scale planning of school provision, but not in developing a particular educational philosophy. Although the "Director of Education" of an English L.E.A. is an extremely influential person, the pivot of the English school system, indeed, is the headmaster or headmistress,[23] who is not, like the American principal, looked upon as an administrator, but as a teacher. The distinction is reinforced by him or her being appointed by a Board of Governors or Managers.[24] Moreover, professional opinion requires that a headmaster once appointed, should be given full freedom as regards the internal organization of his school, its time-table, its syllabuses, and its out-of-school activities. Whilst he is expected to seek his governors' consent to major changes and is expected to listen to their suggestions and comments, he is not expected to shape his policy to fit the educational theories of his lay advisers. His "authority" derives not from them but from well-established sources within the educational structure, notably the universities, which, through their control of major school examinations and their more recently acquired responsibilities for teacher-training, lend their considerable prestige to the underwriting of what is done in the schools.

The division between administration and teaching results, in effect, in their being considered as forming two distinct careers. That is, the ambitious young man in England must decide early whether he is to remain a schoolteacher and strive for a headmastership or whether he is to seek a subordinate post in an education office and work up the administrative hierarchy. It is virtually unknown for a headmaster, for example, to be appointed to a senior administrative post, as it would be felt that his experience was inappropriate. It should be noted, however, that the teaching profession has been sufficiently influential to insist that *senior* administrative officers should have had some actual teaching experience early in their careers.

The third aspect of the educational structure is more difficult to define. In America, there is on the one hand the world of "education" of the elementary schools, the high schools, and the college, and on the other hand, that of the "higher learning," represented by the great postgraduate schools and research organizations. In England, groupings are on a different basis. Here, universities and *selective* secondary schools (that is, publicly maintained grammar schools and independent "public" schools) form very much their own world; and non-selective secondary schools, primary schools, and, to some extent, teacher-training colleges, another. There are two reasons for the English situation: the first is the obvious one—that the duality of the educational system, already mentioned and corresponding to the social-class structure, still persists; the second, closely connected with it, is that teachers in selective secondary schools and in universities in England have virtually identical preparation for their work. That is, the sixth-form English master follows the same courses at his university as those followed by the young university teacher. There is no question of him taking a composite degree with some elements of pedagogy and some elements of English and thus being marked as a high-school teacher of English. His professional training will be limited to one year of professional study after his main university course has been completed. As a result, he identifies himself very closely with the university approach to his subject.

Structure of the Teaching Profession in England and America

We now consider the structure of the teaching profession itself, in each of the two countries, in terms of the formal organization that American and English teachers have set up to defend and promote their general and specific interests.

In America, there is a sharp line to be drawn between the *education association* and the *teachers union*. The former brings together teachers, principals, superintendents, and other professional workers within local and state units; and the great majority of such regional associations form the vast federal structure known as the National Education Association.[25] The teachers unions in America, of which the leading example is the American Federation of Teachers, are more specifically concerned with salaries, superannuation, and other matters relating to conditions of service. Moreover, superintendents are excluded from membership, and the participation of principals and other supervisory personnel is carefully legislated. Most important of all, the American Federation of Teachers is affiliated with the trade-union movement as a whole, in the form of the Combined American Federation of Labor and the Congress of Industrial Organizations.

Developments in England have taken a very different course, partly because of the more readily accepted separation of teaching and administrative functions already discussed and partly because the local administrator emerged after the teachers had already organized themselves.[26]

While teachers in the higher selective forms of secondary education still belong to separate and independent associations for headmasters and headmistresses, assistant masters and assistant mistresses, the National Union of Teachers, which is open to all teachers, is by far the largest of the professional associations. There are separate and distinct associations for teachers engaged in various forms of further education and for lecturers in teacher-training institutions. These separate associations do for particular purposes act in coalition and concert. Administrative officers have their own associations.

Despite its name, the National Union of Teachers is not a trade union and is not affiliated with the trade-union movement nor are any of the other teacher associations. Nevertheless, they all draw to a considerable extent upon the "authority" that underlies the concept of trade unionism and that grows out of the assumption that the conditions of service of workers should be settled by collective bargaining. The nationwide salary scales are settled by negotiations between representatives of the main teacher associations and representatives of the local education authorities, subject to the approval of the Minister of Education.

Teachers in the Social Structure

Through their membership in voluntary associations, political parties, local councils (both as elected members and as co-opted members of education committees),[27] and parliament, teachers are strategically placed in Great Britain to represent the views of their profession. The other great interest groups, which play such an important part in American education —business, labor, religious, and patriotic groups[28]—play a different role in England. Business is of course strongly represented in the Conservative party and labor in the Labour party and businessmen and trade unionists will be found in almost all education committees. Both the Federation of British Industries and the Trades Union Congress have, in the past, developed schemes for educational reconstruction, including even curriculum reforms, and pressed them on political parties and governments. But apart from this they have never sought to interfere with the day-to-day work of individual schools. The Church of England was sufficiently influential, because of its constitutional status, to contend, throughout the nineteenth century, with public bodies for the control of a wide area of elementary education. Even during the period leading up to the passing of the 1944 Education Act it was strong enough to insist on an extension of the teaching of "undenominational" religion in every grant aided school. In schools under the control of the religious bodies (Anglican, Catholic, or Jewish), 75 per cent of capital investment and all running expenses are provided by the state, and religious tests can be imposed on a proportion, but not all, of the teachers. In the publicly provided school (65 per cent of the whole) the conscience rights of teachers occupying all positions are fully secured, but the position of a head teacher is a delicate one since an "act of worship" is required daily, by law, in every school, and is part of the assembly invariably presided over by the headmaster or headmistress. In many schools, and particularly in those with long-standing religious connections, the headmaster or headmistress accepts considerable responsibility for the religious instruction of the older pupils and even prepares them for entry into, or confirmation in, a church. This aspect of the professional life of the teacher in England has no counterpart in the case of the American public-school teacher. The relationship between teachers and the church have not always been amicable, but after the religious settlement of the 1944 Act a state of affairs appears to have been reached where the teacher draws upon the authority of the church while remaining independent of it. Finally, one should note the almost complete absence of pressure from patriotic associations. There have been minor incidents concerning Communist teachers and attempts to strengthen teaching of commonwealth history but these pressures have been far less serious in the life of the English teacher than the American.

The greater authority of the teachers in the English educational structure and their insulation from external pressures is reflected in the classroom situation. There is less need for the British teacher to seek the consensus of his pupils. Parents are either active or passive supporters of teachers in their disciplinary problems, and in the selective grammar schools the system of external public examinations unites teachers and pupils in a common effort to outwit the examiners. Inside the English school there is a gradual drawing of boys and girls, according to age and capacity, into the core of authority within each school. The younger children are given responsibility for things (e.g., duster and chalk); and the older, for the behavior of younger children (e.g., as prefects), or for organizations (e.g., teams and clubs). This differs from the American approach, which rather seeks to minimize age and status differences and to emphasize *sharing* in the *making* of authority through group decisions, rather than to emphasize the *distribution* of authority drawn from custom and tradition. The English teacher is far more cautious in the place that he accords to school and form councils as authority-creating instruments.

As earlier suggested, what has been attempted in this discussion is an examination of the English and American teacher seen within three overlapping frames of reference in which their relationship to major sources of social, educational, and professional authority may be studied. It is true that such an approach obscures the dynamic role of education in relation to social change in modern society. On the other hand, preliminary analysis of this nature is essential if detailed empirical studies are to be effectively planned and interpreted.

NOTES

1. In the not far distant past the term "teacher" in England (at least as far as men were concerned) was associated with the elementary school system and its offshoots. Now, however, and in this study, it is used to cover all teachers in primary and secondary schools of whatever kind. In America, on the other hand, "teacher" has always had a more general significance and it may be necessary to point out that its use here does not embrace teachers in universities, colleges, and other institutions of higher education.

2. See "The Sociology of Education: A Trend Report and Bibliography," *Current Sociology,* VIII (1958), No. 3, 189–91, 224–5, for a bibliography and review of the literature.

3. "The public schools in American society are among our most locally centered, indigenous social institutions. In spite of increasing state and federal financial support, the schools generally remain locally controlled and extremely sensitive to local

public opinion." G. W. Blackwell, "A Sociologist on School-Community Relationships," *Annals of the American Academy of Political and Social Science,* CCCII (Nov., 1955), 134.

4. We are using "authority" in the same sense as H. A. Simon in *Administrative Behavior* (New York: Macmillan Co., 1954) pp. 125–28. " 'Authority' may be defined as the power to make decisions which guide the actions of another. . . . We shall use 'authority' broadly, and comprehend under it all situations where suggestions are accepted without any critical review or consideration." See also E. C. Hughes, *Men and their Work* (Glencoe, Ill.: Free Press, 1958), chap. vi, who distinguishes between "licence" and "mandate"—"an occupation consists, in part, of a successful claim of some people to *licence* to carry out certain activities which others may not, and to do so in exchange for money, goods or services. Those who have such licence will, if they have any sense of self-consciousness and solidarity, also claim a *mandate* to define what is proper conduct of others toward the matters concerned with their work."

5. This generalization would not hold good in other parts of the United Kingdom. For example, Scottish education, though now highly centralized, was at one time very much the concern of each individual parish.

6. George S. Counts, *Education and American Civilization* (New York: Teachers College, 1952), p. 454.

7. Sir Fred Clarke, *Education and Social Change* (London: Sheldon Press, 1940), p. 30.

8. This is put best by W. W. Charters, "It is possible that something which we shall call a 'margin of tolerance' describes the school-community relationship. Citizens of each community may delegate to school personnel the freedom to educate youth according to their professional consciences but freedom within certain well-defined (or ill-defined) bounds. The boundary is composed of values dear to the particular community. If school personnel over-step the boundary, crisis ensues and community values enter into the determination cf school affairs. The margin of tolerance allowed the school may be narrower or broader in different communities . . . however unreasonable or irrelevant the components of the boundary line may seem, *the community is in a position to enforce them.*" "Social Class Analysis and the Control of Public Education," *Harvard Educational Review,* XXIII (Fall, 1953), 268–83.

9. National salary scales, a national superannuation scheme and agreed procedures relating to tenure emerged only slowly as a result of strenuous efforts on the part of teachers' associations and ultimately pressure exercised on the local education authorities by the central government. See A. Tropp *The School Teachers* (London: Heinemann, 1957).

10. See *Annals of the American Academy of Political and Social Science,* CCCII, (Nov., 1955), 74–99, for accounts of the working of educational administration in England.

11. Occasionally, it is true, "independent" and "rate-payer" candidates are elected to local councils but rarely on a strictly education "ticket."

12. See Tropp, *op. cit.,* chap. x. Also E. Eaglesham, *From School Board to Local Authority* (London: Routledge and Kegan Paul, 1956), p. 179.

Compare T. L. Reller on the early history of American education: "There was a strong desire to have the schools close to the people and not too readily responsive to those in positions of influence and power in government. . . . Popular control was intended to ensure an educational program which would provide a basis for a more perfect union rather than for the enhancement of the power of any one group, including public officials. . . . Local government was believed to be "corrupt," and many people wished to remove the schools from this corruption. . . . The legal concept that education was a function of the state supported those who were anxious to eliminate local governmental control of education because of corruption: it was argued that the state should establish separate and independent local Boards of Education to provide and maintain the educational service." "Changing Scenes— Changing Issues," *Annals of the American Academy of Political and Social Science,* CCCII (Nov., 1955), 3.

13. Note the attitude of an extremely distinguished English educational administrator, W. O. Lester-Smith. "A noteworthy feature of English life today is the large number of associations formed to propagate or combat particular causes. Many of them attach great importance to influencing the young, some even have junior sections of their organisation. They are constantly—one or other of them— asking Education Authorities to countenance their lectures or circularise their literature. . . . The normal practice of Local Authorities is to turn a deaf ear to such requests, but they do from time to time make exceptions to their rule." W. O. Lester-Smith, *To Whom Do Schools Belong?* (Oxford: Basil Blackwell, 1946), p. 20.

14. There is a good deal of evidence that community pressure on teacher behavior is declining in the U.S.A., e.g., "The rather rigidly circumscribed life of the teacher in the community has been loosened somewhat partly because of the shortage of teachers, partly because of changes in standards for the culture at large. It is not often possible, for example, to enforce prewar prohibitions against dancing, dating, social drinking, smoking, card-playing, and similar activities, particularly when these activities are socially approved for other professional and managerial groups. Yet some pressures do remain . . . a sizable minority of teachers . . . do feel pressures and a lack of freedom to behave and participate like other professionals." H. Grobman and V. A. Hines, "Private Life of the Teacher," in L. J. Stiles (ed.), *The Teacher's Role in American Society* (14th Yearbook of the John Dewey Society; 1957). But see also D. Riesman *Constraint and Variety in American Education* (New York: Doubleday and Co., 1958), p. 125; and W. S. Elsbree *The American Teacher* (New York: American Book Co., 1939), p. 540.

15. "Many teachers are required by contract or school board regulations to adjure not only politics but all things that might be construed as political. And doubtless even where there are no written regulations, there may be unwritten regulations. . . . The proportion of teachers in legislative bodies is insignificant. . . . Teachers have not been conspicuously in the fore in leading intelligent discussions of political affairs or of speaking out in support of the rights of others. Teachers have been conspicuous by their relative absence even in such non-partisan citizen groups as the League of Women Voters." H. Grobman and V. A. Hines, "Teacher as a Citizen," in L. J. Stiles, *ibid.* See also W. B. Brookover, *A Sociology of Education* (New York: American Book Co., 1955), pp. 238–40.

16. C. F. G. Masterman wrote of the English teaching profession in 1909 that they were "everywhere taking the lead in public and quasi-public activities. They appear as the mainstay of the political machine in suburban districts, serving upon the municipal bodies, in work, clear-headed and efficient; the leaders in the churches and chapels, and their various social organizations. They are taking up the position in the urban districts which for many generations was occupied by the country clergy in the rural districts." *The Condition of England* (London: Methuen, 1909), p. 83. This general description is still true.

17. H. S. Becker "Schools and Systems of Social Status," *Phylon,* XVI (1955), 159–70.

18. "Both parents of two-thirds of the boys and girls who attended selective schools (grammar schools and technical schools) themselves left school at 14, which was in their day the legal minimum leaving-age. Only 12 per cent of the boys and girls came from homes where both parents had had a longer education than the legal minimum." United Kingdom. Ministry of Education. *15 to 18. A Report of the Central Advisory Council for Education (England)* Vol. I. Report. pp. 8–9. (London: Her Majesty's Stationery Office, 1959).

19. See H. S. Becker, *op. cit.* Also H. S. Becker, "The Career of the Chicago Public School Teacher," *American Journal of Sociology,* LVII (March, 1952), 470– 77. "The Teacher in the Authority System of the Public School," *Journal of Educational Sociology,* XXVII, No. 3, 128–41; D. Riesman, "Teachers and Changing Expectations," *Harvard Educational Review,* Spring, 1954.

20. See Tropp, *op. cit.,* pp. 13–15, 177–78. It should be emphasized that the aim of introducing the teacher (recruited from the working and lower-middle classes)

to the world of "culture" and separating him from the parents was in order that he should be able to act as a "missionary" to his class.

21. Certain relatively minor powers of decision as regards the choice of a school of an appropriate religious denomination are reserved to the parent but not powers as regards the kind of secular instruction his child receives.

22. See N. Gross, *Who Runs Our Schools?* (New York: John Wiley and Sons, 1958), for a discussion of the role of school superintendent.

23. G. Baron, "Some Aspects of the 'Headmaster Tradition,'" *University of Leeds Institute of Education. Researches and Studies,* No. 14 (June, 1956).

24. To preserve the individuality of each school, it is customary in England for education committees to appoint governors (for secondary schools) and managers (for primary schools). Such governing bodies are composed partly of committee members and partly of other persons nominated because of their interest in local politics or education. Thus, each school has its "board," which protects it from undue interference by the committee and its officers, but which is limited by them in its own powers.

25. For details and comments on the American teachers unions, see M. Lieberman, *Education as a Profession* (Englewood Cliffs, N.J.: Prentice Hall, Inc., 1956); Commission on Educational Reconstruction, *Organizing the Teaching Profession: The Story of the American Federation of Teachers* (Free Press: Glencoe, Ill., 1955); E. B. Wesley, *NEA: The First Hundred Years* (New York: Harper and Bros., 1957); W. B. Brookover, *op. cit.,* pp. 260–61; W. S. Elsbree, *op. cit.,* chap. xxxiii.

26. Until 1870, the administrative officers concerned with education operated at national level, as members of the Department of Education and the national inspectorate or as secretaries and officials of voluntary societies of national scope. Local control was largely in the hands of local clergy or other amateurs. It was their dependence upon remote sources of authority and their independence of such sources in other respects that made the coming together of various local and denominational bodies of teachers in 1870 and the formation of the National Union of Elementary School Teachers (later the National Union of Teachers) possible. Similarly, secondary schoolteachers came together in their own organizations before any body of officials concerned with secondary education at a local level had come into being.

27. Teachers may serve on "any committee appointed for the purposes of the enactments relating to education" (The Education Act, 1946, s.10), but they may not become members of the *local education authority* that actually employs them.

28. See H. K. Beale, *Are American Teachers Free?* (New York: Charles Scribner's Sons, 1936); Brookover, *op. cit.,* pp. 60–71; M. Starr, *Labor Looks at Education* (Cambridge, Mass.: Harvard University Press, 1946); F. Sparks, "What Management Wants from Our Schools," *Studies in Higher Education,* (Lafayette, Ind.: Purdue University Press, 1944); W. Gellerman, *The American Legion as Educator* (Teachers College Contributions to Education, No. 743; New York: Columbia University Press, 1938).

39 *Definition of the Teacher's Role*

J. KOB

Prefatory Note: The following essay is based on the findings of an inquiry conducted in 1956–1957, intended as a pilot investigation, involving 82 teachers (76 men and 6 women) interviewed in four German secondary schools of different types: two city boys' schools—one "grammar" and the other "modern"; one small-town "modern"; and one residential "modern" school, both co-educational.

Contradictions Inherent in the Professional Role of Secondary Schoolteachers

ANY SOCIOLOGY OF the secondary schoolteacher must present the specific problems of the profession in their relation to the wider society. Apart from the teacher-pupil and teacher-parent relationships, the principal subject-matter of such a sociology is the relationship *teacher-society,* which so far has been almost completely neglected. The sociologist must locate the teaching profession in the wider social structure; he must illuminate the network of relations surrounding the teacher, approaching it from different angles; and, for the time being, at least, must keep aloof from the play of ideas as to what a teacher ought to be, ideas that inevitably influence his pedagogical role. Moreover, it is important to know how the teacher himself conceives of his place in society. With what social areas does he connect his professional position? What other occupations does he feel have the same prestige or similar social functions? How does he imagine that society views and evaluates him?

Under present-day conditions, and given the special character of secondary schoolteaching, it is to be expected that what we might call the professional "self-image" of teachers will be far from uniform. The teacher's position within the educational system, as well as within the social structure, is determined by the contradictory pressures of demands made on him by others as well by himself. Thus, it is not surprising that the character of the profession varies and that there exists a whole series of different "types" of teacher: the self-confident professor and the idealist leader of youth; the man with priestly paternal authority and the deliberately realistic technician; the cultured man of the world and the experienced and deliberately modest "schoolmaster," and so on. Such "types" are of interest

Abridged and translated from J. Kob, *Das soziale Berufsbewusstsein des Lehrers der höheren Schule* (Würzburg: Werkbund Verlag, 1958,) with the permission of the author and the publisher.

to the sociologist because they lend themselves to more than merely psychological interpretation; they are based on the outcome of choices made possible by the very structure of the teaching profession. Thus, their influence is not limited to the practical and technical aspects of teaching; they determine the prevailing public image of the profession, significantly affecting its social prestige and therewith the vocational choice of the rising generation.

The contradiction inherent in any occupation between professional activities, on the one hand, and the extraprofessional enviroment and leisure, on the other—in the case of teaching, between school and society—is, in the case of the teacher, particularly acute and fraught with tension, since it reflects the opposition of the two worlds, of youth and adults. The teacher's specific professional and functional sphere is the world of youth, organized in schools; his belonging to the adult world outside has nothing to do with his profession. This situation is never free of tension unless the individual teacher is willing to let himself be wholly absorbed by the world of youth and to perform a mere guest role in adult society, except, maybe, for his relations with colleagues and former pupils. This case, which would hardly be ideal anyway, is likely to be rare. Normally, the teacher claims a a role in adult society, a role shaped by the facilities offered to him by his milieu, and by interests that he may already have had as a student. But this role is not naturally given, since it is not determined by the structure of professional relations. The result is that the teacher tends to be socially isolated, a fact frequently commented upon with resignation. The tension may also be enhanced by the fact that the pupils, too, live in a society outside school, and the teacher may find one day that in this wider society outside school he has "nothing to say anymore." Our investigation shows that teachers, especially in small urban communities, are frequently conscious of this situation. This particular contradiction between the worlds of youth and adults may induce the teacher to modify his conception of his role, provided he attributes importance to an alternative role outside school, and if he does so, to which alternative role.

A second contradiction derives from the very nature of the teacher's task, and its ultimate effects have to be seen in connection with the first contradiction. Geissler defines what he takes to be the two main tasks of teaching, and considers them as two of the several factors that together, in mutual opposition, constitute the field of tension in school (the *Spannungsfeld der Schule*), within which the teacher has to prove his ability to mediate.[1] For the secondary schoolteacher, these two principal tasks are the teaching of academically based specialized subjects and an all-round shaping of the pupil's personality—"character training." Here, again, there emerges a double commitment of the teaching profession: the teacher is both scholar and educator. The two contrasting tasks tend to be seen as mutually exclusive alternatives, and the individual teacher has to make up his mind whether to view his profession as a scholarly or as a primarily educational activity. The decision he takes is an important determinant of the social grading of his profession. What other occupational group does the secondary schoolteacher consider to be his equals? Other scholars, or the now considerable group of specialists in education? It is well known that considerations of professional policy and of prestige are important in this connection, and that they modify, not so much the teacher's behavior in school, but the image he has of himself—a fact that is expressed, for instance, in his attempts to distinguish himself from elementary, middle, and other schoolteachers. Attempts to level the differences within the profession only intensify the problem in the eyes of the individual teacher.

A third and last contradiction emerges when we examine the individual background of secondary teachers and appreciate the significance of the contrasts we find. The middle position held by the teachers among the higher academic professions insures that the rising generation is recruited from two different social areas. On the one hand, teaching is taken up by individuals coming from families in the lower occupational strata who want to enter the academic professions. The movement may take several generations—teaching is frequently the first stage on the way up to the liberal and scientific top professions. On the other hand, however, teaching is second choice for individuals with specific academic interests and ambitions when these, for one reason or another, prove to be unrealizable. The contrast between these two bases of recruitment is a decisive factor in shaping the inner structure of the secondary schoolteaching profession.

Motives for Taking up Teaching

Secondary schoolteaching frequently represents a second choice of occupation; this was so for a comparatively high proportion of the teachers studied in our investigation.

To identify these "second-choice" teachers we had to apply severe criteria in order to eliminate individuals reporting merely the diffuse professional aspirations that usually precede any definite choice of occupation. Thus, we classed as "second-choices" only those individuals who had received specific training in another profession for at least one year, or who had already worked in a "first-choice" profession. Some modification was necessary in the case of teachers who had opted in the first instance for an academic career. In this case, only those individuals were counted as "second-choice" teachers who had actually worked as university assistants in order to prepare for faculty recognition (*habilitation*), or whose first choice of subject at the university bore no relation whatever to the subjects they were teaching in schools at the time of our inquiry (e.g., Slav languages, Sanskrit, philosophy, etc.) Applying these critera, we found that for some 44 per cent (36) of our sample, teaching represented a "second choice" of occupation. Occupations of first choice were distributed as follows among these "second choice" teachers.

University career		11
Liberal professions:		6
Journalist and writer	3	
Doctor	1	
Lawyer	1	
Playwright, theatrical producer	1	
Engineer with university diploma or scientist employed by industry		5
Officer in the armed forces		5
Businessman		3
Musician (university teacher or conductor)		2
Painter or commercial designer		2
Minister of religion		1
Engineer		1
		36

Twenty-one of these thirty-six individuals (more than 25 per cent of the total sample) had worked for several years in other professions before deciding to become teachers. The following are the professions concerned, in order of frequency:

University teacher or research assistant	5
Officer in the armed forces	4
Journalist, director of publishing company, writer	2
Musician (university teacher, conductor)	2
Businessman	2
Engineer with diploma	2
Playwright, theatrical producer	1
Interpreter	1
Commercial designer	1
Engineer	1
	21

The group of "second-choice" teachers is surprisingly large, particularly in view of the fact that teaching represents a career in the German civil service of relatively high prestige, requiring a prolonged professional training and a prescribed curriculum of studies. Our findings, however, reflect a familiar experience among students of the humanities and the natural sciences: if, on graduating, these students have already decided to become teachers it is often only after having considered other possibilities or even after having realized, at least in part, other professional aspirations.

The nature of the teacher's professional training is largely responsible for this characteristic insecurity as to the choice of occupation. At the beginning of his studies, the student of the humanities or of the natural sciences is not required, in principle, to have his eyes fixed on any professional goal, however vaguely defined. At the end of his studies, he is still offered a wide choice of professions, and even the specialized student is not forced to pursue from the beginning a definite professional goal. This is equally true for teachers of music and the fine arts, studying at the academies of music and art. Thus, it transpires that the factors motivating the choice of subject for university study may be entirely different from those motivating the subsequent choice of profession.

This difference in motivation is not necessarily the rule, however. Thus, 53.6 per cent (44 in number) of the individuals questioned in our inquiry said that they had intended to become teachers from the start, i.e., on entering the university. The remaining thirty-eight had either had no definite, or different professional goals. The difference in the point of time at which the final decision was made by the two groups indicates the further possibility that the motivation was different in kind. The "first-choice" group is likely to have a far stronger attachment to the teaching profession and its basically educational function, an attachment that may be due in part to experiences in the teacher's own school days. Our material reveals that some of these first choices were already made during the individual's early years in secondary school and firmly maintained during later school and university years. The "second-choice" group, on the other hand, showed a primary attachment to other generally academic or even definite professional interests not specifically related to teaching; the decision to become a teacher was secondary and usually based on utilitarian considerations.

These genuine "second-choice" cases have, however, to be distinguished from those whose first choice of profession did not involve university studies and whose decision to become teachers followed a necessary change of occupation (officer) or of a striving for social mobility (small businessmen, engineers): eight out of nine individuals in this position said that they had begun their university studies with the firm intention of becoming teachers. The rest, however, changed their professional aims for purely utilitarian considerations. For them, the primary choice had not lost its attractiveness but had to be abandoned in face of extraneous difficulties. However, inclinations and interests that had motivated the first choice of profession, as well as knowledge and skills acquired during the first training, are usually preserved and made use of as far as possible in the occupation of second choice, i.e., in teaching. Thus, these primary attitudes and attachments form the background of the final choice of teaching, whether this choice is made with the idea that it will provide an economic basis that will enable the individual to continue with his primary interests outside school, or because teaching is considered as a possible field of application for the knowledge and skills already acquired; in this latter case, the teacher's professional attitude is largely determined by his possession of these skills.

Thus, the primary interests that are not at first related to teaching but motivate the choice of university studies, are frequently and deliberately connected with the social as well as the classroom attitude of the teacher. But this is not due to inertia or to the wish to continue to apply at whatever cost the acquired skills and knowledge, but rather to considerations of *maintaining prestige*. For the whole problem of insecurity, so prominent in the choice of the teaching profession, has to be seen in connection with the relative lack of attraction the teaching profession has for university students.

In an investigation in Schleswig-Holstein into the relative prestige of thirty-eight different occupations,[2] K. Bolte arrived at the following picture:[3]

Rank order of occupations among the group of respondents

Adults	University students	Technical students
1. university teacher	university teacher	university teacher
2. doctor	factory director	doctor
3. secondary school teacher	doctor	municipal councillor
4. municipal councillor	landowner	secondary school teacher
5. factory director	municipal councillor	factory director
6. minister of religion	minister of religion	landowner
7. landowner	secondary school teacher	electrical engineer
8. major in the armed forces	electrical engineer	minister of religion
9. opera singer	opera singer	elementary teacher
10. electrical engineer	elementary teacher	major in the armed forces
11. elementary teacher	major in the armed forces	technical designer

This reveals an interesting difference in the ranking of the secondary schoolteacher by the three groups of respondents. The university students do not appreciate him very highly, especially as compared with other academic professions; in their eyes the teaching profession is obviously not very attractive. We shall turn to some of the reasons for this, as revealed by our inquiries, in a latter paragraph. So far as concerns "second-choice" teachers, our findings clearly indicate that the ultimate decision to become a teacher has meant—quite apart from the regretted renunciation of primary professional aspirations—a lowering of prestige claims. This loss is compensated by emphasis on the earlier choice, to which a higher prestige is attributed, in order deliberately to modify the position of the individual within the teaching profession. This modification is usually attempted by insisting that the individual is "not only a teacher" but something else besides, for instance a scientist, an artist, or a musician. The stereotype—emerging time and again in the course of our interviews—"to be not only a teacher" revealed that the need to supplement the notion of his role in this way is very widespread.

The decision to become a teacher is made, although at first reluctantly, on this background of primary interests and individually acquired skills not specifically related to the profession, a background that permits personal and individual prestige to exceed that of the "mere teacher" in general. Thus, even this group is rarely entirely dissatisfied with its professional position, as might have been expected from the lowering of personal professional aspirations. However, these respondents characteristically insisted on the particularity of their own position; thus, they argued, for instance, that the prestige enjoyed by the teacher in his milieu depended on his "personality" and not on his professional status in society.

In brief, then, the differences in the motives underlying the occupational choice of secondary schoolteachers are attributable to the peculiar structure of their professional training, which does not impose on them adherence to a definite professional goal from the beginning, but permits them to change their goal without significant loss of time or money. Furthermore, teaching does not have the same significance for the two differently motivated groups; and this difference also affects the development of the social and professional "self-image" of the teacher; emphasis is different according to the original motivation of the professional choice.

Types of Professional "Self-Image" among Teachers

In order to summarize and compare the data yielded by our inquiry, we will present them by means of a typology. We need not insist on the limited validity of the two types we identify, due not only to the small amount of material but also to our deliberate limitation of our problem.

In establishing our typology, we paid particular attention not only to the fundamental problems of training or motivation of professional choice, but also to the differing estimates of the relative prestige of various branches of teaching, and to the problem of out-of-school activities. In the case of the prestige differences within the profession, it was important to eliminate as far as possible the reserve of respondents deriving from their fear of being put on the same level as the elementary schoolteachers; in formulating our questionnaire we had to keep this problem in mind. The problem of out-of-school activities was equally important, since in the course of our investigation it became clear that out-of-school activities (not mere leisure) are directly connected with the professional "self-image" of teachers. For the secondary school teacher, these activities are not simply hobbies, they have much more the character of voluntarily assumed professional obligations.

We finally established two types; there remained, however, six unclassifiable cases, and it is impossible to say whether with larger numbers something could have been done with these. The classification of particular cases was made not on the basis of single answers, but by the drift or prevailing tendency revealed by all answers.

Two Types of Teacher

This account of our two types of teacher inevitably involves some repetition. Let us observe again that our emphasis is mainly on the "external" aspect of the image the teacher has of his profession—not on types of educational behavior in school.

The professional "self-image" of *type A* is primarily determined by educational functions. Even if the members of this group do not give up academic university training—mainly for reasons of standing and prestige—their interpretation of their professional role is not derived from their academic background but is based on their being teachers; their specific academic training is relative and subordinate to educational functions. The great majority of this group is in favor of a basically pedagogical training, while a minority criticizes any form of educational training, even academic, arguing that pedagogical skills are not a matter of training but of individual disposition and vocation. Both agree, however, that the ability to teach is based on outstanding pedagogical skills, whether these are due to training or to particular educational talents. As a result, the interest in scholarship is relegated to the background. A number of individuals freely admitted that they had chosen their subjects of study for entirely incidental reasons, mainly according to the distribution of good or bad marks they themselves had received in school. Frequently, they added that today they would choose different and more promising educational subjects, for instance German and religion instead of mathematics and natural sciences. They even admitted having been "superficial and careless students," insisted, however, that this had nothing to do with being able teachers. Accordingly, the proportion of graduates in this group, as compared to the following *type B,* is smaller (9 or 25 per cent as against 19 or 47.5 per cent). They distinguished more or less sharply between themselves and the pure scholars; 75 per cent of them had gone up to the university with the firm intention of becoming teachers. Among the second-choice teachers in this group, the profession of officer in the armed forces prevailed as first choice (four out of six cases). Typically, these individuals insisted on the great affinity between the two professions, a fact that according to them facilitated their change from officer to teacher. Most of the individuals belonging to this group are aware of the existence of another group of teachers absorbed by academic interests. Criticisms of this latter group are frequent: "the academics are the worst of teachers." Some two-thirds express the opinion that scholarly but "poor" teachers are not acceptable in school.

If in our material there was to be discovered at all something like a feeling of "unity among all kinds of teachers," it was here in this group A. This is all the more remarkable because of the diversity among them of specific professional interests. In spite of this internal diversity, type A feels a greater affinity to the elementary teacher than to the scholar. "Only because we receive a longer training and educate the élite is our social status one degree higher than that of the elementary teacher." They even recognize the elementary teacher's "superior pedagogical skills," a fact that provokes criticism directed at their own training. Moreover, about 75 per cent are convinced that they have the same pedagogical functions as parents. "The teacher has the same educational function as any other individual; only thanks to his training he is particularly competent." The social and economic position of the secondary schoolteacher nevertheless introduces an element of instability in the professional consciousness of this group. In spite of "downward" argumentation and of comparison with elementary teachers, as soon as questions of prestige are touched upon emphasis shifts again to the traditionally "academic" aspect of the profession and the scholarly university training. In "upward" discussion, however, i.e., with superiors, universities, colleagues, authorities, etc., emphasis is on the educational ethos and function. Within their immediate milieu, members of this group see themselves as "pedagogical experts" in charge of the education of the élite. In defining their role they constrast themselves vigorously with our next *type B*.

The professional "self-image" of type B is based on their academic qualifications and their specialized knowledge in certain subjects. Their conception of their role is determined by their scientific, musical, or artistic background. The proportion of graduates among them is, with 47.5 per cent, considerably higher than in type A. Members of this group refuse to teach subjects in which they have not been trained, while in group A, natural scientists, for instance, insist on teaching German, arguing that teaching German allows for a better realization of their educational aspirations. Type B teachers, on the other hand, prefer to teach only their main subject, giving up secondary subjects that they would be competent to teach but in which they are not interested. Only one-third of them went up to the university with the firm intention of becoming a teacher; two-thirds had other professional aspirations. Typical of this group are the observations made by some on professional designations. They rejected the term "educator," which they attributed to elementary teachers. Observations such as "we are not educators but teachers" made in another context reveal the same attitude. Two of them did not like being called teachers by other people and said they were "glad not to be called teachers." These, however, are extreme cases. For type B teachers, on the whole, do not feel misplaced in school or as teachers; neither do they express a basically negative attitude toward their profession. On the contrary, sure of their academic superiority, they feel highly competent as teachers, a fact that becomes particularly clear when confronted with colleagues of type A: "The educators substitute pedagogical methods for knowledge." Consequently, type B is against intensification of educational training, which means to him, "undue limitation" and "unnecessary specialization." Or: "educational training necessarily interferes with a rigorously scientific level of achievement"; "Educational training may provide certain skills that are necessary but not important; it may supply some teaching tricks" that are of practical value but not essential to the profession.

Outside school, the type B teacher is usually much more active than type A. Eighty per cent of our cases in this group said that their out-of-school activities were intense, as against only 40 per cent in type A, whose activities were mostly hobbies. Type B teachers seem to consider out-of-school activities to be almost, or at least as important, as work in school. In their milieu, members of this type do not appear as "pedagogical experts" but as specialized scholars, painters, or musicians. One of them said that, in looking for an apartment or a house (a difficult matter in Germany) he had told the municipal authorities that he would not only be a teacher but would participate actively in the cultural life of the city; he added that his studies and experience, reaching far beyond the limits of school, particularly equipped him for this. According to him, this had impressed the authorities much more than if he had claimed merely to be a particularly competent educator of youth. Thanks to his out-of-school activities, the type B teacher is socially more secure. He keeps at a distance from the other branches of the profession; he does not consider elementary schoolteachers as his equals, or as different from him only in degree. On the contrary, he feels much nearer to university teachers. Type B teachers do not consider teaching to be the primary and basic task; rather, they see in it a possible field of application for the particular skills and knowledge that in their eyes makes them precisely what they are—outstanding teachers.

So much for the general characterization of our two types of teacher. As has been noted, teachers are aware of their existence and of the contrast they offer, a fact that frequently induces them to reinforce their own adherence to the attitudes of one type or another. Of course, the respective attitudes are held with varying intensity, but this rarely leads to an approximation to the opposite type. On the whole, the two types have to be seen as opposites.

Factors in the Development of Different Types of Teacher

SOCIAL ORIGINS

Teachers of type B frequently try to explain the attitude of teachers of type A. For instance: "many teachers have become what they are because they failed to realize their personal goals." Alternatively type B teachers of type A: "pedagogical techniques are a substitute for knowledge." Apart from the polemical intentions, these statements give some indication of the different "backgrounds" of two types of teachers. Thus, type B teachers, mostly on the way to other professionals and interests, have, as it were, fallen back on the teaching profession. Type A, on the other hand, is characterized by a lower level of academic aspiration and by the firm intention to become teachers. This suggests that they are in process of moving up socially and that the teaching profession is a stage in this process—an inference already drawn from our discussion of different motives for taking up teaching.

A glance at the social origins of respondents seems to confirm the suggestion, although we have to keep in mind the limitations of our material. In the following enumeration of the occupations of the fathers of our teachers, the pedagogical professions—secondary and elementary teaching—are listed separately, showing their substantial contribution to our sample.

Fathers' Occupations	TEACHERS CLASSED AS:			
	Type A	Type B	Unclassified	Total
Academic Professions				
Secondary teachers	2 (5.5)	3 (7.5)		5 (6.0)
Others	3 (8.3)	8 (20.0)		11 (13.5)
Total	5 (13.8)	11 (27.5)		16 (19.5)
Non-academic Professions				
Elementary teachers	8 (22.2)	4 (10.0)	2	14 (17.0)
Independent trade	5 (13.9)	11 (27.5)	1	17 (20.7)
Artisans, manual workers	5 (13.9)	4 (10.0)		9 (11.1)
Others	13 (36.3)	10 (25.0)	3	26 (31.7)
Total	31 (86.3)	29 (72.5)	6	66 (80.5)
All	36 (100)	40 (100)	6	82 (100)

The distribution suggests that, given larger numbers, an analysis of the social origins of teachers might throw light on differences of motive for taking up teaching and their influence on the development of different definitions of the teacher's role. Even in our sample, the contribution of the academic professions to type B is double that to type A. Most interesting is the substantial contribution made by independent trade to type B, and of elementary schoolteachers, medium civil servants, and employees to type A. These latter occupations represent the majority of non-academic professions listed as "others." The smaller contribution of the academic professions of type A suggests the part played by considerations of status. And the character of the non-academic professions —elementary schoolteachers, medium civil servants, and employees —and their sizeable contribution to type A may indicate a connection between father's occupation and the decision to enter the teaching profession—seen as a stage in upward mobility. The pedagogical function of the secondary schoolteacher and his status as civil servant appear to have acted as inducements to recruits from these groups. On the other hand, the contribution of the academic professions and of independent trade to type B, weakens the argument for social climbing as an influence on the recruitment to teaching and explains in part the large number of second-choice teachers in type B. For among the offspring of the traditional academic professions, teaching is not the most attractive occupation; and there is a considerable difference in character and status between independent trading—showing a large contribution to type B—and the teaching profession.

It seems that social origin may provide a partial explanation for the development of different definitions of their role among teachers, and that it exercises its influence through the motivation of occupational choice. The teaching profession acts either as a favorite stage in upward mobility or as a second-choice occupation for university educated individuals.

TEACHING SUBJECTS

In secondary schools, subjects are usually divided into two groups—on the one hand, the "academic" subjects, including the natural sciences, mathematics, and foreign languages; on the other hand, the "moral" subjects including German, art, religion, and sports. It might be expected that teachers of the natural sciences and foreign languages would tend to belong to type B, the rest to type A. This does not altogether hold, however. Type A teachers considered the choice of subjects at the beginning of, as well as during, university studies as of secondary importance—a fact that they partly regretted later—since they were more interested in educational than academic matters. On the other hand, the type B teachers had mostly chosen their subjects for academic reasons. Thus, the choice of subjects does not reflect our division into types. The distribution of different groups of subjects among the two types of teacher in our sample was as follows: (Where the subjects taught by a teacher belonged to more than one group, he was included with teachers of the subject valued most.)

Subject-Groups	Type A	Type B	Unclassified	Total
German (language, history, philosophy, and religion)	12	12	3	27
Languages (ancient and modern)	9	14	3	26
Natural Sciences (including mathematics, biology and geography	11	8		19
Liberal Arts	4	6		10
All	36	40	6	82

Only language teachers showed a slight tendency in the expected direction toward type B. Contrary to expectation, the liberal arts, too, tended toward type B. Teachers of German were equally distributed between both types, and the natural scientists who, according to expectation should tend toward type B, were surprisingly, predominantly type A.

Thus, subjects taught and the definition of their role among teachers do not correspond. We have already said why this was to be expected. However, we should like to consider for a moment the striking fact that teachers of the natural sciences tend toward type A. Since even today, the natural sciences symbolize science as such, at least in public opinion, it might have been expected that academically inclined type B teachers would tend to choose the natural sciences. There is, however, at least one reason for the fact that precisely the contrary is true, viz., that there is a far greater general demand for natural scientists outside teaching than for any other kind of specialist. The probability that a natural scientist will choose to teach is, therefore, small, since industry and commerce offer him other possibilities. Students of philosophy, literature, art, and music, on the other hand, have hardly any attractive alternative of this kind. Thus, it is to be supposed that the natural scientist who decides to become a teacher, is strongly motivated by the educational function of the profession, a fact that probably explains his strength in the group of type A teachers. Moreover, the teacher of natural sciences may find it difficult to adapt himself to the public image of the natural scientist, predominantly modeled on the nuclear physicist who works in the big industrial institutes; he may find it easier to shape his conception of his role by educational rather than scientific-technical standards. In the small urban communities where this kind of public image of the natural scientist is less pronounced and where there are more occasions for the teacher of natural sciences to participate as an expert in outside school activities, the tendency toward self-interpretation in terms of type A was not evident. (Six of the eight natural scientists belonging to type B came from a small city or town.) A third factor may be that the natural scientists teaching at humanistic secondary schools (*Gymnasia*), where the prestige of the natural sciences is generally low, are forced to emphasize their educational function in order to compensate for the lack of prestige of their subjects. For these reasons, the tendency of natural scientists to belong to type A does not come as a surprise.

Besides, it is clear that the broad division into "academic" and "moral" subjects is not accepted by the teachers; their appraisal of the different subjects corresponds more to the *personal self-interpretation of each individual*. Thus, members of type A criticize the classification of their subjects as "academic," emphasizing the great possibilities these subjects offer for the development of the student's personality. Conversely, members of type B object to the label "moral" attached to their subjects; they are afraid of being mistaken for "moralists or preachers" and that pupils may "misunderstand the academic relevance of the subjects taught," the subjects being in this case German and philosophy. In short, the division mentioned above is not accepted by the teachers who strive toward a different functional interpretation of their subjects; in this interpretation, their own professional "self-image" is the important factor. On the whole, therefore, teaching a certain subject is not decisive for the development of any particular definition of the teacher's role.

AGE

Members of type A frequently emphasized that their professional attitude had been directly influenced by the movement for educational reform. In comparison with type B, they feel themselves "progressive," and we may expect to find this difference reflected in the age-structure of the two groups as set out in the following table.

Age-Group	Type A	Type B	Unclassified	Total
Up to 35 Years	8	11	2	21
36–45 Years	4	5	2	11
46–55 Years	18	11	2	31
More than 55 Years	6	13		19
All	36	40	6	82
Average Age	46.5	47.5	40.1	46.6

In both of the highest age groups there are striking differences between types A and B teachers, differences that suggest a direct influence of the educational reform movement. This movement culminated in the universities during the twenties and had its greatest impact on the age group that today is 45 to 55 years old. Teachers over 60, on the other hand, typically tend to type B. This accounts too for the somewhat higher average age of type B. In both of the younger age groups, there is only a very slight predominance of type B (accounted for by the slightly greater total number of individuals classed as type B.)

The fact that type A teachers have felt the reforming impact of the twenties thus finds expression in the age structure of the two types, at least in the two senior age groups. The younger age groups, however, do not reveal any increase of the "progressive" type A; the "traditional" type B seems to be fairly stable.

The historical derivation of type A from the educational reforms of the last seventy years would in fact have been possible on the basis of simple description, i.e., without data about age structure and without knowledge of the personal statements made by teachers of this type. The "educationalization" of the teaching profession, its exclusive concentration on generally humane and specifically educational functions, are some of the reforming ideas typical of type A. This is however not the place to discuss these conceptions in detail.

The historical significance of type B is more difficult to evaluate. At first glance, it seems obvious to oppose him as "traditional" to the "progressive" type. This is, however of doubtful legitimacy, having regard to his persistence as revealed by numerical strength and age structure.

If, however, we take account of the special relation of secondary schools to the movement for educational reform, we may arrive at a partial explanation of the strong conservative resistance and stability of this "traditional" type. Secondary and elementary schools are not affected in the same way by the reform movement. Secondary schools have always played a separate role, different from that of other schools. The reform movement, however, treats them as if they were only one part of the total educational organization, representing only one educational possibility among others. For the elementary school, the reform movement meant from the start higher status, an increased significance in terms not only of quantity but also of quality and prestige. For the secondary schools and their teachers, the matter was different. For them, it was not possible to anticipate clearly the consequences of reform, a fact that sharply divided opinion among reformers. Besides—a passionately discussed question—the secondary schoolteachers were afraid of being put on level with other teachers, so that from the start the whole problem was obscured by questions of prestige. For these reasons, the secondary schools showed little enthusiasm for reform.

There are, however other arguments against designating the type B teacher as "traditional" or "conservative." What distinguishes him from type A and undoubtedly approximates him to the traditional type of teacher criticized by the reformers is his orientation toward outside school world and adult society.[4] This kind of orientation on which he bases his characteristic claim "to be more than a mere teacher" signals his distance from the professional image of teachers as it is held by reform movements: of the teacher who is nothing but an educator directed by pedagogical impulses. But even if the form of this orientation (similar to the one prevailing in the nineteenth century) can be called traditional, the *contents* are no longer so. Science, the basis of type B, has not remained "traditional"; its specific problems as well as its social functions have been fundamentally changed. For these reasons, even those who class themselves as professional scholars, are remote from the old type of *Gymnasiallehrer,* the reformers' principal object of attack. Moreover, our material reveals a frequent deviation from the traditional pattern of occupational choice among potential academics. Thus, an analysis of the primary occupational choices of teachers in our sample shows that technical and industrial professions are chosen as frequently as university teaching; the same is true for the professions already exercised before becoming a teacher. The strong representation of modern journalistic, technical, and industrial professions does not permit us to consider type B teachers—highly attached as we have seen, to primary choices—as predominantly traditional and conservative.

Compared to the type A teacher, strongly influenced by ideas of educational reform and emphasizing his progressive attitudes, the type B teacher appears as "conservative" only in so far as he objects to reforming ideas and bases his definition of his professional role on outside school interests and his role in the wider society. The fact, however, that he is subject to the same changes as these social areas of orientation saves him from getting stuck in traditional ideas and beliefs. This, primarily, accounts for the stability of type B mentioned above in connection with our discussion of the age structure of our sample.

ACTIVITIES OUTSIDE SCHOOL

We will briefly consider now the position of both types of teacher outside school. As we have shown, the type B teacher cannot be understood without attention to this position. In order to get a complete picture of the situation, a direct investigation of the out-of-school sphere would have been necessary; this, however, has not been done. So again, the self-image and personal statements of teachers have served as a basis for our discussion here. Real intensity and degree of engagement in out-of-school activities could not, in many cases, be objectively verified. But the mere statements of teachers about their aspirations and their more or less concealed desires and dreams may serve at least as indications throwing some light on the significance of these problems, which for a larger investigation, it would be worth while to consider.

Out of a total of 82 teachers, 50 described themselves as very active outside school. They were urged to mention only those activities that were more than mere hobbies or usual leisure activities. Type B teachers in particular deplored the lack of time for such activities.

As is to be expected, type B teachers are mainly interested in those activities that, as will be recalled, serve to confirm their professional "self-picture." Out of a total of 50 statements about outside school activities, 32 were made by members of type B, 16 by members of type A, and 2 by the unclassified group. The statements themselves reveal differences of emphasis on different topics during the interviews; on the whole, members of type B put stronger emphasis on out-of-school activities. Moreover, the differences between types are expressed in the different character of the activities discussed. The following table shows the kinds of activities of the two types of teacher; in some cases more than one kind of activity was men-

Out-of-School Activities	Type A	Type B	Unclassified	Total
Scientific work	3	13	1	17
Literature	—	7	—	7
Conferences, adult education courses, etc.	4	8	—	12
Music and art	4	10	—	14
Athletics, etc., and active participation in sports associations	4	—	1	5
Youth work	4	—	—	4
Community and religious work	3	2	—	5

tioned, which accounts for the discrepancy between the following and the above-mentioned figure. The principal activity of type A teachers is in sports and youth work. Both kinds of activities overlap and in most cases there was a direct connection with school; in sports (e.g., rowing) as in youth work, life and work with pupils were simply carried over from school. Moreover, the personal achievement of the teacher in some kind of sport was important. The three type A teachers active in community and mainly religious organizations put the same emphasis on their activities as the sports people. Again, these activities were a mere continuation and expansion of school work. Scientific work, music, artistic work, and conferences were far less emphasized; of eleven type A teachers, only four put a special emphasis on these activities.

Type B teachers are interested neither in youth work nor in sports. The activities listed in the first four categories and related mainly to the individual teacher's special subject predominate. Nine said they were intensely interested in scientific work; either they had already published scientific works, or they hoped to do so soon. Typically, they were continuing work on subjects in which they had been interested since their university days and which frequently had nothing to do with their teaching subjects. Literary work was mainly of journalistic character. Music meant for the most part the conducting of choirs and orchestras mainly composed not of pupils but adults. Theoretical studies of music and composition were less important. The three artistically active teachers—painters and designers—participated in exhibitions of art, thus pursuing the same end of publication.

Appearing in public, type A becomes mainly active as an "educational expert," in sports, youth work, religious circles, etc. For the most part, these activities are directly connected with school, and his pupils take part in them; thus, his out-of-school activities are a mere continuation of school work. For type B, the case is different; he looks, not for an extension of, but for a complement to his profession, whether for reasons of prestige or of genuine interest. He is looking for this complement in the world of adults where he can develop what he is besides being a teacher. Contrary to type A, he does not address himself to youth; neither does he strive to appear as an "educational expert." He claims, rather, to be a scholar, an artist, etc., in a world of adults. There is no doubt that the answers of type B teachers to these questions should be tested as to their validity, since they are likely to exaggerate the scope and intensity of their out-of-school activities. But in any case, there exists in this group a strong need for activities beyond the limits of school, for activities that can be developed independently of school life.

The strength of the social position of the teacher is likely to be determined in a high degree by his out-of-school, i.e., "social" activities. This, not only because these and the social role connected with them have a higher prestige in the eyes of society than the teacher's purely educational function limited to school, but also because these activities permit the development of social relations not connected with school.

The fact that the teacher is, indeed, threatened by social isolation became clear enough in our investigation. He is isolated in particular from the other academic professions, maintaining hardly any social contacts with them. Thirty-three of our respondents (about 40 per cent) considered their social prestige to be low, a fact that they attributed to their low salaries. This reason seems, however, unsatisfactory. Much more important is probably the lack of structured professional relations to adult society; these relations, if they are to exist, must be created by teachers individually on the basis of out-of-school activities. This is illustrated by the fact that type A teachers express much more readily an unfavorable evaluation of their social position—50 per cent of type A, 25 per cent of type B.

In self-criticism, the respondents frequently affirmed the general social insecurity and disorientation of the teacher. To these observations were generally added some references to the normal professional career of the teacher that was said to "spare him any existential confrontation" with adult society. "On leaving school, the teacher goes to the university and after that returns again to school; with the exception of his university years, the usual teacher knows nothing but school." Several individuals claimed that "each teacher should be forced to exercise a liberal profession for some time." This again indicates the "need for a complement" to the profession, a need that is, as we have seen, especially significant for the attitude of type B.

Apart from the reforming ideas, which are still influential in directing the profession toward fundamentally educational goals, the development of professional consciousness is at least as strongly affected by the problem of the teacher's social position related for instance, to motives of professional choice, problems of training, problems of professional policy, and social prestige. The need for wider social activities is in this connection especially important. An obstacle to the satisfaction of this need is, however, the role of the educational expert, the "pedagogical functionary," characterized by scientific sterility and social isolation, a role forced on the teacher by the very organization of school and its claims on his time and working capacity. This definition of his role is one of the main reasons why the professional image of the teacher has lost part of its public prestige.

NOTES

1. The two tasks are termed by Geissler "instruction" (*Geistesbildung*) and "the education of the whole man" (*gesamtmenschliche Bildung*). G. Geissler, "Not und Bewahrung des Lehrers im Spannungsfeld der Schule," *Westermanns pädagogische Beiträge*, VII, No. 2, 55.

2. K. Bolte, *Wandlungen und Strukturen in unserer Gesellschaft: Untersuchungsbericht des soziologischen Seminars der Universität Kiel, 1955.*

3. According to H. von Recum, *Wandlungen der Berufsmobilität im Generations-wechsel und Problematik des sozialen Aufstiegs in unserer Gesellschaft; dargestellt am Beispiel des Volksschullehrerberufes. Untersuchungsbericht Kiel,* 1955.

4. This orientation is not necessarily connected with "un-educational" behavior in the class room. These are not types of educational behavior.

40   *Teachers in Institutions of Higher Learning in Germany*

DIETRICH GOLDSCHMIDT

Prefatory Note: This essay is based on some of the findings of an extensive investigation undertaken in 1953–1954 in West Germany into the past and present situation of teachers in universities and other institutions of comparable standing.

I

IN THE MIDDLE of the nineteenth century the teaching staff of the universities and other institutions of comparable standing in Germany showed a comparatively clear structure: on the one hand, there were the full professors (*Ordinarien*) in charge of most of the academic work; on the other, there was roughly the same number of unsalaried professors by title and lecturers (*Privatdozenten*)—independent scholars licensed by the faculty to teach, who often followed non-academic occupations as free-lance writers or private scholars. At a time when occupations were less specialized and careers less rigid than today, this second group constituted a flexible element in the structure of the university teaching profession, and it was not always a matter for concern that appointment to full professorships were essentially uncertain. There was a comparatively small supplementary staff, as for instance, honorary professors (*Honorarprofessoren*), part-time teachers (*Lehrbeauftragte*), instructors, etc. The number of assistants was small. The full professors were almost exclusively in charge of research and teaching; and they enjoyed all the rights and duties of self-government.

The position is set out in Table 1 and 2. During the winter term 1863–64, the universities of the German Reich were staffed as follows (excluding an unknown number of assistants): full professors—49 per cent; unsalaried professors by title—19 per cent; unsalaried lecturers (*Privatdozenten*)—25 per cent; honorary professors, part-time teachers and instructors—7 per cent.

Today the structure is very different, as can be seen from the figures relating to the position as it was in the winter term 1953–54. The estab-

Translated from H. Plessner (ed.) *Untersuchungen zur Lage der Deutschen Hochschullehrer* (Göttingen: Vandenhoeck und Ruprecht, 1956), Vol. I, with the permission of the author and the publisher.

Table 1.
Teachers in Universities and Comparable Institutions of Higher Learning

	1 Universities				2 Comparable Institutions *		3 All (1(B) & 2)	
	(a) 1863–64 [1]		(b) 1953–54 [1]		1953–54 [2]		1953–54 [2]	
Academic status	n	%	n	%	n	%	n	%
1. Established Staff								
Professors	723	49.3	1,308	26.2	518	27.4	1,826	26.5
Professors extraordinary (a. Readers or Associate Professors)			194	3.8	100	5.3	294	4.3
Total	723	49.3	1,502	30.0	618	32.7	2,120	30.8
2. Non-established Staff, recognized								
Professors by title	277	18.9	937	18.8	142	7.5	1,079	15.6
Lecturers, salaried or otherwise (Privat-dozenten)	364	24.8	1,130	22.6	275	14.6	1,405	20.7
Total	641	43.7	2,067	41.4	417	22.1	2,484	36.0
3. Supplementary Staff, mainly unrecognized Honorary Professors, Visiting Professors, and part-time Teachers[3]	103	7.0	1,430	28.6	854	45.2	2,284	33.2
TOTAL	1,467	100.0	4,999	100.0	1,889	100.0	6,888	100.0
Unrecognized Assistants on contract			2,671	53.4	1,068	56.5	3,739	54.3
Grand Total			7,670	153.4	2,957	156.5	10,627	154.3

* All institutions of higher learning other than universities, excluding the Justus-Liebig-Hochschule, Giessen, and the Medizinische Akademie, Dusseldorf, which here and in the following table are included among the universities; and with the exception of the private Protestant and Catholic theological colleges that remained outside our inquiries.
1. Figures for the German Reich.
2. Figures for the Federal Republic and West Berlin only.
3. And unrecognized (nicht-habilitiert) members of the scientific civil service and instructors, etc.

lished (Planmässig) teachers are in the minority—30 per cent at the universities, 32.7 per cent at other institutions. In the universities, supplementary staff account for almost the same percentage; at the other institutions they even outnumber the established staff. The recognized, but not established, teachers (Nichtordinarien) form the strongest (41.4 per cent) and internally most differentiated group in the university; although at the other institutions they account for only 22.1 per cent of the staff.

Table 2 makes it clear that in this group the "classical" Privatdozent— the unsalaried lecturer living on private means, free to dedicate himself to his scholarly activities—has practically disappeared. Thus, nearly 60

Table 2.

Teachers in Universities: Source of Income

	TOTAL NUMBER	FULL-TIME (MAIN SALARY PAID BY THE UNIVERSITY)		PART-TIME (MAIN SALARY PAID FROM OUTSIDE THE UNIVERSITY)	
		n	%	n	%
1. *Established Staff:*					
Professors, Readers and Associate Professors	1,502	1,490	99.2	12	0.8
2. *Non-established staff: (recognized)*					
(a) Salaried lecturers (Diätendozenten)	385 ⎫				
(b) Counsellors (*Wiss. Rät.*),	⎬		38.1		
Senior Assistants, etc.	402 ⎭				
(c) Assistants on contract	413		20.0		
(d) Status unspecified				159	7.7
(e) Part-time staff from outside the universities				708	34.2
	2,067	1,200	58.1	867*	41.9
3. *Supplementary staff: mainly unrecognized* Honorary professors, Visiting professors, Part-time teachers, Members of the scientific civil service, Instructors	1,430	253	17.7	1,177	82.3
4. *Unrecognized Assistants on contract*	2,671	2,671	100.0		
GRAND TOTAL	7,670	5,614	73.2	2,056	26.8

* Including 426 doctors of medicine.

per cent of the non-established (*Nichtordinarien*) are paid by the universities, more than two-thirds of these holding posts as counsellors (*Wiss. Rät*), senior assistants, assistant on contract or other scientific personnel —although their posts are not on the whole remunerative enough to permit them to devote themselves exclusively to their own academic work. A further 7.7 per cent of this group of non-established teachers, about whose source of income no information is available, are probably dependent on outside funds; whilst 34.2 per cent definitely make their living outside the university altogether, which is often not conducive to good academic work. For some non-established teachers, the fact that they are recognized and belong to a university is valued rather as a symbol of professional prestige than as a step in an academic career, and the universities must rely heavily for the day-to-day conduct of their affairs on the disproportionately large part played by those amongst them who are full-time employees.

Table 1 shows that in addition to the 6,888 recognized teachers (4,999 in the universities and 1,889 in other institutions), there is a group of 3,739 unrecognized (*Nichthabilitiert*) assistants on contract (2,671 in the universities and 1,068 in other institutions). These increase the total teaching strength by 54 per cent, to a total of 10,627 individuals. This means, as can be seen from Table 2, that of a total of 5,614 full-time university teachers, 48 per cent (2,671) are unrecognized assistants. Another 7 per cent (413) are recognized assistants on contract, but hold posts for which recognition is not a necessary qualification; and their numbers should therefore properly be added to those of the unrecognized, making a total of 55 per cent (3,084) in this latter category.

The university clinics and institutes of natural science have employed assistants since long before World War I; but this stratum of assistants, unrecognized but on contract has emerged as a separate status-group only during the last thirty-five years. They are employed today in all branches of the university. Prussian regulations in 1921 and Third Reich regulations in 1939 directed the whole development along orderly and institutionalized channels. Nevertheless, they are still far from being fully integrated into the corporate structure of the university, although, with some exceptions, as civil servants they are adequately paid. The charter of the University of Göttingen, for instance, states only that the assistant "belongs to it" and that his appointment and the supervision of his work lie in the hands of the institute director and of the administrative head (*Kurator*), i.e., they depend on the rank order of public administration and not on the autonomous academic hierarchy.

As a rule, a post as assistant is not obtained immediately on graduation, unless the reserve of gifted young graduates is severely depleted. Usually, the future assistant spends one or two years on a scholarship, as a junior research worker, or holds a temporary post as assistant so that he can prove his capacity for academic work. In the university clinics this is already the rule. There, the assistants of old have been replaced by junior research assistants, subsisting as probationers and helpers on miserable pay or even working voluntarily. At the colleges of advanced technology, several years of practical work are usually required before anybody is appointed to a post as assistant.

In general terms, then, we are witnessing a movement away from traditional ideas about the German university, a movement typical of modern competitive societies in which career structures become increasingly complex. The topmost positions in the universities—the full professorships with directorship of an institute—are being, as it were, steadily elevated; what were formerly considered to be lower-grade posts increase in importance and value and take on an intermediate status, and new subordinate positions are created.

Viewed as a whole, the base of the occupational pyramid of university teachers has been greatly enlarged during the last ninety years or so—a process that will probably continue. The stratification of the profession has become considerably more complex. As a result of the need for longer training to meet the requirements of increasing specialization, of greater "career" differentiation, and under the impact of the events of the thirties and forties the average age of the component groups has risen. The full professors have been obliged to delegate a great part of their activities to younger colleagues or to entrust them with additional research and teaching today expected from them. Their rights, however, have suffered no inroads, and they still constitute the uncontested apex of the pyramid, a position to which everybody making their career in the university or similar institution aspires.

II

The traditionally cherished statutory order and corporate identity of the universities and other institutions of higher learning, as represented by the university faculty and the senate, is threatened by this growth of the teaching staff. In particular, the very faculties that once shaped the spiritual and practical aspects of university life are endangered by swollen numbers. Moreover, the extension of the pyramid has produced problems of hierarchy relatively unknown during the nineteenth century.

The specialized and expensive nature of modern scholarship are the centrifugal sources at work. The clinics and institutes, transformed gradually into large-scale "state capitalist enterprises," threaten to shatter the formal framework of the university. "The 'spirit' that reigns in them is different from the traditional atmosphere of the German universities," says Max Weber. "A deep gulf exists, externally as well as internally, between the 'boss' of a capitalist university enterprise and the full professor of old. As to the inner attitude, too."

But this is not all. In medicine and the natural sciences and, to some extent, in the humanities, the clinics and institutes have become the centers of scientific work. They are poorly integrated into the corporate structure of the university, not only because of the tendency to dissociation, which is a function of their scale, but also because their connection with the university is maintained only tenuously through the institute directors and such of their staff as are recognized teachers. Even the directors, the heads of department, and the senior assistants do not belong as such to the faculty, but only in their capacity as recognized professors and teachers. Created much later than the universities and their charters and constitutions, the institutes and clinics are really autonomous institutions directly dependent on the state. The faculty exerts only an indirect influence on them: it nominates candidates for new appointments as director. And this is the principal cause of the separate status of academic assistants discussed above. Their growing importance follows from the increasingly specialized and costly nature of modern research; neither research nor teaching can dispense with a permanent group of *aides*—very much the reverse of what Humboldt and his friends thought about the university. To some extent, this is even valid for the humanities; here, too, an increasing number of assistants are employed.

The growth of the big clinics and institutes has transformed the scholar of old into the "chief" of a "state capitalist enterprise." The full professor may still be teacher and research-worker, but more and more he becomes an administrative director, a "planner," or "manager." The greater the cost and the scale of the apparatus, the stronger becomes the rational and bureaucratic element that inevitably impregnates academic work. The "chief" becomes the one who stimulates, co-ordinates, disposes of, and presents the research of his colleagues. Even in the humanities, the old dyad of research and teaching has been replaced by the modern triad of research, teaching, and administration.

Many academics are opposed to this state of things, fearing for the scholarly integrity of their work. They complain about the excess of work, but hesitate to delegate their functions. This reluctance to delegate, and the desire to remain academically independent, are largely responsible for the fact that the dependency on institutes and the modern division of labor in the academic field have not yet found expression in university charters or constitutions.

The growth of seminars, institutes, and clinics usually reflects successful pressure on the state or other patrons for financial support. This may even account in some cases for the departmental differences in rates of development which are noticeable in statistics of personnel. The increasing political and economic significance and the great cost of modern research in the natural sciences and technology lend urgency to the demand for the co-ordination of measures for the promotion of scientific endeavor in all fields. Basic and long-term planning, which would also take into account the needs of less fashionable disciplines, is required and would make much difference to the universities—to the structure of their teaching staff as well as to their charters and constitutions. But we cannot pursue this matter here.[1]

A seemingly trivial but not un-important feature of the present situation in the autonomous institutes is the archaic character of facilities for technical and administrative work. Few academics and not even all full professors have succeeded in ridding themselves of inappropriate technical tasks connected with laboratory and clerical work, the library, problems of budget, etc. If they have succeeded, this has usually been at the expense of younger colleagues rather than with the aid of appropriate auxiliary staff. The loosely federated order of institutes and clinics often involves absurdities of separate administrations, telephone connections, mailing arrangements, etc. The rationalization of the "lower" administration and adequate provision of staff would go a long way toward making the universities and similar institutions more attractive to young academics.

III

The university professor today is highly regarded as a disinterested expert and is frequently called upon to act as consultant to outside official and unofficial interests. All university professors—from theologians to engineers—have to take on a novel burden of extraneous public duties involving them in additional work and dissipating their energies. For the most part, they are neither willing nor able to refuse demands of this kind, although they hesitate to acknowledge them formally as legitimate professional obligations. The traditional notion of the professor in his ivory tower no longer fits the new style academic. On the one hand, differentiation of the occupational structure and the specialization and prolonged training characteristic of the so-called academic professions, have raised barriers between these professions. In most disciplines, a change of profession has become so rare that the universities and similar institutions are forced, in the face of the risk of losing recruits, to offer definite "career" opportunities to the younger generation who today are without other means of subsistence. On the other hand, the enormous complexity of the division of labor in modern society results in the academic being needed everywhere as an expert. The importance of science as an instrument for non-scientific purposes has never been so great as today. In this respect, the university professor—far from being in an ivory tower—is in the mainstream of events today.

It emerges from numerous conversations we have had with university teachers in the course of our inquiries that very few among them believe that their opinion—the opinion of an educational élite—should carry special political weight, as was once the progressives' dream. Events between 1933 and 1948 have undermined their self-confidence and at the same time have made them more sensitive to potential threats to traditional values. In this sense, university teachers acknowledge a certain political responsibility. This is true of other academic and non-academic professions too, but the special and comparatively independent position of the university teacher makes it easier for him to raise his voice and make himself heard.

IV

We have to keep in mind the alternative career patterns open to the rising generation of academics, if we wish to understand their difficulties —on the one hand, recognition by the faculty and a teaching appointment;

on the other, a gradual upward climb from temporary to senior assistant, to assistant on contract, to head of department and director.

Academic selection has always been competitive in terms of the chances of being called to a chair, but the growth of the lower and middle ranks in the universities has intensified this competition.

The longer start, i.e., the greater interval between graduation and recognition (*habilitation*), and between recognition and first appointment, is a factor in this situation of course. It is almost impossible today for a doctor, for instance, to be recognized before the age of 32. The average age of recognition among all scholars between 1936 and 1944 was 34.5 years; between 1945 and 1953, 38.5 years. With growing specialization, training requires more time; but this is not the only reason for the longer start. The teaching of large numbers of students, the administration of a modern research institute, and the highly differentiated organization of a modern hospital or clinic all require—as has already been pointed out— considerable personnel in the lower and middle ranges of the hierarchy. These people are not merely in training, but fulfill a professional function as well. This forces them in a greater or less degree, to do specific work and to keep to a timetable; but at the same time it stimulates their desire for an independent position that is more than merely a training job.

In the humanities, the process of integrating young scholars is somewhat different. But even here, to an increasing extent, the route is from junior research assistant, via an assistantship, to a salaried lectureship (*Diatendozent*)—all posts that demand an adequate integration and adaptation and, with the exception of the lectureship, the performance of administrative tasks.

The integration of the young academic under these conditions easily conflicts with the old ideas about scholarly independence. Alongside the acknowledgment of personal achievement, with the faculty license to lecture, and the call to appointment as full professor (also a faculty function), promotion on a "career" ladder becomes increasingly important; this is dependent on the decision of the relevant full professor or director who is usually the only available expert in the matter. Thus, although the recognition and appointment of a young scholar are still a matter for the faculty, his connections with the faculty have much less weight than his "official" relations to his chief. In this respect there are differences between the natural sciences or medicine and the humanities, where the different faculties—especially theology, law, and the social sciences—manifest a lesser degree of institutionalization and a higher degree of internal cohesion.

In the clinics and big institutes, recognition (*habilitation*) is acquiring more and more the character of "promotion" granted according to "seniority." It is ceasing to be an exclusive reward for outstanding scientific achievement. The institutional framework in which the scientist develops is becoming rigid. To shorten the way to recognition by exceptional personal achievements has become practically impossible in many disciplines, as in medicine, for example.

The appointment policy of the faculties follow from this situation. It reflects changes that have taken place inside the different faculties, and possibly, also, bad memories of events after 1933; and it has to take account of the institutionalization not only of university but also of alternative professional careers. Many faculties today eschew the so-called appointment "on credit"; that is, they are afraid of appointing men of promise rather than solid achievement, partly because, owing to the war, the reserve of thirty- to forty-year-old men is small or altogether absent, partly because the old hierarchy of German universities has been levelled in the Federal Republic. Before the war, Rostock, Greifswald, Erlangen, and frequently the Swiss universities were considered as points of departure, while München, Leipzig, Bonn, and especially Berlin represented the final stations.

Only the colleges of advanced technology and the mining academies have conserved a certain flexibility in their appointment policies, and this is mainly attributable to their close connections with practical professional life. Here, the strenuous grind from graduation to recognition, to assistantship or salaried lectureship, is less important than the appointment direct from industry.

There has always been tension between the young scholar, growing old while waiting in a dependent position, and his "chief," who is often, moreover, his former teacher and model. The "young man" has on the one hand to work to order, and on the other to produce evidence for the faculty of independent scholarship, thereby entering into potential competion with his "chief." It seems to be inevitable that the young scholar should suffer and that his feelings toward his master should be mixed. The fact that today the critical feelings prevail reflects not only a decreasing reverence for authority but also the divide between the generations, which events have made much more pronounced than before 1914. The younger generation, in so far as it takes up the academic life, does not rebel, however, but tries to adjust; and some, particularly those over forty, show signs of resignation. Few try to understand their position, and fewer still seriously try to change the conditions of their existence. There are, of course, aspects other than legal and financial to the problem of academics working in clinics and institutes. Nevertheless, the situation we have just described is less grave where personnel and financial resources are adequate or even abundant, as is sometimes the case. As is well known, the older senior assistants, assistants, and the salaried lecturers complain about the insecurity of their tenure, about their unsatisfactory statutory position in relation to the faculty and university, and especially about the scarcity of support granted by the state: there are, for instance, no funds at their disposal for disbursement at their own discretion in accordance with their own plans of research.

The repeated suggestion that risk has its own value, and that recruits to academic life should be required to accept it up to the time of their first appointment—when most of them are at least forty years old—undoubtedly makes for a higher level of achievement on the part of those concerned. The percentage of gifted young people frightened away from universities and similar institutions by this system varies in the different disciplines according to the nature and extent of alternative professional opportunities. On the whole, opportunities for the younger generation to advance in academic life have definitely diminished. The harmful effects of the acute competition in academic "careers" and of the very palpable form the "risk" is taking are becoming obvious. The enlargement of the base of the pyramid —in relation to the number of full professors at the apex—reduces the chances of reaching the goal of the academic career, i.e., the position of full professor. In most disciplines, a considerably smaller percentage than formerly of young recruits can expect the call to a chair.

The element of risk is enhanced by the tendency for specialization, and the institutionalization of professional careers diminishes the possibility of leaving the university for an alternative profession. Only doctors and engineers still enjoy freedom to change. In all the other disciplines—even in chemistry and applied physics—movement is almost impossible after the age of thirty-two to thirty-five, unless people are willing to accept disadvantages. Older persons have either already passed the age limits for other kinds of professional training, or cannot face the difficulties of adaptation involved in beginning again in another profession.

Specialization and attachment to a particular institute often go even so far as to prevent young scientists leaving one institute for another. Apart from professional considerations, this can be due to lack of suitable colleagues or to the attitude of institute directors, whose consent to any move is indispensable—for instance to the exchange of assistants, so much talked about but rarely put into effect. Experience makes it clear, moreover, that young scholars are themselves often unwilling to move; this may be due to the material difficulties of postwar years or to family ties. In short, if staying on after graduation to work at the university helps to improve professional prospects outside, more will do so. And if—as at the moment seems to be the case in medicine—prospects in practice are poor, but are likely to improve with an extended university course, numbers will be particularly large.

Formerly, when the occupational structure was more open, the question of alternative openings for teachers was less important for the university than it has become since World War I. Today, careers are more self-contained, and the young have learned to follow their occupation and advance their careers with more single-minded devotion than before.

Two important points arise here. In the first place, where there are regular outside alternatives to the academic career, as in theology, law, philology (schoolteachers), it should be made possible for the younger generation of academics to acquire the necessary extraneous qualifications, although one does not want to see them unduly hampered in their scientific work and professional development by examinations and prescribed training periods.

Accordingly, as a general rule, the young scholar should be able to see early enough, say, at the age of thirty-two to thirty-five, whether or not he can definitely expect to remain at the university, or whether he must think in terms of another career. The fact that this is rarely possible leads to anxiety about tenure. Since the thirties the universities have tried to solve this problem in face of the shortage of chairs by creating new jobs for, or increasing the number of, salaried lecturers (*Diätendozenten*) and counsellor (*wissenschaftliche Räte*), in particular for non-established teachers.

The younger generation is, of course, concerned about material prospects. Nevertheless, ideas about the future tend to be rather vague, and except for the more hard-headed scientists, as in chemistry, medical clinics, etc., exact knowledge on this score is generally lacking. On the other hand, the actual amount of the present salary, if one is in fact offered, hardly affects the decision whether or not to take up academic work; and the common view that many able young people are deterred from doing so because it is financially unattractive hardly bears inspection.

Only the salaries of research or temporary assistants and students on scholarships approach subsistence level, and this will be true only with reserverations in repect to age and family status. Naturally, the situation is tolerable only in the short run—salaries are, in any case, usually only on a monthly basis. Generally speaking, however, people are willing to put up with the position for short periods at the beginning of their career.

Widespread complaints about the material difficulties of academics have created a false impression of the financial prospects. The prospects of established university teachers, from assistants to full professors, are often visualized as being much worse than they really are. On the other hand, the assistants and salaried lecturers themselves, paid as they are at civil-service rates, rarely complain about their remuneration, and regard themselves as adequately or even satisfactorily paid. As comparisons show, their salaries are indeed—especially in Nordrhein-Westfalen—no worse than those paid to beginners in any comparable profession. On the other hand, the older assistants and lecturers whose upward movement is slow and generally comes to an end at an early stage, do not enjoy the same income increases as do, for instance, senior civil servants, members of the liberal professions, or individuals working in commerce or industry.

To return to fundamental considerations: apart from personal and material questions, under present conditions the young academic is obliged, if he is to preserve his self-esteem, to get through the early stages of his career as quickly as possible. A marked "career consciousness" manifests itself. There are no intermediate stages where he may rest and be respected, as there are, for instance, for lecturers in England. Whoever does not reach his chair considers himself a material and intellectual "failure."

The pressure to achieve, the need to compete, without possibility of escape to alternative professions, and specialization, are increasingly characteristic of academic life in German universities—three features that are often reflected in an isolation and estrangement of the individual more familiar in large-scale industrial or commercial enterprises. And people are suffering from it.

Only some modification of its hierarchical, individualistic and competitive structure can counter the threat to the German university represented by the disappearance of the *Privatdozent,* the independent scholar-teacher for so long the very core and spirit of its existence.

NOTE

1. Since this essay was written, the Federal Republic has established a Standing Committee for Scientific Affairs which has published a comprehensive report on the needs of German universities (*Empfehlungen des Wissenschaftsrates zum Ausbau der Wissenschaftliche Hochschulen.* Bonn: 1960, 535 p.

41 The American Academic Marketplace

THEODORE CAPLOW and REECE McGEE

LIKE MOST SOCIAL systems, the pieces of the academic marketplace fit together, and its workings can be explained. To say this is not to say that it has evolved in the best possible way and could not be improved by rational planning. On the contrary, we submit that the practices which now prevail in the employment of scholars are needlessly damaging to individuals and to institutions.

It may be useful to summarize in one place some of the problems which come to view as we analyze the data. One man's frustration may, of course, be another's felicity, and an element of a social system may be functional for some parts of the system and disfunctional for others, but the existence of a problem for someone in a social system does not mean that someone else automatically benefits. Similarly, the solution of a problem does not mean that a new problem of the same magnitude appears in its place, although it must be admitted that organizational reforms are always likely to have unanticipated consequences.[1] It may be useful to divide this discussion into two parts—the problems of individual scholars and the problems of university administrators. Obviously the administrative problems of universities are of direct concern to faculty members, and the problems of individual scholars ought to be of paramount importance to universities, but the interests of individuals and institutions diverge in some respects, and it is convenient here to look at the same problems from two slightly different viewpoints.

Problems of the Individual Scholar

TEACHING VS. RESEARCH

Perhaps the leading problem for the individual faculty member is the incongruity between his job assignment and the work which determines his success or failure in his own discipline. As we have seen, most faculty members are hired to teach students and to bear their share of responsi-

Reprinted from Theodore Caplow and Reece McGee, *The Academic Marketplace* (New York: Basic Books, 1958), pp. 219–38, with the permission of the publisher.

bility for the normal operation of the university as an educational organization. These are the duties for which they are paid and which they must perform. Although in most occupations men are judged by how well they perform their normal duties, the academic man is judged almost exclusively by
his performance in a kind of part-time voluntary job which he creates for
himself. Not only does his career depend upon these supplementary efforts,
but there is a tendency for his superiors to punish successful performance
of the tasks for which he is hired. It is only a slight exaggeration to say that
academic success is likely to come to the man who has learned to neglect
his assigned duties in order to have more time and energy to pursue his
private professional interests.

Although this inconsistency is most strongly felt in the early stages of
the academic career, it continues to haunt the planning and self-direction
of academic men up to retirement and beyond. It means, for example,
that the best teachers in educational institutions, those at whose feet students come to learn, often restrict themselves to a minimum of participation
in the educational process. It means, further, that a great deal of foolish
and unnecessary research is undertaken by men who bring to their investigations neither talent nor interest. The multiplication of specious or trivial
research has some tendency to contaminate the academic atmosphere and
to bring knowledge itself into disrepute. The empty rituals of research
come to be practiced with particular zeal in unsuitable fields, so that a
published article is regarded as more valuable than skillful teaching in
such expedient sciences as mortuary education and, at the other extreme
of academic respectability, a research paper earns more prestige than a
volume of criticism among professors of modern literature.

INSECURITY

It is generally agreed that intellectual performance is facilitated by a
degree of personal security. This idea is embodied in the almost universal
acceptance of academic tenure and the requirement of fairly long notice
before a nontenure appointment is terminated. The notion that security is
a special requirement of the scholar is based upon various grounds which
are not easy to evaluate objectively—for example, the belief that professors
are, or ought to be, unworldly men, unsuited to cope with problems of
self-advancement in quite the same way as businessmen or officials. Perhaps
more realistic is the perception that intellectual creativity is often cyclical
and sporadic, so that an important piece of work may be accomplished
unevenly over a long period of years, subject to inexplicable breaks and
delays. As many studies have shown, the peak of creativity is reached
early in some fields and late in others and varies also in unaccountable
fashion from one individual to the next. The ideal of academic freedom
includes the assumption that men working on the fringes of established
knowledge will often dissent from the truths of the majority, will appear

unreasonable, eccentric, or disloyal, or will be unable to explain to others their motive for pursuing a particular line of effort.

Beyond these specific reasons for believing that a high degree of security should be a part of the conditions of faculty employment is a more general theory which applies to the employment of civil servants and salaried professionals throughout our occupational system. The public-health physician, the salaried official, the employed artist, are held to have sacrificed the possibilities of high remuneration and conspicuous consumption which their talents might have opened to them in another occupation, or in the fee-taking sectors of their own occupation, in exchange for assured subsistence which enables them to pursue long-term goals in their work without distraction.

It is ironical, in the face of this consensus, that academic employment is often experienced as much less secure than comparable work in industry or private practice. There are three situations in which the academic man is typically beset by insecurity. They correspond in a general way to the early, middle, and late parts of his career. As the data have abundantly shown, there is a high level of both economic and emotional insecurity during the early stages of the academic career before tenure has been achieved. In a major institution, the odds against the promotion of an assistant professor may be five or six to one. This means that the majority of suitably qualified men must anticipate a notice of termination, a traumatic readjustment, and a new start leading quite possibly to a similar outcome. The probationary status of assistant professors becomes more meaningful when it is related to the previous stage of the academic career. As graduate students, they have been tested in many ways and over a period of years for intelligence, persistence, and conformity. The ordeal is sufficient to eliminate the vast majority of graduate students before they reach the doctorate. For those who survive, the habit of insecurity and a certain mild paranoid resignation are standard psychological equipment. These characteristics are often strengthened by the discovery that the criteria which they must meet as faculty members are quite different from those which they have learned to meet in the graduate school. Even their present experiences may not be helpful, since the unsuccessful candidate for academic advancement often is unable to discover why he is rejected.

In the middle stages of the academic career, the chief source of insecurity is what might be called the lack of tenure in a status. Established statuses and established relationships are very frequently disrupted by the exigencies of the market. The bargaining advantage of outside candidates is such as to threaten, at every point of his career, the man who stays in one institution. Because of the intrigues of the cloister and the sporadic tyranny which appears in academic government, only the most eminent members of a faculty are safe against the withdrawal of privileges which they have come to regard as essential or protected against attacks on their prestige. In a profession dominated by prestige orientations, these can be intolerably painful.

The third characteristic situation is the rapid loss of bargaining power, personal influence, and independence which occurs near the midpoint of the normal academic career, as the professor loses the potential mobility which gave him some defense against local pressures. When this decline is gradual, and associated with the movement toward a peaceful retirement, it may be taken as the normal course of events. Often, though, it is abrupt and marked by dramatic incidents. There is a kind of reversal of normal seniority under current conditions, so that younger full professors enjoy unreasonable advantages over their elders.

INEQUITABLE TREATMENT

The ideal of absolute equity is seldom achieved in any occupation, and it is not surprising that professors, like other men, are sometimes treated unfairly. Certain features of the university system, however, sharpen the impact of unfair treatment. Unlike other employers, who may legitimately base the preferment of their employees on seniority or the hazards of office politics, the university is committed to the ideal of advancement by merit. In a community of scholars, scholarly performance is the only legitimate claim to recognition. As we have seen in the foregoing pages, the academic marketplace as a system rests on the assumption that the worth of the academic man can be measured by the quality of his published work. This assumption is so closely woven into the fabric of higher education that, when men of inferior achievements are promoted over their betters, the resulting demoralization is not limited to the persons concerned but tends to affect the entire milieu.

The most striking inequities seem to arise out of the prestige system itself. The mechanisms which allocate graduate students to departments of varying prestige are far less accurate than those which allocate faculty members. The new graduate student has not yet done any professional work by which he can be judged. His previous studies furnish only the roughest indication of his probable capacity as a scholar. If he is one of those whose talents are slow in developing, his record may furnish no relevant information at all. The new graduate student choosing the institution to which he will apply does not usually have access to any current knowledge about the prestige system in the discipline. His choice, professionally speaking, is made almost at random.

Unfortunately, as we have seen, the initial choice of a graduate school sets an indelible mark on the student's career. In many disciplines, men trained at minor universities have virtually no chance of achieving eminence. Even in those disciplines in which the distribution of professional rewards is not tightly controlled by an inner circle of departments, the handicap of initial identification with a department of low prestige is hardly ever completely overcome. Every discipline can show examples of brilliant men with the wrong credentials whose work somehow fails to obtain normal recognition.

This situation appears to be worsening under current conditions. With more activity in the academic marketplace comes the tendency for more rapid advancement through the hierarchy, which, in turn, hastens the fixation of professional reputation. To the men trained in minor departments, and to those who stumble too far down the prestige ladder in their early job seeking, the tendency for reputations to be prematurely determined is an additional handicap. Only if the lists are kept open for half a lifetime or longer, do they have any chance of overcoming their initial disadvantage.

Personal characteristics may become a basis for discriminatory treatment. Women scholars are not taken seriously and cannot look forward to a normal professional career. This bias is part of the much larger pattern which determines the utilization of women in our economy. It is not peculiar to the academic world, but it does blight the prospects of female scholars.

Discrimination on the grounds of religion, particularly against Jews, secondarily against Catholics, and sporadically against Mormons, Unitarians, and others, operates as a selective factor in the predoctoral phases of the academic career and to a limited extent in initial job placement. Thereafter, it ceases to figure importantly, at least in the major universities and in the major disciplines. There is reason to think that religious identification is a far more important factor in the minor universities and colleges and also, as our pilot study suggests, in some of the professional schools.

Discrimination on the basis of race appears to be nearly absolute. No major university in the United States has more than a token representation of Negroes on its faculty, and these tend to be rather specialized persons who are fitted in one way or another for such a role. We know of no Negro occupying a chairmanship or major administrative position in our sample of universities.

Discrimination on the basis of political affiliation has been the subject of much discussion in the past decade and the central theme of a whole series of *causes célèbres*. As things now stand, there is wide variation in the tolerance accorded to senior professors who were formerly Communists, a tolerance depending upon the climate of the campus and the circumstances of the individual's recantation. However, it is plain that the net outcome of the prolonged crisis of academic freedom from 1946 to 1956[2] is a marked restriction of the freedom of professors to engage in politics. According to some of our respondents, political activity of any kind by any faculty member is viewed unfavorably and is likely to bar or delay his advancement. Even when this is not the policy of the institution, it is likely to be construed as such by the junior faculty, with the result that there is extraordinarily little participation in politics by the rising young men of the current academic generation.

The more subtle forms of discrimination are difficult to describe, and we shall note them here only in passing. Our sample includes one case of a candidate who was rejected because of a mannerism in smoking which annoyed the chairman of the selection committee and many other instances in which the evaluation of a candidate was made on arbitrary grounds. Such incidents are perhaps inevitable in an occupation in which merit is so much a matter of other people's opinions and so little susceptible to objective proof.

Indeed, the vast majority of personal problems reported in the interviews have less to do with long-range career opportunities than with the immediate working situation. The typical professor, if such there be, suffers from his acceptance of an ideology which is incongruous with his situation. He tends to see himself as a free member of an autonomous company of scholars, subject to no evaluation but the judgment of his peers. But he is likely to find himself under the sway of a chairman or dean or president whose authority is personal and arbitrary. Academic authority is exercised largely by means of the personal control which the administrator has over the salary, rank, and prerogatives of the working professor.

This control is essentially illegitimate. It serves in default of a workable system of academic government. Like any improvised authority, it can easily become capricious. The assistant professor who offends the dean's wife at a party may be as severely punished for it as the lieutenant who offends the colonel's wife in a similar situation. True enough, with increasing rank and with permanent tenure, some of this helplessness in the face of authority, disappears, but not before habits of obedience have been formed. Even a senior full professor can, as we have shown, be seriously harassed by his superiors, especially toward the end of his career, when it becomes difficult for him to seek another position. The violent opposition between the academic man's image of himself as a kind of oligarch, independent of lay authority, and the galling subjection which he actually experiences is presumably responsible for the combination of private resentment and public submissiveness that so often characterizes the faculty attitude toward administrators.

INADEQUACY OF INFORMATION

Among the immediate problems of the academic man as he moves through his career, the most striking and probably the most remediable is his chronic lack of information. There is no academic discipline, as far as we can discover, in which a listing of vacant associate and full professorships is available to a potential candidate. A few disciplines practice the listing of junior positions, but even in these it is not customary to list the "good" openings—those which carry more than minimum prestige or offer favorable opportunities for advancement. Except at the highest and lowest levels of the discipline, anyone seeking academic employment is ordinarily restricted to those positions which he happens to learn about from his friends and acquaintances. This is seldom more than a small representation of the positions available. As often as not, his choice will lie between undesirable alternatives while the position for which he is best suited waits around the corner for someone else. Moreover, the ban on open solicitation and the automatic depreciation of any candidate who shows excessive interest in a position mean that information about a vacancy may be unusable unless the candidate happens to have the appropriate connections by means of which his informal solicitation can be converted into an inquiry from the employing institution.

Along with inadequate knowledge of vacancies, the academic man is often burdened by a systematic ignorance of his own situation. In one of the universities in our sample, it is considered a serious violation of university policy for a faculty member to disclose his salary to a colleague. In another, the university budget is officially a public document, but most of the members of the faculty have never been able to obtain access to a copy. In a third, the bases on which a promotion is decided are held to be confidential and are not even revealed to the senior members of the department in which the promotion takes place. Quite literally, it is often impossible for a faculty member to discover his relative salary position, the opinion which his superiors have of him, the recommendations which have been made concerning his future, or the criteria on which his current performance is being evaluated.

Although sporadic efforts have been made in the various disciplines to develop comparative information, it is often impossible to obtain accurate reports on salaries, teaching duties, clerical and research facilities, or the normal requirements for promotion, as they compare from one institution to another. Indeed, even the most elementary personnel procedures in academic administration, such as the processing of recommendations for promotion, are often shrouded in a local fog of "security" which cannot be penetrated by the people most directly concerned. Over and above all these specific lacunae in the scholar's image of his own field of operation, there is a great conglomeration of myth and legend and a singular lack of straightforward analysis with regard to the workings of the marketplace.

Problems of the University Administration

TEACHING VS. RESEARCH

The conflicting demands of teaching and research are felt as severely by the institution as by the individual. The identification of teaching with local prestige, and of research with disciplinary prestige, has been pointed out several times in this discussion. With the increasing emphasis on research and disciplinary prestige, the value of the local prestige which the university is able to bestow upon the members of its faculty tends to decline. This is likely to bring about an increasing orientation on the part of faculty to the demands of the discipline and the outside professional audience, and a progressive loss of interest in the curriculum and program of the university. Among the immediate consequences are the neglect of teaching, the devaluation of instructional tasks, and, perhaps most serious, the gradual erosion of the teaching responsibilities of the senior faculty.

The neglect of teaching is not a simple matter. It includes the failure to prepare good classroom lectures and lessons, an indifference to the results of teaching, increasing social distance between teacher and student (so that some professors never make the acquaintance of their undergraduate students as individuals), increased dependence upon mechanical methods of examination, and, at the worst, conventionalized contempt for the student. This pattern is discernible within every major university, but some institutions are notably worse than others. In general, interest in instruction seems to be best maintained in those undergraduate university colleges which are more or less autonomous and whose students enjoy some special status. The fundamental problem, however, is everywhere the same. Despite innumerable committees on the improvement of teaching, annual awards to the best instructor, and an intemperate eagerness in the colleges of education to develop courses in methods of college teaching, the alienation of the university faculty from undergraduate education proceeds apace.

The situation is considerably better with respect to graduate education. The graduate student is identified as a recruit to the discipline, and he participates almost from the beginning in research and related activities which are highly valued by the discipline. As he matures, his achievements contribute to the professional reputation of his sponsors. Only in a few of the largest and most prosperous departments, where graduate students are sufficiently numerous to lose their identity and the burden of graduate instruction is sufficiently great to threaten the working schedule of the faculty, is the graduate student regarded with the same ambivalence as the undergraduate. Unfortunately, this situation tends to occur in just those departments which are most attractive to talented students. It may even be true, as one often hears in departments of the second rank, that the best training cannot be obtained in the best departments because of their overcrowding.

The increasingly precarious position of education in institutions of higher education can be shown by such statistical indexes as the average teaching hours per week of senior staff members. In the two institutions whose statistics we have been able to examine, these indicators have fallen precipitously in recent years. Many factors contribute to the same result. The declining work week has been generally characteristic of salaried employments. The delegation of instructional chores to junior staff is probably a reflection of the increasing status of the academic profession and the increasing independence of its senior members. The gap between the teaching responsibilities of senior and junior staff members reflects, in part, the development of a host of part-time or interim employments—consultantships, fellowships, government assignments, administrative posts in the university—which are intended to be filled by the leading men of the several disciplines.

The basic trend away from teaching and toward research in the major universities is accompanied by minor shifts away from teaching and toward public service, away from undergraduate and toward graduate instruction, away from the general involvement of the faculty in the curriculum and toward specialization. The effects of these trends are mutually reinforcing. An increasing proportion of the faculty regard their teaching duties as obstacles to the performance of essential tasks, and instruction falls more and more into the hands of academics of inferior standing. This is not the place to discuss the emergence of new fields, such as General Education or American Studies, which attempt to redress the balance by adapting the departmental organization to a program centered on undergraduate instruction and to a staff without strong disciplinary connections. In some institutions, this innovation has worked out very well; in others, badly. In either case, there is no reason to believe that the interdisciplinary movement is more than a palliative for the general problem we have been describing. In the long run, the present trends will culminate either in the separation of undergraduate instruction from academic research—a development already visible in the increase of full-time research positions on many faculties—or the establishment of a new balance between the ever-increasing demands and rewards of research and the equally urgent demands of students to be taught.

INSTABILITY

The parallel between the problems of the individual and the problems of the institution is too striking to be overlooked. Corresponding to the insecurity experienced by the individual scholar is the instability of the institutional program which almost inevitably follows.

The borderline between appropriate turnover and excessive turnover is, of course, difficult to determine. Nevertheless, there is good reason to describe the present turnover in many institutions as excessive. Turnover is excessive when senior faculty members appointed to lifetime positions in connection with long-range programs leave after two or three years. With respect to junior staff, the expenditure of time and effort in recruitment is altogether out of proportion to the average duration of appointment for the people recruited. In qualitative terms, turnover may be reckoned as excessive when a university consistently loses members of its faculty whose services are needed and wanted and who cannot be satisfactorily replaced.

The instability and loss of continuity in long-range projects, in graduate instruction, and the development of new curricula which result from excessive turnover can scarcely be exaggerated. A handful of very eminent institutions are protected by the fact that their tenure appointments are usually accepted as permanent. Minor universities are often protected against excessive turnover by the harsh fact that most of the members of their faculties have no other place to go. But for most major universities, the constant comings and goings of professors are a perpetual threat to planning and continuity.

There is a curious complication which haunts the sleep of administrators in these universities—namely, that the hazard of appointing incompetent or idle men to tenure positions increases as the general rate of turnover increases. Inevitably, a certain proportion of all appointments made are poor appointments. In the theoretical extreme case, in which all tenure appointees retained their positions for life, the proportion of "deadwood" on the faculty would be the same as the proportion originally appointed. However, when there is considerable faculty mobility, the ablest members of the faculty will tend to be the most mobile because of their attractiveness to other institutions, and the least competent members will tend to be immobile. For a weak major university, there is a real danger that almost all its superior appointees will eventually be lured away, leaving a permanent cadre which has been rigorously selected for incompetence.

ADMINISTRATIVE FAILURE

There are a number of ways in which the workings of the academic marketplace contribute to administrative failure within each university—for example, by the internal dissension and low morale which follow the appointment of outsiders on unduly favorable terms. As we have seen, candidates for academic positions must normally be attracted from other positions of rather similar characteristics, and some bonus of rank, salary, or perquisites is expected in order to create a difference between the two positions. It is usually thought to be necessary to offer an outsider somewhat better terms as an inducement to move than an insider of exactly the same qualifications could obtain. As we have seen, this practice provides a perpetual incentive for everyone on the academic ladder to circulate among institutions. The result is a vicious circle, whereby the appointment of outsiders on unduly favorable terms causes dissatisfaction among the staff members in place, so that some of them seek their fortunes elsewhere, which requires more new appointments to be made by means of extra inducements, which has a further unsettling effect upon the remaining members of the staff. Meanwhile, the emigrants from this faculty going to their new institutions contribute to the same cycles there. It is possible to find departments which have remained in turmoil for decades through the operation of this mechanism.

A related consequence is the uneven growth or decline of departments or colleges within the university according to the fortunes of the marketplace. It often happens that a department loses two or three men in the same short period by sheer chance—for example, by the simultaneous occurrence of several retirements. When the persons involved are of high standing in the discipline, the fall in the department's prestige is appreciable, and it may result in a scramble of the remaining staff for positions elsewhere. In this way, decades of growth and development can be wiped out in a few months. The reverse process, by which sudden access to resources leads to a sudden spiral of growth, is much more difficult to provoke, but it does occasionally occur at the expense of the other university departments competing for the same resources.

Perhaps the most important problem of this type is the indefinite expansion and proliferation of course offerings and service functions, without much regard for the instructional needs answered, or the quality of the service rendered. Robert Maynard Hutchins has commented vehemently on this tendency.[3]

> With transportation what it is today I do not see why every university should try to teach and study everything. Some subjects do not seem to me to have reached the teaching stage, yet we are ardently engaged in teaching them. Other subjects have not the staff available for instruction everywhere. Others can be adequately dealt with if they are studied in a few places. The present passion for cyclotrons seems to me excessive. The infinite proliferation of courses is repulsive. There is a good deal of evidence, I think, that the educational system as a whole needs less money rather than more. The reduction of its income would force it to reconsider its expenditures. The expectation that steadily increasing funds will be forthcoming justifies the maintenance of activities that ought to be abandoned; it justifies waste.
>
> Some waste is inevitable; but the amount that we find in some universities is disgraceful. These institutions carry on extravagant enterprises that by no stretch of the imagination can be called educational, and then plead poverty as the reason for their financial campaigns. The self-interest of professors, the vanity of administrators, trustees, and alumni, and the desire to attract public attention are more or less involved in these extravagances. Yet the result of them is that the institution is unintelligible, and, in every sense of the word, insupportable.

This problem is not altogether attributable to academic personnel policies. The numerous university self-surveys of recent years have shown a multiplicity of causes. Yet the connection between the academic marketplace and the proliferation of the curriculum is much closer than is generally realized.

The key to the whole problem lies in the fact that it is comparatively easy to add items to the program of a university and almost impossible to remove them once they are established. In the threadbare cliché of the faculty clubs, "No educational experiment ever fails." Almost every new faculty member is sooner or later allowed to add something to the existing curriculum or the existing program of services. This stands like a monument long after his departure. Established courses and functions are regarded as poker chips in the perpetual game of budget distribution. When, to the rule which allows items to be added to the budget but does not allow anything to be subtracted, we add the probability that any existing function will develop into a vested interest, and when we further take into account the enormous distance which separates the modern university administrator from a close view of the departmental program in action, it is easy to understand the ameboid expansion of the curriculum and the shameless appearance of sinecures in the university budget.

IGNORANCE

Like the individual, the university suffers from ignorance and poor communication in an increasingly complex situation which plainly requires knowledge and effective communication. The most salient feature of this ignorance is the inability of the department to obtain anything approaching a complete list of available candidates for vacant positions, or to determine the real availability of candidates under consideration, or to get accurate reports on current supply and demand in the disciplinary market.

Within the university, the problems of communication might well be placed at the head of the agenda for institutional reform. The haphazard character of university government, the prevalence of free-floating authority, the opportunity for intrigue which is created by ill-defined procedures and the habit of secrecy, and, perhaps most of all, the inclination of the working professor to dislike and despise administrators collectively while obeying them obsequiously in individual interaction—all these conditions impede the solution of the university's essential problems of how to discriminate between wise and foolish purposes and how to allocate limited resources to competing goals.

NOTES

1. A delightful exploration of the hypothetical consequences of an academic reform is George J. Stigler's "An Academic Episode," *A.A.U.P. Bulletin,* Vol. 33: 661-5 December 1947. This satire starts with the adoption by a South American university of a rule that in June of each year any member of the faculty can challenge the person immediately above him in rank to a competitive examination. The immediate results were favorable, but in the long run it was observed that faculty members were hoarding knowledge. Therefore, the regulations were amended to grant a bonus to a teacher for any of his students who won a challenge. Another unanticipated consequence appeared in the migration of graduate students to study abroad with the foreign professors who submitted the examination questions. A further effect was the interruption of research and the demotion of men who spent their time in current work instead of cramming. Another amendment was introduced, giving credit for publications, and making the calculations still more complex. ("Cimoor, whose father owned a publishing house, succeeded in getting out two books within the first year, and so influential was his father that many of the reviews were neutral.") At

this point, many of the professors retired by the reform came back to climb the ladder with the aid of their previous writing. Finally, the whole scheme was killed by one more amendment—namely, that a man receiving an offer from another university might be awarded a permanent bonus of any number of points.

2. The deterioration of academic freedom after World War II has been intensively studied by Lazarsfeld, under the sponsorship of the Fund for the Republic, in a large-scale interview study of 2,541 faculty members in 165 institutions. Paul F. Lazarsfeld, assisted by Wagner Thielens, Jr., *The Academic Mind: Social Scientists in a Time of Crises,* The Free Press, 1958. For a detailed account of nine cases in which professors were penalized for their current or former political affiliations, see the special issue on "Academic Freedom and Tenure," *A.A.U.P. Bulletin,* Vol. 44, No. 1, March 1958.

3. *Freedom, Education and the Fund,* Meridian Books, 1956, p. 165.

42 *Recruitment to College Teaching*

MARTIN TROW

I

THE STORY is told that during the Crimean War a committee of inquiry called upon the British Surgeon-General to testify regarding gross inadequacies in the medical services at the front. The Surgeon-General's defense was simple: "Our medical services," he said, "would be perfectly adequate were it not for the casualties." Institutions suffer different kinds of embarrassments; unlike the British Army Medical Corps, ours in higher education is currently not casualties, but a superabundance of enlistments. Nevertheless, to echo the Surgeon-General, our higher educational services would be reasonably adequate were it not that we had to double them in the next decade or so.

This country is already well launched on what seems to be an irreversible movement toward mass higher education. Everyone knows that more and more students will be coming to college in the decades ahead; what is not so widely perceived is that the situation in higher education, at least with respect to numbers, very closely resembles what has been happening in secondary education since just before World War I. In 1910, about 15 per cent of the 14- to 17-year-olds were enrolled in school; the same proportion of the 18- to 21-year-olds were in college in 1940. Between 1910 and 1940 the proportion of the 14- to 17-year-olds in school increased from 15 per cent to nearly 75 per cent.[1] Since World War II, school attendance among the college-age group has been increasing at about the same rate as it did among the high-school-age group between the two wars: the trend in college-going seems to be paralleling the earlier movement to mass secondary education. Behind the figures we can see changes in public conceptions of what constitutes a decent education. The bulk of the population has come to expect a high-school education for themselves or their children. But a large and growing part of the population is also coming to see some time in college as the ordinary, the expected thing. Nearly half of all high school graduates now enter college;[2] that rate has been steadily rising, and there is good reason to believe that we will approach a nearly universal experience with some kind of higher education.[3] This is, I believe, a major fact of life, at once heartening and frightening, the source of high hopes for

Published for the first time in this volume. Revised version of a paper read at the Conference on College Teacher Supply, Demand and Recruitment, sponsored by the New England Board of Higher Education, Boston, Massachusetts, November, 1959.

the future of our civilization and of acute fears for the future of our colleges and universities.

The greater part of this huge growth in the college-student population will be borne by public institutions.[4] In many ways, their problems differ from those faced by private institutions, which can, with some measure of autonomy, determine their own size and shape, choose to grow slowly or not at all. But the tremendous expansion in the student population will be felt—is being felt—by the private colleges as well, even by those most firmly determined to preserve their own distinguishing characteristics. The private colleges will be affected in many ways, but perhaps most directly by having to seek their new college teachers in a market in which the public institutions, often with greater resources, are trying somewhat desperately to meet the ever more urgent demands of increased enrollments. In 1956, the colleges and universities of California employed some 13,000 full-time faculty members, 9,000 of these in the four-year public and private colleges and universities in the state. By 1960, that figure will have increased by about one-third; by 1965, the four-year colleges will be employing an estimated 16,669 full-time teachers, an increase of nearly 8,000 teaching positions in 9 years. In the period 1961–65, four-year colleges and universities in California will have to recruit nearly 9,000 *new* teachers to maintain staff-student ratios in the face of a greatly increased enrollment and to replace the expected retirements, deaths, etc.[5] Given the numbers of new Ph.D.s who go into teaching each year, it is not surprising that the proportions of new teachers in the nation holding Ph.D. degrees have fallen from 31 per cent to 24 per cent in six recent years, with further drops anticipated.[6]

Now it is true that most of the colleges in, say, New England, will not be in *direct* competition for the men and women who will be called to teaching posts in California colleges and universities over the next decade. The national figures on teacher supply and demand are misleading if they are taken to suggest the nature of the staffing problems of any given institution or group of institutions. College teaching is not one profession but many; similarly, there is not one market for college teachers but many, defined in part by region, type of institution, discipline, and many factors of image and reputation about which we know only too little. Moreover, the metaphor of the market may be highly misleading; the recruitment of new staff to some institutions more closely resembles that of a big-league baseball club and its farm teams than it does the classic market of the economists.[7]

But while any particular college may not recruit its teachers in a national market, the staffing of every college goes on within the context of a broad movement toward mass higher education, which cannot help but affect every institution, even those that feel most insulated against it. It is affecting the kinds of people who go to college, the kinds of things they study there, and the conditions they both find and create on campus. It affects what David Riesman has called the "student mix" on a campus:[8] students whose highest aim would have been the local normal school twenty years ago now strike out for the state university, and change the character both of the local institution and the more inclusive one. Their places are filled by students who twenty years ago would not have gone to college—these enter the local normal school to find it upgrading itself to the status of a state college, matching or at least duplicating the offerings of the university in every field, and incidentally creating new teaching positions that have to be filled. Moreover, the coming years will bring larger numbers of applicants to most selective colleges, and higher ratios of applicants to admissions. Many colleges that choose not to grow will be able to be more selective in their admissions, and, if they wish, will be able to raise the average ability level of their student body. These changes in student characteristics may imperceptibly affect the character of staff appointments; moreover, as the reputation of a college changes or is purposefully changed, it begins to draw on a different pool of candidates for faculty appointments.[9] The effects of the tendency toward mass higher education are not restricted to those schools that will bear the direct burden of numbers. Every college will be dealing with the ramified consequences of this great force, and not least when it comes to staffing itself.

Research into the recruitment of college teachers has taken two major forms. On one hand there is the literature on faculty supply and demand, largely statistical and descriptive of the national picture, but with figures broken down over time into such categories as sex, subject area, degree earned, and the like, and with future projections and estimates made of demands and supply in different categories and fields.[10] Some individual states have published even more detailed pictures of the present and anticipated needs for college teachers for the institutions within their borders.[11]

In addition to this literature on supply and demand, there is a growing body of studies of recruitment to college teaching that focuses on the individual and tries to learn something of when and how he makes up his mind to go into teaching, and what factors he perceives as having influenced his decision. The studies by Stecklein and Eckert at Minnesota[12] and by John Gustad at Maryland[13] are good examples of this kind of research. These ways of looking at the problem have been illuminating and, moreover, seem to have fairly clear implications for action. But there are other ways of looking at the whole matter that deserve attention. Two of these perspectives link the issue of the recruitment of college teachers to broad trends in social mobility in the population, on the one hand, and to changing patterns in higher education, on the other. These perspectives raise the following questions: What kinds of people are drawn to college teaching?

What kinds of colleges do they go to? And what happens to them while they are in college? I will thus be speaking first of the social recruitment to college teaching, particularly in the liberal arts and sciences, and then of the value systems on campuses as they affect the quality of the students who go on to become college teachers.

II

First, what kinds of people go into college teaching, and to different areas of it? The kinds of people who staff the junior colleges in California differ in crucial respects—and not least in how they came to be college teachers—from the men in the private denominational colleges of the Midwest; the men who teach in the field of history differ both in their characteristics and in their paths to teaching from the men in the departments of chemical engineering. Our impressions on this point are clear and strong, nor do I think we need doubt them. But for the most part they are impressions; we lack the knowledge that would allow us to specify the nature of these differences, or their bearing on the various paths by which men come to teach in different kinds of institutions and disciplines. The differences among the kinds of men who teach in different kinds of institutions and disciplines are so great that we cannot study "recruitment to college teaching" as if it were a single phenomenon. We must first identify the different patterns that are included within that term, and then study each of these patterns of career choices. We may, for good practical reasons, be interested in "recruitment to college teaching," but we must learn more about the different ways it does happen, rather than impose our practical questions on the complex forces and processes of social life.

Among the complex forces that shape career lines are the manifold influences of social origins. The social and economic class into which one is born, the normative and emotional climate in which one is reared, and the values and orientations of one's family and its subculture heavily affect the kinds of talents a person develops, what he comes to want out of life, and the opportunities he is afforded for pursuing his goals. More specifically, the effects of different social origins can be observed in how one thinks, how well one does in school, what kinds of schools one attends, how far one goes in them, and what one studies there.[14] And the bearing of academic success on whether one becomes a college teacher needs scarcely to be stressed.

The effects of social origins on the nature of intellectual development and academic career can be observed all along a lifeline. Very early, we can see that in some groups and classes a child's curiosity is customarily stimulated and encouraged, in others discouraged and blunted. By the time we get to look at the minority of children who go to college, we can see the bearing of social origins on what colleges they go to, and what they study there. Both of these relatively late "decisions" heavily affect the likelihood that a student will eventually become a college teacher.

Students do not recruit themselves to different fields of study in random ways. Data from a current study of the National Merit Scholarship winners and runners-up show that in this group of gifted and talented youngsters Jewish students are twice as likely as Catholics to major in mathematics and physics.[15] More of the Jewish students study physics than engineering, while among the Catholics almost three times as many are in engineering as are in physics. On the Berkeley campus, the large number of Oriental students are disproportionately represented in engineering, while very few of them are liberal arts majors. Again at Berkeley, over a third of the students in one study who were majoring in the physical sciences came from working-class origins, as compared with only 3 per cent of the students majoring in the life sciences.[16] These facts tell us little in themselves, but they do pose questions: why should this be; how do the values and orientations that we know differ very greatly among people in different social classes and ethnic and religious groups shape the substantive interests and career choices of their sons and daughters?

Simply from what we know of the class and ethnic subcultures in the American population, we can anticipate that the various groups will supply quite different proportions of college teachers in the different areas; and, moreover, that the paths to college teaching will differ very greatly among them. For example, when we look at the social origins of engineering students, a very able group as compared with boys in other major areas, we find them to be disproportionately from lower- and lower-middle-class origins.[17] Their choice of engineering, coupled with what is for many of them a rejection of broader cultural or intellectual interests, represents a distinctive pattern of social mobility—in their case, a vigorous but rather narrowly focused striving for success along rather clearly delineated social and academic paths. We can understand engineers, and engineering education, a good deal better if we know what kinds of people they are, where they have been, and where they are going. I think the same is true for understanding how people come to major, and then to teach, in other fields of study.[18]

What does the recruitment to different fields of study have to do with recruitment to college teaching? The answer is: quite a lot. John Gustad has observed that "the field is chosen long before the occupation,"[19] and some fields are more likely than others to lead to college teaching.[20] Similarly, the recruitment to different kinds of colleges also has considerable bearing on future entry into teaching. The fact is that a student who attends Swarthmore and majors in history is far more likely to end up teaching in college than is a student who studies mechanical engineering at Stevens Institute of Technology. Both the Minnesota study and Gustad report that "the decision to enter college teaching is not a decision at all. It is the end product of drift."[21] But as Gustad immediately notes, "the drift is not accidental," and he finds patterns of motivations underlying the apparent drift. I say "apparent" because what appears to be drift, in the absence of early conscious decision to go into teaching, may actually be rather highly determined by specific early life experiences, and by the broad social statuses that shape those experiences. There are some combinations of class, ethnic, and religious origins that are extremely unlikely to produce college teachers; there are other combinations that seem to be associated with recruitment to different fields of study and different kinds of institutions. But we know almost nothing in detail about these connections between social origins and recruitment to teaching, although the forces may be decisive in shaping the processes of occupational choice—processes of which the participants themselves may be quite unaware and thus unable to report to us.

So little attention has been paid to the social and cultural origins of people in different kinds of colleges and major fields for two reasons. First, because the answers to these questions do not provide very clear directives for action—there is nothing much an administrator can do about the social recruitment of teaching candidates or prospects. In addition, educators are reluctant to talk about the social class or religious or ethnic origins of students, for fear of sounding undemocratic in a society committed to the values of equal opportunties for all, and to rewarding achievement rather than origins. But this confuses the grounds for action with the sources of understanding. A college president may say, "it doesn't matter to me whether a candidate is a Jew or a Catholic or an Oriental, what matters is what he is as a man and a teacher." But this praiseworthy stand does not alter the fact that social origins, and the different kinds of life experience that flows from them, largely determine the kinds of men and women who come to be candidates for teaching positions in different kinds of institutions. In the short run, when we want more teachers and don't much care where they come from, these considerations may seem irrelevant. But in the long run, the numbers and quality of college teachers may depend largely on the movements of broad racial, ethnic, and social strata in the population, and on concomitant changes in their views of education and their conceptions of success.

By and large, as Herbert Hyman and others have shown, lower-class groups value formal education much less than do middle- and upper-middle-class people.[22] But when lower- and lower-middle-class people do come to want their children to go to college, as increasingly they do, they first perceive a college education as purely instrumental, as an advanced vocational training. And their children share these views.[23] But students who view their college education as a vocational training will not contribute the number or, more importantly, the *kind* of college teachers that we want. The view of college education as vocational training usually means that an early choice of career has been made. But becoming a college teacher, as we have seen, is typically the outcome of a deferred career choice. The early career choices of the vocationally oriented usually foreclose the possibilities of their "drifting" into college teaching. In our society, remaining uncommitted and open to the possibilities of teaching college is a social and psychological luxury; the "no nonsense" attitude of many lower- and lower-middle-class families who send their children to college requires that there be some fairly clear and "practical" answer to the question "what are you doing there?" The kind of justification expected is "I'm studying engineering (or education, or business administration)."

Moreover, there is evidence that the hardening of identity that goes with a specific career reduces the impact of college. Norman Miller has very clear data, drawn from the Cornell study of values, showing that vocationally oriented students change far less in their attitudes toward certain civil liberties—are far less likely to acquire the more "liberal" or libertarian views—than are those who see college as primarily a place to acquire a basic education and appreciation of ideas—and this is true both in Ivy League schools and in state colleges.[24] Vocationally or career-oriented students are far less susceptible to influences in college that would modify their opinions or basic life choices. Students whose identities have hardened early cannot be reached as deeply as students who are still engaged in what Erik Erikson calls "identity play,"[25] and particularly not where higher education must reach them deeply enough to make them want to give their lives to it.

In the face of the tremendous demands for college teachers in the future, students with a vocational orientation may increasingly be encouraged to see college teaching as one of the practical careers that can be decided upon early, before a student has experienced the pains and rewards of genuine intellectual work and growth. But the people thus recruited will almost certainly not resemble our better college teachers, who come to it later in their development through their commitment to their field of study.

The increases in college enrollments ahead will be supplied to a great extent by students with a vocational or narrow career orientation. We cannot assume that the college students in an era of nearly universal higher education will resemble the students who have gone to college in the past, or that they will supply a proportionate number of new college teachers. Who will these new students be, how will they view their college education, and—very closely related to that question—how will they view college teaching as a career? The answers to these questions may not give us specific directives for action, but they will define the nature of the staffing problem that American colleges will be living with.[26] By close attention to the social sources of new recruits to different areas of teaching now, we may get clues to the strategies of recruitment demanded by future changes in the character and composition of our student bodies.

III

Another relatively neglected approach to the problem of teacher recruitment is currently gaining increasing attention, and takes this form: under what conditions of life and study are college teachers of high quality most likely to be developed? The focus here is not exclusively on the student and his decision, but is also on the institutions and their characteristics and processes, as these shape career choices.[27] As I have indicated, a number of studies show that the decision to teach in college is characteristically made quite late in the individual's career, in college and graduate school rather than before.[28] This suggests that the impact of higher education is of crucial importance in the development of college teachers. The outcomes of a college education arise from the interplay between the characteristics, values, and orientations that students bring with them to college, and what happens to them there. I have touched on the importance of the characteristics and values that the students bring to college; I would like to turn now to the question of how college affects them.

The general question of what happens in college has been in recent years the subject of considerable study and discussion, the bulk of it focusing on changes in student personality and values during the college years. The pioneering study of Newcomb at Bennington,[29] the work of Nevitt Sanford and his colleagues at Vassar,[30] the extensive studies of student values conducted by a group at Cornell,[31] the report of Jacob on these and other studies,[32] and recent critical reactions to that report[33] are some of the landmarks in the field.[34] Rather than summarize the antecedent research, I would like to focus on one question: under what conditions are able students drawn into college teaching?

It is my impression, and there is some preliminary evidence to support this, that in our best colleges, college teaching appeals to the best students in a highly talented student body. There is, in the schools that recruit students of highest academic ability and that maintain the highest academic standards, a favorable selection to college teaching. At Antioch, Reed, and Swarthmore, good students report that they feel some sense of obligation to go on to graduate school—it is what is expected of them. And the faculty members of those schools often make a conscious effort to recruit their brightest students to an academic career. In those colleges, as elsewhere, relatively few undergraduates are prepared to say outright that they want to teach in college. Rather, the recruitment of the better students on those campuses is to graduate school; but that, of course, is a major step in the making of a college teacher.

Now, the favorable selection to academic life from one section of our college is clearly *not* what we find in secondary education. It is an unhappy fact that there is a decided negative selection, at least among men, to teaching below the college level. Education majors are simply not as talented, lively, or imaginative, by and large, as are majors in other fields. The extensive studies done by the Educational Testing Service and others show this dramatically for a national sample. Education majors scored lowest, and by far, on a comprehensive test of verbal and quantitative competence as compared with majors in every other field.[35] Moreover, a recent study on the Berkeley campus shows the same pattern in much greater detail. At Berkeley, the men who take the education courses—there is no formal education major—have, on the average, poorer grades and less knowledge about public affairs than do men in other majors. (Surprisingly, they also are, as a group, decidedly more illiberal on matters of political tolerance and academic freedom than are men in other areas of specialization.)[36]

I am not here directly concerned with the problems of American secondary education, to which, incidentally, this negative selection may contribute in no small part. But what is true of the secondary schools may well be, or be in the process of becoming, true for some areas of higher education. The immense expansion of higher education that is under way is not merely a growth in numbers, but affects the basic characteristics of the institutions that are responding to that growth. The forces that made for mass secondary education are at work shaping the character of mass higher education, and in similar ways. As this happens, the distance between high school and college narrows; the early years of many colleges come increasingly to resemble the high-school experience; as the latter, with their increased emphasis on college preparation, come to look more like the junior colleges to which an increasing proportion of their graduates and teachers are promoted.[37]

This is a development with far-reaching consequences. One consequence of immediate concern is a possible tendency for a pattern of negative selection of less able, less bold, and less imaginative men to the faculties of the junior colleges and the lower status, mass "people-processing institutions,"[38] which are bearing the brunt of the greatly increased enrollments. This country has developed a highly diversified system of higher education; as T. R. McConnell and his associates have shown in the course of their detailed studies of American colleges, there is a college somewhere for everybody.[39] I am suggesting that the present tendencies may in a sense reduce that diversity by polarizing our colleges into two broad classes: on one hand, a group of selective colleges and universities that maintain traditional standards of excellence, however varied their educational methods, both in their aims and in their practice. They maintain them in large part by having highly selective admissions policies and by refusing to grow rapidly or to any great extent. On the other hand, there is a large body of relatively unselective colleges and universities, which extend educational opportunities very broadly, and which maintain such standards as are compatible with their prior commitment to the extension of educational opportunities. Parallel to, and as a part of, this polarization of American colleges in their basic aims and functions, will, I believe, go two very different processes of recruitment to the staffs of those two different kinds of educational institutions. The first class of schools will as a group continue to educate their own future teachers,[40] and those teachers will represent by and large the better students on those campuses. The second group of schools will also educate the bulk of their own future teachers, but those teachers, I fear, will not be drawn from the better students who pass through them.

There are many reason for this. The very able teachers and the close student-teacher relationships characteristic of the first group of colleges provide a challenging and rewarding image of college teaching to their better students. The frequently less able teachers and the enormous gulf between student and faculty which characterize the people-processing colleges will, I believe, repel the able students on those campuses, and will project an image of college teaching more attractive to timid and less able young men, who look to teaching as a way of avoiding the harsh rigors of the business and professional world.

Another factor, and here the Cornell studies are of interest,[41] is the differing value climates that characterize these different kinds of institutions. In the best liberal arts colleges, the value of intellectual and aesthetic pursuits *for their own sakes* is commonly upheld; in the mass institutions, education is widely perceived as vocational training, or as having its chief value as vocational training, directly in the case of the professional and preprofessional courses, indirectly in the case of the humanities, which also have their prestige and monetary value. Now, where intellectual and aesthetic pursuits are valued for their own sakes, college teaching will appear to be one rewarding way to live out those values and interests, and will appear so especially to those students who have already tasted the rewards of scholarship and scientific inquiry. But on a campus dominated by the values of vocational training, where a college education is primarily a means to other ends, college teaching will be seen as the low status, underpaid, and overworked occupation that on those campuses it too often is. Carl Becker somewhere defines the college teacher as "a man who thinks otherwise." A central task of research is to learn what kinds of life experience, and most especially what kinds of college experience, engender men who think otherwise. The issue of vocationalism versus liberal education is crucial for the recruitment of college teachers, since vocational training cannot help but be primarily a training in received skills, and not in thinking otherwise.

The rise of vocationalism in American mass higher education is a clear and present danger to the recruitment of really able and creative college teachers. The concept of mass higher education is useful for the broad patterns of development in higher education to which it points. But, happily, life is richer and more varied than are the categories of sociologists. Much more is going on in the proliferating junior colleges, the growing state colleges and universities, than I have intimated or know. The first effort of any society to provide higher education for a major part of its population will be full of excitement and surprises, and the life of the new and growing public colleges and junior colleges is in some ways more interesting to study than are the older and stabler processes in the small private colleges about which we know so much more.

Nevertheless, the older, selective liberal-arts colleges simply do not face a problem in maintaining the quality of their faculties anything like that being faced by the schools that are shouldering the main tasks of mass higher education. Most of the discussion of how to recruit college teachers in the future deals primarily with the question of numbers rather than with the kind or quality of teachers to be recruited. The question of numbers is important and urgent, but it is more important for some kinds of colleges than for others. In fact, one basic difference between the two broad categories of colleges I have described is whether the primary concern of those charged with the recruitment of new faculty is numbers or quality. Both considerations are often present, but one or the other usually is the dominating concern. Where the problem of numbers overwhelms a concern with quality in faculty appointments, the kinds of faculty members appointed make it less likely that the best students in those colleges can be drawn toward college teaching. Thus, the same rapid expansion of public colleges and universities, which creates the heightened demand for college teachers, is likely at the same time to reduce the flow of able students from these colleges into academic life.

IV

Even where a concern for the quality of faculty appointments is strong, the pressures of increased enrollments and immediate staffing problems divert attention from the question of the institutional *sources* of able college teachers. That question can be cast as a problem for research in this form: where and under what conditions do we find a favorable recruitment to college teaching, and conversely, where is the recruitment to college teaching a process of negative selection of the less able people? The question thus framed directs our attention to the characteristics of the situation within which the process of selection and self-selection occurs. As we have seen, this typically occurs in a college or graduate school rather than earlier. One of the major forces at the undergraduate level that affects recruitment of the better or the weaker students on a particular campus to college teaching is the relationship among the several major value systems represented on that campus. We can usefully distinguish three broad systems of values in a college:

      a) the college culture;
      b) the youth culture;
      c) the student subcultures.

A crucial question for the impact of higher education—and for the development of college teachers—is, whether the college culture or the mass youth culture dominates the student subcultures on a campus. Let us look at each of these values systems more closely.

a) The college culture is the dominant climate of values that characterizes the institution. It is the system of values affirmed by word and deed by the normative leaders of the institution, its administration, and faculty. It also shapes the *image* of the college that is projected to the students. The crucial question here is to what extent the college is seen as placing primary emphasis on scholarship, art, and science, and on the *intrinsic* importance of those activities, or to what extent it is seen as equally or primarily concerned with extraneous matters—vocational training, public relations, athletic prestige, or whatever. Of course, the "authorities" on a campus may not all share the same views on these matters; faculty and administration may be at odds, or one section of the faculty with another. The essential matter is the dominant tone on a campus: is the college one where serious intellectual and aesthetic pursuits are the center of attention and the touchstone of administration and faculty actions, or not? This is put in either-or terms; of course, colleges vary along a continuum in this regard, and some project diffuse or contradictory images from different parts of themselves. But for most colleges there is a pretty clear answer to that question.

b) By the "youth culture," I mean the special segment of the mass culture that is shared by youngsters of college age. The values of the youth culture comprise the lowest common denominator of American undergraduate life. They are the values and attitudes of college students *qua* students, on the basis of which they can communicate with one another, without knowing one another, across regional, institutional, class, or major subject lines. This is the world of football, popular music, dating patterns—the unrefined and undifferentiated interests and concerns of Americans of college age, unaffected except superficially by their academic environment or higher education. The youth culture is present on every American campus to some degree. How strong it is on a campus, how widely its interests and values dominate the attention and perspectives of a student body, is crucial for the character of the college and the nature of its impact.

c) Third, there are the student subcultures. These vary within and between colleges: they are the distinguishable styles of behavior and attitude, toward education and ideas, toward work and leisure, toward the present and the future, which we can observe among students. Some of these small worlds are familiar enough to have names—there are the worlds of the bohemians and the fraternity boys; the greasy grinds and the highbrows; the politicians and the athletes. And there are myriad tiny student worlds that revolve around interests special to a small group on a campus—a clique of literary men here; a jam of jazz enthusiasts there; a nucleus of physicists at still another place. And they overlap and inter-penetrate in countless ways. It is in these small worlds that norms and values and orientations and ambitions are shaped and changed, if changed at all. They are also where many students begin to acquire the attitudes and orientations that will lead them to graduate school and then into college teaching, in the process which R. K. Merton has called "anticipa-tory socialization."

Now, as we look at these tiny worlds, the crucial question is what shapes the *content* of their interests and values. For, as we know also from studies of other kinds of organization—factories, armies, and hospitals, for example —the informal groupings found in all of them can embody and transmit the values and purposes of the formal organization, or they can sabotage, undercut, and insulate their members against the purposes and values of the larger organization. Or they can simply ignore those purposes, and center on interests that are neither supportive nor subversive of the formal organization.

A small group of students that meet informally to talk about poetry or Plato or politics is clearly furthering the educational purposes of most American colleges. If these or similar subjects occupy some of their atten-tion, whatever may have brought them together, we are still likely to be happy. But if they talk exclusively of dates and football, of automobiles and skiing, they are undoubtedly learning certain skills—perhaps useful ones—but are probably not experiencing the broadening of horizons and sympathies, the sharpening of critical and aesthetic faculties, the develop-ment of independence of mind based on competence of judgment, that are the marks of a liberal education. For the central characteristic of the student subcultures that are dominated by youth-culture values is that their interests are static; they do not deepen, develop, become more dif-ferentiated and refined as their members gain increased competence in an area of interest. Gossip about people, cars, sports has a relentlessly repeti-tive quality; one can break in on it anywhere, any time, any decade, and nothing has changed except the names and the fashionable attitudes. This continuous murmur, the endless bull session, is what Malinowski called "phatic communion," essentially friendly noises by which one indicates that one is a member of the tribe and the kind of person one can get along with. This kind of exchange of sentiments is a very important thing; social life would be a good deal more gritty, perhaps essentially impossible, without it. But it is a part of ordinary social life, and not part of the distinctive ex-perience that is higher education. The question is not *whether* it occurs

—it occurs everywhere, in faculty lounge, as in dormitory or plant locker room or P.X. The question for higher education is the extent to which such talk and such interests dominate and monopolize the relationships among students. Insofar as they do, they serve, and most effectively, to insulate the student against the impact of his formal education, an education that aims to extend his horizons, break through habitual ways of thinking and feeling, and stimulate fresh and independent thought. When subcultures are also organized as formal living groups, and center their interest around the youth culture, they are effective indeed—as Hanan Selvin has shown the sororities on the Berkeley campus to be effective—in insulating their members against the impact of the university climate.[42]

What goes on in these student worlds is a product of the values and interests that the students bring with them to college and the impact the college has on them. The former is very largely a reflection of the values in the students' homes; these vary by social class, ethnic group, and other forces that shape a student's early life experience. The latter, the question of college impact, is a large and challenging problem in itself;[43] the effective size of the institution, the character of its faculty and administration, the quality of student-faculty relations, the image the institution projects to its student body—all are involved here. In some colleges, the special character of the institution—what I have called the college culture—is so strong and clear, so powerfully projected, that it permeates all or almost all of the various subcultures flourishing among the students. This seems to be the case at a college like Reed. In others, the college projects a weak or diffuse image, subcultures vary widely, and many are simply vehicles for the mass youth culture. On some of those campuses, other groups, perhaps supported by live contact with a forceful section of the faculty or a creative group in the community, carry on the informal but genuine education of their members, largely independently of the formal institution of which their members are nominally a part.[44] In those schools where the college culture is weak and there are few alternative points of identification for creative subcultures, where the mass youth culture has the field largely to itself, I doubt if we will find many future college teachers, nor will we find them among the abler students.

To return to this guiding question: whether the better or the poorer students on a college campus are attracted to college teaching is largely an outcome of the interplay of the subcultures on that campus[45] More concretely, where the commitment to college teaching is made by youngsters who are in the process of rejecting the value and perspectives of the mass culture, I think we will find a favorable recruitment. Where the decision to go to college teaching is made without that break, without, if you will, a creative alienation from the concerns and distractions of mass culture, then I think we will find a distinctly negative selection at work. And where are we likely to find the former? I believe in those institutions (a) that project a strong image of serious intellectual and aesthetic purposes, which (b) penetrate the student subcultures, so that in large degree they, or at least some of them, become the carriers or transmission belts for the highest values of academic life, and where for some students the anticipatory socialization to college teaching actually goes on. In these schools and in the subgroups most strongly affected by them, the values of the mass youth culture are relatively weak, in part due to the kinds of student who come from these schools and the kinds of values they absorbed at home, in part due to the relatively powerful competitive influence of the serious intellectual climate on those campuses.

The study of student subcultures has a peculiar fascination of its own, something like the fascination of the exotic, which took anthropologists to remote jungles to study the rich and unfamiliar social systems flourishing there. I suggest that if we can resist the temptation to study student subcultures for their own sakes, we may find that they help us to understand the nature of higher education and its varied outcomes.

Finally, a word on the relation of research to the problems of faculty recruitment. At a recent conference on faculty recruitment, Ruth Eckert made an observation, and added quite appropriately, "now, there is a fruitful area of research." At this point an exasperated college president broke in: "Don't we know enough about this so we do not have to wait for research? We are hungry for teachers *now!*" We may sympathize with the speaker, while believing that he misperceives the right relation between research and practice in this field. We do know enough so that we need not tarry for more research; moreover, the problem will not wait for certified solutions.[46] Yet there are questions whose answers do not directly yield wise and practical suggestions for action, but merely a somewhat fuller knowledge of the nature of higher education and the processes by which it attracts and selects those who give it continuity. We must explore those questions first because they are there. But also we must explore them because the more we know of the varied and complex paths through which men and women become college teachers, the more intelligently can we plan to preserve and create the conditions for a favorable recruitment of college teachers during the rapid expansion of higher education that lies ahead. We must learn what those conditions are, not only to be able to preserve them in the older selective colleges, but also to be able to create and nurture them within the mass relatively unselective institutions. For it is within those institutions, too, that we must find and educate and recruit men and women who, in Max Weber's phrase, live for ideas and not off them. Fundamental inquiry into the forces within student and institutions that work to develop those qualities of mind may paradoxically contribute in direct and practical ways to our efforts to find and recruit college teachers of high quality. Here, as elsewehere, the long way around may be the shortest way.

NOTES

1. *Teachers for Tomorrow* (Bulletin No. 2, The Fund for the Advancement of Education; New York), January, 1956.
2. Henry G. Badger and M. Clemens Johnson, *Statistics of Higher Education: 1955–1956. Faculty, Students, and Degrees* (U.S. Office of Education Biennial Survey [Washington, D.C., 1958]), p. 10.
3. See "Why College Enrollments may Triple by 1970," *College Board Review*, No. 40 (Winter, 1960), pp. 18–19.
4. Between 1947 and 1958, enrollments in public colleges increased by 60 per cent and in private colleges by 15 per cent. In other words, the public colleges absorbed 78 per cent of the total increase in college enrollments in that period. At the beginning of the period, 47 per cent of all four-year college students were in public institutions; at the end of it, the public colleges enrolled 55 per cent of all four-year college students. That trend will almost certainly continue. *A Fact Book on Higher Education* (Washington, D.C.: American Council on Education, not dated), p. 15.
5. Liaison Committee of the Regents of the University of California and the California State Board of Education, *A Study of Faculty Demand and Supply in California Higher Education, 1957–1970* (Berkeley and Sacramento, 1958), p. 26.
6. National Education Association, Research Division, *Teacher Supply and Demand in Universities, Colleges, and Junior Colleges, 1957–58* (Higher Education Series, Research Report 1959–R10 [Washington, D.C., June, 1959]), p. 11.
7. It is not my purpose to consider the institutional networks, the complex connections among institutions of various kinds and levels, which constitute the pipelines through which teachers flow. These relationships—the traditional, personal, intellectual ties among men and institutions—actually define the pool from which new faculty members are recruited; in all cases, that pool is much smaller and more highly delimited than is the total body of people who newly make themselves available for teaching roles, and who constitute the "supply" of new teacher candidates as defined by the national figures. It is important to distinguish the staffing problems of institutions and groups of institutions from the national problem of supply and demand, and it would be of great practical and intellectual importance to study the forces and networks that delimit the roughly exclusive pools of candidates upon which specific institutions and groups of institutions draw. See Theodore Caplow and Reece J. McGee, *The Academic Marketplace* (New York: Basic Books, 1958) [ch. XLI in this volume], which deals with some of these processes of staffing in large universities.
8. David Riesman, "The Academic Career: Notes on Recruitment and Colleagueship," *Daedalus*, LXXXVII (Winter, 1959), 147–69.
9. See Burton R. Clark, "College Image and Student Selection," in *Selection and Educational Differentiation* (Field Service Center and Center for the Study of Higher Education; Berkeley: University of California, 1960), pp. 155–68.
10. See Ray C. Maul, "Requirements of Higher Educational Institutions for Faculty in Science," *Scientific Manpower 1958* (National Science Foundation), pp. 32–37; also National Education Association, Research Division, *op. cit.*
11. See Minnesota Commission on Higher Education, *Higher Education in Minnesota* (Minneapolis: University of Minnesota Press, 1950); *Illinois Looks to the Future in Higher Education* (Report of the Higher Education Commission to the Governor and Legislature of the State of Illinois, 1957); Liaison Committee of the Regents of the University of California and the California State Board of Education, *op. cit.*
12. John E. Stecklein and Ruth E. Eckert, *An Exploratory Study of Factors Influencing the Choice of College Teaching as a Career* (Co-operative Research Program, U.S. Office of Education [Washington, D.C., January, 1958]).

13. John W. Gustad, "They March to a Different Drummer: Another Look at College Teachers," *The Educational Record*, XL (July, 1959), 204–11.

14. On the bearing of social origins on child-rearing, see Daniel R. Miller and Guy E. Swanson, *The Changing American Parent* (New York: John Wiley and Sons, 1958). On class differences in modes of thought, see B. Bernstein, "Some Sociological Determinants of Perception: An Inquiry into Sub-cultural Differences," *The British Journal of Sociology*, IX (June, 1958), 159–74. [See chap. XXIV in this volume (eds.).] For a recent review of the bearing of social origins on educational achievement, see Seymour M. Lipset and Reinhard Bendix, *Social Mobility in Industrial Society* (Berkeley: University of California Press, 1959).

15. This study is currently underway at the Center for the Study of Higher Education, University of California, Berkeley.

16. These data are drawn from a study of students conducted by Hanan Selvin and Warren O. Hagstrom and reported in *The Bulwark of Liberty* (Berkeley: University of California, January, 1959; mimeographed); and in "Determinants of Support for Civil Liberties," *British Journal of Sociology*, XI (March, 1960), 51–73.

17. See Martin Trow, "Some Implications of the Social Origins of Engineers," in *Scientific Manpower 1958* (National Science Foundation), pp. 67–74.

18. I have been discussing some of the factors that may affect the characteristic patterns of social recruitment to a field. But we may equally well ask what are the *consequences* of these patterns of recruitment for the discipline or occupation itself? For example, how is engineering as a profession or field of study affected by the kind of men recruited to it? On this specific question see Trow, "Some Implications of the Social Origins of Engineers." But the more general question can be located in the tradition of thought of the sociology of knowledge.

19. Gustad, *op. cit.*, p. 206.

20. Morris Rosenberg discusses the connection between social origins and career choice in *Occupations and Values* (Glencoe, Ill.: Free Press, 1957), chap. V. Bernard Berelson has data showing the markedly different proportions of Ph.D.'s in different fields who go into college teaching. For example, where less than half of those taking Ph.D.'s in the physical sciences in 1958 went into academic jobs, the proportion was two-thirds for new social-science Ph.D.'s and four-fifths for new Ph.D.'s in the humanities. *Graduate Education in the United States* (forthcoming).

21. Gustad, *loc. cit.* Also, Stecklein and Eckert, *op. cit.*, p. 44.

22. Herbert H. Hyman, "The Values Systems of Different Classes: A Social Psychological Contribution to the Analysis of Stratification," in Bendix and Lipset (eds.), *Class, Status and Power* (Glencoe, Ill.: Free Press, 1953), pp. 426–42.

23. Joseph A. Kahl, "Educational and Occupational Aspirations of 'Common Man' Boys," *Harvard Educational Review*, XXII (Summer, 1953), 186–203 [ch. XXVI in this volume (eds.)].

24. Norman Miller, "Academic Climate and Student Values," paper given at the Fifty-fourth Annual Meeting of the American Sociological Society, September 3–5, 1959, Chicago. One factor working to increase the tendency toward vocational as against liberal education is the marked increase in early marriage and acquisition of children among college students. Elbridge Sibley has noted that "students who face the imminent prospect of having to earn a living for three or more can be expected to choose courses of study that lead to immediate vocational opportunities. Parents who are called upon to contribute to their support while they are still in school will as a rule share that preference. Increased emphasis on vocational training as against liberal education in college and university seems a likely result." "Higher Education and Earlier Parenthood: A Changing Cycle of Family Life," *Antioch Review*, Spring, 1957, pp. 54–55. See also Margaret Mead, "Marrying in Haste in College," *Columbia Forum*, III (Spring, 1960), 31–34.

25. Erik H. Erikson, "The Problem of Ego Identity," *Journal of the American Psychoanalytic Association* IV (January, 1936), 56–121.

26. If the mass unselective colleges do not supply enough recruits to college teaching, one expedient may be the creation of special college-teacher-training institutes, perhaps as adjuncts to existing university departments of education, and similar

in function to the normal schools that were created to supply the great numbers of new teachers required by mass elementary and secondary education. This, I think, would contribute to the polarization of colleges that I spoke of earlier, by creating two basically different routes to college teaching for the two different kinds of institutions. Another alternative is for the older selective colleges to supply a very much larger number of college teachers, to meet not only their own needs but also the needs of the expansion of higher education. But the demands for trained and educated men will be so high from so many sources that this seems unlikely.

27. "Rather marked differences were noted among teachers in the selected subject fields in the kinds of colleges which they had attended as undergraduates. Almost three-fourths (73 per cent) of the teachers in the humanities had done their undergraduate work in private colleges or universities. In contrast, the majority of the persons in the social sciences, the natural sciences, and education had received their baccalaureate degrees from public institutions. . . ." Stecklein and Eckert, *op. cit.,* pp. 34–35.

28. Stecklein and Eckert report that only three per cent of those who later became college teachers had college teaching as a career goal at the time of college entrance; 15 per cent upon receipt of a bachelor's degree; and 48 per cent upon receipt of highest degree. *Op. cit.,* Table 1, p. 9. By contrast, a national survey of law students revealed that 50 per cent had decided to study law at age 19 or less. Wagner Thielens, Jr., "Some Comparisons of Entrants to Medical and Law School," in R. K. Merton, G. E. Reader, and P. T. Kendall (eds.), *The Student-Physician,* (Cambridge, Mass.: Harvard University Press, 1957), p. 132. Medical students tend to make their career decisions even earlier, with 85 per cent having definitely decided to study medicine by age 20, and 44 per cent having decided by the age of 17. Natalie Rogoff, "The Decision to Study Medicine," in R. K. Merton *et al.* (eds.), *The Student-Physician,* p. 115.

29. Theodore M. Newcomb, *Personality and Social Change* (New York: Dryden Press, 1943).

30. Nevitt Sanford (issue ed.), "Personality Development during the College Years," *Journal of Social Issues,* Vol. XII (1956).

31. See Rose K. Goldsen, Morris Rosenberg, Robin Williams, and Edward Suchman, *What College Students Think* (Princeton, N.J.: Van Nostrand, 1960); and Rosenberg, *op. cit.*

32. Philip E. Jacob, *Changing Values in College* (New York: Harper and Bros., 1957).

33. Allen H. Barton, *Studying the Effects of College Education* (Edward W. Hazen Foundation; New Haven, Conn., 1959).

34. See T. R. McConnell and Paul Heist, "Do Students Make the College?" *College and University,* XXXIV (Summer, 1959), 442–52; and also Robert H. Knapp and Joseph J. Greenbaum, *The Younger American Scholar: His Collegiate Origins* (Chicago: University of Chicago Press, 1953); and Martin Trow, "Cultural Sophistication and Higher Education," in *Selection and Educational Differentiation,* pp. 107–23.

35. Henry Chauncey, "The Use of the Selective Service College Qualifications Test on the Deferment of College Students," *Science,* CXVI (July 4, 1952), 75. See also Dael Wolfle and Toby Oxtoby, "Distribution of Ability of Students Specializing in Different Fields," *Science,* CXVI (Sept. 26, 1952), 311–14.

36. Hanan Selvin and Warren O. Hagstrom, *op. cit.*

37. See Burton R. Clark, *The Open Door College: A Case Study* (New York: McGraw-Hill Book Co., 1960.

38. Burton R. Clark, "The 'Cooling-Out' Function in Higher Education," *American Journal of Sociology,* LXV (May, 1960), 569–76, [chap. XXXVI in this volume (eds.)].

39. T. R. McConnell, "Diversification in American Higher Education," prepared for the Voice of America, Center for the Study of Higher Education, Berkeley (mimeographed).

40. "A strong tendency was noted for teachers to return to the same type of institution in which they had done their undergraduate work. Two-thirds (67 per cent) of those teaching in private liberal arts colleges had done their undergraduate

work in this type of institution. The same general situation existed in the public university, where two-thirds (66 per cent) of the teachers had done their baccalaureate work in public universities. Half of the teachers in state colleges had been undergraduates in the same type of school." Stecklein and Eckert, *op. cit.,* p. 31.

41. See Rose K. Goldsen *et al., op. cit.;* also Norman Miller, *op. cit.*

42. Selvin and Hagstrom, "Determinants of Support for Civil Liberties," pp. 68–69.

43. See Jacob, *op. cit.;* and Margaret L. Habein (ed.), *Spotlight on the College Student* (Washington, D.C.: American Council on Education, 1959).

44. This seems to be the case on a large and extremely diversified campus, such as the University of Wisconsin, as described by David Boroff, "On Wisconsin!" *Harper's,* October, 1959, pp. 33–40.

45. It should be made clear that the factors that determine how favorable is the recruitment to college teaching differ from those affecting how many or what proportion of students from a given college go into college teaching. The two variables—numbers and quality—I believe, are quite independent. Numbers (or proportions) are affected by such things as the social origins of the students relative to the social status of college teaching; where students come from very high-status origins, college teaching may not appear particularly attractive compared with the other professional career possibilities open to most of them. However, the students from those campuses, who go into college teaching will be drawn from the more talented students, if the college has the academic standards and cultural qualities discussed above.

46. The program for gifted students recently instituted at the University of Kansas seems to create the close student-faculty relationships characteristic of a small selective college within a state university, which by law is unselective in admission. A large number of students in that program are planning to go on to graduate school, and many of them appear to be on the road to college teaching.

Index of Names